Essentials of Clinical Social Work

ESSENTIALS OF CLINICAL SOCIAL WORK

JERROLD R. BRANDELL

Wayne State University

Los Angeles | London | New Delhi
Singapore | Washington DC

Los Angeles | London | New Delhi
Singapore | Washington DC

FOR INFORMATION:

SAGE Publications, Inc.
2455 Teller Road
Thousand Oaks, California 91320
E-mail: order@sagepub.com

SAGE Publications Ltd.
1 Oliver's Yard
55 City Road
London EC1Y 1SP
United Kingdom

SAGE Publications India Pvt. Ltd.
B 1/I 1 Mohan Cooperative Industrial Area
Mathura Road, New Delhi 110 044
India

SAGE Publications Asia-Pacific Pte. Ltd.
3 Church Street
#10-04 Samsung Hub
Singapore 049483

Acquisitions Editor: Kassie Graves
Editorial Assistant: Elizabeth Luizzi
Production Editor: Brittany Bauhaus
Copy Editor: Michelle Ponce
Typesetter: C&M Digitals (P) Ltd.
Proofreader: Dennis W. Webb
Indexer: J. Naomi Linzer Indexing Services
Cover Designer: Gail Buschman
Marketing Manager: Shari Countryman

Printed in the United States of America

Library of Congress Cataloging-in-Publication Data

Essentials of clinical social work / J.R. Brandell (editor).

pages cm
Includes bibliographical references and index.

ISBN 978-1-4522-9153-6 (pbk. : alk. paper)
ISBN 978-1-4833-1312-2 (web pdf)
ISBN 978-1-4833-2455-5 (epub)

1. Psychiatric social work. 2. Social case work. I. Brandell, Jerrold R.

HV689.E87 2013
362.2′0425—dc23   2013031339

This book is printed on acid-free paper.

13 14 15 16 17 10 9 8 7 6 5 4 3 2 1

BRIEF CONTENTS

DETAILED CONTENTS

ABOUT THE EDITOR

Jerrold R. Brandell, PhD, BCD, is a faculty member at Wayne State University School of Social Work, where he was named a *distinguished professor* in 2008. A former visiting professor of social work at Lund University (Lund, Sweden) and the University of Canterbury, (Christchurch, New Zealand), he has also held appointments at the Boston University and Michigan State University Schools of Social Work. He has led workshops and lectured widely on clinical topics in this country as well as in France, Greece, Israel, Spain, Sweden, New Zealand, and China. Dr. Brandell is a practicing psychoanalyst and social worker psychotherapist, and completed his psychoanalytic training at Michigan Psychoanalytic Council. He obtained his doctorate at The University of Chicago, and his masters at the University of Wisconsin–Madison. He is (founding) editor of the journal, *Psychoanalytic Social Work*, and has published numerous articles and book chapters, as well as 11 books, among them *Psychodynamic Social Work*, *Of Mice and Metaphors: Therapeutic Storytelling with Children*, and *Attachment and Dynamic Practice* (as coauthor). A former chairperson of the AAPCSW National Study Group, he was named a *distinguished social work practitioner* by the National Academies of Practice in 2001. He maintains a small private practice in psychoanalysis and psychoanalytic psychotherapy in Ann Arbor (Michigan) and is also actively involved in clinical supervision and consultation.

ABOUT THE CONTRIBUTORS

Karen Neuman Allen, PhD, is Professor and chair of the Social Work Department at Arkansas State University. Dr. Allen's clinical experience and research involves working with women who have experienced interpersonal violence and individuals with chronic diseases and disabilities. She is the coauthor of "Surviving Domestic Violence" released in 2013.

Maryann Amodeo, PhD, MSW, is professor and chairperson, Clinical Practice Department and codirector of the Center for Addictions Research and Services, Boston University School of Social Work. She has worked in the substance abuse field for more than 20 years as a clinician, educator, and researcher. Her research focuses on the use of evidence-based treatments by substance abuse programs. She is past president of the Association for Medical Education and Research on Substance Abuse.

Martha Bragin, PhD, LCSW, is an associate professor at the Silberman School of Social Work at Hunter College and the Graduate Center, CUNY. She has extensive experience advising governments, international organizations, and United Nations agencies on addressing the psychosocial effects of armed conflict and disaster. She is a member of the IASC reference group on mental health and psychosocial work in emergencies, the international body that establishes standards for practice. Her research explores cultural issues in community resilience.

Margaret O'Kane Brunhofer, PhD, LMSW, is an adjunct professor at the Wayne State University School of Social Work, where she teaches graduate courses in grief and loss and ethics in interpersonal practice. She has extensive clinical experience in the area of grief and loss and specializes in intensive psychoanalytic psychotherapy with survivors of trauma.

Margaret G. Frank, MSSW, BCD, was formerly, coordinator of the Postgraduate Certificate Program in Advanced Child and Adolescent Psychotherapy, Boston University School of Social Work. She maintains a private practice in psychoanalysis and psychoanalytic psychotherapy in Newton, Massachusetts.

Bruce D. Friedman, PhD, ACSW, CSWM, LCSW is a professor at California State University, Bakersfield Department of Social Work Program. He earned his doctorate from Case Western Reserve University–Mandel School of Applied Social Sciences, where he completed a qualitative study examining how homeless shelters address the needs of people who are homeless. His MSW is from Washington University–George Warren Brown School of Social Work, with a dual specialization in families and substance abuse.

Charles Garvin, PhD is professor emeritus, University of Michigan. He is the author or coauthor of such texts as *Contemporary Group Work,*

Interpersonal Practice in Social Work, and *Generalist Practice*, and has edited volumes such as *The Handbook of Social Work with Groups.* He has also written book chapters and journal articles. Currently, he is researching the topic of conflict resolution and working on books dealing with social justice and group work research.

Donald K. Granvold, PhD, LCSW, LMFT is professor of Social Work at the University of Texas at Arlington. He was a 2013 recipient of the NASW Social Work Pioneer Award in recognition of significant contributions to the field. He is currently Professor Emeritus **at University** of Texas at Arlington. Dr. Granvold has been a leader in the advancement of cognitive treatment and constructivist psychotherapy methods particularly as they are applied to couples treatment and divorce. He has authored over 50 book chapters and articles in social work and allied helping profession journals. Dr. Granvold is a founding fellow of the Academy of Cognitive Therapy.

Roberta Graziano, DSW, is professor emerita and former associate dean, Hunter College School of Social Work, where she developed and directed the Aging and Health Work-Study Scholarship Program. Her particular interests are in theory development, particularly trauma theory, and clinical practice. She is a fellow of the New York Academy of Medicine and of the National Academies of Practice and a NASW Social Work Pioneer.

Joan Granucci Lesser, PhD, is adjunct Associate professor at Smith College School for Social Work. Dr. Lesser is founder and practicing clinician with the Pioneer Valley Professionals in Holyoke, MA. Her professional interests include multicultural clinical practice, research and education, neurobiological disorders of children and adolescents, and the treatment of trauma. Dr. Lesser received her MSW from Columbia University and her doctorate from New York University School of Social Work.

Alan J. Levy, PhD is dean of the Chicago Center for Psychoanalysis and the National institute for the Psychotherapies. A social worker psychoanalyst, Dr. Levy is a distinguished scholar and fellow of the National Academies of Practice. Dr. Levy received the Distinguished Career award from Simmons College School of Social Work and the Educator's Award from the National Institute for the Psychotherapies. Dr. Levy maintains a private practice in Northfield, Illinois.

Luz Marilis López, PhD, MSW, MPH joined the faculty at Boston University School of Social Work in 2005. Ms López has 18 years experience in the fields of HIV/AIDS and substance abuse with diverse populations. Her research focuses on the areas of addiction, trauma, HIV prevention, and Latino culture. Dr. López was born and raised in Puerto Rico. She completed her MPH and PhD degree in Social Work from Tulane University in New Orleans, Louisiana.

Randolph L. Lucente, PhD, is a professor, School of Social Work, Loyola University Chicago. Dr. Lucente is a former director of the doctoral program, teaches in the MSW and PhD degree programs, and maintains a part time private practice of psychotherapy in Palatine, Illinois.

Dennis Miehls is professor at Smith College for Social Work. His current research and theoretical interests include relational theory, supervision theory, and neurobiology and clinical social work. Dennis has been named a Distinguished Practitioner by the NAP. He maintains a private clinical practice in Northampton, Massachusetts, specializing in individual and couple therapies with survivors of childhood trauma.

Judith Marks Mishne, DSW, was at the time of her death in 2006, professor and program coordinator of the Doctoral Specialization in Children and Adolescents, New York University Silver School of Social Work. She was the author or editor of nine books, as well as numerous articles and book chapters. Dr. Mishne maintained a private psychotherapy practice in New York City with children, adolescents, and adults.

Laura L. Myers, PhD, is an associate professor and BSW program director at Florida A & M

University. Dr. Myers received her MSW (1992) and PhD (1998) in social work from the University of Georgia. She has published over 24 journal articles, 12 chapters and coauthored *A Social Worker's Guide to Evaluating Practice Outcomes* and *Basic Statistics in Multivariate Research.*

Fredric T. Perlman, PhD, FIPA, is a psychoanalyst in private practice in NYC. He teaches at the Institute for Psychoanalytic Education (affiliated with NYU Medical School) and at the Institute for Psychoanalytic Training and Research where he is a training and supervising analyst and currently president. He is a past President and distinguished life member of the Confederation of Independent Psychoanalytic Societies and a member of the American Psychoanalytic Association and the International Psychoanalytic Association.

Bruce A. Thyer, PhD, LCSW, BCBA-D, is professor and former dean with the College of Social Work at Florida State University. He received his MSW from the University of Georgia in 1978 and his PhD in social work and psychology from the University of Michigan in 1982. He has been active in the national leadership of the Society for Social Work and Research, the Council on Social Work Education, and the American Psychological Association.

Froma Walsh, MSW, PhD is the Mose & Sylvia Firestone professor emerita, School of Social Service Administration and Department of Psychiatry, University of Chicago, and codirector, Chicago Center for Family Health. She is a past president of the American Family Therapy Academy, past editor of *Journal of Marital & Family Therapy*, and a recipient of numerous awards for distinguished contributions in clinical theory and research, with focus on family resilience, contemporary families, and spiritual resources.

INTRODUCTION TO THE ABRIDGED SECOND EDITION

Essentials of Clinical Social Work, which consists of newly updated contributions originally appearing in the second edition of *Theory and Practice in Clinical Social Work* (2011), offers readers a comprehensive introduction to the world of advanced clinical practice. In its 16 chapters, both traditional and newly emerging theories of practice are described in detail, major modalities of treatment are examined, and some of the most critical issues and clinical challenges facing social workers are treated in depth. In each instance, contributions come from well-recognized experts in that particular field of practice.

The clinical social work field continues to change and evolve. These are but a few of the more important developments addressed in this volume:

- There is increasing emphasis on the evidentiary basis for clinical social work practices.
- The neuropsychological basis of behavior and psychopathology may now legitimately be regarded as a framework unto itself, one that is also increasingly associated with models for clinical intervention.

- There is a burgeoning literature on attachment theory and corresponding efforts to incorporate its basic postulates into clinical practice models.
- Conceptions of trauma, trauma survivorship, and treatment models for working with trauma survivors have changed.
- Community violence and terrorism have exerted a dramatic influence on the shape of contemporary social work practice.
- Relational social work models, linked to the relational movement in contemporary psychoanalysis, have gained in prominence.

The basic framework of this abridged second edition remains much the same as that of the original, though new content has been added to each chapter, references have been thoroughly updated, and important new themes have been introduced. Although certain chapters from the complete second edition have not been included, the reader will discover that much of what distinguishes the second edition from the first has been preserved in this abridged version. Indeed, entirely new content areas have been included, many reflecting significant if not transformative shifts in the way clinical social work is now conceived and practiced.

STRUCTURE OF THE CHAPTERS

Although there is some variation across chapters, all contributors were asked to incorporate the following components into their chapters:

- Relevant history—with particular attention to the social work profession—of the theoretical perspective, clinical method, or issue/theme/dilemma
- Discussion and elaboration of important ideas, concepts, and terminology having particular currency for the chapter theme
- Use of well-developed, illustrative clinical examples derived from contemporary practice
- Discussion of important new developments relative to the chapter theme
- Incorporation of content that addresses the clinical evidentiary base

Inasmuch as the principal audience for *Essentials of Clinical Social Work* consists of graduate students and their instructors, contributors were also invited to include supplementary instructional materials (e.g., discussion questions, relevant readings, and Internet sites) in order to maximize student learning of challenging content.

Mary Richmond, a pioneer in the field of social casework, once characterized the clinical process in social work as "the influence of mind upon mind" (Richmond, 1917). Although an enduring truth is captured in Richmond's evocative characterization, made nearly a century ago, the practice of clinical social work continues to evolve and to change. It is our hope that this volume offers essential new knowledge as well as *practice wisdom* to guide the next generation of social work clinicians in meeting the challenges they will face.

REFERENCE

Richmond, M. (1917). *Social Diagnosis*. New York, NY: Russell Sage Foundation.

1

SYSTEMS THEORY

BRUCE D. FRIEDMAN AND KAREN NEUMAN ALLEN

Systems theory enables us to understand the biological, psychological, sociological, and spiritual conditions and dynamics of clients in order to interpret problems and develop balanced intervention strategies, with the goal of enhancing the goodness of fit between individuals and their environments. Systems theory input does not specify a particular conceptual model for understanding problems, and it does not direct the social worker to specific intervention strategies. Rather, it serves as an organizing conceptual framework or metatheory for understanding (Goldstein, 1990; Hearn, 1958; Meyer, 1976, 1983; Siporin, 1980). By looking at the clients holistically, recognizing the context of their life situations and interpersonal concerns of family, work, school, peers, and social support networks that are influenced by broader social and historical conditions, systems theory supports a competency-based assessment to understand the clients' condition (Gray & Zide, 2013). Thus, systems theory for social workers operates in such a way as to capture the person within the context of his or her environment. Gitterman and Germain (2008) have observed:

By immersing ourselves in clients' stories and environments, social workers are in a natural position to describe adaptive and dysfunctional patterns, as well as processes of change. Through detailed and rich descriptions, including direct quotes from clients and significant environmental figures, we capture the whole person within a life course and ecological perspective. (p. 129)

Systems theory, as we know it today, had its origins in sociology and biology (Robbins, Chatterjee, & Canda, 2012). As early as 1887, sociologist Ferdinand Tönnies coined the terms *Gesellschaft* (the individual's self interest) and *Gemeinschaft* (the best interest of the community) in his analysis of urban and agrarian societies. These concepts describe the competing and sometimes balancing of the individual's needs and desires with the morals, values, customs, and expectations of a community. Other sociologists, such as Max Weber and Talcott Parsons, elaborated upon these ideas. However, within social work, systems thinking has been more heavily influenced by the work of the biologist Ludwig von Bertalanffy, and later, by social psychologist Uri Bronfenbrenner, who examined human biological systems within an ecological environment. These ideas ultimately led to our profession's integration and application of systems theory into work with clients. With its roots in von Bertalanffy's systems theory and Bronfenbrenner's ecological environment, the ecosystems perspective provides a framework that permits users to draw on theories from different disciplines in order to analyze the complex nature of human interactions within a social environment.

A *system* is defined as "an organized whole made up of components that interact in a way distinct from their interaction with other entities and which endures over some period of time" (Carter, 2011, p. 4). A familiar demarcation of systems in social work involves the designation of particular social systems as being micro, mezzo, or macrolevel, depending on system size and complexity. Microsystems are understood to refer to small-size social systems, such as individuals and couples. Mezzosystems focus on intermediate-size systems, including groups, support networks, and extended families. Macrosystems focus on large systems, such as communities and organizations. This differentiation of systems by size can be somewhat arbitrary, depending in part on the social worker's perspective as well as the organizational context and purpose in which he or she practices (Greene, 2008). For example, an organization can be viewed from a macroperspective, or it can be viewed as a mezzo unit within the context of its broader community and its political context.

RELEVANT HISTORY

Ludwig von Bertalanffy (1901–1972), as mentioned above, is credited with being the originator of the form of systems theory used in social work. Von Bertalanffy, a theoretical biologist born and educated in Austria, became dissatisfied with the way linear, cause-and-effect theories explained growth and change in living organisms. He thought that change might occur because of the interactions between the parts of an organism, a point of view that represented a dramatic change from the theories of his day. Existing theories tended to be reductionist, understanding the whole by breaking it into its parts. Von Bertalanffy's introduction of systems theory changed that framework by looking at the system as a whole, with its relationships and interactions with other systems, as a mechanism of growth and change. This changed the way people looked at systems and led to a new language, popularizing terms such as *open and closed systems, entropy, boundary, homeostasis, inputs, outputs,* and *feedback.*

General systems theory is likened to a role play of wholeness. Von Bertalanffy (1968) advocated "an organismic conception in biology that emphasized consideration of the organism as a whole or a system" (p. 12). He saw the main objective of the biological sciences as the discovery of organizational properties that could be applied to organisms at various levels for analysis. This led to the basic assumption that "the whole is more than the sum of its parts" (p. 18). Von Bertalanffy's approach is derived from a basic concept that relies heavily on linear-based, cause-and-effect properties to explain growth and change in living organisms. There are two conditions on which these properties depend: (1) that an interaction occurs between parts and (2) that the condition describing the relationship between the parts is linear. When these two conditions are present, von Bertalanffy felt, the interaction was measurable and was subject to scientific inquiry.

Figure 1.1 depicts the linear nature of the system. There are inputs, outputs, and outcomes. However, what happens in the system is somewhat mysterious, and one can only measure the changes by observing the outputs in relationship to the outcomes or goals of the system. Workers can vary or modify the inputs, including their own actions, to create a change within the system.

To measure the interaction, von Bertalanffy applied basic scientific principles to various types of organisms that explain and measure behavior. It is important to understand that von Bertalanffy's original conception of systems theory was one of organization. He saw it as a method of organizing the interaction between component parts of a larger organism. Since it was a way of organizing information rather than explaining observations, it was easily adaptable to many different scientific fields, including psychology, psychiatry, sociology, and social work. The important distinction among the various fields adopting these principles was how they used other theories to explain the interaction within the organism. Thus, systems theory is an organizational theory that looks at interactions between systems: How a field defines the system determines the nature of the interaction. Von Bertalanffy was influenced by a number of sociologists, and their contributions are important to social work. To understand more fully the interactional properties of systems theory, it may be useful to understand the key concepts used by von Bertalanffy and other systems theorists.

Other Contributions to Systems Theory

Von Bertalanffy was influenced by Durkheim and Max Weber, both of whom were early pioneers in the field of sociology. They took early

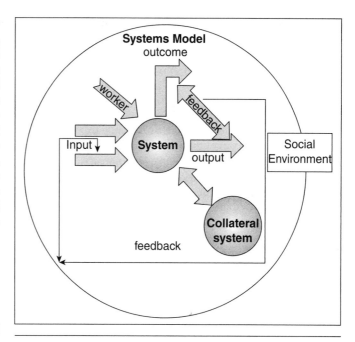

Figure 1.1   Systems Model

systems theory as it was initially applied in the late 1800s and early 1900s to biological organisms and applied it to human social systems. Durkheim was interested in how societies were organized and how they maintained cohesion or group identity over time. He believed that human beings experience a unique social reality not experienced by other organisms, and that order can only be maintained through the consent of individuals within the group who share the same morals and values. In his 1893 doctoral dissertation, later published as *The Division of Labor in Society,* Durkheim (1984) explained that in highly organized systems, the division of labor contributes to the maintenance of societies. In complex societies, individuals perform various roles that, while they lead to specialization and segmentation, also create a high degree of mutual interdependence between units. Although the individuals performing them will change, these roles persist over time and maintain a society (Durkheim, 1984). Durkheim also wrote about crime and suicide, believing both to be a result of disruptions or imbalances in the integration of individuals and society.

Durkheim was particularly interested in how roles and the division of labor maintained society in a macrosense. For example, the role of the police in a society is to protect citizens from criminals and preserve order by enforcing the law. The stability or equilibrium of a society is threatened when the police abuse their authority.

We can also use role theory to judge how well individuals are functioning at a more microlevel. Social workers are often called on to evaluate how well mothers and fathers care for their children. As parents, they are expected to conform to certain norms and role expectations that include providing their young with adequate food, shelter, and medical care and ensuring that their educational needs are met. Severe cases of role disruption can lead to state intervention through protective services. Durkheim is famous for his concept of "anomie," which describes individuals who are alienated because they are unable or unwilling to fit into society through compliance with the normative expectations of the group and thus fail to fulfill expected roles. To a social worker, *anomie* describes situations where there is a severe disruption in the goodness of fit between an individual and his or her social context (Merton, 1938).

These concepts are identified in Figure 1.1, where the system exists within a social environment. Thus, certain factors in the social environment affect the system and its outcomes and outputs. The system also interfaces with other systems or collateral systems. There are expectations on the role and function of the system to conform to standards within the larger social environment. If the system does not subscribe to those norms, then the system is considered dysfunctional.

Max Weber was a contemporary of Durkheim known for his work studying complex social institutions and organizations. In addition to being one of the first sociologists, he was a lawyer, politician, and economist. Unlike Durkheim, who believed that societies are sustained through consensus and the willingness of individuals to comply with normative expectations and roles, Weber believed that governments and bureaucracies are essentially coercive in nature and are maintained through their "monopoly" in the legitimate use of violence or force. He also studied the way in which various types of leaders may influence society. Because they are very often government employees carrying out the policies of the state, it is important for social workers to be mindful of Weber's position that the best interests of the individual or client system they serve may conflict with the interests of those in power.

The work of Durkheim and Weber directly influenced Talcott Parsons (1951), who augmented their work by elaborating on the specific functions of social systems. Parsons was an American philosopher, economist, and sociologist interested in articulating a unified conceptual framework or "grand" theory for sociology. Parsons called his theoretical framework "structural functionalism." Structural functionalism states that social structures involve interaction and relationships among "actors" and are characterized by a functional imperative. This is to say that a defining attribute of a social system is its function in the larger social environment. Parsons delineated four functional states of social systems: (1) adaption (to the external environment), (2) goal attainment or growth, (3) integration (with other social systems), and (4) latency (homeostasis) or pattern maintenance (preservation of interactional patterns, norms, and customs through socialization processes). These states are not mutually exclusive but are integrated.[1]

Adaptation describes the dynamic process in which a given system responds to the demands and pressures of external forces and conditions. It also includes the way in which a system is able to bring in resources from its outside environment. Adaptation involves reciprocal interactions and exchanges between the system and its environment, which ultimately results in both being changed. When a system determines and prioritizes its goals and then obtains and mobilizes resources in directed action to achieve those goals, it demonstrates the function of *goal attainment. Integration* describes the coordination and orchestration of the system's internal components. This leads to a potential conflict where the goal of a member of a (family) system may be in opposition to the goal of the system (Carter, 2011). Finally, *latency* or pattern maintenance describes a system state in which the system is invested in maintaining and transmitting its norms and values (*Blackwell Encyclopedia of Sociology Online,* 2009).

Therefore, when attempting to understand and intervene in social systems, social workers must also consider the functional imperative of the system. Thinking of the function a particular system serves can help social workers to evaluate the extent to which the system is succeeding in fulfilling that purpose and to determine areas of weakness or dysfunction that can be strengthened so that the organization functions properly and supports the individuals and subsystems within it. For example, if we examine the prison

---

[1]Luhmann (Kihlstrom, 2012) expanded on these ideas by looking at the laws and roles of a system that he called society system and included both interaction systems (face-to-face, as in the case of families) and organization systems (formal organizations).

system, we might raise questions about the function of prisons in protecting good citizens from criminals by their removal from society and institutionalization. We might then ask, does a higher rate of incarceration lead to a reduction in criminal activity? However, if we argue that a function of prisons is the rehabilitation of offenders, we may then pose very different questions. What are the recidivism rates for released prisoners? How do they fare once they are released? How well prepared are they to reenter society?

Cybernetics is an interdisciplinary approach that grew in part out of structural functionalism and an interest in understanding how systems create and use processes to regulate themselves. Niklus Luhmann, a contemporary German sociologist, was, like Parsons, attempting to explicate a "grand theory" in sociology that could be applied to all social systems. For Luhmann, all social systems are communication networks, and a particular system selects what kind of information it will accept. This creates and maintains the identity of the system. When studying a particular society, Luhmann (1995) argued, its mass communications and media are its defining features.

All social systems receive inputs from the environment, engage in processes, and generate outputs. In addition to having a structure, social systems serve particular functions. A university receives inputs from society (the student, dollars from the state and from tuition), engages in a process (educating students), and generates an output (educated individuals). A college or university may be considered a social system. It is, moreover, a component of a larger social system or institution—that of higher education. The family is also an essential social system. It serves a variety of functions including socializing and caring for its members. As a system, when change happens to one member of the family, other members of the family system are also affected. Families have structure (roles, boundaries, and rules) and processes (communication and behavioral patterns). Social workers need to address both of these dimensions in working with families (Becvar & Becvar, 2013).

Family systems theory was developed by Murray Bowen (1978). Bowen believed it was necessary to work with extended families inclusive of at least three generations in order to address problems. He identified five characteristics of a family system:

- external and internal family boundaries,
- family rules,
- family role organization,
- power distribution among family members, and
- the communication process.

Communication, as we know, is both verbal and nonverbal, and as social workers, it is an important aspect of our work to facilitate and clarify communication. Communication regulates and either stabilizes or disrupts a system. In the late 1950s, a group of mental health professionals in Palo Alto, California, began to use communication theory and cybernetics to study the origins of schizophrenia. Don Jackson, Gregory Bateson, and Virginia Satir, among others, recognized that communication patterns in dysfunctional family systems were disrupted. Although such patterns were not the cause of schizophrenia, as they had theorized, their contribution to family systems theory has remained an influential one. Bateson (1972) and Bateson, Jackson, Haley, and Weakland (1956) identified a particularly disruptive communication pattern in dysfunctional families. A "double bind" occurs when an individual is placed in a no-win situation through contradictory instructions or expectations. For example, when a child is told to "kiss mommy," but her mother demonstrates rejecting behavior, the child is placed in what is termed a *double-bind* situation. If she doesn't follow the injunction to "kiss mommy," she risks her mother's displeasure. However, she also risks displeasing her mother if she *does* comply.

Virginia Satir (1967) used the term *metacommunication* to describe "communication about a communication." Such metacommunications may be made openly or implicitly by verbal as well as nonverbal mechanisms. The extent to which a message and a message about the message (metamessage) agree with each other is referred to as *congruence* or *incongruence*. Incongruence in communication may result in confusion and anxiety. For example, if a child is told that he performed well on a task but perceives through facial expressions or verbal tones that a parent may be disappointed, he is unable to discern the quality of his performance and the true nature of his parents' approval.

Salvadore Minuchin, a therapist working with young juvenile delinquents, developed structural family therapy, a branch of family systems theory that emphasizes restoring appropriate family roles and boundaries (i.e., structure). In 1967, Minuchin was appointed the director of the Philadelphia Child Guidance Clinic, where Haley and others eventually worked. According to the Minuchin Center for the Family (n.d), structural family therapy recognizes:

- Context organizes us. Individual behavior is a function of our relationships and interactions with others. The structural family therapist looks at what is happening between people rather than the psychology of individuals.

- The family is the primary context, or what is called the "matrix of identity" for individuals. The family is where we develop our sense of self as we interact with other members of the family. The family is constantly changing as members progress through developmental stages and exit and enter the system.

- Family structure is the product of repetitive patterns of interaction that develop overtime as family members interact and adapt to each.

- A family that functions well is not devoid of stress or conflict. Rather, a healthy family is assessed by how effectively it handles them as well as its capacity to respond to the changing needs of individual family members and conditions in the environment.

- A structural family therapist locates, accesses, and amplifies underlying strengths within the family system in order to help the family minimize or eliminate interactional patterns that inhibit its successful adaptation to the needs of individual members and the larger social context.

Structural family therapists use role play, rehearsals, homework, journaling, and other behaviorally based exercises to help restore healthy communication and structure in families (Minuchin, 1974; Minuchin & Fishman, 1981). For example, in Minuchin's work, often the "identified client" was an adolescent who was acting out. In intervening with the family, the structural family therapist helps the parents reclaim their role and authority as parents, providing them with help in communicating appropriate limits and expectations as well as implementing consequences for misbehavior. The adolescent then assumes his or her proper place in the family structure and is relieved of an excess of power. He or she is now free to be a teenager rather than a pseudoadult or parent.[2]

The Terminology of General Systems Theory

Von Bertalanffy believed that all things, living and nonliving, could be regarded as systems, and that systems have properties that are capable of being studied. Each system is a unit of wholeness with a distinct property or structural limitation that delineates it from other systems, a property von Bertalanffy termed the system's *boundary*. The boundary is what makes each system unique and gives it definition. Some boundaries are clearly defined; others may be permeable. In defining a person as a system, one may literally identify the person's skin as the boundary. Access to the person beyond the boundary is through various forms of communication, through the five sensory modalities, or through microorganisms

---

[2]See Chapter 7, "Family Therapy: Systemic Approaches to Practice," for a more detailed discussion of systems theory in relation to family theory and practice.

that find ways of permeating the outer shell, or skin, of the person. However, the structure of the person is clearly defined by his or her physical being.

The boundaries of social systems can be partially defined by norms and customs. For example, a family is a system that defines its boundaries through sociological and legal definitions; groups are social organizations that define their boundary through group membership; and communities are social organizations that define their boundaries through either geographic definitions of community or an ethnic boundary definition, as in ethnic communities. Through this process, it is possible to see that each system has a characteristic boundary and way of defining itself. These invisible boundaries also regulate how individuals enter and exit the system.

A system grows through an exchange of energy between the system and its environment, a process that is possible only if the boundary possesses permeability. This energy can be tangible or intangible. Tangible resources would be food, money, shelter, and other things that contribute to the physical maintenance of the system. An intangible resource could be information, as exemplified when a member of the system is educated or has useful knowledge that helps the system. The amount of information or energy that is permitted to pass through a given system's boundary determines the permeability of that boundary. The more permeable the boundary, the greater the extent of interaction the system has with its environment leading to greater openness.

Von Bertalanffy (1968) differentiated between open and closed systems, observing that "living organisms are essentially *open systems*" (p. 32, italics added). An open system, unlike a closed system, exchanges matter with its environment; *closed systems* "are isolated from their environment" (p. 39). An example of a closed system that may serve adaptive purposes could be an ethnic minority community that has limited access to the majority cultural institutions due to active discrimination directed against its members.

Recognizing that system growth derives from the ability of the system to import energy or system inputs from other systems, openness is a critical quality for system functioning, and possibly even survival. However, there are other times when a system does close as a perceived means of protecting itself. In these instances, the system is exporting (system outputs) more energy than it is able to import. Since systems rely on a flow of energy, with outputs relying on fresh inputs, too much exporting can lead to a state of disorder, referred to as *entropy.* When the system is importing more than it is exporting, it is termed *negative entropy,* or *negentropy,* a state of system growth.

The exchange of information between the system and its environment is regulated by a process called *feedback,* a method of evaluation used to determine whether the system's outputs are consonant with the perceived *outcomes* (goals) that the system has established for itself. In addition to this internal feedback, the system also has a method of measuring responses from the external environment. In both situations, if the system perceives a variance between output and outcome, it can alter the process by varying the level of inputs. A classic example of system feedback and response is the thermostat in your home. The thermostat is set to a certain temperature; the sensors in the device read the room temperature (input) and adjust the furnace (output) to reach the preset temperature. The room temperature is read again in a continual feedback loop that regulates the furnace.

This modifying of levels of inputs and outputs is the form of control that all systems have in their interactions with their environment. In social work terms, an open system would generally (though not invariably) be considered a functional system, while a closed system would be classified as dysfunctional. A functional system interacts dynamically with the larger environment, a need that supports the survival of the system. Because there is a cause-and-effect relationship between the system and the environment, both are constantly changing in consequence of the interaction, so that the open nature of the system is one of constant change. Change does not always relate to disorder. Von Bertalanffy (1968) believed that if a system was working properly, it would achieve a form of dynamic equilibrium with the environment that he called *steady state.* Steady state is achieved through a process of ordering and growth that von Bertalanffy referred to as *negative entropy* (Dale & Smith, 2013).

The concept of steady state is a little misleading; *steady* here does not mean *constant* but a sense of balance between the system and the larger social environment (Anderson, Carter, & Lowe, 1999). To put it slightly differently, the ability of the system to adapt to its environment through changes in its structure leads to states of *equilibrium* and *homeostasis,* both of which relate to different types of balance. Equilibrium is the sense of being in balance. When something is in balance, there is little variability in movement before the state of balance is disrupted. On the other hand, homeostasis is a state of variable balance where the limits to maintaining balance are more flexible (Carter, 2011). These limits are determined by the system and may be likened to the idea of something bending without breaking.

ECOLOGICAL ENVIRONMENT

The concept of ecological environment is credited to Uri Bronfenbrenner (1917–2005). Bronfenbrenner grew up in a state institution for the "feebleminded," where his father was the neuropathologist. Prior to receiving any formal training in psychology, Bronfenbrenner lived on the 3,000 acres of the institution, where patients spent their time working on the farm or in the shops. Through these early-life experiences, combined with his extensive study of the work of theorists such as Kurt Lewin, Bronfenbrenner developed a strong belief in the resilient nature of human beings. He regarded this resiliency as embedded in a cultural context that helped form and shape the individual.

Von Bertalanffy's model assumed a single-dimension cause-and-effect relationship between social units within the environment. Bronfenbrenner, however, had some difficulty with the single-dimension relationship and felt that systems theory did not fully capture the complex dynamics that occur within social systems. In pure scientific situations, all aspects of systems can be carefully controlled for environmental effects. However, Bronfenbrenner (1979) observed that there are a number of additional environmental factors in human social systems, which he referred to collectively as the *ecological environment:*

> The ecological environment is conceived as a set of nested structures, each inside the next, like a set of Russian dolls. At the innermost level is the immediate setting containing the developing person. . . . The next step, however, already leads us off the beaten track for it requires looking beyond single settings to the relations between them. (p. 3)

In essence, this view states that human development cannot be seen in isolation but must be viewed within the context of the individual's relationship with the environment. In addition, each individual's environment is unique. The "person's development is profoundly affected by events occurring in settings in which the person is not even present" (Bronfenbrenner, 1979, p. 3). For example, within the context of a family, there may be forces affecting the parental subsystem that trickle down to affect the children without the children even being aware of them. For example, if a parent is experiencing stress at work and displaces his or her frustration at home by yelling at the children, one may see how events outside the child's immediate environment may exert a pronounced effect on the child's development.

When the concept of ecological environment is introduced into the formula of human development, the result is a complex matrix for defining behavior that not only includes here-and-now circumstances but also involves understanding the historical and cultural factors surrounding the family as well as any biological concerns, hence the bio-psycho-social-spiritual nature of ecological systems. Systems theory, as an organizational theory, can begin to introduce order to this complexity by lending it conceptual clarity.

Figure 1.2 depicts a graphic configuration of the ecological environment. There are individual systems embedded within systems, and those systems interact in a three-dimensional way both vertically and horizontally. Thus, if the unit of analysis is the individual, there are other individuals (horizontal interactions) that relate to him or her. There are also vertical interactions. These vertical interactions may originate from below (in relation to individual biology), or they can come from above (in relation to family or community values or even social policies).

Ecological Systems Theory and Perspective

The juxtaposition of Bronfenbrenner's ecological environment with von Bertalanffy's systems theory leads to the ecological systems perspective that examines transactional relationships between systems. Since von Bertalanffy and Bronfenbrenner developed their theoretical concepts for other disciplines, the connection to social work was not readily apparent. Carol Germain has made strides in applying these concepts to the social work profession.

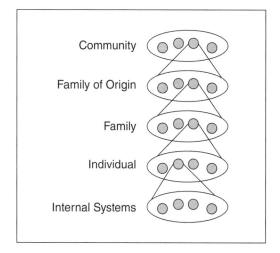

Community
Family of Origin
Family
Individual
Internal Systems

Figure 1.2   Ecological Systems Model

Germain was instrumental in adapting these two theoretical models to an ecological systems perspective with specific applicability to social work. She strongly advocated looking at the bio-psycho-social development of individuals and families within cultural, historical, communal, and societal contexts, a perspective that requires us to look as well at all events in the person's life. Social workers need to go beyond the scope of looking at the individual and rely on public policy, practice, and research to gain the information needed to make an adequate assessment. Germain (1991) characterized the nature of relationships between systems as transactional and "reciprocal exchanges between entities, or between their elements, in which each changes or otherwise influences the other over time" (p. 16). Such relationships are no longer linear but are circular, each system in the interaction affecting the others.

The idea of behavior as a function is adapted from Lewin's field theory, which asserts that an individual can be studied by examining that person in the context of his or her environment. This may be symbolically represented through the equation $B = f(PE)$, where B is the individual's behavior, a function of the interplay between person P and environment E (Lewin, 1935, 1976). Field theory adumbrates aspects of both Bronfenbrenner's theory and Germain's ideas regarding the person-in-environment.

Early social science practice focused on either the behavior of the person or the environment, not the complex interactions between the two (Bronfenbrenner, 1979). The ecological systems perspective, in contrast, is specifically concerned with the nature of such interactions between the individual (or group, family, or community) and the greater environment.

This case demonstrates the interplay of familial values on the individual. There may be times when the individual's goals are at variance with the environmental forces that are acting on the individual and dictate a different path.

This example raises the importance of understanding the interactional quality of person-in-environment relationships. Shulman (2009) refers to this as "client-system interaction" (p. 5)

A case vignette may help illustrate the dual nature of person and environment interactions.

Valerie was a 16-year-old African American high school student who was involved in a program titled Career Beginnings, designed to identify at-risk high school students who had the potential for graduating from high school and then continuing their education at the college level. Valerie showed much promise and was academically successful. Her goal was to pursue a career in medicine.

Everything seemed to be progressing well for Valerie in the program. She had a good job, was responsible, had a good mentor, and maintained a 3.8 grade point average. Shortly before her 17th birthday, she appeared to be gaining weight. When asked, Valerie admitted that she was pregnant. On further exploration, Valerie said that she was the first generation in her family to be close to graduating from high school. She also revealed that she was being pressured by her mother and her grandmother to have a baby. Valerie was a firstborn child, as was Valerie's mother. Both Valerie and her mother were born when their respective mothers were 16. As Valerie approached her 17th birthday, both her mother and her grandmother (who lived with them) began pressuring her to have a child since they viewed motherhood as Valerie's primary role and 16 as the appropriate age to begin to have children. In effect, the family environment did not place the same emphasis on completing high school as did the program.

and describes the need for understanding the context surrounding the individual. In such a process, the worker begins by looking at the client's strengths rather than trying to identify the causes of the problem.

The nature of transactional relationships in the matrix of person-in-environment leads to the following nine assumptions of the ecosystems perspective:

Assumption 1: There is an underlying general order in the world.

Assumption 2: Social ordering is a constant and dynamic process.

Assumption 3: All human social behavior is *purposive.*

Assumption 4: All forms of social organization display self-maintaining and development characteristics.

Assumption 5: All social organizations are greater than the sum of their parts.

Assumption 6: Well-being is the natural state of all humans and human social organization. (This

assumption serves as the foundation of the *strengths perspective.*)

Assumption 7: All forms of social organization can be characterized and studied as social systems.

Assumption 8: The social relationship is the fundamental unit of all social systems.

Assumption 9: The helping process seen in professional social work is the formalization of a natural social process (Dale & Smith, 2013, p. 13).

Germain's (1991) position is that all organisms exist in a particular order in the world. A reductionist approach necessitates the need to understand that order. However, through the ecosystems perspective, it is not necessary to know the order to facilitate systemic change or adaptation; change becomes possible through the identification of the system's strengths.

The ecosystem perspective views individuals as both the cause and the effect of their situation. Since the person is in a dynamic situation, each change he or she makes causes a reactive change in the larger system. Germain (1991) identifies adaptation, life stress, coping, power, and human relatedness as important concepts for understanding the nature of the interactions of person-in-environment.

ADAPTATION

Given the dynamic nature of interactions in person-in-environment relationships, adaptation is the central ecological concept. Adaptation relates to the cause-and-effect relationship between the person and the environment, with change as the inevitable outcome of the interaction.

Adaptation may be directed to changing oneself in order to meet environmental opportunities or demands, or it may be directed to changing the environment so that physical and social settings will be more responsive to human needs, rights, goals, and capacities. (Germain, 1991, p. 17)

Adaptation, as it relates to equilibrium, would provide a short list of choices, whereas in achieving homeostasis, the system would have a more extensive range of options from which to choose. The following case example illustrates the process of adaptation.

Sarah, a 95-year-old woman, suffered from polio since the age of 2.

Throughout her life, she constantly fought both her own body and her inability to access the larger systems that society had to offer. Sarah had undergone a number of spinal fusion procedures that temporarily alleviated some of her more distressing polio symptoms, helping her to adapt somewhat more successfully to the environment. But Sarah did not stop there. As an early activist, she became involved in bringing about awareness of the plight of disabled individuals. She served on her local town's disabilities committee, and when the Americans with Disabilities Act was passed in 1990, she became the director of the town's commission on disabilities. She was recognized as the person who fought for and got the curb cuts installed in the town.

Although confined to a wheelchair because of her polio, Sarah continued to be an active leader in helping businesses in the town become more accessible to the disabled. When Sarah's husband died, she might have become reclusive, since in many respects he was her link to the outside world, chauffeuring her to meetings and otherwise helping her remain connected to the world outside their home. However, because she was able to identify and develop strengths and to adapt to her environmental milieu by using the resources she had helped create, Sarah remained active and involved.

LIFE STRESS

Person-in-environment interaction leads to a normal tension, also referred to as *life stress*. Whenever different entities interact with each other, the ebb and flow between them creates some friction. The system's need to continue to adapt and achieve a state of homeostasis is itself a source of stress:

Life stress encompasses both the external demand and the internal (conscious and unconscious) experience of stress, including both emotional and physiological elements. What is perceived as stressful varies across age, gender, culture, physical and emotional states, past experience, and the perceived and actual nature of the environment. (Germain, 1991, p. 20)

In other words, two people in exactly the same environmental situation may have different experiences owing to their differing perceptions of that situation. For one it may be comparatively stressful, while for the other it could be comparatively stress-free.

Irrespective of the unit of analysis—individual, couple, family, group, or community—the ecosystems perspective is applied in essentially the same fashion, as the following example illustrates.

A group of previously married individuals, Center Singles, consisting of persons in their mid-30s to mid-50s, provided a variety of functions for its members. For some the group symbolized a social outlet, for others it was purely educational, and for still others the group was a means of social support. This was possible since the group's goals were global, with a central focus on the problem of being single again following a divorce or the death of a member's spouse. The global nature of the group's goal was an attraction, since in all likelihood more specific goals would have limited its membership. As a consequence, there were significant differences among group members that represented each person's capacity to cope with that particular life stress.

> Two group members are used as further illustration of this concept. Susan was in her mid-40s and had three children, ranging in age from 14 to 18. Susan's husband had recently told her that he wanted a divorce, to which Susan reacted with surprise and anger. She felt unable to function and had problems concentrating on simple tasks such as addressing envelopes. She was constantly on the verge of tears.
>
> Elaine was also in her mid-40s. She had four children, ranging in age from 13 to 21. When her husband told her that he wanted a divorce, the first thing she did was to look at the want ads and find a job. Both Susan and Elaine were motivated to join the group for similar reasons, yet each dealt with this life stress differently.

Coping

The ability to cope requires both problem solving—what needs to be done to manage stress—and the ability to regulate negative feelings. The outcome of these factors leads to increased self-esteem, which helps diminish the negative feelings caused by a particular stressor.

For a person to cope successfully with stress, the individual must partially block out negative feelings "so that hope is maintained and some problem solving can begin. As problem solving proceeds, self-esteem is elevated, hope is strengthened, and the defenses that were needed at the outset begin to relax" (Germain, 1991, p. 22). Each individual deals with life stress along a continuum in which adaptive coping and maladaptive defenses constitute the extremes.

The locus of the stress is an external source; however, the need to cope and to develop defenses arises from the internal anxiety created by an external stressor. Each person relies on his or her own strengths to cope with stressful situations. When people feel as though their resources have been tapped, their coping ability is reduced, and maladaptive defenses may predominate.

Power

Power has its derivation from a source extrinsic to the individual. Dominant groups in society use their position of power to influence subordinate groups through transactions in which resources are either provided or withheld. Germain (1991) observes, "The abuse of power by dominant groups creates both social and technological pollutions" (p. 24).

The abuse of power by a dominant group can also be a source of tension in person-environment interactions. These tensions affect whole segments of the population, not just one individual. How the individual experiences this tension and

Laurie, a 40-year-old single mother of six, had a history of using drugs and alcohol to cope with the stressors in her life. She needed to supplement her income since the amount that she was earning was not sufficient to feed her family. She began working as a topless dancer but relied on drugs to diminish the shame and anxiety such work stirred up in her. As her financial situation worsened, she supplemented her meager income by performing lap dances and prostituting herself. Increasingly desperate, she turned to shoplifting and passed several bad checks.

By the time Laurie sought help through the Welfare-to-Work program, she had a long rap sheet with multiple convictions for shoplifting, passing bad checks, and welfare fraud. She had already spent some time in jail.

When the worker discussed strategies for potential employment with her, Laurie said that the only things she knew were shoplifting, sex, and drugs. Thus, clinical intervention involved more than simply finding this client a job; it was as important for the worker to promote new coping strategies that would keep her from landing in jail again. Intervention occurred on multiple levels to assist Laurie in developing more adaptive coping strategies for dealing with her financial situation. Other therapeutic foci included building her self-esteem and helping her confront an early childhood trauma stemming from molestation and rape by her maternal uncle when she was 8 years old.

is able to adapt to the tension-producing situation determines that individual's capacity for negotiating power inequities and imbalances. Abuse of power may occur at any systemic level, including within families.

HUMAN RELATEDNESS

Paramount in the concept of person-in-environment is the individual's ability to develop relationships and attachments. Three important relational aspects of person-in-environment interactions have been identified: (1) the attributes of human relatedness, competence, self-direction, and self-esteem, which are all outcomes of the person-in-environment gestalt;

(2) the interdependence of such attributes, each deriving from and contributing to the development of the others; and (3) the apparent absence of cultural bias in such attributes. In other words, every human society, apparently irrespective of culture, values relatedness. Kinship structures and the rules for relating may vary by culture, but the attributes of human relatedness, competence, self-direction, and self-esteem are predictable outcomes of the person-in-environment relationship (Germain, 1991, p. 27).

Since these attributes—human relatedness, competence, self-direction, and self-esteem—exist in all cultures regardless of how the particular culture defines them, it underscores our need to understand the cultural values that contribute to the makeup of each client system.

Joe was a 40-year-old Jewish professional who had recently gone through a messy divorce. In this case, the divorce meant that he had minimal contact with his two sons. This proved especially difficult for Joe since much of his identity as a Jew was linked to culturally prescribed responsibilities as a husband and a father. His lack of contact with his sons was dissonant with his cultural value of fatherhood.

NEW DEVELOPMENTS

Clinical Tools
for Information Gathering

Certain assessment tools can be helpful in gathering information about the client and his or her environment. Three such tools—the genogram, the ecomap, and the social network map—permit a graphic depiction of some aspect of the client's ecological environment, providing important interactional data that can aid the social worker in the assessment process. Such tools can also significantly shorten the traditional case-recording process (Holman, 1983; Sheafor & Horejsi, 2012).

Genogram

The genogram is similar to a family tree. It can describe family relationships in as many generations as the worker and the client wish but is typically limited to three generations. The genogram provides a historical overview of the family and is a useful way of obtaining a sense of the client's historical milieu. By involving the client in helping identify each generation and the characteristics of the people within it, visual pieces of data are created that can be used to great advantage in the assessment process. Such data provide a picture that can often be used by the client to identify previously hidden patterns. Once these historical patterns emerge, the client is much better equipped to develop strategies for behavioral change.

Karen, 42 years old, had been married and divorced three times and was involved in a relationship with a man addicted to drugs and alcohol. A genogram helped Karen and her worker understand that all the men in Karen's life—her grandfather, father, and previous husbands—had been substance abusers with depressive personalities just like that of the man in her current relationship (see Figure 1.3).

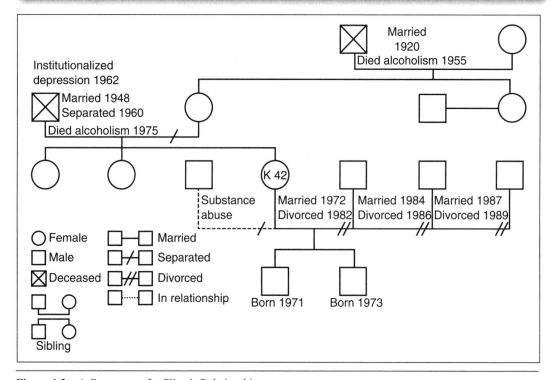

Figure 1.3 A Genogram of a Client's Relationships

Ecomap

Whereas the genogram identifies the historical ecology of the client, the ecomap identifies the client's current social context. The ecomap works by using circles to represent different factors affecting the client and by identifying other systems that have an interface with the client system. An ecomap of a family can also identify the exosystems, or those systems that affect other family members but do not have a direct impact on the identified client. The ecomap is constructed by having the client identify all the organizations that have some impact on his or her life. Each organization is depicted by a circle. The client then identifies the nature and direction of the flow of energy between the organization and self. Because this process meaningfully involves the client in identifying the current situation and pictorially expressing it

through the ecomap, the client may develop a better understanding of his or her situation and ultimately reveal strategies for resolving the dilemma.

Helen was a 39-year-old single mother who had recently moved into the community but continued to have strong ties to her former residence. Her 8-year-old daughter was experiencing problems resulting from the girl's father's decision to move out of the country. An ecomap helped the mother identify resources and supports in her new community (see Figure 1.4).

Social Network Map

A social network map is "a tangible aid that is proffered by social intimates or inferred by their presence and has beneficial emotional or behavioral effects on the recipient" (Gottlieb, 1983, p. 28). The social network map is used in tandem

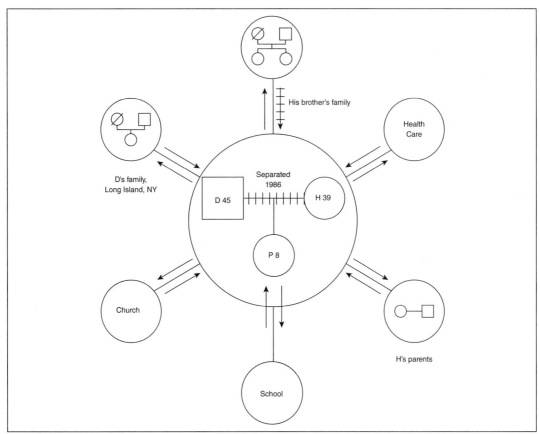

Figure 1.4 Ecomap

with the social network grid to identify and engage the client in defining his or her social supports. Social supports are important and can be classified into five interaction systems necessary for an individual's well-being: emotional integration, social integration, opportunity for nurturance, reassurance of worth, and assistance (Friedman, 1994, p. 16). They enable the individual to negotiate problematic situations and sustain well-being.

The social network map consists of concentric rings, with the client identified as the innermost ring. The client is then asked to identify supports and place them on the map, quantifying the amount of support received through placement in closer proximity to the center of the map—that is, the closer to the center, the greater the amount of support provided to the client. The tandem social network grid is used as a means of quantifying the level of support the client receives from his or her network. This is not an objective measure but is based on the client's subjective perceptions in identifying the valence of the support.

> Mark, 40 years old and homeless, had bounced around from shelter to shelter and was linked to the formal support system. However, he had no informal support system, as a network map revealed. This became a tool in building positive informal supports that helped him sustain a job and independent housing (see Figure 1.5).

CONCLUSION

Social work has been defined as "the professional activity of helping individuals, groups, or communities enhance or restore their capacity for social functioning and creating societal conditions favorable to this goal" (Barker, 2003, p. 357). This definition emphasizes the role of the professional in understanding the client system within its ecological environment to build on client strengths. Social work clinicians need a theoretical framework that will enhance their understanding of person-in-environment interactions, which the ecosystems perspective can provide.

Regardless of the system's size (individual, family, group, or community), an ecosystems perspective provides an interactional view of any system within the context of its environment. The environmental context includes the interplay among multiple influences—biological, psychological, social, and spiritual. The role of the worker is to support the growth of the client system, a perspective that enables the clinician to work on multiple levels, incorporating other theories to develop strategies that address the person-in-environment change process. An ecosystems perspective places the focus on the interaction between the person and his or her environment rather than on one or the other. Since this perspective is not a theory but a method for organizing information, the worker uses other substantive theories, such as psychoanalytic or cognitive and behavioral theories, to help in the analysis of a particular person-in-environment interaction.

Germain, who was an influential social work theorist, adapted von Bertalanffy's and Bronfenbrenner's frameworks and created a social work model to describe person-in-environment interaction. She believed that the best method of analysis was to break down this interaction into its component parts—adaptation, life stress, coping, power, and human relatedness—to gain a clearer picture of client strengths. All systems interact with the environment as both causes and effects of a given situation, and it is important for the worker to understand fully the dynamic nature of this interaction. Just how the social worker chooses to gain that knowledge is left to the worker, since the ecosystems perspective does not dictate which tools to use but relies on the creativity of each worker to assess fully the dynamics of person-in-environment interaction.

Three specific tools—the genogram, the ecomap, and the social network map—were presented as methods for acquiring that knowledge. These tools demonstrate the variety of techniques that can be used to gain information about

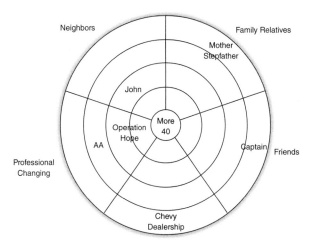

Neighbors — Family Relatives — Mother — Stepfather — John — More 40 — Operation Hope — AA — Captain — Friends — Professional Changing — Chevy Dealership — World Social Association

ID Respondent Name	#	Acess Of Life 1. Household 2. Other family 3. Work school 4. Organizations 5. Other friends 6. Neighbors 7. Professionals 8. Other	Concrete Support 1. Hardly ever 2. Some- times 3. Almost always	Emotional Support 1. Hardly ever 2. Some times 3. Almost always	Information/ Advice 1. Hardly ever 2. Some- times 3. Almost always	Critical 1. Hardly ever 2. Some- times 3. Almost always	Direction of Help 1. Goes both ways 2. You to them 3. Them to you	Closeness 1. Not very Close 2. Sort of close 3. Very close	How Often Seen 1. Few times 2. Monthly 3. Weekly 4. Daily 5. Does not see	How Long Known 1. Less than 1yr. 2. 1-5yr. 3. More than 5 yr.
Operation Hope	01	7	3	3	3	2	3	3	4	1
John	02	5/6	2	3	3	2	1	3	4	1
Chevy Dealership	03	3	3	1	1	1	2	1	4	1
AA	04	7	1	2	2	2	1	2	3	3
mother	05	2	1	1	1	3	2	1	1	3
Stepfather	06	2	1	1	1	3	2	1	1	3
Capital	07	5	1	1	1	2	2	2	4	2
	08									
	09									
	10									
	11									
	12									
	13									
	14									
	15									
1-6		7	8	9	10	11	12	13	14	15

Figure 1.5   Social Network Map

different aspects of systemic interaction. The more knowledge the worker has about person-in-environment interaction, the better informed he or she is and the better able to identify system strengths that will enhance or restore the client's social functioning.

REFERENCES

Anderson, R. E., Carter, I., & Lowe, G. R. (1999). Human behavior in the social environment (5th ed.). New York, NY: Aldine de Gruyter.

Barker, R. L. (2003). *The social work dictionary* (5th ed.). Washington, DC: NASW Press.

Bateson, G. (1972). *Steps to an ecology of mind.* San Francisco, CA: Chandler.

Bateson, G., Jackson, D. D., Haley, J., & Weakland, J. (1956). Toward a theory of schizophrenia. *Behavioral Science, 1,* 251–264.

Becvar, D. S., & Becvar, R. J. (2013). *Family therapy: A systematic integration (8th ed.).* Upper Saddle River, NJ: Pearson Education

Blackwell encyclopedia of sociology online. (2009). Retrieved March 29, 2009 from www.sociologyencyclopedia.com

Bowen, M. (1978). *Family therapy in clinical practice.* Northvale, NJ: Jason Aronson.

Bronfenbrenner, U. (1979). *The ecology of human development: Experiments by nature and design.* Cambridge, MA: Harvard University Press.

Carter, I. (2011). *Human behavior in the social environment* (6th ed.). Piscataway, NJ: Aldine Transaction.

Dale, O., & Smith, R. (2013). *Human behavior in the social environment: A social systems model* (7th ed.). Boston, MA: Allyn & Bacon.

Durkheim, É. (1984). *The division of labor in society* (2nd ed.). New York, NY: Macmillan.

Friedman, B. D. (1994). *No place like home: A study of two homeless shelters.* Ann Arbor, MI: University Microfilms International.

Germain, C. B. (1991). *Human behavior in the social environment: An ecological view.* New York, NY: Columbia University Press.

Gitterman, A., & Germain, C. B. (2008). *The life model of social work practice* (3rd ed.). New York, NY: Columbia University Press.

Goldstein, H. (1990). The knowledge base of social work practice: Theory, wisdom, analogue, or art? *Families in Society: The Journal of Contemporary Human Services, 71*(1), 32–43.

Gottlieb, B. (1983). *Social support strategies: Guidelines for mental health practice.* Beverly Hills, CA: Sage.

Gray, S.W., & Zide, M.R. (2013). *Psychopathology: a competency-based assessment model for social workers* (3rd ed.). Belmont, CA: Brooks/Cole.

Greene, R. R. (2008). *Human behavior theory and social work practice* (3rd ed.). New Brunswick, NJ: Aldine Transactions.

Hearn, G. (1958). *Theory-building in social work.* Toronto, Ontario, Canada: University of Toronto Press.

Holman, A. M. (1983). *Family assessment: Tools for understanding and intervention.* Beverly Hills, CA: Sage.

Kihlstrom, A. (2012) Luhmann's system theory in social work: Criticism and reflections. *Journal of Social Work, 12*(3), 287–299.

Lewin, K. (1935). *A dynamic theory of personality.* New York, NY: McGraw-Hill.

Lewin, K. (1976). *Field theory as human science.* New York, NY: Gardner Press.

Luhmann, N. (1995). *Social systems.* Stanford, CA: Stanford University Press.

Merton, R. K. (1938). Social structure and anomie. *American Sociological Review, 3*(5), 672–682.

Meyer, C. H. (1976). *Social work practice* (2nd ed.). New York, NY: Free Press.

Meyer, C. H. (Ed.). (1983). *Clinical social work in the eco-systems perspective.* New York, NY: Columbia University Press.

Minuchin Center for the family. (n.d). *Structural family therapy.* Retrieved from http://minuchincenter.org/structural_family_therapy

Minuchin, S. (1974). *Families and family therapy.* Boston: Harvard University Press.

Minuchin, S., & Fishman, H.C. (1981). *Family therapy techniques.* Cambridge, MA: Harvard University Press.

Parsons, T. (1951). *The social system.* Glencoe, IL: Free Press.

Robbins, S. P., Chatterjee, P., & Canda, E. R. (2012). *Contemporary human behavior theory: A critical perspective for social work* (3rd ed.). Boston, MA: Allyn & Bacon.

Satir, V. (1967). *Conjoint family therapy: A guide to theory and technique.* Palo Alto, CA: Science and Behavior Books.

Sheafor, B. W., & Horejsi, C. R. (2012). *Techniques and guidelines for social work practice* (9th ed.). Boston, MA: Allyn & Bacon.

Shulman, L. (2009). *The skills of helping: Individuals, families, groups, and communities* (6th ed.). Pacific Grove, CA: Brooks/Cole.

Siporin, M. (1980). Ecological systems theory in social work. *Journal of Sociology and Social Welfare, 7*(4), 5–7, 32.

Tönnies, F. (1887). *Gemeinschaft und Gesellschaft,* Leipzig: Fues's Verlag. (Translated, 1957 by Charles Price Loomis as *Community and Society).* East Lansing: Michigan State University Press.

von Bertalanffy, L. (1968). *General system theory: Foundation, development, application.* New York, NY: George Braziller.

2

BEHAVIORAL AND COGNITIVE THEORIES

BRUCE A. THYER AND LAURA L. MYERS

We don't expect to change human nature, we people of peace, but we do expect to change human behavior.

—Jane Addams (as cited in Linn, 1935, p. 416)

One person changes the behavior of another by changing the world in which he lives. In doing so, he no doubt changes what the other person feels or introspectively observes.

—B. F. Skinner (1974, p. 181)

Behavioral theory is one of the oldest and most extensive theories applied to clinical social work. Over 80 years ago, the distinguished social work educator Virginia Robinson (1930) provided the following observations in this regard:

Two dominant schools of thought may be recognized as differentiating case work approach and treatment at the present time; behaviorist psychology and psychiatric interpretation. The former emphasizes habit training, conditioning and reconditioning in treatment. . . . Illustrations of a partial use of this psychology in treatment are abundant in any case work area. (pp. 83–84)

This was followed by similarly positive remarks from Frank Bruno (1934) in one of the earliest books explicitly dealing with theory for social work practice:

Behaviorism may be described as the theory that learning is the association of a new impression with the circumstances present at the time of receiving it. It has several obvious merits. It integrates emotion and intellect in a manner which realistically reproduces actual experience. It is socially acceptable, in the main, as it places such large faith upon capacity to learn, given the right conditions for association . . . behaviorism affords a first-class technic without specializing in the abnormal. . . . It is invaluable for the social worker in his efforts to understand the conduct of his clients, because it refers him back to the past experiences in which are to be found the particular circumstances which have determined the attitude or the habitual responses for each individual. Thus behaviorism opens up endless possibilities for social work. . . . It is also of value in treatment, for some of the most interesting work of the behaviorists has been in the field of what is called reconditioning. (pp. 197–198)

During the next two decades, behavioral theory was overshadowed by the rise of psychodynamic theorizing within clinical work, but in the 1960s, the behavioral approach reappeared (see Thomas, 1967) as a major orientation, along with cognitive-behavioral theories and therapies (see Werner, 1965), and both can now be considered mainstream perspectives for clinical social work. In a survey of social workers published in 1978, Jayaratne found behavioral approaches to be a preferred theoretical orientation by over one third of the respondents. More recently, Strom (1994) surveyed a random sample of practicing clinical social workers and found that 67% used a cognitive-behavioral orientation in their work and 32% employed a behavioral orientation (respondents could report using more than one theoretical orientation). The behavioral/cognitive-behavioral perspective was employed by more social workers than were respected models such as systems (reportedly used by 53% of the respondents), ecological (11%), task centered (48%), and ego psychology (53%), being exceeded in use only by the psychodynamic (83%) orientation.

Most schools of social work now provide some level of training in behavioral theory and practice (Thyer & Maddox, 1988), and the majority of the controlled-outcome studies on the effectiveness of social work practice that yielded positive results were based on behavioral social work methods (MacDonald, Sheldon, & Gillespie, 1992; Reid & Hanrahan, 1982). More recently, Gorey, Thyer, and Pawluck's (1998) meta-analysis of social work outcome studies similarly concluded that "the empirical social work practice knowledge base is much greater for cognitive-behavioral models" (p. 274).

Reid and Fortune (2003) reviewed 107 published experiments with positive outcomes in social work practice and found that 49% referred to the use of behavioral and/or cognitive interventions. Most general social work practice textbooks contain content on social learning theory (SLT), and a large literature exclusively devoted to behavioral social work now exists (Thyer, 1981a, 1985). Reid (2004) summarized this approach as follows:

> Connections between behavior and its consequences form the central concern of operant theory. The theory is of particular importance in evidence-based social work practice, because it is one of the few theories used in social work that is firmly based in empirical research. (p. 36)

Behavioral and cognitive-behavioral perspectives are sufficiently encompassing as to have applicability to virtually all areas of social work practice, from clinical work with individuals (Thyer, 1988), couples, families, and groups, to community practice (Greene, Winett, Van Houten, Geller, & Iwata, 1987; Rothman & Thyer, 1984), to the formulation of social welfare policies (Thyer, 1996), and to other forms of macrolevel practice (Thyer, 2008). Indeed, the entire Master of Social Work (MSW) curriculum could be centered on contemporary SLT and behavioral-cognitive methods of practice (Thyer & Wodarski, 1990), in a manner similar to that of the singular orientations found in the schools of social work at Smith College (psychodynamic) and the University of Pennsylvania (functionalist) in earlier days. Carey and Foster (2013) recently asserted that " . . . there is perhaps a case to be made that . . . behaviourism . . . has provided a pragmatic and 'common sense' foundation upon which so much social work practice has been consistently applied" (p. 254).

BEHAVIORAL THEORY AND CLINICAL SOCIAL WORK

A behavioral approach to clinical social work rests on a conceptual foundation known as *social learning theory*—that is, learning theories used to explain social behavior. The empirically supported learning theories that comprise SLT involve the processes of respondent conditioning, operant conditioning, and observational learning. Together, these three ways in which human beings learn form a theory of normative human growth and development (Bijou, 1993; Schlinger, 1995; Thyer, 1992a), a framework for conceptualizing so-called psychopathology (Ullman & Krasner, 1969), a comprehensive theory of human personality (Lundin, 1974), and a widely applicable approach to clinical practice (Thyer, 1983).

The general field of behavioral social work can be defined as follows:

> Behavioral social work is the informed use by professional social workers of assessments and interventions based on empirically derived learning theories. These theories include, but are not limited to, respondent learning, operant learning, and observational learning. Behavioral social workers may or may not subscribe to the philosophy of science known as *behaviorism*. (Thyer & Hudson, 1987, p. 1)

Behaviorism is a philosophy of science that contains certain assumptions and positions regarding ontology, epistemology, ethics, determinism, language, and so on (see Thyer, 1999). The axiomatic foundations of behaviorism as a philosophy are much more debatable in terms of their validity than are questions about the effectiveness of behavioral *methods,* such as the value of contingency management in helping drug abusers remain sober. Many practitioners, while appreciating and applying the *methods* of behavioral intervention, remain unconvinced as to the merits of its underlying philosophical foundations. This is of course legitimate, and as long as clients are being effectively served, the philosophical beliefs of the social worker are of less significance.

Setting aside philosophy, the basic empirical principles of SLT are relatively simple and uncontroversial:

1. Human behavior consists of what we do—both observable behavior and unobservable behavior: overt acts, covert speech, thoughts and cognition, feelings, and dreams. All those phenomena that people engage in are considered behavior.

2. To a large extent, much (but not all) of human behavior is learned through life experiences. This learning occurs throughout the life span.

3. It seems very likely that similar fundamental learning processes give rise to individual human behavior across cultures and life circumstances and account for both normative and many so-called dysfunctional actions, feelings, and thoughts.

4. Interpersonal behavior is also a function of these learning processes, giving rise to dyadic, group, organizational, community, and societal phenomena. These larger-scale activities are, to a great extent, a more complex operation of fundamental learning mechanisms.

5. There are at least three major empirically supported learning processes that collectively comprise SLT: respondent learning, operant learning, and observational learning.

Note that *behavior* is defined as what a person does—whether it can be observed or not. Thoughts and feelings are seen as being as much a part of the body's behavior as is publicly observable action. Moreover, all aspects of behavior, overt action, thoughts, and feelings, are seen as strongly influenced by respondent, operant, and observational learning and can potentially be therapeutically modified through the informed, professional use of such learning mechanisms. While it is true that the early behaviorist John Watson defined psychology as the study of overt behavior only, in the 1930s and 1940s, B. F. Skinner attempted to apply learning theory principles to the analysis of private events—phenomena such as thoughts and feelings occurring beneath the skin. It is not true that behavioral practice is concerned only with the client's observable activities. Many aspects of client problems involve affective states (feelings) and thoughts and are a central focus of behavioral assessment and intervention. Also, it is not true that behaviorists claim that all behavior is learned. They do claim that much is learned and that what is learned or not learned through SLT is an empirical question to be answered through data-based experimentation and naturalistic observation, not by theoretical argumentation. (See Thyer, 2005, for a review of common misrepresentations of the behavioral position found in the social work literature and corrective information.)

Behavioral theorists are modest in their claims, quite content that the processes on which they focus are an important part of understanding clinical phenomena but not inherently denying the potential role of other variables (e.g., biology, genetics). It is up to the advocates of other approaches to demonstrate both the validity of their theory and the effectiveness of the clinical social work treatments derived from that theory. To the extent that they do so, in accordance with the empirical, scientific, and analytical approach on which clinical social work is based, it is well and good. The profession is well served, as are clients, which is more important than theoretical squabbles.

Behaviorally oriented clinical social workers do take justifiable pride in noting the close match between SLT and the traditional person-in-environment approach of social work practice. Examine the following quotations. The first three are from the behavioral perspective:

> Men act upon the world and change it, and are changed in turn by the consequences of their action. Certain processes which the human organism shares with other species, alter behavior so that it achieves a safer and more useful interchange with a particular environment. When appropriate behavior has been established, its consequences work through similar processes to keep it in force. If by chance the environment changes, new forms of behavior disappear, while new consequences build new forms. (Skinner, 1957, p. 1)
>
> Most behavioral science emphasizes the power of the environment; it sees environment as constantly controlling behavior, and it sees behavior as constantly affecting the environment. Indeed, the point of most behavior is to affect the environment. (Baer & Pinkston, 1997, p. 1)
>
> Behaviorism's environmentalism does not imply that the organism passively reacts to the environment. The relationship between the organism and the environment is interdependent and reciprocal. . . . That is, although the organism interacts with its environment, its reaction also changes the environment. The organism is then influenced by an environment changed by its own behavior, behaves again, changes the environment again, and so on. Thus the organism's relationship to its environment is one of mutual influence. (O'Donohue & Ferguson, 2001, p. 57)

Here are some quotations from the social work perspective:

> Behavior is the result of the effort of the person to establish himself in his environment in such a way as to give satisfaction to himself. (Bruno, 1934, p. 45)
>
> Flexibility, change, and movement are of the very nature of social interaction. It is no wonder that social workers give close attention to behavior, which is the pulse of the human organism's attempts at adaptation. (Hamilton, 1940, p. 305)
>
> The human being and the environment reciprocally shape each other. People mold their environments in many ways and, in turn, they must then adapt to the changes they created. (Germain, as cited in Bloom, 1992, p. 407)
>
> [The ecosystems perspective is about] . . . building more supportive, helpful and nurturing environments for clients through environmental helping, and increasing their competence in dealing with the environment by teaching basic life skills. (Whittaker & Garbarino, 1983, p. 34)
>
> The ecological perspective makes clear the need to view people and environments as a unitary system within a particular cultural and historic context. Both person and environment can be fully understood in terms of their relationship, in which each continually influences the other within a particular context. . . . Ecological thinking examines exchanges between A and B, for example, that shape, influence, or change both over time. A acts, which leads to a change in B, whereupon the change in B elicits a change in A that in turn changes B, which then changes or otherwise influences A, and so on. (Germain & Gitterman, 1995, p. 816)
>
> A basic assumption . . . is that human behavior is the product of the interactions between the individual and environment. (Northen, 1995, p. 165)

The parallels between the two perspectives are striking, so much so that it would seem that contemporary social workers are reinventing the wheel, autonomously crafting what they call a "P-I-E" perspective while remaining largely ignorant of the SLT antecedents of current models, or are simply choosing to ignore the similarities between the two approaches.

The social learning theorist cites with approval the view of John Howard Griffin (1960), author of *Black Like Me:*

> You place the white man in the ghetto, deprive him of educational advantages, arrange it so he has to struggle hard to fulfill his instinct for self-respect, give him little physical privacy and less leisure, and he would after a time assume the same characteristics you attach to the negro. These characteristics don't spring from whiteness or blackness, but from a man's *conditioning* [italics added]. (p. 89)

We will next turn to a review of the basic principles of SLT. Each type of learning that is described will be followed by an example of its operation in everyday life, then by an illustration of a clinical phenomenon, and finally with one or more brief practice vignettes.

RESPONDENT LEARNING

> The wounded body shrinks even from a gentle touch.
>
> —Ovid

Everyday Examples of Respondent Learning

After the birth of her son John, Laura decided to breast-feed him. When John cried, she would place him at her breast, and he would nurse. After a few moments, her milk would let down and begin to flow. After a week or so, Laura noticed that she experienced milk flow when she picked up the baby as he was crying; it was no longer necessary for him to nurse before she let down. In respondent learning terms, John's nursing at the breast is an unconditioned stimulus, producing the unconditioned response of the release of milk. John's crying (and Laura's picking him up preparatory to nursing) was initially neutral; it had no effect on milk flow. However, after being repeatedly paired in time with the (preceding) physical unconditioned stimulus of nursing, his crying became a conditioned stimulus, which produced the conditioned response of milk flow.

During the winter months, as the air became less humid, Bruce received a shock from static electricity when he touched the car door handle. After this happened a few times, he began hesitating to touch the car door and sometimes had to force himself to do so. Initially, the door handle is a neutral stimulus. After being mildly painfully shocked (an unconditioned stimulus) a few times and snatching his hand away (avoidance, an unconditioned response to the shock), Bruce began avoiding (the conditioned response) touching the door handle (which had now become a conditioned stimulus). As spring approached, Bruce stopped getting shocks when he touched the car door. With repeated touches in the absence of shock, his hesitancy in touching it declined and eventually vanished (until the next winter!). This illustrates the process of respondent extinction.

Clinical Examples of Respondent Learning

Some patients undergoing cancer chemotherapy experience severe nausea after the drugs are intravenously administered. Initially, clinic stimuli (sights, sounds, smells, staff, etc.) are neutral events. The chemotherapy is an unconditioned stimulus for the unconditioned response of nausea and emesis, with the latter being natural or unlearned responses. After a number of episodes of entering the clinic, receiving the medication, and becoming nauseated, some patients become ill prior to receiving the medication, often on entering the clinic itself. In this case, previously neutral aspects of the clinic, paired with the unconditioned stimulus of the medication, become a conditioned stimulus, eliciting the conditioned response of nausea in the absence of the chemotherapy.

In a case reported by a clinical social worker (Shorkey & Taylor, 1973), a child who was hospitalized for the treatment of severe burns was receiving debridement therapy, a very painful procedure. After a number of treatment sessions, which took place in the child's hospital room, the child began screaming and thrashing about when the nurses providing debridement treatments merely entered the room. His severe reaction threatened the healing process and made it very difficult to treat him. The debridement therapy can be viewed as an unconditioned stimulus (he did not learn to feel pain as his severe burns were being treated), and the pain and thrashing about during these treatments can be seen as an unconditioned response (almost everyone withdraws and cries out in response to severe pain). In time, the sight of the nursing staff in their distinctive uniforms became a conditioned stimulus, producing the conditioned response of crying and thrashing.

Clinical Treatment Using Respondent Conditioning

At the age of 67, a retired professor was attacked and severely bitten by a large dog and required emergency room treatment and painful stitches. Subsequently, she developed a severe fear of dogs, meeting the criteria for a specific phobia. Her life became dominated by her fear of dogs, being preoccupied with anticipating situations where she might encounter dogs, even when the dreaded beasts were not around. Treatment consisted of social-worker-assisted gradual exposure to small dogs in the controlled setting of the consulting room and in the natural environment. Using conventional clinical skills (support, encouragement, humor, reinforcement for successive approximations, etc.), the social worker helped her become much less fearful, and she was able to resume her life unimpaired by her morbid fears. (See Thyer, 1981b, for a fuller clinical description of this client's treatment.)

In this true example, the dog was initially a neutral stimulus, and being bitten was an unconditioned stimulus. The unconditioned response is the emotional reaction of fear and avoidance behavior. After the attack, dogs in general had become a conditioned stimulus, evoking the conditioned responses of fear and avoidance, even if they were nonthreatening. Gradual real-life exposure therapy has such an impressive degree of empirical support that it can be considered a first-choice treatment for phobic disorders (Nathan & Gorman, 2007; Wilson, 1989).

Patients experiencing pretreatment nausea following cancer chemotherapy have been taught progressive relaxation (PR) training skills. Relaxation inherently inhibits nausea, and by first learning PR techniques with the social worker outside the chemotherapy clinic, patients can then practice them in the clinic itself. Pairing relaxation with clinic stimuli can reduce or eliminate respondently learned pretreatment nausea (see Boynton & Thyer, 1994). Thyer (2012a) provides a lengthier exposition of respondent learning theory, with both everyday and clinical examples, than can be presented here.

OPERANT LEARNING

> Verily there is a reward for the righteous.
>
> —Psalms 58:11

The concept of positive reinforcement has entered our everyday lexicon, but even well-trained clinicians are sometimes confused by the distinctions among positive and negative reinforcement, positive and negative punishment, and extinction. Inasmuch as these are conceptually and practically different learning processes, it is worth distinguishing between them.

Colloquially, positive reinforcement can be labeled as *rewarding*. It occurs when a consequence is presented (hence, the word *positive*), and the behavior rewarded subsequently increases (becomes stronger, more frequent, or is maintained) in the future (with such strengthening giving rise to the word *reinforcement*). Negative reinforcement can be familiarly construed as *relief*. If a behavior's consequence consists of removing something unpleasant and the behavior is subsequently strengthened, then negative reinforcement is involved.

Positive punishment occurs when a behavior's consequence consists of presenting something aversive, which results in a decrease in the likelihood of that behavior. Because something is presented, the term *positive* is used. Because the result is a decrease in behavior, the operation is called *punishment*. As you might suspect, negative punishment involves the removal (hence, *negative*) of something pleasant, resulting in a decrease (hence, *punishment*) in the future probability of that behavior. Colloquially, think of negative punishment as operating similarly to a fine. The following illustrations describe these different behavioral operations more concretely. It is common for social workers to think that the terms *punishment* and *negative reinforcement* mean the same thing. They do not. Negative reinforcement is good. People like getting reinforced, whereas virtually no one likes being punished.

Operant extinction can occur with behaviors being maintained through reinforcement. If the reinforcers are discontinued, the behavior may strengthen temporarily (this is called an *extinction burst*) but will then decline and ultimately cease entirely. Interestingly, behaviors maintained with a continuous schedule of reinforcement (every time a behavior occurs, reinforcement follows) are easier to extinguish than behavior with a history of being reinforced only every now and then. Behaviors that occasionally yield reinforcing consequences are sometimes very durable and quite resistant to extinction. People will persist in repeating a particular behavior for long periods of time if in their past this sometimes resulted in reinforcement (particularly if the reinforcers are particularly powerful ones).

Examples of Positive Reinforcement

A child volunteers to answer in class and is praised by her teacher for answering. Volunteering is strengthened. Here, praise and social approbation are functioning as a reinforcing consequence.

A youth desirous of being accepted by a street gang must pass an initiation test—perhaps stealing something from a local shopping mall. He commits the crime and is lavishly praised by the established members of the gang. Here, social praise is serving to positively reinforce dysfunctional (in the long run) behavior.

Smoking crack produces an immediate and intense rush, a highly pleasurable sensation that lasts for a few minutes and then subsides. Almost anything that enables one to gain access to crack will be strengthened by this positively reinforcing experience. Burglary, prostitution, and robbery are examples of behaviors that can be maintained in part by the positive consequences of smoking crack.

Clinical Practice Using Positive Reinforcement

In a group home for chronically mentally ill individuals, the activity therapist provided the clients with an exercise bicycle, hoping they would voluntarily ride it. Instead, it gathered dust, despite its strategic location in the TV room. After one week, she arranged to positively reinforce riding short distances on the exercise bike with contingent low-calorie snacks. The miles ridden by the residents soared. This was continued for a week and then discontinued for 7 days to see if maybe they would now ride on their own. Instead, bike riding plummeted. During the fourth week, contingent snacks were once again made available for riding the exercise bike, and mileage once again dramatically increased. The contingent snack program was thereafter left in place as a regular part of the group home's programming to encourage the clients to get some aerobic exercise (see Thyer, Irvine, & Santa, 1984, for additional data and details).

Examples of Negative Reinforcement

You step out into the bright sunlight, and your eyes hurt. Putting on sunglasses alleviates the pain. In the future, you are more likely to put on your sunglasses in bright light.

A crack addict has gone for a prolonged period without using the drug. A profound dysphoric mood and unpleasant physical sensations occur, caused by the drug's withdrawal symptoms. Reusing crack temporarily produces relief from these noxious sensations and moods. Using crack is thus also negatively reinforcing (producing relief) the drug-seeking behavior in the established addict who is experiencing withdrawal.

Clinical Practice Using Negative Reinforcement

Barth (1986, p. 155) describes a practice vignette where brief periods of time-out or social isolation are used with a disruptive boy in a group work setting. If he sits still and is quiet for a brief period, he is allowed to rejoin the group. In this illustration, if it is assumed that being in time-out is aversive, then being released from time-out contingent on appropriate behavior is used to negatively reinforce such behavior.

Examples of Positive Punishment

A child uses a curse word in front of a parent and is slapped hard across the mouth. In the future, the child uses that curse word less often in front of that parent. In this case, an aversive stimulus (the slap) is presented, and the subsequent effect on behavior is a reduction.

A husband carefully prepares a gourmet meal and serves it to his wife when she returns home from a hard day at the office. Instead of praising his efforts, she throws the meal at him, heats up a microwave dinner, and pops open a beer while criticizing his culinary efforts. If gourmet cooking for his wife declines in frequency, it can be said that his spouse positively punished such behavior through her contingent aversive criticism and by her throwing the hot food at him.

Clinical Practice Using Positive Punishment

An 11-year-old boy, Mark, who lived in a Salvation Army group home, swore profusely at the dinner table. Despite the efforts of the cottage parents, coaxing and other forms of verbal persuasion had no effect on reducing Mark's profanity. After consultation with a social worker, the cottage parents took an unobtrusive baseline of the frequency of Mark's swearing during the 30-minute dinner period. After 5 days, Mark was informed that he would have to wash cottage windows for 10 minutes each time he swore. Failure to complete his window washing assignments satisfactorily could result in a curtailment of other privileges. After one day of the window-washing contingency, he virtually stopped swearing. After 2 weeks with little profanity, the contingent chore was discontinued, and regrettably, his swearing quickly increased, so after 5 days, window washing was reinstated. His swearing dropped to near-zero again, and it remained very low for the rest of the year. Because the aversive chore of window washing was presented to Mark, contingent on swearing, and the result was a decrease in the frequency of profanity, this procedure is appropriately labeled positive punishment (see Fischer & Nehs, 1978, for data and further details).

Examples of Negative Punishment

You are speeding along the highway, en route to the monthly meeting of the local clinical social work society, and you are pulled over by a policewoman because you were going too fast. The net result is that you lose a large sum of money (the fine). If you exceed the speed limit less often in the future, then speeding can be said to have been negatively punished.

A clinical social worker accurately records a client's diagnosis on insurance forms. Because of her truthfulness in revealing a marital problem as the focus of treatment, in lieu of a formal clinical disorder, the insurance company demands that the honest social worker repay some of the reimbursements already provided. If in the future the social worker becomes less truthful in completing insurance forms, telling the truth can be said to have been negatively punished.

Clinical Practice Using Negative Punishment

Young children meeting the criteria for attention deficit disorder with hyperactivity were given academic assignments to work on in class. If they stayed focused on their tasks, they had access to 20 minutes of playtime at the end of the work period. If their attention wandered and they were seen to

(Continued)

(Continued)

be not completing their assignments, the teacher flipped over a card on a stand, indicating that 1 minute of free time was deducted from their recess. Additional episodes of off-task behavior resulted in additional minutes being deducted from playtime. Compared with baseline levels of work and time on task during medication treatment (Ritalin), the response cost contingency (or fine) greatly promoted the children's attention to academic work, as well as accuracy. In this instance, something pleasant (playtime) was reduced contingent on undesirable behavior. While such contingencies were in effect, the undesirable behavior was greatly reduced; hence, this is an illustration of negative punishment (see Rapport, Murphy, & Bailey, 1982, for a complete description of this program).

Examples of Operant Extinction

Every time in your life you have turned on a light switch in your bathroom, the light turns on. One night, you go into the bathroom and flip the switch, but nothing happens. You will perhaps flip it a few more times but will eventually give up (and engage in some other more reinforcing behavior, e.g., changing the light bulb).

If you were so fortunate as to have won a large prize in your state's lottery, you might persist for many months or years in buying lottery tickets, particularly if sometimes you won another $5, $10, or $20. If you never won and never knew anyone else who ever won, it is likely that your lottery participation would drop off and stop completely (which is why states so cleverly arrange schedules of reinforcement of lottery winnings and widely advertise them to induce people to continue playing). There is a large literature on the power of various types of schedules of reinforcement; Ferster and Skinner (1957) is a good place to begin learning about these principles in detail.

Clinical Practice Using Operant Extinction

Anthony, an 11-year-old Black child, was severely intellectually disabled and lived in a residential facility because of his history of severe aggression. Any time anyone got within a few feet of Anthony, he would hit, kick, bite, scratch, or spit in an effort to get the person to move away. This behavior made it impossible for his parents to keep him in their home. To make a complex story very brief, assessment determined that Anthony found the close proximity of others to be aversive, and his aggression was speculated to be a negatively reinforced operant response. When he aggressed, he got what he wanted: People moved back and left him alone.

A trial treatment program was devised whereby the social worker (Bruce, wearing heavy clothes and gloves) would enter the playroom, which was well stocked with toys, and attempt to engage Anthony in play, all the while remaining within a couple of feet of him. No matter what aggressions Anthony performed (and they were many), Bruce did not move away or indicate pain. This treatment was construed as involving the principle of operant extinction. The reinforcers maintaining maladaptive behavior (aggression) were tentatively identified (people backing away, other reactions by

Anthony's victims), and it was hypothesized that stopping this pattern of negative reinforcement would lead to a reduction in aggression.

Detailed records were made of the frequency of Anthony's aggression, and over the 45-minute experimental treatment session, aggression dramatically declined. This result also occurred during a second 45-minute treatment session and justified several subsequent daylong treatments involving multiple staff. Similar results were obtained during these lengthier sessions, and after several such programs, Anthony's aggression was greatly reduced. Facility records of his aggression in nontreatment settings (e.g., school, dorm) revealed reductions in aggression following this treatment program. No punishment was ever employed in Anthony's treatment (see Figueroa, Thyer, & Thyer, 1992, for details on this case).

Here is another simple narrative example of the general approach called applied behavior analysis, drawn from the social work literature of over 40 years ago:

During the initial phases of a project integrating orthopedically handicapped children into groups of nonhandicapped children, no specific instructions were given to the group leaders regarding the degree of special attention they were to provide the handicapped children. After a few sessions, it was noticed that one leader appeared especially overprotective: Every time the handicapped child approached this leader, he was treated with excessive warmth and openness. At the direction of his supervisor, the leader observed the results of this interaction carefully. It became apparent that the leader was, in effect, rewarding passive, dependent behavior and that this was detrimental to the integrative attempts.

On the basis of this observation, the leader predicted that if he were to respond more critically to this behavior, that is, to redirect the handicapped child whenever feasible and realistic, the child would become less passive and more independent and would interact more with his peers (at this point, a hypothesis has been developed and a prediction made wherewith to test the hypothesis). The leader adopted this approach, and his prediction was borne out, namely, that a more objective response did affect the specific elements of behavior under consideration in a desirable fashion (Holmes, 1967, pp. 95–96).

This example illustrates the operant assessment and intervention process of conducting a functional analysis—carefully observing client behavior in its natural environment and then formulating initial ideas about what environmental consequences precede and follow both functional and dysfunctional behavior. Test these ideas by deliberately altering these antecedents and consequences and measure their effects on behavior, if any. If behavior can be regularly changed by changing the client's environment (e.g., providing reinforcement for a desired behavior resulting in it increasing or extinguishing an undesired behavior by removing its reinforcing consequences), this can provide valuable leads to more formal treatment planning, perhaps involving one or more of the approaches described by Stuart (1967):

> The client can learn to alter his responses to existing forces . . . in the environment. . . . The client can learn to alter his environment so that existing behaviors can yield desirable outcomes. . . . The client can learn to alter both his responses and his environment. (pp. 27–28)

Wong (2012) provides a very good overview of operant theory prepared from the perspective of social work practice, as does Reid (2004). Sundel and Sundel (2005) remains perhaps the best introductory textbook on the application of operant theory and therapy in the human services.

OBSERVATIONAL LEARNING

> For behaviour, men learn it, as they take diseases, one of another.
>
> —Francis Bacon

The use of observational learning, also known as *learning via imitation,* is a widespread method in behavioral social work. Modeling can be used to help a client acquire a new behavior through observing someone else perform the behavior, as opposed to instructing the client verbally without an actual demonstration of what is expected. Modeling and its associated practices of role playing and behavioral rehearsal can be used to help clients acquire social skills, assertiveness, daily living skills, and other adaptive behavior. The advancement of a well-articulated theory of observational learning has lagged behind the development of some well-established empirical principles regarding effective models. For example, people are more likely to imitate models who resemble them, imitating real-life models is more effective in producing behavior change than imitating written descriptions of behavior to

be modeled, models who are seen by clients being rewarded for displaying certain behaviors will likely be more effective in inducing the client to display the desired actions, and models who are seen to display imperfect performance initially and gradually become more competent are more effective than models who exhibit perfect behavior on the first attempt (see Rosenthal & Bandura, 1978).

Observational learning was a major component in the assertiveness training approach developed by social workers Eileen Gambrill and Cheryl Richey (1976) and Sandra Sundel and Martin Sundel (1980). Modeling was also used by Butterfield and Parson (1973) to help parents teach their mentally disabled child to develop skills in chewing solid food. Sheldon Rose has published a series of outcome studies on social work with groups, with the group work serving as the context in which members role-play, model, rehearse, and practice new interpersonal skills (see Gammon & Rose, 1991, for one such example). Modeling is widely used as a component of behavioral marital and family therapy, for social skills training in a variety of clinical contexts, and for helping clients overcome pathological fears (e.g., Komhaber & Schroeder, 1975).

There does remain controversy over whether observational learning is a distinct method of acquiring new behavior or if it is a special form of operant learning (Baer & Deguchi, 1985). Certainly, it is a fundamental method of acquiring behavior. It appears that humans have the capacity of learning through imitation virtually from birth, and observational learning is well documented among animals (see Thyer, 1992a; Zentall, 2006). It makes sense that if modeled behavior is reinforced, both the new behavior and the likelihood of imitation are strengthened. Beginning this process as infants, it would seem that generalized skills in observational learning would become well established by the time one reaches adulthood (which is typically the case). Many experiments with humans have shown that if imitated behavior is reinforced, the likelihood of imitation is greatly strengthened. If imitated behavior never produced reinforcing consequences, would imitation continue? It seems unlikely.

Keep in mind that it is not people who are reinforced, punished, or extinguished, it is behavior. It is not correct to state, "I reinforced the client"; the correct statement is "I reinforced the client's self-disclosure" (or some other action).

SUMMARY ON SOCIAL LEARNING THEORY

The illustrations and case presentations discussed so far represent extremely simple examples of behavioral phenomena influenced by SLT and their practical applications to clinical social work. However, by building on these elementary principles, researchers have developed sophisticated theoretical accounts for some very complex clinical phenomena. For example, social worker Richard Stuart (1980) has put forth a conceptual model of marital discord and an extensive model of marital therapy based almost exclusively on operant principles, and Gerald Patterson (1982) has similarly employed this approach in conceptualizing and intervening in dysfunctional families.

Using SLT, Ivar Lovaas developed and tested a psychosocial intervention for autistic youth, which, when applied early and intensively enough, resulted in normative emotional and intellectual functioning for about 50% of the clients when followed up some years later (Lovaas, 1987; McEachin, Smith, & Lovaas, 1993). Gordon Paul devised and rigorously evaluated a psychosocial treatment for persons with chronic mental illness (schizophrenia), which resulted in earlier discharge from the hospital, less recidivism, less aberrant behavior, and virtually no use of psychotropic medications, compared with standard treatment (Paul & Lentz, 1977; Paul & Menditto, 1992). Nathan Azrin has tested a community reinforcement approach to helping alcoholics, with dramatic positive results in terms of long-term abstinence (Azrin, 1976). Clearly, it would be a mistake to discount behavioral methods as appropriate only for developing

theoretical models of simple problems such as enuresis or phobia. Some of the most difficult and recalcitrant issues social workers deal with are being effectively addressed using behavioral methods, and this conceptual framework has much to offer the field (Thyer, 2012b).

COGNITIVE THEORY

> People are disturbed not by things, but by the views they take of them.
>
> —Epictetus

Cognitive theory has been a viable model of clinical social work practice for over three decades, beginning with Harold Werner's (1965) early work describing the applications of Albert Ellis's rational emotive therapy (RET) approach to the field. Most practice textbooks that address behavioral social work practice either subsume cognitive therapy in the behavioral chapter or deal with it as a separate chapter in its own right (e.g., Werner, 1979). What exactly distinguishes cognitive therapy from mainstream behavior therapy is sometimes a confusing issue, because almost all cognitive theory is an expansion or extension of SLT rather than its repudiation. Cognitive therapists do not disavow the validity of the principles of respondent, operant, and observational learning. Rather, they claim that there are additional elements that need to be considered in arriving at an etiological understanding of clients, in assessment, and in devising treatments. A number of these elements follow (Scott, 1995, p. 123):

1. Individuals respond to cognitive representations of environmental events rather than to the events per se.

2. Learning is cognitively mediated.

3. Cognition mediates emotional and behavioral dysfunction.

4. At least some forms of cognition can be monitored.

5. At least some forms of cognition can be altered.

6. As a corollary to Assumptions 3 to 5, altering cognition can change dysfunctional patterns of emotion and behavior.

7. Both cognitive and behavioral therapeutic change methods are desirable and can be integrated.

There are four major types of interventions in cognitive therapy (Fischer, 1978, pp. 177–187):

1. Changing misconceptions, unrealistic expectations, and other faulty ideas

2. Modifying irrational statements to oneself

3. Enhancing problem-solving and decision-making abilities

4. Enhancing self-control and self-management

Wodarski and Bagarozzi (1979) note that "all models assume that cognitive behaviors comply with the same laws that influence the control of overt behaviors" (p. 200), while Werner (1982) states that "the cognitive therapist fully supports the use of a learning theory (behavior modification) approach" (p. 61). Albert Ellis (1994), the founder of the widely popular *rational emotive therapy,* later changed the name of his model to rational emotive *behavior* therapy, which he said more accurately reflected his views on the relationship between cognitive and behavioral therapy, and Aaron Beck's seminal work on cognitive therapy for clinically anxious clients describes mainstream behavior therapy procedures such as assertiveness training, breathing exercises, exposure therapy, modeling, and homework exercises (Beck & Emery, 1985).

The difference between behavior therapy and cognitive therapy has been succinctly stated by Werner (1982): "The cognitivist says that the primary determinant of emotion and behavior is thinking" (p. 3). Accordingly, much of cognitive therapy consists of carefully listening to clients, asking them to describe significant events in their lives and what happened both externally and internally, in an attempt to isolate possible irrational or other dysfunctional ways of thinking

that purportedly mediate maladaptive overt actions and covert emotions.

The cognitive theory of RET postulates the following:

> People usually create self-defeating feelings and behaviors by constructing irrational or self-defeating beliefs. . . . RET holds that when people take their strong preferences or desires for success, love or comfort, and define them as musts and commands, they tend to make themselves grandiosely anxious, depressed, hostile, and self-pitying. (Kendall et al., 1995, p. 170)

Originally, in the 1950s and 1960s, Ellis (see Ellis & Grieger, 1977) developed a listing of 11 or so major categories of irrational beliefs derived from his clinical experience, a list that rapidly grew to several hundred specific types. More recently, he refined these into a much smaller number of central core irrational cognitions, which are maintained to be etiologically related to certain emotional, cognitive, and behavioral disorders, as can be seen from the following examples:

1. I must be thoroughly competent, adequate, achieving, and lovable at all times, or else I am an incompetent worthless person.

2. Other significant people in my life must treat me kindly and fairly at all times, or else I can't stand it, and they are bad, rotten, and evil persons who should be severely blamed, damned, and vindictively punished for their horrible treatment of me.

3. Things and conditions absolutely must be the way I want them to be and must never be too difficult or frustrating. Otherwise, life is awful, terrible, horrible, catastrophic, and unbearable. (Kendall et al., 1995, p. 172).

Treatment in Ellis's model (Ellis & Grieger, 1977) consists of listening to the clients describe events in their lives wherein they became angry, fearful, depressed, and so forth and in inquiring as to the thoughts that occurred following these ostensibly upsetting events. RET uses an ABC model of cognitive theory, with A being the activating event (what happened in the client's life), B being the irrational beliefs the client said to herself, and C being the consequence—the emotions, other thoughts, and behaviors following the reiteration of the irrational belief(s). In most cases, the therapist can elicit the client's having made one or more irrational self-statements of the type described. The social worker can then educate the client to the effect that it was not the environmental events that upset her but rather what she had covertly told herself regarding those events. Further work involves teaching the client to construct more rational self-statements and to practice these during daily life when encountering troubling events. The theory is that as rational self-talk replaces irrational beliefs, pathological behavior, affect, and thoughts will be eliminated. To a large extent, RET consists of a deliberate psychoeducational effort at producing a profound philosophical reorientation on the part of the client, aligning the person with new, more rational core beliefs to replace the irrational ones causing distress. This approach is not without controversy, of course. Who decides what constitutes a "rational" belief? The usual collection of dead European men? Albert Ellis? The social worker? The client?

Cognitive theory as developed by Aaron Beck (see Beck & Emery, 1985) has produced another well-developed model of practice that, like RET, enjoys a strong tradition of empirical research support as being highly effective for a growing number of clinical disorders. Originally developed for work with seriously depressed clients, Beck's version of cognitive theory is being applied to nearly the entire spectrum of *Diagnostic and Statistical Manual of Mental Disorders* (*DSM*) defined conditions, including affective disorders, anxiety disorders, and personality disorders. Rather than postulating irrational beliefs as the etiological source of pathology, Beck claims the existence of a construct he calls "cognitive sets" (the distinctions between Beck's and Ellis's views continue to elude the finest brains in psychotherapy). As in RET, clinicians using Beck's cognitive theory help patients in an educational and instructional process to identify covert faulty thinking using a variety of verbal tools. Among these are "counting automatic thoughts" (e.g., "There's another fearful thought. I'll just count it and let it go"), asking questions (e.g., "Where is the logic?" "Are you thinking in all-or-none terms?"), generating alternative interpretations, and normalizing anxiety (or depression, or something else), among quite literally dozens of specific techniques (see Beck & Emery, 1985, for a review).

Other specific approaches to therapy that rely on some variation of cognitive theory include Meichenbaum's stress inoculation training, D'Zurilla and Goldfried's problem-solving training, Rehm's self-control therapy, Barlow's panic control treatment, and Linehan's dialectical behavior therapy for persons meeting the criteria for borderline personality disorder (see Hollon & Beck, 1994, for a review).

There are a large number of clinical assessment instruments designed to measure clients' reports of irrational cognitions (there is no way to measure cognitions directly, of course), and considerable correlational research has demonstrated associations between reported irrational beliefs and client problems (e.g., Himle, Thyer, & Papsdorf, 1982). Such studies corroborate (but do not prove) the hypothesis that irrational beliefs cause pathological states.

Cognitive theory (and its associated therapies) has spawned a number of professional organizations and journals. Both Ellis and Beck established official training programs for their versions of cognitive therapy, with various levels of qualifications available. Most large cities now have some type of specialty clinic offering cognitive therapy, whose practitioners may or may not be affiliated with one of the training institutes. The journal *Cognitive Therapy and Research* was founded in 1976, followed by outlets such as the *Journal of Cognitive Psychotherapy.* In 1994, the Association for Advancement of Behavior Therapy (AABT), which had published the journal *Behavior Therapy* since 1970, founded the journal *Cognitive and Behavioral Practice.* In 1990, *Behavior Therapy* added the subtitle *An International Journal Devoted to the Application of Behavioral and Cognitive Sciences to Clinical Problems,* with these developments reflecting the increasing emphasis within AABT of cognitive research and practice on its original behavioral orientation. And, of course, there have long been theoretical journals (as opposed to practice ones) devoted to cognitive phenomena (e.g., *Cognitive Development, Cognitive Psychology,* and *Cognitive Science*). Tamie Ronen and Arthur Freeman's (2007) social work textbook, *Cognitive Behavior Therapy in Clinical Social Work Practice,* is one of the best discipline-specific resources for social workers to become familiar with, and Borcherdt (1996) is also another good cognitive-behavioral text written by a social worker. Other recent additions to the oeuvre of cognitive behavioral social work include a chapter by Garland and Thyer (2013) and Brian Sheldon's (2011) book *Cognitive Behavioral Therapy.*

A LOOK TOWARD THE FUTURE

Is SLT going cognitive? Cognition is sometimes erroneously differentiated from behavior, with cognitive therapy said to deal with changing cognitions and behavior therapy said to be limited to changing overt behavior while ignoring the client's thinking processes and feelings. Recall from the definition of behavior that cognition is behavior, itself to be explained by the principles of SLT. The National Association of Social Workers (NASW) *Social Work Dictionary* reflects this perspective:

> *Behavior:* Any action or response by an individual, including observable activity, measurable physiological changes, cognitive images, fantasies, and emotions. Some scientists consider even subjective experiences to be behaviors.

> *Behavior therapy:* Application of behavior modification principles in clinical settings to assess and alter undesired behaviors . . . using techniques based on empirical research.

> *Cognitive theory:* A group of concepts pertaining to the way individuals develop the intellectual capacity for receiving, processing, and acting on information.

> *Cognitive therapy:* Clinical intervention using cognitive theory concepts that focus on the client's conscious thinking processes, motivations, and reasons for certain behavior. (Barker, 1995, pp. 33, 34, 65)

For the behavior analyst, cognition (and feelings) are behaviors of the body that require explanation in the same manner as overt, publicly observable actions are accounted for. Rather than postulating, as does cognitive theory, that environmental events happen, that these are cognitively processed, and that, based on this cognition, overt behavior and affect result, the behaviorist hypothesizes that environmental events occur and that this results in overt behavior, affect, and cognition. These results may not be concurrent— some may occur before others—but regardless of this temporal ordering, all are seen as largely a function of environmental experiences.

Recall the client who was bitten by a dog. Later in life, when she avoided dogs, feared them, and could narrate negative thoughts about them, the cause of the overt behavior, the fear, and the cognitions was the experience of being bitten. Her later negative thoughts are not held to cause her to fear and flee dogs. Rather, being bitten caused all three behavioral phenomena. Thus, mainstream behavior analysis postulates a thorough environmental determinism, whereas the cognitive theorist maintains a largely mental determinism, influenced to some extent by the environmental factors favored by the behaviorist. This issue is not moot, however. If one believes in largely environmental determinants, then social work intervention will more likely have an environmental focus, alleviating aversive conditions and deprivations; reinforcing adaptive abilities; teaching, shaping, and coaching functional life skills; working with the client in real-life contexts; and so forth. If one subscribes to a cognitive account, then social work practice is more likely to take the form of office-based Socratic argumentation, uncovering irrational self-statements, repeating affirmations, and other verbally oriented mechanisms of changing clients' mentation. The reader may make his or her own appraisal about which approach seems most consistent with social work's person-in-environment perspective.

The causal role of cognition has been an important topic of philosophical debate for several millennia, and social workers will not likely resolve the issue to the satisfaction of everyone. As a practical matter, Bandura (1977) has long noted that the most effective method of changing cognitions is through engaging in overt behavior. If you want to help a phobic think more rationally about dogs and be less fearful, helping the client experience a series of harmless (perhaps even pleasant) encounters with dogs may be more effective in improving affect and cognition and in reducing avoidance than verbal cognitive therapy conducted in an office. And cognitive therapy is eclectic: "RET also employs many behavioral methods, most commonly reinforcement, response cost, assertiveness and skill training, and in vivo extinction and implosion to fearful stimuli" (Kendall et al., 1995, p. 180). Thus, for the clinical social worker using these theories, it is not a question of doing cognitive therapy or behavior therapy; most employ both approaches. Even the behavior analyst may employ so-called cognitive therapy techniques, but she or he would likely (privately!) construe them in SLT terms rather than accept mentalistic accounts of their mechanism of action.

To a large extent, behavior theory has always been concerned with explaining cognitive phenomena. Throughout his career, B. F. Skinner wrote incisive works theorizing about private events such as thinking, self-control, self-talk, and emotions (see Thyer, 1992d, for references). In one of his last books, Skinner (1989) wrote chapters with titles such as "The Place of Feeling in the Analysis of Behavior," "The Origins of Cognitive Thought," "The Initiating Self," and "The Listener."

In addition to explaining cognitive processes, behaviorists have always focused on treating cognitive and affective disorders with behavior analysis and therapy. Behavior therapy never was exclusively focused on changing overt actions. For example, the earliest behavior therapy method ever rigorously tested was Wolpe's technique of systematic desensitization (SD; see review by Fischer, 1978). SD was developed in the 1950s, the dawn of formal behavior therapy. It was explicitly designed to treat pathological affective states, originally those related to clinical anxiety, and was eventually applied to most so-called neurotic conditions.

Part of the error, of course, lies in the very terms *behavior therapy* and *cognitive therapy,* inasmuch as we are not accustomed to the technical term *behavior* subsuming cognition and affect. But such has been the case for decades, and it is time to stop perpetuating the myth that these are two different fields (Thyer, 1992b). Behavior theory is cognitive theory. Behavior therapy *is* cognitive therapy.

As a further practical matter, both behavior therapy and cognitive therapy have impressive track records of empirical support for a wide variety of formal disorders and problems in living. For example, cognitive therapy, as developed by Beck, seems very effective in the treatment of major depression, perhaps as effective as conventional antidepressant medications. Panic disorder, generalized anxiety disorder, phobias, anorexia and bulimia, delusional behavior and other clinically important aspects of schizophrenia, posttraumatic stress disorder, obsessive-compulsive disorder, alcoholism, and sexual dysfunctions are but a few of the formal disorders for which cognitive and/or behavior therapy have considerable research support in the form of numerous well-controlled outcome studies (see reviews by Emmelkamp, 1994; Hollon & Beck, 1994; Nathan & Gorman, 2007).

These developments have profoundly influenced social work theory and intervention models. During the past three decades, a large number of methodologically sound outcome studies have been conducted on clinical social work practice.

Here are some of the conclusions of review articles summarizing this body of evidence:

> Turning now to the vital question of which methods are most strongly correlated with positive outcome we see that behavioural and cognitive-behavioural methods (whether deployed in groups, or with individuals) sweep the board. . . . The majority of positive results within research of an experimental and quasi-experimental kind are accounted for by behavioural and cognitive-behavioural approaches. (MacDonald, Sheldon, & Gillespie, 1992, p. 635)
>
> Social workers are generating an empirical basis that supports claims to effectiveness for a broad range of problems. . . . The influence of the behavior modification movement is apparent and pervasive. The majority of the experiments involve evaluation of skills training or contingency contracting within the frame of reference of learning theory. (Reid & Hanrahan, 1982, pp. 338, 329)
>
> Most of the studies with unequivocally positive outcomes test forms of practice that relied heavily on problem-solving and task-centered methods, usually in conjunction with behavioral methods. (Rubin, 1985, p. 474)

A recent survey of licensed clinical social workers (LCSWs) conducted across 34 states found that the top five most frequently used interventions were cognitive-behavior therapy (used by 43% of practitioners), solution-focused therapy (23%), psychodynamic therapy (21%), cognitive-therapy/restructuring (18%), and behavior modification/evaluation (12%) (See Pignotti & Thyer, 2009), so it is clear that these behavioral and cognitive approaches have had a considerable impact on our actual practices. This trend extends beyond social work, as a recent survey of the therapeutic orientations of faculty in doctoral-level counseling and clinical psychology programs revealed (Heatherington et al., 2013). In clinical psychology, of 54 programs described as focusing their training in clinical science, 80% of the faculty described themselves as having a cognitive-behavioral therapeutic orientation, versus 7% who subscribed to a psychodynamic perspective. The same trend was evident, to a lesser extent, in counseling psychology, wherein 42% reported a cognitive-behavioral orientation, versus 19% maintaining a psychodynamic one.

Behavioral and cognitive interventions are closely linked to their underlying theoretical conceptualizations. It would be a mistake in logical reasoning to assume that the effectiveness of the interventions proves the validity of the theory (see Thyer, 1992c), but a greater danger is for the profession to ignore or misrepresent SLT, which often happens (Thyer, 1992b, 2005). Respondent, operant, and observational learning elements are a significant component of many of the psychosocial and interpersonal problems encountered in practice. Knowledge of these elements is essential for effective clinical social work.

REFERENCES

Azrin, N. H. (1976). Improvements in the community-reinforcement approach to alcoholism. *Behaviour Research and Therapy, 14,* 339–348.

Baer, D. M., & Deguchi, H. (1985). Generalized imitation from a radical-behavioral viewpoint. In S. Reiss & R. R. Bootzin (Eds.), *Theoretical issues in behavior therapy* (pp. 179–217). New York, NY: Academic Press.

Baer, D. M., & Pinkston, E. M. (Eds.). (1997). *Environment and behavior.* Boulder, CO: Westview Press.

Bandura, A. (1977). Self-efficacy: Toward a unifying theory of behavioral change. *Psychological Review, 84,* 191–215.

Barker, R. L. (1995). *The social work dictionary* (3rd ed.). Washington, DC: NASW Press.

Barth, R. P. (1986). *Social and cognitive treatment of children and adolescents.* San Francisco, CA: Jossey-Bass.

Beck, A. T., & Emery, G. (1985). *Anxiety disorders and phobias: A cognitive perspective.* New York, NY: Basic Books.

Bijou, S. W. (1993). *Behavior analysis of child development* (2nd ed.). Reno, NV: Context Press.

Bloom, M. (1992). A conversation with Carel Germain. In M. Bloom (Ed.), *Changing lives: Studies in human development and professional helping* (pp. 406–409). Columbia: University of South Carolina Press.

Borcherdt, B. (1996). *Fundamentals of cognitive-behavior therapy.* New York, NY: Haworth Press.

Boynton, K. E., & Thyer, B. A. (1994). Behavioral social work in the field of oncology. *Journal of Applied Social Sciences, 18,* 189–197.

Bruno, F. (1934). *The theory of social work.* New York, NY: D. C. Heath.

Butterfield, W. H., & Parson, R. (1973). Modeling and shaping by parents to develop chewing behavior in their retarded child. *Journal of Behavior Therapy and Experimental Psychiatry, 4,* 285–287.

Carey, M., & Foster, V. (2013). Social work, ideology, discourse, and the limits of post-hegemony. *Journal of Social Work, 13,* 248-266.

Ellis, A. (1994). Radical behavioral treatment of private events. *Behavior Therapist, 17,* 219–221.

Ellis, A., & Grieger, R. (Eds.). (1977). *Handbook of rational-emotive therapy.* New York, NY: Springer.

Emmelkamp, P. (1994). Behavior therapy with adults. In A. E. Bergin & S. L. Garfield (Eds.), *Handbook of psychotherapy and behavior change* (pp. 379–427). New York, NY: Wiley.

Ferster, C. B., & Skinner, B. F. (1957). *Schedules of reinforcement.* New York, NY: Appleton-Century-Crofts.

Figueroa, R. G., Thyer, B. A., & Thyer, K. B. (1992). Extinction and DRO in the treatment of aggression in a boy with severe mental retardation. *Journal of Behavior Therapy and Experimental Psychiatry, 23,* 133–140.

Fischer, J. (1978). *Effective casework practice: An eclectic approach.* New York, NY: McGraw-Hill.

Fischer, J., & Nehs, R. (1978). Use of a commonly available chore to reduce a boy's rate of swearing. *Journal of Behavior Therapy and Experimental Psychiatry, 9,* 81–83.

Gambrill, E. D., & Richey, C. A. (1976). *It's up to you: Developing assertive social skills.* Millbrae, CA: Les Femmes.

Gammon, E. A., & Rose, S. D. (1991). The coping skills training program for parents of children with developmental disabilities: An experimental evaluation. *Research on Social Work Practice, 1,* 244–256.

Garland, E., & Thyer, B. A. (2013). Cognitive-behavioral approach. In M. Gray & S. Webb (Eds.). *Social work theories and methods* (2nd edition, pp. 159–172). Thousand Oaks, CA: Sage.

Germain, C. B., & Gitterman, A. (1995). Ecological perspective. In R. L. Edwards (Ed.), *Encyclopedia of social work* (pp. 816–824). Washington, DC: NASW Press.

Gorey, K. J., Thyer, B. A., & Pawluck, D. E. (1998). Differential effectiveness of social work practice models. *Social Work, 43,* 269–278.

Greene, B. F., Winett, R. A., Van Houten, R., Geller, E. S., & Iwata, B. A. (1987). *Behavior analysis in the community: 1968–1986.* Lawrence, KS: Society for the Experimental Analysis of Behavior.

Griffin, J. H. (1960). *Black like me.* New York, NY: Signet.

Hamilton, G. (1940). *Theory and practice of social casework.* New York, NY: Columbia University Press.

Heatherington, L., Messer, S. B., Angus, L., Strauman, T. J., Friedlander, M. L., & Kolden, G. G. (2013). The narrowing of theoretical orientations in clinical psychology doctoral training. *Clinical Psychology: Science and Practice, 19,* 362–374.

Himle, D. P., Thyer, B. A., & Papsdorf, J. D. (1982). Relationship between irrational beliefs and anxiety. *Cognitive Therapy and Research, 6,* 219–223.

Hollon, S. D., & Beck, A. T. (1994). Cognitive and cognitive-behavioral therapies. In A. E. Bergin & S. L. Garfield (Eds.), *Handbook of psychotherapy and behavior change* (pp. 428–466). New York, NY: Wiley.

Holmes, D. (1967). Bridging the gap between research and practice in social work. In National Conference on Social Welfare (Ed.), *Social work practice, 1967* (pp. 94–108). New York, NY: Columbia University Press.

Jayaratne, S. (1978). A study of clinical eclecticism. *Social Service Review, 52,* 621–631.

Kendall, P. C., Haaga, D. A. F., Ellis, A., Bernard, M., DiGiuseppe, R., & Kassinove, H. (1995). Rational-emotive therapy in the 1990s and beyond: Current status, recent revisions, and research questions. *Clinical Psychology Review, 15,* 169–185.

Komhaber, R. C., & Schroeder, H. E. (1975). Importance of model similarity on extinction of avoidance behavior in children. *Journal of Consulting and Clinical Psychology, 43,* 601–607.

Linn, J. W. (1935). *Jane Addams: A biography.* New York, NY: Appleton-Century-Crofts.

Lovaas, O. I. (1987). Behavioral treatment and normal educational and intellectual functioning in young autistic children. *Journal of Consulting and Clinical Psychology, 55,* 3–9.

Lundin, R. W. (1974). *Personality: A behavioral analysis.* New York, NY: Macmillan.

MacDonald, G., Sheldon, B., & Gillespie, J. (1992). Contemporary studies of the effectiveness of social work. *British Journal of Social Work, 22,* 615–643.

McEachin, J. J., Smith, T., & Lovaas, O. I. (1993). Long-term outcome for children with autism who received early intensive behavioral treatment. *American Journal of Mental Retardation, 97,* 359–372.

Nathan, P. E., & Gorman, J. (Eds.). (2007). *A guide to treatments that work* (3rd ed.). New York, NY: Oxford University Press.

Northen, H. (1995). *Clinical social work knowledge and skills* (2nd edition). New York, NY: Columbia University Press.

O'Donohue, W., & Ferguson, K. (2001). *The psychology of B. F. Skinner.* Thousand Oaks, CA: Sage.

Patterson, G. R. (1982). *Coercive family process.* Eugene, OR: Castalia.

Paul, G. L., & Lentz, R. J. (1977). *Psychosocial treatment of chronic mental patients: Milieu versus social-learning programs.* Cambridge, MA: Harvard University Press.

Paul, G. L., & Menditto, A. A. (1992). Effectiveness of inpatient treatment programs for mentally ill adults in public psychiatric facilities. *Applied & Preventive Psychology, 1,* 41–63.

Pignotti, M., & Thyer, B. A. (2009). Use of novel unsupported and empirically supported therapies by licensed clinical social worker: An exploratory study. *Social Work Research, 33,* 5–17.

Rapport, M. D., Murphy, H. A., & Bailey, J. S. (1982). Ritalin vs. response cost in the control of hyperactive children. *Journal of Applied Behavior Analysis, 15,* 205–216.

Reid, W. J. (2004). The contribution of operant theory to social work practice and research. In H. E. Briggs & T. L. Rzepnicki (Eds.), *Using evidence in social work practice: Behavioral perspectives* (pp. 36–54). Chicago, IL: Lyceum Press.

Reid, W. J., & Fortune, A. E. (2003). Empirical foundations for practice guidelines in current social work knowledge. In A. Rosen & E. Proctor (Eds.), *Developing practice guidelines for social work intervention: Issues, methods, and research agenda* (pp. 59–79). New York, NY: Columbia University Press.

Reid, W. J., & Hanrahan, P. (1982). Recent evaluations of social work practice: Grounds for optimism. *Social Work, 27,* 328–340.

Robinson, V. R. (1930). *A changing psychology in social casework.* Durham: University of North Carolina Press.

Ronen, T., & Freeman, A. (Eds.). (2007). *Cognitive behavior therapy in clinical social work practice.* New York, NY: Springer.

Rosenthal, T., & Bandura, A. (1978). Psychological modeling: Theory and practice. In S. L. Garfield & A. E. Bergin (Eds.), *Handbook of psychotherapy and behavior change* (pp. 621–658). New York, NY: Wiley.

Rothman, J., & Thyer, B. A. (1984). Behavioral social work in community and organizational settings. *Journal of Sociology & Social Welfare, 11,* 294–326.

Rubin, A. (1985). Practice effectiveness: More grounds for optimism. *Social Work, 30,* 469–476.

Schlinger, H. D. (1995). *A behavior analytic view of child development.* New York, NY: Plenum Press.

Scott, W. D. (1995). Cognitive behavior therapy: Two basic cognitive research programs and a theoretically based definition. *Behavior Therapist, 18,* 122–124.

Sheldon, B. (2011). *Cognitve-behavioural therapy: Research and practice in health and social care* (2nd edition). New York, NY: Routledge.

Shorkey, C. T., & Taylor, J. E. (1973). Management of maladaptive behavior of a severely burned child. *Child Welfare, 52,* 543–547.

Skinner, B. F. (1957). *Verbal behavior.* Englewood Cliffs, NJ: Prentice Hall.

Skinner, B. F. (1974). *About behaviorism.* New York, NY: Knopf.

Skinner, B. F. (1989). *Recent issues in the analysis of behavior.* Columbus, OH: Merrill.

Strom, K. (1994). Social workers in private practice: An update. *Clinical Social Work Journal, 22,* 73–89.

Stuart, R. B. (1967). Application of behavior theory to social casework. In E. J. Thomas (Ed.), *The socio-behavioral approach and applications to social work* (pp. 19–38). New York, NY: Council on Social Work Education.

Stuart, R. B. (1980). *Helping couples change: A social learning approach to marital therapy.* New York, NY: Guilford Press.

Sundel, M., & Sundel, S. (2005). *Behavior change in the human services* (5th ed.). Thousand Oaks, CA: Sage.

Sundel, S. S., & Sundel, M. (1980). *Be assertive: A practical guide for human service workers.* Beverly Hills, CA: Sage.

Thomas, E. J. (1967). *The socio-behavioral approach and applications to social work.* New York, NY: Council on Social Work Education.

Thyer, B. A. (1981a). Behavioural social work: A bibliography. *International Journal of Behavioural Social Work and Abstracts, 1,* 229–251.

Thyer, B. A. (1981b). Prolonged in-vivo exposure therapy with a 70-year-old woman. *Journal of Behavior Therapy and Experimental Psychiatry, 12,* 69–71.

Thyer, B. A. (1983). Behavior modification in social work practice. In M. Hersen, P. Miller, & R. Eisler (Eds.), *Progress in behavior modification* (pp. 173–226). New York, NY: Plenum Press.

Thyer, B. A. (1985). Textbooks in behavioral social work: A bibliography. *Behavior Therapist, 8,* 161–162.

Thyer, B. A. (1988). Radical behaviorism and clinical social work. In R. Dorfman (Ed.), *Paradigms of clinical social work* (pp. 123–148). New York, NY: Guilford Press.

Thyer, B. A. (1992a). A behavioral perspective on human development. In M. Bloom (Ed.), *Changing lives: Studies in human development and professional helping* (pp. 410–418). Columbia: University of South Carolina Press.

Thyer, B. A. (1992b). Behavioral social work: It is not what you think. *Arete, 16*(2), 1–9.

Thyer, B. A. (1992c). Social work theory and practice research: The approach of logical positivism. *Social Work & Social Sciences Review, 4*(1), 5–6.

Thyer, B. A. (1992d). The term "cognitive-behavior therapy" is redundant [Letter]. *Behavior Therapist, 15,* 112–128.

Thyer, B. A. (1996). Behavior analysis and social welfare policy. In M. A. Mattaini & B. A. Thyer (Eds.), *Finding solutions to social problems: Behavioral strategies for change* (pp. 41–60). Washington, DC: American Psychological Association.

Thyer, B. A. (Ed.). (1999). *The philosophical legacy of behaviorism.* Dordrecht, the Netherlands: Kluwer.

Thyer, B. A. (2005). The misfortunes of behavioral social work: Misprized, misread, and misconstrued. In S. A. Kirk (Ed.), *Mental disorders in the social environment: Critical perspectives* (pp. 330–343). New York, NY: Columbia University Press.

Thyer, B. A. (2008). Evidence-based macro practice: Addressing the challenges and opportunities. *Journal of Evidence-Based Social Work, 5*(3/4), 453–472.

Thyer, B. A. (2012a). Respondent learning theory. In B. A. Thyer, C. N. Dulmus, & K. M. Sowers (Eds.), *Human behavior in the social environment: Theories for social work practice* (pp. 47-81). New York, NY: Wiley.

Thyer, B. A. (2012b). Behavioral social work practice. In E. Mullen (Ed.). *Oxford Bibliographies Online: Social Work.* Retrieved from http://www.oxford-bibliographies.com/view/document/obo-9780195389678/obo-9780195389678-0040.xml?rskey=hvWGWW&result=1&q=Thyer#firstMatch.

Thyer, B. A., & Hudson, W. W. (1987). Progress in behavioral social work: An introduction. *Journal of Social Service Research, 10*(2/3/4), 1-6.

Thyer, B. A., Irvine, S., & Santa, C. (1984). Contingency management of aerobic exercise by chronic schizophrenics. *Perceptual and Motor Skills, 58,* 419–425.

Thyer, B. A., & Maddox, K. (1988). Behavioral social work: Results of a national survey on graduate curricula. *Psychological Reports, 63,* 239–242.

Thyer, B. A., & Wodarski, J. S. (1990). Social learning theory: Towards a comprehensive conceptual framework for social work education. *Social Service Review, 64,* 144–152.

Ullman, L. P., & Krasner, L. (1969). *A psychological approach to abnormal behavior.* New York, NY: Prentice Hall.

Werner, H. D. (1965). *A rational approach to social casework.* New York, NY: Association Press.

Werner, H. D. (1979). Cognitive therapy. In F. J. Turner (Ed.), *Social work treatment* (2nd ed., pp. 243–272). New York, NY: Free Press.

Werner, H. D. (1982). *Cognitive therapy.* New York, NY: Free Press.

Whittaker, J., & Garbarino, J. (1983). *Social support networks: Informal helping in the human services.* New York, NY: Aldine.

Wilson, G. T. (1989). Behavior therapy. In American Psychiatric Association (Ed.), *Treatments of psychiatric disorders* (pp. 2026–2036). Washington, DC: American Psychiatric Association.

Wodarski, J. S., & Bagarozzi, D. A. (1979). *Behavioral social work.* New York, NY: Human Sciences Press.

Wong, S. E. (2012). Respondent learning theory. In B. A. Thyer, C. N. Dulmus, & K. M. Sowers (Eds.), *Human behavior in the social environment: Theories for social work practice* (pp. 83–128). New York, NY: Wiley.

Zentall, T. R. (2006). Imitation: Definition, evidence, and mechanisms. *Animal Cognition, 9,* 335–353.

3

PSYCHOANALYTIC THEORY

FREDRIC T. PERLMAN AND JERROLD R. BRANDELL

The historical relationship between clinical social work and psychoanalysis is both fascinating and extremely complex. Classical psychoanalytic theory and, later, ego psychology stand in relation to social work theory and practice in much the same way as the theory of relativity stands in relation to modern theoretical physics. In each case, the introduction of a new and radical theory has had far-reaching ramifications for the existing framework of knowledge.

In this chapter, psychoanalytic ideas and their unique contributions and adaptations to the practice of clinical social work will be discussed and explored in depth. Psychoanalytic theory, of course, is not a unified body of knowledge; rather, it is composed of multiple theories, models, and schemata pertaining to development, psychopathology, and clinical method and technique. It is a literature of vast scope whose evolution spans an entire century.

PSYCHOANALYSIS AND CLINICAL SOCIAL WORK: A CONCISE HISTORY

The earliest historical influence of psychoanalytic ideas on the social work field seems to have occurred in the late 1920s. Strean (1993) observes that the professional climate in social work favored the introduction of psychoanalytic ideas at this time, inasmuch as caseworkers had begun to recognize the limitations of advice giving, moral suasion, and manipulation of the environment in their work with clients.[1] Beginning in the early 1920s, with the advent of the child guidance movement and work with clinical populations such as the shellshock victims of World War I, the context for social work practice shifted dramatically. Many social workers began to work in hospitals and clinics, thereby extending their exposure to psychiatrists and psychiatric thinking (Goldstein, 1995). The influence of psychiatric thinking so dominated social work

---

[1]Psychoanalysis offered a radically new perspective, one that augmented and complemented the caseworker's understanding of how social forces contribute to the client's maladjustment, with a unique emphasis on the client's motives, conflicts, disturbing wishes, defensive adaptations, and personal history (Strean, 1993, pp. 6–7).

during this period that it led one historian to describe it as the "Psychiatric Deluge" (Goldstein, 1995; Woodroofe, 1971). Freud's theories, in particular, stimulated great interest among many social workers.

Psychoanalytic theory placed emphasis on the individual and imputed meaning to pathological symptoms. It presumed the existence of an unconscious and of universal experiences in early-childhood development (such as the Oedipus complex) that, failing adaptive resolution, might persist into later development and serve as a basis for psychopathology. It also provided a model for understanding the tendency of individuals to translocate and to repeat early-childhood conflicts in adult relationships, even extending to the relationship between client and worker (Goldstein, 1995).

Annette Garrett, in a publication that appeared in 1940, became one of the first social work authors to comment on the transformative impact of Freud's work on social work theory and practice. She observed that the concepts of *social diagnosis* and *social treatment,* originally derived from the pioneering work of Mary Richmond, had gradually evolved into *psychosocial diagnosis* and *psychosocial treatment.* The incorporation of Freudian ideas into social work practice thus enabled social workers to individualize the person-in-environment configuration; each client was regarded as having a unique set of personal experiences, specific strengths and weaknesses peculiar to him or her, and highly individualized, idiosyncratic ways of operating in the world (Strean, 1993).

During the past 80+ years, psychoanalysis has exerted a powerful and, at times, revolutionary influence on the field of clinical social work, a phenomenon paralleled in other social and behavioral sciences. Although it can be argued that the impact of psychoanalytic thinking has pervaded a variety of clinical social work approaches, three classical approaches to social casework may illustrate this influence most clearly: (1) the diagnostic or psychosocial school, (2) the functional school, and (3) the problem-solving approach.

The Diagnostic or Psychosocial School

Although Mary Richmond is often credited with having originated the diagnostic or psychosocial approach to casework, there were a number of other early contributors.

Gordon Hamilton, Bertha Reynolds, Charlotte Towle, Fern Lowry, Marion Kenworthy, Betsey Libbey, Annette Garrett, and Florence Hollis are among those whose teaching and scholarship helped shape this approach to casework (Hollis, 1970).

An important link between psychoanalysis and the psychosocial approach is in the latter's use of Freudian personality theory as a basic organizing framework. According to Hollis (1970, p. 36), dynamic personality theory, augmented by ego psychological principles, provided the most useful approach to an understanding of the individual and his or her relative success or failure in adaptive functioning.

Sigmund Freud, Karl Abraham, Anna Freud, Thomas French, Franz Alexander, August Aichom, Ernst Fedem, Abram Kardiner, Erik Erikson, Heinz Hartmann, Ernest Kris, Rudolf Loewenstein, Rene Spitz, Margaret Mahler, W. R. D. Fairbairn, Donald Winnicott, Harry Guntrip, Edith Jacobson, Robert White, Otto Kernberg, and Heinz Kohut (Hollis, 1970, p. 39; Woods & Hollis, 1990, pp. 31–32) are psychoanalytic theorists whose work has had particular influence on the psychosocial school.

The influence of psychoanalytic theory is especially evident in the psychosocial school's view of diagnosis. Diagnosis is conceived of as having three equally important facets: (1) *dynamic diagnosis,* in which the individual's interplay with others in his or her environment is examined; (2) *etiological diagnosis,* where the focus is on both current and historically remote features of the person-environment matrix; and (3) *classificatory diagnosis,* in which an effort is made to classify various aspects of the individual's functioning, typically including a clinical diagnosis (Hollis, 1970, p. 52). Other psychoanalytic ideas, such as resistance, transference, and countertransference, have also been integrated into the psychosocial perspective.

The Functional School

The functional theory of casework, developed by Virginia Robinson and Jessie Taft at the Pennsylvania School of Social Work in the 1930s, was also linked to psychoanalysis. The functionalists, however, rejected the classical psychoanalytic ideas that the psychosocial school had embraced, characterizing them as "mechanistic, deterministic view(s) of man . . . [who is seen as] . . . prey to the dark forces of an unconscious and . . . the harsh restrictive influences of internalized parental dicta in the early years" of development (Smalley, 1970, pp. 82–83). Freud's disciple, Otto Rank, whose theories emphasized human growth, the development of the self, and the will as a controlling and organizing force, became an important force in functional theory as a member of the teaching faculty at the University of Pennsylvania. Rank's work also emphasized ideas such as the use of relationship to facilitate growth and the significance of time as a factor in the helping process, ideas that Taft and others used as the basis for the functional model.

One of Rank's unique contributions, according to Smalley (1970), was his theory of birth trauma:[2]

> Rank emphasized the development of life fear and death fear out of the birth experience and saw all individuals as experiencing and expressing these two fears throughout life . . . the fear of not living, not experiencing, not realizing potential which

may be thought of as the death fear; and the fear of separation, of independent existence outside of the womb. (pp. 92–93)

Functional theory has also drawn from Erik Erikson's model of psychosocial and psychosexual development and, to some extent, from the work of Karen Horney and Erich Fromm. Although fundamental tenets of the functional approach such as the function of agency and the use of time as a dimension in the casework relationship are not especially psychoanalytic, the emphases on separation and individuation and on developmental crises and adaptations appear to have an unmistakable psychoanalytic cast.

The Problem-Solving Model

The problem-solving model was developed by Helen Harris Perlman in the 1950s at the University of Chicago. Perlman's model has been described by one author as an effort to traverse the often contentious debate that had erupted between the functional school and the diagnostic school by the 1950s, although she was largely unsuccessful in achieving this objective (Goldstein, 1995, p. 37). Perlman's model of casework is very closely tied to ego psychological theory, and she views the casework process itself as demonstrating a "striking parallel" with "the normal operations of the ego in its problem-solving efforts" (Perlman, 1957, p. 85). With the use of concepts such as *partializing* (breaking down large problems into smaller, more manageable tasks), Perlman (1970) attempted to "translate ego psychology into action principles" (p. 135).

The problem-solving model also emphasized the significance of relationship, and Perlman did write of relational phenomena such as transference and countertransference. However, she was always careful to make clear distinctions between casework and depth psychology. Casework always aimed to "maintain the relationship on

---

[2]Rank's (1924/1973) book *The Trauma of Birth* was at first favorably received by Freud (Jones, 1957). Within 2 years, however, with the publication of *Inhibitions, Symptoms, and Anxiety* (Freud, 1926), Freud had completely reversed himself, rejecting Rank's thesis in toto.

the basis of reality," to keep client and caseworker firmly anchored in their joint purpose, aware of "their separate and realistic identities" and their goal of achieving "a better adaptation between the client and his current problem-situation" (Perlman, 1957, p. 78). Such goals stand in marked contrast to those of psychoanalysis and psychoanalytic psychotherapy, where there is considerably greater emphasis and attention given to remote or distal causes of intercurrent symptoms and failures in adaptation and to the intrapsychic basis of conflict in general. Furthermore, whereas the transference relationship is promoted in psychoanalysis and in certain psychoanalytic psychotherapies, the effort in the problem-solving approach is to "manage the relationship and the problem-solving work so as to give minimum excitation to transference" (Perlman, 1957).

FOUNDATIONS OF THEORETICAL PSYCHOANALYSIS

Psychoanalysis is the creation of Sigmund Freud (1856–1939), a Viennese neurologist whose pioneering studies of hysteria, obsessional illness, and other obscure disorders of unknown etiology led him from the practice of neurology to the creation of a new form of treatment based on the investigation of the individual sufferer's mental life. Freud discovered that certain mental illnesses occurred when the sufferer's personality was permeated by the intrusion of powerful and mysterious impulses from deep within the psyche. At one time, Freud thought that these mysterious impulses were delayed reactions to traumas, especially sexual traumas that had been experienced in early childhood and then dissociated. He soon discovered, however, that these mysterious impulses were not merely the reactions to untoward events of childhood; rather, they were expressions of instinctual drives at the core of the psyche. Normally, these instinctual forces are repressed, Freud wrote, but in neurosis they rise up like demonic forces from the deep.

Neurotic symptoms such as hysterical paralyses, amnesias, obsessions, and phobias could be seen as the battleground where the forces of the invading instinctual drives were locked in combat with the defending forces of the embattled personality.

Freud devoted his life to the study of these invading instinctual forces—of their origins in the mind and their influence on mental life. He came to think of the mind as an organization of hierarchically ordered mental systems, in which higher systems, which are associated with mature development, regulate the activity of lower systems, which are more primitive. Instinctual forces, he believed, emanated from the great darkness at the center of psychic life, which he called *the unconscious* or, later, the *id.* He endeavored to identify the elemental instinctual forces, to trace their development, and to discern their influence not only on the individual but also on the cultural life of humankind. During the course of his career, Freud continually modified his investigative-therapeutic techniques and wrote extensively about his discoveries, applying them not only to the problems of psychopathology and pathogenesis but also to the psychology of dreams, mythology, creativity, and love and to critical issues in anthropology, developmental psychology, religion, and political science.

The structure of Freud's psychoanalytic enterprise was exceedingly complex. Freud conceived of psychoanalysis as a research method, a therapeutic technique, a theory of mental functioning, a theory of psychopathology, and a theory of human development. Each of these theories was intimately connected with each of the others. As a result of clinical discoveries, the entire network of theories was continually modified. In the course of his lifetime, Freud propounded three theories of the instincts (1905, 1914b, 1920), two theories of anxiety (1895a, 1926), and two different models of the mind (1900, 1923).

One of the most important trends in the development of Freudian theory was the progressive expansion of his focus from the study of instinctual drives and of the unconscious to the investigation of higher strata of the mind responsible for processing and regulating the instincts in accordance with realistic and moral considerations. Freud initially was little interested in the higher functions of the mind, which he thought were easily understood through introspection. His expanding clinical experience, however, yielded new data that dramatically disconfirmed this naive assumption. Many clients, he learned, suffered from feelings of guilt of which they were utterly unaware and over which they could exert no control. He also discovered that defensive functioning was largely unconscious. These discoveries revealed that the higher stratum of the mind was largely unconscious and far more complex in its functioning than he had originally recognized. Freud's early work may be characterized as a *psychology of the id* or *depth psychology,* while the later work is usually summarized by the term *ego psychology.*

One of the extraordinary features of Freud's scientific style was that he never systematized his ideas or categorically renounced any of his earlier points of view, even when he propounded new ideas that contradicted the old. As a result, his students could hold different "Freudian" positions, each the product of a different phase of Freud's theoretical development.

In the years since Freud's death, psychoanalysts around the world have reshaped Freud's theory in accordance with their own views and empirical data.[3] The result has been a proliferation of psychoanalytic theories, a process paralleled by efforts to identify their most salient common characteristics. Some have paid special attention to the problem of object relations,[4] characterizing these theories as having either a drive/structure or a relational-structure basis (Greenberg & Mitchell, 1983). Others have grouped psychoanalytic theories into several dominant psychologies or orientations of psychoanalytic thought, which collectively have been referred to as the *four psychologies of psychoanalysis* (Pine, 1988). Although each of these psychological systems or orientations—drive theory, ego psychology, object relations theory, and the psychology of the self—has certain distinctive features, it is arguable as to whether any of the four can be thought of as an essentially separate psychological system (Pine, 1990).

We have based the following discussion on somewhat different premises. It is our understanding that the impetus for the development of each major school of psychoanalytic thought has typically involved certain fundamental questions believed to be irreconcilable within the framework of existing theory. Each of these schools has retained certain features of traditional or mainstream psychoanalytic theory, so that in most instances, the differences among these major schools reflect processes that are both qualitative and evolutionary. We therefore prefer to speak of the continuities and discontinuities of the respective schools. Because the discontinuities between traditional psychoanalytic theory and later developments in ego psychology are somewhat less pronounced than are, for example, those between traditional psychoanalytic theory and psychology of the self, traditional psychoanalytic theory, and later, ego psychology are presented in the same discussion. This same rationale permits us to separate the discussion of the various object relations theories, both British and American, from self psychology and relational psychoanalysis.

---

[3]Psychoanalysis is properly regarded as an empirical science, although it is also a naturalistic one; it is most usefully thought of as *postdictive*—seeking to explain behavior and its antecedents rather than making any attempt to predict behavior (Holzman, 1995, p. 5).

[4]Defined as the "individual's interactions with external and internal (real and imagined) other people, and to the relationship between their internal and external object worlds" (Greenberg & Mitchell, 1983, pp. 13–14).

Classical Psychoanalytic Theory

Classical psychoanalytic theory derives from the *structural model* or viewpoint of psychoanalysis (Freud, 1923).[5] It represents an integration of Freud's theories of instinctual life with his later understanding of the ego and ego development. Classical psychoanalytic treatment techniques emphasize self-knowledge or insight as the essential curative factor in psychotherapy. Classical psychoanalytic theory has been refined in each generation of Freud's followers. The most influential proponents of the classical position have included theorists such as Otto Fenichel, Anna Freud, Annie Reich, Bertram Lewin, Leo Rangell, Jacob Arlow, and Charles Brenner. Much of the following exposition of classical theory derives directly from Freud. The more contemporary views discussed here derive largely from the views of Charles Brenner and his collaborators. Because Brenner's thinking includes a number of significant modifications, it is often characterized as *contemporary classical* or *contemporary structural theory.*

Psychoanalytic theory posits that the mind is a product of evolutionary development, which functions to ensure adaptation and survival. Mental activity is governed by a fundamental propensity to seek pleasure and avoid pain. Freud called this the *pleasure-unpleasure principle,* or sometimes simply the *pleasure principle.* It is likely that the pleasure principle is favored by natural selection because pain is associated with injury, which threatens survival, while pleasure is associated with the satisfaction of needs, which promotes survival. Organisms failing to seek pleasure and avoid pain would probably be prone to extinction.

Freud held that the mind is moved to activity by the pressure of inborn motivations, or instinctual drives, whose satisfaction is pleasurable. The automatic pursuit of pleasurable satisfactions is modified by successive developmental experiences in which pleasure seeking is paired with aversive contingencies that provoke affects of unpleasure. This is exemplified by the normal experiences of socialization in which primitive infantile pleasures are disrupted by parental discipline. Socialization challenges the pleasure principle by creating situations in which the child learns that the pursuit of instinctual pleasures will be met by aversive contingencies such as punishment or the withdrawal of affection. As a result, urges to pursue those instinctual pleasures trigger contradictory affective signals motivating contradictory tendencies toward both approach and avoidance. This approach-avoidance dilemma may be characterized as a condition of psychic conflict.

Psychoanalytic research reveals that mental life is characterized by the pervasive presence of psychic conflict. This is a consequence of the prolonged dependency of the child on his or her parents and, later, on the extended family and wider social environment. As a result of this extensive dependency, a child undergoes a protracted process of development and socialization during which many innate desires for pleasurable activity and human relatedness are subject to the idiosyncratic responsiveness and disciplinary reactions of the child's significant caretakers. When these responses to the child's behavior are repetitive and painful, they eventually precipitate psychic conflict in the child, who wants to gratify his or her pleasurable inclinations yet avoid the painful consequences he or she expects the behavior to elicit. Psychic conflict challenges the mind to produce new patterns of pleasure seeking that will gratify desires while avoiding or minimizing the expected aversive consequences.

Freud discovered that psychological symptoms and character pathologies are complex structures, unconsciously produced by the mind to avoid or minimize unpleasure. He characterized these structures as *compromise formations.* The concept of compromise conveys the discovery that psychological symptoms and character problems, however painful or crippling, are

---

[5]Explained in the section on metapsychological viewpoints.

intended to achieve a measure of pleasure while averting a measure of pain.

At one time, psychoanalysts believed that psychic conflict and compromise formation were features of mental illness while mental health was characterized by the absence of psychic conflict. Psychoanalytic data, however, have revealed this to be an inaccurate view of mental health. Analysis of the healthy aspects of any individual's mental functioning, such as a happy vocational choice or the pursuit of a pleasurable hobby, regularly reveals the influence of the same desires and conflicts that determine the client's symptoms and character pathology (Brenner, 1982).

CONFLICTS, COMPROMISE FORMATIONS, AND THEIR AFTERMATH

The analysis of compromise formations requires a familiarity with their basic anatomy. Psychoanalytic data reveal that compromise formations regularly include wishes of childhood origin that are associated with, and therefore arouse, aversive affects, such as anxiety and guilt, and psychological defenses that function to reduce the unpleasure of these aversive affects. This section will provide a more detailed description of these components.

Wishes of Childhood

Childhood wishes are formed by the interaction of biological and social-experiential factors. In the first days of infancy, biologically rooted needs produce tension states that are devoid of psychological content. These diffuse tensions acquire structure when caretakers provide experiences of satisfaction appropriate to the infant's actual need. As a result, diffuse tensions are gradually transformed into wishes to repeat these experiences of satisfaction (Freud, 1900). Because these experiences entail specific activities with specific persons, wishes always include representations of these activities and persons.

These aspects of the wishes are called their *aims* and *objects*. Every individual's wishes are unique and personal because they are formed by unique personal experiences.

Psychoanalysts have traditionally employed a theory of drives (or instinctual drives) to conceptualize the biological sources of mental life. The psychoanalytic concept of instinctual drives differs from the ethological concept of instincts. In lower animals, instincts are "specific action potentials" with genetically determined, prestructured patterns of action (Thorpe, 1956). The evolution of higher vertebrates, however, includes the progressive substitution of learned behavior for these preprogrammed action patterns (Lorenz, 1937/1957). In psychoanalytic theory, instinctual drives give rise to tensions but not to specific programs for action. Wishes, which arise when these tensions are structured by experiences of satisfaction, are specific schemata for action. Because they represent the motivational pressure of drives, wishes are also referred to as *drive derivatives*. Drives themselves, however, are not observable and must be regarded as hypothetical constructs (Brenner, 1982). Psychoanalytic theory has traditionally employed the related idea of drive energy to conceptualize the driving force of wishes in mental life. Although some contemporary theorists reject these energetic ideas (Greenberg & Mitchell, 1983; Klein, 1976; Mitchell, 1988), many analysts find them useful because they provide a means for conceptualizing the fluctuating intensities with which wishes are invested.

Psychoanalytic theorists since Freud have wrestled with the challenge of identifying and classifying the basic drives. Many different drives have been suggested over the years. Freud himself posited basic drives for sex and self-preservation (1905) and, later, for life and for death (1920). Other theorists hypothesized drives for power and masculinity (Adler, 1927), individuation (Jung, 1916, 1917), aggression (Hartmann, Kris, & Lowenstein, 1949), mastery (Hendricks, 1942), attachment (Bowlby, 1969), effectance (White, 1963), safety (Sandler, 1960), empathy (Kohut, 1971, 1977), and so on. Are all these drives primary motivations, or may some be better understood as derivative expressions of more basic drives? Most theorists believe that science is best served if primary drives can be identified. To date, no scientific consensus about primary motivations has been achieved. A consistent feature of all psychoanalytic schools of thought, however, has been the tendency to identify some motivations as primary and others as indirect or subordinate expressions of those primary motivations (Eagle, 2012). Most traditional analysts recognize the existence of two primary drives: the sexual and the aggressive. This classification is based on clinical findings that regularly reveal the prominent role of sexual and aggressive wishes in the psychodynamics of symptoms and other pathology.

The Sexual Drive

In psychoanalytic thought, *sex* has a broader meaning than it does in everyday discourse. In psychoanalysis, the word *sexual* connotes a broad range of pleasures that are not necessarily connected with sexual intercourse or even with overtly sexual conduct. The semantic extension of the terms *sex* and *sexuality* highlights the plasticity of the sexual drive and the continuity of sexual development from childhood to adulthood. Human sexuality does not arise in adulthood or even in adolescence but in early childhood. Although the sexual wishes of childhood differ from those of adulthood, they are predecessors of adult sexuality, and their motivational influence is discernible when the sexual wishes of adulthood are studied. Although adult sexuality supersedes childhood sexuality, it does not entirely replace it. Childhood sexual wishes are absorbed into the larger network of adult desires and in some cases may substitute for adult desires. Because some childhood sexual wishes are inevitably conflictual, their role in adult sexuality often results in disturbances in sexuality and love life. Adult sexuality, then, cannot be adequately understood without an appreciation of its roots in the sensual desires of childhood.

Childhood sexuality (or *infantile sexuality*) is composed of numerous sensual pleasures,

experienced in relation to sensitive parts of the body, such as the skin, the mouth, the anus, and the genitals (the *erogenous zones*). Freud believed that these pleasures are initially stimulated by the activities of baby care, such as holding, feeding, touching, and bathing, and then subsequently pursued as ends in their own right. He also believed that the maturation of the sexual drive through childhood entailed a sequenced intensification of oral, anal, and phallic (clitoral) sexual wishes (Freud, 1905). Between the ages of about 3 and 6, these sexual wishes give rise to the formation of the *Oedipus complex.*

The Oedipus complex is a configuration of psychological forces characterized by the concentration of sexual wishes on one parent, usually of the opposite sex, and the emergence of hostile feelings for the remaining parent, who is now the child's rival in love. Numerous variations in this typical pattern occur under different familial conditions. Siblings, for example, may become objects of oedipal desire, through early displacement away from a loved parent or when a child's relations with parents thwart typical oedipal development (Abend, 1984; Sharpe & Rosenblatt, 1994). The Oedipus complex typically entails feelings of inadequacy, fears of the rival parent's retaliation, and usually feelings of defeat. These painful consequences normally motivate a retreat from oedipal strivings and efforts to limit awareness of persisting oedipal desires, a process that initiates the latency phase, during which sexual wishes are relatively dormant. The Oedipus complex actually consists of both positive oedipal and negative oedipal strivings. The positive Oedipus complex reflects the child's wish for a sexual relationship with the opposite-sex parent and a concomitant wish for the demise of the same-sex parent. Due to the child's sense of vulnerability and fundamental ambivalence, however, negative oedipal strivings coexist with the positive ones. In effect, the child also desires sexual union with the parent of the same sex, a wish that gives rise to feelings of rivalry with the opposite-sex parent for the former's affections. In most instances, the positive Oedipus complex supersedes the negative Oedipus complex, a condition that traditional psychoanalytic theory stipulates is necessary for the emergence of a heterosexual orientation and a cohesive identity in adulthood (Moore & Fine, 1990). Sexual desire reemerges as a prominent motivation under the hormonal impetus of adolescence, which introduces the genital pleasure of orgasm. The sexual wishes of adulthood provide a context for the gratification of childhood sexual wishes as well. These are normally evident in the activities of foreplay, which typically include kissing, touching, anal stimulation, and other such features that derive from childhood sensual experience. The influence of infantile sexual wishes is also evident when the person chosen as a partner in adulthood (*object choice*) resembles a primary object of childhood sexuality.

The Aggressive Drive

Most psychoanalysts recognize that destructive wishes play an important role in mental life. Although there is little dispute about the centrality of aggression, there is widespread disagreement about how best to understand it. Analysts differ on whether the aggressive drive exerts a continuous pressure for discharge, as does the sexual drive, or whether aggression is a "reactive instinct" (Fine, 1975), triggered by frustration, perceived threats, or other noxious conditions. Freud and many of his followers believed that the aggressive drive generates a more or less continuous flow of destructive impulses (Freud, 1920; Hartmann et al., 1949). Friedman and Downey (1995) have recently argued that aggression is related to the organizing influence of male hormones on the fetal brain and is thus a typical feature of male psychology, evidenced by the rough-and-tumble play among boys. They suggest that aggression in males may express genetically determined strivings for dominance over other males. Other important theorists conceptualize aggression as

a reaction to threats or injuries to self-esteem (Kohut, 1972; Rochlin, 1973), to physical or mental pain (Grossman, 1991), to the experience of "ego weakness" (Guntrip, 1968), to the frustration of dependency needs (Fairbairn, 1952; Saul, 1976), to "the internally felt experience of excessive unpleasure" (Parens, 1979), and so on.

Psychological data support the view that hostile aggression is a reaction to pain, frustration, and feelings of endangerment. These mental states can be episodic and situational, but they may also be chronic features of mental life. Traumatic events, for example, often leave emotional lesions, which give rise to a continuous stream of aggressive wishes. Captain Ahab's unrelenting hatred for Moby Dick, the great whale that bit off his leg, is a good example. All children experience frustrations and disappointments and are prone to feel small, powerless, damaged, or unloved, at least at times. Oedipal strivings, for instance, normally entail feelings of anxiety and guilt, which may persist as feelings of doom or endangerment. The ultimate failure of oedipal ambitions often leaves a feeling of inferiority. In this view, aggression is an inevitable aspect of mental life since everybody suffers to some extent from the painful residue of childhood conflicts. It is likely that aggression may become a central motivation of mental life in accordance with the degree to which such painful states dominate subjective experience. It may also be observed that people who endure a great deal of pain or frustration as a result of maladaptive compromise formations are also prone to be aggressive as a consequence of their unhappiness. Aggression is not only a component of psychic conflict; it may also be a consequence of it.

Unpleasures

Psychic conflict occurs when wishes become associated with painful affects of *unpleasures* in the course of development. Freud (1926) discovered that childhood wishes were regularly associated with anxiety (i.e., fear). He found that these fears fall into one of four basic categories, each representing a specific danger: (1) loss of the object (mother or primary caretaker), (2) loss of the love of the object, (3) punishment, especially by genital mutilation (castration), and (4) fear of being a bad child who deserves to be punished (fear of conscience, or *superego*). When a wish is associated with any of these dangers, the impulse to enact it triggers mounting anxiety. This may reach traumatic levels if not alleviated by the reassurance of protective caretakers or by independent measures. Over time, the child gradually learns various ways to reduce anxiety, called *defenses.* One important defense is repression, which entails a shifting of attention away from tempting but dangerous wishes. As awareness of the wish diminishes, the associated fear is also reduced. Eventually, the child learns to recognize the onset of anxiety and to employ defenses to curtail its development. When anxiety is employed as a signal of danger, it is called *signal anxiety.*

Contemporary psychoanalysts have offered many additions and refinements to Freud's 1926 theory. Many theorists have proposed additions to the classification of psychological dangers and anxieties: fear of loss of the personality, or "aphanisis" (Jones, 1911); fear of being eaten (Fenichel, 1929); fear of ego disintegration (A. Freud, 1936); engulfment by persecutory objects (Klein, 1946/1975a); ego dissolution (Bak, 1943); narcissistic injuries, such as humiliation or disillusionment with an ideal object (Kohut, 1966); dissolution of self (Frosch, 1970); fragmentation anxiety (Kohut, 1971); separation anxiety (Mahler, 1968, 1972); and annihilation anxiety (Freedman, Hurvich, & Ward, 2011; Hurvich, 1989, 1991, 2011, in press), to name a few. There is no arbitrary limit to the number of childhood fears that may be identified, although any proposal should conform to childhood psychology. Fear of one's own death, for example, is not regarded as a fear of early childhood since young children have no concept of death. In children's thought, death signifies known dangers, such as bodily damage or separation from loved

ones. The study of childhood fears is complicated by the fact that some fears are disguised expressions of more basic anxieties. The theoretical desideratum is to identify the elemental fears. At present, this remains an unsettled issue.

An important theoretical innovation follows from the discovery that anxiety is not the only painful affect with which childhood wishes are associated. Brenner (1975) has demonstrated that *depressive affects* (or *miseries*) also instigate psychic conflict. He has proposed an important revision in the psychoanalytic theory of affects and their relation to psychic conflict (Brenner, 1975, 1982). In his view, all affects are composed of two components: (1) sensations of pleasure and unpleasure, which are innate potentials, and (2) ideas of gratification and calamity, which derive from experience. Pleasurable affects include sensations of pleasure in conjunction with ideas of gratification. Unpleasurable affects include sensations of unpleasure in conjunction with ideas of misfortune or calamity. The ideational component also entails a temporal dimension: Gratification or calamity may occur in the future, in the present, or in the past. Happy reminiscences, for example, pertain to past gratifications, while excited anticipation pertains to future expectations. Similarly, anxiety includes the anticipation of future calamities, while depressive affect includes calamities that have occurred. In Brenner's view, the ideational components of anxiety and depressive affect are identical. These are the four dangers Freud described, conceptually reformatted as the calamities of childhood (Brenner, 1982).

Brenner's revised theory expands the explanatory range of dynamic thinking and better explains certain clinical data. In Brenner's view, both anxiety and depressive affect are regularly occurring components of psychic conflict. Psychic conflict occurs when wishes are associated with depressive affect, just as when they are associated with anxiety (Brenner, 1982). This is a normal aspect of the mourning process, during which every wish for reunion with the lost object elicits a wave of misery. It is also typical of many pathological conditions, especially depressive conditions, in which psychic conflict is characterized by prominent feelings of loss, of being unloved, of being punished or morally condemned, or of being inferior (Brenner, 1982). Both anxiety and depressive affect typically include ideas pertaining to more than one calamity. A child who fears that he will be viciously attacked by a punitive parent, for example, is also likely to feel either anxious or miserable about the loss of the parent's love. Insofar as depressive affect is a motivational factor in psychic conflict, the term *signal anxiety* should be replaced by the term *signal affect* (Jacobson, 1994).

Defense

The third component of psychic conflict is defense. The theory of defense is a cornerstone of psychoanalytic theory (Freud, 1894). The theory of defense has undergone numerous changes and revisions, and like the other aspects of psychoanalytic theory, it is subject to numerous controversies. Defenses may be defined as psychological activities that reduce the unpleasure of psychic conflict by blocking, inhibiting, or distorting awareness of disturbing mental contents. Defenses are traditionally conceptualized as methods for blocking or disguising the expression of the drive derivatives that arouse unpleasure. Contemporary theorists, however, recognize that the unpleasure associated with drive derivatives may be warded off independent of the drive (Abend, 1981; Brenner, 1981, 1982). This is particularly important in clinical work with impulsive clients who habitually forget about the consequences of their conduct. Of course, defenses against negative affects may also be adaptive—for example, in situations where anxieties are unrealistic and unduly inhibiting or in circumstances that require courage or fortitude in the face of unpleasure.

The traditional concept of defense mechanisms entails the assumption that defenses are discrete mental functions that can be observed and classified. In the course of his career, Freud described at least 10 different defenses. In her pioneering study of the ego, Anna Freud (1936) listed 9 different defenses: (1) regression, (2) repression, (3) reaction formation, (4) isolation, (5) undoing, (6) projection, (7) introjection, (8) turning against the self, and (9) reversal, to which intellectualization and identification were eventually added. In the years that followed, this list grew to include 22 major and 26 minor defenses (Laughlin, 1979). Contemporary structural theory explains this proliferation as a consequence of the idea that defense requires special mechanisms. In fact, what are cited as defense mechanisms are simply ego functions that are deployed in situations of psychic conflict to reduce unpleasure.

> Whatever ensues in mental life that results in diminution of unpleasurable affects—ideally in their disappearance—belongs under the heading of defense . . . the ego can use for defense whatever lies at hand that is useful for the purpose. (Brenner, 1981, p. 558)

Affects, ideas, attitudes, alterations of attention, and even wishes (drive derivatives) may serve as defenses. Brenner thus concludes, "Modes of defense are as diverse as psychic life itself" (p. 561).

THE GENESIS OF PSYCHIC CONFLICTS AND COMPROMISE FORMATIONS

The analysis of psychological conflicts and compromise formations also requires knowledge of the genesis of psychic conflict. Psychic conflict comes into existence during the course of individual development as a result of childhood experiences and the way that they are interpreted by the child. Childhood normally entails many pleasurable experiences, which give rise to wishes for an expanding variety of pleasures. These are often felt as desires of great urgency and power and are often irresistible to the immature child. Even as these wishes reach new levels of intensity, however, every child must undergo a succession of socialization experiences, such as weaning and toilet training, in which their expression is limited, restricted to special circumstances, or utterly forbidden.

Discipline often entails punishment and temporary withdrawals of the parent's loving attentiveness, interactions that are threatening to the child. The character of the child's subjective perception may be quite distorted because of the child's emotional reactions to discipline and as a result of his or her immature cognitive functioning. Whenever a parent punishes a child or restricts a child's pleasure, especially a pleasure in which the child is highly invested, the child is prone to become frustrated and angry. The angrier the child becomes, the more likely he or she is to believe that the parent is equally angry. Parents who discipline, even lovingly, may thus come to be perceived as fantastical figures of devastating power. These distorted representations of the parent's aggressive intentions are an aspect of the child's *psychic reality.*

Psychic reality is the true context of existence from the child's point of view (Freud, 1900). Psychic reality is only partially determined by objective events. Wishes, affects, and related cognitive distortions result in the formation of a privately constructed universe in which highly unrealistic wishes, such as the wish to be both sexes or the wish to marry the parent, may appear quite reasonable. Accompanying these wishes, fears of horrendous dangers, such as abandonment or castration, may appear equally real and imminent. Sometimes aspects of psychic reality may be recognized as fantastical in nature, an insight that dissipates their compelling quality. The situation is more complicated when the construction of psychic reality includes memories, however fragmentary, disguised, or elaborated, of seduction and incest or of other threatening or horrifying events. When psychic reality has been shaped by such objective events, fantastically exaggerated elaborations of these memories tend to exert a persistent influence over the person, based on an enduring sense of actuality. Psychic conflicts are thus bound to be particularly damaging and intractable when parents are actually abusive or when childhood is characterized by the occurrence of unusual traumas, such as a death in the family, an accident, an illness, or surgery.

No matter how entangled in psychic conflict a child's wishes may be, they exert a persistent pressure toward gratification, thus motivating an unending succession of efforts to achieve fulfillment, in both fantasy (imaginary action) and action. In the course of these efforts, childhood wishes are shaped and reshaped by the impact of aversive contingencies on the one hand and by the discovery of pleasurable substitutes on the other. Repetitive trials eventually produce compromise solutions. The best compromises confer a maximum of pleasure with a minimum of unpleasure. These compromises are valued and retained as preferred schemata or blueprints for future gratifications of the wish. They may be repeated with numerous variations whenever the wish arises, in both fantasy and action. Of course, the inexorable process of socialization soon imposes new restrictions and unpleasures, which in turn necessitate new compromise formations.

Pine (1970) illustrates this developmental process with regard to the transformation of anality (pleasure related to bowel functioning) and scopophilia (pleasure in looking at others). He describes the compromise formations of two 8-year-olds who are intensely invested in anal wishes. One talks incessantly about bathroom odors and the need to avoid them, a pattern that keeps these thoughts in mind. A second vigorously sprays the toilet with aerosol spray, thus creating a potent new odor to enjoy. Two other 8-year-olds desire to look at their mother's naked body but are frightened of the sight of her penis-less genitals. Each takes every opportunity to look, but each allays anxiety differently. One simply looks through his mother; the other gleefully points at his mother's fat. In each case, the scopophilic wish may be enjoyed while the desire to look is disguised or denied. In each of these cases, the primary wish of childhood has given rise to derivative forms, new editions that minimize their aversive emotional consequences. The continuing development of each childhood wish thus entails the creation of successive compromise formations, each represented by particular patterns of conduct and corresponding anthologies of private fantasies (Arlow, 1969). By the time adulthood is reached, mental life will include numerous layers of developmentally stratified compromise formations. All are rooted in the primary wishes and conflicts of childhood. These are the hidden organizers of psychic life.

THE METAPSYCHOLOGICAL PERSPECTIVES

What is referred to as the Freudian *metapsychology* is actually a collection of six axiomatic principles that serve as the explanatory basis for Freud's most important formulations about human behavior and psychopathology. The term *metapsychology* came to be used to refer to this framework because it emphasized phenomena that went beyond the extant psychological systems of Freud's time. The six viewpoints or perspectives are the topographical, structural, dynamic, economic, genetic, and adaptive. Some authors have suggested that the genetic and adaptive perspectives, unlike the first four perspectives, were not as clearly explicated by Freud as by later theorists, although there is a general consensus that these two perspectives are nevertheless implicitly represented in Freud's writings (Moore & Fine, 1990).

The Topographical Perspective

According to the topographic model (Freud, 1900), the mind is composed of three systems: (1) the system unconscious, (2) the system preconscious, and (3) the system conscious. The system *unconscious,* which represents the primitive core of instinctual strivings, functions entirely according to the pleasure principle and is incapable of delaying or inhibiting pleasure seeking. It generates desires for which it seeks representation in conscious thought and fulfillment in action. The unconscious is developmentally superseded by a higher system, the preconscious, which functions in tandem with the system conscious. The *preconscious* is composed of contents and thought activities that are readily identifiable and accessible to consciousness, and it is therefore

also referred to as the preconscious-conscious. The preconscious is capable of realistic thought, moral self-evaluation, and conscious regulation of pleasure seeking according to the reality principle. Most important, the preconscious inhibits the primitive impulsivity of the unconscious by blocking the mental representations of unconscious desires through repression and other defenses. The preconscious performs this function because certain primitive impulses, which are pleasurable in the system unconscious, are experienced as unpleasurable in the (more realistic) system preconscious. Finally, the system *conscious* is conceptualized as a sense organ, capable of perceiving outer stimuli, bodily sensations (including emotions), and the mental contents of the preconscious. In this early formulation, Freud conceptualized psychic conflict as occurring between the unconscious and the preconscious-conscious.

The Structural Perspective

Freud employed the topographic model until it became clear that it did not accurately match the clinical data. The topographic model predicts that the anti-instinctual activities of the preconscious should be accessible to conscious awareness. Clinical data revealed, however, that some aspects of defensive and moral functioning (unconscious defenses and unconscious guilt), both anti-instinctual features of the preconscious, are in fact inaccessible to consciousness. Accordingly, Freud (1923) developed a revised model, which has come to be known as the *structural model.* According to the structural model, the mind is constituted by three agencies—the id, the superego, and the ego—each of which serves a different set of functions. *Id* is a new term for the older *system unconscious,* which continuously generates primitive impulses that press for satisfaction. The superego, a mental system composed of internalized representations of parental authorities, functions as an inner supervisor, providing love and approval for moral behavior, as well as condemnation and criticism for immoral desires and conduct. The ego is the executive system of the mind, responsible for the organization of mental life and the management of social conduct. The ego functions to integrate the demands of the id and the superego with the conditions and contingencies of external social reality. The ego is the seat of consciousness, although the aspects of ego functioning (unconscious thoughts, ego defenses) are unconscious. The structural model permits the conceptualization of psychic conflict between the three systems, each of which pursues potentially contradictory aims. In accordance with the structural model, the terms *unconscious, preconscious,* and *conscious* may be used as adjectives to describe the accessibility to consciousness of specific mental contents rather than as nouns to denote mental systems.

The Dynamic Perspective

The dynamic perspective, which can be traced to *Studies on Hysteria* (Breuer & Freud, 1893–1895), postulates that behavior is motivated; it is lawful, has an identifiable cause, and is purposive (Holzman, 1995). The dynamic perspective is necessary to understand not only neurotic symptoms and other forms of psychopathology but also the neurotic meaning of ostensibly insignificant behavioral acts associated with everyday living (also termed *parapraxes*),[6] such as slips of the tongue, the forgetting of names, misreadings, and bungled actions (Freud, 1901; Holzman, 1995). It is an especially important and facilitative viewpoint in psychoanalytic efforts to understand the latent meaning of dreams.

In *The Psychopathology of Everyday Life* (Freud, 1901), the dynamic perspective is brought to life by literally hundreds of examples of parapraxes. A representative vignette follows:

> I forbade a patient to telephone to the girl he was in love with—but with whom he himself wanted to break off relations—since each conversation served only to renew the struggle about giving her up. He was to write his final decision to her, though there were difficulties about delivering

letters to her. He called on me at one o'clock to tell me he had found a way of getting round these difficulties, and amongst other things asked if he might quote my authority as a physician. At two o'clock he was occupied in composing the letter that was to end the relationship, when he suddenly broke off and said to his mother who was with him: "Oh! I've forgotten to ask the professor if I may mention his name in the letter." He rushed to the telephone, put through his call and said into the instrument: "May I speak to the professor, please, if he's finished dinner?" In answer, he got an astonished: "Adolph, have you gone mad?" It was the same voice which by my orders he should not have heard again. He had simply "made an error," and instead of the physician's number he had given the girl's. (p. 222)

The Economic Perspective

It is not possible to explain mental life solely on the basis of qualitative variables. All the motivations already described vary in their intensities at different times, resulting in an endless shifting in the balance of psychological forces within the mind. The economic perspective is an outgrowth of Freud's observations concerning the strength of the drives and other mental phenomena that seemed to require a quantitative explanation. In his early clinical work, Freud had been impressed by the power of intrusive ideas and the compelling character of rituals in obsessive-compulsive neurosis, the refractory nature of conversion symptoms to even the most aggressive medical interventions, and the potency of paranoid delusions. These forms of psychopathology, as well as his experience with the resistance of his neurotic clients, convinced him that a quantitative factor underlies much of behavior, pathological or otherwise (Holzman, 1995). The mechanisms of displacement and condensation, both of which Freud had originally discussed in connection with the concepts of primary and secondary process and dream analysis (Freud, 1895b, 1900, 1911), were also conceived of quantitatively. Displacement is

---

[6]From the Greek, literally translated as "abnormal or faulty actions."

the intrapsychic operation whereby the intensity or interest of an idea that is anxiety generating is shifted onto a second idea that has an associative connection to the first but is less anxiety arousing. Condensation is an unconscious defensive operation through which a single image, as in a dream, actually serves to represent multiple ideas or meanings.

The Genetic Perspective

The genetic point of view, like the topographical, economic, and dynamic viewpoints, is anchored in Freud's earliest papers and several lengthier works, for example, *Studies on Hysteria* (1893–1895) and *The Interpretation of Dreams* (1900). The genetic viewpoint asserts that a meaningful psychological understanding of the adult is of necessity predicated on a thorough comprehension of that person's childhood experiences. Stated in slightly different terms, the genetic perspective postulates that the past persists into the present (Holzman, 1995). This particular viewpoint, which has been expropriated by popular culture to a greater degree than perhaps any other, has given rise to the somewhat simplistic notion that dysfunctional behavior and psychopathology in adulthood are almost invariably linked to unhappy childhood experiences.

Freud actually never regarded past experiences as the sole criterion for the development of later psychopathology. He did propose that the historical legacy of experiences acquired meaning as a consequence of a "mutual interaction between and integration of constitutional factors and environmental events" (Holzman, 1995, p. 56). In other words, constitutional factors such as the strength of the drives and various individual endowments and capabilities exert influence and are, in turn, influenced by the nature of the individual's experiences in his or her environmental milieu.

The Adaptive Perspective

The adaptive perspective, chiefly concerned with the relationship of the individual to the surrounding environment, highlights the influence of both interpersonal and societal forces. This has been termed the individual's "commerce with the real world" (Holzman, 1995, p. 58). Although the adaptive perspective was present in a nascent form in Freud's early formulations of drive theory (1900, 1905), it was not until his publication of *The Ego and the Id* (1923) that the importance of the extramural environment was emphasized. The development of Freud's concept of the ego and its relationship to the environment opened the way for dramatic developments in psychoanalytic theory.

EGO PSYCHOLOGY

In a sense, our exploration of ego psychology has already begun with the discussion of compromise formations, defense theory, and metapsychological perspectives. In the early stages of his career, Freud was primarily concerned with exploring the depths of the mind in an effort to discover its primordial origins. He saw mental life as the refracted expression of primitive strivings. His first view of the curative process in psychoanalysis rested on the assumption that bringing these strivings to life (i.e., making the unconscious conscious) would permit them to be dealt with in a more adaptive way. Accordingly, he had little interest in studies of consciousness, which he regarded as superficial. With the introduction of structural theory in 1923, the importance of the preconscious was expanded, and the psyche was depicted as having greater complexity.

The 1923 formulation of structural theory was epochal, permitting various problems in normal development as well as the influence of environmental variables and the character of the infant's earliest relationships with caregivers to be studied in entirely new ways. At the same time, ego psychological theorists have managed to preserve more or less intact Freudian drive theory, which may differentiate this school from either object relational or self-psychological theories (Mitchell & Black, 1995). The more prominent architects of ego psychology are Anna Freud, Heinz Hartmann, Rene Spitz, Margaret Mahler, Erik Erikson, and Edith Jacobson. It is to certain of their contributions that we now turn.

Anna Freud and Defense Theory

Perhaps Anna Freud's most significant contribution to ego psychology was her clarification of defense theory and specification of the principal mechanisms of defense. She was also considered a pioneer in the field of child psychoanalysis and devoted much energy to studying the psychoanalytic treatment process and to developing research instruments such as the Hampstead Profile, a comprehensive, developmentally based instrument for assessing a client's ego functioning and object relations. Anna Freud's efforts to explicate the structural model and Sigmund Freud's (1926) revised theory of anxiety, and to make these consonant with a superordinate focus on the ego and its functions, led her to consider problems such as the "choice of neurosis" and "motives" for defense. In fact, she distinguished four principal motives for defense against the drives: (1) superego anxiety (or guilt), (2) objective anxiety (in children), (3) anxiety about the strength of drives, and (4) anxiety stemming from conflicts between mutually incompatible aims (A. Freud, 1936). On the basis of her extensive observations of and psychoanalytic work with young children, Anna Freud later developed the concept of developmental lines (A. Freud, 1963), a variegated developmental schedule that permitted the clinician-researcher to follow important changes in sexual, aggressive, and social developmental "lines" from infancy to adolescence.

The Ego and Adaptation

Heinz Hartmann's contributions were designed to enhance and expand the scope of psychoanalytic theory, with the objective of transforming it into a system of general psychology (Goldstein, 1995; Mitchell & Black, 1995). A central argument of Hartmann's most important work, *Ego Psychology and the Problem of Adaptation* (1939), was that the human infant was born with innate "conflict-free ego capacities" that would be activated in an "average expectable environment," thereby ensuring the infant's survival and adaptation. The capacities to which Hartmann (1939) referred included language, perception, memory, intention, motor activity, object comprehension, and thinking. Hartmann's notion of conflict-free ego capacities contrasted with more traditional psychoanalytic ideas, where adaptation is achieved only as an outcome of frustration and conflict. Hartmann also proposed the twin concepts of *alloplastic adaptation,* the individual's efforts to alter external realities to meet various human needs, and *autoplastic adaptation,* which refers to the individual's efforts to accommodate to external realities.

The Developmentalists: Rene Spitz, Margaret Mahler, and Erik Erikson

Spitz and Mahler, both of whom began their professional careers as pediatricians, are well recognized for their important contributions to developmental ego psychology. Working as a consultant in a foundling home during World War II, Spitz first described the dramatic sequelae of a syndrome that exacted a profound developmental toll on the infants he studied. Although the nutritional needs of these infants were met quite adequately and care was provided for them in hygienic environments, they were deprived of interaction with maternal caregivers. Seemingly as a direct consequence of the absence of mother-infant interaction, they became withdrawn, failed to achieve developmental milestones, and had very high morbidity and mortality rates (Spitz, 1945).[7] Spitz characterized this syndrome as *anaclitic depression* (depression associated with

---

[7]If the infant's mother was able to resume her maternal functions during the first 3 months, the downward spiral that otherwise often led to retardation, marasmus, and death could be reversed.

thwarted dependency needs). Spitz (1965) later identified what he termed the *three psychic organizers:* (1) the baby's social response at approximately 3 months, (2) the emergence of stranger anxiety at 8 months, and (3) the child's "no" response, first observed at about 15 months. Spitz's greatest contribution may have been his systematic effort to identify the particular facilitative environmental conditions that spur the development of the "innate adaptive capabilities" Hartmann had previously described (Mitchell & Black, 1995).

Mahler's work was also principally with young children, although the original focus of her clinical research was psychotic youngsters. Mahler believed that the nature of the ego pathology she observed in psychotic children was inadequately addressed within the traditional framework of drive theory. She proposed that these children suffered from defects or failures in the organization of internalized self and object representations and experienced a corresponding difficulty in differentiating self from not self; in consequence, such children were largely incapable of acquiring an enduring sense of self that is distinct and separable from others. This, in turn, suggested to Mahler that the infant's "mediating human partner," as Spitz had also maintained, had a highly significant role in the evolution of the infantile ego. Ultimately, Mahler turned to the study of normal infant development. Mahler's theory of the separation-individuation process, recent criticisms notwithstanding (Homer, 1985; Stern, 1986), introduced a schema that not only transformed the study of infant pathology but has also served as the

theoretical basis for a psychoanalytic approach to the psychotherapy of adults with borderline personality disorder (Masterson & Rinsley, 1975).[8] On the basis of her longitudinal investigations of mother-infant pairs in a nursery setting, Mahler portrayed a process that begins at birth and continues into the child's fourth year (Mahler, Pine, & Bergmann, 1975). Characterizing infants as essentially nonrelated or objectless at birth (the autistic phase), she described their gradual emergence via a period of mother-infant symbiosis into four relatively discrete stages of separation and individuation: (1) differentiation (5 to 9 months), (2) practicing (9 to 15 months), (3) rapprochement (15 to 24 months), and (4) the development of object constancy (24 to 36 months and beyond).

Erikson's greatest contributions to ego psychology involved his theory of psychosocial and psychosexual epigenesis[9] and the detailed attention he gave to the concept of ego identity. Whereas Spitz and Mahler focused their attentions on the earliest developmental processes of the infant's emerging ego, Erikson's psychosocial epigenetic theory examined ego development across the entire life span and highlighted social-environmental factors to a greater degree than any existing ego psychological model. In Erikson's view, healthy ego development was contingent on the mastery of specific developmental tasks and normative crises associated with each of eight life cycle stages he identified:

1. *Basic trust versus basic mistrust:* This stage is coterminous with Freud's oral phase; the principal experiential mode in this stage is oral

---

[8]Masterson and others have hypothesized that adolescents and adults with borderline pathology have experienced a derailment in the normal separation-individuation process during the critical rapprochement phase; this leads to what has been described as the core dilemma of the borderline character: fear of loss of self versus fear of loss of the other.

[9]*Epigenesis* is a term that Erikson expropriated from the field of embryology. It is defined as "the predetermined sequential development of the parts of an organism" (Holzman, 1995, p. 160). Each part follows an internal organismic timetable, permitting it to emerge and then to become successfully integrated with the rest of the organism. In such a developmental schema, the earliest stages of growth have an inherently greater vulnerability to disruption than the later ones, since the effect of such disruption on the early stages will thereby influence all subsequent ones.

receptive. In optimal circumstances, there is a preponderance of positively valenced experiences with one's mother, which culminate in basic trust.

2. *Autonomy versus shame and doubt:* This stage coincides with the anal stage in Freud's model of the libidinal stages. The emphasis is on the child's newly emerging autonomy, coextensive with the increased radius of locomotor activity and maturation of the muscle systems. Success in this phase results in the child's pleasure in independent actions and self-expression, and failure results in shame and self-doubt.

3. *Initiative versus guilt:* This stage corresponds to Freud's phallic stage. Sexual curiosity and oedipal issues are common, competitiveness reaches new heights, and the child's efforts to reach and attain goals acquire importance. Danger arises when the child's aggression or manipulation of the environment triggers an abiding sense of guilt.

4. *Industry versus inferiority:* This stage occurs during the latency period in Freud's model. It is associated with the child's beginning efforts to use tools, his sense of being productive, and of developing the capability to complete tasks.

5. *Identity versus identity diffusion:* This stage is ushered in by adolescence. It is perhaps the most extensively developed in the Eriksonian model. Stable identity requires an integration of formative experiences "that give the child the sense that he is a person with a history, a stability, and a continuity that is recognizable by others" (Holzman, 1995, p. 163). Erikson (1959) also enumerated seven aspects of identity consolidation that are critical codeterminants of success or failure in this stage: (1) a time perspective, (2) self-certainty, (3) role experimentation, (4) anticipation of achievement, (5) sexual identity, (6) acceptance of leadership, and (7) commitment to basic values.

6. *Intimacy and distantiation versus self-absorption:* The major developmental task of this phase, which occurs during early adulthood, is the individual's capacity for healthy sexual and nonsexual intimacy while still retaining a firm sense of personal identity. Should such intimacy be impossible, there is a "regressive retreat to exclusive concern with oneself" (Holzman, 1995).

7. *Generativity versus stagnation:* This penultimate phase of the adult life cycle involves the adult in the critical tasks and responsibilities of parenting. Parenthood is not inextricably tied to generativity, however; just as there are adults who relinquish or are otherwise unable to fulfill parental responsibilities, so too are there childless adults whose generativity involves the pursuit of creative or artistic initiatives.

8. *Integrity versus despair and disgust:* Ego integrity is the culmination of ego identity (Erikson, 1959; Goldstein, 1995). It reflects a level of maturity signaling the individual's acceptance of the past, particularly past disappointments and mistakes.

Jacobson: The Self and the Object World

The daunting task of summarizing the considerable scope of Edith Jacobson's contributions to the psychoanalytic literature has been previously discussed (Greenberg & Mitchell, 1983). Jacobson attempted to integrate the Freudian emphasis on constitutional factors in development (including instinctual drives) with the growing recognition of the potent imprint of life experience. In a series of papers that culminated in the publication of *The Self and the Object World* (1964), Jacobson revised and reformulated Freud's theory of psychosexual development and various aspects of classical metapsychology, particularly the economic principle. Although she never actually disputed the primacy of the drives, she theorized that the mother-infant relationship had complementarity with innate maturational forces and, furthermore, that the distinctive features of the infant's instinctual drives acquire meaning only within the milieu of the caregiving relationship. In Jacobson's model of early development, a complex reciprocal interchange between the infant's ongoing experience with caregivers and the maturational unfolding of the drives leads to the formation of self images and object images. These images have different hedonic valences, and it is the infant's gradual capacity for integrating good and bad experiences of objects and of self that is finally necessary for mature affectivity. The phenomenology of affective disorders was also of considerable interest to Jacobson, whose book *Depression: Comparative Studies of Normal, Neurotic, and Psychotic Conditions* (1971) continued her exploration of the complex relationship between affectivity and the inner representational world.

OBJECT RELATIONS THEORY

None of the psychoanalytic theory groups discussed in this chapter actually constitutes a fully separate psychoanalytic psychology. This is perhaps especially true of object relations theory, a general heading under which is subsumed several distinct groups of theories, each possessing distinctive theoretical premises and complementary approaches to psychoanalytic treatment.

Grotstein (1996) traces the psychoanalytic use of the term *object* to a series of six papers written by Freud: (1) "Three Essays on the Theory of Sexuality" (1905), (2) "Family Romances" (1909), (3) "On Narcissism: An Introduction" (1914a), (4) "Mourning and Melancholia" (1917), (5) "A Child Is Being Beaten" (1919), and (6) "The Ego and the Id" (1923). In the original use of this term, Freud (1905) had sought to minimize the importance of the infant's caretakers, who were viewed more with respect to their inhibition or facilitation of the child's instinctual wishes than as human beings in their own right. Gradually, however, Freud demonstrated increasing interest in the role of objects, which we can glean from "his conception of the ego-ideal, the superego, and the Oedipus Complex itself . . . contributions [where the object is conceived] as being incorporated into the psychic structure" (Grotstein, 1996, p. 91). In Freud's (1917) essay on the mourning process,

there was further exploration of the relationship between external object loss and the internal process through which the object is established as an identification in the mourner's ego. Freud also made use of object relations ideas in his examination of the role that sadism and masochism played in pathological narcissism.

A number of theorists have shaped object relations thinking since Freud: Karl Abraham (1924/1948), whose model of object relations was embedded in an eloquent paper on the development of the libido; Sandor Ferenczi (1913/1950), whose postulation of an infantile desire to return to a prenatal symbiotic state anticipates the work of Margaret Mahler; Ian Suttie (1935/1952), who wrote that the infant comes into the world with an innate need for companionship, nonsexual love, and security, all of which evolve in the mother-infant relational matrix (Mishne, 1993); Imre Hermann (1933, 1936), who hypothesized that there was a human instinct to cling that paralleled the instinctual behavior of other primates;[10] and Michael Balint and Alice Balint, among whose theoretical contributions were the instinct of "primary object love" (M. Balint, 1937/1949)[11] and "the basic fault" (A. Balint, 1937/1949), a concept that designated a primary breach in the ego arising during the preoedipal period.

Contemporary object relations theories, however, have been especially influenced by several major theorists: Harry Stack Sullivan, Melanie Klein, and Donald Winnicott.

Interpersonal Psychoanalysis: The Work of Harry Stack Sullivan

Interpersonal psychoanalysis derives from the clinical work and theoretical formulations of

---

[10]Grotstein (1996, p. 95) observes that Hermann's work seems to have adumbrated the well-known experiments of H. F. Harlow (1959) in this regard.

[11]In their assertion of such an instinct, the Balints repudiated Freud's concept of primary narcissism and the idea that infants only gradually develop attachments to objects (Grotstein, 1996).

Harry Stack Sullivan (1892–1949), an American psychiatrist who pioneered the psychotherapeutic treatment of severely disturbed individuals. Sullivan, who studied medicine in Chicago, was greatly impressed by the exciting intellectual developments in philosophy and the social sciences at the University of Chicago. He was particularly influenced by the work of social thinkers such as George Herbert Meade, Edward Sapir, John Dewey, and other proponents of the American pragmatist school of philosophical thought. Sullivan's distinctive approach to psychotherapy and psychiatry reflected his profound immersion in this intellectual milieu (Chapman, 1976; Mullahy, 1970; Perry, 1982).

Sullivan was deeply dissatisfied with existing psychoanalytic theory. He distrusted the abstract, metaphorical concepts of Freudian theory, which, in his view, pertained to mental systems and structures that are not observable and are, hence, only hypothetical in nature. In contrast to Freudian theorists, Sullivan (1953, 1956), who was greatly influenced by Bridgman's (1945) "operationalism," believed that psychiatric theories should, to the greatest extent possible, employ "operational" terms with definable and empirical referents. Sullivan also found that Freudian theory (as it existed during his formative years of psychiatric practice) was inadequate to the understanding and treatment of the severely mentally ill clients with whom he worked. As a result, Sullivan's clinical and theoretical contributions to psychiatric and psychoanalytic thought are strikingly original and couched in his own highly idiosyncratic terminology.

Over the years, Sullivan came to reject the basic features of Freudian theory. Most important, Sullivan repudiated Freud's belief that human motivations are determined by instinctual drives. In opposition to Freud's classical drive theory, Sullivan posited that human motivations are primarily interpersonal in nature, determined by interpersonal relationships, especially the relationships of childhood and adolescence, and understandable only in terms of such relationships. Sullivan believed that human beings respond to two sets of motivations. One

set is characterized as the satisfaction of bodily and emotional needs, including sexuality and intimacy. A second set of motivations is related to the experience of anxiety and related strivings for security. Both the satisfaction of needs and the achievement of security are interpersonal events occurring in relation to other persons. In contrast to the Freudian conception of personality as the characteristic way the individual organizes the competing claims of id, ego, and superego, Sullivan conceptualized personality as the characteristic ways in which the individual interacts with other people in the pursuit of satisfactions and security. Mental illness, he argued, can best be understood as a disturbance of interpersonal relations. Sullivan's efforts to employ operational concepts and his concomitant emphasis on interpersonal relations gradually gave rise to a new psychoanalytic orientation in which the primary focus was on interpersonal relations rather than intrapsychic events.

Sullivan's approach to treatment reflected this shift of emphasis. If mental illness and other malformations of personality are the consequence of pathogenic interpersonal relationships, he reasoned, mental health may best be promoted by the creation of healthy interpersonal relationships. In the late 1920s, Sullivan implemented this idea at Sheppard and Enoch Pratt Hospital in Baltimore, where he developed an unusual inpatient psychiatric unit for male schizophrenics in which ward staff were specially trained to interact with the patients and to foster comfortable and emotionally rewarding interpersonal relationships with them in order to help correct their unhealthy relationship patterns. Sullivan also developed a distinctive method of conducting individual therapy with clients. Abandoning the free-association method of classical psychoanalysis, Sullivan employed a conversational approach to clients, conceptualizing his role as that of a participant-observer in the relationship with the client. His goal was to engage the client in a collaborative study of the client's interpersonal relationships so that the client's unhealthy patterns of relating to others could be discovered and understood. Most important, Sullivan stressed the importance of establishing a healthy relationship with the client to correct habitual maladaptive interpersonal patterns. Employing these techniques, Sullivan achieved unparalleled therapeutic gains with clients who had previously been regarded as hopeless and untreatable. As his work became known, Sullivan became one of America's most respected and admired psychiatrists. He acquired a growing circle of collaborators that included some of the leading thinkers in psychoanalysis, such as Clara Thompson, Erich Fromm, and Frieda Fromm-Reichmann, all of whom contributed to the development of the interpersonal school of psychoanalysis.

Sullivan never attempted to establish a comprehensive theoretical system, and contemporary therapists working within the interpersonal tradition have introduced their own technical and theoretical innovations (Arieti, 1974; Chrzanowski, 1977; Fromm-Reichmann, 1950; Havens, 1976, 1986; Levenson, 1972; Thompson, 1964; Witenberg, 1973). Interpersonal psychoanalysis is best described as "a set of different approaches to theory and clinical practice . . . with shared underlying assumptions and premises" (Greenberg & Mitchell, 1983, p. 79). These include Sullivan's rejection of Freudian instinct theory, his basic view of psychopathology as a disturbance of interpersonal relationships, his belief in the interpersonal roots of mental illness, and his emphasis on the curative importance of healthy interpersonal relationships. Interpersonal psychoanalysis has often been criticized by exponents of traditional psychoanalysis as superficial or lacking in depth because of its focus on the interpersonal field and its rejection of drive concepts. However, Sullivan's ideas are now believed to have exerted a profound and far-reaching influence on contemporary psychoanalytic thinking (Havens & Frank, 1971).

An overarching theme in Sullivan's writings is that the human infant is born into a relational milieu; relational configurations in his theoretical model evolve out of actual experience with others. Sullivan (1931) repeatedly underscored the assertion that human beings can be understood only within the "organism-environment complex"[12] and consequently are incapable of "definitive description in isolation." In Sullivan's developmental model, a superordinate importance is placed on the interpersonal field, together with the efforts that children devise to maintain relatedness with significant others.

Needs for satisfaction are "integrating tendencies" that impel the individual to seek physical and emotional contact with others. The integration of relationships in the pursuit of satisfactions is complicated, however, by the arousal of painful affective states that Sullivan characterizes as anxiety. Sullivan's notion of anxiety differs from Freud's view of anxiety in two principal ways. In his mature formulation (Freud, 1926), Freud conceptualized anxiety as a form of fear related to specific typical danger situations of childhood (loss of the mother, loss of the mother's love, castration, and guilt). Sullivan used the term *anxiety* to include any form of mental suffering, distress, or anguish aroused in an interpersonal situation. A second difference pertains to the manner in which anxiety is generated. In Freudian theory, anxiety is a signal of danger, typically aroused by the mobilization of repressed wishes associated with specific danger situations. Accordingly, "Drives and reality are inextricably linked as sources of danger to the ego" (Holzman, 1995, p. 143). In Sullivan's theory, the infant's experience of anxiety is aroused by anxiety (in its more narrowly defined sense) or by other strong affects of distress in the caregiver. Babies are exquisitely sensitive to the moods of others and, through a phenomenon Sullivan termed *empathic linkage,* experience the caregiver's anxiety as if it were their own. While needs for satisfaction are integrating tendencies that foster relatedness, anxiety and other forms of

---

[12]It is not difficult to see a clear parallel between Sullivan's use of this term and the social work emphasis on the person-in-environment matrix; interestingly, however, Sullivan is not often cited by social work historians as having had a significant influence on the development of social work theory.

emotional suffering are aversive experiences that impair interpersonal relations. Excessive anxiety in infancy and childhood predispose the affected individual to experience anxiety in the context of his or her adult relationships. This vulnerability to anxiety contributes to disturbances of interpersonal relationships that are usually referred to as psychopathology or mental illness.

Sullivan believed that the most basic differentiation for the infant was "not between light and dark, or between mother and father, but between anxious states and non-anxious states" (Mitchell & Black, 1995, p. 68). During development, the child forms schematic impressions or "personifications" of self and mother. Pleasurable experiences give rise to impressions of the "good mother" and the "good me," while experiences of anxiety produce impressions of the "bad mother" and the "bad me." Extremely painful or terrifying interpersonal situations elicit representations of the "evil mother" and the "not me." The memory of such experiences is vigorously avoided and may be terrifying when aroused. "Evil mother" and "not me" experiences are associated with severe mental illness.

Sullivan introduced the term *self-system* to collectively characterize the myriad psychological activities that the individual employs to avoid anxiety ("bad me" and "not me") and to ensure feelings of security ("good me"). In Sullivan's writing, security is defined as the *absence of anxiety*. The self-system is an expansive system of mental states, symbols, and coordinated activities that function to promote feelings of security by assessing the safety of interpersonal situations, anticipating the arousal of anxiety, and minimizing anxiety through the activation of security operations. Security operations roughly parallel the concept of defense in the traditional Freudian system: They operate covertly, out of the individual's awareness, serving to diminish anxiety and other feelings of emotional distress associated with the "bad me" or "not me" and to restore feelings of security and well-being that are the affective concomitants of the "good me." The concept of security operations also differs from the traditional Freudian concept of defenses, however, in

significant ways. In classical Freudian theory, defenses are mental activities designed to reduce anxiety arising from intrapsychic conflict (i.e., conflict between the id, ego, and superego). In Sullivan's theory, security operations are intended to diminish the anxiety and emotional distress that arise from disturbances in interpersonal relationships. While defenses are best understood as intrapsychic phenomena, security operations entail an interpersonal dimension. Security operations promote relatedness and facilitate the satisfaction of emotional needs by preserving security in interpersonal situations.

Security operations develop and become increasingly sophisticated as the child matures. Typical security operations of early childhood include apathy and somnolent detachment, both of which reflect a process of disengagement from an anxiety-arousing interpersonal situation, such as an anxious or anguished mother. As the child develops progressive cognitive capabilities, other security operations become possible. A typical security operation of later development is selective inattention, a tactical redeployment of focal attention from disturbing aspects of interpersonal experience to aspects that enhance the individual's feelings of self-esteem or security. As a result of selective inattention, disturbing aspects of interpersonal phenomena are excluded from experience and memory. An individual's security operations include complex patterns of interpersonal activity that manifest as typical aspects of the individual's interpersonal relationships. For example, habitual compliance or placating behavior, aggressive bullying or dominating, emotional withdrawal or constriction, and pomposity and self-centeredness may be conceptualized as complex security operations intended to avoid anxiety in interpersonal situations, that is, to maintain the vulnerable individual's sense of comfort and security. Sullivan (1953) summarizes patterns of interpersonal conduct such as the dramatization of roles, or the repetitive enactment of emotionally safe relational configurations, interpersonal patterns that he calls *me-you patterns.*

In sum, Sullivan's interpersonal approach to psychoanalysis is prototypical of psychoanalytic schools of thought that diverge from classical Freudian theory by positing that human motivations and personality structure derive from the interpersonal experiences of development rather than from the unfolding influence of instinctual drives. Other psychoanalytic theorists who shared this point of view are Fairbairn (1952) and Guntrip (1968, 1971). Greenberg and Mitchell (1983) group these schools of thought together as the relational theories of psychoanalysis.

In addition to his enduring impact on psychoanalytic theory, Sullivan's (1962) contributions have had a major impact on the understanding and treatment of schizophrenia. Sullivan was passionate in his arguments against professional "objectivity" and "detachment" in the psychotherapy of schizophrenic clients, since he believed that the distorted interpersonal relations of the schizophrenic originally developed from a matrix of disordered relationships between the client and members of the client's family. Although a relational approach to the psychotherapy of schizophrenia has enjoyed less popularity since the recent ascendancy of biological psychiatry, Sullivan's emphasis on the social context of psychopathology remains a viable theoretical premise.

The Work of Melanie Klein

Some have asserted that Melanie Klein (1882–1960) and her theory of object relations have exerted an influence on the contemporary world of psychoanalysis second only to that of Freud (Mitchell & Black, 1995). Though this claim is arguable, most would concede that Klein's theoretical positions were at the center of a protracted debate in the British psychoanalytic establishment that ultimately led to the creation of three separate schools of psychoanalysis in that country. Klein was also the first psychoanalyst to treat children with the psychoanalytic method, "a project . . . long overdue . . . [that] aroused considerable interest in the psychoanalytic community," when her first paper was published in 1919 (Greenberg & Mitchell, 1983, p. 119). Although the history of psychoanalysis

is replete with controversies over theory and technique, perhaps none has attained the notoriety and divisiveness or equaled the profound ramifications of the prolonged disagreement between Melanie Klein and Anna Freud.

The schism that developed between Klein and Anna Freud began in the mid- to late 1920s over issues of technique in child analysis. A fundamental premise of Klein was that the play of young children was equivalent to the free associations of adult clients; so long as the meaning of their play was interpreted to them, children, like adults, were suitable subjects for psychoanalytic treatment. Anna Freud's position, however, was that small children could not be analyzed owing to an inherently weak and rudimentary ego that would be incapable of managing deep interpretations of instinctual conflict (Mitchell & Black, 1995). Klein published a number of theoretical and clinical papers and several books over a period of some 40 years. Although she steadfastly maintained that her observations and psychoanalytic work with children were intended as confirmations and extensions of Freud's hypotheses, her discoveries led her to portray the mind "as a continually shifting, kaleidoscopic stream of primitive, phantasmagoric images, fantasies, and terrors," a vision that seemed very unlike that of Freud (Mitchell & Black, 1995, p. 87). In Freud's model of the mind, the Oedipus complex has a developmentally profound, transformative impact on the psyche that yields the creation of new conflict-mediating structures (the mature ego and superego) that have stability and coherence. An almost inexorable progression of the libido culminates in the 6-year-old's genital sexuality and the accompanying oedipal dilemma; this, for Freud, constitutes the core conflict or nuclear complex of the neuroses. In fact, Klein never questioned the primacy of the Oedipus complex but located it at a much earlier point in development than did traditional psychoanalytic theory. Klein's fundamental view of the nature of oedipal phenomena also differed from the traditional perspective. For Klein, "The very nature of the Oedipus complex changed from a struggle over illicit pleasures and the fear of punishment, to a struggle for power and destruction and the fear of retaliation" (Greenberg & Mitchell, 1983, p. 123).

Sigmund Freud had theorized that infants proceed from a state of primary narcissism to object love via autoerotism; in effect, true object love is not possible until the libido progresses to the oedipal stage. The Kleinian infant, by contrast, is both psychologically separate and object seeking from the moment of birth (Grotstein, 1996; Klein, 1935). Klein went further, however, proposing that infants as young as 3 weeks of age are subject to a primitive anxiety state, which she called *persecutory anxiety.* She believed that this configuration of anxiety was linked to schizoid mechanisms (e.g., splitting, projective identification, idealization, and magic omnipotent denial) and that such intrapsychic experience resulted in the infant's first developmental organizer, the paranoid-schizoid position (Klein, 1935):

> *Paranoid* refers to the central persecutory anxiety, the fear of invasive malevolence, coming from the outside. . . . *Schizoid* refers to the central organizing defense: splitting, the vigilant separation of the loving and good breast from the hating and hated bad breast. (Mitchell & Black, 1995, p. 93)

The infant who is operating out of the paranoid-schizoid position has a bifurcated and fragmented experience of objects; "the child attempts to ward off the dangers of bad objects, both external and internal, largely by keeping images of them separate and isolated from the self and the good objects" (Greenberg & Mitchell, 1983, p. 125). Relations with objects are, by definition, always partial and either all good or all bad but never composed of both good and bad parts. According to Klein (1964), however, the infant gradually begins to integrate the experiences of good and bad breast-other, so that whole-object relations ultimately become possible. Klein has termed

this important shift in intrapsychic experience, which begins at approximately 3 to 4 months, the *depressive position.*

The depressive position (the second developmental organizer of infancy) is initiated by the infant's growing concern for the welfare of the libidinal object who has been the recipient of hateful fantasies of vengeance and annihilation characteristic of the paranoid-schizoid position.[13] Concomitant with the infant's newly emerging capacity for whole-object relations is an ability to experience ambivalence or both good (loving) and bad (hateful) feelings toward the same object. Although this represents a critical developmental achievement for the infant, it simultaneously creates new dangers since

> the whole mother who disappoints or fails the infant, generating the pain of longing, frustration, desperation, is destroyed in the infant's hateful fantasies, not just the purely evil bad breast (with the good breast remaining untouched and protected). The whole object (both the external mother and the corresponding internal whole object) now destroyed in the infant's rageful fantasies is the singular provider of goodness as well as frustration. In destroying the whole object, the infant eliminates her as a protector and refuge . . . [which leads to] . . . intense terror and guilt. (Mitchell & Black, 1995, p. 95)

The target of the infant's destructive urges is also a deeply loved figure toward whom the infant feels profound gratitude (Klein, 1935). These feelings, coupled with the child's regret and sorrow over his or her destructiveness, serve as the basis for fantasies of reparation. Such fantasies are intended to repair the damage and transform the annihilated object into a whole object once again.

The concept of projective identification, which some believe to be a sine qua non for the understanding and treatment of borderline and other severe personality disorders, is also attributed to

---

[13]In Kleinian theory, the regulation and containment of aggression has the quality of a leitmotif, though with specific meanings at various developmental stages.

Klein (1946/1975a, 1952/1975b). Projective identification not only represents a strategy of defense but is a significant though developmentally primitive mode of interaction. In projective identification, the subject projects unwanted parts of the self into others for "safekeeping." Ogden (1982), a contemporary Kleinian, has defined the concept in the following manner:

> Projective-identification is a concept that addresses the way in which feeling states corresponding to the unconscious fantasies of one person (projector) are engendered in and processed by another person (the recipient), that is, the way in which one person makes use of another person to experience and contain an aspect of himself. (p. 1)

Klein and her theories have been criticized for a number of reasons. A basic premise of Klein is that the infant is capable of a complex fantasy life from birth, a contention that receives little support from either cognitive psychology or the neurosciences (Tyson & Tyson, 1990). Others have noted that in Klein's framework, where mental life is viewed as fragmented and chaotic, there is "considerable fuzziness concerning the relationship between fantasy and the establishment of character or psychic structure" (Fairbairn, 1952; Kernberg, 1980; Mishne, 1993). At the same time, the magnitude of Klein's influence is indisputable.

For those interested in studying the work of Melanie Klein, there are a number of excellent introductory volumes, including Hanna Segal's short classic (1979), as well as more elaborate expositions by Hinshelwood (1994), Likierman (2001), Kristeva (2001), and Petot (1990, 1991). For readers who prefer a more concise account, we highly recommend Britton's (2012) cogent description of Klein's original ideas and their subsequent elaboration by Wilfred Bion.

The Middle Tradition and D. W. Winnicott

There was considerable divisiveness within the British psychoanalytic community by the early 1940s, principally due to theoretical differences between Anna Freud and Melanie Klein, which had given rise to an increasingly contentious and acrimonious professional environment. At the time, Ernest Jones[14] was the official head of the psychoanalytic movement in Britain, and he had worked diligently to foster a professional climate of "creative exploration, inclusiveness, and openness to emerging ideas," an ambience that had made possible relative quiescence, if not harmony, between Melanie Klein and adherents of mainstream psychoanalysis—at least until the arrival of the Freuds from Vienna in 1938 (Borden, 1995). As relations between those faithful to Anna Freud's views and those who pledged loyalty to Melanie Klein began to deteriorate, Jones worked to uphold the integrity of the British Psycho-Analytical Society. In 1943 and 1944, he organized what have come to be known as the "Controversial Discussions," a series of formal theoretical debates the original intent of which was to provide Melanie Klein with an opportunity to clarify her position on Sigmund Freud's metapsychology (Borden, 1995; Kohon, 1986; Mishne, 1993) and to explore the nature of theoretical differences between the Kleinians and (Anna) Freudians. The result of these discussions,[15] which failed to resolve the deep theoretical differences between the two camps, was the organization of the British psychoanalytic community into three distinct groups: (1) the Kleinians, (2) the Freudians, and (3) a middle or independent group.

The independent group consisted of a number of seminal thinkers, among them D. W. Winnicott,

---

[14]Ernest Jones (1879–1958), a pioneer in the early psychoanalytic movement, was a close friend and disciple of Freud. The contribution for which he is most often remembered is his three-volume biography of Freud (Jones, 1953, 1955, 1957).

[15]See King and Steiner (1991) for a detailed account of these meetings.

W. R. D. Fairbairn, John Bowlby, Michael Balint, and Harry Guntrip. Each of these theorists developed object relations theories based on Klein's basic postulate of an infant who is object seeking from the moment of birth. At the same time, "They also all broke with Klein's premise of constitutional aggression . . . proposing instead an infant wired for harmonious interaction and non-traumatic development but thwarted by inadequate parenting" (Mitchell & Black, 1995, pp. 114–115). D. W. Winnicott (1896–1971) is regarded by many as the best-known representative of the independent group (Borden, 1995; Grotstein, 1996). Winnicott, like Spitz and Mahler, was originally trained as a pediatrician and spent more than 40 years working with infants and mothers. His careful observations of infants and their mothers led him to assert that "there is no such thing as an infant. There is only the infant and its mother" (Winnicott, 1960/1965b, p. 39). This declaration, which is truly axiomatic for Winnicott, underscores the critical importance that he attributed to the earliest object relations between infant and caregiver.

Winnicott is especially well-known for his ideas about primary maternal preoccupation, good-enough mothering, and the holding environment; his formulation of the true self and the false self; and the concept of the transitional object.

Primary Maternal Preoccupation, Good-Enough Mothering, and the Holding Environment

Winnicott believed that the emergence of a health-promoting psychological milieu for each human infant depends on his or her mother's capacity for what Winnicott termed *primary maternal preoccupation.* The state of *primary maternal preoccupation,* which gathers considerable momentum in the last trimester of pregnancy, reflects each mother's natural absorption with the baby growing inside her. The expectant mother becomes

> increasingly withdrawn from her own subjectivity . . . and more and more focused on the baby's movements, on the baby's vitality. . . . The mother

finds her own personal interests, her own rhythms and concerns fading into the background. (Mitchell & Black, 1995, p. 125)

Winnicott (1965b) has also characterized this as the mother's identification with the infant.

Good-enough mothering, which commences with the mother's primary maternal preoccupation, initially requires that the mother meet the symbiotic needs of her newborn. If she is well attuned to her baby, whatever she offers the baby is provided at the "right time" for her baby rather than being timed to meet her own needs. As her baby faces experiences that evoke frustration, aggression, or loss, the good-enough mother is able to provide empathically attuned support, or *holding.* Winnicott stresses that good-enough mothering is a natural and spontaneous process that evolves out of each mother's intuitions and leads to the creation of a *facilitative* or *holding environment* on which each infant depends. He also observed that the extensive adaptations and accommodations that a mother makes for her infant gradually diminish; the result is brief lapses that teach the baby that the mother is not omnipotent (Moore & Fine, 1990). Such maternal failures in empathy are coterminous with significant advances in the infant's psychomotor development; while infantile omnipotence is lost, there is newfound delight in the infant's exciting forays into the object world outside the infant-mother matrix (Winnicott, 1958/1965a, 1960/1965b).

True Self and False Self

Winnicott wrote that all individuals begin life with a true self, an "inherited potential" that represents the infant's core self or essence. In a facilitative environment, the true self, which has been equated with the spontaneous expression of the id, continues to develop and becomes firmly established. The false self, on the other hand, is a facade that the infant-child erects so as to achieve compliance with the mother's inadequate adaptations, whether these maternal failures are in the form of deprivations or impingements on the child's growth (Goldstein, 1995). Infants exposed to such repeated depri-vations or impingements are able to survive, but in Winnicott's estimation, they are able to do so only at the cost of "living falsely" (Mishne, 1993; Winnicott, 1960/1965b). Although Winnicott emphasized that the partition or distribution of self-experience into "true" and "false" is always present in varying degrees (even in normal infants), the false self has an almost palpable presence in various forms of child and adult psychopathology. Winnicott treated a number of clients with basic pathology of the self, individuals who might have been diagnosed with schizoid or borderline disorders. What impressed him most about such clients was their profound inner alienation. In such clients, "subjectivity itself, the quality of personhood, is somehow disordered" (Mitchell & Black, 1995, p. 124). Winnicott gradually came to understand that these adult clients suffered from "false self disorders," and the bridge he "constructed between the quality and the nuances of adult subjectivity and the subtleties of mother-infant interactions provided a powerful new perspective for viewing both the development of the self" and the process of treatment (Mitchell & Black, 1995, p. 125).

The Transitional Object

Winnicott's concept of the transitional object is perhaps the best known of his theoretical ideas, though its popularization may have contributed to a blurring of its original meaning (Mitchell & Black, 1995). The transitional object is typically a blanket, a teddy bear, or some other inanimate but nevertheless cherished possession of the infant. The soothing and calming qualities with which it is endowed are especially evident during stressful separations from caregivers and at bedtime (Winnicott, 1951/1958). Its odor and tactile characteristics hold a special significance, in that they are believed to be reminiscent of the child's mother. In the mother's absence, it is the transitional object that enables the infant to sustain the illusion of a calming, comforting mother. Because the transitional object is a creation of the infant and, unlike the mother, remains under his or her control, it serves to promote the infant's increased autonomy and independence

(Moore & Fine, 1990). The blanket or teddy bear, however, is not simply a symbolic re-creation of the mother, designed to facilitate the infant's transition from symbiotic merger to relative autonomy; it is, rather, a "developmental way station,"

> a special extension of the child's self, halfway between the mother that the child creates in subjective omnipotence and the mother that the child finds operating on her own behalf in the objective world. The transitional object . . . cushions the fall from a world where the child's desires omnipotently actualize their objects to one where desires require accommodation to and collaboration of others to be fulfilled. (Mitchell & Black, 1995, p. 129)

Although Winnicott (1951/1958) originally presented the concept of the transitional object and transitional experience in the context of early infant development, he later broadened this framework to include aspects of adult experience. The transitional experience for the child is embedded in a capacity for play, whereas for the adult, transitional experience is a "protected realm" where there exists opportunities to "play with" new ideas and fantasies and cultivate one's own creative impulses (Greenberg & Mitchell, 1983).

Winnicott's theories, unlike those of Freud, Klein, or Sullivan, have never attained the status of a school of thought, nor did Winnicott ever make the claim that his theories, taken together, represented "a comprehensive theory of object relations" (Bacal & Newman, 1990, p. 185). His papers, many of which were originally presented as talks (Greenberg & Mitchell, 1983), have a stylistic informality and poetic quality that at times can be almost seductive to the reader; at other times, however, these same inherent ambiguities and his idiosyncratic, discursive style make Winnicott difficult, even frustrating, to read. Despite this, and despite recent criticisms of Winnicott's distortion of traditional psychoanalytic ideas (Greenberg & Mitchell, 1983; Williams, 2012), his influence has remained strong. Winnicott's vision has enriched our understanding not only of infant development but also of the significant relationship between environmental failures in early life and the phenomenology of certain disorders of adulthood.

THE PSYCHOLOGY OF THE SELF

The psychology of the self, introduced by Heinz Kohut, has only recently emerged from a vigorous and at times rancorous debate within psychoanalytic circles. The evolution of Kohut's self psychology is represented in a series of books and papers published between 1959 and 1984. Kohut originally introduced "his theoretical and technical innovations within the framework of classical drive theory" (Greenberg & Mitchell, 1983, p. 357) but subsequently presented a significantly expanded and revised framework (Kohut, 1977, 1984) that has become the basis for an important and distinctive theory of psychoanalytic psychology.

Heinz Kohut (1913–1981) received a traditional psychoanalytic education and worked for many years in the classical tradition with his analytic clients. The original impetus for the development of his theory came from his clinical experiences with clients, particularly those who seemed unable to make use of the interpretations that followed the classical formulas. Kohut had noted that despite his most concerted efforts, these clients frequently evinced no benefit from his interpretive work, and in many cases, their symptoms actually became worse (Leider, 1996). After repeated efforts to revise and refine his formulations proved unsuccessful, Kohut surmised that the essential difficulty was not that he had timed his interpretations poorly or that the focus was either too narrow or too global, but that the fault lay with the fundamental theoretical assumptions of classical theory. These theoretical premises, Kohut argued, were useful in the treatment of the classical neuroses (e.g., hysterical, obsessive-compulsive, and phobic disorders), but by the latter part of the 20th century, such cases were no longer seen with the same frequency as they had been in Freud's day. If classical neurotic cases were modal in the 1920s,

clients with borderline and narcissistic personality disorders, in particular, seemed to be diagnosed with increasing frequency by the 1960s and 1970s.

Kohut's vision of the human condition gradually evolved into something quite different from that of Freud. The Freudian view of humankind can be characterized as an ongoing battle between primitive desires and civilized precepts for behavior, a struggle that is repeated anew with each succeeding generation. In such a perspective, guilt represents a supreme accomplishment, a painful though essential ingredient for the renunciation of instinct, which is a sine qua non for civilized behavior. Kohut, on the other hand, addressed himself not to battles but to

> isolation . . . painful feelings of personal isolation. . . . Kohut's man in trouble was not riddled with guilt over forbidden impulses; he was moving through a life without meaning. . . . He looked and acted like a human being, but experienced life as drudgery, accomplishments as empty. Or he was held captive on an emotional roller coaster, where exuberant bursts of creative energy alternated with painful feelings of inadequacy in response to disrupting perceptions of failure. The creative process was short-circuited. . . . Relationships, eagerly, even desperately pursued, were repeatedly abandoned with an increasing feeling of pessimism at ever getting what one really "needs" from another. (Mitchell & Black, 1995, p. 149)

Kohut asserted that one of the most fundamental distinctions between self psychology and classical psychoanalytic theory concerned human nature. Kohut (1977) believed that classical psychoanalysis was chiefly concerned with Guilty Man, "whose aims are directed toward the activity of his drives . . . and who lives within the pleasure principle," attempting "to satisfy his pleasure-seeking drives to lessen the tensions that arise in his erogenous zones" (p. 132). Kohut's concept of Tragic Man, however, illuminates "the essence of fractured, enfeebled, discontinuous human existence" (p. 238). It represents Kohut's effort to explain clinical phenomena such as the schizophrenic's fragmentation, the pathological narcissist's efforts to cope with diffuse and painful vulnerabilities, and the despair of those approaching old age with the recognition that important ambitions and ideals remain unrealized.[16]

Kohut and his adherents have introduced several terms and concepts that are associated with psychoanalytic self psychology, each of which we shall explore in some detail: mirroring, idealizing, and partnering selfobjects; the tripolar self; the self types; empathy and transmuting internalization; cohesion, fragmentation, and disintegration anxiety; and compensatory structures.

Mirroring, Idealizing, and Partnering Selfobjects

Kohut used the term *selfobject* to refer to a particular kind of object relationship in which the object is actually experienced as an extension of the self, without psychological differentiation. Kohut (1971) observed that

> the expected control over such [selfobjects] . . . is then closer to the concept of control which a grownup expects to have over his own body and mind than to the . . . control which he expects to have over others. (pp. 26–27)

He believed that infants are born into an interpersonal milieu that optimally provides them with three distinctly different though equally necessary kinds of selfobject experiences. One kind of experience calls for mirroring selfobjects, "who respond to and confirm the child's innate sense of vigor, greatness and perfection." A second variety of selfobject experience requires the powerful and reassuring presence of caregivers "to whom the child can look up and with whom he can merge as an image of calmness, infallibility, and omnipotence" (Kohut & Wolf, 1978, p. 414).

Kohut later introduced a third selfobject realm, referred to as *alter ego* or *partnering selfobjects.* This third variety provides a range of experiences through which children acquire a sense of belonging and of essential alikeness within a community of others.

The Tripolar Self

The tripolar self is the intrapsychic structure over which are superimposed the three specific selfobject experiences we have described. The first pole, that of grandiose-exhibitionistic needs, is associated with the need for approval, interest, and affirmation (mirroring). The second pole, the idealizing pole, is associated with developmental needs for closeness and support from an (omnipotent) idealized other (Leider, 1996).[17] The third pole is that of the alter ego, and it involves the ongoing need for contact with others who are felt to bear likeness to the self. These three poles are "structures that crystallize as a result of the interaction between the needs of the self and the responses of those important persons in the environment who function as selfobjects" (Leider, 1996, p. 141).

The Self Types

Kohut and other exponents of psychoanalytic self psychology believe that the self is most usefully understood within the intersecting matrices of developmental level and structural state. Four principal self types that have been identified are (1) the *virtual self,* an image of the newborn's self that originally exists within the parent's mind and evolves in particular ways as the parental "selfobjects emphatically respond to certain potentialities of the child" (Kohut, 1977,

---

[16]Erikson had, of course, addressed this particular phenomenon (though from an ego psychological perspective) in his description of "ego integrity versus despair," the eighth and final normative crisis in the human life cycle.

[17]Kohut has referred to this as the need for "uplifting care," both literally and figuratively speaking, from the idealized selfobjects.

p. 100); (2) the *nuclear self,* a core self that emerges in the infant's second year, serving as the basis for the child's "sense of being an independent center of initiative and perception" (Kohut, 1977, p. 177); (3) the *cohesive self,* the basic self-structure of a well-adapted, healthily functioning individual, characterized by the harmonious "interplay of ambitions, ideals, and talents with the opportunities of everyday reality" (Leider, 1996, p. 143); and (4) the *grandiose self,* a normal self-structure of infancy and early childhood that develops originally in response to the selfobject's attunement with the child's sense of himself or herself as the center of the universe.

Empathy and Transmuting Internalization

Kohut, whose theoretical contributions have focused on development of the personality, psychopathology, and psychoanalytic technique, placed a great deal of emphasis on the role of empathy in human development.[18] Self psychology defines *empathy* as "vicarious introspection," the immersion of oneself into the experience of an other; the capacity for empathic attunement in the child's selfobject milieu is considered to be of the utmost importance. At the same time, a critical impetus for healthy self-development involves what are described as minor, relatively nontraumatic lapses in parental empathy. Such lapses, because they are optimally frustrating, serve as a catalyst for the child's development of transmuting internalizations. Transmuting internalization is an intrapsychic process whereby the child gradually "takes in" functions associated with the selfobject, which may range from self-calming and self-soothing to pride, humor, and

stoicism in the face of adversity. In other words, through an almost imperceptible, bit-by-bit process of translocation, these functions gradually become enduring parts of the child's own self-structure, though they are transformed to "fit" the child's unique self.[19]

Cohesion, Fragmentation, and Disintegration Anxiety

Cohesion is the term used in self psychology to refer to a self state that serves as the basis for robust, synchronous, and integrated psychological functioning. Self-cohesion makes possible the harmonious interplay of ambitions, ideals, and talents in the context of everyday realities. It also protects the individual from regressive fragmentation in the face of adversity or obstacles that may interfere with the satisfaction of object or selfobject needs (Leider, 1996). Individuals who are fragmentation prone (who tend, under stress, to develop symptoms such as hypochondriasis, hypomanic excitement, or disturbances in bodily sensation and self-perception) have been unable to acquire stable, consolidated, and enduring self-structures. Whether this is a consequence of parental pathology, environmental vicissitudes, or a combination of the two, it is invariably associated with the unavailability of parental selfobjects to perform important selfobject functions. Such developmental deficiencies are associated with self or selfobject disorders (e.g., narcissistic pathology, borderline states, depression, and psychosis). Disintegration anxiety is defined as the fear of the breaking up of the self, which, according to Kohut, is the most profound anxiety a human being is capable of experiencing. A related term, *disintegration products,* refers to various

---

[18]Akhtar (1988) also notes that self psychology has made contributions to the study of sociopolitical processes and the philosophy of human nature.

[19]The key elements in the sequence of transmuting internalization are, in order, optimal frustration, increased tension, selfobject response, reduced tension, memory trace, and development of internal regulating structure.

symptoms produced by an enfeebled, disharmonious self (e.g., paranoia, narcissistic rage, exhibitionism, and other paraphilias).

Compensatory Structures

When in the course of early development, the parental selfobjects fail to respond adequately to a particular constellation of selfobject needs (whether for mirroring, idealizing, or partnering), it is sometimes possible to compensate for these deficiencies through more intensive structuralization of a second set of selfobject needs. As an example, an individual who has experienced developmental arrest in the area of ambitions (perhaps due to chronic disappointments in his or her efforts to evoke mirroring responses from a parent) may find the same selfobject to be far more accessible for the fulfillment of idealizing or partnering needs. The evolution of compensatory structures is motivated by the individual's need to rise above developmental obstacles and to repair defects in self-structure (Leider, 1996). Compensatory structures, however, are regarded as normative, and as Kohut (1984) observes, "There is not one kind of healthy self—there are many kinds" (p. 44).[20]

RECENT DEVELOPMENTS IN SELF PSYCHOLOGY

Self psychology is no longer the unitary theory it was during Kohut's lifetime, though most who are identified with his theories continue to subscribe to two basic features of his work: (1) the central importance of the therapist's sustained, empathic immersion in the subjective experience of the client and (2) the concept of selfobjects and the selfobject transference

(Mitchell & Black, 1995; Terman, 2012). There has been considerable divergence and ferment within self psychology in recent years, a situation that has prompted one well-known theorist to observe that "self psychologists no longer have a common language" (J. Palombo, personal communication).

The analyst and infant researcher Joseph Lichtenberg (1983, 1989) has addressed himself to Kohut's developmental concepts and their particular meaning in light of important new developments in the field of infant research. Infant research has also been of interest to Lachmann and Beebe (1992, 1994), who have paid special attention to self-psychological notions of self-regulation and transmuting internalization, expanding and extending Kohut's original formulations. Stolorow's intersubjectivity theory (Stolorow, Brandschaft, & Atwood, 1987), while based on the organizing framework of Kohut's system, represents a more revolutionary paradigm. "Rather than the individual, isolated self, Stolorow's emphasis is on the fully contextual interaction of subjectivities with reciprocal, mutual influence" (Mitchell & Black, 1995, p. 167). Bacal (1995) and Basch (1986, 1988), and others too numerous to mention, have also shaped the burgeoning literature of psychoanalytic self psychology.

RELATIONAL PSYCHOANALYSIS

Relational psychoanalysis is a relatively new and rapidly evolving school of psychoanalytic thought. Considered by its founders to represent a paradigm shift in psychoanalysis, the relational approach was initiated by the publication of Jay Greenberg and Stephen Mitchell's book *Object Relations in Psychoanalytic Theory* in 1983. This work, and the relational movement

---

[20]*Defensive structures,* another term Kohut used, are differentiated from compensatory structures in that the former "cover over" the primary defects in the self, whereas compensatory structures actually compensate for the defect rather than simply disguise it.

that followed it, brought together various strains of psychoanalytic theorizing, all of which were seen to assign primary importance to real interpersonal relations, rather than to instinctual drives, in their understanding of human motivation and personality. The relational approach thus began as a work of selective integration of compatible psychoanalytic models and approaches, particularly the interpersonal school of Harry Stack Sullivan (the psychoanalytic tradition in which both Mitchell and Greenberg were educated), British object relations theory, and the self-psychological theory of Heinz Kohut, among others. Each of these schools of thought were seen to be conceptually rooted in a relational premise that differed from the fundamental drive premise of traditional Freudian psychology.

Greenberg and Mitchell characterized all these theoretical systems as "relational models," creating both a theoretical umbrella and, eventually, an organizational context for dialogue and collaboration among "relational" theorists and practitioners from otherwise differing backgrounds. It should be evident in this context that relational psychoanalysis did not originate as a single school of thought and cannot therefore be neatly summarized by a comprehensive set of theoretical propositions to which all relational psychoanalysts subscribe. *Relational psychoanalysis* refers to a spectrum of psychoanalytic theories and theorists brought together on the basis of a common set of fundamental premises about human nature. These schools of thought all diverge from traditional Freudian conceptualizations of human motivation and the nature of the mind. Some of the theorists brought together under the relational rubric, such as Harry Stack Sullivan and Ronald Fairbairn, were explicit in the criticism of Freud's drive theory. Others, such as Donald Winnicott and Hans Loewald, fit their novel ideas into a traditional psychoanalytic framework, using drive terminology to express ideas that, on a relational construal, actually differed from those of Freud.

The relational movement gained its first institutional foothold when it became a separate (and among candidates studying in the program, an instantly popular) official orientation within the New York University Postdoctoral Program in Psychotherapy and Psychoanalysis in 1988. In 1991, a scholarly journal, *Psychoanalytic Dialogues: A Journal of Relational Perspectives,* devoted to the development of the relational school of thought was launched under the editorship of Stephen Mitchell. This journal immediately became a well-respected and influential publication, attracting submissions from around the world. Relational ideas quickly grew in influence, especially in New York, and have had a worldwide influence in Italy and other European countries, in Israel, and elsewhere.

The most influential relational psychoanalyst has been Stephen Mitchell, whose writings provide the primary, though not the only, source for this brief overview of relational theory. Between the time he published his 1983 volume with Jay Greenberg and his sudden and untimely death in December 2000, Stephen Mitchell authored or coauthored several subsequent, widely read books (e.g., Mitchell, 1988, 1993b, 1997, 2000). Mitchell's account of relational theory is the primary source for this overview. His enormous output following the publication of his book with Greenberg, along with the contributions of a growing circle of relational psychoanalysts, transformed the relational model from a product of selective integration into a vibrant international movement, producing an exciting original literature, nurtured by developments in research and adjacent schools of thought (e.g., attachment research, intersubjectivity, mentalization), and giving rise to new training institutes and professional psychoanalytic organizations.

The Relational Challenge to Drive Theory

The core challenge of relational theory has, from its inception, been directed toward Freudian drive theory and the drive/structure model of mental life posited by Freud (Greenberg & Mitchell, 1983). To articulate the relational objections of

Freudian theory, it is necessary to outline those tenets of Freudian theory that are the subject matter of their critique. In the following paragraphs, then, we review these features of Freud's theorizing as they are seen by their relational critics. The rendition is accurate so far as it goes, but it is selective, emphasizing only those features that are relevant to the relational challenge, namely, the mechanistic and biological components of the theory, and omitting other aspects, which are outside the scope of this focus.

From its inception, psychoanalytic theory concerned itself with the motivations that underlie mental life and behavior. Freud (1905) conceptualized the primary motivations that "drive" human behavior as "instinctual drives," formed by the phylogenetic experiences of the human race and rooted in the elemental constitution of every human being. Early in his theorizing, Freud construed the primary motivations as the sexual and self-preservative drives, often epitomized as "sex and hunger" (1905, 1915a). Some years later, Freud (1920) linked both these drives within a larger notion of "Eros" or the life instinct. At the same time, he posited a "death instinct" which, in his view, gave rise to an aggressive drive. While many analysts rejected the idea of a death instinct (e.g., Simmel, 1944), virtually all analysts since Freud have recognized both sex and aggression as important motivations in mental life, a notion often characterized as the dual-drive theory (e.g., Hartmann et al., 1949).

In Freud's formulations, instinctual drives have their source in the body but are represented in the mind as tension states, or states of "unpleasure," that can only be relieved through an action that satisfies the instinctual demand (Freud, 1905, 1915a). If sexual needs, originating in the sex organs, produce a tension state in the mind, only a sexual action (e.g., an action leading to orgasm) will dissipate it. Such action, leading to "drive discharge," produces a subjective feeling of relief, or "pleasure." Patterns of successful drive discharge (actions that reduce unpleasure) are represented in the mind as "wishes" or, more broadly, as "desire." Because sexual drives (and often aggressive drives, as well) require the

involvement of another person (formally characterized as the drive's "object," in Freudian terminology), drive discharge motivates interpersonal events and engagements. Interpersonal relations are thus seen as "drive derivatives."

Instinctual drives were seen by Freud (1915a) as perpetually pressing the individual to action in the service of drive discharge, the intensity of the pressure they exert increasing or decreasing in accordance with the biological processes at their source. The realities of social life, however, make it impossible for anyone to gratify all their wishes all the time. As a result, patterns of drive discharge must be fashioned to fit a social context. The foregoing view may be summarized by observing that human behavior is orchestrated by drives that are modified by the constraints imposed by the social world. In the relational view, these social constraints, derived from interpersonal relationships, were far less important to Freud and his followers than the drives they constrained.

Relational theorists challenge this view of human motivation, decisively rejecting the idea that human beings seek out interpersonal relationships for the primary purpose of gratifying instinctual sexual or aggressive drives. A cornerstone of all relational theory is the premise that human beings are born with a primary need for relatedness and communication with other human beings. This need is seen as fundamental to the human organism, and its satisfaction is held to be necessary for normal development and survival. In the relational perspective, then, social experience is primary as a motivation and as an organizer of mental life. It is social experience, not biological preformed instinctual drives, that shapes our personalities.

Evidence for the existence of a primary need for relationships is drawn from multiple sources. Children who are abused or neglected by their parents are seen to be intensely attached to their hurtful and frustrating parents, despite the fact that these relationships are a source of suffering rather than of pleasure. Similarly, adults may seek out relationships with others that repeat traumatic injuries and frustrations. Traditional analytic theory has explained such self-injurious behavior by reference to faulty ego functioning, primitive defenses, latent sexual meanings and pleasures embedded in painful experience, the repetition compulsion, and the death instinct. Relational theorists, on the other hand, who do not regard all behavior as motivated by the pursuit of pleasure, can readily explain such maladaptive attachments as satisfying a primary need to maintain human relatedness and preserve or repeat important relationships, despite the pain these relationships entail.

Relational theorists also cite very substantial evidence from attachment research (Bowlby, 1969, 1973, 1975) as well as infant research (Lichtenberg, 1983) that points to the primacy of a need for interpersonal relationships. Reviewing a large body of such research, Lichtenberg writes, "Study after study documents the neonate's pre-adapted potential for direct interaction—human to human—with the mother" (cited by Mitchell, 1988, p. 24). Daniel Stern (2005) points to the existence of "mirror neurons" as evidence that human beings are innately equipped to understand each other's experience and, thus, to relate to each other in a psychologically meaningful way (p. 80). Mirror neurons are neurons situated in the motor cortex that fire when another is observed in various kinds of behavior. Notably, their pattern of firing replicates the neural activity that would occur if the observer were engaged in the same behavior. Mirror neurons are thus seen as an innate neural foundation for our empathic understanding of the actions and intentions of others. Iacoboni (2008) suggests that the absence of sufficient mirror neurons is the cause of autism, whose pathognomonic feature is "mind-blindness," or the inability to understand the minds of others.

The relational claim that human beings seek connection with others as an end in itself, rather than as a means to gratify instinctual drives, accords with contemporary ideas about the evolution of human beings. As early social life became more complex, natural selection would have favored those of our ancestors who were capable of forming good relationships

with others and negotiating the demands of social life successfully. As cultures become increasingly complex, greater social intelligence is needed to survive. "In a sense," writes the anthropologist Clifford Geertz, "the brain was selected by culture" (quoted in Mitchell, 1988, p. 18). The relational view is also supported by ethological studies, such as those cited by Bowlby (1969), who construed attachment behavior as ensuring the proximity of the mother to the child and thus enhancing the child's likelihood of survival. Mitchell (1988) concludes as follows:

> The infant does not become social through learning or through conditioning, or through an adaptation to reality . . . the infant is programmed to be social. Relatedness is not a means to some other end . . . the very nature of the infant draws him into relationship. In fact, relatedness seems to be rewarding in itself. (p. 24)

Relational Configurations and the Nature of the Mind

As described above, human beings are motivated by an innate desire to establish interpersonal relationships with others. The character of the relationships we seek to form and also those we seek to avoid are determined not by preformed instinctual patterns but by actual experiences with other people. Early experiences with parenting figures give rise to expectations about how we will be treated by others. These expectations, in turn, motivate our subsequent relational strivings. Our interpersonal experiences thus give rise to the motivations that impel us to form further relationships. Mitchell (1988) and other relational theorists view the mind as composed not of instinctual drives but of "relational configurations" (p. 3).

Relational configurations are models of interpersonal or "relational" experiences that we seek with others as well as those painful or frightening experiences that we seek to avoid. As noted above, relational configurations are formed on the basis of actual life experiences, but they are not necessarily veridical representations of those experiences, as all encounters of the objective world are experienced through a prism of representations and fantasies, formed on the basis of yet earlier experience. Like life experiences themselves, relational configurations are posited to include three dimensions: (1) the self, (2) the object, and (3) the psychological space in which the two interact. "These dimensions are subtly interwoven, knitting together the analysand's subjective experience and psychological world" (Mitchell, 1988, p. 33). In the relational model, interpersonal experience and the relational configurations to which they give rise are the building blocks of the mind. Insofar as the mind is structured through interactions with others, it is impossible to conceive of a mind in isolation, outside of a context of interpersonal relationships. Relationships are the "stuff" of the mind, Mitchell writes.

Relational configurations determine our perceptions of others, our expectations of their attitudes and responses to us, and our interpersonal behavior toward them. Although relational configurations are stable and repeated, producing a feeling of continuity and consistency of life experience, they are also normally subject to the influence of new experiences with others. Thus, while relational configurations shape our experience of others, they are, in turn, also shaped by our actual interpersonal experiences through life. The potential openness of relational configurations to change on the basis of new interpersonal experience is fundamental to the relational view of psychotherapeutic treatment.

Relational configurations also shape our experience of ourselves. Relational theorists do not view the self as a unified structure located outside a social or relational field. The self is a network of impressions that we form of ourselves in the context of our relationships with others. Harry Stack Sullivan (1940) wrote that the self is formed, at least in part, by the "reflected appraisals" of others (p. 22). Kohut (1971, 1977), writing many years later, would similarly refer to the importance of "mirroring" in the development of the self. For Sullivan,

Kohut, and the relational theorists who followed, the notion of self is meaningful only within the context of our relationships with other people, including current interpersonal relationships in the real world as well as those we preserve within our memories and imaginations.

Psychopathology in the relational perspective is characterized by relational configurations that are conducive to painful relationships; constrictions in our capacity for authenticity, mutual intimacy, and love; and impairments in the quality of self-experience. Although relational configurations are normally susceptible to transformation in the context of new experience, this mutability is more limited in psychopathological conditions. Psychopathology is characterized by the maladaptive character of relational configurations, by the rigidity of those configurations, and, importantly, by persistent attachments to painful or frustrating relationships with primary figures (as in the case of abused children, noted above). As will be seen below, the clinical practice of relational psychoanalytic therapy not only features the creation of novel and more adaptive relational configurations through the therapeutic interaction but also entails, to one degree or another, the elucidation and interpretation of those persistent relational configurations that limit the client's relational potential and happiness.

Sex and Aggression in Relational Thought

Although the relational model is a vigorously environmental model of personality functioning, positing that personality organization is structured by interactions with others, it is not, on that account, exclusively or naively environmental. As seen above, our motivation for human interaction, as well as our preadapted capacity for complex human relationships, can be traced to evolutionary pressures. In this sense, relational theory is no less Darwinian than Freudian theory. Similarly, although relational theory does not construe sexuality or aggression as drives, sex and aggression are both prominent features of human life, and relational theory acknowledges and accounts for both from within its own perspective (Mitchell, 1988, 1993a).

Theoretical Roots and Developments of Relational Ideas

While relational psychoanalysis was organized as an umbrella movement, "American interpersonal" psychoanalysis, as propounded by Harry Stack Sullivan, has clearly been the dominant theoretical influence on its development. British object relations theory, as represented especially by the writings of Ronald Fairbairn and Donald Winnicott, has also been very influential, as has the work of infant researchers, postmodern philosophy, and, to some extent, the writings of Heinz Kohut. Sándor Ferenczi, one of the first generation of psychoanalysts following Freud, has also come to be appreciated as a pioneer who introduced many ideas and clinical approaches later adopted and developed by relational psychoanalysts. Concise reviews of relational theory, including current assessments of the basic premises, contemporary concerns, and future directions of this new tradition in psychoanalysis, are found in Harris (2011) and Aron and Lechich (2012).

Basic Clinical Tenets of Relational Psychoanalysis

Relational psychoanalysis is not a unified theory and contains no unitary theory of psychoanalytic technique. Because the relational school includes practitioners from a wide diversity of backgrounds, each with its own treatment traditions, it is impossible to articulate a single approach that characterizes all. Sullivanian interpersonalists are apt to be more active in their approach than, say, object relations therapists or self psychologists. Some are more freewheeling, others less so. Some challenge their clients, insistently confronting rigid schemata, while others take an attitude of passive receptivity or empathic immersion.

In general, however, analysts and therapists committed to a relational approach engage the therapeutic situation with a few clinical propositions in mind: (a) Personality is formed through interpersonal interactions, (b) the clinical situation is inherently intersubjective and shaped by mutual influence and must be conducted in a way that incorporates this fact, and (c) the client needs some kind of authentic personal engagement from the therapist. These assumptions suggest a model relational approach, characterized, to one degree or another, by the following features: (a) The relationship between client and therapist typically takes center stage, in part as a source of information about the client's subjective life but, more important, as an interpersonal context within which habitual relational configurations are transformed, characteristic relational patterns are renegotiated, rigid expectations are called into question, and new relational potentials are actualized; (b) the therapist seeks to understand and articulate the interpersonal field as a whole, including the ongoing and resonating impact of each participant on the other, rather than observing the client as an isolated entity whose mind is unaffected by the ongoing interaction; (c) the therapist pursues understanding in collaboration with the client, engaging the client as an equal partner, and the therapist's observations and interpretations are offered in a spirit of mutual discovery and inquiry—as possibilities rather than as objective pronouncements; and (d) the therapist is attentive to the pervasive mutual influences exerted in the therapeutic interaction, to the mutual evocation of emotional states and impressions, and is open to recognizing, acknowledging, and articulating his or her own role in creating conflicts and impasses.

CONCLUSION

This chapter began by exploring the relationship between clinical social work and psychoanalysis in some depth, examining particular social work treatment theories and their incorporation of various psychoanalytic concepts.

We also summarized a range of psychoanalytic systems, from traditional Freudian theory to relational psychoanalysis. Various models of development have also been included, principally because psychoanalytic developmental theories are typically closely linked to psychoanalytic theories of psychopathology. Finally, we have labored to explicate major theoretical disagreements in order to reveal the richness and complexity of this vast body of literature. We hope that this chapter has provided a useful overview of important psychoanalytic theories and controversies and the unique relationship between them and clinical social work.

REFERENCES

Abend, S. (1981). Psychic conflict and the concept of defense. *Psychoanalytic Quarterly, 50,* 67–76.

Abend, S. (1984). Sibling love and object choice. *Psychoanalytic Quarterly, 53,* 425–430.

Abraham, K. (1948). A short study of the development of the libido. In *Selected papers on psycho-analysis* (D. Bryan & A. Strachey, Trans., pp. 418–450). London, UK: Hogarth Press. (Original work published 1924)

Adler, A. (1927). *The practice and theory of individual psychology.* New York, NY: Harcourt.

Akhtar, S. (1988). Some reflections on the theory of psychopathology and personality development in Kohut's self psychology. In J. Ross & W. Myers (Eds.), *New concepts in psychoanalytic psychotherapy* (pp. 227–252). Washington, DC: American Psychiatric Press.

Arieti, S. (1974). *Interpretation of schizophrenia.* New York, NY: Basic Books.

Arlow, J. (1969). Unconscious fantasy and disturbances of conscious experience. *Psychoanalytic Quarterly, 38,* 1–27.

Aron, L., & Lechich, M. I. (2012). Relational psychoanalysis. In G. O. Gabbard, B. L. Litowitz, & P. Williams (Eds.), *Textbook of Psychoanalysis* (pp. 211–224). Washington D.C: American Psychiatric Publishing.

Bacal, H. (1995). The essence of Kohut's work and the progress of self psychology. *Psychoanalytic Dialogues, 5,* 353–356.

Bacal, H., & Newman, K. (1990). *Theories of object relations: Bridge to self psychology.* New York, NY: Columbia University Press.

Bak, R. (1943). Dissolution of the ego: Mannerism and delusions of grandeur. *Journal of Nervous and Mental Diseases, 98,* 457–464.

Balint, A. (1949). Love for the mother and mother-love. *International Journal of Psychoanalysis, 30,* 251–259. (Original work published 1937).

Balint, M. (1949). Early development states of the ego: Primary object love. *International Journal of Psychoanalysis, 30,* 265–273. (Original work published 1937).

Basch, M. (1986). "How does analysis cure?" An appreciation. *Psychoanalytic Inquiry, 6,* 403–428.

Basch, M. (1988). *Doing psychotherapy.* New York, NY: Basic Books.

Borden, W. (1995). *Making use of theory in practice: Legacies of the independent tradition.* Unpublished manuscript.

Bowlby, J. (1969). *Attachment and loss: Vol. 1. Attachment.* New York, NY: Basic Books.

Bowlby, J. (1973). *Separation: Anxiety and anger.* New York, NY: Basic Books.

Bowlby, J. (1975). *Loss: Sadness and depression.* New York, NY: Basic Books.

Brenner, C. (1975). Affects and psychic conflict. *Psychoanalytic Quarterly, 44,* 5–28.

Brenner, C. (1981). Defense and defense mechanisms. *Psychoanalytic Quarterly, 50,* 557–569.

Brenner, C. (1982). *The mind in conflict.* New York, NY: International Universities Press.

Breuer, J., & Freud, S. (1893–1895). *Studies on hysteria* (J. Strachey, Trans., Vol. 2). London, UK: Hogarth Press.

Bridgman, P. W. (1945). Some general principles of operational analysis. *Psychological Review, 52,* 246–249.

Britton, R. (2012). Klein and Bion. In G. O. Gabbard, B. L. Litowitz, & P. Williams (Eds.), *Textbook of Psychoanalysis* (pp. 185–197). Washington D.C: American Psychiatric Publishing.

Chapman, A. H. (1976). *Harry Stack Sullivan: The man and his work.* New York, NY: Putnam.

Chrzanowski, G. (1977). *Interpersonal approach to psychoanalysis.* New York, NY: Gardner Press.

Eagle, M. (2012). Theories of motivation. In G. O. Gabbard, B. L. Litowitz, & P. Williams (Eds.), *Textbook of Psychoanalysis* (pp. 38–53). Washington D.C: American Psychiatric Publishing.

Erikson, E. (1959). *Identity and the life cycle: Vol. 1. Selected papers, psychological issues.* New York, NY: International Universities Press.

Fairbairn, W. (1952). *An object relations theory of the personality.* New York, NY: Basic Books.

Fenichel, O. (1929). Dread of being eaten. In H. Fenichel & D. Rapaport (Eds.), *The collected works of Otto Fenichel, first series* (pp. 158–159). New York, NY: W. W. Norton.

Ferenczi, S. (1950). Stages in the development of the sense of reality. In *Sex in psychoanalysis* (E. Jones, Trans., pp. 213–239). New York, NY: Basic Books. (Original work published 1913)

Fine, R. (1975). *Psychoanalytic psychology.* New York, NY: Jason Aronson.

Freud, A. (1936). *The ego and the mechanisms of defense.* London, UK: Hogarth Press.

Freud, A. (1963). The concept of developmental lines. *Psychoanalytic Study of the Child, 18,* 245–265.

Freud, S. (1894). The neuropsychoses of defense. In J. Strachey (Ed. & Trans.), *The standard edition of the complete psychological works of Sigmund Freud* (Vol. 3, pp. 45–61). London, UK: Hogarth Press.

Freud, S. (1895a). On the grounds for detaching a particular syndrome from neurasthenia under the description "anxiety neurosis." In J. Strachey (Ed. & Trans.), *The standard edition of the complete psychological works of Sigmund Freud* (Vol. 3, pp. 87–113). London, UK: Hogarth Press.

Freud, S. (1895b). Project for a scientific psychology. In J. Strachey (Ed. & Trans.), *The standard edition of the complete psychological works of Sigmund Freud* (Vol. 1, pp. 283–387). London, UK: Hogarth Press.

Freud, S. (1900). The interpretation of dreams. In J. Strachey (Ed. & Trans.), *The standard edition of the complete psychological works of Sigmund Freud* (Vols. 4 & 5, pp. 1–715). London, UK: Hogarth Press.

Freud, S. (1901). The psychopathology of everyday life. In J. Strachey (Ed. & Trans.), *The standard edition of the complete psychological works of Sigmund Freud* (Vol. 6, pp. 1–291). London, UK: Hogarth Press.

Freud, S. (1905). Three essays on the theory of sexuality. In J. Strachey (Ed. & Trans.), *The standard edition of the complete psychological works of Sigmund Freud* (Vol. 7, pp. 125–245). London, UK: Hogarth Press.

Freud, S. (1909). Family romances. In J. Strachey (Ed. & Trans.), *The standard edition of the complete psychological works of Sigmund Freud* (Vol. 9, pp. 235–241). London, UK: Hogarth Press.

Freud, S. (1911). The handling of dream interpretation in psycho-analysis. In J. Strachey (Ed. & Trans.), *The standard edition of the complete psychological works of Sigmund Freud* (Vol. 12, pp. 89–96). London, UK: Hogarth Press.

Freud, S. (1914a). On narcissism: An introduction. In J. Strachey (Ed. & Trans.), *The standard edition of the complete psychological works of Sigmund Freud* (Vol. 14, pp. 67–102). London, UK: Hogarth Press.

Freud, S. (1914b). Remembering, repeating, and working-through. In J. Strachey (Ed. & Trans.), *The standard edition of the complete psychological works of Sigmund Freud* (Vol. 12, pp. 147–156). London, UK: Hogarth Press.

Freud, S. (1915a). Instincts and their vicissitudes. In J. Strachey (Ed. & Trans.), *The standard edition of the complete psychological works of Sigmund Freud* (Vol. 14, pp. 117–140). London, UK: Hogarth Press.

Freud, S. (1917). Mourning and melancholia. In J. Strachey (Ed. & Trans.), *The standard edition of the complete psychological works of Sigmund Freud* (Vol. 14, pp. 237–260). London, UK: Hogarth Press.

Freud, S. (1919). "A child is being beaten": A contribution to the study of the origin of sexual perversions. In J. Strachey (Ed. & Trans.), *The standard edition of the complete psychological works of Sigmund Freud* (Vol. 17, pp. 175–204). London, UK: Hogarth Press.

Freud, S. (1920). Beyond the pleasure principle. In J. Strachey (Ed. & Trans.), *The standard edition of the complete psychological works of Sigmund Freud* (Vol. 18, pp. 7–64). London, UK: Hogarth Press.

Freud, S. (1923). The ego and the id. In J. Strachey (Ed. & Trans.), *The standard edition of the complete psychological works of Sigmund Freud* (Vol. 19, pp. 12–66). London, UK: Hogarth Press.

Freud, S. (1926). Inhibitions, symptoms, and anxiety. In J. Strachey (Ed. & Trans.), *The standard edition of the complete psychological works of Sigmund Freud* (Vol. 20, pp. 75–175). London, UK: Hogarth Press.

Friedman, R., & Downey, J. (1995). Biology and the Oedipus complex. *Psychoanalytic Quarterly, 64,* 234–264.

Freedman, N., Hurvich, M, & Ward, R., with Geller, J. D. and Hoffenberg, J. (2011). *Another kind of evidence: Studies on internalization, annihilation anxiety, and progressive symbolization in the psychoanalytic process.* London, UK: Karnac.

Fromm-Reichmann, F. (1950). *Principles of intensive psychotherapy.* Chicago, IL: University of Chicago Press.

Frosch, J. (1970). Psychoanalytic considerations of the psychotic character. *Journal of the American Psychoanalytic Association, 18,* 24–50.

Goldstein, E. (1995). *Ego psychology and social work practice.* New York, NY: Free Press.

Greenberg, J., & Mitchell, S. (1983). *Object relations in psychoanalytic theory.* Cambridge, MA: Harvard University Press.

Grossman, W. (1991). Pain, aggression, fantasy, and concepts of sadomasochism. *Psychoanalytic Quarterly, 60,* 22–52.

Grotstein, J. (1996). Object relations theory. In E. Nersessian & R. Kopff (Eds.), *Textbook of psychoanalysis* (pp. 89–125). Washington, DC: American Psychiatric Press.

Guntrip, H. (1968). *Schizoid phenomena, object relations, and the self.* New York, NY: International Universities Press.

Guntrip, H. (1971). *Psychoanalytic theory, therapy and the self.* New York, NY: Basic Books.

Harlow, H. (1959). Love in infant monkeys. *Scientific American, 200,* 68–74..

Harris, A. (2011). The relational tradition: Landscape and canon. *Journal of the American Psychoanalytic Association, 59:* 701–735.

Hartmann, H. (1939). *Ego psychology and the problem of adaptation.* New York, NY: International Universities Press.

Hartmann, H., Kris, E., & Lowenstein, R. (1949). Notes on the theory of aggression. *Psychoanalytic Study of the Child, 3/4,* 9–36.

Havens, L. (1976). *Participant observation.* New York, NY: Jason Aronson.

Havens, L. (1986). *Making contact.* Cambridge, MA: Harvard University Press.

Havens, L., & Frank, J., Jr. (1971). Review of P. Mullahy. *Psychoanalysis and Interpersonal Psychiatry, 127,* 1704–1705.

Hendricks, I. (1942). Instinct and the ego during infancy. *Psychoanalytic Quarterly, 11,* 33–58.

Hermann, I. (1933). Zum Triebleben der Primaten. *Imago: Zeitschrift füer Psychoanalyse auf die Geist-wissens-chaften, 19,* 113.

Hermann, I. (1936). Sich-Anklammern-Auf-Suche-Gehen. *International Zeitschrift Psycho-Analyse, 22,* 349–370.

Hinshelwood, R. D. (1994). *Clinical Klein: From theory to practice.* New York, NY: Basic Books.

Hollis, F. (1970). The psychosocial approach to the practice of social casework. In R. W. Roberts & R. H. Nee (Eds.), *Theories of social casework* (pp. 33–75). Chicago, IL: University of Chicago Press.

Holzman, P. (1995). *Psychoanalysis and psychopathology.* Northvale, NJ: Jason Aronson.

Homer, T. (1985). The psychic life of the young infant: Review and critique of the psychoanalytic concepts of symbiosis and infantile omnipotence. *American Journal of Orthopsychiatry, 55,* 324–344.

Hurvich, M. (1989). Traumatic moment, basic dangers, and annihilation anxiety. *Psychoanalytic Psychology, 6,* 309–323.

Hurvich, M. (1991). Annihilation anxiety: An introduction. In H. Siegel, L. Barbanel, I. Hirsch, J. Lasky, H. Silverman, & S. Warshaw (Eds.), *Psychoanalytic reflections on current issues* (pp. 135–154). New York: New York University Press.

Hurvich, M. (2011). New developments in the theory and clinical application of the annihilation anxiety concept. In A. B. Druck, C. Ellman, N. Freedman, & A. Thaler (Eds.), *A new Freudian synthesis: Clinical process in the next generation.* London, UK: Karnac.

Hurvich, M. (in press). *Annihilation anxiety: Clinical, theoretical and empirical implications.* London, UK: Karnac Press.

Iacoboni, M. (2008). *Mirrroring people: The new science of how we connect with others.* New York, NY: Farrar, Strauss & Giroux.

Jacobson, E. (1964). *The self and the object world.* New York, NY: International Universities Press.

Jacobson, E. (1971). *Depression: Comparative studies of normal, neurotic, and psychotic conditions.* New York, NY: International Universities Press.

Jacobson, J. (1994). Signal affect and our psychoanalytic confusion of tongues. *Journal of the American Psychoanalytic Association, 42,* 15–42.

Jones, E. (1911). The psychology of morbid anxiety. In E. Jones (Ed.), *Papers on psychoanalysis* (4th ed.). London, UK: Bailliare, Tindall, & Cox.

Jones, E. (1953). *The life and work of Sigmund Freud, 1856–1900: The formative years and the great discoveries* (Vol. 1). New York, NY: Basic Books.

Jones, E. (1955). *The life and work of Sigmund Freud, 1901–1919: Years of maturity* (Vol. 2). New York, NY: Basic Books.

Jones, E. (1957). *The life and work of Sigmund Freud, 1919–1939: The last phase* (Vol. 3). New York, NY: Basic Books.

Jung, C. G. (1916). *Collected works of C. G. Jung: The relations between the ego and the unconscious* (Vol. 7, pp. 1–201). Princeton, NJ: Princeton University Press.

Jung, C. G. (1917). *Collected works of C. G. Jung: On the psychology of the unconscious* (Vol. 7, pp. 202–406). Princeton, NJ: Princeton University Press.

Kernberg, O. (1980). *Internal world and external reality.* Northvale, NJ: Jason Aronson.

King, P., & Steiner, R. (Eds.). (1991). *The Freud-Klein controversies, 1941–1945.* London, UK: Routledge.

Klein, G. (1976). *Psychoanalytic theory: An exploration of essentials.* New York, NY: International Universities Press.

Klein, M. (1935). A contribution to the psychogenesis of manic-depressive states. *International Journal of Psychoanalysis, 16,* 145–174.

Klein, M. (1964). *Contributions to psychoanalysis, 1921–1945.* New York, NY: McGraw-Hill.

Klein, M. (1975a). Notes on some schizoid mechanisms. In M. Masud & R. Khan (Eds.), *Envy and gratitude and other works, 1946–1963* (pp. 1–24). New York, NY: Delacorte Press. (Original work published 1946)

Klein, M. (1975b). Some theoretical conclusions regarding the emotional life of the infant. In M. Masud & R. Khan (Eds.), *Envy and gratitude and other works, 1946–1963* (pp. 61–93). New York, NY: Delacorte Press. (Original work published 1952)

Kohon, G. (Ed.). (1986). *The British school of psychoanalysis: The independent tradition.* London, UK: Free Association Books.

Kohut, H. (1966). Forms and transformations of narcissism. *Journal of the American Psychoanalytic Association, 14,* 243–272.

Kohut, H. (1971). *The analysis of the self.* New York, NY: International Universities Press.

Kohut, H. (1972). Thoughts on narcissism and narcissistic rage. *Psychoanalytic Study of the Child, 27,* 360–400.

Kohut, H. (1977). *The restoration of the self.* New York, NY: International Universities Press.

Kohut, H. (1984). *How does analysis cure?* Chicago, IL: University of Chicago Press.

Kohut, H., & Wolf, E. (1978). The disorders of the self and their treatment: An outline. *International Journal of Psychoanalysis, 59,* 413–425.

Kristeva, J. (2001). *Melanie Klein.* New York, NY: Columbia University Press.

Lachmann, F., & Beebe, B. (1992). Representational and selfobject transferences: A developmental perspective. In A. Goldberg (Ed.), *New therapeutic visions: Progress in self psychology* (Vol. 8, pp. 3–15). Hillsdale, NJ: Analytic Press.

Lachmann, F., & Beebe, B. (1994). Representation and internalization in infancy: 3 principles of salience. *Psychoanalytic Psychology, 11*(2), 127–166.

Laughlin, H. (1979). *The ego and its defenses.* Northvale, NJ: Jason Aronson.

Leider, R. (1996). The psychology of the self. In E. Nersessian & R. Kopff (Eds.), *Textbook of psychoanalysis* (pp. 127–164). Washington, DC: American Psychiatric Press.

Levenson, E. (1972). *The fallacy of understanding.* New York, NY: Basic Books.

Lichtenberg, J. (1983). *Psychoanalysis and infant research.* Hillsdale, NJ: Analytic Press.

Lichtenberg, J. (1989). *Psychoanalysis and motivation.* Hillsdale, NJ: Analytic Press.

Likierman, M. (2001). *Melanie Klein: Her work in context.* New York, NY: Columbia University Press.

Lorenz, K. (1957). The nature of instincts. In C. Schiller (Ed.), *Instinctive behavior* (pp. 129–175). New York, NY: International Universities Press. (Original work published 1937)

Mahler, M. (1968). *On human symbiosis and the vicissitudes of individuation.* New York, NY: International Universities Press.

Mahler, M. (1972). The rapprochement subphase. *Psychoanalytic Quarterly, 41,* 487–506.

Mahler, M., Pine, F., & Bergmann, A. (1975). *The psychological birth of the human infant.* New York, NY: Basic Books.

Masterson, J., & Rinsley, D. (1975). The borderline syndrome: The role of the mother in the genesis and psychic structure of the borderline personality. *International Journal of Psychoanalysis, 56,* 163–177.

Mishne, J. (1993). *The evolution and application of clinical theory.* New York, NY: Free Press.

Mitchell, S. (1988). *Relational concepts in psychoanalysis.* Cambridge, MA: Harvard University Press.

Mitchell, S., & Black, M. (1995). *Freud and beyond: A history of modern psychoanalytic thought.* New York, NY: Basic Books.

Mitchell, S. A. (1993a). Aggression and the endangered self. *Psychoanalytic Quarterly, 62,* 351–382.

Mitchell, S. A. (1993b). *Hope and dread in psychoanalysis.* New York, NY: Basic Books.

Mitchell, S. A. (1997). *Influence and autonomy in psychoanalysis.* Hillsdale, NJ: Analytic Press.

Mitchell, S. A. (2000). *Relationality: From attachment to intersubjectivity.* Hillsdale, NJ: Analytic Press.

Moore, B., & Fine, B. (1990). *Psychoanalytic terms and concepts.* New Haven, CT: Yale University Press.

Mullahy, P. (1970). *Psychoanalysis and interpersonal psychiatry.* New York, NY: Science House.

Ogden, T. (1982). *Projective identification and psychoanalytic technique.* Northvale, NJ: Jason Aronson.

Parens, H. (1979). *The development of aggression in early childhood.* Northvale, NJ: Jason Aronson.

Perlman, H. (1957). *Social casework: A problem-solving process.* Chicago, IL: University of Chicago Press.

Perlman, H. (1970). The problem-solving model in social casework. In R. W. Roberts & R. H. Nee (Eds.), *Theories of social casework* (pp. 129–179). Chicago, IL: University of Chicago Press.

Perry, H. S. (1982). *Psychiatrist of America: The life of Harry Stack Sullivan.* Cambridge, MA: Harvard University Press.

Petot, J.-M. (1990). *Melanie Klein, Volume I: First discoveries and first system (1919–1932).* Madison, CT: International Universities Press.

Petot, J.-M. (1991). *Melanie Klein, Volume II: The ego and the good object (1932–1960).* Madison, CT: International Universities Press.

Pine, F. (1970). On the structuralization of drive-defense relationships. *Psychoanalytic Quarterly, 39,* 17–37.

Pine, F. (1988). The four psychologies of psychoanalysis and their place in clinical work. *Journal of the American Psychoanalytic Association, 36,* 571–596.

Pine, F. (1990). *Drive, ego, object, and self.* New York, NY: Basic Books.

Rank, O. (1973). *The trauma of birth.* New York, NY: Harper & Row. (Original work published 1924)

Rochlin, G. (1973). *Man's aggression: The defense of the self.* Boston, MA: Gambit.

Sandler, J. (1960). The background of safety. *International Journal of Psychoanalysis, 41,* 352–365.

Saul, I. (1976). *The psychodynamics of hostility.* Northvale, NJ: Jason Aronson.

Segal, H. (1979). *Melanie Klein.* New York, NY: Viking Press.

Sharpe, S., & Rosenblatt, A. (1994). Oedipal sibling triangles. *Journal of the American Psychoanalytic Association, 42,* 491–523.

Simmel, E. (1944). Self preservation and the death instinct. *Psychoanalytic Quarterly, 13,* 160–185.

Smalley, R. (1970). The functional approach to casework practice. In R. W. Roberts & R. H. Nee (Eds.), *Theories of social casework* (pp. 77–128). Chicago, IL: University of Chicago Press.

Spitz, R. (1945). Hospitalism: An inquiry into the genesis of psychiatric conditions in early childhood. *Psychoanalytic Study of the Child, 1,* 53–73.

Spitz, R. (1965). *The first year of life.* New York, NY: International Universities Press.

Stern, D. (1986). *The interpersonal world of the infant.* New York, NY: Basic Books.

Stern, D. (2005). Intersubjectivity. In E. S. Person, A. M. Cooper, & G. O. Gabbard (Eds.), *Textbook of psychoanalysis* (pp. 77–92). Washington, DC: American Psychiatric.

Stolorow, R., Brandschaft, B., & Atwood, G. (1987). *Psychoanalytic treatment: An intersubjective approach.* Hillsdale, NJ: Analytic Press.

Strean, H. (1993). Clinical social work: An evaluative review. *Journal of Analytic Social Work, 1*(1), 5–23.

Sullivan, H. (1931). Socio-psychiatric research: Its implications for the schizophrenia problem and for mental hygiene. *American Journal of Psychiatry, 87,* 977–991.

Sullivan, H. (1940). *Conceptions of modern psychiatry.* New York, NY: W. W. Norton.

Sullivan, H. (1953). *The interpersonal theory of psychiatry.* New York, NY: W. W. Norton.

Sullivan, H. (1956). *Clinical studies in psychiatry.* New York, NY: W. W. Norton.

Sullivan, H. (1962). *Schizophrenia as a human process.* New York, NY: W. W. Norton.

Suttie, I. (1952). *The origins of love and hate.* New York, NY: Matrix House. (Original work published 1935).

Terman, D. M. (2012). Self psychology. In G. O. Gabbard, B. L. Litowitz, & P. Williams (Eds.), *Textbook of Psychoanalysis* (pp. 199–210). Washington D.C: American Psychiatric Publishing.

Thompson, C. (1964). *Interpersonal psychoanalysis: The selected papers of Clara Thompson.* New York, NY: Basic Books.

Thorpe, W. (1956). *Learning and instinct in animals.* London, UK: Methuen.

Tyson, P., & Tyson, R. (1990). *Psychoanalytic theories of development.* New Haven, CT: Yale University Press.

White, R. (1963). *The ego and reality in psychoanalytic theory.* New York, NY: International Universities Press.

Williams, P. (2012). Object relations. In G. O. Gabbard, B. L. Litowitz, & P. Williams (Eds.), *Textbook of Psychoanalysis* (pp. 171–183). Washington D.C: American Psychiatric Publishing.

Winnicott, D. (1958). Transitional objects and transitional phenomena. In *Through paediatrics to psycho-analysis* (pp. 229–242). London, UK: Hogarth Press. (Original work published 1951)

Winnicott, D. (1965a). The capacity to be alone. In *The maturational process and the facilitating environment* (pp. 29–36). New York, NY: International Univer-sities Press. (Original work published 1958)

Winnicott, D. (1965b). The theory of the parent-infant relationship. In *The maturational process and the facilitating environment* (pp. 37–55). New York, NY: International Univer-sities Press. (Original work published 1960)

Witenberg, E. (Ed.). (1973). *Interpersonal explorations in psychoanalysis: New directions in theory and practice.* New York, NY: Basic Books.

Woodroofe, K. (1971). *From charity to social work in England and the United States.* Toronto, Ontario, Canada: University of Toronto Press.

Woods, M., & Hollis, F. (1990). *Casework: A psychosocial therapy.* New York, NY: McGraw-Hill.

4

NEUROBIOLOGY AND CLINICAL SOCIAL WORK

DENNIS MIEHLS

This chapter elucidates the burgeoning influence of neurobiology on clinical social work practice. Contemporary literature from the broad fields of infant research, child development theory, contemporary attachment theory, trauma theory, cognitive neuroscience, relational theory, and psychodynamic clinical theory is converging in a synergistic and interesting manner that supports the notions that human beings are resilient and that change is possible across the life cycle, even if individuals have experienced unfortunate traumatic beginnings. In its broadest sense, the term *neurobiology* is used here to discuss current research findings on brain function(s); a summary of the literature, which suggests that relationships have the capacity to build and rebuild certain parts of the brain that influence our social and emotional lives and responses to others, is offered. I agree with Louis Cozolino (2006) when he suggests that there is no such thing as a "single brain" and that one's social brain is fundamentally shaped in interaction with other people. There are many implications to this statement; this chapter illuminates some of these implications, especially as they are related to clinical social work that uses

relationships as a central component to practice with a diverse range of clients.

This chapter first gives a brief introduction to the main concepts of contemporary neurobiological literature; the focus is on findings that have direct relevance to clinical social work practice. The potential of reparative relationships is emphasized, as well as how the integration of neurobiology affects contemporary clinical practice. The influence of right brain activities frames this discussion, and clinical examples are used to illustrate these concepts. Next, the chapter discusses how disrupted attachment and traumatic events affect brain development. Clinical examples are used to support the conceptual framework that is discussed. Last, the future implications of using neurobiological understandings of human behavior as they are relevant to clinical social work practice is explored.

AN INTRODUCTION TO NEUROBIOLOGY: KEY AREAS TO CONSIDER

The following is a thumbnail sketch of current literature that describes brain functions that are related to change processes in the context of human relationships, including clinical social work interventions with clients. In addition to the information in this chapter, the reader is encouraged to explore the ever-expanding literature in sources such as those found in the recently published texts by Applegate and Shapiro (2005), Badenoch (2008), Cozolino (2006), Doidge (2007), Iacoboni (2008), Montgomery (2013), Schore (2003a, 2003b), Siegel (2007), and Siegel and Hartzell (2004). In these texts, readers will find excellent descriptions of brain physiology that complement the following material.

At the outset, it is important to recognize that our study and knowledge of how the brain functions is rapidly expanding. Current technology such as magnetic resonance imagery (MRI) and positron emission tomography (PET) facilitates research that illuminates where particular brain activity is occurring under certain conditions (Applegate & Shapiro, 2005; Basham & Miehls, 2004). Researchers are able to trace the parts of the brain that are activated during different experiences, and we can hypothesize how mental processes affect one's subjective experiences. The work of Schore (2003a, 2003b) and other infant and trauma researchers (Cozolino, 2006; Siegel, 1999, 2007) has extended our working knowledge of brain functions related to affect regulation, normative development, and interrupted development. Studying the effects of disrupted attachment on the developing emotional security of infants and children has been particularly useful in understanding the essential components of brain physiology that contribute to overall positive mental health.

Generally, we understand that individuals develop mental health symptoms as a result of a combination of genetic vulnerabilities that lead to alterations in which neurotransmitters and hormones are produced within the individual's body; this leads to further alterations in brain functions and to the development of disorders. Consider the interactive effects on brain physiology for individuals who experience depression. Depressed individuals likely have a combination of neural deficits with some potential damage to the body-brain functions as a result of feelings of hopelessness. In other words, there is a reciprocal effect of genetic vulnerability interacting with the emotional world of depressed individuals that leads to actual change in brain physiology and the nature of certain brain functions. See the section below that discusses right and left brain hemisphere functions for a fuller description of the brain functions of depressed individuals.

It is important to recognize that parts of the brain interact to create not only resilience but also mental health problems. Three parts of the brain are intricately connected, referred to as the *triune brain* (Levine, 1997). This concept is later expanded, but in a basic sense, the triune brain is a combination of the reptilian brain, the limbic system, and the neocortex. The reptilian brain is that part of our brain that is instinctual and the most basic; it promotes our basic survival. Our limbic system is the site of our emotions and feelings, and the neocortex is that part of our brain that is the thinking, cognitive, and perceptual processing center. If we have a vertical integration of the reptilian, limbic, and neocortex, then we have the capacity to sense the ebb and flow of empathic connection in our own bodies (Badenoch, 2008). However, if the natural flow of our triune brain is interrupted (e.g., as a result of trauma), one has difficulty in integrating the various functions of the brain, and one's capacity to experience and hold complex affective states is compromised. Compromised individuals develop a range of symptoms and responses to stimuli that fundamentally shape their interactions with the world around them, including their relationships with others.

Of particular relevance for this chapter, brain physiology is summarized in terms of *plasticity*, the different functions of the *right and left brain hemispheres*, the role of the *hippocampus* and *amygdala* in understanding memory systems, and how *attachment experiences* shape these key brain functions. This is followed by a discussion of how these brain functions are activated and used in a clinical relationship, one that leads to repair of earlier disrupted attachment or traumatic events. The focus here will be on those aspects of brain physiology that have particular relevance for mental health and clinical social work practice.

PLASTICITY

Simply put, *plasticity* refers to the brain's capacity to reshape itself in response to new experience (Badenoch, 2008; Baylis, 2006). As a living system, the brain is continuously shaped by the activity of the basic units of the nervous system, referred to as *neurons*. Neurons are "cells that transmit signals to one another via chemical messengers" (Cozolino, 2006, p. 38). Following a survival of the fittest notion, brain functions are strengthened when connections are made between neurons. Neurons seek out neighboring cells in which to form alliances; in this process, certain associations within the brain become used and systematized within the individual, and "neurons that fail to communicate with other neurons die off through a process called apoptosis" (Cozolino, 2006, p. 39). Infants and young children have tremendous potential to take in messages that set the foundations for brain activity. Research in neurobiology increasingly demonstrates the importance of the relational matrix in shaping individual response to internal and external stimulation. We now know that secure attachment relationships both shape the infant's ability to tolerate impingements and are central in the infant's development of the capacity to regulate affective experiences. In other words, secure attachment fosters the development of neural circuits that assist the child in developing sound interpersonal relationships. Traumatic events alter the child's ability to stay regulated, and brain functions become focused on survival, resulting in less optimal footings in mental health. However, researchers and clinicians now recognize that the power of the professional relationship can assist individuals to modify actual brain function. Rather than assuming that individuals are destined to carry the templates of brain physiology with them throughout life, findings in neurobiology suggest that even the most frightening and painful experiences of individuals can be altered by activity both within one's mind and, more important, as a result of activity between minds. Cozolino (2006) notes,

> Relationships not only add to the development and expansion of neurons, but provide the added energy for their growth and survival. The effect of good parenting is to provide an optimal metabolic environment for growth through biochemical stimulation and the enhancement of neuroplastic processes. (p. 43)

Right and Left Brain Hemisphere Development and Functions

The brain is divided into a right and a left side. Common parlance often refers to individuals as either "right brained" or "left brained." This phrase is often used to dichotomize individuals in a general sense as being either more feeling/ artistic or more intellectual/ rational. These characterizations do have some foundation in the neurobiology of brain hemispheric characteristics and functions. Increasingly, we are able to distinguish the complexity of functions of the two hemispheres and understand how the brain creates mechanisms that aid integration of experiences on multiple levels (Badenoch, 2008; Cozolino, 2006; Siegel, 2007).

There are similar structures in both halves of the brain. The two hemispheres are essentially mirror images of each other, although the information that each processes and the means of processing information differ. A connecting tissue, called the *corpus callosum*, connects the two hemispheres. Because of its leading role in language development, the left hemisphere was considered the dominant hemisphere for understanding emotions until recently. However, our understanding of the characteristics and functions of the twin hemispheres has deepened in the past 20 years. Cozolino (2006) notes that "although it remains true that the left hemisphere takes the lead in semantic and conscious processing, social and emotional dominance leans toward the right" (p. 66). The right hemisphere develops most actively during the first 2 or 3 years of life, while the left hemisphere is mostly developed around the second year of life (Siegel, 2007).

Right-brain-hemispheric activity is broadly characterized as being experienced in a holistic and nonlinear manner. The links between emotion and bodily experiences affect the autonomic processes within the individual. The right hemisphere is "specialized for perceiving and processing visual and spatial information—such as sending and receiving nonverbal signals, the centerpiece of social understanding" (Badenoch, 2008, p. 19). Nonverbal interactions such as observing the facial expression of another and sensing danger from another are processed in the right hemisphere. These reactions develop early, and infants and young children sense the relative feeling of safety or danger from the nonverbal behaviors of parental or caregiver figures. From these experiences, individuals develop symbolic internal representations of themselves and others. We also develop a sense of relationships from right-brain-hemispheric activity.

It is important to note that right brain activities often happen without conscious awareness. This implies that right brain responses process emotional responses based on past experiences. We develop a template of responses that are beyond our awareness, and as Cozolino (2006) notes, "because the right brain develops first, it organizes and stores many emotional experiences that can emerge in later relationships, especially when we are under stress" (p. 68). Innumerable interactions with attachment figures during the first 18 months of life shape right brain circuitry, and the infant learns to recognize and appraise the relative safety or danger of others. This is directly related to the infant's burgeoning abilities to regulate emotions. This is not an individual experience; the infant develops its right brain circuitry while in connection with the right brain of the attachment figure. In other words, the "linking of right hemispheres is accomplished through eye contact, facial expressions, soothing vocalizations, caresses, and exciting exchanges"

(p. 72). The attuned parent knows when to engage or disengage so that the infant can begin to regulate his or her own emotional states without being overwhelmed. Disrupted attachment and traumatic events play havoc with right brain development and the achievement of emotional regulation. This is discussed later in more detail.

The left hemisphere develops somewhat later and is often characterized as serving the executive functions of logic, language, and linearity. The left hemisphere makes sense of situations and "specializes in identifying and processing the details of a situation and is therefore superior in processing the semantic aspects of language, making causal connections between phenomena, and coordinating fine motor movements (Applegate & Shapiro, 2005, p. 8). In other words, the left hemisphere takes the lead in consciously processing information that is accessible to the individual's memory. The left brain forms language to explain, order, and characterize experiences.

When there has been healthy and synchronized attunement from an attachment figure, the infant or toddler begins to integrate the functions of the two hemispheres. Badenoch (2008) refers to this synchronization of the two hemispheres as *vertical integration*. Individuals with vertical integration of the two hemispheres have the capacity to fluidly move between the functions of the two hemispheres. This ability leads one to have the capacity to verbalize affective states while in the midst of experiencing states of nonconscious activation of bodily sensations. Recall that the right brain responses are activated through a range of nonverbal activities, and these activities are often encoded on an unconscious basis. The left brain, then, begins to bring forth conscious ideas to the individual that help explain the autonomic responses of the right brain. For example, an adult who experiences panic when he sees a barking German Shepherd will be able to calm himself when the left brain accurately remembers and brings into conscious thought a childhood experience of being terribly frightened by a large dog. This individual has achieved vertical integration of the two hemispheres. However, if the child had been unable to feel safe in the childhood experience, the right brain response will dominate the current experience and the logic and calming messages of the left brain will be mute. In other words, emotions experienced in the present are altered not only in response to the intensity of the original childhood experience but also based on the historical ability of an attachment figure to help the frightened child mediate this experience.

We now turn to the role of emotions, certain sections of the limbic system, and the autonomic nervous system to further explore how individuals process information and make meaning of their experiences. In addition, the different types of memory and how these are formed and retrieved are also explored.

Information Processing and Memory

As noted, the right and left brain hemispheres function collaboratively to ensure healthy adaptation to the internal and external stimuli that a child experiences. When the hemispheres are working well together, the left brain is able to organize experiences in such a way that the individual does not feel threatened, and as such, is able to continue to explore novel situations and enjoy the positive emotions associated with growth and development. However, if the child feels overtly threatened and is not in the presence of a calming, affectively balanced attachment figure, certain templates of responses become more powerfully ingrained in the individual's experience. As noted above, these templates influence the response and the meaning system of individuals. Cozolino (2006) notes that "states of stress, anxiety, fear, trauma, and pain all result in heightened activation in right-sided structures" (p. 74). We tend to use the defense strategies of fight, flight, or emotional distancing of ourselves from something or someone when we experience negative emotions. Right brain activation tends to be biased toward negative emotions, while left brain activation tends to be biased toward positive emotions. Citing Keenan et al. (1999), Cozolino suggests the following:

An unfortunate artifact of the evolution of laterality may be that the right hemisphere, biased toward negative emotions and pessimism, develops first and serves as the core of self-awareness and self-identity. To be human may be to have vulnerability towards shame, guilt, and depression. (p. 75)

This process is particularly heightened if the individual has experienced disrupted attachment or traumatic events in early development.

Increasingly, we know that childhood stress and trauma lead to difficulties in the development of explicit memory and affect regulation, healthy interpersonal relationships, healthy identity development, and the ability to creatively engage in exploration of the world and other people (Cozolino, 2002; Inbinder, 2006; Schore & Schore, 2008; Shapiro & Applegate, 2000; Teicher, Andersen, Polcari, Anderson, & Navalta, 2002). In terms of neurobiology, how does all this work? We know that repetitive stressors and traumatic events force individuals to find adaptive coping mechanisms. When an individual feels threatened, the *amygdala* appraises the severity of the situation and initiates actions of fight or flight. Memory is the means by which the brain responds to experiences, and connections are made that lead to either *implicit* or *explicit* memory.

Recall that right brain activity dominates in an infant's experiences until approximately 18 months of age. As such, the experiences of the infant are encoded as *implicit memories*. Siegel and Hartzell (2004) note that "implicit memory results in the creation of the particular circuits of the brain that are responsible for generating emotions, behavioral responses, perception, and probably the encoding of bodily sensations" (p. 22). In other words, implicit memories are nonverbal memories that become activated on an unconscious basis. What was encoded as an infant in certain situations becomes stimulated when the adult experiences similar circumstances or experiences. The infant has encoded a memory of similar events and automatically develops emotions, behaviors, perceptions, and even bodily sensations in reaction to current data. Badenoch (2008) explains, "When implicit memories are activated in our day-to-day experience, they have no time stamp, so we interpret the emotional, visceral, perceptual, behavioral surge as being entirely *caused by something occurring in the present moment*" (p. 25). (This is discussed later.) An essential goal of clinical intervention is to assist individuals in transforming implicit memories to *explicit* memories.

Another important part of the brain, the *hippocampus*, becomes active and operational in the second year of an infant's life. The hippocampus is the site of one's ability to articulate the experience of emotions, and it is also the site of explicit memory. "There are two components of explicit memory: *semantic, or factual,* memory, which becomes available at around a year and a half of age, and *autobiographical* memory, which begins to develop sometime after the second birthday" (Siegel & Hartzell, 2004, p. 23, italics added). The later development of the hippocampus explains why all individuals universally experience what is termed *childhood amnesia* and why humans are not able to remember details of the experiences of their first 2 years of life. Explicit memory is encoded consciously, and in fact, one must focus conscious attention on a situation to develop explicit memory. Autobiographical memory links the hippocampus and the front part of the brain, called the *prefrontal cortex.* Siegel and Hartzell (2004) suggest that "the prefrontal cortex is extremely important for a wide range of processes, including autobiographical memory, self-awareness, response flexibility, mindsight, and the regulation of emotions" (pp. 24–25). Research demonstrates that the development of the prefrontal cortex is profoundly influenced by interpersonal relationships. As such, secure attachment relationships contribute to sound development of the functions associated with the prefrontal cortex. Autobiographical memory allows individuals to begin to narrate their stories and to make sense or meaning of their experiences. Badenoch (2008) emphasizes that this type of remembering is related to empathic connections. She says,

"*Empathic attunement is the key factor that fosters this all-important integrative step in children,* and it is also part of the reason that solid therapy can rewire the brain so efficiently" (p. 28, italics in original). Siegel (2007) has drawn together research findings and lists nine integrative functions of the middle prefrontal cortex:[1] (1) regulation of the body, (2) attuned communication, (3) emotional regulation, (4) response flexibility, (5) empathy, (6) insight, (7) fear modulation, (8) intuition, and (9) morality.

Studying the brains of depressed individuals offers some interesting data that suggest that brain functions are altered with certain mental health conditions. Citing Bremner et al. (2002), Badenoch (2008) says that "recent neuroimaging studies have revealed that the *medial orbitofrontal cortex* of people who suffer from *major depression* is 32% smaller than in nondepressed people" (p. 122, italics in original). This suggests that these individuals have less capacity to integrate cognitive and emotional processes and are also more challenged than nondepressed individuals in regulating their body and emotions. The functions of the prefrontal cortex noted above are significantly altered in the depressed individual. Badenoch also suggests that the volume of the hippocampi of depressed individuals is 19% less than in individuals without depression. Recalling that the hippocampus is that part of the brain that helps the individual to have explicit and declarative memories, we then understand that depressed individuals have a physiological reason for experiencing memory and cognitive deficits during their depressive episodes. Badenoch also suggests that depressed individuals have heightened amygdalae arousal, and this contributes to fearing others or perceiving others as threats to their emotional safety and well-being. The overactive amygdalae of depressed individuals also leads to difficulty sleeping, as these individuals are on alert even during sleep periods.

---

[1]For a more detailed description of Siegel's work, the reader is encouraged to review Siegel (2007).

There is increasing evidence that demonstrates the interface of trauma on brain development so that if an infant experiences traumatic events or disrupted attachments, the development of the prefrontal cortex is compromised. This leads to many unfortunate outcomes, as the previously mentioned nine functions are underdeveloped. We now turn to the impact of trauma on these functions of brain activity.

The Influence of Trauma on Brain Development

Humans are resilient beings. However, certain traumatic events shape the response of individuals in particular ways, depending on their experiences. It is important to recognize that trauma is a relative concept, and that there will be variability in individual responses to certain types of disrupted attachment, neglect, abuse, and extreme stressors. We discuss how these sorts of traumatic events influence one's ability to remember events and to process these events in an adaptive manner. Recall that memory is implicit or explicit. When individuals experience symptoms of posttraumatic stress disorder, including dissociation, their capacities to work through aspects of trauma are compromised.

The adult brain regresses to an infantile state when the adult experiences stressors or traumatic events. Van der Kolk (1996) points out that traumatic memories are not encoded in narratives; rather, individuals store unprocessed traumatic events in somatic, bodily sensations. When an individual is flooded by feelings after being reminded of past traumatic events, the limbic system of the individual and certain functions of the brain work together to modulate or control the emotional responses of the individual. Basham and Miehls (2004) note as follows:

First, the psychophysiological effects following trauma include extreme autonomic responses that are reminiscent of the actual trauma. Alternating patterns of hyperarousal and numbness plague trauma survivors, who are disturbed regularly by startle responses, lowered thresholds to sound intensities, and a reduced electrical pattern in cortical events. (p. 76)

The amygdala of the trauma survivor is excited by the sympathetic regulatory system when there is a familiar traumatic stimulus coming toward the individual. Citing Cahill and McGaugh (1998), Cozolino (2002) says that the "activation of the amygdala (and the related physiological and biological changes) is at the heart of the modulation of emotional and traumatic memory" (p. 271). The heightened arousal of the amygdala disrupts the ability of the hippocampus to participate in the memory process of the event. In other words, the functions of the hippocampus, which are related to understanding the event, attaching language to it, and consciously remembering the event, are hijacked by the trauma survivor's amygdala.

An individual processes the relative danger or safety of situations in rapid fashion. Any new stimulus is appraised by right brain functions, which read the facial expressions, body language, and posture of the other participant. If the behavior or stimulus is familiar to the individual and has previously been experienced as benign, then the individual moves forward with the interaction with increasing complexity. If the hippocampus is unfamiliar with the situation, then a message is picked up by the brain essentially saying "Be alert" or "Wake up," that something is going on that needs to be tended to and controlled. Then, the amygdala takes over, implicit or iconic memories are predominant, and the individual experiences sensorimotor or bodily responses to the stimuli. The explicit or declarative memory functions cease operation. This explains why trauma memories are often encoded outside the conscious awareness of the trauma survivor. The current situation reminds the individual of a previous traumatic event that was not processed and encoded as explicit or declarative memory. Rather, the event was remembered through sensorimotor memory. In clinical social work, then, *the therapeutic process aids the individual in translating these implicit memories into more readily accessible conscious explicit memories.*

Often, the trauma survivor will try to make sense out of these sensorimotor memories by talking to family (e.g., to confirm the history of the event), to friends, or to clinicians. An individual will suffer less and become less likely to repeat traumatic patterns when he or she attaches words to these experiences. Making meaning of the events and categorizing and schematizing them will diminish the strength of the previous traumatic events.

Two other experiences of trauma survivors fit with this understanding of brain functions. An unfortunate clinical manifestation of trauma survivorship is the experience of flashbacks, which are powerful and intrusive images of previous traumatic events. Cozolino (2002) suggests the following:

> Traumatic flashbacks are memories of a quite different nature than are those of nontraumatic events. To begin with, they are stored in more primitive circuits with less cortical and left-hemisphere involvement. Because of this, they are strong somatic, sensory, and emotional, as well as inherently nonverbal. (p. 272)

Here too, the amygdala fear networks are activated. Clinical interventions help the trauma survivor to begin to mediate the intensity of the flashback experience.

Finally, it is important to note that the part of the brain that is related to the development of speech and language (*Broca's area*) also is rendered nonfunctional for many trauma survivors. Thus, we can understand the experience of trauma survivors who appear frozen or are given to silence, speechless terror, and a sense of numbness. Cozolino (2002) suggests the following:

> This inhibitory effect on Broca's area will impair the encoding of conscious memory for traumatic events at the time they occur. It will then naturally interfere with the development of narratives that serve to process the experience and would otherwise lead to neural network integration and psychological healing. (p. 274)

Here too, clinical work can assist survivors in attaching words and meaning to the experiences that paralyze them and enhance their capacity to talk about such experiences.

So with these basic fundamentals of brain neurobiology understood, we now turn to some clinical examples in which the understanding of these concepts facilitated forward movement for clients in their journey toward becoming less controlled by the traumatic events of their past. The clinical examples elucidate interventions and emphasize the importance of right brain activities that are stimulated between the client and the clinician. In addition, work with borderline-personality-disordered individuals, sexually addicted clients, and social anxiety/phobic clients is also presented.

CLINICAL IMPLICATIONS OF NEUROBIOLOGY THEORY

The following clinical examples illustrate some of the concepts discussed in the first part of this chapter. Clinicians who pay attention to neurobiological theory understand the importance of setting a therapeutic environment conducive to the exploration of subtle and overt shifts in the client's behavior—and to everything in between. Clinical social workers have the capacity to enable their clients to alter patterns of attachment, and a crucial component of the therapeutic effort is the recognition, acceptance, and active construction of secure and consistent relationships with clients.

It is useful to note that clinical social workers have historically emphasized the healing restorative capabilities of the treatment relationship. As early as 1917, Mary Richmond emphasized that the professional relationship was absolutely crucial in helping the client initiate his or her own change process. Richmond was a central figure in shifting the focus of social work away from simply a process of charity and caregiving in the friendly visitor role. Rather, she developed a more scientific approach to the study and diagnosis of clients within their environment. Richmond recognized the significance of the client-worker relationship and viewed it as a linchpin of the helping process. Goldstein, Miehls, and Ringel (2009) note, "Richmond made repeated references to the teaching functions of the relationship, which she thought should embody such qualities as simple friendliness, tact, good will, deep respect, a loving attitude, and mutuality" (p. 2).

The historical emphasis on relationship as a restorative foreshadowed the importance of attachment relationships and their healing capacities for neurobiological and emotional changes in individuals. The use of a neurobiological approach to understand the essential cornerstones of treatment emphasizes that an individual's psychopathology is essentially viewed as deficits in affect regulation (Schore, 2003b, Schore, 2012). Secure attachment relationships, which offer the opportunity for increasingly complex abilities for regulating highly charged affective states, aid optimal development in children. They also facilitate optimal change processes for our clients. Neurobiological theory explains that empathy is created as a result of both left and right brain connections between client and clinician. Crucial for the development of trust in the treatment relationship, the clinician understands that her right brain nonverbal attunement with her client's right brain activity leads to satisfying and healing affect-synchronizing activities. The clinician is more active in helping the client recognize, feel, and manage affective states in the early part of the treatment process. As the client becomes more aware of the range of her affective states, she becomes more able to self-regulate emotions while in the clinician's presence. The clinician titrates her involvement based on the client's ability to recognize and regulate her emotional world. These interventions are formulated as a result of understanding infant research that has demonstrated that parents need to help modulate the primitive affective states of their children (Beebe & Lachmann, 2002; Stern, 1985). With increasing ability to modulate right brain experiences, the clinician is able to shift to left brain activity that promotes insight and the creation of new narratives to reshape the client's internal object relations

world. Clients can alter their internal representations of relationships and redesign their views of self and others—all while reshaping their brain structures.

In recognizing the strength of right brain activity in understanding behavior, the social worker needs to accept that the client is picking up her affect and the state of her internal world via, for example, observations of facial expression, tone of voice, and posture. In addition, the clinician's own affective responsiveness to a client may reveal powerful unconscious aspects of the client that were previously unrecognized. Many social workers have been trained to conduct clinical work as a predominantly left brain activity. They have been taught to encourage clients to verbalize, seek insight into, and update memories. While these are all important activities, Badenoch (2008) suggests that there are potential risks in staying focused on only left brain activities when working with a client. One drawback may be that the client follows the lead of the clinician in staying left brain focused and thus misses opportunities to experience and use the bodily sensations stimulated in the right brain as sources of information. Second, clinicians who ignore their own right brain responses may limit or reduce their capacity to receive information about their clients' right brain experiences— which are so crucial in affect regulation. Increasingly, authors suggest that our understanding of our clients' experiences is enhanced when we, as clinicians, pay attention to our own embodied responses. Marks-Tarlow (2012) argues that clinical intuition plays a central role in change processes in psychotherapy. She suggests that "by grounding ourselves in inner sensory, emotional, and imaginal faculties, we can tap into a receptive mode of consciousness. This prepares the mind, brain, and body for the possibility of deep connections with patients that coexist with deep connections with ourselves" (p. 11). She emphasizes that paying attention to our body's responses (right brain experiences) opens up pathways for discovery into our clients' internal worlds. Similarly, the Boston Change Process Study Group (2010) discusses that change occurs in ways beyond representational processes that are semantic—these rely on symbolic representation in language. The second kind of representation that it discusses is *implicit relational knowing*. These authors note that therapeutic dyads also develop procedural representations in the clinical relationship. The client and the clinician develop ways of procedural representations that "are rule-based representations of how to proceed, of how to do things. Such procedures may never become symbolically coded" (p. 31). This group of clinicians suggests that powerful moments of change can occur when the usual procedural code is interrupted in the therapeutic encounter. At these

moments, which they term *now* moments, the therapeutic dyad needs to reconfigure their notion of the therapeutic process. These authors see these moments as opportunities for change, in contrast to an impasse or some sort of resistance to the treatment process. It is clear that many authors are discovering the power of paying attention to one's right brain activities while conducting psychotherapy.

The following example illustrates a clinician's ability to use his right brain responses in a clinical situation. Recognition of this reaction aided the further development of the clinical work.

Clinical Vignette 1

Ken[2] was a 28-year-old professional who had requested psychotherapy to help him deal with his performance anxiety. He experienced a great deal of public anxiety, and this anxiety was interfering with his ability to comfortably teach his classes at the community college in which he was employed. His anxiety was so debilitating that he was considering shifting his career, but he decided to engage in psychotherapy before he made such a major life decision. We agreed that we would have specific goals that would be focused on the alleviation of his anxiety. While we agreed that a cognitive-behavioral approach would be most beneficial for him, Ken was also open to exploring developmental/historical issues if they emerged as defenses to the therapeutic work.

His family history revealed that he was the eldest of four boys, raised in a rural area of western Massachusetts. He noted that his parents had what appeared to be a happy marriage, and that they worked well together to provide for him and his brothers both emotionally and practically. He did not reveal any traumatic events in his past during the data-gathering phase of the clinical work. Ken was a good student and had moved through college in a facile and accomplished manner. He had been employed at the community college for 18 months, having completed a PhD in his chosen field of study. He married his high school sweetheart, and he reported that he and his wife were happy together. They intended to have children after they were more established in their respective careers.

Ken made good use of the psychotherapy and was slowly and consistently gaining some relief from his acute anxiety as a result of practicing some mindfulness and relaxation techniques. He also began to challenge some of his cognitive distortions related to his own competencies; he tended to

(Continued)

[2]Although all clinical material has been disguised (through the use of composite case material) to protect client confidentiality, the clinical process issues represented here are consistent with the author's clinical practice.

(Continued)

be somewhat depressed at times, and his self-concept was distorted as a result of a harsh belief system. While the client seemed to be moving along in his treatment, I became aware that my anxiety level was heightened when in session with Ken. I began to have some difficulty staying focused on the content, often feeling a sense of nausea or some dizziness. Certainly puzzled by my response, I reflected on my own history and previous therapy to ascertain how and why I was affected in this way by the client's presentation. I recalled my own public speaking anxiety that I had worked through in my own therapy a number of years earlier. I imagined that I was identifying with Ken and that perhaps I was even holding his anxiety during the sessions.

While this insight offered some temporary relief to my symptoms of anxiety, I continued to be aware of how uncomfortable I was during the sessions with Ken. When I began to wonder how long Ken would stay in treatment, I recognized that my anxiety was a potential interference to our continued treatment alliance. I wondered if our unconscious (right brain activity) was being mutually stimulated in our dialogues. I understood that I needed to bring my anxiety response into the room—without being self-indulgent or losing the focus of the needs of the client. In the next session, Ken was reporting continued success in his teaching experiences. He was getting good feedback from some of his students, and he seemed to be growing into his role as a lecturer. As I supported the changes in him outside the therapy office, I asked him if he felt anxiety during his sessions. (On the surface, he appeared calm and comfortably engaged in the relationship with me.) His knee-jerk reaction was to deny that he felt any anxiety between us. I cautiously shared with him that I was puzzled with my own reactions to him. I briefly said that I sometimes experienced discomfort during the sessions with him, noting my bodily responses of nausea and dizziness. I emphasized that I wasn't blaming him for this response, but that I was curious whether he ever experienced such symptoms during our sessions.

Ken reflected on this idea for a while and then reluctantly admitted that he was increasingly terrified of coming in for his appointments. He acknowledged that he was very respectful of me, and that he knew his fears were ill-founded, but he said that he was worried that I was going to "attack" him. I listened quietly and suggested that this must be very uncomfortable for him. Our appointments were in the early morning, and there was typically no one else in the building when we met for his sessions. I asked him if he thought I would hurt him physically. He said uncomfortably, "No, not physically but sexually—I am afraid you are going to force me into something sexual." Sensing his acute anxiety and shame, I asked him if he could talk more about this. Ken agreed and then disclosed to me that he was having increasing difficulty managing his uncomfortable feelings related to an incident that he had experienced as a young adolescent. He reported that had he idealized three boys who were 3 or 4 years older than he. These were boys from his neighborhood he had tried to hang out with during his free time. He said that he wanted to participate with them in various activities, such as fishing and other sports activities. On one summer evening, the other boys permitted him to tag along with them—something that was usually denied to Ken. He accompanied them to a secluded fishing spot near their homes, where the boys sexually assaulted him. He had never disclosed this to anyone, and he had tried to suppress the memory of the event. However, he also reported that he was having a number of disturbing dreams related to this event and that he felt nauseated and dizzy when these images came back to him. It seemed as if he was experiencing some flashbacks of the event.

I suggested that Ken might be looking up to me, paralleling the idealization of his neighborhood chums. I also noted that it must be scary to think that I would turn on him as his companions had done. He replied by saying that he should have told me about this history when we first started our work together; he wanted to avoid this, but he also had an inkling that his performance anxiety was perhaps connected to this sexual assault. He noted that he knew his thoughts were illogical, but he wondered if others (e.g., in his classes) would see him as a pathetic male who could not protect himself. Ken and I spent the remainder of the hour processing what he might feel like afterward, in light of this revelation. He was able to acknowledge that he would feel embarrassed or worry about what I would think of him. We ended the session with an invitation to call me in between sessions if he wanted to touch base; we also acknowledged that his goals for therapy would include further discussion and working through of this traumatic event.

As noted above, often right brain activity, which is characterized by nonverbal but somatic representations, is passed unconsciously between client and clinician. In many instances, it is important that the clinician convey a sense of calmness and offer a holding environment to help quiet a dysregulated client who has stored traumatic events in the right brain domain of implicit and somatic memories. In this example, the clinician used his own somatic responses to help the client unearth a traumatic event. Ken had few explicit memories of the traumatic event; however, he was able to use his somatic responses to open up pathways for further discussion of the event. As his therapy progressed, he began to experience further symptomatic relief when he attached more explicit memories and verbalizations to this unfortunate event in his history.

The following is a particularly poignant example of how my client John stored an implicit memory of traumatic physical and verbal abuse, experienced at a young age. Farber (2008) describes a similar clinical experience, that of a client who had retained the image of her father hovering over her crib, "telling her that children are very beatable, which frightened her, as did the shadows in her room which looked like a large terrifying thing lurking over her bed" (p. 67).

Clinical Vignette 2

John and I had been working together for some months when he disclosed what he termed as an unusual and unexplained reaction that he experienced on certain partially cloudy days. John, a 28-year-old PhD student at a local college, had sought therapy as he was having difficulties in forming an intimate relationship. He dated frequently, but he acknowledged his difficulty in trusting the

(Continued)

(Continued)

young women he dated. He seemed to become more distrusting of others the longer he knew them. His beginning treatment with me was punctuated with a number of missed appointments; he seemed to be enacting a pattern in which he perceived that I would become frustrated with him and terminate our relationship. He had some conscious awareness that he was setting this scenario up, and he seemed to gain some trust in me as we were able to talk through this pattern. He also had started to see the patterns in his relationships with his girlfriends, and he was beginning to notice how he set himself up to be rejected or rejecting in these dynamics.

John was raised primarily by his mother, who lived alone for most of John's childhood. She occasionally had boyfriends, but John did not have many memories of any of these men. John's biological father had left the relationship with John's mother when she discovered her pregnancy. She was a college student at the time, and she decided to leave college in order to support herself and John. John was aware that his mother had lived with a man when he was an infant and a toddler, but he did not know much about this man and did not have any explicit memories of him.

As noted above, John reported to me that he wanted to talk about an unusual anxiety that he experienced. With a sense of shame, he reported that he became acutely anxious on partially cloudy days when there was a distinct pattern of sun and cloud. He commented that he had a reaction of fear whenever the sun would be covered with clouds, and that the days in which there was a lot of sun-cloud activity were particularly difficult for him. I reassured John that this experience seemed to be originating from some sort of implicit memory, and I explained some of the ideas concerning implicit and explicit memory. I also explained that he may have had some experiences as a young child that he had stored implicitly and that we might be able to better understand this response if he could look for other examples when he felt as he did on partially cloudy days. Our exploration of his reactions to storms, winds, and other weather patterns seemed to hold little meaning for him, and we agreed to keep this anxiety in mind as other situations arose.

Three or four sessions later, John reported that he had had another experience that echoed the "cloudy-day feeling"—we had developed this as a form of short-cut communication that both of us understood as his acute anxiety in these situations. He reported that he was sitting in a seminar room awaiting his colleagues and his professor. He was enjoying his spot at the table as the sun was coming in, and he welcomed the warmth on the chilly spring morning. As others started to come in they crossed between him and the window, casting a shadow—this paralleled the experience of the sun going behind clouds. John experienced this with four or five people as they came into the room, and he was aware of his acute anxiety. He became so distraught that he decided to move, telling his colleagues that the sun was bothering him.

He continued to think about this experience until he came in for his session, and he said that he was still shaken by it. The experience was now grounded in an interpersonal situation, and this was most upsetting for him. I gently asked him if he was ever aware of any person being cast in a shadow like this when he was a small child. He wasn't sure, but he said that he had a vague memory that his crib was positioned in his room so that the light from the hallway off of his bedroom would cast a shadow when someone would enter his room. He described the physical space of his childhood bedroom, and he could clearly reconstruct how someone entering his room was scary for him. I commented that often children feel safety when a parent comes into their room to comfort them or to cover them up, as examples. John clearly stated that this was not good for him. He suggested that he was going to talk to his mother about this to see if she could help him understand this response.

John left a message for me later that evening indicating that his mother was quite distraught when John initiated a conversation about his bedroom and shadows and the like. She tearfully disclosed that her boyfriend who lived with them when John was between 1 and 3 years of age would often go into John's room to quiet him down. She reported that John was often a restless and tearful young child, and that her boyfriend would become particularly irate with John's behavior. She described how he would "fly into" John's room, yelling at him to shut up; at times, he would spank John so as to try to get John to stop. Recognizing the importance of this conversation, I phoned John back, and we agreed to meet the next day as our schedules permitted this extra session.

In the session, John described his mixture of strong feelings. Though he felt saddened and angry about hearing this part of his history, he also felt some relief. He actually was calm when he spoke about his conversation with his mother. I commented on his demeanor. He acknowledged that he felt calm as he finally had some way to understand his "cloudy-day anxiety." We acknowledged that he would likely continue to have some anxiety on those days but that he could begin to put the experience in perspective. Not surprisingly, we started to talk about his fear of men and his general distrust of others. This example demonstrates how both an interrupted attachment and traumatic events are stored in the right brain, implicit memory banks.

We now explore some specific diagnostic disorders (borderline personality disorder, sexually addictive behavior, and social anxiety) and apply the concepts of neurobiology to these disorders. Disrupted attachment relationships are at the core of many mental health disorders. As such, a primary affective state of troubled individuals is *shame*. The two preceding examples clearly demonstrate the phenomenon of shame. Since shame is the visceral experience of being shunned, clinicians need to be particularly conscious of engaging clients in an open, nonshaming, nonblaming stance. This is often difficult when working with difficult clients who trigger our own responses, but again, it is useful to continuously monitor our own nonverbal responses to clients. This may be particularly true while working with borderline clients, who often stimulate countertransference responses within clinicians.

BORDERLINE PERSONALITY DISORDER

The relationship patterns of borderline personality disordered individuals are often chaotic and fraught with tremendous interpersonal conflict. Borderline individuals often have difficulty in modulating or controlling their affectivity, and such persons often become enraged when they feel hurt and misunderstood. In addition, these individuals often develop self-destructive behaviors in their efforts to manage their chaotic internal worlds. Boschert (2007) quotes Gabbard and suggests that "understanding some of the neurobiologic underpinnings of borderline personality disorder can help psychoanalysts weather the year or more that it takes to see significant changes in a patient" (p. 15). He reported that borderline individuals have a hyperactive amygdala and, more generally, impaired regulation of the amygdalae; hippocampal abnormalities; and smaller prefrontal cortices than do nonborderline clients. Borderline individuals often attribute negative intentions to others around them, often despite evidence to the contrary. This inability to read facial expressions is a direct result of right brain dysfunction and will often be an impediment to the formation of a solid treatment alliance.

Boschert (2007), quoting Gabbard, observes the following:

> MRI studies suggest that hippocampal and amygdalar volumes are smaller in borderline patients than in people without the disorder. . . . [R]educed volume of the medial and orbital prefrontal cortices in borderline patients, compared with controls, may be associated with the increased impulsiveness seen with the disorder. (p. 15)

These deficits compromise the borderline individual's ability to achieve a healthy sense of mentalization. *Mentalization* is a term used to describe one's ability to make sense of the mental states in oneself and others (Fonagy, Gergely, Jurist, & Target, 2002). Borderline individuals have great difficulty understanding the intentionality of others' behavior, and this leads to much conflict in interpersonal relationships. Their inability to understand both their own internal states and the internal states of others pushes borderline clients to act out their internal worlds in exaggerated and often enraged behaviors. Unfortunately, this acting-out behavior often pushes people away from the borderline individual, which may in itself lead to either actual or perceived abandonment, one of the borderline individual's greatest fears. Badenoch (2008) also suggests that the chronic state of emptiness experienced by borderline individuals and their identity diffusion experiences "no doubt have neural correlates in the inability of the middle prefrontal cortex to manage smooth state transitions in the midst of overwhelming limbic upset" (p. 141). Put somewhat differently,

the borderline individual does not have a sense of vertical integration in either right- or left-brain-hemispheric functions.

Borderline individuals often enact self-harm or suicidal behaviors. Here too, neurobiological findings help us understand the mechanisms involved in the self-perpetuation of such behaviors. Cozolino (2002) explains this by suggesting that acting-out, borderline individuals usually bring caretaking people into their interpersonal world. Family members or clinicians become quite protective when the borderline client makes suicidal threats, gestures, or attempts, or indulges in self-harm behaviors such as cutting. Cozolino suggests that endogenous opioids are generated in the borderline individual when caregivers begin to take notice and try to protect the individual. He says, "This same chemical system mediates the distress calls of the baby primates and mothers' response to these calls. Infants become distressed when their mothers are absent, and are soothed and calmed upon their mother's return" (p. 278). The mother's return is correlated with the release of endorphins, thus creating a sense of well-being in the infant (p. 278). The response of caregivers to the borderline individual's behavioral acting-out or suicidal gestures is also correlated with the release of endorphins— a consequence that unfortunately contributes to the likelihood of *further* acting-out behavior. In other words, such individuals are reinforced, neurochemically speaking, for their acting-out behavior. Clinical work with the borderline individual is arduous and often necessitates long-term treatment. The use of empathic connection while building structure and consistency is essential. The clinician needs to actively help the borderline client become aware of and tolerate stimuli in the right brain hemisphere. Beginning to name and regulate affective states is essential as the borderline client begins to form a trusting relationship with the clinician. Bateman and Fonagy (2004) encourage clinicians to be aware that the aggression of the borderline client is likely an indicator of anxiety, and the clinical task becomes one of having the borderline client identify the source of the anxiety—often related to fear of abandonment.

SEXUALLY ADDICTIVE BEHAVIOR

As noted earlier in the chapter, there is a great deal of plasticity in the human brain—our brain has the ability to continuously change and rebuild itself. While we have discussed the positive benefits of relationships that foster neuroplasticity, it is important to consider that *addictive* behaviors, including alcohol and gambling addictions, are also subject to plasticity. In this instance, changes occur in an escalating manner, and the need for further stimuli to satisfy the addict's needs leads to a negative cycle of interaction. This can become debilitating and interpersonally destructive, which is especially evident in sexually addictive behavior. Doidge (2007) explicates the process of sexually addictive behavior for many who have been seduced by the allure of ever-accessible pornography on the Internet. He notes, "All addiction involves long-term, sometimes lifelong, neuroplastic change in the brain" (p. 106). I currently have a number of male clients who fit the picture of the sexual addict. They describe an increasing use of pornography that leads them to increasingly compulsive behavior in which they spend many hours surfing the Internet for pornographic sites that will satisfy their sexual addiction. Many describe spending countless hours on the computer, compulsively masturbating. Often these men put their jobs at risk as their employers become aware of the behavior; indeed, they appear to be incapable of controlling such behaviors, despite negative consequences such as job loss or interpersonal dissatisfaction with their partners.

Studying the effects of Internet addiction, Rendi, Szabo, and Szabo (2007) note "that addicts used the internet on the average 38 hours per week for non-educational and non-employment-related objectives that had significant negative effects on exam performance among students, conflict among couples, and also reduced performance among workers" (p. 223). Their study also documents an increased tolerance, leading to even greater efforts to achieve satisfaction via increased exposure. Recognizing the neurochemical aspects of sexual addiction, Keane (2004) suggests that sexual activity releases endorphins, which leads to a "trance-like euphoria" (p. 196). She goes on to say that "sex has a significant addictive potential because it has both adrenaline and analgesic-like qualities—it both stimulates and soothes" (p. 196).

Doidge (2007) also observes that sexual addicts continuously reinforce their need for increased stimulation in order to be sexually excited and satisfied. As with drugs, the sexual addict becomes desensitized to the behavior, which necessitates a further escalation of behavior to move past the tolerance level. Thus, individuals who were initially excited by images of consensual sexual activity may search out images depicting sadomasochistic or bondage activities. Their sexual fantasies while engaged with real partners may include this sort of imagery; they become unable to perform sexually with a partner, as their partners can never live up to the imagery of the pornographic material. Their partners become dissatisfied, and this may lead to further dissatisfaction for the addicted male.

This escalation of sexual imagery speaks to the plasticity of the brain. Doidge elaborates: "The content of what they found exciting changed as the Web sites introduced themes and scripts that altered their brains without their awareness" (p. 109). Unfortunately, sexual addicts often become less and less attracted to their real partners. As with other addictions, the only real solution to this negative, escalating cycle is for the addict to stop the compulsive behavior cold turkey. If the addict is able to stop the escalating behavior, he will be able to readjust his pleasure system to engaging with his real partner again. The following vignette is an example of this difficulty.

Clinical Vignette 3

Jeffrey sought therapy as his wife was threatening to leave their marriage unless he was able to deal with his sexually addictive behavior. She had recently discovered a very expensive phone bill—Jeffrey had been spending a great deal of time and money engaged in phone sex activities. He reluctantly reported to me that the phone sex was only part of the picture. He was a self-employed professional who worked out of a home office. Surfing the Internet for hours, Jeffrey's work productivity was very compromised, and he was increasingly behind in completing his work for clients who sought his accounting services. He also admitted that he had started to cruise the downtown streets, looking for prostitutes. His wife only knew of the phone sex activities, and Jeffrey was certain that she would leave him if she knew of the other sexual acting-out behavior. He acknowledged that the intensity and type of pornography that he was attracted to were increasing; he also admitted that his search for a prostitute was most exciting to him. The actual sex with the prostitutes was less satisfying, but he reported that he was intensely aroused when searching for the "right" prostitute. He offered that the "right" prostitute fit the image of the women who were depicted in pornography, including sadomasochistic activities.

Jeffrey was pessimistic at the start of treatment. He did not think that he could alter his sexual behavior, and he admitted that he was no longer interested in having sex with his wife. He felt trapped by his need for ever-increasing dangerous behavior. He knew that prostitution was illegal, was not safe in terms of sexually transmitted diseases, and would mean certain separation from his wife if she discovered this behavior. Jeffrey was ambivalent, at best, about engaging in psychotherapy. He was uncertain if he wanted to, or could, alter his sexual behavior. After completing a thorough assessment, I recommended to Jeffrey that his therapy would be complemented if he started to attend Sexual and Love Addiction Anonymous (SLAA). This 12-step group program follows principles similar to those of Alcoholics Anonymous and other 12-step programs.

In addition to offering some ego-supportive work and building a treatment alliance with Jeffrey, I began to discuss with him some basic brain physiology principles. Using psychoeducation, I began to help Jeffrey understand how he had wired his brain to require increasingly graphic sexual images in order to be satisfied sexually. Using this cognitive model with Jeffrey appealed to his rather obsessive thinking style. It also offered an explanation for his behavior that was not laden with shame and guilt. He was an able learner, and he started to read further material about plasticity and sexual behavior from references that I supplied to him. He was reluctant to stop his compulsive behavior cold turkey, but after three or four attempts to do this, he was able to maintain his sobriety, refraining from the use of phone sex, Internet pornography, or prostitutes. He also needed to retrain himself to find sexual pleasure and excitement with his wife; this was a lengthy process, and I referred him and his wife to a couple therapist to help them rebuild their relationship. Jeffrey did not disclose the extent of his acting-out behavior to his wife, but he was able to reengage with her in all aspects of their intimacy with the benefit of individual and couple therapy. As an interesting aside, couple therapists are well-advised to understand that intimate partners can also be sparked by right brain connections and that clinical work often needs to unearth these nonverbal interactions that lead to discord between partners (Shimmerlik, 2008).

SOCIAL ANXIETY/PHOBIA

As noted in the case of Ken, described above, social anxiety can be a highly uncomfortable condition that often compromises the individual's ability to maintain satisfying personal or professional relationships. Cozolino (2006) suggests that "the automatic and unconscious activation of shame continues to shape our self-image and social behavior into adulthood. For some, coping with shame and the anxiety it evokes is a crippling and lifelong struggle" (p. 242), leading to the development of social phobia. Numerous studies (Asmundson & Stein, 1994; Eastwood et al., 2005; Straube, Kolassa, & Glauer, 2004) as cited in Cozolino (2006) suggest that social phobics turn their attention to information that is socially evaluative and that "they are biased toward anticipating, detecting, and remembering negative and angry responses by others" (Cozolino, 2006, p. 244). Cozolino (2006) also points out that socially phobic people have a diminution in Broca's area of the brain, the center of the brain that aids verbalization. This appears to offer an explanation for the socially phobic person's difficulty in finding words to describe his or her inner world. Cozolino also notes the correlation of social phobia with the fear of public speaking.

The anxious person has a heightened amygdala response, which then activates the basic fight or flight function of the socially phobic individual. Each new encounter or person is negatively appraised, and the right brain functions accelerate the self-protective qualities of fight or flight; ultimately, the socially phobic client withdraws into herself or himself with a sense of shame. I currently have a young client who is convinced that even strangers encountered in the shopping mall are evaluating his appearance. Each time he appears in public (including attending high school), he agonizes over what clothes to wear. He often becomes so immobilized that he avoids school and social events. In consequence of his missing school, his parents and teachers make negative evaluations of him, thus reinforcing his sense that others are critical of him and angry with him. This circular pattern often underscores the universal anxiety that social phobics experience—that is, that others are scrutinizing them and are critical of them. Clinical intervention is aimed at helping the social phobic become less activated by novel situations and people by trying to counterbalance the initial impression of negativity that overrides left brain functioning. Here too, the development of a caring treatment relationship aids the rewiring of the social phobic's brain functions so as to minimize the acute activation of the amygdala. Forming a secure attachment relationship with the social phobic over time, the clinician aids in the modulation of the initial fight or flight response of the client. Understanding the neurobiology of this disorder specifically leads the clinician to certain interventions formed with the intention of helping alter brain functions. It is often very useful to educate our clients about basic brain functions so they can also begin to actively interrupt default patterns formed in their early attachment relationships or activated as a result of other traumatic events (as in the case of Ken above).

CONCLUSION

In concluding this chapter, I am aware of the burgeoning literature on human neuroscience and how it has influenced clinical social work practice in a variety of ways. In addition to clinical work with individuals, other authors (Lapides, 2011; Shimmerlik, 2008) also suggest that the concepts found in this chapter can be utilized in couple therapy. There seems to be little doubt that neurobiology will continue to have a major impact on clinical work over the next decades. While much of neurobiological theory feels intuitively correct to clinical social workers, we are in an exciting time in which some brain functions can be observed through research and with the use of brain imaging tests and devices.[3] Of importance, the role of secure attachment relationships as being reparative of our clients' distress is very consistent with the social work profession's understanding of the clinical relationship as having considerable power in terms of facilitating change processes. This is consistent and integrative with contemporary relational theories (Goldstein et al., 2009) that also recognize the crucial importance of being connected with others and that these connections are necessary to facilitate change. Neurobiological theory is therefore a hopeful theory, recognizing the plasticity of brain function and the capacity for change across the life cycle. Right brain connection between people has tremendous potential to foster change. Some might suggest that change can even happen without insight or shifts in cognition (Boston Change Process Study Group, 2008). The reader is encouraged to use this chapter as a beginning guide to the exploration of the links between neurobiology and clinical social work—an area of investigation that will continue to yield interesting and important findings to help us become more caring, empathic, and competent clinical social workers.

REFERENCES

American Association of Psychoanalysis in Clinical Social Work. (2009, March 1). Re: How learning about neuroscience changed practice [LISTSERV]. Retrieved from LISTSERV Posting March 1, 2009.

Applegate, J., & Shapiro, J. (2005). *Neurobiology for clinical social work: Theory and practice.* New York, NY: W. W. Norton.

Asmundson, G. J. G., & Stein, M. B. (1994). Selective processing of social threat in patients with generalized social phobia: Evaluation using a dot-probe paradigm. *Journal of Anxiety Disorders, 8,* 107–117.

Badenoch, B. (2008). *Being a brain-wise therapist: A practical guide to interpersonal neurobiology.* New York, NY: W. W. Norton.

Basham, K., & Miehls, D. (2004). *Transforming the legacy: Couple therapy with survivors of childhood trauma.* New York, NY: Columbia University Press.

Bateman, A., & Fonagy, P. (2004). *Psychotherapy for borderline personality disorder: Mentalization-based treatment.* London, UK: Oxford University Press.

Baylis, P. (2006). The neurobiology of affective interventions: A cross-theoretical model. *Clinical Social Work Journal, 34*(1), 61–81.

Beebe, B., & Lachmann, F. M. (2002). *Infant research and adult treatment: Co-constructing interactions.* Hillsdale, NJ: Analytic Press.

Boschert, S. (2007). Let neurobiology guide borderline treatment. *Clinical Psychiatry News, 35*(4), 15–18.

---

[3]This chapter was originally written during a rich and sophisticated discussion conducted on the LISTSERVof American Association for Psychoanalysis and Clinical Social Work (AAPCSW), which focused on the practical implications of contemporary neuroscience. Moderator, Joel Kanter, initiated dialogue on this topic when he asked readers to describe, "how learning about neuroscience changed, or even transformed, my practice" (AAPCSW, 2009). Many responses illustrated the impact of neuroscience on the respondents' practice, and my hope is that this chapter will also add to the growing literature that applies neurobiological thinking to clinical social work practice.

Boston Change Process Study Group. (2008). Forms of relational meaning: Issues in the relations between the implicit and reflective-verbal domains. *Psycho-analytic Dialogues, 18,* 125–148.

Bremner, J. D., Vythilingam, M., Vermetten, E., Nazeer, A., Adil, J., & Khan, S. (2002). Reduced volume of orbitofrontal cortex in major depression. *Biological Psychiatry, 51,* 273–279.

Cahill, L., & McGaugh, J. L. (1998). Mechanisms of emotional arousal and lasting declarative memory. *Trends in Neurosciences, 21,* 294–299.

Cozolino, L. (2002). *The neuroscience of psychotherapy: Building and re-building the human brain.* New York, NY: W. W. Norton.

Cozolino, L. (2006). *The neuroscience of human relationships: Attachment and the developing social brain.* New York, NY: W. W. Norton.

Doidge, N. (2007). *The brain that changes itself: Stories of personal triumph from the frontiers of brain science.* New York, NY: Penguin Books.

Eastwood, J. D., Smilek, D., Oakman, J. M., Farvolden, P., van Ameringen, M., Mancini, C., et al. (2005). Individuals with social phobia are biased to become aware of negative faces. *Visual Cognition, 12,* 159–181.

Farber, S. (2008). Dissociation, traumatic attachments, and self-harm: Eating disorders and self-mutilation. *Clinical Social Work Journal, 36,* 63–72.

Fonagy, P., Gergely, G., Jurist, E., & Target, M. (2002). *Affect regulation, mentalization, and the development of the self.* New York, NY: Other Press.

Goldstein, E., Miehls, D., & Ringel, S. (2009). *Advanced clinical social work: Relational principles and techniques.* New York, NY: Columbia University Press.

Iacoboni, M. (2008). *Mirroring people: The new science of how we connect with others.* New York, NY: Farrar, Straus & Giroux.

Inbinder, F. (2006). Psychodynamics and executive dysfunction: A neurobiological perspective. *Clinical Social Work Journal, 34*(4), 515–529.

Keane, H. (2004). Disorders of desire: Addiction and problems of intimacy. *Journal of Medical Humanities, 25,* 189–204.

Keenan, J. P., McCutcheon, B., Freund, S., Gallup, G. G., Sanders, G., & Pascual-Leone, A. (1999). Left-hand advantage in a self-face recognition task. *Neuropsychologia, 37,* 1421–1425.

Lapides, F. (2011). The implicit realm in couples therapy: Improving right hemisphere affect-regulating capabilities. *Clinical social work journal, 39,* 161–169.

Levine, P. (1997). *Waking the tiger: Healing trauma.* Berkeley, CA: North Atlantic Books.

Marks-Tarlow, T. (2012). *Clinical intuition in psychotherapy: The neurobiology of embodied response.* New York, NY: W.W. Norton.

Montgomery, A. (2013). *Neurobiology essentials for clinicians: What every therapist needs to know.* New York, NY: W.W. Norton.

Rendi, M., Szabo, A., & Szabo, T. (2007). Exercise and Internet addiction: Commonalities and differences between two problematic behaviors. *International Journal of Mental Health Addiction, 5,* 219–232.

Richmond, M. (1917). *Social diagnosis.* New York, NY: Russell Sage.

Schore, A. (2012). *The science of the art of psychotherapy.* New York, NY: W.W. Norton.

Schore, A. (2003a). *Affect dysregulation and disorders of the self.* New York, NY: W. W. Norton.

Schore, A. (2003b). *Affect regulation and the repair of the self.* New York, NY: W. W. Norton.

Schore, J., & Schore, A. (2008). Modern attachment theory: The central role of affect regulation in development and treatment. *Clinical Social Work Journal, 36,* 9–20.

Shapiro, J., & Applegate, J. (2000). The neurobiology of affect regulation: Implications for clinical social work. *Clinical Social Work Journal, 28,* 1–28.

Shimmerlik, S. M. (2008). The implicit domain in couples and couple therapy. *Psychoanalytic Dialogues, 18,* 371–389.

Siegel, D. (1999). *The developing mind.* New York, NY: Guilford Press.

Siegel, D. (2007). *The mindful brain: Reflection and attunement in the cultivation of well-being.* New York, NY: W. W. Norton.

Siegel, D., & Hartzell, M. (2004). *Parenting from the inside out: How a deeper self-understanding can help you raise children who thrive.* New York, NY: Penguin Books.

Stern, D. N. (1985). *The interpersonal world of the infant: A view from psychoanalysis and developmental psychology.* New York, NY: Basic Books.

Straube, T., Kolassa, I. T., & Glauer, M. (2004). Effect of task conditions on brain responses to threatening faces in social phobics: An event-related functional magnetic resonance imaging study. *Biological Psychiatry, 56,* 921–930.

Teicher, M. H., Andersen, S. L., Polcari, A., Anderson, C. M., & Navalta, C. P. (2002). Developmental neurobiology of childhood stress and trauma. *Psychiatric Clinics of North America, 25,* 397–426.

van der Kolk, B. (1996). The body keeps score: Approaches to psychobiology of posttraumatic stress disorder. In B. van der Kolk, A. McFarlane, & L. Weisaeth (Eds.), *Traumatic stress: The effects of overwhelming experience on mind, body and society* (pp. 214–241). New York, NY: Guilford Press.

5

CLINICAL PRACTICE WITH CHILDREN

ALAN J. LEVY AND MARGARET G. FRANK

The dimensions of clinical work with children have changed markedly in recent years. Political and economic factors have affected mental health and social services settings, greatly constraining child therapists by limiting the scope and time they can devote to their clients, many of whom are in dire need of more intensive treatment. This environment has fostered the medicalization of child mental health services with a consequent atomization of how children's difficulties are conceptualized. One effect of this development has been narrowing the way that therapy itself is conceptualized and limiting goals for child therapy regardless of need. Ironically, just as these developments have denuded child mental health services, there have been concurrent developments in psychoanalytic approaches to the treatment of children in light of new knowledge of neurobiological factors affecting children's functioning and of the nature of development itself.

This chapter addresses clinical practice with children in this context. Child therapy is considered through an amalgam of psychoanalytic theories. These include: object relations theories such as those of Melanie Klein and D. W. Winnicott, the American interpersonalist school developed by Harry Stack Sullivan among others, through intersubjective and psychoanalytic self psychology developed by Heinz Kohut and Robert Stolorow, and by means of contemporary relational psychoanalytic theories exemplified by the work of Aron, Mitchell, and Benjamin. The premise of this chapter is that treatment that is informed by psychoanalytic theories helps therapists more mindfully navigate the current treatment environment and to understand child treatment in its complexity. The combined impact of time pressures, social attitudes, and new mandates impinging upon social workers often militates against the establishment of a deeply therapeutic relationship, and clinicians struggle to explain and justify their work under these conditions. Paradoxically, knowledge about the ways in which life events can shape children's development and their adaptations, combined with awareness of the nonlinearity of developmental and therapeutic growth enables clinicians to maintain and strengthen their therapeutic focus on the child. Further, clinical work that is informed by this approach helps practitioners truly help the children and families that they serve.

THEORETICAL CONSIDERATIONS

Psychoanalytic theories begin with the perspective that clinicians must develop an intimate knowledge of children's development in the physical, cognitive, social, and emotional realms, as well as the contexts within which children function. Such knowledge requires understanding the nature and processes of typical development. Current thinking about growth and development has moved toward recognizing the essentially interconnected nature of biological, social, and emotional processes. These factors collectively propel children in the direction of becoming adults with a deeper sense of themselves and others as individuals, and who consequently develop into more fully related human beings. Child development researchers and psychoanalytic theoreticians now view growth as a process of developing the ability to form attachments and to use one's experiences with others to construct a sense of oneself (Beebe, Knoblach, Rustin, & Sorter, 2005; Beebe & Lachmann 1988; Stern, 1985; Tronick, 2007). This progression is emblematic of how psychoanalytic models of development are continually reworked in light of new knowledge.

Each advance contributes to our knowledge of development and forms the basis for subsequent treatment innovations. Development can be seen as a process of navigation toward increasing differentiation and elaboration through intimate relationships with others. It plays an essential role in deepening one's sense of individuality and those of others as subjective human beings. The process then is one of ongoing redefinition of how to attach to others while acquiring a dynamic sense of autonomy and relatedness. This is a lifelong process indeed. One might say that a hallmark of a well functioning adult is one in which individuals are able to be intimate and relate to another without fear of loss of self. Well functioning adults maintain their sense of differentiation relatively unimpeded by the threat of psychologically losing relatedness with those upon whom

they construct their sense of themselves. Current thinking also sees successful development as maintaining a dynamic balance and congruence between the internal representation of self and other with the recognition of each as independent centers of subjectivity (Benjamin, 1995). Despite their differences, psychoanalytic theories of development reveal a common focus upon the representational world (Beebe & Lachmann, 1988; Tronick, 2007; Tyson, 2002). Each posits that the formation of a subjective sense of self and other is constructed from relational experiences derived from a complicated matrix of forces within which children's innate endowments encounter the qualities and aptitudes of caretakers and others in the environment (Beebe et al., 2005; Beebe & Lachmann, 1988; Tronick, 2007).

Modern developmental theories generally have moved beyond specific stage-sequence models of development. As a result, many psychoanalytic child therapists have begun to move away from a strict understanding of development as organized by an invariant sequence. This is well summarized by Demos (2007) who states that:

The value of a stage theory approach and its general appeal have been that it has organized vast amounts of data into a few general categories. But it did so by overvaluing homogeneity and treating individual variation as noise, and by overvaluing the end product as represented by performance on defined tasks, thereby ignoring the competence of the organism and the processes by which the organism defines relevant tasks at all ages. Both of these stances obscured the importance of context and the dynamic nature of the match occurring in the transactions between the organism and the context. Finally, it has always been difficult for stage theories to account for the emergence of new behaviors and to articulate the process of change, namely what causes an organism to go from one stage to the next, without recourse to vague notions of maturation or changes in the brain. (pp. 136–137)

While Demos (2007) asserts that early emotional learning can have long-lasting effects on psychological functioning, their sequelae can be modulated and regulated by continued developments (p 143).

This notion is echoed by Tyson and Tyson (1990) who note the systemic nature of development. They state that "the formation of intrapsychic structures from innate and experiential elements is characterized by forward spurts and backward slides. Thus it is a discontinuous process" (p. 29). These authors state, further that "The development process accordingly takes place through the differentiation, transformation, and reorganization of a variety of networking, branching, and interrelated systems. In every system, the form taken at each stage is affected by the development of all the other systems in interaction with the environment" (p. 32). One might add that development also is predicated upon the state of the system and associated systems prior to the point of transformation.

While specific events remain crucial for understanding development, the complexity of human beings as social individuals necessitates a view of development that allows for multiple pathways to development (Thelen, 2005; Tyson, 2002). Thus, contemporary psychoanalytic scholars and clinicians now understand development as more complex than was conceptualized previously. It now is common to observe elements of several intermixed developmental phases at one point in time. Further, the sense of self and other is now seen as inextricably linked. This sense is seen as developing throughout life, though early childhood experiences lay the foundation for the course of later self/other development. Children construct a relational matrix comprised of organizations of their experiences of self and others (Mitchell, 1988). Representations of self and other typically are infused with affect and they necessarily involve expectations of how others will act and how one will experience others. Benjamin (1995) describes the dialectical tension between the subjective construction of objects (i.e., mental representations of others that are constructed by individuals that are based upon their experience; they form part of the relational matrix) with the recognition of others as centers of subjective experience that are independent from one's own. This dialectic fosters the development of both.

Implications for Treatment of Children

Therapy aims to foster the development of affect regulation. The process of affect regulation entails helping children establish and differentiate emotional representations through "sensitization to emotion-specific patterns of internal state cues." (Fonagy, Gergely, Jurist, & Target, 2004). That is, helping children to register emotional cues is one facet of affect regulation. The process of symbolization of affective experiences also is a component in the development of affect regulation since it marks affects as different from actual external events. Fonagy et al. (2004) state that markedness is conveyed by nonverbal elements such as meaningful looks, prosody, partial or exaggerated actions of action schemes, and so on:

> The non-consequentiality of the situation thus is communicated and the actions that are anticipated as a consequence . . . do not ensue. This permits the decoupling of the symbol from actuality. The child feels safe in this subjunctive world because there is no threat of actual danger. As a result, a child and caretaking other may play with reality and develop potential space. The process of developing marked externalizations and that of affect mirroring fosters the capacity for affect regulation. The child is free to experience painful affect memories and thus re-encode them so that their newly developing symbolic features become integrated with non-symbolic affective components such as visceral and procedural elements. (p. 296)

This process permits emotional symbolization of experience. One result is that higher cortical functions can modulate emotional experience. As shall be seen later in this chapter, the safety of the play frame paradoxically permits psychically dangerous material to emerge.

Contemporary developmental theories allow for multiple historical and contemporaneous factors in shaping one's experience and forming the experience of self and others. While parents and other caretakers certainly have been involved fundamentally in the formation of self and object representations, the full dimensions of children's emotional development cannot be placed solely at their feet. Constructions of self and other more or less undergo changes to the degree that children have new relational experiences. As such, early experiences are formative, but they are not necessarily determinative. Loewald (1980) states that, in psychoanalysis, "inasmuch as re-enactment is a form of remembering, memories may change under the impact of present experience" (p. 360). Loewald's view is in close agreement with the notion that memories and other forms of representation are more or less altered and re-encoded each time they are activated. It also acknowledges the essential role of immediate experience with others in forming and reforming one's experiences of self and other.

Experiences during various developmental phases therefore have a dispositional influence on self/other representations. Self/other representations generate scenarios that are reenacted in some way in the world at large and, most important for the clinician, within the treatment relationship. Psychoanalytic child clinicians infer self/other representations from various sources. Primary among them is the therapist's experience of a child's behavior in treatment sessions. Indeed, much of the quality of self/other experiences is communicated implicitly (i.e. asymbolically). Thus, in addition to the content of children's words or play, the ways by which children communicate with therapists also are as important in informing therapists' inferences. Therapists' constructions of their clients' self/other representations also are informed by other sources. Reports by caretakers and others, historical accounts of children's development, and direct observations of child clients in other contexts also inform these constructions. Psychoanalytic child therapists attempt to construct their models of their clients' self/other representations in order to capture their complexity and nuances. They utilize this understanding to foster children's awareness of their nature and functions. It is of equal importance that therapists use their understanding to engage children in order to foster new relational

experiences. As with other forms of psychoanalytic treatment, child therapy is based upon a spirit of inquiry whereby the experiences of the therapeutic dyad form the basis for a deeper exploration of child's self/other representations (Lichtenberg, Lachmann, & Fosshage, 2002). In this model, therapeutic change derives from direct relational experiences of child clients with their therapists coupled with the dyadic formation of these experiences. The therapeutic enterprise is therefore based upon ongoing iterations of relational experiences between child and therapist and their mutual investigation of their possible meanings.

THE ROLE OF PLAY

Play is a primary medium for child psychotherapy. It has been a subject of interest to psychoanalysis since its inception (Altman, Briggs, Frankel, Gensler, & Pantone, 2002; Levy, 2008). Traditionally, psychoanalytic views of the functions of play are that it serves to develop a sense of mastery, allows for wish fulfillment, permits the assimilation of overpowering experiences, transforms experience of the individual from passivity to activity, is a vehicle for temporarily moving away from demands of reality and the superego, and is a route for fantasizing about real objects (Waelder, 1976). Contemporary analysts have extended these views to the relational and neurobiological spheres (Altman, 1994, 2004; Barish, 2004a, 2004b; Bonovitz, 2004; Frankel, 1998; Levy, 2008, 20011b). Benjamin (1988) acknowledges the importance of symbolic play in expressing the tension that exists in the acceptance of conflicting feelings between self and others, that is, between complementarity and recognition. She asserts that play constitutes an essential element in the developmental process of dismantling one's sense of omnipotence and in promoting mutual understanding. In this way, play facilitates the development of the capacity to relate to the other as both object and subject. She notes that play creates the first dialogic forms of mutual recognition.

Play is seen as a form of transitional phenomenon because it opens potential space in which a child can symbolically destroy, differentiate from, and use the therapist. In the frame of play, anything is possible because the play partners are free to enact any scenario, wish, fear, or self-state. The play partners are able to do this because, within the frame of play, there are no consequences to one's actions since play isn't strictly real. Rather, it is marked as a form of subjunctive communication—that is, possible, but not actually true (Pizer, 1998). Play permits psychologically dangerous thoughts and feelings to be acted upon and then be plausibly denied by the child (Levy, 2008). While not strictly real, play in psychoanalytic psychotherapy is linked very powerfully to a child's subjective experiences (Levenson, 1985), and in this way play may be more emotionally resonant than in other domains of a child's life. The duality of actual experience occurring in the subjunctive play frame paradoxically permits deeply held feelings and thoughts to emerge and to be engaged therapeutically within the frame of play. Play thus derives its therapeutic value; it fosters integration of diverse modes of processing experience. In order to play, children must engage and coordinate a variety of sensory, perceptual, cognitive, affective, and behavioral processes. Since it encompasses action as well as thought and feeling, play engenders experience of emotionally vivid self-states within the relatively secure relationship with the therapist (Levy, 2011a, 2011b).

BEGINNING TREATMENT

There are guiding principles covering the many ways one might start the treatment process. It is important for therapists to carefully consider who they may represent to the client. Therapists act in partnership with their child clients, helping children to construct their own stories. In other words, they coconstruct new meanings through their relationship (Saari, 1991). It is essential that therapists genuinely have an extraordinary interest in their child clients in part because it can engender new relational experiences. Such experiences may serve as a template for the construction of new models of self and others or alter existing ones to foster a sense of self integrity, cohesion, and interpersonal security.

An ability to accept a measure of uncertainty due to the relative ambiguity that play entails also is an essential attribute of child therapists (Levy, 2008; Sutton-Smith, 1997). Child therapists must learn to cultivate patience and let the therapeutic relationship emerge and evolve. In addition, therapists must be prepared to tolerate uncomfortable states that may be painful, hard to imagine, or even repulsive. These feeling states are seen as a form of implicit communication of the child's experiences and constitute key constituents of the therapist's formulation of the child's experiences. In this way, much information regarding children's organization of experiences is embodied in the play relationship. It is important to engage children in creating and recreating their own stories and become a co-investigator of their experience.

THERAPEUTIC RELATIONSHIP

The concept of the therapeutic alliance in psychoanalytic child treatment has evolved with new developments in child development, neurobiology, family dynamics, and in psychoanalysis. With child therapy in particular, the therapeutic alliance generally has moved to a more collaborative approach within the therapeutic dyad (Aron, 1996; Levy, 2008). Because play allows children's experience to be embodied and enacted in a less than real play context, child clients express and explore facets of themselves in a facilitating relationship. Formation of a holding environment paradoxically permits a sense of security, allowing unacceptable, psychically dangerous feelings to emerge and to be addressed in more productive ways (Levy, 2011b; Pizer, 1998; Winnicott, 1971). In short, the relationship needs to be safe but not too safe (Bromberg, 2006). The therapeutic alliance especially is complicated in psychoanalytic child treatment since the therapist must maintain working alliances with the child's caretakers, teachers, school-based mental health professionals, and others. Child therapists therefore must respond to the multiple pulls emanating from sources beyond the child her or himself. One needs to embrace this state of affairs and balance one's approach based upon these multiple inputs. Indeed, child therapists must develop working alliances with other adults while also keeping the needs and subjectivity of their child clients alive.

All clients, both children and adults, enter treatment with some measure of ambivalence. For children, this ambivalence is colored by the fact that they rarely self-refer for treatment. Decisions to seek or end treatment usually are made by adults with varying degrees of input from children themselves. An additional complication lays in the fact that many children have a limited understanding of what psychotherapy is, or they have had experiences with other forms of treatment. Another major point of departure from treatment of adults is children's dependence upon their parents. Discordant and painful feelings about children's parents may become the focus of therapeutic work. The fact that children must then see their parents just after a session can be a powerful influence on the therapeutic alliance. The therapeutic relationship therefore must be negotiated continually with this in mind.

There will be a variety of different styles with which children engage their therapists. For example, they may present as oppositional, they may isolate themselves and wall themselves off from therapists, or lose the therapeutic frame of play and act in provocative ways. Each style is a form of engagement (even the walled-off style), and it is incumbent upon therapists to try to understand this behavior from the vantage point of children's self/other constructions, relational histories, and current therapeutic settings. Children's styles of engagement inevitably will be an amalgam of these and other elements. Since the relationship is comprised of elements that often are contradictory, therapists become aware of the inherent paradoxes that they must negotiate as an essential part of the therapeutic relationship (Pizer, 1998). Therapists, thus, must implicitly and at times explicitly hold contradictory self-states in order to help children come to terms with them and integrate their experience to form a more complex personality organization.

Sam, a boy of 9, came to the therapist with a diagnosis of pervasive developmental disorder. Neuropsychological evaluations indicated that Sam was intellectually gifted, but that he presented with fundamental difficulties in understanding the reactions of others, cognitive rigidity, especially in ambiguous situations. There was also evidence that Sam had deficits in executive functions. Over the years, Sam's parents enrolled him in a number of therapies designed to address one or another of Sam's difficulties. Sam expressed antipathy towards his parents for what he perceived as controlling his life, for their restrictions on his free time, curbs on his viewing movies that his peers had already seen, and so on. He experienced periods of severe emotional dysregulation when the perceived impingements were especially intrusive. Sam enjoyed saying inappropriate things, especially when he was with his parents, who reacted angrily to his behavior. Sam's parents had him receive cognitive behavioral therapy since age 2 to help him with this. That therapy focused on redirecting Sam to more prosocial activities and on helping Sam to employ techniques to prevent dysregulation.

Sam approached psychoanalytic therapy with understandable apprehension. Early on, Sam began to say things that he thought were inappropriate to the therapist. Rather than stop him from speaking, the therapist engaged him by exploring how others reacted when he said these things. They laughed together at how people became upset at these comments, and the therapist acknowledged that it might feel good to upset people who he felt upset him. They spontaneously began to compose plays that included material that became increasingly outrageous. At Sam's request, the therapist dutifully recorded them and even offered measured suggestions for the plot and for dialogue. Sam began to anticipate his sessions eagerly. He was careful to make sure that the therapist hid their plays when the sessions were over.

Intermixed with this activity, Sam began to mention the ways that his parents angered him and talked about fantasies that he had about punishing them and others who he felt had wronged him. Concurrent with these events, Sam's behavior became more regulated, and he appeared more relaxed and even happy. Sam then engaged the therapist in competitive board games. This afforded the therapeutic dyad opportunities to address issues of aggression, dominance, defeat, and self-esteem. Because Sam chose games that required a good deal of strategy, his deficits in executive functions were evident. His expressed desire to destroy the therapist in the game, along with his fantasies of omnipotent domination of the therapist, and of the entire world, were also directly expressed and experienced through the game. The therapist accepted these feelings and playfully responded with acknowledgements of Sam's intentions. Sam would become visibly anxious when he seemed to be losing the game. He would become silly, say that he lost interest in the game, or giddily flick his pieces across the board and knock down as many of the therapist's pieces as he could. The therapist recognized how frustrating the game could be and permitted these otherwise forbidden feelings and behaviors to be expressed through the game. Sam's ability to tolerate periods when it appeared that he would lose the game improved, and he began to laugh with the therapist when he became frustrated by his moves.

In contrast to approaches that emphasize elimination of problematic behavior, psychoanalytic child therapy aims to engage these behaviors and associated thoughts and feelings within the relatively secure frame of therapeutic play. Negative consequences are minimized within the frame of play, and the atmosphere is one of acceptance so long as the difficulties occur within this frame. Dissociated self-states are permitted to emerge in the context of the therapeutic relationship so that they can become better integrated within the child's personality (Bromberg, 1998). Change occurs through a combination of insight derived from the therapeutic encounter and the development of new ways of "implicit relational knowing"

(Lyons-Ruth, 1999; Boston Change Process Study Group, 2002). In this way, play is an essential element in psychoanalytic child therapy.

In child treatment, the therapist must be prepared to be symbolically destroyed within the treatment relationship in more concrete ways than is typical for treatment with adults (Levy, 2011b). Destruction in a treatment relationship often is a developmentally necessary step for a client progressing from relating to internal objects to using people as independent centers of subjectivity (Winnicott, 1969). The immediacy of child treatment invites the client/therapist dyad to enter into enactments in especially visceral ways (Levy, 2011b). In these times especially, the current treatment becomes infused with past self-other organizations.

Often, prior events inadvertently become the focus of treatment.

Megan, an 11-year-old girl, was referred for treatment due to angry outbursts at school and at home. She would become so frustrated and frustrated with others and in her inability to regulate and effectively communicate her feelings, that at times she would physically hurt herself (one time she took a soft drink can and smashed it on her forehead, requiring sutures to close the wound).

Over time, Megan and her therapist developed a close relationship that consisted of playful banter. She frequently said that the therapist was not truly interested in her and was only following the rules prescribed in a therapy book. Megan's therapist assessed that her anger conveyed her disappointment in key relationships and surmised that she unconsciously wished for a relationship that felt more genuine and empathic. Megan told her therapist that she must be a horrible mother to her two sons, after all, she was seeing her in the evenings and was not available to care for them. The therapist viewed Megan's behavior as a projection of her feelings of worthlessness and of her experience of others as empty and disingenuous. At the time, the therapist was unmarried and not yet a parent.

Through this exchange, the therapist was able to challenge Megan's deeply held views about herself and the world. She questioned why Megan thought that she wouldn't care about her. Her therapist also wondered aloud about Megan's denigrating therapy and allowed Megan to feel more comfortable and avoid feeling closer to the therapist, because "God forbid someone worthwhile actually might care for you. I mean, what would you do if you actually started to (care) about me?"

Of course, it seemed that Megan already was beginning to care about her therapist. This would pose a problem for Megan in several ways. First, her sense of self-cohesion would be threatened. Second, through a new relationship with her therapist her hunger for a generative relationship would become apparent. This would be very disruptive to her emotional equilibrium. All of the narcissistic injuries that she had experienced, her attachment to the very people upon whom she constructed her sense of herself and the world, would be called into question. Third, her sense of interpersonal security would be threatened. Past overtures for emotional engagement with her depressed and self-absorbed parents were rebuffed. She risks a similar fate now with her therapist. Therefore, there is a dread of repeating past patterns but also a fear of facing new relational scenarios.

Psychoanalytic treatment of children inevitably aims to engage children on their terms and earnestly attempts to understand and to respond sensitively to their needs. Engagement of children occurs through a mixture of play and verbal discussion. The opportunity to act upon and struggle with problematic self/other constructions is the essence of contemporary psychoanalytic treatment (Mitchell, 1988; 1997). It is an ongoing process of directly experiencing these constructions in the treatment relationship and then genuinely trying to understand the experience of clients. It entails attempting to communicate with children authentically, based upon therapists' understanding of their clients' experience. Through this process, new relational experiences develop, modifying earlier self/other constructions and creating new ones. This is not easy to accomplish. Despite all of its known limitations and pitfalls, children's constructions of self and other form the basis of their sense of themselves and of how the world works. There is order even in the disorder. The treatment process never is simple or easy, since children protect the ways that they organize themselves and the world. While their lives may be deeply painful, at least children know who they are and how to engage the world. The possibility that this sense might be lost is terrifying, and it often trumps the development of more satisfying self/other organizations.

Trust is a state of being that emerges during the beginning of treatment, but it is never constant. As new issues emerge, children's anxiety and mistrust of the process, their therapist, or both, can arise anew.

Sometime later in treatment, Megan learned from her mother, who worked in an allied field, that her therapist was getting married. Megan raised this during the following session. She tearfully said that the therapist hadn't been truthful with her and let her believe that she was married with children of her own. She said that the therapist let her go on and on about what a bad mother she was with her sons when she knew that this was untrue. Megan said that she embarrassed her and probably enjoyed it. The therapist forced herself to listen to Megan and knew that his behavior had unwittingly resulted in Megan experiencing her as empty and shallow as others. Once Megan stopped and the emotional intensity had died down a bit, the therapist asked Megan why she thought she didn't reveal that she had no children. Megan said that she just let her feel this way because it didn't matter to her. All that mattered was some "stupid therapy thing" that she tried. The therapist explained that at the time she thought that it was important that her status as a parent not interfere with the opportunity for Megan to express her feelings about the therapist. She continued that she now knows how hurtful this was to Megan and apologized to her. Megan's therapist said that this was just the sort of thing that Megan experienced before. Right then she could feel what it must have been like for Megan. She told Megan that she knew that it would take time for Megan to feel comfortable with the therapist again.

It is a paradox of therapy that by acknowledging such ruptures in the therapeutic relationship and responding sensitively, clients can become more trusting of the relationship. Therapists who put their discomfort and needs on the back burner communicate that they indeed are reliable partners.

Assessments of children's relational histories and the ways by which they organize their sense of self and other are essential components in guiding therapists in engaging child clients. For example, if children present with a narcissistic organization and have placed themselves behind an emotional force field, therapists must balance these children's need for self protection with their need to engage the therapist. If children try to control the situation, therapists will have to permit this (within bounds) and ultimately attempt to learn the reasons for their need for control. As therapists' relational dilemmas acquire both consciousness and greater clarity, they may then share these with the children.

In one case, a therapist began to work with a 9-year-old girl who viewed her parents as intrusive. She told her mother that she wouldn't answer any questions that her new therapist asked her. Upon encountering the client, the therapist, who knew of the girl's concerns remarked, "You know, I have a problem. I think privacy is very important, and I know that questions can make people uncomfortable. I hope that when you feel like letting me know a little about yourself that you will help me get to know you."

Such interventions address a number of dimensions. Children are left with the control and are encouraged to use it to resolve their relational dilemmas. The therapist allies herself with the child's dislike of intrusiveness, and at the same time, offers a goal for the beginning of treatment. The therapist, by wondering whether the child simply could tell her anything about herself that she wished to tell, obviated her need to ask questions. The need simultaneously to hold and balance paradoxical relational elements, such as the need for self-protection and the need to be understood, are guiding principles for the therapist. By using this approach, control was not wrested from the child so that she was enabled to pursue the task at hand. At the end of her first session, the child announced to her mother, who had been waiting for her, "I told her a lot about me, and she never asked one question." The therapist learned a great deal from the child because there are many ways that children communicate beyond words.

These are guiding principles for beginning treatment and for mutually setting the stage for children to tell and enact stories of their experience and their unique points of view. Each child client may present with different needs and relational styles, but all need the opportunity to communicate the subjective essence of their experiences. Therapists inaugurate a unique process by which a mixture of old and new experiences emerge (Pizer, 1998). This process inherently engenders a shift where the experience of being with their therapist serves as a template for children to construct new self/other representations. Therapists' interest in and responses to children's words, affects, and actions shape this evolving therapeutic process.

TREATMENT SETTING

Therapists aim to develop a holding environment with their clients (Winnicott, 1958), a space with physical, psychological, and affective dimensions that facilitate their clients' development. A holding environment is a product of the therapeutic relationship and, thus, is a mutual construction of both child clients and their therapists. It is a context wherein children can experience heretofore intolerable self states. This becomes possible when therapists remain in emotional contact with their clients while maintaining their own emotional regulation.

Much of what has just been discussed belongs to the dimension of psychological space. It is important to view the physical setting from the point of view of one's clients. Therapists must be consciously aware of the messages that they give to children through their physical setting, their child supplies, and their demeanor. How children communicate their experiences is as important as what they say and do, because it often reveals implicit emotional and relational elements that are essential in understanding children and guiding therapists. A holding environment provides the safety and space necessary for the emergence of the children's relational scenarios. Therapists need to observe and know themselves well enough to guard against impinging upon their clients' self-development by asserting their own needs and interests too strongly.

ASSESSMENT PROCESS

A discussion of the initial phase of treatment must include some aspects of child assessment. While diagnostic labels have their place in clinical communication, assessment entails close observation of children's behavior and formulating hypotheses about how they organize themselves and others. Direct assessment begins at the moment of meeting. This includes assessment of children's development in a variety of domains, including physical, cognitive, and emotional development. Therapists attempt to assess how development has been blocked or skewed. It is also important to note discrepancies in level of development among various domains. For example, children who are advanced in their cognitive development but are age typical in their emotional functioning, may be more likely to develop anxiety as they are able to abstract and become aware of material that is emotionally overwhelming.

> Jordan is a 9-year-old boy who was referred by his pediatrician because he was restless and anxious. He would try to stay awake for as long as he could in order to guard his family from earthquakes, tornados, and other natural disasters. When the therapist engaged Jordan in a discussion of his anxiety, Jordan said that his family lived along a seismic fault line and in an area where tornados were not unusual. He asked how he could know whether or not tornados could strike his family.

While there were many other factors that contributed to Jordan's anxieties, his therapist noted his great intelligence and natural curiosity about the world and how it works. He was a thoughtful boy whose family encouraged asking questions. Jordan's intellectual development led him to raise plausible questions about scary events. However, emotionally, he was still a 9year-old-boy who depended upon his parents and felt very vulnerable.

Developmental mismatches also can exacerbate difficulties relating to peers.

> Scott was a 7-year-old boy who also was referred for treatment for his anxiety. His younger brother was assessed as intellectually gifted. Scott's brother also showed great athletic prowess from an early age and was being groomed as a possible Olympian. Although intelligent and athletic himself, Scott was not viewed as a prodigy. The son of two mental health professionals, Scott appeared to be highly empathic and aware of the feelings of others. One day, while he was at practice for his sport, a boy approached Scott and, in a provocative tone, asked Scott if he felt badly about himself because he is in the average group while his brother was receiving special training from the head coach. Scott replied that he knew that the boy was trying to make him jealous of his brother, but it wouldn't work. He said that he was proud of him for his accomplishments, and that he felt good about himself, too, so the boys' taunts weren't going to work. While one might admire Scott's emotional maturity in this situation, the boy, frustrated in his attempt to make him feel badly about himself, punched Scott and escalated his verbal assault. Developmental maturity at times can be a liability in the context of one's peers.

Assessment focuses upon how self and other are organized. Therapists need to observe whether children's sense of separateness and relatedness is developing adaptively. Separateness refers to ones view of self and others as independent and unique beings and not to physical distance or proximity. Different cultures shape the nature and quality of self/other differentiation. It is somewhat easier to assess psychological separateness in adults. For example, adult clients who proceed to talk as if their therapists already know the characters to which they refer in session or seem to assume that they know what has happened to them during the week lack psychological separateness. It is as if therapists are part of them and have somehow been with them outside of the treatment setting.

Assessments should always contextualize children's behavior and their development in order to more accurately account for their behavior. Factors such as cultural background, family structure and history, and the neighborhood in which they reside, provide essential information to guide therapists' formulations. In addition, all assessments need to take strengths as well as obstacles into account. Good therapy capitalizes on individual and environmental strengths as it addresses the difficulties faced by children.

The assessment process is inextricably related to the initial direction that treatment takes. However, since therapy is a complex, nonlinear process, one cannot accurately predict the ultimate course of treatment from the outset. That said, all forms of psychoanalytic treatment involve work on how feelings are managed, how self and other are organized, and their concomitant self/other scenarios. In sum, with child clients, therapists carefully attempt to construct how their unique life experiences and capacities influence their functioning.

Therapists currently have much less time to thoughtfully assess cases. The authors assert that, for treatment to be sensitive to the needs of each child client, and for a rich therapeutic relationship to develop, time must be found for such work. Therapists must think carefully and critically about their cases, regardless of the context in which they practice. It is essential to good treatment. Therapists learn more with time, and this enables them to affirm or discard hypotheses that inform treatment. While treatment is affected by limited time, still it is possible to provide a therapeutic experience even in a single encounter. This can be of enormous help. However, for more profound growth to occur, longer term, intensive treatment is required.

CORE TREATMENT CONSIDERATIONS

Although divisions of phases in the treatment process are artificial and not distinct, there also is a flow to treatment where certain considerations such as assessments, terminations, and others are more salient. Treatment themes are always present over the full course of treatment. They are never totally settled. The core treatment phase usually follows a period of settling in during which the therapeutic dyad is focused upon how to engage one another. During the core phase, there is an elaboration and deepening of themes and relational dilemmas.

TRANSFERENCE/COUNTERTRANSFERENCE AND ENACTMENTS

Over time, the nature of transference and countertransference and their roles in therapy have developed as their conceptualization has expanded. A contemporary understanding of transference is as a present manifestation of self/other constructions originally drawn from earlier life experiences that are more or less intermixed with the current context (Hoffman, 1998; Tyson, 2002). Therefore, although present experiences of self and other more or less have evolved from early life experiences, they always include experiences in the context of the current relational field. While these relational dynamics are similar to those formed with others, they are not enacted in exactly the same ways within the therapeutic dyad. Thus, the therapeutic relationship encompasses an admixture of old and new elements. Cognitive neuroscience now holds that when something is remembered, it is altered to some extent each time it is remembered. Therefore, memories are constructed in the present (Levy, 2011a; Tyson, 2002). With transference and countertransference, therefore, the past always resides in the present, and the present always inhabits the past.

For the purposes of this discussion, the term *countertransference* refers to all feelings, thoughts, and actions on the part of therapists in relation to their clients. Earlier conceptualizations of countertransference defined the phenomenon as primarily unconscious pathological material from therapists' own personalities that has been activated in response to their clients. Countertransference in this earlier model almost always is an impediment to therapeutic progress, and therefore, it should not impinge upon the therapy. A more contemporary understanding of countertransference has countered the notion that countertransference is antithetical to therapeutic progress. It no longer is a subject for shame, nor does it necessarily imply pathology in the therapist.

Contemporary views of transference and countertransference hold that it is impossible to disentangle sources for the actions of therapist and client (Aron, 1996; Hoffman, 1998). As with transference, it both is too neat and inaccurate to posit that some countertransference reactions do come from the personality of therapists while others are prompted by clients. A blend of the two always is the case. What is essential are the ongoing attempts by therapists to know themselves and raise questions in order to understand how their experiences inform and affect treatment.

Contemporary views of the transference/countertransference nexus, thus, are far more complex. As a consequence, guidelines for therapists' handling of these phenomena consequently are less straightforward. It requires even more attention as well as more tolerance for their inherent ambiguity. Therapists' reactions can now be seen as a tool of great value, and its therapeutic utility is enhanced when therapists attempt to separate the foundations of their own reactions from those of their clients. They become a different experience when therapists are willing and able to discuss the here and now in the transference and consider with their clients the parallels to their earlier experiences.

Seth was a 10-year-old boy who was referred to the therapist by his school principal because he engaged in physical fights almost daily. He was raised by his mother, who is intellectually challenged. Seth never knew his father. His mother had relationships with several other men, all of whom were substance abusers. Two of these men fathered Seth's two younger half siblings. One of these paramours was gang involved, and Seth recalls observing him physically assaulting his mother. Seth felt powerless and unable to rescue his mother. This man also threatened to kill Seth, and on more than one occasion pinned Seth to the floor and held a gun to his head.

Seth and his mother went from one unstable living situation to another. At one point, the electricity was turned off during the winter due to nonpayment of the bill. Seth remembers sitting with his mother huddled around candles and using the oven to heat the apartment. At this point, 6 months prior to the referral, Seth's maternal grandmother told Seth that he would be spending the weekend with her and to pack what he needed for the visit. Upon arriving at his grandmother's house in the suburbs, Seth learned that his grandmother obtained guardianship, and that he would only return to his mother's home for brief visits. Seth continues to feel responsible for his mother's welfare, and she continues to rely on him for support and advice.

Seth engaged his therapist in play sessions, during which Seth regaled him with stories of his phenomenal athletic prowess. As treatment progressed, Seth regularly made disparaging comments about just about everything his therapist did. The therapist would make comments like: "You must really think that I stink!" and "I can't seem to do anything right!" to which Seth would emphatically and playfully make comments such as "That's right, you do stink." Seth then would follow this comment by ordering the therapist to serve him by retrieving the balls with which he was playing, clean up messes, and so on. When the therapist commented that Seth thought that he should serve him, Seth would agree, and say that the therapist indeed was his slave, and that he was the master.

This case illustrates how an understanding of children's relational histories and context informs therapists about the possible meanings of the client's behavior. It also is an example of how relational patterns manifest themselves between child and therapist during play. It should be noted that material which would not easily be revealed can be enacted within the frame of play. Since play permits this material to emerge because it isn't strictly real, trust develops between the therapeutic dyad so that each knows that reprisals for play behavior is unlikely to be provoked by the appearance of this material. Seth's therapist withheld interpreting the connection to Seth's history of violence and terror and his need to be in control and humiliate the therapist, as Seth felt that he had been earlier in his life. Such interpretations, while accurate, serve to make children self-conscious, and thus, may interrupt the playful nature of the interaction. Rather, the therapist let Seth control and belittle him because it was done in the frame of play. In addition, the therapist kept in mind that, for the therapist to become a usable object to Seth, Seth must first psychologically destroy the therapist and they both must survive the destruction (Winnicott, 1971). More formal reflection by the therapist occurred after the affective danger was diffused by the repetitive procedural processing of this scenario. Further, the therapist's reflection about Seth's experience enhanced Seth's ability to regulate painful and heretofore dysregulating affect (in this case, his anger and the terror of feeling out of control).

Despite his best efforts to hide it, Seth clearly was growing attached to the therapist. He resisted ending sessions by stalling and negotiating for more time. The therapist tried to be sensitive to Seth's needs and acknowledged his wish for more time but expressed his regret that it could not be met in action. Seth would respond by telling the therapist how cheap he was for not extending the hour. The therapist often responded back by playfully saying that it was a shame that Seth was stuck with such a withholding therapist. Seth agreed and added that the therapist was a real asshole. The therapist said that right now he may be an asshole in Seth's eyes but added that he was Seth's asshole. Seth then smiled and ended the session.

The closeness that was developing in their relationship became uncomfortable for Seth. He wanted more than the therapist was able to provide. This was a familiar state of affairs to him. Seth began to express his anger over his unmet needs playfully, all the while maintaining the construction of the therapist as incompetent. The therapist he liked was incompetent and uncaring. Note the playful, paradoxical response of the therapist here. He did not challenge Seth's characterizations verbally, but the way he responded to them communicated his acceptance of Seth's heretofore intolerable feelings and his implicit understanding of their sources. The therapist's response assured Seth that his anger toward the therapist would not disrupt their relationship.

How therapists communicate to their child clients, particularly when responding to disappointments and pain expressed in the treatment relationship is as important as *what* therapists say about it. The relational context and emotional tone of a communication lies primarily in nonverbal cues. For therapists to respond in a therapeutic manner, they must be able to communicate their understanding from within the therapeutic dyad as well as from without. Therapists, although immersed in the treatment relationship, need to have developed working hypotheses about the meanings of their clients' behavior. These constructions serve to guide therapists' implicit communications so that they resonate emotionally with the verbal content of their communications.

As treatment progressed, and Seth's tolerance for painful affect increased, the therapist would comment that it seemed that Seth wanted his therapist to be with him all the time, and that controlling the therapist would keep the therapist with him, doing everything that he wished for. Seth agreed with his usual "That's right. I do". The therapist commented how he could understand how important this was to Seth since he knew that there were many times that Seth hadn't been able to count on people he needed. Rather than agreeing verbally with the therapist, Seth acknowledge what the therapist said by his facial expression. The therapist then said that he wished that one day Seth would feel that he's been able to get what he needs from other people and not feel that he has to control them in order to get it. The session ended with Seth adopting this usual jocular persona when he joined his grandmother for the trip home.

Treatment relationships evolve over time, usually in ways that cannot be predicted from the outset. As Seth and his therapist continued to work together, their relationship developed to where Seth could tolerate acknowledging his attachment to his therapist. The therapeutic relationship held Seth so that his feelings could be addressed more directly. Seth's therapist then was able to tie the transferential elements of Seth's behavior to his experiences outside of the therapy setting. In contrast to the mixed verbal and nonverbal responses that he made earlier, Seth's response to the therapist was nonverbal. Acknowledgements of tender issues tend to be replete with nonverbal elements. This interpretation was implicitly communicated with the therapist's earnest wish for Seth.

Countertransference and Enactments

The therapist was aware of really liking Seth and admired how well he managed the complexities of his life. He also identified with his sense of vulnerability and his courage in soldiering on. The therapist observed how deeply perplexing it was for Seth when there were angry outbursts, and his attempt to keep his anger under wraps in order to maintain his equilibrium and his sense that his status was tenuous. He saw Seth essentially as a gentle boy who was struggling to reconcile his anger and vulnerability with other facets of his personality organization. The therapist was aware of parallels between Seth's dilemma and his own struggles as a child, although the details of his history were quite different from those of Seth.

The therapist became aware of other facets of the transference/countertransference nexus as treatment progressed. This became apparent following an enactment that occurred between them.

During one session, Seth and the therapist were engaged in their usual activity. Seth attempted ever more difficult shots with the foam basketball, all the while extolling his phenomenal talent and skill. His berating of the therapist was unusually harsh. He resisted his therapist's attempts to explore this issue by making even more harsh comments about the therapist. At one point, Seth attempted to make a shot that he had tried unsuccessfully many times before. On this occasion, the therapist, who

(Continued)

(Continued)

was standing by the basket to retrieve the ball reached out and caught the ball just before it went into the basket. It should be noted that the therapist is not particularly adept at catching balls, so it was even more significant that he caught the ball so effortlessly on this particular occasion.

To the therapist, his action was reflexive, and it felt as though someone else had caught the ball. The therapist felt awful and knew immediately that his action would injure Seth emotionally. Seth indeed was devastated by the therapist's action. On the verge of tears, Seth asked the therapist why he did this. After some fumbling around between them, the therapist remarked that catching the ball did seem like a hostile act. He told Seth that he didn't plan to catch the ball. It just happened. The therapist then said that maybe he didn't realize how Seth's berating him might have affected him. He speculated that maybe he was having trouble feeling this way because he also felt close to Seth. The therapist then said that it can be hard for people to feel angry at people that they're close to. Seth's response was that even if this was so, the therapist really hurt him. The therapist said that he knew that he hurt Seth and was genuinely sorry about it. He said that while he wished that he could take it back, he knew that he couldn't. Seth said "That's right, you can't". The therapist then said that he guessed that this was a familiar situation for Seth, being angry at someone that he cared about. He added that maybe they could find a way to feel angry with each other without it being so devastating. Seth began to relish seeing his therapist unsettled and remorseful.

It is apparent that this session, in part, reflected Seth's difficult history. Enactments provide an opportunity for therapists and clients to engage each other differently. The heightened sense of emotion, the sense of immediacy that punctuates such interchanges brings their enacted nature into bas-relief. During these times the relational dynamics and self-states that have been so destructive to the client are ascendant and are more amenable to modification even as they appear to be closed off and not open to change. It was only after this session that the therapist realized how, like Seth, his anger burst through in an unsettling and perplexing way. He began to consider how he had experienced the very elements from which Seth sought to dissociate himself. The therapist saw his reactions as a projective identification (Ogden, 1986), that is, Seth's unarticulated dissociated elements were projected onto the therapist and were enacted in the treatment relationship but as the therapist's and not Seth's reactions. Since the line between

transference and countertransference, between historical and contemporary influences, are unclear the therapist's own difficulties also were an essential constituent of the interchange. Participation by the dyad necessarily is nonlinear in nature, and, as such, the outcome of any particular form of engagement cannot be predicted in a reliable way (Levy, 2011a).

How a therapist reacts in these situations can be of great therapeutic value. Black (2003) states that enactments "in their interactional fluidity and capacity to engage deep unarticulated psychic content hold the potential to free mental processes" p. 651. This certainly seemed to be the case between Seth and his therapist. Bromberg (1998) states that

The analyst's role, however—his ability to bridge therapeutically the nonverbal and verbal domains of experience—is created not simply by his natural empathic giftedness with regressed patients but by his use of the patient's ongoing enacted interchange with him. If he pays attention, this often unsettling feedback will teach him how to be the 'primary object' in an ever-evolving way that *allows him to be emphatic as well as empathic.* (Italics included in the original, p. 145)

He also asserts that "the importance of the analyst's ability to communicate his own subjective survival as a real object in order to be available as a usable primary object for the patient" (p. 145).

Black (2003) notes that opening potential space at these times

> requires the analyst's regaining an internal capacity to hold imagery, affect, and experience in a generative, open, nonpedantic manner. Ultimately, that the analyst can still think may be more important than *what* the analyst thinks. The degree to which the patient is able to stay in the fluidity of the enactment energy, in the session and beyond it, relies in part on her being reassured that 'using' the analyst in this way will not destroy the analyst's mind. (p. 640)

Black (2003) also states that, during enactments, the motion and experience of participating in the enactment together with clients is the most defining aspect of such encounters. The process of destabilizing one another results in an energy that may move patients away from rigidity and toward generative change. The key is to tolerate the experience because it lends "experiential reality to our patient's sense of being joined in this risky journey" (p. 647).

Both child client and adult therapist inevitably participate in enactments. Each projects unbearable dissociated parts of themselves in ways that are experienced by the other, finding the other's vulnerability in the process. What makes enactments so insidious, so necessary, and inevitable is that each part of the child client/therapist dyad is only partially aware of these elements (Stern, 2003, 2004). In effect, each may see the part that the other plays in it, but at best, is only dimly aware of his or her own contributions to the enactment. This was the case with Seth. The therapist was aware of Seth's need for control, of his need to make the

therapist subservient to him, thereby rendering him relatively harmless. He knew how scared Seth was of his own aggression. This made sense to the therapist given Seth's history of witnessing violence by adult males. By not responding aggressively to Seth, the therapist was permitting Seth's aggression to emerge in the treatment relationship so that it could be experientially recognized, reflected upon, and put in a historical context—ultimately, allowing Seth to develop new ways of relating.

But what may Seth have seen in the therapist? Seth knew (at least implicitly) that the therapist was attempting to contain his own anger and aggression toward Seth. After all, Seth was pretty disparaging and dismissive of the therapist, albeit in a playful way. Also, having witnessed domestic violence as a child, the therapist survived by accommodating to his unstable, violent parents. In order to do this, the therapist had to dissociate his own anger. Seth certainly didn't know this about the therapist's history. However, it became clear that Seth implicitly knew that, in order to remain so accommodating to him, the therapist had to have dissociated his anger. The therapist simply *was* too good to be true.

This enacted pattern of permitting Seth's aggression to enter the treatment relationship while the therapist dissociated his own, continued until it culminated in the episode where the therapist sadistically caught the ball and deprived Seth of the joy in making an epic shot. It was only then that *both* Seth *and* the therapist began to confront their enactment.

The importance of therapists understanding the ways in which developmental experiences are woven into the fabric of self/other constructions and scenarios cannot be overemphasized. These insights must be communicated in ways that child clients are able to grasp. In addition, child therapists must continually reflect upon their experiences with clients and contextualize them (in terms of their own life experiences as well as those of their child clients) in order to be able to endure being seen in ways that are uncomfortable and even painful.

TERMINATION

Termination is far more complicated in child therapy than it is with treatment of adults. The question of when a child no longer is in need of treatment, who makes this decision, and how termination is implemented merits careful consideration. Further, it has become more prevalent to end treatment in response to therapeutic progress. It therefore is incumbent upon therapists to examine the basis of these decisions carefully, with concern for the sensitivities of their child clients.

Therapists should keep goals and objectives for treatment of particular children in mind throughout the course of therapy, even though therapy rarely goes as one predicted at its outset. While the aims of treatment goals may become unclear at times, it is essential that therapists guard against treating children without regard for goals. Further, especially for child treatment, therapists need to consider the developmental trajectories and risks incurred by the children they treat. While it is not possible to protect children from every possible future risk factor, therapists need to realize that therapy can play an essential component in preventing the occurrence of future difficulties.

There are several factors to consider when assessing whether termination is indicated. One important consideration is whether children's development is now approaching that of their peers and whether their ability to manage developmental challenges is adequate. Assessment of development must occur with regard for children's biological and environmental contexts. If children appear to be functioning well, it is incumbent upon a clinician to consider whether termination is indicated. Children should be free to engage others in affirmative ways, with confidence in their abilities and enjoyment of life. Although the main goals of psychoanalytic treatment are broader than symptom removal, assessment of children's development naturally includes whether symptomatic behavior is lessened with respect to severity, frequency, and duration.

Another factor to consider in termination is whether the environment is able to facilitate development of child clients. In particular, it is essential to assess whether caretakers and other key people in the life space of children are able to respond in ways that promote children's growth. While it is difficult to conclusively determine the readiness of extra-therapy resources to nurture children, therapists should guard against expecting perfection and bear in mind Winnicott's formulation of "good enough" parenting.

A third factor to consider lies in the relationship between therapist and child. At times, children who were anxious to attend therapy sessions may begin to avoid coming to appointments and even view treatment as impingements in their lives. This may be an indication that children have developed friendships and interests outside of treatment, and that they are now acting in ways that are typical for their age and situation. One proviso to consider is whether children's reluctance to attend sessions is indicative of other factors. These may include resistance to factors pertaining to the treatment relationship or the material that is being addressed in treatment. If this seems to be the case, generally treatment should not be terminated, and the identified factors must be addressed.

Changes in the nature of the therapeutic relationship itself can be an indication that termination should be considered. These changes typically are characterized by the formation of an easy, friendly relationship that is devoid of the energy that stemmed from relational conflicts. Likewise, play in treatment sessions also shifts. Play scenarios lack the powerful themes that once characterized treatment.

If therapists determine that termination may be indicated, it should be taken up with parents (or other caretakers) prior to initiating termination directly with children. Therapists and parents should mutually assess the current status of the child and review the course of treatment then. If termination of treatment is mutually agreed upon, therapists need to discuss the vicissitudes of the termination process with parents. This should include typical reactions that children have to termination and the possible ways that their child might respond. Termination, even under the best of circumstances, activates for all clients (and their therapists) a range of feelings about loss. Key themes of treatment, anticipated difficulties as children grow, and information on what to do should parents have concerns in the future should also be discussed. It is essential for therapists to stress the importance of therapists themselves actually raising termination with clients. The reactions of the treatment dyad are essential material to be addressed during this period. This should not be pre-empted or diluted by parents introducing termination to their children. Therapists need to be cognizant of the fact that this is a termination of sorts for parents as well, and they must be sensitive to their concerns.

Termination must be planned with regard for children's needs, their developmental level, and the nature of the treatment relationship. Child therapists must consider differences in children's sense of time when planning termination. The duration of the termination process should be long enough to permit feelings of loss, anger, and anxiety to surface but not so long that the process is dragged out unnecessarily or so the actual termination date is so far off that it is meaningless for children.

When therapists introduce termination with child clients, it should be in the context of reviewing the original reasons for the referral and the assessment with children of their progress. The therapist should couch termination in a progressive frame and in terms that children can understand, such as a graduation. Children then should be free to express their feelings so that therapists can respond to them. Expressing one's own reactions prematurely runs the risk of crowding out those of the client. The number of remaining sessions should be reviewed with children to avoid denial of the imminent loss. Younger children or older children whose development has been compromised substantially may need visual cues to assist them in keeping track of the number of remaining sessions. Children and therapists often

draw termination calendars together. Each time children come to their sessions, they cross off one session. Therapist and client then count the number of remaining sessions in order to maintain the frame of termination.

For the final sessions, therapists should plan a termination celebration with their clients. Often, hitherto unexpressed wishes may surface for therapeutic work. Parents may be encouraged to bring a camera to the last session to take photos of therapist and child together. Therapists should gently cue children about the amount of time that remains in order to ensure that time is left for goodbyes. It should be stressed that the last several minutes of the final session should be reserved for client and therapist to spend alone together. Therapists should prepare parting generative wishes for their clients prior to the final session. They should be communicated at this time. It should be noted that terminations rarely progress as planned. Therapists should try to let the process flow as naturally as possible. In order to ensure a therapeutic termination, the elements should be kept in mind and encouraged, but they should not be forced upon clients.

Many times, termination of treatment is not initiated by therapists. It is, of course, best to avoid terminations initiated prematurely (at least in the view of the therapist) by maintaining a close working relationship with parents and other caretakers. However, some parent-initiated terminations are unavoidable. In such cases, therapists should strive to arrange a meeting with parents to address their concerns (whether they are unconscious, unexpressed, or explicit), and if termination still appears imminent, therapists should assert the importance of the therapeutic termination process. Should a parent refuse to engage in such a process, therapists must insist upon a final session in order to say goodbye to their clients. Often therapists in this situation must deal with their own feelings of anger and helplessness that are engendered by this state of affairs. Therapists should, therefore, carefully consider how they will present the termination to their clients. They must be careful to avoid criticizing and otherwise undercutting a child's parents while preserving the essence of the therapy and relationship with their client.

Given the increased mobility of people, therapists often find that they must initiate termination of treatment due to their own personal reasons, such as accepting a new position, moving to a new region, or so on. Regardless of the impetus for premature terminations, untimely endings of treatment evoke strong feelings of desertion for the client and those of failure by the therapist. Negative self representations frequently are activated, such as "This wouldn't be happening if I weren't so bad." Too often therapists who experience guilt about an inappropriate termination wish to shield themselves from anger expressed by children. Consequently, therapists may deflect anger by blaming external factors such as agency policy, shortage of funding, their own need to search for another position, and so on. The intensity of their countertransference, thus, may interfere with the importance of receiving, containing, and responding therapeutically to their clients' feelings. There are, of course, no acceptable reasons for the child. Essentially it boils down to the conviction that "if you really cared about me, you would not let this happen." The child feels helpless, and frequently this is mirrored in the therapist's own reactions. It is essential that therapists bear in mind that they have much to offer their clients during these times. By eliciting fantasies and feelings associated with this loss, the entire experience of parting may offer something previously unknown to child clients: an experience of ending that is respectful of their feelings and promotes their integrity.

Paul and his therapist were ending treatment because his therapist was graduating from his master's program. Paul never knew his father. He had abandoned Paul, his older sisters, and his mother shortly after Paul's birth. Paul's mother subsequently had a succession of short-term relationships with men. He had grown close to a few of them, only to be abandoned by them when their relationships with Paul's mother ended. He was referred for therapy because of his angry, sullen behavior. Paul railed against treatment and his therapist throughout their sessions. His therapist tried to engage him but was rebuffed at every turn. Paul's therapist grew discouraged and felt devalued and unimportant to Paul, but he continued to be available to Paul and attempted to understand the sources of his anger.

When the therapist informed Paul that he would be leaving the clinic, Paul replied: "Good! I hated seeing you, and now I can stay home and watch TV in peace!" Paul denied any feelings of attachment to his therapist, and asserted that his therapist was "a pain in the ass". The therapist accepted Paul's feelings and tried to continue to understand their sources. He also tried to contain his own painful reactions. During the final session, with only a few minutes to the end, the therapist told Paul:

We have only a few minutes left together and I wanted to say that I know how difficult it's been for you to see me these past months. I know that there have been many men who have left you over the years, some of whom you cared for and many of whom you disliked. There are a lot of reasons for this, but I wanted you to know that, despite how difficult it's been for us, I will think of you over the years and hope that you'll find people who will stick with you and who you can feel truly care about you. I'll be thinking of you and wishing that you'll find this in your life.

At that, Paul, for the first time during the session, looked directly at his therapist. He was silently crying. Paul then said: "You made me cry, you asshole!" The therapist responded that he knows that

Paul was angry at him, but he needed Paul to know that his anger didn't change his wishes for Paul, and that he'll wonder how he's doing over the years. As they said goodbye, for the first time in their relationship, the tone became sad and wistful. It should be noted that Paul's treatment terminated over 30 years ago, and his therapist still remembers Paul and wishes him well.

CONCLUSION

As our knowledge has grown, psychoanalytic treatment of children has grown more complicated, replete with multiple influences and meanings. The complexities inherent in child treatment have crystallized the essential ambiguity of the treatment situation and the nonlinearity of therapeutic change. This requires even more careful attempts at clarity even though the enterprise essentially is impossible. Therapists need to continually get their bearings and remain open to new understanding throughout therapy. In addition, therapists must strive to use their knowledge deliberately and deliberatively and yet authentically engage their clients. The struggle to understand, to genuinely know one's client, often is more important than a static formulation of the case. Indeed, new experiences inform our understanding so that it evolves over the course of treatment.

Regrettably, there are fewer and fewer clinicians equipped with the knowledge and skills that permit them to provide the depth and sensitivity that so many children desperately need. Moreover, agencies, clinics, hospitals, and private practitioners are pressured to restrict the availability of quality treatment for children. Ironically, one can scarcely think of other endeavors that are as essential, emotionally demanding, and ultimately rewarding as treating children. It is our sincere hope that others will commit themselves to this venture.

REFERENCES

Altman, N. (1994). A perspective on child psychoanalysis: The recognition of relational theory and technique in child treatment. *Psychoanalytic Psychology, 11*, 383–395.

Altman, N. (2004). History repeats itself in transference-countertransference. *Psychoanalytic Psychology, 14*, 807–815.

Altman, N., Briggs, R., Frankel, J. Gensler, D., & Pantone, P. (2002). *Relational child psychotherapy*. New York, NY: Other Press.

Aron, L. (1996). *A meeting of minds: Mutuality in psychoanalysis*. Hillsdale, NJ: The Analytic Press.

Barish, K. (2004a). What is therapeutic in child therapy? *Psychoanalytic Psychology, 21*(3), 385–401.

Barish, K. (2004b). The child therapist's generative use of self. *Journal of Infant, Child, and Adolescent Psychotherapy, 3*(2), 270–284.

Beebe, B., & Lachmann, F. (1988). The contribution of mother-infant mutual influence to the origins of self and object representations. *Psychoanalytic Psychology, 5*, 305–337.

Beebe, B., Knoblach, S., Rustin, J., & Sorter, D. (2005). *Forms of intersubjectivity in infant and adult treatment*. New York, NY: Other Press.

Benjamin, J. (1988). *The bonds of love: Psychoanalysis, feminism, and the problem of domination*. New York, NY: Pantheon.

Benjamin, J. (1995). *Like subjects, love objects: Essays on recognition and sexual difference*. New Haven, CT: Yale University Press.

Black, M. (2003). Enactment: Analytic musings on energy, language, and personal growth. *Psychoanalytic Dialogues, 13*(5), 633–655.

Bonovitz, C. (2004). The cocreation of fantasy and the transformation of psychic structure. *Psychoanalytic Dialogues, 14*(5), 553–580.

Boston Change Process Study Group (BCPSG). (2002). Non-interpretative mechanisms in psychoanalytic therapy–the 'something more' than interpretation. *International Gestalt Journal, 25*, 37–71.

Bromberg (1998). *Standing in the spaces: Essays on clinical process, trauma, and dissociation*. Hillsdale, NJ: The Analytic Press.

Bromberg, P. M. (2006). *Awakening the dreamer: Clinical journeys.* Hillsdale, NJ: The Analytic Press.

Demos, E.V. (2007). The dynamics of development. In Craig Piers, John P. Muller, and John P. Brent (Eds.), *Self-organizing complexity psychological systems.* Lanham, MD: Jason Aronson.

Fonagy, P., Gergely, G., Jurist, E., & Target. M. (2004). *Affect regulation, mentalization, and the development of the self.* New York, NY: Other Press.

Frankel, J. (1998). The play's the thing: How the essential processes of therapy are seen more clearly in child therapy. *Psychoanalytic Dialogues, 8*(1), 149–182.

Hoffman, I. Z. (1998). *Ritual and spontaneity in the psychoanalytic process.* Hillsdale, NJ: The Analytic Press.

Levenson, E. (1985). *The ambiguity of change: An inquiry into the nature of psychoanalytic reality.* Northvale, NJ: Jason Aronson.

Levy, A. (2008). The therapeutic action of play in the psychodynamic treatment of children: A critical analysis. *Clinical Social Work Journal, 36*, 281–291.

Levy, A. (2011a). Psychoanalytic approaches to play therapy. In Charles. E. Schaefer (Ed.), *Foundations of play therapy* (2nd ed., pp. 43–59). Hoboken, NJ: John Wiley.

Levy, A. (2011b). Neurobiology and the therapeutic action of psychoanalytic play therapy with children. *Clinical Social Work Journal, 39*, 50-60.

Lichtenberg, J. D., Lachmann, F. M., & Fosshage, J. L. (2002). *A Spirit of inquiry: Communication in psychoanalysis.* Hillsdale, NJ: The Analytic Press.

Loewald, H.W. (1980). *Papers on psychoanalysis.* New Haven, CT: Yale University Press.

Lyons-Ruth, K. (1999). The two-person unconscious: Intersubjective dialogue, enactive representation, and the emergence of new forms of relational organization. *Psychoanalytic Inquiry, 19*, 576–617.

Mitchell, S. (1988). *Relational concepts in psychoanalysis: Integration.* Cambridge, MA: Harvard University.

Mitchell, S. (1997). *Influence and autonomy in psychoanalysis.* Hillsdale, NJ: The Analytic Press.

Ogden, T. (1986). *The matrix of the mind: Object relations and the psychoanalytic dialogue.* Lanham, MD: Rowman & Littlefield.

Pizer, S. A. (1998). *Building bridges: The negotiation of paradox in psychoanalysis.* Hillsdale, NJ: The Analytic Press.

Saari, C. (1991). *The creation of meaning in clinical social work.* New York, NY: The Guilford Press.

Stern, D. B. (2003). The fusion of horizons: Dissociation, enactment, and understanding. *Psychoanalytic Dialogues, 13*, 843–873.

Stern, D. B. (2004). The eye sees itself: Dissociation, enactment, and the achievement of conflict. *Contemporary Psychoanalysis, 40*, 197–237.

Stern, D. N. (1985). *The interpersonal world of the infant.* New York, NY: Basic Books.

Sutton-Smith, B. (1997). *The ambiguity of play.* Cambridge, MA: Harvard University Press.

Thelen, E. (2005). Dynamic systems theory and the complexity of change. *Psychoanalytic Dialogues, 15*, 255–283.

Tronick, E. (2007). *The neurobehavioral and social-emotional development of infants and children.* New York, NY: W. W. Norton and Co.

Tyson, P. (2002). The challenges of psychoanalytic developmental theory. *Journal of the American Psychoanalytic Association, 50*, 19–52.

Tyson, P., & Tyson, R. (1990). *Psychoanalytic theories of development.* New Haven, CT: Yale University Press.

Waelder, R. (1976). The psychoanalytic theory of play. In Samuel A. Guttman (Ed.), *Psychoanalysis: Observation, theory, application.* New York, NY: International Universities Press.

Winnicott, D.W. (1958). *Through pediatrics to psychoanalysis.* New York, NY: Basic Books.

Winnicott, D.W. (1969). The use of an object. *International Journal of Psycho Analysis, 50*, 711–716.

Winnicott, D.W. (1971). *Playing and reality.* New York, NY: Routledge.

6

CLINICAL SOCIAL WORK WITH ADOLESCENTS

RANDOLPH L. LUCENTE AND JUDITH MARKS MISHNE

INDIVIDUAL TREATMENT

Psychotherapy

The term *psychotherapy* was used by Freud, and the theory and techniques of individual psychotherapy have been enriched by the use of classical and newer psychoanalytic theories of mental functioning and psychopathology. These theories reflect the evolving conceptions of psychoanalytic foci: drive theory, ego psychology, object relations theory, self psychology, and attachment theory and the amplifications, modifications, and extensions of all these theory bases that are informed by inclusion of data that are, in turn, derived from infant research, neurobiology, and communication theory; a contemporary philosophy of science; and the intersubjective interplay between the two differently organized subjective worlds of clinician and client.

Alexander (1953) reminds us that psychotherapy is older than psychoanalysis and, while originally the traditional domain of psychiatry, is now shared with other clinicians, notably social workers, psychologists, and psychoanalysts:

> While it is customary to divide individual psychotherapeutic procedures into two categories, the *supportive* and *insight-oriented* psychotherapies, it must be borne in mind that supportive measures are knowingly or inadvertently used in all forms of psychotherapy; and conversely, some degree of insight is rarely absent from any sound psychotherapeutic approach. (p. 270)

Intensive Insight-Oriented Individual Therapy and Supportive Individual Therapy

The literature on technique and choice of interventions addresses two broad classifications: (1) supportive psychotherapy and (2) insight-oriented psychotherapy. Intensive uncovering, insight-oriented individual treatment seeks to increase the ego's capacity to tolerate emotionally conflictual situations that are partially or completely repressed. These

127

situations commonly originate in early childhood, and their later reverberations are precipitated by subsequent actual life situations and relationships. The principal therapeutic tool is the transference. Transference occurs when the client relives early personal relationships in the treatment because old patterns and reactions are transferred, or displaced, onto the therapist and then repeated through the regression that is commonly characteristic in intensive, uncovering therapy. In contrast, supportive individual treatment is indicated as follows:

> Whenever the functional impairment of the ego is of temporary nature caused by acute emotional stress. In such cases the therapeutic task consists, first of all, in gratifying dependent needs during the stress situation, thus reducing anxiety. Another important therapeutic device consists of reducing emotional stress by giving the client an opportunity for emotional abreaction. (Alexander, 1953, p. 281)

Commonly, support involves a review and examination of the client's stress situation and offering advice and clarification to assist in judgment and clearer assessment of stressors. If the continual involvement in external life situations proves beyond a client's coping capacities, environment manipulation might well be required.

Supportive treatment goals include the improvement of ego functions to promote better adaptation to the inner and outer worlds, the provision of symptom reduction and relief, and overt behavioral change without attempts to modify the personality or greatly reduce unconscious conflict. Repression can be maintained because the therapy focuses on preconscious and conscious elements of mental life.

> It is always the ego in its various functions that is supported in psychodynamically-oriented individual supportive therapy. Support can be accomplished directly by focusing on problematic ego functions, or indirectly, by decreasing the pressure or strain on the ego from drives, superego prohibitions and external reality. (Rockland, 1989, p. 8)

The concept of adaptation is crucial in supportive therapy. Some authors base recovery on the empowerment of the client and the creation of new connections (Herman, 1992; Kardiner & Spiegel, 1947; Saleebey, 2000; Symonds, 1982), whereby there is a reformation of faculties such as the capacities for trust, autonomy, initiative, competence, identity, and intimacy (Erikson, 1963).

In general, supportive techniques—those that primarily stabilize, maintain, and soothe—attempt to keep current functioning optimal and prevent regression. These techniques include universalization, whereby clients are helped to feel that their responses, emotionally, are typically what others would feel under similar circumstances, thus sharing a similarity to the rest of humankind rather than feeling isolated or disconnected. Other interventions include subtle suggestion, offering advice, posing alternative constructions, and exploring the psychosocial surround. The focus in all these supportive measures is on understanding and dealing with current feelings and exploring interpersonal relationships with family, friends, and authority figures. Effectively operationalized, these supportive procedures enable the client to keep an even keel, both strengthening mature defenses that possess adaptive value and lessening the use of primitive mechanisms that tend to be self-defeating in the long run. Supportive techniques have been described as *here-and-now* interventions that attempt to reduce distortions of self experience, promote reality-oriented appraisals of others' behaviors, and minimize all good/all bad concrete thinking. Encouragement to go on and the instillation of confidence (hope) that therapy will be of benefit, albeit with hard-won rewards, also have their place in the supportive treatment arsenal.

By comparison, the goals of insight-directed intensive psychotherapy are more ambitious than in the case of supportive treatment. In intensive therapy, the clinician attempts to help the client achieve greater self-awareness and some degree of underlying personality change. The immediate relief of symptoms is secondary and should not be used as a guideline to consider termination of therapy. The goal is to make the underlying conflict conscious, thereby permanently staving off later or subsequent symptom formation or symptom substitution. Insight-oriented procedures focus on the interior mental and emotional life of the client and deal with representations of internalized experience that reside primarily in the unconscious. The techniques of uncovering, insight-oriented psychotherapy bring unconscious and preconscious focus into consciousness; this includes conscious comprehension of drives and drive derivatives, as well as the preconscious and unconscious superego and ego functions, especially the ego's defenses.

The distinction between supportive and insight-oriented psychotherapy can be blurred, and while differences between the two approaches abound, so do their points of intersection. For example, it would be unimaginable that a successful, 2-year-long insight-oriented psychotherapy would fail to include preparatory work with supportive procedures to foster the development of a therapeutic alliance. Generally, the frequency of appointments—twice a week versus once a week—is one recognized criterion of distinction. Individual supportive treatment is a mode of therapy focused less on unconscious intrapsychic conflicts and generally more on interpersonal and environmental conflicts. It is a therapeutic intervention in which less regression is encouraged than in insight-oriented uncovering treatment. The focus on the here-and-now, rather than on early infantile conflicts, generally dictates that the clinician assume a more active stance than the nongratifying, nondirective neutral clinician, providing uncovering, insight-oriented treatment.

> "Neutral" means that the therapist does not take sides in the client's inner conflicts or try to direct the client's life decisions. . . . The . . . neutral stance is an ideal to be striven for, never perfectly attained. (Herman, 1992, p. 135)

In supportive treatment, the clinician's stance of neutrality is less than in insight-oriented therapy. In the context of a frequently needed, reflective,

educative, advising therapeutic role, active support is provided. Basic character change is not a goal; rather, supportive treatment aims to increase the client's capacity for reality testing, strengthen object relations, and loosen fixations. With these aims in mind, supportive individual treatment is always an element of adolescent psychotherapy. Supportive individual treatment is the most appropriate intervention for many adolescents and other clients living amid considerable chaos; in some situations, outreach; collaborative contacts with family members, teachers, and others; and even environmental manipulations are necessary, in conjunction with direct work with the client. Generally, supportive treatment is of shorter duration than uncovering, insight-directed psychotherapy. The therapist who is providing supportive treatment will comment and reflect on apparent behavior patterns, reactions, and relationships, leaving some areas deliberately untouched and unexplored, so as not to assault needed defenses.

Insight-oriented, uncovering individual treatment is the optimal intervention for clients suffering from internal conflict—conflict unrelated to environmentally generated chaos and traumata. The conflict, commonly originating in the past, is not accessible to conscious awareness and problem-solving efforts. The client's problems are intrapsychic; if interpersonal conflicts or academic or work problems are apparent and are to be treated by analytic uncovering techniques, they must be transformed into intrapsychic problems. At this level, insight-oriented procedures are probably an element of the vast majority of all long-term adolescent psychotherapies. Complaints about interpersonal, intrafamilial, and work-related difficulties are common presenting problems. These stresses must be due to circumscribed basic intrapsychic conflicts, in contrast to those caused by constitutional or environmental failures. This method of therapy is best suited for suffering individuals who nevertheless possess a fairly intact psychic structure. Clients who present basic ego weakness or deficits commonly manifest poor frustration tolerance, poor impulse control, a meager capacity for drive modulation, inadequate self/other distinctions, inadequate reality testing, impaired object relations, and defects in regulating affects, all of which interfere with a capacity to develop transference and contain acting out. Such individuals who have suffered greater injury are best treated in supportive individual therapy, in contrast to the more intact client, who possesses the ego strength to tolerate and profit from uncovering treatment through more complete working through of basic conflicts. Generally, working through evolves out of reenactment in the transference of repetitive object choices and comprehension of the repetition compulsion (repeated self-injurious behaviors), via insight and introspection.

Treatment technique in insight-oriented therapy is predicated on abstinence—absence of advice and active support. In a climate of empathic attunement, the principal tool is interpretation, reflection, and demonstration of the connection of the early traumas with the current presenting problems. The hallmark of an insight-oriented approach to the client's conflicts is the use of interpretation. Through interpretation, the client has the same mental representation in two separate regions of the mind in two different forms: (1) the conscious memory of the therapist's words and (2) the unconscious memory, in symbolic or condensed form, of an experience, event, thought, attitude, wish, fear, or feeling. The closer the repressed content is to consciousness, rather the ease with which it may be moved to the preconscious and beyond the repression barrier and censor to consciousness, the less likely it will be subject to resistance and returned to the dynamic unconscious: However, to have listened to something and to have experienced it are psychologically two different processes, even though the described content is the same (Freud, 1912). Over time, interpretations provide connections: (a) from the present to the past and to represented inner experience and (b) from the unconscious to the preconscious-conscious systems. Interpretive activity, fostering insight and increased client self-observation, is contingent on the therapist's capacity for empathy and the ability to regress with the client's clinical material through an attitude of "evenly suspended attention" (Freud, 1912). The bipersonal, relational field—a therapist-client mutually "shared unconscious" (Lyons-Ruth, 1999)—is the forum that permits the clinician to come to some kind of understanding based on deduction, induction, or an intuitive hunch via a clinically valid, subjective fact (Ogden, 1994), which he or she then shares with his or her client.

Interpretations are not dogmatic statements of indubitable truth. They are, rather, phrased tentatively and speculatively as if asking for a response from the client to a question. As such, they are always imprecise and seek to reveal or uncover a new, hidden meaning. The thrust of interpretive work conveys to the adolescent that experiences have meanings, that what is experienced as outside is represented on the inside, and that the external world of reality is connected to the internal world through constructions of these personal meanings. A useful guideline for beginning an insight-oriented strategy is to start, first, with interpretations of the behaviors and motivations of significant others as they affect the client and, second, with interpretations of the adolescent's affects as they spontaneously emerge in treatment, feelings that often reside outside conscious awareness. At a later stage after the relationship has deepened, through the emergence of the therapeutic alliance, interpretations of defense are appropriate, working with such defenses rather than confronting them directly. As the therapist comes to know the client better, developing a working model of the mind of the adolescent in interaction with his own subjective self, the clinician may operate on the basis of "conjecture" (Brenner, 1982), which then becomes the working hypothesis as to the nature of many earlier conflicts emanating from misalliances, absences, inconsistencies, trauma, or failures of parental support or empathy. This later agenda would include interpretations aimed at addressing early developmental arrests and clarifying complex affect states, and related characterological and interpersonal styles of relating, that are ingrained, repetitive, and maladaptive. As uncovering, insight-oriented treatment progresses, the adolescent relives the psychodynamic past in the present, organizes a more integrated narrative of his autonoetic history,[1] and develops new capacities for mindsight into self and others (Allen, Fonagy, & Bateman, 2008; Fonagy, Gergely, Jurist, & Target, 2002; Schore, 2003; Siegel, 1999).

Social work authors in the tradition of a psychodynamic approach to psychotherapy include Woods and Hollis (2000), whose research and writings have informed clinical social work practice for half a century. While offering an initial typology that separated sustainment from insight-oriented procedures, the clinicians' repertoire of clarification, explorations of the psychosocial surround, and interpretation was expanded to include person-situation reflection, dynamic reflection, and developmental reflection. A later analogue study using the Woods and Hollis typology of interventions found that an uncovering, interpretive psychotherapeutic approach was preferred by clinicians in the treatment of clients diagnosed as neurotic, whereas clients with borderline personality organization were more likely to improve with supportive treatment (Lucente, 1980).

Some clinicians tend to minimize the significance of genetic interpretations, believing that they divert attention from the immediacy of transference feelings. In many instances, "pushing the present back into the past, can serve as a defense for the analyst against painful countertransference feelings" (Giovacchini, 1987, p. 253). In sum, the degree of needed abstinence or emotional holding and support the client is provided is determined by the original assessment, which emphasizes ego functions and the nature of transference manifestations.

A careful diagnostic assessment and appraisal of the patient's strengths, life circumstances, psychological mindedness, and intrapsychic structure determines which level of intervention is appropriate. A misappraisal may have serious consequences if too much regression is encouraged and the patient becomes overwhelmed and despairing,

feeling that hopes for "cures" have been betrayed. (Mishne, 1993, p. 89)

Dewald (1964) reflects on complications when clinicians confuse methods, goals, and the readiness of clients to handle material that is unconscious, and he cites massive inappropriate regression, therapeutic stalemates, and severe, dangerous acting out when abstinence and insight-uncovering approaches are misapplied to clients who need more active direction and support. The importance of a skilled assessment cannot be overemphasized.

Assessment

The evaluation and diagnostic label is not meant as a pejorative depreciation or stigmatizing effort. Diagnoses, rather, are shorthand descriptions of presenting problem(s) and symptoms, underlying character structure, physical state, and nature of milieu and environmental stressors. Diagnosis should offer information about the strengths and weaknesses of the client and family, thereby providing guidelines for optimal treatment planning. The distinction between evaluation and treatment is not merely a semantic one. A basic confusion is introduced when initial contacts are regarded as treatment before any insight is gained about the structure, nature, and history of the problem. Clients cannot genuinely engage in contracting and mutual goal setting before they have a better understanding of their presenting problems and the reasons they have been offered a particular therapeutic modality. They need to comprehend the nature of the prescribed therapy, including an estimate of the time and cost involved:

Beginning treatment before formulating a diagnosis is analogous to prescribing antibiotics indiscriminately for any undiagnosed physical disease.

---

[1]*Autonoetic consciousness* may be defined as the capacity of the individual to relive experiences in his or her past, resulting in a subjective sense of familiarity or knowing.

There are various modalities of ongoing intervention, but few agencies and clinics provide the full range. Without a diagnostic assessment, clients may simply be forced into whatever modality a given agency offers, with no differentiation of case need. The reality that an agency cannot be all things to all people, and rather should, on appropriate occasions, refer clients elsewhere, underscores the need for assessment as a separate and distinct phase. (Mishne, 1983, p. 27)

Anna Freud (1962) believed that the diagnostic approach provides data to determine a decision for or against treatment, the choice of therapeutic model, and treatment aims and goals, based on distinguishing transitory from permanent pathology:

Accordingly, it becomes the diagnostician's task to ascertain where a given child stands on the developmental scale, whether his position is age-adequate, retarded or precocious, and in what respect; and to what extent the observable internal and external circumstances and existent symptoms are interfering with the possibilities of future growth. (pp. 149–150)

In determining what holds individuals back, consideration must be given to fixation and regression. In situations of fixation, there remains a potential in psychic development for residuals of earlier phases to acquire and retain cathexes, strong charges of psychic energy. Arrests or fixations of development occur in instinctual, super-ego, and ego organization, and this causes various degrees of persistence of primitive, often child-like ways of thinking, reasoning, and relating to people to attempt to derive satisfaction or retain an old sense of danger and fear (Freud, 1965). In addition to insufficiently understood constitutional reasons for fixation, there are early experiences in which the child's developing immature ego was overwhelmed by stress. These traumatic experiences, such as parent loss, separations, and critical illness, usually involve an unfortunate combination of excessive frustration and excessive gratification. (A bereaved young mother, suffering from her spouse's untimely death, allows their 3-year-old son to sleep with her; thus,

the child suffers the pain and frustration due to the loss of the father and excessive gratification from inordinate closeness and overstimulation from the mother.) With disturbances of development and conflict over current functioning, regression to earlier behavior and functioning occurs. (Thus, the boy, arrested and too tied to his mother, may seek overindulgence and inappropriate closeness with her when facing adolescent stressors.)

Regression presents itself in two forms: libidinal and ego regression. Libidinal regression is a retreat to an earlier phase of psychosexual organization, especially of the infantile period. Such a retreat or falling back occurs when a predetermined maturation step presents the individual with difficulty that he or she is unable to master. A simple example of libidinal regression is evident at instances of serious emotional stress; for example, a 12-year-old child resumes thumb sucking, a habit previously abandoned. In ego regression, the mind may revert to modes of functioning typical of an earlier period of life. The concept of regression is intimately related to the hypothesis that in the course of attaining adulthood, an individual passes through a series of epigenetic phases, each with a phase-appropriate mental organization. The makeup of each such organization is inferred from the way instinctual drives discharge, ego functions operate, and the conscience and ideals guide. Under stress or trouble with successful management of age-appropriate maturational stages, there is disruption of mental functioning, and regression occurs. A college senior who was achieving well in school fears graduation and career choices and regresses into earlier dysfunctional patterns and poor academic performance, the original presenting problems that necessitated therapy. Despite enormous therapeutic and academic gains for 3 years, the demands of adult life after college pose a threat sufficient to cause substantial regression.

Psychological testing may be another assessment tool but generally is not a standard diagnostic procedure. However, academic problems, developmental delay, and suspicions of learning disabilities may be better understood by means of intelligence and projective testing. An appraisal of an adolescent's physical condition is essential during the assessment process, and this may or may not require the attention of physicians for a physical or neurological exam, or both, when organic pathology is suspected. Concerns about child abuse and substance abuse commonly require assessment efforts by psychologically and medically trained clinicians. When assessment is positive for abuse or neglect, reporting via mandated reporter statutes to the appropriate state departments of children and family services is always indicated.

Throughout the evaluation processes, it is crucial to note how parents and adolescents share material. The importance is far beyond factual data, such as the child's developmental history, accounts of illness and separation, or the adolescent's articulation of presenting problems. The child and the parent's emotional attitudes, feelings, and style of relating to each other and to the clinician are often more telling than hard data and facts. The clinician must be alert to affects of depression, anger, anxiety, aloofness, and indifference. Do the members of the family present apathy, anger, helplessness, enthusiasm, or empathy? Parental style, the nature of parenting provided, and parental motivation are probably key prognostic issues that serve as guidelines for the ongoing planning for therapy (Mishne, 1983).

The process of the assessment phase involves listening, exploration, and efforts to begin to form an alliance with family members. Clinicians must be alert to becoming overidentified with the teenager or the parents, becoming infected by parental anxieties, or feeling pressed to provide premature advice and recommendations before the depth and true nature of the presenting problems are understood. The process of the diagnostic study stresses the importance of observation and verbal communication in therapeutic work, diminishes any aura of mystery or magic about such procedures, and enables the parents and the adolescent to feel actively involved and to focus their attention on the work ahead. Often, an assessment affords

relief for parents' guilt and anxiety as they secure help for their child and themselves. In collecting information, the diagnostician must recognize and respect parental resistance or the adolescent's resistance. Parents may object to a necessary school inquiry, questions about their marriage, and explicit expectation that they remain actively involved on behalf of their child. Adolescents may and often do displace any and all problems onto their parents or teachers, feel stigmatized about needing help, and thereby oppose any idea of ongoing contact. If there is no working through of the parents' and adolescent's resistance, it frequently increases, resulting in a disinclination to complete the assessment phase or to begin treatment. In many situations, strong parental resistance offers a clear diagnostic message of where treatment interventions should begin—with them. In other situations, a child's resistance reflects parental uncertainty, covert resistance, or ineffective parenting; that is, the parent is afraid or otherwise unable to set limits and expectations. A young child cannot be permitted to make decisions about the need for treatment, and in some instances, this may be equally true for the adolescent client. Ideally, the adolescent is allowed considerable input into the decision to seek help. This is obviously not the case, however, when the teenager is a nonvoluntary client, perhaps referred by the juvenile court, school, or some other such agency of power.

It is unrealistic for a clinician to expect resistances and defenses such as denial or projection to be surrendered quickly or easily. Parents and adolescents may project all difficulties onto teachers and the school; time is needed for them to arrive at a more realistic understanding of the legitimate reasons for insistent referrals by school personnel. Teenagers are not allowed autonomy regarding attendance at school or with regard to medical or dental needs. Similarly, they are often not able to make wise decisions regarding psychotherapy contact. In such situations, where the clinician faces intense resistance, ambivalence, or parental ineffectiveness, it is wise to remain firm and patient, clarifying the situation rather than allying with the regressive infantile stance of the parents or teenager or identifying with parents' covert rejection and helplessness. Firm limits, outreach, and persistence often constitute a form of caring that overwhelmed parents have not been able to provide their child. When the referral is nonvoluntary, the clinician is well-advised to inform the adolescent about expectations and reality and take a therapeutic stance that will not permit collusion; for example, if the teenager misses appointments, this reality will not be kept in confidence and withheld from parents, the school, the juvenile court, the probation department, or other relevant authority (Mishne, 1986).

During the early part of the assessment process, and especially in the evaluation of the early-phase adolescent, parents may require assistance in preparing their adolescent for the diagnostic study, and at the conclusion, children as well as parents need a follow-up or informing interview. This is necessary to communicate the diagnosis and recommendations, to cope with any anxiety and resistances, and to motivate family members to act on the recommendations. Sharing findings and recommendations requires skill and sensitivity on the part of the clinician. Parents and adolescents should receive the clinician's explanation of the conflicts confronting the child and where and why the child seems stuck developmentally. The significance of the adolescent's conflict and its potential impact on the teenager's long-range development and future adjustment must be estimated. Recommendations and findings need to be presented simply and clearly, minus the jargon of the profession. The parents, adolescent, and clinician frequently need time and several appointments to consider the emotional significance of the recommendations. Professionals often lose sight of the impact of therapy on a child and his or her parents, minimizing the investment of time and energy and the effect on the family (Mishne, 1983). In cases involving adolescents, there are a number of situations where a therapist surmises that although a child presents some problems, the child's problems serve as an entree for parents

with either marital or individual problems. A recommendation for marital or individual treatment of the parent may indeed be the outcome, accompanied by no recommendation of any therapy for the teenager. There are instances where an adolescent who is not seen directly benefits greatly by improvement of the family milieu or by improvements in parents, through the provision of parent guidance or individual therapy to a parent.

For the older adolescent, especially for those who self-refer, a briefer evaluation process that relies less on parental inputs and more on the details generated in individual interviews may be possible. The axes of the expanded *Psychodynamic Diagnostic Manual* (PDM Task Force, 2006), which incorporate findings from neurobiology and the attachment research literature; the six areas of inquiry that reflect the biopsychosocial point of view (Meeks & Bernet, 2001); and other systems of assessment, for example, Brandell (2004), all offer plans for the orderly collection of the data necessary for treatment planning.

The model most frequently used for the diagnosis of conditions in adolescence is the one developed by Meeks and Bernet (2001). The six arenas for assessment are framed with questions the diagnostician seeks to answer. The first involves the role of the constitution—the extent to which psychopathology may be related to biochemistry or an inherited familial pattern. Examples include the symptoms of an underlying bipolar disorder, learning disabilities or minimal brain dysfunction, attention deficit disorders, and schizophrenic illness.

The second arena for investigation relates to the question "What is the highest level of psychological development the adolescent has achieved?" This question seeks to establish fixation points or serious arrests in developmental stages to which the adolescent regresses when experiencing pressure related to a maturationally timed crisis. A careful historical look, backward in time, may establish unmastered tasks from the oral, anal, or phallic phases; trauma, for instance, in the processes of attachment or separation-individuation; or a clear miscarriage of transmuting internalizations of selfobject needs in developing a cohesive self.

The third arena attempts to formulate the most characteristic interpersonal style of relating in the adolescent's object relations with others. For instance, is he or she primarily narcissistic, manipulative, withdrawing, shy, dependent, rebellious, paranoid, or inappropriately intrusive?

Meeks and Bernet's fourth arena asks the question "Why does the adolescent appear to be disturbed now?" It may be that the current symptomatology in reality reflects long-standing conflict that has heretofore eluded diagnosis. A 16-year-old suffering serious abandonment trauma at the age of 2, evidencing varying degrees of an anaclitic depression that has waxed and waned for 10 years, only now presents with a crisis of suicidal ideation subsequent to a breakup with a romantic partner who had served as a secure holding environment.

The fifth question has to do with the extent to which the adolescent displays a sense of being distressed or conflicted: "Are the symptoms of dysfunction experienced as ego alien or ego syntonic?" If they are of the former valence, the potential client will be more motivated to accept a recommendation for treatment based on a hope for relief, for instance, from the painful affects of anxiety, depression, or guilt. If the symptoms are of the latter valence, considerable pressure from the family may be necessary to deal with the initial resistance to treatment.

The sixth and final question asks, "If the adolescent accepts the treatment recommendation, to what extent will the family be able to accept it and the implications for supporting the changes the adolescent will be making in his or her life?"

Incorporating all the above six elements of the Meeks and Bernet assessment profile, a recent contribution to the literature frames four additional questions, expanding and modifying the original schedule (McKenzie, 2008). First, are the adolescent's defenses primarily mature or immature, adaptive and sublimatory or maladaptive with projection, acting out, or denial everywhere in evidence? Second, what is the nature of the family system? Third, are there significant areas of diversity (ethnicity, race, spirituality, oppression, socioeconomic status [SES], or cultural beliefs) that permeate the psychosocial surround? The last has to do with the availability and nature of the resources, both internal and external, that speak to the adolescent's resilience or vulnerability to stress.

Another equally viable approach to assessment of the adolescent client is Brandell's psychodynamic model (2004), which lists eight distinct components covering the regulatory personality structures, for example, ego functions, affects, and the self system, as well as specific areas of competence and effectance. Irrespective of the diagnostic system chosen to guide this aspect of the initial phase past referral, however, the pivotal issue is that the assessment model should be inclusive, comprehensive, and multifaceted in the organization of data involving observation, clarification, and the use of nomenclature (American Psychiatric Association, *Diagnostic and Statistical Manual of Mental Disorders*, fourth edition, text revision [*DSM-IV-TR*], 2000), the underlying principle being that in a psychodynamic formulation of conflicts, most symptoms of psychological dysfunction are profoundly overdetermined in their etiology and expression rather than being unitary or static.

The informing interview should generally be done with the adolescent alone, after the interview with the parents. In general, the approach used with the parents is also appropriate for the adolescent. The clinician should share with the teenager the assessment observations, impressions, and recommendations and should help the adolescent deal with anxiety and resistance. The recommendations should be presented as logically fitting with the presenting problems and in age-appropriate language. Adolescents should always be seen for a follow-up interview. Often, children want to know about their parents' reactions and responses, which frequently can be shared openly. However, if the parents have been very resistive to the recommendations, the clinician must not reveal all, since it is not useful to create dissension between adolescent and parent(s). When the clinician and parents differ, this fact can be recognized with the teenager while careful attention and respect are given to the parents' opinions.

The Recommendation for Individual Treatment

The criteria for determining indications and contraindications for individual, family, or group therapy are many and varied. There are a number of fundamental theoretical struggles in the clinical field, and in some cases, decisions are made on the basis of clinician bias, philosophy, orientation, and training. Some clinicians, trained in several methods of intervention, are more open to issues of diagnosis and considerations of criteria for determining the optimal modality. Offer and Vanderstoep (1975) reflect on the conflicts regarding treatment recommendations and cite the psychoanalytic and systems analysis perspectives. The psychoanalytically oriented practitioner considers several interventions, in contrast to family systems analysts, who generally believe "that the question of indications and contraindications is a 'non-question'" (p. 145). The psychoanalytically oriented practitioner uses a nosological classification and views individuals and families from a psychodynamic point of view; according to this view, certain problems are suitable for treatment by family therapy and others are not. Systems analysts in the field of family therapy make no distinctions and strongly object to considerations of indication and contraindication; some believe that assessment is merely a device to deal with the therapist's anxiety and advocate an action-oriented point of view. Such a view leads therapists to engage in rearranging the family system, since the unit of attention is not the individual but the family system itself.

A psychoanalytic perspective and affirmation of a diagnostic process requires distinctions and cautions regarding indications and contraindications. The presence of severe psychotic-like depression; severe masochistic character pathology; hardcore psychopathology, child abuse, or domestic violence; perversion; criminality; a firm

decision for divorce; or unyielding prejudice against family or group therapy points to a clear recommendation for individual treatment. Similarly, highly narcissistic individuals who lack empathy and are fixated in struggles regarding self-esteem or self-regard are inappropriate candidates for group therapy. Adolescents with deficient controls generally cannot be effectively treated in group or family therapy. Suggestive clients who are easily led become stimulated to excessive acting out in group treatment (Heacock, 1966). Ginott (1961) enumerates several other criteria to exclude specific children and teenagers from group therapy, among them, those experiencing intense sibling rivalry who require one-to-one attention; sociopathic adolescents who present shallowness, cruelty, persistent stealing, intense selfishness, impulsivity, or lack of empathy; those with accelerated drive expressions; highly sexualized or extremely aggressive children; children eroticized due to their exposure to perverse sexual activities or as the result of sexual victimization; and children traumatized by overt catastrophes. All such adolescents need supportive individualized treatment.

In sum, individualized insight-oriented therapy is optimal for teenagers with discrete areas of internal conflict, a strong basic ego structure, psychological mindedness, and a capacity for insight. More damaged adolescents who suffer from constitutional, perceptual, and cognitive deficits or whose families present severe pathology need active and supportive treatment. Supportive treatment is appropriate for severely disturbed adolescents who present habit disorders in eating, discipline, and sleeping, related to a lack of appropriate parental direction or environmental structure, limits, and boundaries. Some adolescents with adequate personality development can be helped by a brief course of supportive treatment following trauma due to surgery, divorce, or death of a parent. In supportive work, attention should be focused on the present, with efforts toward improving rational control, diminishing anxiety and depression, and reinforcing secondary ego processes. Adolescents who are considered less than neurotic, with diagnoses of borderline or narcissistic personality organization, often can be engaged only by individual supportive interventions; sometimes they can move into a more uncovering, insight-oriented treatment.

The Treatment Relationship

Individual treatment can be behavioral, supportive, uncovering, reconstructive, or interpretive and reflective. Mistakes, failures to assess the client properly, or the inflexible provision of one modality or form of treatment to all clients can cause a teenager to become more disturbed. Some clinics offer short-term treatment exclusively; others provide only individual treatment and in cases of adolescent clients omit necessary family work with parents; still others provide only a family or group form of intervention. Too frequently, slogans, panaceas, agency bias, or dictates from third parties via insurance companies control practice, with the result that there is little demonstrated respect for the individual. The burgeoning managed care industry has dramatically affected the provision of treatment services to adolescents and their families over the course of the past 15 years. Currently, more than 50% of the population is enrolled in these organizations, where case management practices restrict both the independence and decision making of clinicians who treat and the right of free choice among clients to select their own therapists. Being an unregulated industry means the obvious: There are no uniform standards or procedures that govern the relationship with treatment providers relative to reimbursement schedules, length of treatment and its frequency, and expected treatment outcomes. A recent study of a randomly drawn sample of National Association for Social Worker (NASW) professionals found that the majority of respondents reported pressure from managed care organizations (MCOs) to alter their original diagnoses and shorten the recommended course of treatment at the behest of utilization reviewers (Bennett, Naylor, Perri, Shirilla, & Kilbane, 2008). Concerns about lowering their fees abounded as did ethical dilemmas relative to client confidentiality

and the inherent problems with a system that contains cost at the expense of providing service to those in need.

The genuine nature of the problems and, in many instances, severely rationed care lead to a revolving door effect, with client needs remaining unmet and crises unresolved, with clients continually returning for needed ongoing attention. The treatment process and the nature of the treatment recommended (supportive or insight oriented) are nevertheless regulated to varying degrees by these outside forces today. Even more insidious is the subtle effect of MCO policies on the relationship between clinicians and their administrators in agency-based practice. Pressured to conform by abbreviating treatment, young clinicians are encouraged to focus on alleviating overt behaviors, concretizing symptom formation at the expense of developing a therapeutic relationship. This is true in both private and agency-based practice and thus cannot be ignored. These outside forces, in dictating the length of the care provided, determine, in fact, whether an actual therapeutic relationship can or cannot be established.

The Therapeutic Alliance

In a genuine treatment process (one that is not merely an extended diagnostic evaluation concluding with directions for overt behavior change), the therapeutic alliance is the single most important element in the treatment relationship. The literature on psychotherapy outcomes, studied and researched for decades, has consistently demonstrated that establishing and maintaining the therapeutic alliance in the treatment relationship correlates significantly with client improvement (Lawson & Brossart, 2003). Studies of the therapeutic alliance as a process (e.g., Frieswyk, Allen, & Colson, 1986) related to outcome (Luborsky et al., 1980) and as a scaled, measurable research variable (Marziali, Marmar, & Krupnick, 1981) pointed to two more recent, evidentiary meta-analytic research studies that have confirmed the therapeutic alliance as central to the effectiveness of practice

(Horvath & Symonds, 1991; Martin, Garske, & Davis, 2000).

The therapeutic alliance is seen as emanating out of the client's "conscious or unconscious wish to cooperate and his readiness to accept the therapist's aid in overcoming intense difficulties and resistances" (Sandler, Kennedy, & Tyson, 1980, p. 45). While the alliance in child psychotherapy arises out of the wish for pleasure in the treatment situation, the alliance for the adolescent involves a genuine comprehension of problems and the need to deal with them. The alliance is not an end unto itself but rather a means to an end, a way of facilitating the treatment process. According to Basch (1980), it is based on a new and corrective relationship, "a fund of trust" (p. 133), that adolescent client and therapist mutually share with one another. Alongside this rapport and positive feeling the adolescent develops for the therapist, the alliance is also based on an accurate appraisal of a need for understanding and for gratification in being understood. Adolescent clients will look to therapy for relief only if they have the capacity for self-observation and some awareness that there are significant problems.

The therapeutic alliance is the larger, subsuming context of psychotherapy that encompasses the treatment relationship: what is transferred as well as "real," the working-through process in the middle phase, and the decision to eventually terminate. As the alliance goes, so goes every aspect of the psychotherapy. The alliance emerges gradually as the therapist becomes a good-enough object, an auxiliary ego, in a supportive holding environment where the client's capacity for self-observation and reflection increases in consonance with the clinician's ongoing encouragement and timely interpretation of the adolescent's feelings underlying behavior. These emotional states, for instance, of impatience, frustration, sadness, helplessness, shame, and embarrassment, and the categorical affects (Tomkins, 1962, 1963), many of which frequently operate out of conscious awareness, are observable in facial displays, body language, and posture or can be inferred, as coded, in the manifest language used to describe experience.

These interventions that target emotions are employed because of the adolescent's tendency to act in order to avoid awareness of feelings. This interpretive pattern of therapeutic activity serves to connect thoughts, attitudes, emotions, and behavior in the client's present life situation.

Not all teenagers have sufficient inner ego structure for self-observation and self-awareness. Severely disturbed clients may not regard their symptoms as painful, projecting blame onto parents or experiencing their self-injurious behaviors as ego syntonic. In the absence of feelings of guilt, anguish, or anxiety in the adolescent, it is the parents and other concerned adults who suffer and worry, and they must insist on the teenager's involvement in treatment. In such cases, the parents usually make the initial alliance, which then supports and sustains the treatment.

Most adolescents simply will not relate to a distant authority figure who keeps his client at the end of a 10-foot pole. Therefore, the effective engagement of the client in this early stage of therapy will be modeled on the therapist as a special guide, an older adult friend, or a favorite aunt or uncle. This experience-near form of relating in the therapeutic alliance, which may include timely and appropriate clinician self-disclosures, permits the adolescent client to begin a controlled regression to the pathogenetic nuclei of internalized conflicts (Blos, 1970), the residues of unmastered developmental tasks from which the current symptoms emanate. The development of the alliance can be gauged by the adolescent's increased capacity for self-observation and by the therapist's subjectively felt experience of relief that the treatment effort has finally begun to be shouldered by the client as well as himself.

The developing alliance witnesses an increase in the young client's capacity for self-observation, which will become the basis for a successful working through of conflicts. In this regard, being thoughtfully self-analytical and reflective begins to resemble the adult's capacity for reality testing and advanced reasoning based on formal operational thought (Piaget, 1950). At the other extreme, there are also elements of the child therapy situation, where play vehicles support the simple enjoyment of hobbies, games, crafts, and sports. For the young adolescent, especially, board games, the easel and chalkboard, or Nerf basketball may occupy a significant portion of the 55-minute hour. To the extent that the treatment relationship affords some partial gratification of drives and the release of pleasurable feelings, this aspect of the alliance supports the mature sublimation of libidinal and aggressive strivings. At still another level, the adolescent's experiencing ego, coupled with the normative immersion in teen peer culture activities, literally mandates initiation into new social roles with concomitant expectations for performance and mastery in myriad new forums—team and solo sports and membership in extramural school clubs and social networks, for example, the debate team, theater and the performing arts,

band and orchestra, or the pom-pom squad. All four of these dimensions involve self-expression and agency as the adolescent contributes to the therapeutic alliance with a sharing of his or her subjective world and its multiple personal meanings. In this fashion, these four dimensions—the reality ego, the pleasure ego, the observing ego, and the experiencing ego—represent the structural/functional elements that promote and strengthen the adolescent's contributions to the alliance and reciprocally interact with the clinician's timely interventions, that is, a mix of insight-oriented and supportive procedures. The outcome of a successful engagement with the adolescent client in building the therapeutic alliance is a beginning identification with the therapist and a strengthening of the adolescent's ego ideal (Lucente, 1986).

Case Illustration

Fifteen-year-old Abby was referred to me[2] by her parents on discharge from a psychiatric inpatient service after a 3-day period of observation for depression with suicidal ideation. I had treated her mother 20 years earlier and followed her as an outpatient in long-term insight-oriented psychotherapy spanning a period of 3 years, which also included an individual brief treatment of her husband and some marital therapy. Initial sessions with Abby included her thoughts on the similarity of her current symptoms of depression with her mother's past history and her decision to enter outpatient treatment with her mother's former therapist. In these regards, she freely volunteered that I might see her in stereotypical fashion as merely a replica of her mother and that I might miss her uniqueness and individuality. While thoughtful and intelligent, she was clearly subdued and conveyed little pleasure in her daily routine, which had previously included active, joyous participation on the high school volleyball team. In addition to elaborating on her current interests, activities with peers, and childhood experiences, she slowly began to hint at the depth of her anger, lurking just beneath the surface, which attached to the three crucial recent events in her life that had contributed to her suicidality: (1) the change in her previously close relationship with her father, (2) a breakup with a close female friend and peer who had betrayed her trust, and (3) her mother's attempts to "smother" her. During this time, I experienced Abby as hesitant to acknowledge and disclose these emerging

(Continued)

---

[2]Abby was treated by Dr. Lucente.

(Continued)

preconscious feelings of frustration and angry impatience. I also noted her defensive avoidance and nonresponse to any of my positive comments on her achievements, talents, and resiliencies. I sensed that the potential for a therapeutic alliance was hanging in the balance or, worse, that it might actually be lost. Feeling at odds with my own self-created pressure to engage, I began to struggle in session to maintain an evenly suspended attention to Abby's material. Finally, she described in detail an altercation with her mother later in the week after our session. Her mother had "smother mothered me once again," demanding that she accompany her to the wake and funeral of one of her college friends, a woman whom Abby barely knew. At the same time, Abby pointed out that her newfound friends had planned a sleepover slumber party for that very same Friday, that the event had been on the family calendar for more than 2 weeks, and that the Saturday events included mall shopping, a movie, and a light afternoon restaurant meal. Struggling with the intensity of her mother's insistence that she meet her mother's needs at the expense of her own, and noting her own escalating argumentativeness and disrespect, Abby said that a picture of my face had suddenly flashed through her mind as she wondered what I would do if I were in this situation and in her shoes. In a split second, she had become more focused and more caring toward the hurt in her mother's voice as she offered a solution to their dilemma. She would attend the wake that Friday afternoon and evening with her mother but would be dropped off at her friend's house in time for the get-together and evening sleepover. In the morning, she agreed to check in with her mother before setting out for the mall and movie later in the day.

Our "shared two-person unconscious" (Lucente, 2008; Lyons-Ruth, 1999; Stern, 1983) actually contained unconscious elements, represented in each of our memory systems, of Abby's mother as my client and as her parent. With some reflection, I came to understand, through Abby's vivid description of the argument with her mother—of being pressured to perform as a parent's dutiful daughter and "smothered"—that I had unwittingly recreated the very same dynamics based on my own unverbalized high expectations of her performance as my client. In subsequent sessions over the next few weeks, I noticed myself becoming increasingly more comfortable and less preoccupied with plans to make the alliance happen. My further reflections on Abby's selfobject deficits aided me in tracing them to my understanding of her mothering, through my working model of her mother's mind, as the source of these problems. This self-correcting, mentalizing review of Abby's mother—as lacking mirroring and idealizing functions—was followed by an increase in Abby's self-observing and reflective functioning, as evidenced by her report of the following dream, which I interpreted, silently to myself, as a significant, tacit statement that she had accepted me as her therapist and that I was no longer her mother's.

I am alone in this large, white three-story house with many rooms on each floor and a picture of someone with white hair in one of the third-floor bedrooms. There is scaffolding on one of the exterior walls as if a work crew is making much needed repairs, and I am trying hard to use the scaffolding to look into the rooms from the outside, but I am having trouble climbing to the next level.

Abby's associations to her dream are (a) that her dream house is a very different house from the modern, split-level one in which she currently resides; (b) that the man in the picture with the white hair seems to resemble her grandfather, who died a year ago and with whom she had been extremely close throughout her childhood; (c) that variations on this same dream have been recurrent for the past 2 years of her life, since entering adolescence; and (d) that this is the first time she has been outside the house and the first time scaffolding has been part of the manifest content.

My understanding of Abby's dream begins with the white house as a metaphoric image of her evolving adolescent identity information. (1) The rooms, some of which she already knows, as well as the new ones that she will eventually decorate in conformance with her individuality, symbolize her many "me selves" (Erikson, 1968), as the various components of her identity representations. (2) Her initial feelings of excitement, turning to worries and trepidations of the unknown, suggest the ambivalence that is endemic to the adolescent stage as a passage to self-knowledge and a revised narrative. (3) That she is alone implies its opposite, that is, there is a work crew of valued others—consisting of her therapist and a father whose hair is prematurely white, linked to the picture of her paternal grandfather, an internalized object of identification who occupies one of the rooms in her white house—all of whom serve the purpose of guides, assisting her in putting her house in order. (4) Starting at the ground floor, with the scaffolding at the foundation, signifies the vertical complexity of the structure of the building as well as her psyche and points to a hierarchy of functions from id to ego, from unconscious to conscious mentation, and from one epigenetic stage to the next. Furthermore, starting with her foundation indicates a willingness to regress in the service of a therapy contract. Finally, that she is for the very first time on the outside looking in and finding it hard going attests to her willingness to self-observe and reflect on the psychological interior of her edifice. The themes in this single dream pointed to the foci of treatment for the next year: character formation, identity, and a second separation-individuation.

Transference

In his early considerations of transference, Freud (1912, 1915, 1916–1917) stated that all people unconsciously displace and transfer the libidinal aspects of their primary object relationships to current object relationships. The term *transference*, derived from adult psychoanalytic therapy, refers to the views and relations the client presents about significant early-childhood objects: parents, siblings, and significant caretakers. Transference phenomena are expressed in the client's current perceptions, thoughts, fantasies, feelings, attitudes, and behavior with regard to the therapist (Sandler et al., 1980). In the classic sense, transference phenomena involve the reliving of the client's psychodynamic past—internalized, conflictual relationship experiences—in the current and present object relationship with the therapist. It is these repressed wishes and fears that continue to shape the client's expectations of the therapist, as well as his behavior toward him and his perceptions of him, as a replica of primary objects from the past. Not infrequently, unconscious wishes and fears return with a change from passive to active. For example, there may be an active and conscious wish for closeness and intimacy and an equally active but more powerful unconscious fear that were this closeness to occur, rejection would surely follow—wearing a chip on the shoulder, out of conscious awareness, almost guarantees that the stated goal will never be attained by rejecting an intimate relationship before it has a chance to develop.

Self psychology posits different transference phenomena for clients with structural deficits, who suffer faulty self-esteem, and who are incapable of making clear self/other distinctions. They develop a "selfobject transference," which must be distinguished from the classic definition and understanding of transference. Selfobject transferences are not displacement phenomena but rather a use of the therapist to provide a missing part of the self for the client. Because adolescents typically continue to reside with their significant early objects, they generally do not displace feelings, defenses, and perceptions from their past in the classic model of the repetition compulsion. More generally, they demonstrate what have been called *transference subtypes*: (a) where there is an extension of or a defensive displacement from the current relationship with the primary objects or (b) where past experiences, that is, conflicts involving drive, wishes, and defense, are revived as a consequence of clinical work and are displaced onto the therapist in the manifest or latent preconscious imagery (Sandler et al., 1980, pp. 78–104).

Another transference phenomenon commonly demonstrated by children and adolescents is that of externalization in the transference. Children and adolescents often do battle with their environments and use the therapist to represent a part of their personality structure. During the adolescent upheaval, externalization and projections are common defenses with which the teenager wards off inner conflict; the superego function is relegated to outside authority figures whom the teenager defies but also invites to control or punish him for disobedience and defiance (Furman, 1980):

> However, the externalization not only changes an inner battle into an outer one, it also supplants a very hard inner threat into a usually milder punishment from the outside. The visible misbehavior is seen as less of a violation than the inner forbidden activity or wish, for example, masturbatory activity or sexual or aggressive feelings toward forbidden objects. (p. 271)

In addition to these subtypes of transference manifested by adolescents and children, many have noted specific types of adolescent transference patterns related to the adolescent's habitual style of relating. These patterns can tax or disrupt the therapeutic alliance and also obstruct ego growth, thus requiring identification and active management (Meeks & Bernet, 2001). Meeks has noted four patterns: (1) the erotic transference, (2) the omnipotent transference, (3) the negative transference, and (4) the superego transference—the therapist as superego. Management of these varied transference phenomena includes acceptance of the adolescent's feelings, avoidance of counterattack, and a firm refusal to accept unrealistic blame and excessive criticism. As the adolescent is helped to explore and comprehend his or her anger, the empathic therapist tries to reflect a recognition of how things appear and to feel from the client's perspective. The therapist does not try to force his or her views on clients, but

> neither does he attempt to avoid his responsibility as an adult to offer his ethical conclusion. . . . Such openness in discussions also encourages the adolescent to think about his own assumptions and to use his own powers of logic to the best possible advantage. (Meeks & Bernet, 2001, p. 135)

Self psychology views these transference patterns more as narcissistic transference, common in adolescence, which is a time of heightened narcissism and self-regard. These three core structures that make up the tripolar self (idealizations, grandiosity, and twinship) all undergo significant change during this phase of development and will be observable in transference related phenomena in the treatment of many adolescent clients. Idealization and de-idealization of the therapist are common, and Goldberg (1972) recommends that the therapist not confront but

> accept the narcissistic disorder of the adolescent client as existing alongside a relative paucity of object love and not try to change narcissistic investment into object love. Treatment consists of a gradual undermining of the grandiosity and

exhibitionism of the client as well as a diminution of his search for unattainable ideals. (p. 5)

In all, the therapy focuses on recognition and acceptance of the adolescent's narcissism in a nonjudgmental fashion, using the transference to demonstrate the use of the clinician as a regulator and modulator of self-esteem. In these regards, a lengthy clinical vignette describes the process of an empathic attunement in the psychotherapy of a 14-year-old whose idealized parental imago and internalized grandiose self poles were mobilized in a transference relationship that enabled him to overcome a debilitating sense of inferiority and to develop a capacity for increased self-regulation (Lucente, 2012).

Transference phenomena can be particularly intense in individual psychotherapy. In group and family therapy, there can be considerable dilution or diminution because of the presence of other family or group members. When others are present, clients commonly conceal more private feelings, hopes, and fantasies. Some adolescents, struggling for age-appropriate self-presentation, tend to be less open in the presence of others about any productions in treatment in the realm of play, poetry, or painting; they may be similarly disinclined to reveal feelings of anger, omnipotence, grandiosity, or dependency longings. Such feelings are generally most easily shared by adolescents in the privacy of individual psychotherapy.

Countertransference

Countertransference, like *transference*, is an overused term that commonly covers any and all feelings and reactions from the therapist in response to the client. In fact, there are varied and conflicting definitions that reflect differing perspectives regarding the legitimate domain of this term. Dewald (1964), for example, states that countertransference arises not out of a client's behavior alone but from unconscious and preconscious forces within the therapist that cause the therapist to react to the client in ways that are inappropriate to the current reality of the therapeutic relationship. Such unrealistic, unprovoked reactions are viewed as displacements from significant early relationships with the therapist's siblings and parents. Giovacchini (1985) differs with this formulation and offers a broader definition:

I believe countertransference is ubiquitous; it is found in every analytic interaction in the same way transference is. Everything a therapist or a client thinks, feels or does can be viewed as being on a hierarchal spectrum, one end dominated by unconscious, primary process elements, and the other end dominated by reality-oriented, secondary process factors. When a client directs his feelings toward the therapist, the primary process elements of the spectrum represent transference, and in a similar fashion that part of the analyst's responses that stems primarily from the more primitive levels of his psyche can be viewed as countertransference. (p. 450)

Some clinicians make distinctions along Giovacchini's spectrum, designating reality-oriented factors as counterreactions and those that emanate out of unconscious primary-process variables as countertransference. Marcus (1980) defined countertransference as a reaction to a specific client, to the client's transference response, or to other components of the client's material. When used defensively, it can interrupt or disrupt the therapist's analyzing function because it "activates a developmental residue and creates or revives unconscious conflict, anxiety and defensiveness" (Marcus, 1980, p. 286). When not used defensively, it can be a valuable diagnostic tool and an effective treatment response in which a clinician is led to reflect and undertake a frank examination of his or her aroused feelings in order to avoid or resolve various therapeutic impasses or stalemates.

There are appropriate and all but universal countertransferences or counterreactions (according to one's definition of therapists' responses) to specific clients—those who are very impulsive, acting out, highly narcissistic, extremely aggressive, unmotivated and resistive, or suicidal. Such adolescents arouse understandable anxiety, fears, and frustration in all therapists. Furthermore, there is a wide variation in the client-therapist fit. One cannot work with equal effectiveness with all of one's clients.

> Rather than viewing treatability only in terms of the client's limitations, it is more realistic to consider the patient/therapist relationship as the axis that determines treatability. A patient may not be treatable by a particular therapist, but that does not make that patient untreatable. (Giovacchini, 1985, p. 450)

Some adolescent clients provoke anger, rejection, and hostile demands for compliance; others cause therapists, like parents, to feel anxious, overwhelmed and helpless, or ashamed and professionally mortified. Clients who are productive and promising may please and gratify the therapist, who unconsciously uses the client as a narcissistic extension, as a source of pride and praise. Signs of countertransference problems are the therapist's lateness, boredom, overinvolvement, fear, anger, mistakes about scheduling, and so on. The therapist must be self-observing and self-aware and seek appropriate sources of help and support to minimize the potentially negative impact such countertransference reactions may otherwise have. Supervision, consultation, and personal treatment help the therapist stay in touch with and control his or her unconscious and pre-conscious early conflicts and properly modulate conscious behaviors and responses. The goal is to provide a safe holding environment, one that is characterized by restraint, appropriate containment of drive expression, attunement, an absence of nihilistic pessimism, and a continuous sense of concern and compassion, based on the clinician's ability to remember the adolescent's history. This enables the therapist to see that earlier injuries and pain have in fact produced unpleasant defenses such as denial, projection, and externalization.

Empathy is crucial in all treatment relationships. Kohut, the founder of self psychology, included it as a central concept in his seminal psychoanalytic papers on psychoanalytic therapy. In 1975, Kohut pronounced psychoanalysis as the science of empathy par excellence. Earlier, Kohut discussed introspection as the process of self-observation of the inner world of fantasies, feelings, and wishes and empathy as the process in which others were similarly understood. He used the phrase *vicarious introspection* to denote that through empathy one observes vicariously the inner world of another. Empathy is a central concept in self psychology, and Kohut (1971, 1978a, 1984) conceived of it as curative in the treatment process. He called it "a value neutral method of observation attuned to the inner life of man" (1984, p. 395).

Clearly empathy is a critical ingredient in countertransference, and accurate empathy is composed of affective and cognitive components (Kohut, 1978b). Empathy is not used to satisfy or gratify client needs, nor is it the same as sympathy or support. "Rather, empathy informs the individual as to what is needed or yearned for by the other" (Lynch, 1991, p. 16). Ornstein (1978) notes that Kohut summarized his understanding of empathy with the following propositions:

> (1) Empathy, the recognition of the self in the other, is an indispensable tool of observation without which vast areas of human life, including man's behavior in the social field, remains unintelligible. (2) Empathy, the expansion of the self to include the other, constitutes a powerful psychological bond between individuals which, more perhaps than love, the expression and sublimation of the sexual drive, counteracts man's destructiveness against his fellows; and (3) Empathy, the accepting, confirming and understanding human echo evoked by the self, is a cherished nutriment without which human life as we know it and cherish it could not be sustained. (p. 84)

In the context of the treatment relationship using a self psychology perspective, efforts by the therapist must evoke efforts at empathic immersion, to gain understanding of each client's demands, hopes, fears, ambitions, and symptomatic behavior. "The theory of self psychology removes the focus from the client's faulty functioning in favor of learning to understand the underlying structure responsible for the faulty functioning" (Basch, 1980, p. 409). Interpretations are offered following the achievement of understanding, to assist in structure building, that is, "compensatory structures where development was earlier interrupted and thwarted by traumatic empathic failure" (Basch, 1980, p. 404). While better cognition and insight might occur, a goal of treatment is to open a path of empathy between self and selfobject and deepen the client's capacity for self-acceptance. A further treatment goal is the development of a cohesive self, through a process Kohut called *transmuting internalization.* Transmuting internalization occurs incrementally as clients develop capacities to self-soothe, self-regulate, increase self-regard, and mirror and "to accept the hurts that are caused by failures of optimal responses by important others" (Solomon, 1991, p. 132). Kohut (1984) viewed treatment as a corrective emotional experience, and it is generally agreed that the expanded theoretical constructs of self psychology, as a model of deficits versus conflicts, have been particularly useful in consideration of countertransference and for working with the more fragile populations. It is especially productive in clinical work with adolescents.

The Real Relationship

Alexander (1963) was one of the first to challenge the concept of analytic neutrality. He stated emphatically that the analyst's values are subtly learned by the client through verbal and nonverbal communications and by the experience of genuineness, warmth, and respect in a corrective emotional experience with a real person. Empathic warmth and active participation in the treatment process, include the judicious use of self-disclosure, particularly in work with adolescent clients who clearly respond to their therapist's gender, age, appearance, style, humor, and other characteristics. While psychoanalysis is an intensive, in-depth process of uncovering that requires the client to lie on a couch, in psychotherapy, the emphasis is primarily on the here-and-now and the manifestations of transference, which may or may not be addressed in any depth. Thus, the real relationship may well dominate over the transference relationship.

The approach of self psychology, based on Kohut's expanded views of empathy, is predicated on the therapist's greater emotional availability and spontaneity, resulting in a "generally calmer and friendlier atmosphere." In individual psychotherapy with adolescents, support, reflections, enhancement of self-esteem, education, and guidance in a talkative and responsive interchange are more frequent interventions than interpretations of the transference or of defenses, or the elaboration of fantasies and unconscious primary-process material, as is the case in analysis.

THE MIDDLE PHASE OF TREATMENT

Resistance, Working Through, Intersubjectivity, and Psychoneurobiology

The beginning phase of treatment consists of assessment, selection of appropriate intervention, initial engagement, and contracting, which it is hoped will culminate in the development of a working alliance that is based on the growing treatment relationship between the adolescent client and the therapist. Resistance, commonly dealt with in the middle phase of treatment, is defined as any obstruction that evolves in the process of treatment and in the treatment relationship. Character resistances are present from the beginning of treatment and can be distinguished from the opposition that arises in the course of therapy. Such opposition arises because internal conflict is defended, and there is always some degree of resistance to removing these defenses. Dewald (1964) noted that resistances emerge during the treatment process at varying levels of consciousness. They are caused by the client's fear of change or gratification arising from regressive infantile drives, early patterns, or infantile relationships, and the need to maintain repression of the unconscious conflicts that produce anxiety and guilt. A complete lack of defenses and resistance is an ominous sign, suggesting a lack of psychic structure, possible decompensation, or a propensity for merger and indiscriminate compliance. It is important to understand why, what, and how the client is avoiding. Therefore, resistances and defenses should not be assaulted with confrontational or intellectualized reflections and interpretations.

Anna Freud (1958, 1978) discussed the inability or unwillingness of children and adolescents to maintain a stable therapeutic alliance, tolerate frustrations, and translate feelings into words rather than actions. There is a "type of juvenile patient who does not allow anxiety to find expression in thought or words but constantly negates it" (Sandler et al., 1980, p. 58). Adolescents often demonstrate resistance before and during the course of therapy because of their wish for autonomy and their fear that the therapist—the agent of the parents—will attempt to transform them in accord with the parents' needs and not the adolescent's preferences. Silences, broken appointments, tardiness, action rather than verbalization, passive-aggressive behavior, impatience, boredom, and resentment are standard adolescent manifestations of resistance.

Defenses are commonly used in the service of resistance. *Defense* is a term used to describe struggles of the ego, unconsciously employed, to protect the self from perceived danger. The threat of recognition or conscious awareness of repressed wishes or impulses causes anxiety and guilt and must be avoided. Assessment and diagnosis determine whether the defenses demonstrated are age adequate, primitive, or precocious and whether they prove to be effective in binding impulses and anxiety to promote coping and adaptation. The defenses employed shape the individual's personality and style of coping with reality. Some clients' defenses are ineffectual and create secondary interference with reality functioning and consequent disequilibrium, for example, denial, projection, and acting out. Others reflect more adaptive, mature accommodations to external reality and internal ego structure, for example, sublimation and undoing. Splitting defenses become more object bound as the adolescent undergoes a second separation-individuation. More adaptive projective identification mechanisms—where part self and part object representations, and their associated affects, are projected onto others to replicate unresolved conflicts with introjects—eventually replace primitive splitting. Interpersonal reenactments frequently involve role reversals with aggressive, affirming, or rejecting part selves and bad part objects.

The defenses must be recognized, understood, and accepted as the client's needed protection against anxiety. Many adolescent clients are often objectionable, assaultive, draining, and provocative, yet despite this reality, a nonpunitive therapeutic stance must be maintained. The discussion of countertransference and counter-reactions suggested ways to maintain therapeutic calm, objectivity, and ongoing commitment to the adolescent client.

Working Through

The term *working through* was originally used by Freud to describe the continuing application of analytic work to overcome resistances that persisted after interpretation of repressed instinctual impulses. The goal of working through is to make insight effective in order to bring about significant and lasting change. When longer-term therapy is possible, it can strengthen the working-through process, after the client's attainment of earlier treatment gains (e.g., mastery of reality, the enactment of age-appropriate life roles and tasks). Introspection and insight are linked with working through, which occurs when the client's ego identifies with the therapist, so that the client may share in the therapist's understanding and take part in the therapeutic effort.

Adolescent efforts are not typically directed toward understanding the past because of their intense preoccupation with current real difficulties and apprehensions about the future. It is usually not until late adolescence that young clients internalize the analyzing, observing, and reflecting function of their therapists, and they begin to acquire and retain an understanding of the genesis of their difficulties. Many teenagers who are provided treatment may require additional therapy later in adulthood, when more genuine working through is possible.

It is critical to bear in mind that even insight has limitations. Self-understanding produces neither magical change nor relief. Working through and resolution of both internalized and externalized conflicts require considerable time and repeated encounters with and recognition of newly learned truths. Many clinicians believe that "sufficient working through has taken place when the [young client] has moved to the next level of development and established himself there" (Sandler et al., 1980, p. 184). This progression would involve an alteration of balance among the defenses, neutralization of resistances, formation of new identifications, reconstruction of the ego ideal (Campbell, 1981), and more adaptive character traits.

INTERSUBJECTIVITY AND PSYCHONEUROBIOLOGY

The paradigm shift that has been emergent for the past decade and a half in contemporary psychoanalytic thought is now complete. Informed by psychoneurobiology research, this new model, with its overarching umbrella of intersubjectivity, is a synergistic blend that includes attachment (e.g., Atwood & Stolorow, 1999; Bowlby, 1969; Main & Solomon, 1986; Sander, 2002) and object relations theory (e.g., Mahler, Pine, & Bergman, 1975; Winnicott, 1951, 1956, 1960), relational and narrative approaches, constructivism, and the traditional theories, for example, drive and ego psychology, self psychology, and systems theory. This paradigm shift has dramatic implications both for the conduct of psychotherapy, especially with adolescents, and for understanding change processes, choice of interventions, and expected treatment outcomes.

The clinical relationship provides an experience-near opportunity for the adolescent to understand and regulate emotions. Primary emotional experience (Brown, 1993), the foundation of and precursor to a more advanced and expanded awareness of feeling states and their self-management, emerges as an initial capacity

from internalizations of intersubjective episodes in the early holding environment (Winnicott, 1960, 1967) and is represented in neural networks, that is, it is encoded as implicit memories in the affect centers—the limbic system, the amygdala, and the prefrontal orbital cerebral cortex—in the right hemisphere of the asymmetric and bilateral human brain (Schore, 1994, 2003; Siegel, 1999, 2007). These early experiences of intersubjectivity and affect sharing, for example, "feeling felt," serve as a substrate for all later close relationships, including the dialogue in treatment between therapist and client as the two subjective selves mutually interact with one another (Attwood & Stolorow, 1999). When empathically mirrored, the infant self evolves with structure, cohesion, and stability. However, where misalliances, attunement ruptures, and other empathic failures have occurred in the holding environment, the adolescent's therapy must be directed toward their repair in the working-through, middle phase of treatment. At issue here is the development of the affect regulation and reflective functions in the context of an insecure attachment. Impaired IWMs (Internal Working Models), with a potential for internalized representations as an "alien self" are consequences of caretaking that lacks the "markedness" of an accurate perception (the mirroring signal) of the infant's affect state with a clear, "secondary representation" of the infant's actual experience versus that of the caregiver's (Bateman & Fonagy, 2004; Rossouw, 2012, p.133). Because the adolescent phase revisits separation-individuation for the second time, a psychotherapeutic focus on maintaining the alliance throughout this middle phase almost ensures that areas of arrest will be addressed and reworked. Treatment in the middle phase focuses on developing mindsight (Siegel, 1999, 2007), affect regulation (Allen et al., 2008; Fonagy et al., 2002; Panskepp & Biven, 2012; Schore, 1994, 2003), and understanding the adolescent's current relationships in the context of peers and the primary objects of childhood. The mentalizing strategy, as operationalized interventions, starts with the clinician's attitude of active curiosity about the workings of the adolescent mind, as well as his own, and encouragement to explore the working model of the minds of others (Allen et al., 2008; Fonagy et al., 2002). Techniques include the use of metaphorical thought and analogies, exploring fantasies and engaging in the playful, "let's pretend mode" to develop a capacity for safely exploring the more complex emotions, motivations, thoughts, and impulses of self and others. Maintaining an "evenly suspended attention" (Freud, 1912) to the adolescent's productions is essential in a mentalizing therapy because the clinician's default mode, for knowing the minds of others, is egocentric, that is, his or her own. Allen et al. (2008) recommend that the clinicians "quarantine" their own affects as much as possible to ensure that they do not discover in the client only what they expected to find anyway. In this fashion, quarantining one's own affects serves to self-correct the tendency to assume that we know the emotional lives of others solely on the basis of our own feelings. Underscoring the complexity of bringing evidence based practice interventions into the real world of psychotherapy, Cunningham, Foster, and Warner (2010) describe a process research model for multisystem therapy (MST) with difficult to engage African-American adolescents in the juvenile justice system. This validation study included interview data with expert clinicians and a coding system that permitted trained judges to evaluate within-session therapeutically beneficial behaviors (e.g., empathy/validation, mutual storytelling, and strength focus/building hope), as well as statistical measures of reliability, all of which were preparatory for a more elaborate analysis of audio tapes of clinician-client narrative for further content validation of categories describing clinician interventions and client responses.

Schore, D. J. Siegel, Fonagy, and numerous recent theorists, for example, J. P. Siegel (2007), Brown (2008), and Barth (2008), have identified the significance of internalized, unmetabolized, raw affect states (Kernberg, 1985)—the result of alliance ruptures, misattunements, and mirroring failures in early object relations—that become the basis for defensive splitting and projective identification mechanisms as the prototype mode for all close future attachments. An intersubjective, affect-regulating treatment approach naturally activates these projective identification processes in therapy, signifying a reciprocal invitation from one unconscious mind to another to engage in a shared state of affect attunement (Schore, 2003). As the clinician and client pair at this level of the unconscious affect engagement, the synchronous matching of the two right brain hemispheres of client and therapist permits a transfer of accurately mirrored emotions that modifies what had been previously encoded, in implicit memory, as misattuned (Lyons-Ruth, 1999; Trevarthen, 1996). Mentalizing interventions with these projective identification mechanisms in the middle phase of therapy alter the manner in which self and object images, and the attendant affect states, are represented. In this manner, therapeutic empathy detoxifies raw affects, which are reinternalized by the client in a more benign, metabolized, and de-aggressivized representational form (Ogden, 1986, 1994).

TERMINATION

The topic of termination has received relatively scant attention in the clinical literature. Some believe this is due to the fact that the concluding phase of treatment produces the greatest amount of stress and difficulty. Related transference reactions, counterreactions, and countertransference problems, though common, have received little attention as a consequence. How the therapeutic process is brought to a conclusion may in fact be the most important aspect of the entire treatment process, solidifying gains or, if unsuccessful, weakening and undoing the therapeutic work. Ferenczi (1927/1955) was the first to focus specifically on the concluding phase of treatment and noted that completion is attainable "only if unlimited time is at one's disposal" (p. 82). The next significant examination was Freud's (1937/1950) seminal paper, titled "Analysis Terminable and

Interminable," in which he offered guidelines and criteria for concluding analytic work. He emphasized relief of the client's suffering, the conquering of anxieties and inhibitions, and the therapist's conviction that treatment be successful enough to ensure against relapse and repetition of the client's symptoms and pathology. He emphasized sufficient intrapsychic structural change to permit optimal functioning.

Under optimal conditions, when individual psychotherapy has been of sufficient duration to effect a meaningful treatment relationship and corrective emotional experience, the termination phase is of utmost significance. It entails loss and separation, emancipation and growth, and it always reactivates earlier losses and separations that the client has endured. Ideally, the client will conclude treatment feeling strengthened and fortified by the experience of mastering the current loss. Termination can offer an opportunity to rework and modify earlier separation problems; it can evoke panic and rage, guilt and grief, or a sense of accomplishment and mastery.

The classic criteria for termination generally exclude decisions based solely on symptom relief; rather, there is an emphasis on movement beyond points of arrest or fixation and demonstration of the capability to handle ongoing and predictable future developmental and environmental problems. Psychotherapy, in contrast to psychoanalysis, focuses primarily on the here-and-now and on the interaction and interpersonal relationship of client and clinician. Less attention is given to early conflicts, and instead, the focus is on the capacity for reality testing; stronger, more age-appropriate object relationships; and loosened fixations. Particularly with children and adolescents, the young person's failure to develop progressively (or damage that interferes with such growth) is the most significant feature in undermining future mental health (A. Freud, 1962).

Dewald (1964) suggested that for clients treated in insight therapy, indications for termination are some structural change in the personality, the lessening or elimination of symptoms, or evidence of improved capacity to tolerate specific symptoms and conflicts. Other indicators are improvements in relationships, work life, academics, and, more generally, self-awareness and self-control. For those seen in supportive therapy, indications for appropriate termination would be reduction of symptoms, better management of drive expression, improved self-esteem, and cessation of the prior regressive pull. Decisions about termination may be determined by external factors, such as change of locale of the family or the therapist, change of jobs, or conclusion of an internship for a clinician who has been in training.

Clients' reactions to termination are many and varied. With some, conflicts intensify during the conclusion of therapy due to resistance to facing old losses, sadness, and grief. Mourning is often masked by a facade of anger and denial, which may break down, revealing intense grief, sadness, and anxiety. Some clients try to stave off the date of scheduled termination with denial, regression, and resumption of old symptoms.

Countertransference dilemmas are frequent during this phase of treatment. A therapist's overly intense attachment, dislike of a client, therapeutic overambition, or overidentification will interfere with an effective termination. Therapist and client are both affected by the termination phase, the reasons for conclusion of treatment, and the nature of the therapeutic gains achieved and maintained. The real relationship is usually more evident at the conclusion of treatment, since termination connotes a separation between two individuals whose relationship has been in the nature of a collaboration on a precious enterprise (Hurn, 1971). This real relationship must have professional parameters in accord with the prior treatment relationship.

Clinical social work has a long and storied history with research that examines the effectiveness of practice—both long term and brief—with all its myriad service delivery systems, populations, and intervention methods. Significant controversy still exists over the merits of long-term as opposed to short-term treatment (Reid & Shyne, 1968). The most recent literature on these two broad classifications confirms the practice wisdom that long-term, dynamically informed therapies are needed to address complex dysfunctions; further, they produce better results, that is, client improvements, than short-term treatment. Long-term treatment will benefit clients whose multifaceted depressions and chronic symptoms of anxiety (*DSM-IV-TR*, 2000, Axis I) are comorbid with character pathology (*DSM-IV-TR*, 2000, Axis II) and who, therefore, possess serious potential for more than just mild dysfunction relative to social, familial, and occupational responsibilities (Fonagy, Roth, & Higget, 2005; Gabbard, Gunderson, & Fonagy, 2002). Leichsenring and Rabung (2008) subjected this hypothesis to rigorous computer analysis. They compared the outcomes of treatments that were defined as long-term, psychodynamically oriented, and relationship-based with brief treatments using cognitive behavioral therapy (CBT), family therapy, crisis management, supportive psychiatric treatment as usual, or dialectical behavior therapy (DBT). They located 23 such studies in the literature from 1960 to 2007 that conformed to their rigorous inclusion criteria, for example, random assignment of clients to the experimental and comparison conditions or clinical observation/measurement packages with multiple instruments for collecting data and statistical analysis at Times 1 and 2. The long-term treatments were self-defined as psychodynamic (e.g., attachment oriented, ego psychology, or self psychology) and of at least 50 weeks' duration, and interventions comprised a mix of insight-oriented and supportive procedures. Of the more than 1,300 clients (adolescents and young adults) treated in these 23 studies and subsequently subjected to meta-analytic review, fully 96% were better off at the end of their long-term treatments compared with the control clients receiving short-term therapy. Finally, of the 23 outcome research reports that were subjected to this critical review, those adolescent and young adult clients with borderline personality organization receiving mentalization-based, long-term treatment (Bateman & Fonagy, 2001) had the second highest improvement scores of all. In sum, from the

above evidence-based literature, it can be reasonably inferred that mentalizing-based, longer-term psychotherapy would be appropriate for many clinical populations of adolescents. This would include those with depression, anxiety, and other symptoms reflecting a broad range of potential character dysfunctions, because it is in this stage of development that adolescents normatively begin to demonstrate greater maturity in their self-reflective and affect-regulating functions.

The population of adolescents from the above research, which includes teens who evince borderline functioning, those with acting out, externalizing behaviors and conduct disorders, those exhibiting serious depressions and impulsive suicidality, and those with affect dysregulation and nonreflective working models of self and other, have been subjects of a psychotherapeutic model referred to as mentalization-based treatment of adolescents (MBT-A) (Midgley and Vrouva, 2012). MBT-A provides a treatment focus on the adolescent client with weekly individual sessions from trained clinicians, and family therapy conducted at least monthly. It also consists of an extended initial assessment followed by three stages of treatment. This manualized and structured treatment model specifies interventions and goals that are clearly stated: increased capacities for mentalization, enhanced awareness of affect states, and improvements in social cognitions and empathic understanding of the intentions of self and others, that is, a theory of mind (Rossouw, 2012). The MBT-A model both illustrates the complexity of research attempting to measure practice outcomes, and exemplifies therapeutic best practices based on the reciprocal interrelationship of empirical evidence informed by theory and clinical practice.

LATE ADOLESCENCE

Late adolescence is viewed as a stage of consolidation and stabilization. We anticipate and expect clarity and purposeful actions, productivity, constancy of emotions, stable self-esteem, and more mature functioning. Narcissism has lessened, and there is a greater tolerance for frustration, compromise, and delay. In his seminal work on adolescence, Blos (1962) noted that the adolescent strives for

1. a highly idiosyncratic and stable arrangement of ego functions and interests,

2. an extension of the conflict-free sphere of the ego (secondary autonomy),

3. an irreversible sexual position (identity constancy), and

4. the stabilization of mental apparatuses. (p. 129)

Anna Freud (1958) described the five central issues of adolescence as (1) impulses—acceptance versus rebellion, (2) love versus hate of parents, (3) revolt versus dependency, (4) idealism versus narcissism, and (5) generosity versus narcissism. Finally, being "on the way to consolidating" identity for the late-stage adolescent (Lucente, 1996, 2008) involves the following: (a) an adultomorphic body image rooted in one's core gender as unambiguously male or female (Stoller, 1968); (b) mature psychosexual drive organization, that is, genitality and a sexuality that expresses itself via arousal for a preferred erotic object (Erikson, 1959; Freud, 1905, 1923, 1924); (c) autonomous, independent functioning, that is, a second separation-individuation with capacities for object and self-constancy; (d) moral reasoning using hypothetico-deductive thought and internalized ego ideals (Gilligan, 1982; Kohlberg, 1976); (e) an evolved, superordinate ego-superego system that organizes the various components of the personality (Blanck & Blanck, 1974, 1986); and (f) a maturing capacity for affect regulation and related processes, for example, autonoesis, mindsight, and empathy (Allen et al., 2008; Fonagy et al., 2002; Schore, 2003; Siegel, 1999).

Current social realities and the enhanced awareness of the length of time involved in pre-adult personality consolidation, plus adolescents' extended financial dependency and their lengthier academic preparation, have expanded our concept of adolescence and the coextensive mastery of age-appropriate tasks beyond the teenage and even college years. This expanded perspective of adolescence, including Erikson's concept of "moratorium" (a time for continued education, contemplation, role experimentation, or work or travel), has redefined the adolescent stage of life in contemporary Western society.

Beth, an Older Adolescent[3]

Based on this expanded contemporary view of adolescence, Beth, a 21-year-old college graduate from an upper-middle-class, Midwestern Jewish family, may be viewed as an older adolescent. She had not resolved what Anna Freud (1958) noted as the five central issues of adolescence described earlier.

Beth was referred for treatment by her father's previous therapist, following her father's request. She agreed with her father's concerns and seemed motivated for therapy at the onset of contact. She expressed an immediate sense of relief to "be doing something positive now" and was clearly pleased by the natural fit between herself and this clinician (Dr. Mishne). Beth had just moved into the city following college graduation. She was employed at her first job in the fashion industry and, subsidized

(Continued)

---

[3]Beth was treated by the late Dr. Mishne.

(Continued)

by her father, resided in a comfortable semiluxury apartment that she shared with a roommate. She presented as a wholesome and very attractive young woman, with athletic interests and abilities. She described a wide circle of friends from college to whom she was devoted. Much of her time and energy involved friends and shared activities, such as health club daily workouts, jogging, rollerblading, skiing, charity fund-raisers, group gatherings, group summer and ski houses, and going to dinner and clubs with these friends. Beth was devoted to her family and communicated with them constantly, which involved daily calls with her father at his office, frequent evening calls to Dad and his second wife, as well as calls to her older sister, and stormy weekly conversations with her mother.

A combative and conflictual relationship with her mother was a major presenting problem. Weight management and control of her eating was also of real concern. Beth acknowledged a long-standing reading disability, struggles with some academic work, and well-concealed poor self-esteem, secondary to her history of academic problems. This made her uncertain about whether to pursue graduate studies in business, an area of interest and one in which she had achieved notable mastery, given her competence with figures and numbers. Because of her reading disability, Beth shamefully revealed that she was completely unable to engage in many intellectual pursuits and could not even peruse the newspaper by herself at home. She knew that she was an attractive and engaging young person but often felt empty and too eager to keep "busy busy" to distract herself.

Beth dated these feelings back to elementary school. Her academic difficulties surfaced in the fourth grade, at the time of her parents' divorce. Both Beth and her sister were provided psychotherapy as children, and Beth took responsibility to have clinical reports and summaries of her childhood treatment forwarded to me. Following an assessment, she committed herself to biweekly individual psychotherapy, which her father agreed to underwrite. She wanted to work on the problems she had with her mother, weight management, her history of romantic problems with boyfriends, and feeling better about herself. She easily entered into a treatment contract and soon developed a therapeutic alliance.

The process of treatment was a mix—initially supportive, then, insight-oriented psychotherapy, as Beth became less concerned about her present circumstances and future and could reflect on her earlier experiences and observe their later reverberations. Beth was able to move from a posture of rage, disregard, and contempt for her mother to a position whereby she felt and demonstrated greater empathy and compassion for her mother and for herself. As her controls improved, there was a decided improvement in her transactions with her mother and diminution of the long-standing guilt that had always followed her explosions and rebelliousness. Beth's mother, who was self-employed, was described as a warm and intelligent woman who was very attractive despite her being grossly overweight. She was overly dependent on her own parents and seemed to be stuck in self-defeating patterns that had prevented her from remarrying or becoming romantically connected with a genuinely available partner since her divorce.

Beth's anger and shame about her mother's life appeared to be a natural outcome of her mother's long-term involvement with a married man and her inability to sever this connection. Beth's mother was unable to break off this relationship despite her supposed personal aspirations and years of promises to Beth that she would do so. Beth's greater enjoyment of time with her father and stepmother generated eternal conflicts between Beth and her mother. It also gave rise to demands and accusations from her mother, followed by Beth's explosive verbal abuse, and finally Beth's reactive guilt. As she reflected on the long-standing nature of their conflict, Beth came to recognize her lack of complete and genuine separation-individuation from her mother; furthermore, she seemed to mirror her mother in weight management problems and in her unwise romantic choices of boyfriends who did not treat her well.

The manifest transference was one of idealization, with the therapist being perceived as the all-good, empathic idealized maternal object. The corresponding counterreaction or countertransference (Marcus, 1980) can be best described as a positive maternal one, with the therapist taking care and attention not to impose her personal values or goals (e.g., enrollment in graduate school) on Beth. Using a self psychology perspective, interpretations were offered to assist in structure building. In addition to better cognition and insight, the goals of Beth's treatment involved the opening of pathways of empathy between Beth and her mother and the deepening of Beth's capacity for self-acceptance and empathy for herself and her mother. A further objective was the development of greater self-cohesion, which evolved through transmuting internalization, that is, the internal changes that occur as clients develop a "capacity to accept the hurts that are caused by failures of optimal responses by important others" (Solomon, 1991, p. 132).

After 2 years of therapy, Beth appeared to demonstrate a significant degree of working through. As a consequence, it seemed unlikely that she would regress to the earlier mother-daughter rageful battles or food management difficulties. Out of identification with the therapist and the therapeutic work, she made substantial gains. She became less impulsive and less erratic with food management, resolved her feelings of love versus hate for her mother, was more realistic and less worshipful of her father, and assumed greater responsibility for her finances. She was able to increase her earnings and savings, was more independent of her father (save for therapy bills), and was idealistic and generous about giving, emotionally, to all in her family, as well as her friends. She made additional gains in romantic relationships, and although she was not involved in an exclusive attachment, she enjoyed far better relationships with boyfriends of late.

Termination was decided on by Beth, based on her feeling strengthened and fortified by the treatment experience. She felt ready "to graduate" because of the elimination of symptoms and presenting problems and improvements in her relationships, work performance, self-esteem, and self-control. The real relationship was more evident during the planned termination phase, with Beth's commenting on the closeness and support she felt she had received. She indicated comfort at the thought that she could and would return at any point if she found it necessary. Beth appeared to have resolved the tasks of late adolescence at the conclusion of therapy. Accordingly, no objections or questions were raised about her decision, since it is crucial to effect an appropriate letting go of adolescent clients based on the therapist's surrender of omnipotent hopes of safeguarding the adolescent client against future dangers, life's vicissitudes, and regression. One must allow the adolescent the opportunity to take the chance of independent passage (Ekstein, 1983).

REFLECTIONS ON THE TREATMENT PROCESS

Work with Beth was supportive and empathic, and the self psychology perspective was employed. In a warm and friendly ambience, the therapist permitted and encouraged emotional availability and spontaneity, and the treatment process focused on techniques of understanding, explanations, and interpretations of Beth's demands, hopes, ambitions, struggles, and symptomatic behaviors. Beth's lack of separation and individuation from her mother was viewed not from the perspective of oedipal anxiety or fears of oedipal victory but rather as the effects of disintegration anxiety, mild learning disability, and the mortification inherent in the lack of early mastery of academics. Beth's aggression and adhesive negative attachment to her mother were redefined, not ignored, and the therapist, through interpretive linkages and genetic reflection, enabled Beth to understand her bond of anger as the result of her shame over her mother's weight, poor self-control, and long involvement with a married man. Interpretations, when offered, focused on Beth's low self-esteem and embarrassment about herself and her mother rather than her overadmiration and idealization of her father, the more competent and effective parent. There was no focus on Beth's faulty functioning but rather an effort to understand the underlying structure responsible for the faulty functioning. By providing experience-near explanations of Beth's self-experiences, she was aided in developing self-soothing techniques and understanding more accurately her retaliatory responses to her mother's repeated traumatizing empathic failures. The self psychology approach avoided critical confrontation with Beth's evasions, demands, and excitability; the therapist's reflections instead focused on providing the origins and explanations of her actions and behavior.

The goal of enhancement of Beth's self-perceptions was achieved, as evident in her growing capacity to empathize with herself and her mother and better understand the shortcomings in their selfobject bond. She demonstrated insight into her mother's relationship with Beth's maternal grandparents and was thereby able to experience greater tolerance and compassion toward her mother. Additional educational interventions addressed her learning disability and its short-term and long-term effects on her self-esteem. Greater understanding enabled Beth to exert better self-control and tone down her affective exchanges with her mother and her boyfriends. In addition, she began to consider the possibility of graduate school courses. She also demonstrated improved performance at her job, evident from the promotions and increased responsibility given to her.

In the transference, Beth idealized the therapist as the good mother who is consistently patient, calm, and empathic. Through identification and transmuting internalization, Beth felt less frantic or overwhelmed and increasingly could engage in well-modulated and controlled deliberations and problem solving. With better self-control and self-understanding, she was also able to surrender her tough demeanor, which she came to understand as her defensive facade in disagreements. When disappointed by her mother or a boyfriend, Beth learned to relate in a more benign and less reactive manner; imperfections and small slights from others now could be experienced as manageable. With better self/other distinctions, learned in treatment, Beth felt less provoked and personally diminished by the inconsiderate behavior of others. She came to see herself and the other more realistically and, with this enhanced self-acceptance, was better able to accept her imperfect mother and the shortcomings of her friends. Beth's mother was able to respond positively to Beth's improved mode of relating to her, and this was vividly demonstrated when Beth required surgery. Beth's mother as well as her father came to be with her, and her mother functioned in a considerate parental fashion, with a noticeable absence of the explosive arguments, accusations, and childish demands that Beth's mother typically made of her.

Beth's treatment was initially supportive and then shifted to an insight-oriented focus. Beth seemed to benefit and grow from the curative effect of the "correctional emotional experience" (Kohut, 1984, p. 78). The improvements seemingly evolved out of a therapeutic dialogue that provided understanding and explanations of what went wrong in Beth's early childhood and throughout her adolescence.

CONCLUSION

Adolescents are generally recognized as one of the most difficult age-groups to treat. Some clinicians and researchers do not believe that adolescents can actually engage in and maintain a therapeutic alliance. Others believe that only short-term periods of therapy are possible, with adolescents coming for help periodically when stress becomes overwhelming. A number of writers recommend the setting of only moderate goals, specifically to increase the ego's tolerance for conflicts and to improve reality testing. Since teenagers attempt to disengage from their parents, many resist any dependent relationship with an adult parental figure. The decathexis from parental love objects often results in impoverishment of the ego because of the pain and mourning associated with the loss of the close and loving parent-child ties. This mourning process may leave little ego energy for attachment to an individual therapist. Frequently encountered treatment obstacles in work with adolescent clients have consisted of a lowered threshold for frustration, a preference for action rather than verbalization of feelings, and new weaknesses and immaturities of ego structure. Because of adolescent narcissistic withdrawal, many teenagers have little if any libidinal energy available with which to explore their past or relate in the present. Because of all these realities and the specific vulnerabilities of adolescents, supportive, empathic treatment is the best beginning intervention, and some judicious, therapeutic self-disclosures may be very appropriate in facilitating engagement (Lucente, 2012). Insight-oriented psychotherapy may later be possible if the alliance is positive and when the teenager is motivated to seek greater self-understanding and mastery of age-appropriate tasks.

The adolescent therapist is cautioned regarding the use of confrontation to avoid the possibility of regressive fragmentation. Many adolescents are not candidates for group or family therapy, because of the stressors in the family or because some are unable to empathize with peers or tolerate public self-exposure due to their shaky self-esteem or self-regard. Group and family interventions can be threatening to many adolescents who are very sensitive to criticism and self-conscious with peers. Individual psychotherapy is appropriate for the widest range of adolescents: the severely disturbed, the teenager in a traumatic home situation, or one who presents a habit disorder, ego deficits, or developmental disability.

Specialization in adolescent therapy can begin only during formal clinical education. Adolescents present special demands; their communications are frequently unclear, and they are reticent, resistance prone, and rebellious, with a propensity for action rather than words and the sharing of feelings. Work with this population requires lengthy, ongoing training, experience, and supervision.

In addition, to be able to do intensive psychotherapy with adolescents, aspiring therapists, regardless of discipline, may require some personal treatment in order to develop a therapeutic, objective, empathic response that both embodies self-awareness and self-observation and controls against regression and countertransferential acting out with adolescent clients. We may or may not have encountered, struggled with, or lived through the identical pain and stresses that our clients experience, but as adolescents, we once all engaged in the same developmental struggles for autonomy, separation, and individuation. We have also suffered the same fears of narcissistic injury and failure as our teenage clients. We once encountered with alarm, anxiety, and excitement our first love, erotic arousal, and sexual and emotional intimacy. Thus, clinical work with adolescents strikes continuous, responsive chords in all therapists in a unique, though stressful manner, which must be recognized and contained.

REFERENCES

Alexander, F. (1953). Current views on psychotherapy. In *The scope of psychoanalysis: Selected papers of Franz Alexander, 1921–1961* (pp. 276–289). New York, NY: Basic Books.

Alexander, F. (1963). The dynamics of psychotherapy in the league of learning theory. *American Journal of Psychiatry, 120,* 440–448.

Allen, J. G., Fonagy, P., & Bateman, A. W. (2008). *Mentalizing in clinical practice.* Washington, DC: American Psychiatric.

American Psychiatric Association. (2000). *Diagnostic and statistical manual of mental disorders* (4th ed., text rev.). Washington, DC: Author.

Atwood, G., & Stolorow, R. (1999). *Faces in a cloud: Intersubjectivity in personality theory.* Northvale, NJ: Jason Aronson.

Barth, D. F. (2008). Hidden eating disorders: Attachment and affect regulation in the therapeutic relationship. *Clinical Social Work Journal, 36*(4), 355–366.

Basch, M. (1980). *Doing psychotherapy.* New York, NY: Basic Books.

Bateman, S. W., & Fonagy, P. (2001). Treatment of borderline personality disorder with psychoanalytically oriented partial hospitalization: An 18 months follow-up. *American Journal of Psychiatry, 158*(1), 36–42.

Bateman, S. W., & Fonagy, P. (2004). *Psychotherapy for borderline personality disorder: Mentalization-based treatment.* Oxford: Oxford University Press.

Bennett, C. C., Naylor, R. B., Perri, C. S., Shirilla, R. G., & Kilbane, T. (2008). Managed care's influence on clinical decision making. *Praxis, 8*(8), 57–68.

Blanck, G., & Blanck, R. (1974). *Ego psychology: Theory and practice.* New York, NY: Columbia University Press.

Blanck, G., & Blanck, R. (1986). *Beyond ego psychology: Developmental object relations theory.* New York, NY: Columbia University Press.

Blos, P. (1962). *On adolescence.* New York, NY: Free Press.

Blos, P. (1970). *The young adolescent: Clinical studies.* New York, NY: Free Press.

Bowlby, J. (1969). *Attachment and loss: Vol. 1. Attachment.* New York, NY: Free Press.

Brandell, J. R. (2004). *Psychodynamic social work.* New York, NY: Columbia University Press.

Brenner, C. (1982). *The mind in conflict.* Madison, CT: International Universities Press.

Brown, D. (1993). Affect development, psychopathology, and adaptation. In S. L. Ablon, D. Brown, E. J. Khantzian, & J. E. Mack (Eds.), *Human feelings: Explorations in affect development and meaning* (pp. 5–66). Hillsdale, NJ: Analytic Press.

Brown, W. G. (2008). Failure to mentalize: Defect or defense? *Psychoanalytic Social Work, 15*(1), 28–42.

Campbell, R. J. (1981). *Psychiatric dictionary* (5th ed.). New York, NY: Oxford University Press.

Cunningham, P. B., Foster, L. F., & Warner, S. E. (2010). Culturally relevant family-based treatment for adolescent delinquency and substance abuse: Understanding within-session processes. *Journal of Clinical Psychology: In session. 66*(8), 830–846. Wiley.

Dewald, P. (1964). *Psychotherapy: A dynamic approach.* New York, NY: Basic Books.

Ekstein, R. (1983). The adolescent self during the process of termination of treatment: Termination, interruption or intermission. In M. Sugar, S. Feinstein, J. Looney, A. Swartzberg, & A. Sorosky (Eds.), *Adolescent psychiatry: Vol 9. Developmental and clinical studies* (pp. 125–146). Chicago, IL: University of Chicago Press.

Erikson, E. H. (1959). Identity and the life cycle: Selected papers. In G. S. Klein (Ed.), *Psychological issues* (Vol. 1, pp. 18–171). New York, NY: International Universities Press.

Erikson, E. H. (1963). *Childhood and society* (2nd ed.). New York, NY: W. W. Norton.

Erikson, E. H. (1968). Theoretical interlude. In E. Erikson (Ed.), *Identity: Youth and crisis* (pp. 208–231). New York, NY: W. W. Norton.

Ferenczi, S. (1955). The problem of the termination of the analysis. In M. Balint (Ed.), *Final contributions to the problems and methods of psychoanalysis* (pp. 77–86). New York, NY: Basic Books. (Original work published 1927)

Fonagy, P., Gergely, G., Jurist, E., & Target, M. (2002). *Affect regulation, mentalization, and the development of the self.* New York, NY: W. W. Norton.

Fonagy, P., Roth, A., & Higget, A. (2005). Psychodynamic therapies, evidence-based practice, and clinical wisdom. *Bulletin of the Menninger Clinic, 69*(1), 1–58.

Freud, A. (1958). Adolescence. *Psychoanalytic Study of the Child, 13,* 255–278.

Freud, A. (1962). Assessment of childhood disturbances. *Psychoanalytic Study of the Child, 17,* 149–158.

Freud, A. (1965). Normality and pathology in childhood: Assessment of development. In *The writings of Anna Freud* (Vol. 6, pp. 3–7). New York, NY: International Universities Press.

Freud, A. (1978). The role of insight in psychoanalysis and psychotherapy: Introduction to the Anna Freud Hampstead Center Symposium, held at the Michigan Psychoanalytic Society, March. In H. P. Blum (Ed.), *Psychoanalytic explorations of technique: Discourse on the theory of therapy* (pp. 29–40). New York, NY: International Universities Press.

Freud, S. (1905). *Three essays on the theory of sexuality.* In J. Strachey (Ed. & Trans.), *The standard edition of the complete psychological works of Sigmund Freud* (Vol. 7). London, UK: Hogarth Press.

Freud, S. (1912). The dynamics of transference. In J. Strachey (Ed. & Trans.), *The standard edition of the complete psychological works of Sigmund Freud* (Vol. 12, pp. 97–108). London, UK: Hogarth Press.

Freud, S. (1915). Observations on transference love. In J. Strachey (Ed. & Trans.), *The standard edition of the complete psychological works of Sigmund Freud* (Vol. 12, pp. 157–171). London, UK: Hogarth Press.

Freud, S. (1916–1917). Introductory lectures on psychoanalysis. In J. Strachey (Ed. & Trans.), *The standard edition of the complete psychological works of Sigmund Freud* (Vol. 12, pp. 15–16). London, UK: Hogarth Press.

Freud, S. (1923). The ego and the id. In J. Strachey (Ed. & Trans.), *The standard edition of the complete psychological works of Sigmund Freud* (Vol. 19, pp. 1–66). London, UK: Hogarth Press.

Freud, S. (1924). The passing of the Oedipus complex. In J. Strachey (Ed. & Trans.), *The standard edition of the complete psychological works of Sigmund Freud* (Vol. 19). London, UK: Hogarth Press.

Freud, S. (1950). Analysis terminable and interminable. In J. Strachey (Ed. & Trans.), *Collected papers* (Vol. 5, pp. 316–357). London, UK: Hogarth Press. (Original work published 1937)

Frieswyk, S. H., Allen, J. G., & Colson, D. B. (1986). Therapeutic alliance: Its place as a process and outcome variable in dynamic psychotherapy research. *Journal of Consulting and Clinical Psychology, 54,* 32–38.

Furman, E. (1980). Transference and externalization in latency. *Psychoanalytic Study of the Child, 3*(5), 267–284.

Gabbard, G. O., Gunderson, J. G., & Fonagy, P. (2002). The place of psychoanalytic treatments within psychiatry. *Archives of General Psychiatry, 59*(6), 505–510.

Gilligan, C. (1982). *In a different voice.* Cambridge, MA: Harvard University Press.

Ginott, H. (1961). *Group psychotherapy with children.* New York, NY: McGraw-Hill.

Giovacchini, P. (1985). Countertransference and the severely disturbed adolescent. In M. Sugar, S. Feinstein, J. Looney, A. Swartzberg, & A. Sorosky (Eds.), *Adolescent psychiatry: Vol 12. Developmental and clinical studies* (pp. 449–467). Chicago, IL: University of Chicago Press.

Giovacchini, P. (1987). *A narrative textbook of psychoanalysis.* Northvale, NJ: Jason Aronson.

Goldberg, A. (1972). On the incapacity to love: A psychotherapeutic approach to the problem in adolescence. *Archives of General Psychiatry, 26,* 3–7.

Heacock, D. R. (1966). Modification of the standard techniques for out-patient group psychotherapy with delinquent boys. *Journal of the National Medical Association, 58,* 41–47.

Herman, J. L. (1992). *Trauma and recovery.* New York, NY: Basic Books.

Horvath, A. D., & Symonds, B. D. (1991). Relation between working alliance and outcome in psychotherapy: A meta-analysis. *Journal of Counseling Psychology, 38,* 139–149.

Hurn, H. T. (1971). Toward a paradigm of the terminal phase. *Journal of the American Psychoanalytic Association, 19,* 332–348.

Kardiner, A., & Spiegel, A. (1947). *War, stress and neurotic illness: The traumatic neuroses of war* (Rev. ed.). New York, NY: Hoeber.

Kernberg, O. (1985). *Borderline conditions and pathological narcissism.* Northvale, NJ: Jason Aronson.

Kohlberg, L. (1976). Moral stages and moralization: The cognitive-developmental approach. In T. Lickona (Ed.), *Moral development and behavior* (pp. 31–53). New York, NY: Holt, Rinehart & Winston.

Kohut, H. (1971). *The analysis of the self.* New York, NY: International Universities Press.

Kohut, H. (1978a). Introspection, empathy and psychoanalysis: An examination of the relationship between mode of observation and theory. In P. H. Ornstein (Ed.), *The search for the self: Selected writings of Heinz Kohut, 1950–1978* (Vol. 2, pp.

205–232). New York, NY: International Universities Press.

Kohut, H. (1978b). The psychoanalyst in the community of scholars. In P. H. Ornstein (Ed.), *The search for the self* (Vol. 2, pp. 685–721). New York, NY: International Universities Press.

Kohut, H. (1984). *How does analysis cure?* (A. Goldberg & P. Stepansky, Eds.). Chicago, IL: University of Chicago Press.

Lawson, D. M., & Brossart, D. F. (2003). Link among therapies and parent relationship, working alliance, and therapy outcome. *Psychotherapy Research, 13,* 383–394.

Leichsenring, F., & Rabung, S. (2008). Effectiveness of long term psychodynamic psychotherapy: A meta-analysis. *Journal of the American Medical Association, 300*(13), 1551–1565.

Luborsky, L., Mintz, J., Auerbach, A., Christoph, P., Bachrach, H., Todd, T., et al. (1980). Predicting the outcome of psychotherapy: Findings of the Penn Psychotherapy Research Project. *Archives of General Psychiatry, 37,* 471–481.

Lucente, R. L. (1980). *An analog study of clinical social work processes: Ego diagnosis and psychosocial treatment.* Ann Arbor, MI: University Microfilms International.

Lucente, R. L. (1986). Self-transcending and the adolescent ego ideal. *Child and Adolescent Social Work Journal, 3*(3), 161–176.

Lucente, R. L. (1996). Sexual identity: Conflict and confusion in a male adolescent. *Child and Adolescent Social Work Journal, 13*(2), 97–114.

Lucente, R. L. (2008). Affectivity: Regulation, identity formation, and metaphorical thought. *Psychoanalytic Social Work, 15*(1), 1–27.

Lucente, R.L. (2012). *Character formation and identity in adolescence: Clinical and developmental issues.* Chicago, IL: Lyceum.

Lynch, V. J. (1991). Basic concepts. In H. Jackson (Ed.), *Using self psychology in psychotherapy* (pp. 15–25). Northvale, NJ: Jason Aronson.

Lyons-Ruth, K. (1999). Two person unconscious: Intersubjective dialogue, enactive relational representation, and the emergence of new forms of relational organization. *Psychoanalytic Inquiry, 19,* 576–617.

Mahler, M., Pine, F., & Bergman, A. (1975). *The psychological birth of the human infant.* New York, NY: Basic Books.

Main, M., & Solomon, J. (1986). Discovery of an insecure-disorganized/disoriented attachment pattern. In T. B. Brazelton & M. Yogman (Eds.), *Affective development in infancy* (pp. 95–124). Norwood, NJ: Ablex.

Marcus, I. (1980). Countertransference and the psychoanalytic process in children and adolescents. *Psychoanalytic Study of the Child, 35,* 285–298.

Martin, D. J., Garske, J. P., & Davis, K. K. (2000). Relation of the therapeutic alliance with outcome and other variables: A meta-analytic review. *Journal of Consulting and Clinical Psychology, 68,* 438–450.

Marziali, E., Marmar, D., & Krupnick, J. (1981). Therapeutic alliance scales: Development and relationship to psychotherapy outcome. *American Journal of Psychiatry, 138,* 361–364.

McKenzie, F. R. (2008). *Theory and practice with adolescents.* Chicago, IL: Lyceum Books.

Meeks, J., & Bernet, W. (2001). *The fragile alliance* (5th ed.). New York, NY: Krieger.

Midgley, N., & Vrouva, I., Eds. (2012). *Minding the child: Mentalization-based interventions with children, young people, and their families.* London, UK: Routledge.

Mishne, J. (1983). *Clinical work with children.* New York, NY: Free Press.

Mishne, J. (1986). *Clinical work with adolescents.* New York, NY: Free Press.

Mishne, J. (1993). *The evolution and application of clinical theory: Perspectives from four psychologies.* New York, NY: Free Press.

Offer, D., & Vanderstoep, E. (1975). Indications and contraindications for family therapy. In M. Sugar (Ed.), *The adolescent in group and family therapy* (pp. 145–160). New York, NY: Brunner/Mazel.

Ogden, T. H. (1986). *The matrix of the mind.* Northvale, NJ: Jason Aronson.

Ogden, T. H. (1994). The analytic third: Working with intersubjective clinical facts. *International Journal of Psychoanalysis, 75,* 3–19.

Ornstein, P. (1978). *The search for the self: Selected writings of Heinz Kohut 1950–1978* (Vol. 1). New York, NY: International Universities Press.

Panskepp, J., & Biven, L. (2012). *The archaeology of the mind: Neuroevolutionary origins of human emotions.* New York, NY: W. W. Norton.

PDM Task Force. (2006). *Psychodynamic diagnostic manual.* Silver Springs, MD: Alliance of Psychoanalytic Organizations.

Piaget, J. (1950). *The psychology of intelligence.* London, UK: Routledge & Kegan Paul.

Reid, W. J., & Shyne, A. W. (1968). *Brief and extended casework.* New York, NY: Columbia University Press.

Rockland, L. H. (1989). *Supportive psychotherapy: A psychodynamic approach.* New York, NY: Basic Books.

Rossouw, T. (2012). Self-harm in young people: Is MBT the answer? In N. Midgley & I. Vrouva (Eds.). *Minding the child: Mentalization-based interventions with children, young people, and their families.* London, UK: Routledge.

Saleebey, D. (2000). Power in the people: Strength and hope. *Advances in Social Work, 1*(2), 127–136.

Sander, L. W. (2002). Thinking differently: Principles of process in living systems and the specificity of being known. *Psychoanalytic Dialogues, 12*(1), 11–42.

Sandler, J., Kennedy, H., & Tyson, P. L. (1980). *The technique of child psychotherapy: Discussions with Anna Freud.* Cambridge, MA: Harvard University Press.

Schore, D. N. (1994). *Affect regulation and the origin of the self: The neurobiology of emotional development.* Hillsdale, NJ: Lawrence Erlbaum.

Schore, D. N. (2003). *Affect regulation and the repair of the self.* New York, NY: W. W. Norton.

Siegel, D. J. (1999). *The developing mind: How relationships and the brain interact to shape who we are.* New York, NY: Guilford Press.

Siegel, J. P. (2007). The role of affect regulation in a case of attempted maternal-filicide suicide: Commentary on an act of despair. *Clinical Social Work Journal, 35*(4), 223–228.

Solomon, M. F. (1991). Adults. In H. Jackson (Ed.), *Using self psychology in psychotherapy* (pp. 117–133). Northvale, NJ: Jason Aronson.

Stern, D. B. (1983). Unformulated experience: From familiar chaos to creative disorder. *Contemporary Psychoanalysis, 19*(1), 71–99.

Stoller, R. (1968). *Sex and gender: On the development of masculinity and femininity.* New York, NY: Science House.

Symonds, M. (1982). Victim responses to terror: Understanding and treatment. In F. Ochberg & D. Soskis (Eds.), *Victims of terrorism* (pp. 95–104). Boulder, CO: Western University.

Tomkins, S. (1962). *Affect, imagery, consciousness: Vol. 1. The positive affects.* New York, NY: Springer.

Tomkins, S. (1963). *Affect, imagery, consciousness: Vol. 2. The negative affects.* New York, NY: Springer.

Trevarthen, C. (1996). Lateral assymetries in infancy: Implications for the development of the hemispheres. *Neuroscience and Biobehavioral Reviews, 20,* 571–586.

Winnicott, D. W. (1951). Transitional objects and transitional phenomena. In *Through pediatrics to psychoanalysis* (pp. 229–242). New York, NY: Basic Books.

Winnicott, D. W. (1956). Primary maternal preoccupation. In *Through pediatrics to psychoanalysis* (pp. 300–315). New York: Basic Books.

Winnicott, D. W. (1960). The theory of the parent-infant relationship. In *The maturational process and the facilitating environment* (pp. 37–55). New York, NY: International Universities Press.

Winnicott, D. W. (1967). *The location of cultural experience: Playing and reality.* New York, NY: Basic Books.

Woods, M., & Hollis, F. (2000). *Case work: A psychosocial therapy.* New York, NY: McGraw-Hill.

7

FAMILY THERAPY

Systemic Approaches to Practice

FROMA WALSH

FAMILY SYSTEMS THEORY AND PRACTICE

Family systems theory has become an essential framework to understand human functioning and dysfunction in context. Over recent decades, family therapy theory and practice have become more responsive to the growing diversity and complexity of families in our changing world. This chapter first summarizes core concepts in a family systems orientation, with a focus on the interaction of biopsychosocial-spiritual influences, a multigenerational family life cycle perspective, and a conceptual model of family stress and resilience. Family assessment guidelines are offered, including a framework identifying key processes in family functioning and resilience to inform strengths-oriented family intervention. An overview is provided of foundational models of family therapy and more recent collaborative, community-based approaches and evidence-based models. Current practices include varied intervention formats with individuals, couples, and families, from consultation and brief therapy to multisystemic approaches, multifamily groups, and more intensive family therapy.

EVOLUTION OF THE FIELD

The family and larger social forces have been recognized as major influences in individual functioning from the early focus in social work on the person-in-environment. In the mid-20th century, with the ascendancy of the psychoanalytic model in the mental health field, attention narrowed to the early mother-child bond, with maternal deficiencies blamed for individual disturbances throughout life. The richness and complexity of family life tended to be reduced to a pathogenic role of the mother, who was seen in practice, if at all, apart from the treatment of the primary client. A paradigm shift occurred in the late 1950s with the development of general system theory, communications theory, and cybernetics (Bateson, 1979; Watzlawick, Beavin, & Jackson, 1967). Direct observation of whole families in studies of schizophrenia shifted attention from etiological questions of problem origin to ongoing transactional processes that reinforced disturbed behavior or distress. Therapeutic interventions were designed to alter dysfunctional patterns in family sessions. The rapid expansion of theory and family approaches to treat a wide range of problems led to the emergence of foundational models in the 1970s, each with distinct views of problem maintenance, change processes, and techniques to achieve objectives.

Over recent decades, family therapy theory and practice have been reformulated and expanded by a new generation of family systems scholars and practitioners. With a broad biopsychosocial systemic perspective, greater attention is given to biological and sociocultural influences. Issues concerning race, class, gender, and sexual orientation, neglected in earlier models, are addressed. Systems approaches have become more responsive to the growing diversity of families and the complexity of their challenges. Focus has been redirected from family deficits and dysfunction to family challenges and resources in collaborative approaches aiming to strengthen family functioning and resilience. Although family therapy approaches vary, they share a common grounding in systems theory.

Family Systems Orientation

The practice of family therapy is grounded in a set of basic assumptions about the mutual influence of family members and the interplay of individual, family, and sociocultural processes. Ecological and developmental perspectives are interwoven in viewing the family as a transactional system that functions in relation to its broader sociocultural context and evolves over the multigenerational family life cycle. Stressful events and problems of an individual member affect the whole family as a functional unit, with ripple effects for all members and their relationships. In turn, family processes—in relating and handling problems—contribute significantly to positive adaptation or to individual and relational dysfunction.

Systemic Lens: Relational and Interactional Perspective

Family therapy is not simply a therapeutic modality in which all members are seen conjointly.

A family systems approach is distinguished less by who is in the room and more by the clinician's attention to relationships and systemic patterns in assessment and intervention. Therapists consider (a) how family members may contribute to and are affected by problem situations, (b) how they can be resources in solving problems, and (c) how family bonds and functioning can be strengthened for greater well-being and positive growth.

Regardless of the source of problems, therapists involve key family members who can contribute to needed changes. Individuals may be seen separately or brought together for some sessions in different combinations, depending on therapeutic aims. Therapy may focus on strengthening a couple relationship; it might combine individual and conjoint sessions, as with an adolescent and parents. Siblings, grandparents, and other key extended family members might be involved in some sessions. Family interventions aim to modify dysfunctional patterns, tap family resources, facilitate communication and problem solving, and strengthen both individual and family functioning.

Mutual Influences and Accountability

Family members are interconnected such that each individual affects all others, who in turn affect the first member in a circular chain of influence. Every action is also a reaction: A father's harsh response to a child's tantrum may exacerbate his or her out-of-control behavior. Ongoing conflict between parents over the handling of an adolescent's misbehavior can make matters worse. Parents can become polarized, one overly strict and the other overly lenient, each in reaction to the other. In tracking the *sequence of interactions* around a presenting problem, therapists note repetitive patterns. Whenever parents start to argue, a child—or a pet—demands attention. Regardless of how a sequence began, family members can be helped to pull together as a team in order to handle stresses and problems more effectively. Skilled intervention involves interrupting vicious cycles to promote virtuous cycles and problem resolution.

Although processes may be circular, not all participants have equal power or influence. Feminist critique of early systems therapy brought recognition of the culturally based, gendered power differential, as well as the generational hierarchy, in families and society, which contributes to abuse of women and children (McGoldrick, Anderson, & Walsh, 1989). Family therapists have become alert not to take a neutral stance or a no-fault circular influence position, which can perpetuate abuse. It is imperative to hold an offending individual accountable for harmful behavior. Therapists also are cautioned not to endanger a partner or children by pressing them to reveal mistreatment in the presence of an offender, who may punish them after the session. The safety and security of vulnerable family members is always a top priority in all family therapy.

Biopsychosocial-Spiritual Orientation

The practice of family therapy, grounded in biopsychosocial systems theory (Bertalanffy, 1968), increasingly addresses the complex interplay of individual, family, and social processes. The profound influence of biological influences in medical and psychiatric conditions and in psychosocial well-being is well established. Yet research finds strong mutually interactive effects of genetic and neurobiological influences with environmental factors (Siegel, 2012; Spotts, 2012). Family relationships and significant interpersonal transactions can have a strong mediating influence over the life course.

Putting an ecological perspective into practice, individual or family distress is understood and treated in sociocultural context. A systemic approach addresses the family's interface with larger systems, such as school, workplace, justice, and health care systems. It attends to cultural, political, and socioeconomic influences and addresses harmful social and institutionalized discrimination, injustice, and marginalization, based on race, ethnicity, religion, class, gender, sexual orientation, age, or disabilities (McGoldrick & Hardy, 2008). Where problems are primarily biologically based, as in autism, or are largely fueled by social, political, or economic conditions, family distress may result from unsuccessful attempts to cope with an overwhelming situation. For instance, conflict between the parents of an adolescent with bipolar disorder may be fueled by repeated unsuccessful attempts to deal with their child's emotional outbursts. A systemic assessment guides intervention focus on most relevant system levels, with the family as an essential partner in achieving aims.

The significant role of religion and spirituality in physiological and psychosocial distress, healing, and resilience has been documented in a growing body of research on faith beliefs and practices, such as prayer and meditation (Koenig & King, 2012). In family therapy, multifaith as well as multicultural perspectives can guide respectful inquiry to understand spiritual sources of distress and identify potential spiritual resources that fit the client's belief systems and preferences (Walsh, 2009b; Walsh, 2010). Incorporating the spiritual dimension of human experience in theory and practice expands the systemic lens to a biopsychosocial-spiritual orientation.

With multiple influences, clinicians need to be careful not to presume a family causal role in individual symptoms or relational distress. Parents often feel blamed for a child's problems and shamed for their inability to resolve them. Sensitive family intervention addresses family stress and helps members tap resources and find more effective ways to approach their challenges.

MULTIGENERATIONAL FAMILY LIFE CYCLE PERSPECTIVE

In a systemic model, individual and family developments are seen to coevolve over the life course and across the generations (McGoldrick,

Garcia- Preto, & Carter, 2014). Relationships grow and change, boundaries shift, roles are redefined, and new members and losses require adaptation. Each developmental phase poses new challenges. Distress often occurs around major transitions, such as the birth of the first child, entry into adolescence, the launching of young adults, retirement, or elder care challenges. Divorce, single parenting, and stepfamily integration pose additional challenges for many families. The growing diversity of family forms, lifestyle options, and timing of nodal events makes it imperative that no single model or life trajectory be deemed essential for healthy development (Walsh, 2012). Over an expanded life course, family members are increasingly likely to transition in and out of single status, couple bonds, and varied family configurations, adding complexity to all relationships.

Family history and relational patterns are transmitted across the generations, influencing future expectations, hopes, and dreams. Some families become stuck in the past; others cut off emotionally from painful memories and contacts. Well-functioning families are better able to connect their past, present, and future direction. Family therapists help clients make linkages, reconnecting with valued aspects of family and cultural heritage and learning from the past as they chart their future course.

Family Stress, Coping, and Resilience

Individual symptoms and family distress are often triggered by a serious crisis, trauma, or loss within the family or in the larger community, such as the death of a loved one, job or home loss, or major disaster. Distress may be fueled by a disruptive transition, such as migration, family separation, divorce, or stepfamily formation. Families can become overwhelmed by a pileup of stressors or the cumulative impact of recurrent or persistent challenges with chronic illness or harsh conditions of poverty. Major stressors affect the entire family,

often contributing to conflict, abuse, divorce, and both relational and residential instability. Some families are shattered, yet others adapt and even grow stronger out of adversity. The family response can make a difference.

Individual counseling that attends only to a symptomatic member may leave other family members and the family unit at risk. For instance, combat-related trauma can generate secondary trauma for a spouse, marital conflict, and distress for children and other members through ongoing transactions affected by posttraumatic stress;. When the family support system is strengthened, individual and relational healing are fostered. As another example, research finds that the death of a child heightens risk of parental estrangement and divorce. Yet when partners are helped to support each other through the healing process, their bond is strengthened, with positive ripple effects to relationships with children and other family members (Walsh & McGoldrick, 2004).

Family resilience is the ability of the family to rebound from life crises and persistent challenges, emerging strengthened and more resourceful (Walsh, 2003). It involves dynamic processes that foster positive adaptation in the context of significant adversity (Rutter, 1987). The concept of family resilience expands focus beyond a dyadic view—seeing a family member as a resource for individual resilience—to a systemic perspective on risk and resilience in the family as a functional unit (McCubbin, McCubbin, McCubbin, & Futrell, 1998; McCubbin, Thompson, Thompson, & Fromer, 1998; Walsh, 2003).

The concept of family resilience extends theory and research on family stress, coping, and adaptation (McCubbin & Patterson, 1983). A basic premise is that stressful life challenges have an impact on the whole family, and in turn, key family processes mediate the recovery—or maladaptation—of all members and their relationships. Thus, the family's response is crucial. Major stressors can derail the functioning of a family system, with ripple effects for all members and their relationships. Key processes and extrafamilial resources enable the family to rally in times of crisis, to buffer stress, to reduce the risk of dysfunction, and to support optimal adaptation.

Family resilience entails more than coping, managing stressful conditions, shouldering a burden, or surviving an ordeal. It involves the potential for personal and relational transformation and growth that can be forged out of adversity. By tapping key processes for resilience, families that have been struggling can emerge stronger and more resourceful in meeting future challenges. Members may develop new insights and abilities. A crisis can be a wake-up call, heightening their attention to core values and important matters. It often becomes an opportunity for families to reappraise life priorities and stimulates greater investment in meaningful relationships. In studies of strong families, many report that through weathering a crisis together their relationships were enriched and became more loving than they might otherwise have been.

Research on resilience in families can usefully inform clinical practice. For instance, the presumption that divorce inevitably damages all children has been countered by over a decade of studies finding that fewer than one fourth do poorly. Most children rebound relatively well, and one third are remarkably resilient, thriving in all measures of functioning and well-being (Greene, Anderson, Forgatch, DeGarmo, & Hetherington, 2012). Multiple variables influence children's adaptation, including the predivorce climate, postdivorce parental conflict or cutoff, and financial pressures. Helping parents navigate the divorce process can make a significant difference in risk and resilience. Such studies identifying key family processes can inform collaborative divorce counseling and mediation approaches for positive adaptation (Ahrons, 2004; Bernstein, 2007). Similarly, stepfamily formation is fraught with challenges, contributing to a 60% divorce rate. Research on successful stepfamily processes can inform interventions to lower risks and facilitate integration (Pasley & Garneau, 2012)

ASSESSMENT OF FAMILY FUNCTIONING

Mapping the Family System

In clinical practice, a broad conception of family is needed to encompass the wide range of family structures, relationship options, and cultural diversity in contemporary society (Walsh, 2012). With the aging of society, attention to multigenerational relationships is increasingly important (Walsh, 2014). Clinicians need to be mindful of cultural, personal, and professional assumptions and biases when assessing families, since views of the normal family are socially constructed. The idealized nuclear family model with gendered breadwinner/homemaker roles now is found in only a small band on the wide spectrum of families, yet social expectations can compound a sense of deficiency and failure for those who don't fit that model, especially single parents (Anderson, 2012). Those who don't conform to cultural or religious standards for marriage and family, such as same-sex couples and lesbian, gay, bisexual, and transgendered (LGBT) parents, are gaining wider acceptance yet still face stigma and inequalities (Green, 2012). Studies over the past two decades have found abundant evidence that children can thrive in a variety of family arrangements, including gay parenting (Walsh, 2012). What matters most are stable, caring, and committed relationships and effective family processes.

In the first session, it is important to learn who is in the family system. This includes all household members, nonresidential parents, steprelations, and the extended kin network, as well as other significant relationships (e.g., intimate partner, informal kin, godparents, and caregivers). The *genogram* (McGoldrick, Gerson, & Petry, 2008) (see Chapter 1, "Systems Theory," this volume) and timeline are essential tools for mapping the family system, diagramming relationship and system patterns to guide intervention. Key information is noted, such as alliances, conflicts, triangles, cutoffs, substance abuse, violence, sexual abuse, illness, and traumatic death or losses. In families that have complex relationships, such as different fathers for several children, it is especially valuable for the clinician—and family members—to see all key members and how they are related on one page. It can bring some coherence to chaotic systems for intervention planning.

A resilience-oriented assessment searches for positive influences and potential resources, positive models, and mentors, as well as problematic patterns and troubled relationships. Inquiry about a family's organizational shifts and coping strategies in response to past stressors, such as major losses, can help one illuminate the family's meaning making, coping, and adaptation with current challenges, such as recent or threatened loss. It is important to identify strengths, such as courage, faith, and perseverance, in the midst of ongoing and past struggles and to draw out positive stories and experiences in overcoming adversity (Walsh, 2006).

Family functioning is assessed in the context of the multigenerational system moving forward over time. It is important to ask about recent and anticipated stressors and disruptive events that may contribute to presenting problems. A family timeline can be sketched to note the timing, sequence, or pileup of stressors and family tensions. Frequently, symptoms coincide with stressful family transitions, relationship changes, additions, or losses and in the context of stressful events, such as the death of a loved one. Because family members may not initially mention such connections, the genogram and timeline can guide inquiry and reveal patterns for further exploration.

Although all change is stressful, strain increases exponentially when current stressors intersect with sensitive multigenerational issues. Nodal events are likely to reactivate past conflicts, particularly when similar challenges are confronted. An impending separation may reactivate past losses. Families may conflate current situations with past adverse experience, generating catastrophic fears. One mother became anxiously preoccupied that her 16-year-old daughter would become pregnant, as she had at the same age. In another case, a husband's conflict over

his wife's desire to have a second child became more understandable on learning that his mother had died in childbirth with his younger sibling: He feared losing his beloved wife. Family intervention explores such covert linkages and untold stories, helping families to heal and draw lessons from their past in order to make positive choices in their current relationships.

Even in brief present and future-focused intervention, it is crucial to note past trauma, such as combat or refugee experience and family histories of traumatic loss, which can contribute to depression, substance abuse, and self-destructive behavior (Walsh, 2007; Walsh & McGoldrick, 2004). Critical events that occurred at the same age or current nodal point in the family system may be particularly relevant. A teenager's drug overdose was incomprehensible to his parents until, in a family session, he revealed his deep bond with his older brother, who had died in a car crash at age 16. For years he had tried to take his place to ease his parents' grief, but, turning 17, he no longer knew how to be, except to join him in heaven.

ASSESSING KEY PROCESSES IN FAMILY FUNCTIONING AND RESILIENCE

Family process research over the past three decades has provided considerable empirical grounding for assessment of family functioning (Lebow & Stroud, 2012; Walsh, 2012). The family resilience framework in Table 7.1 was developed as a conceptual map for clinicians to assess family functioning and to target and strengthen key processes that foster positive adaptation (Walsh, 2003, 2006). This framework, informed by social science and clinical research, identifies key processes for effective family functioning in three domains: (1) family belief systems, (2) organization patterns, and (3) communication processes. Cultural differences must be kept in mind, and any assessment must consider functioning in context, relative to each family's values, resources, and life challenges.

Table 7.1 Key Processes in Family Resilience

Belief Systems

1. **Making Meaning of Adversity**

   View resilience as relationally based
   Normalize and contextualize distress
   View crisis as a meaningful, comprehensible, and manageable challenge
   Appraise adverse situations, options, and future expectations

2. **Positive Outlook**

   Hope, optimistic bias; confidence in overcoming barriers
   Encouragement; affirm strengths and potential
   Active initiative and perseverance
   Master the possible; accept what can't be changed

3. **Transcendence and Spirituality**

   Larger values and purpose
   Spirituality: faith, rituals / practices, and congregational support
   Inspiration: new possibilities, dreams; creative expression; social action
   Transformation: learning, change, and growth from adversity

Organizational Patterns

4. **Flexibility**

   Adapt to meet new challenges, rebound, and reorganize
   Regain stability, continuity, and dependability through disruption
   Strong authoritative leadership: nurture, guide, and protect members
   Varied family forms: cooperative parenting/caregiving teams
   Couple/coparent relationship: equal partners; mutual respect

5. **Connectedness**

   Mutual support, collaboration, and commitment
   Respect individual needs, differences, and boundaries
   Seek reconnection and reconciliation of troubled relationships
   Social and economic resources
   Mobilize kin and social and community networks; recruit mentors
   Financial security; work-family balance; institutional supports

Communication/Problem Solving

6. **Clarity**

   Clear and consistent messages (words and actions)
   Clarify ambiguous information; truth seeking/truth speaking

7. **Open Emotional Expression**

   Share range of feelings (joy and pain, hopes and fears)
   Mutual empathy; tolerance for differences
   Responsibility for own feelings and behavior; avoid blaming
   Pleasurable interactions, respite; humor

8. **Collaborative Problem Solving**

   Creative brainstorming; resourcefulness
   Shared decision making; negotiation; resolve/repair conflicts
   Focus on goals, concrete steps: build on success; learn from failure
   Proactive stance: prevent crises; prepare for future challenges

Family Belief Systems

Shared belief systems are at the core of all family functioning. Relationship rules, both explicit and unspoken, provide a set of expectations about roles, actions, and consequences that guide family life and members' behaviors. Shared values and assumptions are constructed through transactions with significant others and the larger social world. They are strongly influenced by cultural and spiritual beliefs, which are transmitted across generations. In immigrant families, traditional cultural beliefs, for instance, about spirit possession or faith healing practices, may not be mentioned unless a therapist inquires respectfully about them (Falicov, 2007, 2012, 2013). Multigenerational stories become encoded into family scripts that can rally efforts or fuel catastrophic fears when facing a challenge.

Meaning making, hope, and transcendence. It is important to explore and facilitate family efforts to make meaning of the problem situation: how it came about and how it might be improved. Therapists aim to understand constraining beliefs and narratives and to expand those that open possibilities and facilitate positive change (Freedman & Combs, 1996). Research suggests that clinicians can foster resilience by helping distressed families to (1) view a crisis as a shared challenge that is comprehensible, manageable, and meaningful to tackle; (2) (re)gain a hopeful, positive outlook that fuels initiative and perseverance, with a focus on mastering what is possible; and (3) draw on larger transcendent/ spiritual values, purpose, and connection. Families do best when they share a larger worldview, most often through cultural and spiritual beliefs, practices, and community involvement. Spiritual nourishment, transformation, and growth are also found through nature, the expressive arts, and service or social action to benefit others.

Family identity and convictions are conveyed through shared rituals, including celebrations of holidays, traditions, rites of passage, and marriage or commitment ceremonies, as well as routine interactions (e.g., family dinner, bedtime stories). Rituals provide continuity and also facilitate painful transitions and losses, especially at death, with funeral rites and memorials. Family therapists (Imber-Black, 2012) often use rituals in therapeutic intervention to foster healing and transformation. They are especially valuable where a loss, such as a stillbirth, has not been adequately marked.

Family Organizational Patterns

Family functioning requires effective organization to maintain integration as a family unit, foster healthy development of members, and master life challenges. Varying family structures, such as a two-earner two-parent family, a single-parent family, a divorced joint-custody family, a stepfamily, and a three-generational household must organize family roles and relationship patterns in varied ways to fit their circumstances.

Adaptability—a counterbalance of *flexibility* and *stability*—is required for effective family functioning and resilience. Families need strong leadership with predictable and consistent rules, roles, and patterns of interaction. Families must also adapt to changing conditions or new developmental priorities. Without this flexible structure, families at dysfunctional extremes tend to be either overly rigid and autocratic or chaotically disorganized, unstable, and leaderless. In times of crisis, such as a medical emergency, or disruptive transitions, such as a changing household, flexibility must be counterbalanced by efforts to restabilize, reorganize, and reestablish patterns in daily living. Significant losses may require major adaptational shifts to ensure continuity of family life. For instance, when a breadwinner father is laid off or becomes disabled, family roles change as the mother becomes the sole earner, and he assumes most homemaking and child-rearing responsibilities.

Connectedness, or cohesion, is vital for family functioning and resilience. To function well, families need to balance closeness with respect for separateness and individual differences.

Extremes of enmeshment or disengagement tend to be dysfunctional. However, with varying cultural norms, personal preferences, and situational demands, clinicians must be cautious not to presume that a highly connected couple or family pattern is dysfunctionally enmeshed. Many cultures value high cohesion and prioritize the needs of the family over individual preferences (Falicov, 2012).

Role relations often must be renegotiated in families. Increasingly, couples are striving for equal partnership in marriage and family life, with both spouses in the workplace and sharing child-rearing and household responsibilities. Still, more traditional patriarchal values and role divisions are often upheld by older generations, recent immigrants, and adherents of fundamentalist religions. Research shows that an equitable sharing of authority, responsibility, and privilege in the couple/parental unit fosters healthy relationships (Knudsen-Martin, 2012). In kinship care, when grandparents step in to raise grandchildren, or become legal guardians, renegotiation of roles, relationships, and households is required (Engstrom, 2012). The complexity of divorced and stepfamily configurations poses challenges to sustain workable parenting coalitions across households and to knit together biological and steprelations, including extended kin.

Family structural boundaries need to be clear and firm yet permeable (Minuchin, 1974). Interpersonal boundaries promote differentiation and autonomous functioning. Generational boundaries maintain hierarchical organization in families for effective functioning, leadership, and authority. Children gain competencies by assisting parents with responsibilities, and their role may be vital in single-parent and large families and in cases of parental illness or disability. However, rigid role expectations can sacrifice a child's own development needs. Generational boundaries are blurred when a parent abdicates leadership or uses a child as a parental surrogate. When boundaries are breached most destructively in sexual abuse (Sheinberg & Fraenkel, 2001), it is imperative to strengthen family structure with clear leadership, authority, and protective boundaries.

The concept of the *triangle* and the dysfunctional process of *triangulation* (Bowen, 1978) refers to the pattern when two members (e.g., spouses/parents) draw in or scapegoat a third person to deflect rising tension. A couple may avoid conflict by uniting in mutual concern about a symptomatic child. A child may serve as peacemaker or go-between for warring parents, balancing loyalties and regulating tension. In high-conflict divorces, one parent may draw a child into a loyalty bond against the other parent. A grandparent-child coalition may be formed against a parent. In more troubled families, such patterns tend to be rigid and replicated in interlocking triangles throughout the system.

Kin and community resources are vital lifelines for family functioning, especially for support through hard times and for multistressed, underresourced families. For transnational families, adaptation and resilience are facilitated by finding ways to sustain connection with loved ones and the community left behind (Falicov, 2007). Friendship networks are especially important for adults living alone and in the families of choice formed in gay and lesbian communities. Faith communities offer valued resources to many families by means of congregational support, spiritual practices, communal rituals, clergy guidance, and involvement in a range of programs and service to others (Walsh, 2009b). Clinicians are encouraged to become acquainted with faith-based resources in their communities.

Communication Processes

Communication processes facilitate all family functioning. Family therapists attend to both content and relational aspects of verbal and nonverbal messages. It is important for family members to communicate openly about practical, emotional, and relational issues. Clinicians should be mindful of varied cultural norms regarding directness and expressivity of opinions and feelings.

Clarity. Clear and congruent messages conveyed in words and actions are important. In ambiguous situations, such as an unclear medical prognosis or the threat of divorce, anxiety is heightened. When communication is blocked, children sense anxiety, imagine the worst, and commonly express fears through somatic or behavioral symptoms.

Open emotional expression. A climate of mutual trust encourages open expression of a range of feelings and empathic responses, with respect for differences. Troubled families tend to perpetuate mistrust, blaming, and scapegoating. Highly reactive, destructive cycles of conflict can escalate into violence. Cascading effects of criticism, stonewalling, contempt, and mutual withdrawal contribute to despair and divorce. It is important to address with sensitivity areas of conflict and toxic subjects where communication is blocked or distorted, as well as constraints of gender-based assumptions. Expectations that men should be tough problem solvers and not reveal vulnerability, fear, or soft emotions can block their ability to address significant emotionally laden issues and to give and receive emotional support. It is useful to reframe vulnerability as inherent in the human condition and expression of difficult feelings as strength rather than shameful weakness.

Collaborative problem solving is crucial for family functioning and is facilitated in all approaches to family therapy. Systemic assessment attends to the decision-making process and addresses power struggles and control issues. Negotiation and conflict management skills can be honed in therapy. Fairness, respect for differences, and reciprocity are vital for long-term relational harmony.

Families need to master instrumental problems, such as juggling job and child care demands, and meet the socioemotional needs of members, as by comforting anxious children. They can falter at various steps in the problem-solving process (Lebow & Stroud, 2012): identifying the problem; communicating about it and brainstorming possible solutions; or deciding on an approach, taking action, following through, and evaluating its effectiveness. The family's resilience is strengthened by building on small successes and viewing mistakes as learning experiences. Families become more resourceful as therapy focuses proactively to anticipate, prepare for, and avert future problems.

Family Functioning in Context

Families with diverse values, structures, resources, and life challenges forge varied pathways in coping, adaptation, and resilience. Whether patterns are functional or dysfunctional depends on the *fit* between family processes, the demands of their problematic situation, and their resources. Family-centered institutional policies, structures, and programs of larger systems are essential to support optimal family functioning, from health care, to child and elder care, to workplace flexibility and retirement benefits. It is not enough to help vulnerable families overcome the odds for family resilience; social policy must also change the odds against them in order for families to thrive (Seccombe, 2002).

MAJOR APPROACHES TO FAMILY THERAPY

Table 7.2 presents an outline of major models of family therapy, their views of functioning and dysfunction, change processes, and therapeutic goals. Reflecting the mental health field's focus on psychopathology, foundational family therapy models tended to focus on changing dysfunctional family patterns in the maintenance of individual symptoms. Over the past three decades, the field of family therapy

Table 7.2 Major Approaches to Family Therapy

Family Therapy Model	View of Problems	Therapeutic Goals	Process of Change
Intergenerational/Growth-Oriented Approaches			
Psychodynamic/ Intergenerational Boszormenyi-Nagy Framo Byng-Hall	Symptoms due to shared family projection process; unresolved past conflicts, and losses, loyalty, trust issues in family of origin	Resolve family-of-origin issues ↓ Family projection processes ↑ Individual and relational growth	• Insight-oriented, link past / present dynamics • Facilitate resolution of issues in current transactions • Encourage mutual empathy
Bowen Model Bowen Carter McGoldrick	Functioning impaired by unresolved family-of-origin issues, losses: • Poor differentiation • Anxiety (reactivity) • Triangles • Cutoffs, conflicts	↑ Differentiation of self ↑ Cognitive functioning ↓ Emotional reactivity Detriangle: Repair cutoffs, conflicts	• Survey multigenerational system (use genogram, timeline) • Plan, coach focused interventions to change self with family • Detoxify, use humor
Experiential Satir Whitaker	Symptoms are nonverbal messages expressing current communication dysfunction in system	Direct, clear communication Genuine expression of feelings Individual & relational growth	• Facilitate direct communication • Experiential techniques to reveal conflicts, needs • Catalyze change process
Problem-Solving Approaches			
Structural Minuchin Philadelphia Child Guidance Clinic	Family structural imbalance: • Malfunctioning hierarchy, boundaries • Maladaptive reaction to developmental/ environmental changes	Reorganize structure: • Parental leadership, authority • Clear, flexible subsystems, boundaries • Promote adaptive coping	Shift interaction patterns: • Join family • Enactment of problem • Map structure, plan restructuring • Tasks and directives

Family Therapy Model	View of Problems	Therapeutic Goals	Process of Change
Strategic/Systemic Palo Alto group Haley, Madanes Milan approach	Symptoms maintained by family's unsuccessful problem-solving attempts	Solve presenting problem; specific behavioral objectives • Change symptom-maintaining sequence to new outcome	Pragmatic, focused, action-oriented: • Interrupt feedback loop • Relabeling, reframing, paradox • Circular questions; curiosity
Postmodern Solution-focused Berg & de Shazer **Narrative** White & Epston H. Anderson Freedman, Combs	• Normality is socially constructed • Problem-saturated narratives • Constrained, marginalized by dominant discourse	• Envision new possibilities; take positive steps to attain • Facilitative meaning-making • Re-author, thicken life stories	• Future-oriented potential • Search for problem exceptions • Collaborative, respectful • Externalize problems to overcome
Behavioral, Cognitive-Behavioral Patterson Alexander, Sexton Epstein, Baucom Datillio	Maladaptive, symptomatic behavior reinforced by • Family reward • Negative interaction cycles • Core beliefs (schemas)	• Concrete, behavioral goals • Improved communication and problem solving • Cognitive restructuring of misperceptions	• Therapist guides, shapes • Change interpersonal assumptions • Reward desired behavior • Negotiation, problem-solving skills
Psychoeducational C. Anderson McFarlane	• Biologically based disorders; stress/diathesis • Adaptational challenges (e.g., chronic illness, single parents)	• Optimal functioning ↓ stress, stigma, isolation • Master adaptational challenges	• Multifamily groups, social support • Provide useful information • Offer management guidelines • Respectful collaboration
Multisystemic Santistaban et al. Liddle et al. Henggeler	Family, social, larger systems influence adolescent conduct disorders, substance abuse	• Reduce risks, problem behaviors • Promote positive youth adaptation	• Family-centered • Collaborative involvement of peers, schools, community programs

has expanded the theory and application of family systems interventions and has refocused attention from family deficits to family strengths. (For a fuller description of models, see Goldenberg & Goldenberg, 2013.) The approaches differ in focus on particular aspects of functioning and well-being: multigenerational patterns and relational dynamics, structural patterns, communication, problem solving, and language and meaning systems. Despite many differences, family systems approaches attend to ongoing transactional processes and relational connections.

Intergenerational Approaches

Early in the field of family therapy, growth-oriented intergenerational approaches to family therapy sought to bridge psychodynamic, object relations, and family systems theories. In *psychodynamically oriented approaches,* therapists attend to the web of dynamic processes in the family network of relationships. In theory, a shared projection process, based on complementarity of needs, influences mate choice as well as couple and parent-child relationship patterns. Unresolved conflict or loss interferes with realistic appraisal and response to other family members. Current life situations are interpreted in light of the parents' inner object world and role models, contributing to distortion, scapegoating, and irrational role assignment. Symptoms can result from attempts by spouses/parents to reenact, externalize, or master through current relationships their intrapsychic conflicts originating in the family of origin.

Assessment and intervention explore the complex multigenerational family patterns and their connection to disturbances in current functioning and relationships. Extended family members may be included in family sessions, or individuals may be encouraged to work on changing key relationships between sessions (Framo, 1980). The therapeutic aim is for family members to deal with one another directly in order to work through unresolved conflicts and losses rather than by analysis of transference patterns with the therapist. The therapist actively encourages members' awareness of intense conflictual emotions, interprets their sources and consequences, and identifies shared defense mechanisms. The therapist takes charge in preparing, guiding, and processing such highly charged work. Covert family processes are made overt and accessible to resolution through insight and action for emotional working through. The conjoint process builds empathy and mutuality, strengthening couple and family bonds. In application of *attachment theory,* therapists facilitate couple and parental efforts to provide a secure family base for stable, trusting relationships (Byng-Hall, 1995) and emotional attunement (Greenberg & Johnson, 2010).

The *contextual approach* of Boszormenyi-Nagy (1987) emphasizes the importance of covert but powerful family-of-origin loyalty patterns with the aim of reconstruction and healing of wounded relationships. Therapy focuses on the ethical dimension of family relationships, examining the transgenerational legacies of parental accountability and filial loyalty. The therapist seeks to resolve issues and repair relational injuries or injustices through understanding and negotiation of grievances. Families are strengthened by efforts toward trustworthiness and relational equitability.

The *Bowen model* (Bowen, 1978) is a theory of the family emotional system and a method of therapy based on the view that functioning is impaired by poor differentiation, characterized by anxiety and emotional reactivity. This commonly produces conflict, triangulation, or cutoffs in highly charged relationships. Stresses on the family system, especially those caused by death, can decrease differentiation and heighten reactivity. Improved functioning results when emotional reactivity no longer blocks cognitive processes, and there is more genuine relating. The therapeutic goal is to assist individuals in repairing troubled relationships, achieving a higher level of differentiation and reduced anxiety in direct contact. Through a coaching process

(Carter & McGoldrick, 2001), which can be done in individual therapy, a client is coached to change his or her own behavior in relation to other family members, in contacts between sessions. In couple therapy, partners are encouraged to work on their own extended family relationships that are blocking, or intruding into, their relationship. In family therapy, separate and conjoint sessions may be combined, as with an adolescent and parents or stepparents or with adult siblings, around conflicts related to their family of origin. The therapist serves as consultant and coach, preparing and guiding change efforts and toning down reactivity to toxic family issues and contact.

Initially, a family evaluation surveys the entire family field. A genogram and timeline are constructed to diagram the network of relationships, important facts, relationship information, and major events. Client and therapist gain a working knowledge of the family system before undertaking change with an individual or a part of the family. Clients are encouraged to contact family members to clarify obscured or missing information, gaining new perspectives on parents, other members, and family history. Opportunities are pursued in meetings, visits, holiday gatherings, and reunions, as well as letters, phone calls, and Internet contacts. In the process of change, clients redevelop more differentiated personal relationships with family members, repairing cutoffs and changing their own part in emotionally charged cycles. Individuals are encouraged to take an "I position," asserting their own thoughts and feelings without attacking, defending, or withdrawal. Humor is used to detoxify emotional situations. Techniques of detriangling and reversals (expressing the unacknowledged other side of an issue) are two of the many means employed to open up rigid patterns. Sessions may start at weekly or biweekly intervals and be spaced out as work proceeds. Follow-through is essential, given the anxiety generated and the need to handle others' self-correcting reactions that can undermine change. Even when others do not change, clients' own efforts can be empowering and healing, benefiting other relationships in their lives. Carter and McGoldrick (2001) have expanded this approach to address the impact of larger cultural forces, such as sexism, racism, and social class disparities.

Experiential Approaches

Experiential approaches to family therapy were developed by two leading pioneers, Virginia Satir (1972), who blended a communication approach with a humanistic frame of reference, and Carl Whitaker (1992), who practiced an idiosyncratic style of intervention. Experiential approaches are highly intuitive and relatively atheoretical. As the natural consequence of life experience, old pains can be aroused by current interaction, regardless of awareness or intent. The aim of these growth-oriented approaches is fuller awareness and appreciation of oneself in relation to others, achieved through an intense, affective experience with open communication of feelings and differences. In a phenomenological approach to assessment and intervention focused on the immediate experience, the therapist elicits important information in transactions. The approach encourages exploration, experimentation, and spontaneity of members' responses to each other. Experiential exercises, such as family sculpting and role play, are used to catalyze this process. The therapist is facilitative, following and reflecting family processes and stimulating nondefensive, genuine relating.

PROBLEM-SOLVING APPROACHES

Structural Model

Structural family therapy, developed by Minuchin (1974) and colleagues at the Philadelphia Child Guidance Center, emphasizes the importance of family organization for the functioning of the family unit and the well-being of members. The model focuses on the patterning of transactions in which symptoms are embedded. Problems are viewed as an indication of imbalance in family organization, particularly a malfunctioning hierarchy with unclear parent and child subsystem boundaries. Commonly, symptoms are a sign of a maladaptive reaction to environmental or developmental changes. Child-focused problems often detour conflict between parents or between a single parent and a grandparent.

Therapy is brief, aiming to strengthen the family structural foundation by modifying dysfunctional patterns for better functioning and coping with life stresses. Presenting problems, a symptom of family distress, usually are resolved as this reorganization is accomplished. Therapy involves three processes: (1) *joining,* (2) *enactment,* and (3) *restructuring.* First, the therapist joins the family in a position of leadership of the therapeutic system, connecting with family members, especially parents, to engage them in the change process. Second, the therapist assesses the family transactions as members enact presenting problems in the interview. Third, based on an interactional diagnosis and structural mapping of the immediate family field, the therapist uses tasks and directives to restructure the family around its handling of problems. The therapist is active in sessions, shifting triangular patterns, blocking dysfunctional coalitions, and promoting healthier alliances. Directives, or tasks involving structural change, are assigned to be carried out between sessions. Efforts are directed to strengthen the parental subsystem (couple, single parent, or parent-grandparent) and reinforce appropriate generational boundaries. Live observation of sessions through a one-way mirror facilitates training and intervention.

The structural model was developed to work effectively with poor, inner-city, multiproblem families presenting child or adolescent concerns. It is especially useful with single-parent and underorganized families. It was also applied successfully to psychosomatic and eating disorders. More recent efforts have also been directed to change traditional child welfare and foster care

systems, criticized for "dismembering families" in fragmented approaches, toward practices that support children's ongoing connections and knit together biological and foster or kinship care family systems (Minuchin, Colapinto, & Minuchin, 2006).

Strategic/Systemic Approaches

Early strategic and systemic approaches to family therapy were developed by the Mental Research Institute (MRI) group in Palo Alto (Haley, 1976; Weakland, Fisch, Watzlawick, & Bodin, 1974), and by the Milan team (Boscolo, Cecchin, Hoffman, & Penn, 1987). These models regard presenting problems as both a symptom of and a response to current stresses, a communicative act within a repetitive sequence of interactions. Therapy focuses on how a family has attempted to solve its problems, because a misguided attempt may make matters worse. Families often do what they do because they believe it is the best way to approach a problem or the only way they know. The therapeutic task is to interrupt ways of handling the problem that are not working. Therapy focuses on altering the interactional feedback loop that maintains symptomatic behavior. Early strategic approaches assumed that symptoms serve a function in the family and that change depends more on indirect means of influence than on insight or simply improving communication. The therapist's stance was remote, yet active and pragmatic, planning and carrying out a strategy to achieve specific objectives.

Several techniques are widely used. *Relabeling, reframing,* and *positive connotation* involve strategic redefinition of a problem situation to cast it in a new light. They are commonly used to redefine what has been viewed negatively as a well-intentioned attempt to adapt or to protect other family members. These techniques can be useful in shifting a family's rigid view or response, altering an unproductive blaming process, or overcoming barriers to change. In the reformulation of a problem, new solutions can become more apparent. *Directives* are carefully designed behavioral tasks for families to carry out between sessions. They are useful in gathering direct information about the ways family members interact and how they respond to change efforts. When well formulated and well timed, they can be highly effective in structural and behavioral change. *Indirect techniques* are seemingly in opposition to objectives but actually serve to move toward them. In paradoxical instruction (no longer widely used) a therapist might prescribe the symptom or direct clients to do the opposite of their intended goal.

The *Milan approach* stresses the importance of learning a family's language and beliefs, seeing the problem through various members' eyes and appreciating the values and expectations that guide their handling of problems and inability to change. The approach follows three principles in conducting family interviews and obtaining useful information for change: (1) *Working hypotheses* are formed about the connection of symptoms with family relationships; (2) *circular questioning* elicits various members' perspectives about relationship patterns, such as who is more connected or concerned about an issue; and (3) *neutrality* was initially advised for the therapist's avoidance of judgment, criticism, or moral alignment with any part of the system. Recognition that therapists can never be neutral led to a therapeutic stance of *respectful curiosity* (Cecchin, 1987).

Behavioral and Cognitive-Behavioral Approaches

Behavioral approaches to family therapy developed from behavior modification and social learning traditions (Patterson, Reid, Jones, & Conger, 1975). Families are viewed as critical learning contexts, created and responded to by members. Therapy attends to transactional rules, behaviors, and conditions under which social behavior is learned, influenced, and changed. Following social exchange principles,

family interactions offer many opportunities for rewarding exchanges likely to enhance relationships. In well-functioning families, maladaptive behavior is not reinforced, and adaptive behavior is rewarded through attention, acknowledgment, and approval. Poor communication and reliance on coercive control exacerbates maladaptive behavior and relationship distress.

Intervention objectives are specified in concrete observable behavior. The therapist guides family members in a straightforward way to learn more effective modes of dealing with one another by changing the interpersonal consequences of behavior (contingencies of reinforcement). Individuals learn to give each other approval and acknowledgment for desired behavior instead of reinforcing maladaptive behavior by attention or punishment. The therapist builds communication skills in negotiation and problem solving, increasing adaptability in varied situations. Within a positive alliance, the therapist assumes a role as educator, model, and facilitator. Numerous studies have documented the effectiveness of this approach with adolescent conduct disorders, particularly the functional family therapy model developed by Alexander and colleagues (Sexton & Alexander, 2003). More recent cognitive-behavioral approaches (Dattilio, 2005) restructure family schemas along with behavioral change and are also effective with couple conflict.

RECENT DEVELOPMENTS IN STRENGTHS-BASED APPROACHES

The field of family therapy has shifted increasingly from a deficit to a strengths perspective and from a hierarchical stance of the therapist as expert to a respectful collaboration with family members. Assessment and intervention are redirected from problems and how they are maintained to solutions and how they can be attained. Therapeutic efforts aim to identify and amplify existing and potential competencies and resources. Therapist and clients work in partnership to see new possibilities in a problem-saturated situation and to overcome impasses to change and growth. This positive, future-focused stance shifts the emphasis of therapy from what went wrong to what can be done for enhanced functioning and well-being.

These approaches oppose assumptions that symptoms necessarily serve ulterior functions for the family and reject the notion that the therapist must use clever techniques to overcome family resistance to change. Therapists attribute benign intent to all clients, assume that they really do want to change, and strive to overcome constraints. The therapeutic relationship eschews the hierarchical power-based position of earlier approaches. Instead, it is built on trust and respect of families and oriented toward recognizing and amplifying their positive strengths and resources and their untapped potential.

Postmodern Approaches

Postmodern perspectives have heightened awareness that clinical views of normality, health, and pathology are socially constructed. Clinicians and researchers inescapably bring their own values and biases and thus coconstruct the patterns they discover in families. Moreover, therapeutic objectives are influenced by both family and therapist beliefs about healthy functioning (Walsh, 2012). Clinicians and researchers need to be aware of their own implicit assumptions, values, and biases embedded in cultural norms, professional orientations, and personal experience.

Postmodern approaches are based in constructivist and social constructionist views on the subjective experience of reality (Hoffman, 1990). These approaches were influenced by earlier strategic-systemic models but broke away from many core principles. While people are thought to be constrained by their narrow, pessimistic views of problems, limiting the range of alternatives, therapy refocuses from problems and the patterns that maintain them to solutions and the processes that enable them. Use of the *reflecting team* (Andersen, 1987) in consulting team observation of live sessions fosters a more collaborative approach, whereby families, after the session, can observe the team in discussion of their session and then offer their own reflections.

Narrative and conversational approaches emphasize the therapeutic conversation and process of "restory-ing" a problematic experience (Anderson, 1997; Freedman & Combs, 1996; White & Epston, 1990). At the core of therapy is the postmodern view that reality is subjective and is socially constructed through language. A basic premise is that people strive to make meaning of their experience. The clients' stories are the primary focus. Meanings are coconstructed in the therapy process. Therapist views, as well as those of clients, are subjective, influenced by culture, personal experience, and professional orientation and assumptions. Therefore, therapists eschew the role of expert in interpreting their clients' lives; rather, their skills are in listening well to client narratives, being curious about their stories, asking questions to thicken descriptions, and wondering about alternative constructions to expand possibilities. Therapy attends to the ways in which language and meaning reflect cultural values and the larger social context. Space is opened for voices that have not been heard or views that have been marginalized by a dominant discourse. The objective is to construct new narratives, or life stories, that are less constraining and more empowering and satisfying.

The technique of externalization (White & Epston, 1990) serves as a means through language to reframe problem situations toward more empowering constructions that encourage problem resolution. Essentially, it shifts conversation to separate the problem from the symptom bearer, most often a child, lessening internalized guilt, shame, and defensiveness. An external force may be defined as wreaking havoc on their lives. The therapist aligns with the child and parents, or with a couple, as a therapeutic team who, together, will gain control over and defeat this negative force. Clients are accountable for the choices they make in relation to their problems. The goal is for clients to feel successful and victorious in conquering their problems.

Solution-focused approaches avoid complex formulations when simple assumptions will lead more quickly to change (de Shazer, 1988), contending that complicated problems do not necessarily require complicated solutions. This brief approach generally does not assess or address the impact of stress events or broader family and contextual influences. Therapists search for exceptions to immediate problems: solutions that have worked in other situations and might work now and in the future. Formulaic techniques, such as *scaling* (client ratings to concretize aims and progress) and asking the *miracle question,* are used to refocus from complaints to desired outcomes and the steps needed to reach them. Berg (1997) has described useful applications of this approach for social service settings.

Family Psychoeducational Approach

Family psychoeducational approaches have been empirically demonstrated to be an essential component of effective treatment for schizophrenia (Anderson, Reiss, & Hogarty, 1986) and find valuable application with a range of chronic mental and physical conditions (Gonzalez & Steinglass, 2002; Lefley, 2009; McFarlane, 2002; Miklowitz, 2010; Rolland, 1994). This approach provides family education and support to foster coping and adaptation, with concrete guidelines for crisis management, problem solving, and stress reduction. The rationale is explicitly based on the importance of practical information, social support, and problem-solving assistance through the predictably stressful periods that can be anticipated in

the future course of a chronic illness or major life transition.

With major mental illness, families are engaged as valued collaborators in the treatment process, with respect for their challenges. This approach does much to correct the marginalization and blame-laden causal attributions experienced by many families of the mentally ill in traditional psychiatric settings. In the controlled study by Anderson and colleagues (1986), family intervention combined with drug maintenance and social skills training dramatically reduced relapse rates and improved functioning of individuals with chronic schizophrenia and also reduced family distress. The approach is based on a stress-diathesis model: Environmental stresses interact negatively with a core biological vulnerability to produce disturbed cognitions and behaviors. Assisted by information and support, families are viewed as important caregiving resources for the long-term management of the condition. A highly structured, family-oriented program was designed to avoid treatment dropout, to sustain functioning in the community, and to decrease family stress and relapse rates. Anxiety and tensions in patient-family interactions decrease as families gain knowledge about the illness and confidence about their ability to manage it. The approach focuses on solving immediate problems one at a time, measuring success in small increments, and maintaining family morale.

Family psychoeducational interventions have been adapted to a number of formats, including periodic family consultations, workshops, and brief time-limited or ongoing multifamily groups (McFarlane, 2002). Group formats decrease family isolation and the stigma associated with mental illness as they offer mutual support, sharing of experience, and exchange of useful ideas among families struggling with similar challenges. Brief psychoeducational "modules" timed for critical phases of an illness (Rolland, 1994) support families in digesting manageable portions of a long-term coping process and in handling periodic flare-ups. Such cost-effective approaches are especially useful with families at high risk of maladaptation or relapse of a serious condition.

Multisystemic Approaches With Adolescent Conduct Disorder

Several evidence-based, multisystemic and multidimensional intervention models offer highly effective approaches with high-risk and seriously troubled youth by involving families and larger-community systems (Henggeler, Clingempeel, Brondino, & Pickrel, 2002; Liddle, Santisteban, Levant, & Bray, 2002; Santisteban et al., 2003; Sexton & Alexander, 2003; Szapocznik & Williams, 2000). These approaches with adolescent conduct disorder and drug abuse also yield improvements in family functioning, including increased cohesion, communication, and parenting practices, and are significantly linked to more positive youth behavioral outcomes than in standard youth service. Multisystemic interventions may take a variety of forms and involve school counselors, teachers, coaches, and peer groups; they may work with police officials, probation officers, and judges to address adolescent and family legal issues. They might help a youth and family access vocational services, youth development organizations, social support networks, and religious group resources.

With families that are often seen as unready, unwilling, or unmotivated for therapy, these approaches engage family members in a strengths-oriented, collaborative alliance. They develop a shared atmosphere of hope, expectation for change, a sense of responsibility (active agency), and empowerment. Rather than seeing troubled youths and their families as resistant to change, attempts are made to identify and overcome barriers to success in the therapeutic, family, and social contexts. Therapeutic contacts emphasize the positive and draw out systemic strengths and competencies for change. Clinicians maintain and clearly communicate an optimistic perspective throughout the assessment and intervention processes.

Collaborative Family Health Care

Family-centered health care is a rapidly growing practice arena. Research has demonstrated that a collaborative team approach—including health and mental health care providers, patients, and their families—fosters optimal biopsychosocial care (Campbell, 2003; McDaniel, Hepworth, & Doherty, 2007). Preventive and integrative approaches to mental health and health care are most effective when supported by families. For military service members with disabilities, particularly posttraumatic stress disorder (PTSD) and traumatic brain and orthopedic injuries, spouses and family members are essential partners for optimal recovery. For persons suffering from serious mental illness, family consultation and psychoeducation facilitate a collaborative approach to treatment, with mutual understanding of aims and concerns (McFarlane, 2002). Strengthening the family support system is crucial for inpatient discharge planning, medication compliance, and optimal community living. Families benefit, as well, when linked with local support groups, online resources, and consumer organizations such as the Multiple Sclerosis Foundation and the National Association for the Mentally Ill (NAMI).

With advances in medicine and the aging of society, families increasingly confront long-term challenges of chronic illness and caregiving. Family systems approaches expand the customary model of individual caregiver (predominantly female), for whom overload can compromise health and well-being, to a *caregiving team* approach, involving siblings and other key family members (Walsh, 2006; 2014). Dementias, particularly Alzheimer's disease, with accompanying ambiguous losses, are especially agonizing for family members (Boss, 1999). End-of-life decision making, as well, poses difficult relational, ethical, and spiritual dilemmas for loved ones. With bereavement, a family-systems approach attends to the reverberations of a significant loss for all members and their relationships and facilitates family healing and adaptation (Walsh & McGoldrick, 2004). A family approach is especially valuable with complicated losses: those that are sudden and unexpected, untimely (e.g., the death of a child), violent (e.g., a car crash, deliberate harm), stigmatized (e.g., suicide, HIV/AIDS), or not socially supported (e.g., perinatal death, same-sex partners, loss of a pet) (Walsh, 2007, 2009a).

The family systems illness model, developed by Rolland (1994, 2012) and applied in numerous studies, provides a useful framework for consultation, therapy, psychoeducational workshops, and multifamily groups with families facing chronic illness, disability, and loss. Most families lacking a psychosocial map for this experience benefit enormously from information and support in coping with and adapting to a family member's serious illness. Family dynamics, stress and coping, and supportive relationships can influence compliance, disease course, and the well-being of the sick person, caregivers, and others. Therefore, a brief family consultation near the initial diagnosis, at hospital intake and discharge, and at major nodal points and transitions over the course of the illness (e.g., recurrence or progression of the illness, transfer to hospice) facilitates patient and family adaptation and support. With the new era of genomics, family consultation will be needed increasingly for a broad spectrum of medical and psychiatric conditions around genetic testing, living with risk information, making life decisions, and informing other at-risk family members.

Practice Applications of a Family Resilience Framework

A family resilience practice approach aims to strengthen family capacities to overcome adversity. It addresses symptoms of distress and family functioning in the context of serious crisis, trauma, and loss; disruptive life transitions; and stress-laden chronic conditions. Practice applications draw on strengths-based systemic practice principles and methods described above, focusing on therapeutic and preventive efforts for

fostering family coping, adaptation, and positive growth in dealing with life challenges. A basic systemic premise guiding this approach is that individual or shared crises and persistent adversity have an impact on the whole family, and in turn, key family processes can facilitate the recovery and resilience of all members and their relationships. Facilitating the family's ability to master its immediate crisis situation also increases its resourcefulness in meeting future challenges. A number of programs developed by faculty at the Chicago Center for Family Health (Walsh, 2006, 2013) illustrate the wide range of valuable applications of a family-resilience-oriented approach in clinical and community-based intervention and prevention:

- Illness, disability, end-of life, and caregiving challenges
- Complicated traumatic loss, healing, and resilience
- Family-school partnership program for success of at-risk youth
- LGBT challenges with stigma, inequalities
- Positive adaptation to divorce; stepfamily integration
- Job loss, unemployment, and financial hardship
- Combat-related trauma and military family resilience
- Major disasters: facilitating family and community resilience
- Refugee trauma and resilience: multifamily groups for Bosnian and Kosovar refugees
- Complex trauma in war-torn regions: Kosovar Family Professional Education Collaboration (KFPEC)
- Los Angeles Gang Reduction/Youth Development (GRYD) Prevention Program

Such programs in many settings can be designed in varied formats: family consultation, brief or intensive family therapy, multifamily groups, family networks, and community forums. A number of family systems therapists have developed their own resilience-oriented approaches to respond to community-wide disasters (e.g., Saul, 2013). Landau (2007) has designed a consultation model (LINKS) to build family and community resilience in situations of natural disaster and conflict in many parts of the world.

Strengthening Resilience in Vulnerable Multistressed Families

Many families in poor communities, disproportionately minorities, are buffeted by frequent crises and persistent stresses that overwhelm their functioning (Aponte, 1994). Traumatic losses, abrupt transitions, and chronic stresses of unemployment, housing, discrimination, and health care can fuel despair. With neighborhood crime, violence, and drugs, parents worry constantly about their children's safety. Bleak life prospects, making it hard to break the cycle of poverty, leave parents defeated by repeated frustration and failure. Intertwined family and environmental stresses contribute to school dropout, gang activity, and teen pregnancy. Too often, agencies and schools have viewed multistressed families through their deficits and written them off as unreachable and untreatable.

A family resilience approach is most needed and beneficial with vulnerable multistressed families (Walsh, 2006). When therapy is overly problem focused, it grimly replicates families' problem-saturated experience. Empowering interventions that enhance positive interactions, supporting coping efforts, and building resources are more effective in reducing stress and enhancing pride and more effective functioning. A compassionate understanding of their struggles can engage parents in efforts to break dysfunctional cycles. By tapping family resources and potential, strengthening bonds for mutual support, and encouraging their best efforts, families can be encouraged to gain hope, confidence, and new competencies to overcome their life challenges. Maintaining a family focus involves a systemic view that addresses their problems, repairs and strengthens bonds, and supports efforts for positive growth (Madsen, 2009; 2011; Minuchin et al., 2006; Ungar, 2004).

Disruptions and losses in relationships with foster or kinship care and reunification increase the risk of youth adjustment problems. A systemic approach is needed to address the shifts, sustain connections, and resolve conflicts in role relations, as the following case vignette illustrates.

Terrell, age 8, was seen in individual therapy for anxiety and poor concentration in school 3 months after he was returned to the custody of his mother, a single parent, following her recovery from drug addiction. Terrell and his siblings had been living with their maternal grandmother, in her guardianship for 2 years. In regaining their mother, the children had now lost their grandmother. Although the grandmother lived nearby, the mother cut off all contact between them, still angry at her for initiating the court-ordered transfer of the children. Now becoming overwhelmed by job and child care demands, she risked losing custody again.

A systemic approach was needed to guide intervention efforts. Sessions with the mother and the grandmother were held to calm the transitional upheaval, repair their strained relationship, and negotiate their changing roles. The therapist facilitated their collaboration across households, with the mother in charge as primary parent. It was crucial to reframe the grandmother's role—not rescuing the children from a deficient mother but supporting her daughter's best efforts to succeed with her children and her job. The children's vital bond with their grandmother was renewed in her after-school child care, thereby also relieving pressure on the mother. The mother's sister, Terrell's godmother, was included in a session, to explore how she might also be a resource. She invited Terrell to play with his cousins on Saturday afternoons, which pleased him and gave his mother the needed respite.

AN EXPANDING FIELD OF PRACTICE

Family-systems-based interventions are finding broad application in community-based services for a broad diversity of clients and a wide range of problems. Despite some differences in strategies and techniques, systemic approaches focus on direct assessment and change to improve individual and relational functioning, well-being, and resilience. Clinicians with a family systems orientation increasingly integrate elements of various models (e.g., Scheinkman, 2008), and most see individuals, couples, and family members in varied combinations depending on particular situations. Cell phones and the Internet offer new possibilities for family contact and involvement. Therapists increasingly use their systemic perspective to collaborate with schools, workplaces, health care, justice, and other larger systems. Growing numbers of family therapists work with low-income and minority families and at-risk youth. Multicultural approaches address the intersections of race, class, gender, and culture in clinical practice (McGoldrick & Hardy, 2008). Therapists address the concerns of LGBT clients (e.g., Green, 2012), immigrant and refugee families (Falicov, 2007), and others suffering discrimination and marginalization in the larger society. Family therapists work to promote social policy and institutional changes needed for families and their members to thrive. Many devote attention and expertise to address social justice and humanitarian concerns in our society and worldwide. Many strive to foster family and community recovery and resilience in regions affected by natural disasters, war, and ongoing conflict. With a systemic orientation, it is essential not only to help families overcome obstacles to their well-being but also to address the hardships and remove the barriers that block their ability to thrive.

A common question, "When is family therapy indicated?" requires reconceptualization. Family therapy is the practice of a systemic orientation, guided by the assumption that an individual's problems can best be understood and changed in their relational and social context. Positive changes in stressful transactions will facilitate individual change and growth. A systemic lens can enrich all forms of intervention, from a biomedical model to cognitive-behavioral approaches. Family consultations can facilitate engagement, collaboration, and building of family resources by direct contact with key members in the kin network. For instance, foster care is facilitated when important family members are involved, like a family council, to discuss placement options and collaborate in decision making and ways of supporting children's experience (Minuchin et al., 2006).

In systemic intervention approaches, therapists aim to promote change directly with significant family members, during or outside sessions. Therapy may selectively focus on specific problems and include those members most crucial for problem solving. More intensive family therapy may be needed in cases of multiple, complex, or entrenched difficulties. With the recognition that complex biopsychosocial problems are often not resolved by a single approach, combined modalities are often indicated. For serious mental illness, research documents the combined effectiveness of psychotropic interventions with individual, family, and group approaches, as noted above. Treatment models for substance abuse, violence, and sexual abuse also require a multimodality approach. Careful planning, timing, and focus are important.

Finally, our knowledge base and practice approaches are informed and enriched through the contributions of both quantitative and qualitative research on family processes and therapeutic process (Lebow & Stroud, 2012; Sprenkle, Davis, & Lebow, 2009; Walsh, 2012). Given the broad diversity of families and their challenges, no single model fits all. Most important, at the heart of the therapeutic endeavor is our common humanity and compassionate relationship with the families we serve, supporting their best potential and positive strivings.

CONCLUSION

This chapter provides an overview of family systems concepts and methods. In recent decades, the theory and practice of family therapy has expanded to respond to increasing cultural diversity, challenging socioeconomic conditions, varied family forms, changing gender roles, and variable and extended life courses. As the very definition of the family has broadened, so too has the definition of family therapy, to encompass a wide variety of approaches and formats, including family consultation and brief therapy, more intensive family therapy, individual coaching approaches, multifamily groups and workshops, and collaboration with school, workplace, health care, and other larger systems. In all direct practice, a developmental, systemic orientation is valuable as an integrative framework, fostering an understanding of each person in family and sociocultural contexts and facilitating respectful collaboration with families in clinical and community-based interventions for optimal functioning, well-being, and resilience.

REFERENCES

Ahrons, C. (2004). *We're still family.* New York, NY: HarperCollins.

Andersen, T. (1987). The reflecting team: Dialogue and meta-dialogue in clinical work. *Family Process, 26,* 415–428.

Anderson, C.M. (2012). The diversity, strengths, and challenges of single-parent households. In F. Walsh, (Ed.), *Normal family processes: Growing diversity and complexity* (4th ed., 128–148). New York, NY: Guilford Press.

Anderson, C. M., Reiss, D., & Hogarty, G. (1986). *Schizophrenia and the family.* New York, NY: Guilford Press.

Anderson, H. (1997). *Conversation, language, and possibility: A postmodern approach to therapy.* New York, NY: Basic Books.

Aponte, H. (1994). *Bread and spirit: Therapy with the new poor.* New York, NY: W. W. Norton.

Bateson, G. (1979). *Mind and nature: A necessary unity.* New York, NY: Dutton.

Berg, I. (1997). *Family-based services: A solution-focused approach.* New York, NY: W. W. Norton.

Bernstein, A. (2007). Re-visioning, restructuring, and reconciliation: Clinical practice with complex postdivorce families. *Family Process, 46*(1), 67–78.

Bertalanffy, L. von. (1968). *General system theory: Foundation, development, applications.* New York, NY: Braziller.

Boscolo, L., Cecchin, G., Hoffman, L., & Penn, P. (1987). *Milan systemic family therapy: Conversations in theory and practice.* New York, NY: Basic Books.

Boss, P. (1999). *Ambiguous loss.* Cambridge, MA: Harvard University Press.

Boszormenyi-Nagy, I. (1987). *Foundations of contextual family therapy.* New York, NY: Brunner/ Mazel.

Bowen, M. (1978). *Family therapy in clinical practice.* New York, NY: Jason Aronson.

Byng-Hall, J. (1995). Creating a secure family base: Some implications of attachment theory for family therapy. *Family Process, 34*(1), 45–58.

Campbell, T. (2003). The effectiveness of family interventions for physical disorders. *Journal of Marital & Family Therapy, 29*(2), 263–281.

Carter, B., & McGoldrick, M. (2001). Advances in coaching: Family therapy with one person. *Journal of Marital & Family Therapy, 27,* 281–300.

Cecchin, G. (1987). Hypothesizing, circularity, and neutrality revisited: An invitation to curiosity. *Family Process, 26,* 405–414.

Dattilio, F. M. (2005). The restructuring of family schemas: A cognitive-behavioral perspective. *Journal of Marital & Family Therapy, 31*(1), 15–30.

de Shazer, S. (1988). *Clues: Investigating solutions in brief therapy.* New York, NY: W. W. Norton.

Engstrom, M. (2012). Family processes in kinship care. In F. Walsh (Ed.), *Normal family processes* (4th ed., 196-221). New York. NY: Guilford Press.

Falicov, C. J. (2007). Working with transnational immigrants: Expanding meanings of family, community and culture. *Family Process, 46,* 157–172.

Falicov, C. (2012). Immigrant family processes: A multidimensional framework. In F. Walsh (Ed.). *Normal family processes* (4th ed., pp. 297–322). New York, NY: Guilford Press.

Falicov, C. J. (2013). *Latino families in therapy: A guide to multicultural practice.* (2nd ed.). New York, NY: Guilford Press.

Framo, J. (1980). Family of origin as a therapeutic resource for adults in marital and family therapy: You can and should go home again. *Family Process, 15,* 193–210.

Freedman, J., & Combs, G. (1996). *Narrative therapy: The social construction of preferred realities.* New York, NY: W. W. Norton.

Goldenberg, I., & Goldenberg, H. (2013). *Family therapy: An overview* (8th ed.). Belmont, CA: Brooks/Cole.

Gonzalez, S., & Steinglass, P. (2002). Application of multifamily groups in chronic medical disorders. In W. F. McFarlane (Ed.), *Multifamily groups in the treatment of severe psychiatric disorders* (pp. 315–341). New York, NY: Guilford Press.

Green, R. J. (2012). Gay and lesbian family life: Risk, resilience, and rising expectations. In F. Walsh (Ed.). *Normal family processes* (4th ed., 172–195). New York, NY: Guilford Press.

Greenberg, L., & Johnson, S. (2010). *Emotionally focused therapy for couples.* New York, NY: Guilford Press.

Greene, S., Anderson, E., Forgatch, M. S., & DeGarmo, D. S., & Hetherington, E. M. (2012). Risk and resilience after divorce. In F. Walsh (Ed.), *Normal family processes* (4th ed., pp. 102–127). New York: Guilford Press.

Haley, J. (1976). *Problem-solving therapy.* San Francisco, CA: Jossey-Bass.

Henggeler, S. W., Clingempeel, W., Brondino, M. J., & Pickrel, S. G. (2002). Four-year follow-up of multisystemic therapy with substance-abusing and substance-dependent juvenile offenders. *Journal of the American Academy of Child & Adolescent Psychiatry, 41*(7), 868–874.

Hoffman, L. (1990). Constructing realities: An art of lenses. *Family Process, 29,* 1–13.

Imber-Black, E. (2012). The value of rituals in family life. In F. Walsh (Ed.), *Normal family processes* (4th ed., pp. 483–498). New York, NY: Guilford Press.

Knudsen-Martin, C. (2012). Changing gender norms in families and societies: Toward equality and complexities. In F. Walsh (Ed.), *Normal family processes* (4th ed., pp. 324-346). New York, NY: Guilford Press.

Koenig, H., & King, D. (Eds.). (2012). *Handbook of religion and health* (2nd ed.). New York, NY: Oxford University Press.

Landau, J. (2007). Enhancing resilience: Families and communities as agents for change. *Family Process, 46*(3), 351–365.

Lebow, J., & Stroud, C. (2012). Assessment of couple and family functioning: Prevailing models and instruments. In F. Walsh (Ed.). *Normal family processes* (4th ed., pp. 501-528). New York, NY: Guilford Press.

Lefley, H. (2009). *Family psychoeducation for serious mental illness: Evidence-based practices.* New York, NY: Oxford University Press.

Liddle, H. A., Santisteban, D. A., Levant, R. F., & Bray, J. H. (Eds.). (2002). *Family psychology: Science-based interventions.* Washington, DC: American Psychological Association.

Madsen, W.C. (2009). Collaborative helping: A practice framework for family-centered services. *Family Process, 48,* 103–116.

Madsen, W. C. (2011). Collaborative helping maps: A tool to guide thinking and action in family-centered services. *Family Process, 50,* 529–543.

McCubbin, H., McCubbin, M., McCubbin, A., & Futrell, J. (Eds.). (1998). *Resiliency in ethnic minority families: Vol. 2. African-American families.* Thousand Oaks, CA: Sage.

McCubbin, H., Thompson, A., Thompson, E., & Fromer, J. (Eds.). (1998). *Resiliency in ethnic minority families: Vol. 1. Native American and immigrant families.* Thousand Oaks, CA: Sage.

McCubbin, H., & Patterson, J. M. (1983). The family stress process: The double ABCX model of adjustment and adaptation. *Marriage and Family Review, 6*(1/2), 7–37.

McDaniel, S., Hepworth, J., & Doherty, H. (2007). *Medical family therapy: Psychosocial treatment of families with health problems* (2nd ed.). New York, NY: Basic Books.

McFarlane, W. (Ed.). (2002). *Multi-family groups in the treatment of severe psychiatric disorders.* New York, NY: Guilford Press.

McGoldrick, M., Anderson, C., & Walsh, F. (Eds.). (1989). *Women in families: A framework for family therapy.* New York, NY: W. W. Norton.

McGoldrick, M., Garcia-Preto, N., & Carter, B. (Eds.). (2014). *The expanded life cycle: Individual, family, and social perspectives* (5th ed.). Needham Heights, MA: Allyn & Bacon.

McGoldrick, M., Gerson, R., & Petry, S. (2008). *Genograms: Assessment and intervention* (3rd ed.). New York, NY: W. W. Norton.

McGoldrick, M., & Hardy, K. (Eds.). (2008). *Revisioning family therapy: Race, culture, and gender in clinical practice* (2nd ed.). New York, NY: Guilford Press.

Miklowitz, D., (2010). *Bi-polar disorder: A family-focused treatment approach.* (2nd ed.). New York, NY: Guilford Press.

Minuchin, P., Colapinto, J., & Minuchin, S. (2006). *Working with families of the poor* (2nd ed.). New York, NY: Guilford Press.

Minuchin, S. (1974). *Families and family therapy.* Cambridge, MA: Harvard University Press.

Pasley, K., & Garneau, C. (2012). Remarriage and stepfamily life. In F. Walsh (Ed.). *Normal family processes* (4th ed., pp. 149-171). New York, NY: Guilford Press.

Patterson, G. R., Reid, J. B., Jones, R. R., & Conger, R. E. (1975). *A social learning approach to family intervention.* Eugene, OR: Castalia.

Rolland, J. S. (1994). *Families, illness and disabilities: An integrative treatment model.* New York, NY: Basic Books.

Rolland, J. S. (2012). Mastering family challenges in serious illness and disability. In F. Walsh (Ed.), *Normal family processes* (4th ed., pp. 452–482). New York, NY: Guilford Press.

Rowe, C. L., & Liddle, H. A. (2008). When the levee breaks: Treating adolescents and families in the aftermath of Hurricane Katrina. *Journal of Marital & Family Therapy, 34,* 132–148.

Rutter, M. (1987). Psychosocial resilience and protective mechanisms. *American Journal of Orthopsychiatry, 57,* 316–331.

Santisteban, D. A., Coatsworth, J., Perez-Vidal, A., Kurtines, W. M., Schwartz, S. J., LaPerriere, A., et al. (2003). Efficacy of brief strategic family therapy in modifying Hispanic adolescent behavior problems and substance use. *Journal of Family Psychology, 17*(1), 121–133.

Satir, V. (1972). *Peoplemaking.* Palo Alto, CA: Science and Behavior Books.

Saul, J. (2013). *Collective trauma, collective healing.* New York, NY: Springer.

Scheinkman, M. (2008). The multi-level approach: A road map for couples therapy. *Family Process, 47,* 197–213.

Seccombe, K. (2002). "Beating the odds" versus "changing the odds": Poverty, resilience, and family policy. *Journal of Marriage and the Family, 64*(2), 384–394.

Sexton, T., & Alexander, J. (2003). Functional family therapy: A mature clinical model for working with at-risk adolescents and their families. In T. Sexton, G. Weeks, & M. Robbins (Eds.), *Handbook of family therapy* (pp. 323–363). New York, NY: Brunner-Routledge.

Sheinberg, M., & Fraenkel, P. (2001). *The relational trauma of incest: A family-based approach to treatment.* New York, NY: Guilford Press.

Siegel, D. (2012). *The developing mind.* (2nd ed.). New York, NY: Guilford Press.

Spotts, E. (2012). Unraveling the complexity of gene-environment interplay and family processes. In F. Walsh (Ed.), *Normal family processes: Growing diversity and complexity* (4th ed., pp. 529–552). New York, NY: Guilford Press.

Sprenkle, D., Davis, S., & Lebow, J. (2009). *Common factors in couple and family therapy.* New York, NY: Guilford Press.

Szapocznik, J., & Williams, R. A. (2000). Brief strategic family therapy: Twenty-five years of interplay among theory, research and practice in adolescent behavior problems and drug abuse. *Clinical Child and Family Psychology Review, 3*(2), 117–134.

Ungar, M. (2004). The importance of parents and other caregivers to the resilience of high-risk adolescents. *Family Process, 43*(1), 23–41.

Walsh, F. (2003). Family resilience: A framework for clinical practice. *Family Process, 42*(1), 1–18.

Walsh, F. (2006). *Strengthening family resilience* (2nd ed.). New York, NY: Guilford Press.

Walsh, F. (2007). Traumatic loss and major disasters: Strengthening family and community resilience. *Family Process, 46*(2), 207–227.

Walsh, F. (2009a). Human-animal bonds II: The role of pets in family systems and family therapy. *Family Process, 48*(4), 481–499.

Walsh, F. (Ed.). (2009b). *Spiritual resources in family therapy* (2nd ed.). New York, NY: Guilford Press.

Walsh, F. (2010). Spiritual diversity: Multifaith perspectives in family therapy. *Family Process, 49,* 330–348.

Walsh, F. (Ed.). (2012). *Normal family processes: Growing diversity and complexity* (4th ed.). New York, NY: Guilford Press.

Walsh, F. (2013). Community-based practice applications of a family resilience framework. In D. Becvar (Ed.), *Handbook of family resilience* (pp. 65-82). New York, NY: Springer.

Walsh, F. (2014). Families in later life: Challenges, opportunities, and resilience. In M. McGoldrick,

N. Garcia-Preto, & B. Carter (Eds.), *The expanded family life cycle* (5th ed.). Boston, MA: Allyn & Bacon.

Walsh, F., & McGoldrick, M. (Eds.). (2004). *Living beyond loss: Death in the family* (2nd ed.). New York, NY: W. W. Norton.

Watzlawick, P., Beavin, J., & Jackson, D. (1967). *Pragmatics of human communication.* New York, NY: W. W. Norton.

Weakland, J., Fisch, R., Watzlawick, P., & Bodin, A. (1974). Brief therapy: Focused problem resolution. *Family Process, 13,* 141–168.

Whitaker, C. (1992). Symbolic experiential family therapy: Model and methodology. In J. K. Zeig (Ed.), *The evolution of psychotherapy* (pp. 13–23). Philadelphia, PA: Brunner/Mazel.

White, M., & Epston, D. (1990). *Narrative means to therapeutic ends.* New York, NY: W. W. Norton.

8

COGNITIVE-BEHAVIORAL THERAPY WITH ADULTS

DONALD K. GRANVOLD

Cognitive-behavioral therapy (CBT) has continued to evolve as the leading evidence-based practice treatment methodology. Several factors may account for this reputation. First, CBT methods lend themselves to empirical evaluation. Specific CBT procedures have been developed and implemented for the treatment of myriad psychological problems and disorders. Many intervention procedures have been conducted repetitively and evaluated for efficacy. Furthermore, many cognitivists are researchers and have sought not only to implement their interventions but to conduct controlled outcome evaluations of their efforts. The result is a large body of research lending support to the efficacy of CBT. Finally, the influence of the CBT movement has been considerable, such that the sheer numbers of those doing CBT may now exceed the adherents to many other approaches to treatment.

Cognitivism emerged during the mid- to late 1950s, when behaviorism was strongly challenging psychoanalytic theory. So profound has been the cognitive movement that it has been described as revolutionary in its impact on both the conceptualization of human functioning and human change interventions (Baars, 1986; Dember, 1974; Ingram & Kendall, 1986; Ingram & Siegle, 2001; Mahoney, 1977). Professionals with a background in psychoanalytic theory and many who were trained in behaviorism have actively participated in this movement, and the influence of both schools of thought can be discerned in various cognitive-behavioral methods. This movement has had a discernible influence on social work theory and practice (Berlin & Marsh, 1993; Brower & Nurius, 1993; Cobb, 2008; Franklin, 1995; Franklin & Nurius, 1998; Granvold, 1988, 1989, 1994a, 1996, 1999, 2007, 2009a, 2009b; Nurius, 1991; Nurius & Berlin, 1994; Nurius & Majerus, 1988; Regehr, 2001; Richey, 1994; Ronen & Freeman, 2007; Saleebey, 2006; Vonk & Early, 2009). Twenty years ago, Mahoney and Lyddon (1988) identified more than 20 distinct varieties of cognitive therapy (CT). CBT has continued to be expanded, enhanced, and elaborated, resulting in a variety of conceptualizations of human distress and treatment models. The predominant focus of cognitive methods is on the private inner experience of the individual. These phenomena are ascribed a central role in the etiology, maintenance, and treatment of human disturbance, distress, and maladaptive behaviors. Furthermore, the meaning-making function of humans directly influences the ways individuals experience the vicissitudes of life across the life span. These same meaning-making capacities enable humans to reconstruct the past, redefine the present, and creatively construe a future of possibilities.

While cognition is recognized as highly viable for intervention, most cognitivists believe in reciprocal determinism (Bandura, 1978)—the view that cognitions, behavior, personal factors (emotions, motivation, physiology, and physical factors), and social-environmental factors are interactive. Consistent with this view, early in the cognitivist movement, behavioral factors were specified for incorporation in the design of assessment and treatment methodologies. Cognitive intervention thus evolved to cognitive-behavioral intervention, a more accurate descriptor for the interventions practiced by most cognitivists.

The two original cognitive interventions, Albert Ellis's (1962) rational-emotive therapy (RET) and Beck's (1976) CT, focused specifically on the examination of existing beliefs on the basis of rationality and validity. Both approaches sought cognitive change through cognitive restructuring. Both promoted behavior change along with cognitive change efforts. A. T. Beck has recommended behavioral activation as one of the first steps in the treatment of depressed clients (personal communication, January 1999). Although behavior change has been integral to the treatment models of Ellis and Beck, cognitive change is central to their conceptualizations of human distress and psychotherapeutic treatment. The cognitive-behavioral interventions developed by behaviorally trained theorists are markedly different. The intention with these methods has been the development of strategies to teach specific cognitive skills rather than to restructure existing cognition (Hollon & Beck, 1994). Self-instruction training, stress inoculation training (Meichenbaum, 1977), and problem-solving training (D'Zurilla & Goldfried, 1971;

D'Zurilla & Nezu, 1999, 2001) represent these latter behaviorally oriented cognitive-behavioral approaches. Thus, although both approaches incorporate cognitive and behavioral methods, they go about it differently. As the methods have evolved, the distinctions between them have become increasingly fuzzy. Furthermore, many more cognitive-behavioral approaches have been developed, often designed to treat specific populations (Barlow, 2002; Dattilio & Freeman, 2007; Ellis, Sichel, Yeager, DiMattia, & DiGiuseppe, 1989; Epstein & Baucom, 2002; Follette & Ruzek, 2006; Kingdon & Turkington, 1994; Linehan, 1993; Wells, 1997; Wright, Thase, Beck, & Ludgate, 1993). Hollon and Beck (1994) significantly state that "although it is clear that differences in process and procedure do exist [among all cognitive-behavioral approaches], it is still not known whether these variations have implications for efficacy" (p. 430). While this statement was made some 15 years ago, research seeking comparative outcomes between cognitive-behavioral methods is ongoing. Furthermore, cognitive-behavioral interventions continue to be developed, expanded, and modified, providing myriad opportunities and challenges for practitioners and researchers to determine comparative efficacy.

EFFECTIVENESS OF COGNITIVE-BEHAVIORAL INTERVENTIONS

Cognitive-behaviorists have emerged as a driving force in the multidisciplinary field of psychotherapy. Cognitive-behavioral approaches are among the most frequently used intervention procedures. This distinction is well deserved given the established efficacy of the methods. In this age of evidence-based practice, social workers and other mental health professionals seek proven procedures, those on which they believe they can rely to produce both rapidly effective and resilient (long-lasting and relapse-resistant) change. A mass of findings supports the efficacy of cognitive and cognitive-behavioral methods in the treatment of a broad range of clients experiencing personal, interpersonal, and social issues and problems (Barlow, 2002, 2008; Beck, 1995; Brower & Nurius, 1993; Clark, Beck, & Alford, 1999; Craighead, Craighead, Kazdin, & Mahoney, 1994; Dattilio & Freeman, 2000, 2007; Dobson, 2001; Follette & Ruzek, 2006; Freeman & Dattilio, 1992; Freeman, Pretzer, Fleming, & Simon, 2004; Granvold, 1994a; Hollon & Beck, 1986, 1994; Kuehlwein & Rosen, 1993; Leahy, 2004; Scott, Williams, & Beck, 1989; Whisman, 2008).[1]

The broad base of support for CBT methods extends to applications across diverse populations. Clients from various socioeconomic backgrounds and educational levels have been effectively treated. Procedures have been designed and modified for application to all ages, from preschoolers to the elderly. Treatment formats have included individual, group, couple, and family interventions. In recent years, CBT has been applied to many at-risk populations, including a broad range of trauma survivors (Dattilio & Freeman, 2007; Follette &

Ruzek, 2006), victims and perpetrators of partner violence (Hamberger & Holtzworth-Munroe, 2007; Holtzworth-Munroe, Meehan, Rehman, & Marshall, 2002), victims of rape and sexual abuse (Muran, 2007; White, 2007), suicidal clients (Freeman, Martin, & Ronen, 2007; Reinecke, 2000; Reinecke, Washburn, & Becker-Weldman, 2007), and divorcing or divorced clients (Granvold, 1994b, 2000a, 2000b, 2008b, 2009b). Although clinicians have enjoyed remarkable success in applying cognitive-behavioral procedures to an array of populations and problems, further applications to at-risk populations with which social workers so often come into contact are ripe for development.

THEORETICAL DEVELOPMENTS IN COGNITIVE PSYCHOTHERAPIES AND PRACTICE IMPLICATIONS

Behavior therapy (BT) is considered to be the first wave in the development of more scientifically

---

[1]Treatment efficacy has been demonstrated in the treatment of *anxiety and panic disorders* (Barlow, 2002; Beck, Sokol, Clark, Berchick, & Wright, 1992; D. M. Clark et al., 1994; D. M. Clark et al., 1999; Craske & Barlow, 2008; Dattilio & Kendall, 2000; Loerch et al., 1999), *social phobia* (Antony & Rowa, 2008; Clark et al., 2003, 2006; Heimberg et al., 1998; Stangier, Heidenreich, Peitz, Lauterbach, & Clark, 2003; Turk, Heimberg, & Magee, 2008), *depression* (Barlow & Hofmann, 1997; Clark, Beck, & Alford, 1999; Hollon & DeRubeis, 2004; Hollon, Thase, & Markowitz, 2002; Young, Rygh, Weinberger, & Beck, 2008), *personality disorders* (Beck, Freeman, & Associates, 1990; Bienenfeld, 2007; Davidson, 2008; Linehan, 1993; Pretzer & Beck, 2004; Sperry, 1999), *posttraumatic stress disorder* (Clark & Ehlers, 2004; Dancu & Foa, 1992; Mueser et al., 2008; Resick, Monson, & Rizvi, 2008; Riggs, Cahill, & Foa, 2006), *schizophrenia* (Basco, Kingdon, Turkington, & Wright, 2009; Kingdon & Turkington, 1994; Pfammatter, Junghan, & Brenner, 2006; Rathod, Kingdon, Weiden, & Turkington, 2008; Rector, 2004; Turkington et al., 2008), *child sexual abuse victimization* (Cloitre & Rosenberg, 2006; McDonagh et al., 2005; Resick, Nishith, & Griffin, 2003), *obsessive-compulsive disorder* (Clark, 2004a, 2004b; Franklin & Foa, 2008), *anger control* (Beck & Fernandez, 1998; Fernandez & Beck, 2001; Novaco & Chemtob, 1998), *chronic pain* (Evers, Kraaimaat, van Riel, & de Jong, 2002; Keefe et al., 1990; Thorn, 2004; Turk & Gatchel, 2002), *eating disorders* (Agras et al., 1992; Agras, Telch, Arnow, Eldredge, & Marnell, 1997; Ball & Mitchell, 2004; Craighead & Agras, 1991; Epstein & Sloan, 2005; Fairburn, Cooper, Shafran, & Wilson, 2008; Fairburn & Harrison, 2003; Mitchell et al., 2004; Myers, 2007; Telch, Agras, Rossiter, Wilfley, & Kenardy, 1990; Wilson, Grilo, & Vitousek, 2007), *medical disorders* (Andrasik & Walch, 2003; DiTomasso, Martin, & Kovnat, 2000), *substance abuse* (Beck, Wright, & Newman, 1992; Beck, Wright, Newman, & Liese, 1993; Higgins, Sigmon, & Heil, 2008; Irvin, Bowers, Dunn, & Wong, 1999; McCrady, 2001; Newman, 2004), *couple problems* (Baucom, Shoham, Mueser, Daiuto, & Stickle, 1998; Epstein, 2004; Epstein & Baucom, 2002; Granvold, 2007; Granvold & Jordon, 1994), and *family problems* (Bedrosian & Bozicas, 1994; Dattilio, 2000, 2004; Dattilio & Epstein, 2005).

based treatments. An array of behavioral methods were developed and applied to various problems and populations. Some of the behavioral procedures used today were developed during the BT movement and have remained viable. CT represents the second wave of development, spearheaded by Beck, Ellis, and Kelly. The two waves have been effectively merged into cognitive-behavior therapy. Hayes (2004) has described the recent developments in these therapies as the third wave of BT:

> Grounded in an empirical, principle-focused approach, the third wave of behavioral and cognitive therapy is particularly sensitive to the context and functions of psychological phenomena, not just their form, and thus tends to emphasize contextual and experiential change strategies in addition to more direct and didactic ones. These treatments tend to seek the construction of broad, flexible, and effective repertoires over an eliminative approach to narrowly defined problems, and to emphasize the relevance of the issues they examine for clinicians as well as clients. The third wave reformulates and synthesizes previous generations of behavioral and cognitive therapy and carries them forward into questions, issues, and domains previously addressed by other traditions, in hope of improving both understanding and outcomes. (p. 658)

The therapies of the third wave are different but share some common characteristics, including "focus on mindfulness, acceptance, diffusion, the patient's values in life, relationships, the rationale for how the treatment works, and the client-therapist relationship" (Ost, 2008, p. 297). The most prominent third-wave therapies are a heterogeneous group of treatments including dialectical behavior therapy (Koons, 2008; Linehan, 1993; Linehan & Dexter-Mazza, 2008; Linehan & Koerner, 2012; Robins, Fenwick, Donnelly, & Lacy, 2008), integrative behavioral couples therapy (Jacobson & Christensen, 1996), mindfulness-based cognitive therapy (Germer, Siegel, & Fulton, 2005; Segal, Williams, & Teasdale, 2002), behavioral activation (Dimidjian et al., 2006; Dobson et al., 2008; Hopko et al., 2011; MacPherson et al., 2010; Martel,

Dimidjian, Herman-Dunn, 2010; Snarski et al., 2011), acceptance and commitment therapy (ACT) (Hayes, 2012; Hayes, Strosahl, & Wilson, 1999; Hofmann & Asmundson, 2008), and schema therapy (Arntz & van Genderen, 2009; Young, Klosko, & Weishaar, 2003). Some assumptions central to cognitive-behavior therapy have come under scrutiny and challenge with the development of these treatment approaches. ACT has caused the greatest controversy within CBT circles. It is noteworthy that, while relatively new to the field, ACT has been applied to a broad range of problems and populations. A number of empirical studies have been undertaken to evaluate the efficacy of ACT, some making direct comparisons of CT with ACT (Bohlmeijer, Fledderus, Rokx, & Pieterse, 2011; Dalrymple & Herbert, 2007; Forman, Herbert, Moltra, Yeomans, & Geller, 2007; Lappalainen et al., 2007). Preliminary results provide support for the efficacy of the model. See Kahl, Winter, & Schweiger (2012) for a review of the third wave of cognitive behavioral therapies.

Constructivist Theory and Practice

A postmodernism movement is also under way within and outside the CBT circle. Although not widely embraced, the constructivist and social constructionist philosophies of human functioning and human change processes merit special attention. Although the following consideration is focused on constructivism, social constructionism shares much in common with constructivism (Gergen, 1991, 1994). In 1993, Mahoney noted an evolution within the CT revolution resulting in a philosophical bifurcation among cognitivists. He went on to state that constructivism is the source of "the first major conceptual debate in the field" (p. 189). Constructive metatheory or constructivism has emerged in contrast to traditional or orthodox CT. Constructivism represents a philosophic departure from the ontological realist stance of most early cognitivists and carries with it an array of practice implications. (Ontology is the study of the nature of reality and existence.)

Constructivist metatheory was spawned in an intellectual environment significantly shaped by the influence of postmodernism (Neimeyer, 1995). The postmodern perspective rejects the view of an objective reality in favor of the intersubjectivity of all human experience. It is assumed that people are active participants in meaning making. Reality is subjective, the cocreation of the individual and the stimulus condition. Meanings are socially embedded and are constructed out of life experience. Reality is a dynamic rather than a static condition. Consequently, while some meanings are rather inexorable over time, other meanings are highly subject to reconstruction. The passage of time, altered circumstances, and selfhood changes have a tremendous potential impact on meaning reconstruction. Socialization promotes the tendency in people to form rather restrictive, often singular views of complex life events, circumstances, and processes. Furthermore, negative constructions often prevail over more positive meanings. These simplistic, absolutistic, and negative biases in human meaning making are considered to be readily challengeable psychotherapeutically (Granvold, 2007).

As noted above, constructivism stands in contrast to realism ontologically. According to realism, there is a singular, stable, external reality that can be known. Truth objectively exists, and cognitions can be checked against this reality. Such a correspondence theory of truth (validity) is rejected by constructivists in favor of a conceptualized personal reality, unique to the individual, which can be appraised on the basis of viability. Here, viability is a function of the consequences for the individual adopting the conceptualization and the "overall coherence with the larger system of personally or socially held beliefs into which it is incorporated" (R. A. Neimeyer, 1993a). Epistemologically, constructivism is based on a motor theory of the mind in which "the mind appears as an active, constructive system, capable of producing not only its output but also to a large extent the input it receives, including sensations that lie at the base of its own constructions" (Guidano, 1988, p. 309). Knowledge is an evolutionary result and an interactive process. This view is in contrast to the sensory theories, which hold that information flows inward through the senses to the mind, where it is maintained, a view Popper (1972) referred to as "the bucket theory of the mind."

On the basis of these philosophic differences, constructivists approach clinical practice in a markedly different way from traditional cognitivists:

1. Individual life span development is explored. Particular attention is paid to attachment processes across the life cycle.

2. Individuals are viewed from a systems perspective in which a client's experience produces a series of perturbations to the equilibrium of the self-system. These perturbations are viewed as inherent to the process of change and development. Thus, rather than framing client concerns as problems, a process orientation is adopted. The goal of therapy based on a problem view is corrective—to modify, minimize, or eliminate the problem. The process orientation goal is to explore clients' personal meanings and guide the transformation of these meanings into more highly viable meaning constructs (Lyddon, 1990). A problem is conceptualized as a discrepancy between a client's current capacity and the developmental challenges being experienced.

3. Emotional expressions are considered by constructivists to be integral to the personal meaning and personal development processes of the individual. Rather than exercising efforts to control, diminish, or terminate emotional expressiveness (viewed as potentially counterproductive), clients are encouraged to explore, experience, and express their emotions.

4. Selfhood processes: The self is not singular or fixed but rather is a multifaceted and ever-changing system of identity meanings. Selfhood is a process reflecting a history of development and accumulated meanings forged through tacit and explicit cognitive operations (Guidano, 1987, 1988). The evolutionary elaboration of self results in a multifaceted self comprising self-schemas that are variably activated in a social context. Since schemas are seldom purged from

our memory system, we have ever-increasing sets of self-conceptions. Due to cognitive limitations, only a partial set of self-schemas can be activated at a given time. The activated "self" is the one that "reflects meaningful links between the demands of the situation and self-conceptions related to those cues" (Nurius & Berlin, 1994, p. 255). Thus, the socially embedded nature of self-schemas plays a powerful role in the activation of one set of self-conceptions over another. From the above conceptualization, it can be concluded that multiple possible selves exist among stored schemas (Markus & Nurius, 1986). One's active sense of self is *never* a complete representation of one's being. Furthermore, one's sets of self-conceptions are continuously expanding as the experience of life is translated into selfhood development.

5. Activity: Humans are active participants in their own evolution, not merely "passive pawns in life" (Mahoney & Granvold, 2005, p. 75). Individuals are seen as ripe with potential to assume a proactive role in their experiencing of life. The past may be revisited and given new meaning through the application of current perspectives and preferential ways of construing past realities. Life in the moment reflects the intersection of external demands and human choice. While not within total human control, individual agency is a powerful influence on the meaning and experience of life in the moment. As with the past and the present, constructive focus on the future is biased with hope, possibilities, and rejuvenation. Constructive conceptualizations of human change emphasize client awareness and expression of creative potential, self-efficacy, and activity. Life and psychotherapy are about possibilities—those realized but perhaps lacking form, recognition, or acknowledgment—and possible futures with the potential for achievement, revitalization, and revisioning of self and life experience.

6. While both constructivist and traditional cognitive therapists promote a collaborative relationship with the client, seeking an understanding of the idiosyncratic meanings the client brings to therapy, constructive therapists tend to be far less active-directive in the disputation of distorted, unrealistic, or irrational beliefs and opt rather to invite the client to construct an alternative view, or they challenge the viability of the views held. Constructivists tend to be more metaphoric, approximate, exploratory, and intuitive (R. A. Neimeyer, 1993b).[2]

The constructivist movement is strong within the cognitivist ranks. Most cognitivists are philosophical constructivists, and although constructive psychotherapy approaches may be evident in their clinical procedures, many continue to practice predominantly traditional CBT.

The remainder of this chapter is devoted to the explication of traditional CBT procedures. It should be emphasized, however, that the boundaries between constructivism and traditional cognitivism are fuzzy. The content that follows may be representative of the actual practice behaviors of both persuasions at various points.

COMMON FEATURES OF COGNITIVE-BEHAVIORAL TREATMENT

Although there is great variability in the way CBT is practiced, there are distinguishing features that set cognitive-behavioral intervention apart from other approaches. The following features are

---

[2]See the following sources for a more comprehensive and in-depth exposure to constructivist psychotherapies: Granvold (1996, 1999, 2008a, 2008b), Guidano (1984, 1991, 1995), Guidano and Liotti (1983, 1985), Kuehlwein and Rosen (1993), Mahoney (1991, 1995, 2003), Mahoney and Granvold (2005), G. J. Neimeyer (1993), R. A. Neimeyer (1993a, 1993b, 1993c, 1995, 2009), Neimeyer and Raskin (2000, 2001), Raskin and Bridges (2002, 2004, 2008), and Rosen and Kuehlwein (1996).

generally agreed on by cognitive-behaviorists and are reflected in the ways clinical practice is performed.

Idiosyncratic Subjective Experience

The unique private meanings the client holds in relation to the problem and its context are the focus of the collaborative treatment experience. The therapist seeks to understand (1) the specific meanings of life events and corresponding emotional responses; (2) the perceptual patterns, information-processing patterns, beliefs, and belief structures that are operative in organizing reality; and (3) the causal connections the client makes between stimuli in his or her world and responses either experienced personally or observed in others (attributional thinking). Attention to these phenomena validates the client and provides the shared awareness and meaning base from which the client and the therapist collaboratively proceed. Self-report data are relied on heavily in developing an understanding of the client's issues, concerns, and problems and their etiology.

Collaborative Effort

Counseling is a collaborative effort between the client and the therapist. The client provides specific content related to views of self, others, and the world; implements the strategies developed in a session; and reports the outcomes of the efforts. The therapist provides structure, assessment measures and guidelines, characteristic information related to the client's problem and its treatment, alternative intervention strategies for selection and implementation, and evaluation tools and procedures for measuring the outcomes. The generation of a treatment strategy is a team effort in which the client and the therapist join forces against the problem. Trust, an important ingredient in the therapeutic alliance, is built through the collaborative approach. The objective is not only for the client to trust the therapist (and his or her honesty, caring, and

expertise) but for the client to develop and expand trust in self. The collaborative effort may also focus on the client's motivation to change and the personal and social barriers to change. Many involuntary clients proceed with limited motivation to engage or make meaningful change. Other clients who may not qualify as involuntary possess psychological characteristics or exist in interpersonal circumstances that challenge potentially effective change strategies (e.g., cognitive schemas) (Leahy, 2001, 2003). Change-resistant issues such as addictions, strong obsessive-compulsive behaviors, and poor impulse control also pose challenges to treatment compliance and effective, resilient change (Beck et al., 1993; Fairburn et al., 2008; Franklin & Foa, 2008; Freeman & Storie, 2007; Wilson & Pike, 2001).

Unconditional Regard for Self and Others

The therapist represents the view that all humans are worthy as a given and acts to promote the adoption of this philosophy by the client (Ellis, 1977b; Fulton, 2005; Granvold, 1994c). Unconditional regard for oneself and others is based on self-acceptance—acknowledgment that each of us has strengths and limitations, skills and talents offset by ineptness and error proneness, knowledge and ignorance, exceptional traits and flaws, and fallibilities. Self-esteem (which is all too often conditionally founded) is discarded in favor of self-acceptance. It is in the context of accepting oneself with one's flaws and shortcomings as inherently human that the assumption of worthiness can be reconciled as unconditional. To make worthiness anything but unconditional is a formula for failure given the imperfect nature of human beings. This standard of acceptance is applied across the board to all humankind in the form of unconditional regard for others. All are worthwhile *with* their imperfections. Rating one's own traits and behavior and that of others is considered to be acceptable if the rating is not generalized to represent worth, value, or dignity. Nor does this stance promote a disappreciation of excellence, a lack of interest in competence, or a lack of enthusiasm for achievement and development of skills. It is healthy to work toward goals and objectives, to cultivate and hone skills, to limit ignorance through study, and to unleash creativity through experimentation and practice. These activities, however, are in no way measures of self-worth or personal value.

Structured and Directive Approach

Traditional CT is focused on a specific problem that may be cognitive, emotional, behavioral, physical-physiological, social-environmental, or a combination of these areas. In whatever way it is conceptualized, the therapist and the client specifically define issues, concerns, or problems and target them for change. The therapist is responsible for the course of treatment and may act to influence the process by setting treatment guidelines and limits, maintaining a strategic focus on treatment goals or targeted change, and attending to issues such as marginal compliance or noncompliance with agreed-on actions, power struggles, and preparation to end treatment. Although a pervasive spirit of collaboration is sought with the client, the ultimate responsibility for the conduct of treatment resides with the therapist.

Active Approach

The client is expected to take an active role both within and outside the treatment setting. Freeman and Dattilio (1992) noted that the client does not come in to be "therapized" but instead actively participates in resolving the problem. After the strategy for change is formulated collaboratively, the client puts the change effort into effect and gathers outcome data. Homework assignments are used to promote the transfer of gains from the treatment setting to the client's natural environment and to produce more resilient change (Granvold & Wodarski, 1994). Homework is graduated in level of demand and

is structured to facilitate generalization across populations, settings, and circumstances within given settings. The assessment and outcome data that the client gathers are brought to the therapist for collaborative consideration in evaluating the effectiveness of the treatment strategy and the modification of the change effort.

Education Model

CT involves didactic instruction, along with techniques such as bibliotherapy, written assignments, the use of audiotapes and videotapes, and attendance at lectures and seminars. Early in treatment, it is necessary to present the cognitive-behavioral model to the client. The interactive nature of cognitive, emotional, behavioral, physical-physiological, and social-environmental factors and their contribution to emotional disturbance and maladaptive behavior is explained and discussed. The antecedent-behavior-consequence approach to assessment and intervention is identified and applied. The client's misconceptions about the problem and its treatment are addressed early in treatment. The nature of the therapeutic relationship is discussed, with attention focused on the expected collaboration between the therapist and the client. Empirical practice procedures are delineated. Throughout treatment, the therapist educates the client with problem-specific information and content relevant to the treatment process. For example, the concept of relapse prevention is introduced early in treatment, and procedures for the prevention of relapse are presented and discussed at strategic intervals. The development of the client's knowledge and understanding of the issues, concerns, or problems and his or her conceptual grasp of CBT is critical to the collaborative enterprise between the client and the therapist.

Socratic Methods

The use of Socratic questioning is one of the key features of CBT. Far greater results can be expected through the use of the Socratic method than through direct suggestions, explanations, or directives. Skillful questioning facilitates the disclosure of critical cognitive phenomena and leads the client through a process of self-discovery and reasoning. The Socratic method (1) stimulates the client's development of self-awareness and self-observation; (2) facilitates the shift from vague, ill-defined concerns to focused definitions of the problem; (3) opens up topic areas rather than leaving them minimally explored; (4) gives the therapist access to the client's characteristic patterns of perceiving, reasoning, information processing, and problem solving; (5) exposes the client's belief system; (6) exposes the client's coping mechanisms and tolerance of stress; and (7) is effective in the therapist's modeling of reasoning, the challenging of irrational beliefs, and problem solving (Granvold, 1994c, 2009a; Wells, 1997). Questioning also facilitates the client's active participation in the treatment experience, fosters the collaborative effort, and limits the therapist's authoritarian role, which is typical of some treatment approaches.

Empirical Focus

The client and the therapist embark on an empirical investigation of the client's cognitive functioning as it relates to his or her emotional and behavioral responses. Once precepts, ideas, beliefs, attitudes, and expectations are identified, an attempt is made to validate them in a systematic way. The process involves the generation of hypotheses that, when tested, will prove that targeted cognitions are either valid, rational, and adaptive or lack support. These experiments may be in-session exercises in logic, reasoning, or recall of life experiences or may involve in vivo experiments. Disproved hypotheses are revised on the basis of evidence and then retested. Outcome measures are used to document the cognitive, emotional, and behavioral changes that the client experiences as a result of the process. These measures not only are meaningful in evaluating specific cognitive restructuring and

behavior change but also serve to document the success of the treatment and the efficacy of the methods that are used.

Time-Limited Treatment

The therapist's provision of structure to the treatment experience and the active participation of the client shorten the length of time required for effective results. CBT is an efficient approach, and the inherent generalizability of cognitive change combined with behavior change promotes lasting effects. The comparative brevity of CBT methods makes for a comfortable fit with the time limits set by managed care and third-party payer systems.

Relapse Prevention

For treatment to be considered successful, the results must be sustained long after treatment is terminated. In the past, change efforts that showed convincing signs of success at the point of termination often failed to be sustained for a significant period after termination. In short, the methods showed short-term efficacy but were not resilient against posttreatment challenges. Rather than discard the proved methods, a series of strategies to prevent relapse were developed and incorporated in treatment along with the original procedures.

Marlatt (1985) described relapse prevention as "a self-management program designed to enhance the maintenance stage of the habit-change process" (p. 3). Relapse-prevention strategies are integral parts of cognitive treatment for all categories of problems (Antony, Ledley, & Heimberg, 2005; Marlatt & Gordon, 1985; Wilson, 1992). Procedures aimed at maintenance and relapse prevention include self-efficacy development, coping skills training, knowledge of and inoculation against relapse, environmental planning (stimulus control procedures), self-monitoring, lifestyle change, social system support, fading, early detection of relapse cues, and follow-up contacts and booster sessions (Granvold & Wodarski, 1994).

These and other procedures promote clients' sustained mastery of the cognitive, emotional, and behavioral skills developed in treatment and better prepare clients to cope with future challenges to their well-being.

ASSESSMENT

Assessment and intervention have been described as flowing imperceptibly into one another (Weiss & Margolin, 1977). Among the meanings one can draw from this caveat is that assessment itself may effect change (unless it is accomplished totally unobtrusively) and assessment drives intervention. Franklin and Jordan (1999) describe the dual functions of assessment as discovery and change. Ethical treatment obligates the therapist to engage in an assessment process that has structure, design, and strategy yet is flexible enough to allow for spontaneous assessment opportunities.

Cognitive-behavioral intervention relies on assessment that is comprehensive and specific, historic and contemporary, and initial and ongoing. Furthermore, assessment should focus on the therapeutic relationship and the process of therapy. Seeking an understanding of the client requires an exploration of cognitive functioning, behavior in the context of antecedents and consequences, emotional functioning, physical and physiological data (including medical and medication/drug information), and social-environmental functioning. Such an assessment is based on the view that these factors are reciprocally influential (Bandura, 1978), and thus, the cause of the client's condition is multiple and interactionally determined. It is out of a global understanding of the client that specific treatment goals can be identified. Treatment goals may be defined in the following terms: problem or process; individual, social, or environmental; or cognitive, emotional, behavioral, or physical/physiological. In whatever terms they are stated, treatment goals are to derive from a comprehensive yet specific understanding of the client.

Assessment is both historic and contemporary. Family-of-origin content, developmental events, remarkable life events (e.g., trauma, successes), and the factors that have prompted counseling are viable explorations. This content often serves to elucidate the client's current concerns, coping capacity, and change potential. Traditional cognitive-behavioral therapists tend to be highly here-and-now focused (with the exception of their approach to issues such as posttraumatic stress disorder of a historic nature), and thus, the time spent on history is far less than the time devoted to current functioning. Furthermore, historic determinations are integrated with the meanings derived from presenting problems and current behavior.

Assessment is initial and ongoing. Initial assessment findings shape the early phase of intervention. It is necessary to continue to assess the client over time both to gain a more comprehensive or in-depth understanding of the client in his or her social and environmental context and to track ongoing change throughout treatment and at points beyond termination. Berlin and Marsh (1993) provide an excellent description of the range of considerations to guide the therapist in the process of continuous assessment.

Assessment of the therapeutic relationship and the therapy process provides valuable feedback regarding the client's assessment of the therapist as a collaborator in the change effort and the client's appraisals of the methods being implemented and the outcomes achieved. Both client and therapist are involved in constructing and reconstructing an understanding (Berlin & Marsh, 1993), a process that may remain at a highly inferential level if it is not made explicit.

Assessment serves to guide the selection of appropriate interventions and to provide evaluative criteria to determine the efficacy of the therapeutic intervention implemented (Jacobson & Margolin, 1979). As clinical problems are specified, client and therapist collaborate in the assessment process. Although comprehensive assessment relies on exploration in various domains, the utility and relevance of these different domains vary among clinical problems specified for change (Craighead et al., 1994). Thus, for example, some targeted problems may be more environmentally influenced, while others are more specifically cognitive-emotional-behavioral.

Cognitive functioning is recognized as only one ingredient in the dynamic puzzle of human functioning. CBT, however, relies heavily on the assessment of cognitive functioning and the influence of social learning factors on the clinical problem. In the material that follows, the process of cognitive assessment will be presented in detail. (For information on behavioral assessment, refer to Barlow, 1981; Berlin & Marsh, 1993; Ciminero, Calhoun, & Adams, 1986; Craighead et al., 1994; Dimidjian, Martell, Addis, & Herman-Dunn, 2008; Fischer & Corcoran, 1994; Haynes, 1978; Hersen & Bellack, 1976; Hudson, 1990; Nay, 1979.)

Cognition is not a single phenomenon. Its meaning is variable, and therefore, different assessment devices and formats are used depending on the component of cognitive functioning under scrutiny. Cognitive targets of assessment can be subclassified into three categories:

1. *Cognitive content* (also referred to as cognitive products): This includes thoughts, self-verbalizations, decisions, accessible beliefs, values, attributions, images, and recognition-detection meanings attached to stimuli (Ingram & Kendall, 1986).

2. *Cognitive process,* the mechanism by which information is selected (input), transformed, and delivered (output): Included are functions such as selective attention, perception, encoding, storage, and retrieval.

3. *Schema,* a term used to represent two aspects of cognition: First, it denotes cognitive structure—the way in which information is organized and internally represented (Ingram & Kendall, 1986); structure is the mechanism that serves to store information (iconic-sensory phenomena and beliefs) and comprises associative linkages and networks of meaning and memory nodes. Information processing is guided by these activities. Second, schema represents cognitive propositions stored in cognitive structures. Schemas are inflexible, general rules or silent assumptions (beliefs, attitudes, concepts) that develop as enduring concepts from past (early) experiences and form the basis for screening, discriminating, weighing, and coding stimuli and for categorizing, evaluating experiences, and making judgments and distorting reality situations (Riso, du Toit, Stein, & Young, 2007; Rush & Beck, 1978; Young, 1990). The individual's perceptual filters; one's views of self, others, and the world; and cohesive factors that form the bases of appraising and judging are all based on schemas. Young et al. (2003) identified 18 early-forming maladaptive schemas grouped in five domains: (1) disconnection and rejection, (2) impaired autonomy and performance, (3) impaired limits, (4) other-directedness, and (5) over-vigilance and inhibition. Maladaptive schemas may lie dormant only to be activated and displace adaptive schemas when human crises are experienced (e.g., the death of a loved one, divorce, job loss, victimization).

Cognitive Content

The assessment of cognitive content (products) is typically conducted through an interview, with paper and pencil or a computer. An extensive array of standardized measures has been developed for problem areas in which clients' self-statements, thoughts, satisfaction, expectations, and beliefs are sought. In addition to standardized measures, forms for monitoring and recording faulty cognitions and associated responses have also been developed (e.g., the Daily Record of Dysfunctional Thoughts by Beck, Rush, Shaw, & Emery, 1979, and the Rational-Emotive Therapy Self-Help Form by Ellis & Dryden, 1987). These forms may be used as homework, thereby producing individualized data that may not be exposed by standardized measures.[3]

---

[3]For additional information on the assessment of cognitive content, see Blankstein and Segal (2001), Kendall and Hollon (1981), Merluzzi and Boltwood (1989), Merluzzi, Glass, and Genest (1981), Michelson and Ascher (1987), Schwartz and Garamoni (1986), Segal and Shaw (1988), and Young et al. (2008).

Cognitive Process

The assessment of cognitive-process functions is more difficult to accomplish than is the assessment of cognitive content. The assessment of information processing is most frequently accomplished through interview procedures. Beck et al. (1979) described faulty information processing, such as arbitrary inference, selective abstraction, and overgeneralization, as characteristic of depressed clients. They detailed the use of Socratic questioning to expose the process and to validate or invalidate the thinking and thus to arrive at specific information-processing errors. The assessment of cognitive process functions through this interview format has been applied to an array of problems, including anxiety (Beck & Emery, 1985; Blankstein & Segal, 2001; Freeman & Simon, 1989; Guidano & Liotti, 1983; Turk et al., 2008), agoraphobia (Barlow & Craske, 2006; Craske & Barlow, 2008; Michelson, 1987; Thorpe & Burns, 1983), depression (Beck et al., 1979; Blankstein & Segal, 2001; Freeman, 1990; Young et al., 2008), personality disorders (Beck et al., 1990; Beck, Freeman, & Davis, 2003; Linehan & Dexter-Mazza, 2008; Rothstein & Vallis, 1991), anorexia nervosa (Fairburn et al., 2008; Garner & Bemis, 1985), and substance abuse (Beck et al., 1993; Higgins et al., 2008).

Another cognitive-process assessment procedure, developed by Mahoney (1991), is stream of consciousness, "an exercise in which the client is invited to attend to and, as best one can, report ongoing thoughts, sensation, images, memories, and feelings" (p. 295).

Schemas

Assessment of schemas is conducted through probing and Socratic exploration, questionnaires, and personal journals. The objective is vertical exploration, the accessing of core meanings— views about self, others, the world, and the future. Examples of structured assessment methods for use in the interview include the *downward arrow technique* (Burns, 1980; Neimeyer & Neimeyer, 1993), in which a chain of meanings is derived from a triggering event or a cognition considered possibly to stem from a maladaptive schema; *laddering* (R. A. Neimeyer, 1993c), in which a personal construct ladder is elicited to explore meanings surrounding identity and core constructs; and *repertory grid* (Kelly, 1955), a means of eliciting a client's significant constructs through the development of a matrix of elements important in his or her domain (personal meaning networks and interpersonal relationships).

Access to schematic functioning may be done through the use of paper-and-pencil methods, which allow more open-ended or subject-directed reporting of cognitions. Useful questionnaires for this purpose are the Dysfunctional Thought Record (Beck et al., 1979), Thought Listing (Cacioppo & Petty, 1981), and Think-Aloud (Genest & Turk, 1981) techniques.

The personal journal can be a useful assessment technique for various aspects of cognitive functioning. Mahoney (1991) suggests alternative formats, including current events, memories, a structured "life review project," dreams and fantasies, and reflective "notes to myself." The content recorded can produce insights into the client's "web of associations" and expose core meaning structures. Neimeyer and Neimeyer (1993) suggest bringing the journal into treatment to be read aloud by the client or the therapist. Journal content, in addition to being highly meaningful in itself, may stimulate therapeutic discussions, producing highly salient content. Young et al. (2003) recommend the use of lengthy life history assessment forms providing "a comprehensive assessment of the patient's current problems, symptoms, family history, images, cognitions, relationships, biological factors, and significant memories and experiences" (p. 74). Also, Young developed the Young Schema Questionnaire (YSQ-L2) (Young & Brown, 1990, 2001), a self-report measure that provides the therapist with a strength score associated with specific schemas. High-scored items are used clinically by the therapist in probing for further information about the relevant schema. Leahy (2003) developed the Leahy Emotional Schema Scale to access the client's "theory about emotions." The information gleaned is useful in discussing clients' views of their perceived capacity to cope with and modify unappealing emotions and their judgments about specific emotions (e.g., depression is shameful).

INTERVENTIONS

Cognitive-behavioral therapists use an array of techniques in their treatment strategies and target cognition, behavior and, to a lesser degree, emotions as entry points in the change process. The ways in which cognitive and behavioral elements are integrated and the processes believed to mediate change differ across approaches (Hollon & Beck, 1994). Some approaches are more strongly cognitive, with a focus on the cognitive restructuring of peripheral cognitions and on uncovering and modifying core meaning structures and self-schemas. Others are oriented toward cognitive development: the teaching of new cognitive skills. Cognitive-behaviorists also consider physical and physiological factors and social and environmental influences on client functioning. Although it is not specifically addressed here, treatment strategies may include intervention in these components of human functioning as well. The following is a presentation of several major CBT approaches.

Cognitive Restructuring

Cognitive restructuring encompasses a set of procedures with the common goal of challenging, disputing, modifying, and changing existing cognitions (peripheral beliefs, schemas) or cognitive processes (perception, information processing). Typically, the rationality or validity of cognitive constructs (or processing) is examined. Many approaches to cognitive restructuring use the Socratic method to guide the client in the identification, exploration, modification, and elaboration of cognitions (Beck, 1995, 2005; Granvold, 2009a; Wells, 1997). Other approaches use imagery and guided discovery and in vivo behavioral procedures to test out and modify

beliefs (Beck & Weishaar, 2008; Granvold, 2009a). The goal of cognitive restructuring is to guide the client in the exposure of cognitions influencing untoward, unappealing, discomforting, or dysfunctional outcomes and to modify them through further exploration, disputation, or elaboration. In traditional CBT, clients are guided in the use of logic or evidence to examine and modify their exaggerated, distorted, or ill-founded beliefs. That is, does logical or empirical evidence exist to support the client's belief or cognitive processing? The two major interventions with a cognitive restructuring focus are Ellis's rational-emotive behavior therapy (REBT) and Beck's CT.

The constructivist approach to cognitive change is markedly different from traditional cognitive restructuring. No determination is sought as to whether a cognition is *rational* or *irrational*; rather, the focus is on the consequences of the construct under consideration. Many cognitive restructuring efforts are designed to reframe a specific cognition, to replace one thought with another. In some circumstances, it may be undesirable to replace a thought or even to directly attempt to reduce its strength even though it may stimulate unappealing responses and mood states. Furthermore, a client may be unwilling to abandon a given thought. Cognitive elaboration is an alternative approach to cognitive restructuring in which the focus is on the generation of alternative thoughts, views, or meaning constructions without the expectation that the original view be abandoned (Granvold, 1996, 2008a). This approach is particularly useful with clients who hold strongly to a specific belief although the consequences are very negative, emotionally challenging, or unappealing. For example, there may be logical evidence to support clients who maintain a sense of responsibility for an accident or the death of a loved one. The therapist's challenge of the belief may be met with great resistance, incredulity, or offense. Use of cognitive restructuring honors the client's current construct while seeking other meanings, other ways of viewing the stimulus.

Rational-Emotive Behavior Therapy

RET was founded in 1955 by Albert Ellis. Disenchanted with the ineffectiveness and inefficiency of psychoanalytic methods (in which he was trained), Ellis turned to philosophy, an early love, from which he derived his pioneering cognitive treatment method. The bedrock of RET lies in the works of early philosophers (e.g., Epictetus, Aurelius, Socrates) through 20th-century philosophers (e.g., Heidegger, Tillich) and many in between (e.g., Kierkegaard, Kant, Spinoza, Schopenhauer), whose common set of beliefs

> hold that emotional upsetness largely originates in illogical, unrealistic, and irrational thinking and that humans have the distinct ability to monitor this kind of thinking, to reflect on it, and to change it, so that they significantly help themselves solve their everyday problems and their fairly severe disturbances. (Ellis, 1989, p. 7)

In addition to drawing on philosophy, Ellis also turned to BT methods, which he had used to treat himself for severe fear of public speaking and social anxiety about dating. Thus, behavior rehearsal procedures and extra-session behavioral activation have come to be incorporated in RET from its early beginnings, prompting Ellis (1989) to proclaim himself to be the first cognitive-behavioral therapist. RET was renamed REBT in 1993 on the grounds that RET has always stressed and made use of behavioral components (Ellis, 1993).

REBT is a logico-empirical method of psychotherapy in which human disturbance is viewed as largely the product of faulty beliefs, as outlined in Ellis's early work *Reason and Emotion in Psychotherapy* (1962). Ellis clearly stated the integral interrelationship of thinking and emotion and professed that sensing, moving, emoting, and thinking are not experienced in isolation. While stressing the interactive view of human psychological processes, Ellis has accorded cognition a special role in human psychological processes and points to, in particular, the evaluative role thought plays in psychological health and disturbance (Dryden & Ellis, 2001; Ellis & Dryden, 1987).

Rationality and Irrationality

The concept of rationality is central to REBT. Humans are viewed as biologically predisposed to think irrationally, and this tendency has a notable bearing on psychological disturbance. Ellis defines *rational* as "that which aids and abets people achieving their basic goals and purposes" (Dryden & Ellis, 2001, p. 298). These goals and purposes are products of long-term hedonism instead of short-term hedonism in the psychologically healthy human being. In other words, those who delay the immediate satisfaction of their desires in favor of the promotion of ultimate valued and physically healthy consequences are viewed as functioning rationally. *Irrational* means that which prevents people from achieving these ultimate goals. Ellis (1984) notes that "even if everybody had had the most rational upbringing, virtually all humans would often irrationally escalate their individual and social preferences into absolutistic demands on (a) themselves, (b) other people, and (c) the universe around them" (p. 20). Hence, Ellis concludes that there is a human tendency toward irrationality. To elucidate further the issue of rational versus irrational thinking, Ellis posits that rational beliefs "are evaluative cognitions of personal significance that are preferential (i.e., nonabsolute) in nature. They are expressed in the form of 'desires,' 'preferences,' 'wishes,' 'likes,' and 'dislikes'" (Ellis & Dryden, 1987, p. 5). Irrational beliefs differ in two respects from rational beliefs:

> First they are absolute (or dogmatic) in nature and are expressed in the form of "musts," "shoulds," "oughts," "have-to's," etc. Second, as such they lead to negative emotions that largely interfere with goal pursuit and attainment (e.g., depression, anxiety, guilt, anger). (Ellis & Dryden, 1987, pp. 5–6)

The ABCs of REBT

REBT is known for its ABC model of human disturbance, a model that has been labeled the *expanded ABC theory* (Ellis, 1991;

Ellis & Bernard, 1986). A stands for activating event, B represents the individual's belief(s) about the event, and C denotes the person's emotional and behavioral responses or consequences, which derive from B. Ellis's model that posits that restructuring the belief(s) at B, which means changing from irrational to rational thinking through disputation—D—will produce greater emotional well-being—E. According to REBT theory, A is not merely an external reality but the individual's perception of A. While A appears to cause emotional and behavioral consequences directly, the contention is that Bs serve as mediators between A and C. The client, through Socratic dialogue, is taught to challenge his or her irrational thinking and to replace it with rationality.

To illustrate this model, consider the family member of a hospitalized patient who is upset (angry, frustrated, agitated) when a physician fails to meet with the patient and family at an agreed-on time:

1. A. The failure of the physician to appear for the consultation

2. B. "The doctor must honor his or her commitments in a timely fashion."

3. "I can't stand it when people make idle commitments."

4. "Doctors have no feelings for their patients or their patients' families and should be punished for their lack of caring."

5. "My sick family member and I must not matter to the doctor."

6. C. Emotions: anger, hostility, frustration, resentment

7. Behavior: Client angrily confronts the social worker and nursing staff regarding the doctor's irresponsibility, swears and threatens to change doctors or hospitals or call an attorney.

8. D. "Why must the doctor keep the appointment?"

9. "Where is it written that doctors must be on time?"

10. "Even though I am upset, where is the evidence that I can't stand it?"

11. "How does the physician's failure to keep the appointment make him or her an uncaring person?"

Disputation of the beliefs is accomplished through Socratic dialogue.

Derivatives of Irrational Beliefs

Irrational beliefs tend to be rigid, absolutistic, demanding expectations and judgments: "Things must be a certain, fixed way" or "Things must go my way." Three major derivatives flow from irrational beliefs: (1) something is awful (catastrophization); (2) "can't stand it" (demandingness and low frustration tolerance); and (3) damnation ("What a no-goodnik *you* and *I* must be for such treatment!"), which constitutes rating self and others as subhuman.

Ellis (1962, 1994) has identified 11 major illogical, irrational, and self-defeating ideas with which most people in our society have been directly or indirectly indoctrinated. The list is acknowledged as being neither inclusively definitive nor nonoverlapping:

1. It is a dire necessity for adult humans to be loved or approved by virtually every significant other person in their community.

2. One absolutely must be competent, adequate, and achieving in all important respects, or else one is an inadequate, worthless person.

3. People absolutely must act considerately and fairly, and they are damnable villains if they do not. They are their bad acts.

4. It is awful and terrible when things are not the way one would very much like them to be.

5. Emotional disturbance is mainly externally caused, and people have little or no ability to increase or decrease their dysfunctional feelings and behaviors.

6. If something is or may be dangerous or fearsome, one should be constantly and excessively concerned about it and should keep dwelling on the possibility of its occurring.

7. One cannot and must not face life's responsibilities and difficulties; it is easier to avoid them.

8. You must be quite dependent on others and need them and cannot mainly run your own life.

9. One's history is an all-important determiner of one's present behavior; if something once strongly affected one's life, it should indefinitely have a similar effect.

10. Other people's disturbances are horrible; one must feel very upset about them.

11. There is invariably a right, precise, and perfect solution to human problems; it is awful if this perfect solution is not found.

While receiving extensive confirmation from clients and colleagues that these self-defeating beliefs are often operative when an individual is emotionally distressed, Ellis (1994) does not consider them to be a panacea against human disturbances and states that with some people they actually may have limited applicability.

Unconditional Regard for Self and Others

Another salient component of REBT is unconditional regard for self and others (Ellis, 1962, 1973, 1977b). Ellis contends that negative self-rating is a major cause of human disturbance and presents innumerable problems that result when people fail to value themselves very highly (Ellis, 1977b). Among the consequences are diminished appraisal of their successes, a strong demand to prove themselves, intense seeking of approval, self-sabotage of their potential achievements, obsessive comparisons with others, intense performance anxiety, short-range hedonism, a lack of self-discipline, defensiveness, hostility, depression, withdrawal, lack

of self-confidence, and self-berating. Ellis (1977b) makes a profound distinction between self-esteem and self-acceptance when he writes that self-esteem "means that the individual values himself because he has behaved intelligently, correctly, or competently" (p. 101). Hence, conditions are placed on self-esteem that evolve from an appraisal of performance. Obvious flaws in this process result from characteristics such as the imperfect nature of human functioning; changes in skill level over time; extreme, unrealistic performance standards; and the unrealistic expectation that one can exert control over uncontrollable factors.

In addressing the unconditional acceptance of self, Ellis and Dryden (1987) write that "the person accepts herself and others as fallible human beings who do not have to act other than they do and as too complex and fluid to be given any legitimate or global rating" (p. 18). Self-acceptance, or unconditional self-regard, involves the acknowledgment and acceptance of one's strengths and limitations. One's knowledge, talent, skills, and aptitudes are counterbalanced by one's ignorance, incompetence, ineptness, and lack of potential in specific areas. Inasmuch as all humans possess a ledger of strengths and limitations, it is unrealistic to expect to perform with exceeding competence in all areas of life. In short, accepting oneself with one's flaws and limitations is tantamount to the psychologically healthy acceptance of self as human.

Detecting and Disputing Irrational Beliefs

The key to detecting irrational beliefs is in looking for "shoulds," "musts," and "ought to's." Although not all irrational beliefs include *should, must,* or *ought to,* most do. Others may be merely unrealistic or unempirical statements (Ellis, 1977a). By asking, "What is it about A that is causing you C?" the client's unique view (e.g., evaluation, expectation, judgment) of the activating event is uncovered. The likely consequence of this process is the discovery of an irrational thought. A client who is upset (angry, frustrated, hurt, resentful, jealous) over his failure to receive a raise at work could be queried as follows:

Therapist: What is it about not getting a raise that is upsetting to you?

Client: I believe that I deserve a raise.

Therapist: Let's assume that you do. Why must you get what you deserve?

Client: Because if you do what you're supposed to do, you should get what you have coming.

Therapist: It sounds as if you are saying that you should be treated fairly.

Client: Yes, that's it.

Therapist: Why must you be treated fairly?

Client: I guess, because I just should . . . that's what's right.

Therapist: I agree with your desire to be treated fairly, but what evidence do you have that people, you included, are always treated fairly?

Client: None really, I guess. Unfairness seems to be more typical, or at least real common.

In this way, the therapist guides the client in reaching the awareness that his emotional distress is the product of an expectation of fairness, and furthermore, the client articulates an acknowledgment that unfairness is somewhat common:

Therapist: A desire for fairness is a reasonable expectation. But given the commonplace occurrence of unfair treatment in our world, do you think you can legitimately expect to always be treated fairly?

Client: No, not really.

Therapist: What could you tell yourself about being treated unfairly that would allow you to feel less upset?

Client: I guess I could say that I'd like to always be treated fairly, but it's not reasonable to expect to always be treated fairly.

Therapist: Excellent. You've shifted from a demand statement to a preference. Now when you make this shift, how do you feel about not getting a raise?

Client: Upset . . . but less upset, I guess. I still don't like it.

This client has gained an initial awareness of the irrational thought (demand for fairness). The ABCDE model of REBT could be taught at this time and, in many cases, bibliotherapy recommended for more effective knowledge development. It takes repeated bombardment of irrational thoughts with logico-empirical disputation to promote effective change. Furthermore, it is likely that a given client functions with a range of irrational beliefs under an array of circumstances. Therefore, it is necessary in treatment sessions to apply REBT methods repetitively to various activating events.

Cognitive Homework

Clients are assigned various forms of cognitive homework. Alternative methods, formal and informal, may be employed to facilitate disputing of irrational beliefs. Written disputing forms, audiotape disputing, and unstructured in vivo rehearsal are all useful options. Bibliotherapy and prerecorded audiotapes are used to expand the client's understanding and to reinforce rational thinking. A number of imagery techniques, including rational-emotive imagery (Ellis, 1979; Goodman & Maultsby, 1974; Maultsby, 1977, 1984; Maultsby & Ellis, 1974), are taught in session and practiced as homework. Clients gain experience in modifying emotional responses through changing their beliefs while vividly imaging the activating event.

After a brief period during which the therapist instructs the client in relaxation, the client is asked to re-create the activating event in his or her mind (or to imagine the worst thing that could happen to him or her), implode his or her extreme emotional responses, and shift feelings from unhealthy extreme emotions to more appropriate emotive responses, such as disappointment and frustration, through altering the belief(s) underlying the emotions. The therapist may verbally instruct the client to shift his or her thoughts from irrational to rational beliefs while imaging: "Rather than thinking that it's terrible to be laid off your job, think that it's only unfortunate." After the client is given time to achieve the shift, the therapist asks the client to report any changes in emotional intensity or in the actual emotions being experienced.

Emotive Techniques

REBT is known for its use of emotive evocative methods, particularly "shame-attacking" exercises, in which clients publicly act "shameful" (e.g., walk in public with a banana on a string to draw negative attention as a means of developing a tolerance for judgmental and negative feedback and a reduction in approval needs), feel the associated feelings, and become desensitized (tolerate and reduce the discomfort) (Dryden & Ellis, 2001; Ellis, 1969; Ellis & Becker, 1982; Ellis & Dryden, 1987). Clients are encouraged to evoke their emotions creatively for the purpose of in vivo disputing of associated irrational beliefs or to "prove" that the actual consequences are less negative than expected.

Behavioral Techniques

Behavioral assignments have been used in REBT since its inception in recognition of the effect behavior change can have on cognitive change (Dryden & Ellis, 2001; Emmelkamp, Kuipers, & Eggeraat, 1978). Clients are consistently encouraged to revisit the activating event for the purpose of in vivo desensitization and to do so floodingly if it is therapeutically appropriate (Ellis, 1979; Ellis & Dryden, 1987).

Ellis used various behavioral methods to overcome resistance and to reinforce the practice of cognitive change. Rewards and penalties are employed to promote the performance of challenging, emotionally discomforting assignments. Clients are taught to use the Premack principle (Premack, 1965, 1971), in which the performance of homework is a contingency for doing high-reward activities such as watching television, pleasure reading, going online, or talking on the telephone.

Skill training is often used in REBT when a client evidences deficiencies in skills central to or in support of a change effort. Verbal and communication skills, assertiveness, parenting skills, and behavioral skills to enhance sexual functioning (e.g., noncoital sensate pleasuring techniques) are examples of skills areas that may be taught in therapy (or assigned for development outside therapy) to meet performance deficiencies.

To illustrate skills training, consider Martha, a recently divorced woman, whose former husband, Roger, often told her of his recent dating activities when returning the children to her care after visitation. Martha felt deeply hurt when he made these disclosures (since she continued to feel love and attachment toward him). In a role play, the therapist played Martha, while Martha took the role of Roger. The therapist assertively stated,

> "Roger, I have no desire to hear about your dating activities. When you pick up or return the children, the only information we need to discuss is that related to the children. I would appreciate your cooperation in honoring this request."

After several iterations, during which Martha (role-playing Roger) became increasingly argumentative, the roles were reversed. Similarly, the therapist (role-playing Roger) began with an accepting response to the assertive stance taken by Martha. With each subsequent rehearsal, however, Martha's assertiveness was met with greater resistance from the therapist. Martha was given the homework assignment to assert herself with Roger consistent with the rehearsal in session.

Cognitive Therapy

CT (Beck, 1970, 1976; Beck et al., 1979; Beck & Weishaar, 2008) posits that the treatment of an emotional disturbance or a behavioral problem is achieved through accessing and modifying "the cognitive content of one's reaction to the upsetting event or stream of thought" (DeRubeis & Beck, 1988, p. 273). The cognitive content includes peripheral thoughts, beliefs, attitudes, appraisals, values, causal attributions, and meanings that may be accessed relatively easily through client self-report. Schemas constitute a second component of cognitive content.

First, consider the peripheral beliefs that make up the content of the cognitive reaction to an upsetting event. Beck and his colleagues (Beck, 1995; Beck et al., 1979; Beck & Weishaar, 2008; DeRubeis & Beck, 1988; DeRubeis, Tang, & Beck, 2001) encourage the client to view this cognitive content as a hypothesis (rather than a fact) and to scrutinize and appraise the belief carefully. This process tends to produce a different view, which strengthens over time. For example, the belief that "husbands and wives should agree" may commonly operate to prompt emotional upset in a marital partner when there is disagreement between mates. This belief may be modified under scrutiny to "it's okay for husbands and wives to disagree," followed by repeated application of the alternative view when disagreement occurs. Over time, the strength of the latter belief is expected to increase, along with a reduction in the degree of emotional and behavioral reactivity when disagreement is experienced.

The second component of cognitive content comprises core beliefs or schemas (underlying meaning structures), which form the basis for categorizing, evaluating, judging, and distorting reality situations (Rush & Beck, 1978) and are considered to be the core of the cognitive disturbance. Core beliefs are not readily accessible and are identified through the common themes that run through the individual instances of disturbance (DeRubeis & Beck, 1988). These themes are then evaluated on the bases of their utility (the consequences of holding them, both positive and negative) and validity (their fit with logic or concrete evidence). This is done through Socratic dialogue and produces client awareness of the core meanings implicitly underlying the client's cognitive, emotional, and behavioral responses to life events. Thus, a causal connection is made between these schemas and emotional disturbance and maladaptive behaviors. Through this process, the therapist guides the client in considering an alternative view, one of far greater utility and validity. Repetitive challenge of faulty core beliefs and replacement with alternative views is achieved to promote the client's shift in commitment to core meanings that produce greater emotional well-being and adaptive functioning. Many related and unrelated life events that have historically stimulated episodes of emotional distress are considered to promote generalization, and the therapist provides verbal reinforcement for effective cognitive restructuring.

In addition to addressing cognitive content factors as they relate to human disturbance, Beck and his colleagues also address the process of cognitive functioning. Various types of thinking errors (information-processing errors) are identified, and their contributions to clients' distortions and ultimate disturbance and dysfunction are explicated. These errors, along with peripheral and core beliefs, are targeted for intervention. The following definitions, taken from Beck et al. (1979), describe common information-processing errors:

1. *Absolutistic/dichotomous thinking* is evidenced in the tendency to view experiences, objects, and situations in a polarized manner: good/bad, right/wrong, or strong/weak. ("I am a total failure." "Life's a bitch.")

2. *Overgeneralization* "refers to the pattern of drawing a general rule or conclusion on the basis of one or more isolated incidents and applying the concept across the board to related and unrelated situations" (Beck et al., 1979, p. 14). ("I am a poor tennis player. I'm just no good at sports." "I didn't meet anyone or enjoy singles

Sunday school. Singles groups just don't work for me.")

3. *Selective abstraction* involves focusing on the negative in a situation, ignoring other positive (sometimes more salient) features, and viewing the entire experience as negative based on the selective view. ("My work performance evaluation was terrible," stated by one whose evaluation included a few average or below-average ratings but, comparative with the work group, was an overall high rating.)

4. *Arbitrary inference* refers to the process of reaching a specific conclusion when there is no evidence to support it; when the evidence is circumstantial, vague, or unclear; or when there is evidence to the contrary. Freeman (1983) describes two forms of arbitrary influence: (1) *mind reading* ("She thinks I'm weak, I know it." "They think I'm great!") and (2) *negative prediction,* which involves imagining or anticipating that something bad or unpleasant is going to happen without adequate or realistic support for the prediction. ("I'm going to do terribly at this job interview." "I'll never have a love relationship again," stated by a recently divorced person.)

5. *Magnification and minimization* involve errors in evaluating the significance or extent of a behavior, condition, or event that are so extreme as to constitute a distortion. For example, a husband finds out that his wife forgot to take the dog to the veterinarian for a routine visit and becomes extremely upset and chastises her (magnification). After 12 years with her law firm, Mary Ann becomes one of the 15% to be promoted to partner. She believes and says that "anyone could have done it" (minimization).

6. *Personalization* is the act of relating a negative event or situation to oneself without the adequate causal evidence to make the connection. People may take the view that they are the cause or object of a negative event. "If I had been home with Dad, he wouldn't have had the heart attack" (cause). "They made the college degree requirements more stringent just because I'm enrolling" (object).

Learning these common errors allows the client to label his or her problematic cognitive processing and in so doing to become more aware of flawed thinking even as it is happening. Clients quickly learn to discount their initial thinking (when an error in information processing is recognized) and rapidly replace it with sounder conclusions.

Behavioral methods are used to enhance and support cognitive change and to produce a change in beliefs. Another reason for using behavioral methods is to change behavior. Methods designed specifically to target behavior change (cognitive change may well follow) include contingency management techniques, response prevention, skills training, desensitization, and flooding (Cobb, 2008; Farmer & Chapman, 2008). Beck and his colleagues (Beck & Weishaar, 2008; DeRubeis & Beck, 1988) identified a range of behavioral techniques useful in CBT, including *homework, hypothesis testing, exposure therapy, behavioral rehearsal and role playing, diversion techniques, activity scheduling, self-monitoring,* and *guided-task assignments.* Among the many behavioral methods in CT, two frequently used approaches will be covered: self-monitoring and scheduling activities.

Self-monitoring is assigned to the client whereby an hour-to-hour record of activities, associated moods, and other pertinent data is completed for at least 1 week, and often much longer (DeRubeis & Beck, 1988). The record is useful in hypothesis testing, becoming a repository of evidence with which to judge hypotheses more accurately than with mere memory. It provides content for in-session exploration and facilitates acknowledgment of the relationship between mood and activities.

DeRubeis and Beck (1988) identify the purpose of *scheduling activities* in CT as twofold: "(1) to increase the probability that the client will engage in activities that he or she has been avoiding, and (2) to remove decision-making as an obstacle in the initiation of an activity" (p. 279). For example, mastery and pleasure activities are assigned to the depressed client to interfere behaviorally with depressive symptomatology, or the anxious client may be given graded-task assignments that expose him or her to low-demand, anxiety-provoking situations in vivo. The success of CT lies, in part, in the creative use of the extensive time between treatment sessions.

To summarize, in CT the client is guided in the identification of information-processing functions (errors), causal attributions, (exaggerated) expectations, and beliefs (peripheral or core) associated with the disturbance. The therapist prompts the client in stating these cognitions as hypotheses, and together, client and therapist seek evidence (logical or empirical) to support the hypotheses. In light of little or no evidence to support the hypotheses, new meanings are generated. These new meanings undergird and reinforce a more positive view of self, enhanced self-efficacy, greater emotional self-control, a more realistic view of available life opportunities, and a greater sense of hope for the future. Behavioral procedures are used to test out, enhance, and promote change in cognitive functioning; to stimulate emotional change; to effect behavior change; and to achieve the transfer of change from the therapeutic environment to the client's natural environment.

To illustrate the cognitive restructuring of a negative causal attribution, consider Joe, a client whose 15-year-old stepdaughter, Linda, is in residential treatment for extreme acting-out behavior (incorrigibility, fighting with peers, truancy, and promiscuity). Joe has been highly critical of Linda throughout the 10 years he has known her and has tended to interpret her motives as negative and manipulative. One of his goals in therapy is to learn to see the positive in Linda and to give her the benefit of the doubt. Joe, Linda, and May, Linda's mother, have all been taught the cognitive model; thus, Joe has initial awareness that his thoughts, beliefs, and ways of processing information are highly influential in shaping meanings, eliciting emotions, and prompting behavioral responses to given stimulus conditions. The following is a family therapy excerpt:

Joe: Linda was home for visitation last weekend, and she was up to her usual tricks. I asked her to mow the yard, which she did—except that she left the parking strip unmowed. I know that she skipped mowing at the curb just to spite me.

Linda: I did not, Dad! I just forgot. It was the first time I've ever mowed the yard!

Therapist: Linda, while you sound angry, what are you feeling right now?

Linda: I am angry. He's always putting me down. I can never do anything right in his eyes.

Therapist: You feel as if you can't measure up to his expectations?

Linda: No, I can't!

Therapist: And you feel criticized by your dad much of the time?

Linda: Yes, I do.

Therapist: Besides anger, what other emotions are you experiencing? Anything else?

Linda: Yes, I guess I feel hurt, too . . . and disappointment . . . because I do try [stated with marked sadness].

Therapist: I think that I understand your feelings here, Linda, and what you're thinking. [Turning to Joe] Joe, what is your reaction to what Linda has just said?

Joe: Well, right now I'm feeling a little sad for her because I can be a difficult person to work for. Even the men at the plant tell me so. . . . I have a reputation as a hard driver. [After a brief interchange in which Linda and Joe are guided by the therapist in clarifying their respective intentions, sharing their feelings, and expressing their mutual caring and desire to get along better, the focus shifts to Joe.]

Therapist: Joe, how do you feel when you think of Linda as acting spitefully toward you?

Joe: Angry and disgusted. I feel as if she's never going to behave responsibly.

Therapist: Do you like these feelings?

Joe: No, not at all. I have been hoping that my relationship with Linda would improve, but my anger and resentment toward her just seem to make it worse.

Therapist: This may seem obvious, but do you want to change your feelings toward Linda?

Joe: Certainly . . . yes, I really do.

Therapist: And, as we've discussed before, you're willing to do the work to change the mental habits that may be operating to hurt your relationship?

Joe: Yes, I really am.

Therapist: That's great, Joe. I'm pleased, too, that you are willing to put time and effort into the process. Joe, suppose we test out your statement that Linda failed to mow the parking strip just to spite you.

Joe: Okay.

Therapist: Where's the evidence to support that view?

Joe: I guess there really isn't any hard evidence. It is what I think.

Therapist: Can you think of any other explanation for Linda's behavior besides being spiteful?

Joe: Yes. Perhaps she just forgot, or maybe she didn't see it. The parking strip is on the other side of the sidewalk—a little removed.

Therapist: These are plausible explanations, Joe. Now how do you feel toward Linda when you attribute her behavior to these factors rather than to her being spiteful?

Joe: I don't really feel so angry or resentful—more just frustrated with her that she couldn't complete the job right.

Therapist: So you have identified alternative, plausible explanations for Linda's failing to mow the parking strip, views that compete with the thought that she acted out of spite for you.

Joe: That's right.

Therapist: Now, which views serve you better in achieving the goals you have for your relationship with Linda?

Joe: That she's not acting out of spite. Rather, she just made a mistake—human error, I guess you could call it.

Therapist: That's a great way to put it, Joe. We humans are all error prone, even you and me!

Cognitive Skills Training Methods

Behaviorally trained theorists developed cognitive-behavioral interventions designed to teach specific cognitive skills, in contrast to those whose focus is to restructure existing cognitions. Most of these methodologies have been developed to treat specific disorders rather than as general treatment methodologies for broad application. Two notable exceptions are Meichenbaum's self-instruction training (Meichenbaum, 1977; Meichenbaum & Goodman, 1971) and problem-solving training (D'Zurilla, 1988; D'Zurilla & Goldfried, 1971; D'Zurilla & Nezu, 2001). Due to space limitations and the current limited utilization of cognitive self-instruction, the following discussion is focused on problem-solving training.

Problem Solving

Problem solving has been classified alternatively as a behavioral procedure and a cognitive-behavioral procedure. D'Zurilla and Goldfried (1971) define problem solving as

a behavioral process, whether overt or covert in nature, which (a) makes available a variety of potentially effective response alternatives for dealing with the problematic situation and (b) increases the probability of selecting the most effective response from among these various alternatives. (p. 108)

D'Zurilla (1988) has modified this definition, specifying problem solving as "a cognitive-affective-behavioral process through which an individual (or group) attempts to identify, discover, or invent effective or adaptive means of coping with problems encountered in everyday living"

(p. 86). According to this model, problem-solving deficiencies may result in a failure to resolve stressful life problems. The results of the problem-solving deficiency may be anxiety, depression, anger, or the development of other problems (D'Zurilla & Nezu, 2001). Problem-solving deficiencies have been found to be associated with a variety of personal and interpersonal problems (Dobson & Dobson, 1981; Jacob, Ritchey, Cvitkovic, & Blane, 1981; Kazdin, Esveldt-Dawson, French, & Unis, 1987; Nezu & Carnevale, 1987; Vincent, Weiss, & Birchler, 1976; Weisz, Weiss, Wasserman, & Rintoul, 1987), and training in problem solving has been found to improve the functioning of various clinical populations (Bedell, Archer, & Marlow, 1980; Chaney, O'Leary, & Marlatt, 1978; D'Zurilla & Nezu, 1999; D'Zurilla, Nezu, & Maydeu-Olivares, 2004; Ewart, Burnett, & Taylor, 1983; Jannoun, Munby, Catalan, & Gelder, 1980; Mynors-Wallis, Gath, Lloyd-Thomas, & Tomlinson, 1995; Nezu, 1986; Nezu, D'Zurilla, & Nezu, 2005; Nezu, Nezu, & Houts, 1993).

Problem-solving training has been used effectively with both children and adults, and it can be used alone or in conjunction with other methods. There are several approaches to problem solving, but the most widely accepted is the five-step model of D'Zurilla and Goldfried (1971): (1) problem orientation, (2) problem definition and formulation, (3) generation of alternative solutions, (4) decision making, and (5) implementation and verification of solutions. Problem orientation relates to the cognitive set of the individual in relation to problem solving and coping with life situations. D'Zurilla (1988) identifies the significant problem orientation factors as follows: "problem perception, causal attributions, problem appraisals, beliefs about personal control, and values concerning the commitment of time and effort to problem solving" (p. 89). Step 2, problem definition and formulation, involves assessment of the problem and establishment of an achievable goal. The third step involves brainstorming to generate alternative solutions to the problem. At Step 4, the alternatives are evaluated, and a solution is selected for implementation. The final component of the process is designed to determine the effectiveness of the problem-solving effort and, if the solution is found to be lacking, to promote modification of the original solution or a return to Step 3 to select another promising alternative solution.

The goal of problem solving is to treat life problems that are antecedents of maladaptive responses and are considered to be causally related to these responses. Only when these antecedent problems are difficult to define or change is the approach to be applied to the maladaptive responses (D'Zurilla, 1988). The following are examples of problem-solving issues:

- How can I make better use of my time?
- How can my husband and I do more novel activities?
- How can I reduce the disruptive behavior of my children at the table?
- How can I get my aging father to take better care of himself?
- How can I reduce the stress of my job?

The effectiveness of problem solving can be extended through the use of adjuncts such as cognitive restructuring and training in social skills, assertiveness, self-control techniques, and coping skills.

CONCLUSION

The principles and practice of cognitive-behavioral therapy have been subject to misunderstanding and misinterpretation. This chapter has focused on the elucidation of features common to the methodology and to the specification of assessment and treatment procedures. The presentation has been heavily weighted on the cognitive component of CBT given the more recent development of cognitive procedures. It should be emphasized that behavior change strategies not only are powerful adjuncts to the cognitive methods presented but also produce significant change independently of associated cognitive and/or emotive change (Farmer & Chapman, 2008; Martell, Dimidjian,

& Herman-Dunn, 2010; Wilson, 2008). The combined cognitive and behavioral procedures presented are highly applicable to the clinical challenges confronting social work practitioners. Cognitive-behavioral intervention appears to be effective in the treatment of a broad range of adult and child issues, challenges, and problems. Empirical support for CBT continues to increase. In this era of evidence-based practice, cognitive-behavioral methods merit strong consideration for application in clinical and nonclinical social work settings.

The cognitive-behavioral landscape is changing with the development of third-wave procedures and paradigm-challenging approaches to human distress and treatment rooted in postmodernism. The bedrock of CBT is not one of granite; rather, it is one of shifting sand. One may contend that this is a good thing. Long ago, this author's mentor challenged him by declaring, "You will know that you have 'arrived' when you quit asking yourself if you are getting the right answers and begin asking yourself if you are asking the right questions." Current approaches to CBT may well represent some *right* answers. However, these right answers derive from the current dominant trends in psychological theory and clinical practice. The most unsettling aspect of these conceptualizations is the remarkable focus on problems, deficits, distress, and disorder, with limited attention to client coping capacities, resiliency, support system resources, creativity, and a multitude of client strengths and possibilities. The critical practitioner will seek to effectively apply best-practice methods while continuing to question the assumptions (limiting to expansive) explicitly and implicitly inherent in those practices.

REFERENCES

Agras, W. S., Rossiter, E. M., Amow, B., Schneider, J. A., Telch, C. F., Raebum, S. D., et al. (1992). Pharmacological and cognitive-behavioral treatment for bulimia nervosa: A controlled comparison. *American Journal of Psychiatry, 149,* 82–87.

Agras, W. S., Telch, C. F., Arnow, B., Eldredge, K., & Marnell, M. (1997). One-year follow-up of cognitive-behavioral therapy for obese individuals with binge eating disorder. *Journal of Consulting and Clinical Psychology, 65,* 343–347.

Andrasik, F., & Walch, S. E. (2003). Headaches. In A. M. Nezu, C. M. Nezu, & P. A. Geller (Eds.), *Handbook of psychology: Vol. 9. Health psychology* (pp. 245–266). Hoboken, NJ: Wiley.

Antony, M. M., Ledley, D. R., & Heimberg, R. G. (Eds.). (2005). *Improving outcomes and preventing relapse in cognitive-behavioral therapy.* New York, NY: Guilford Press.

Antony, M. M., & Rowa, K. (2008). *Social anxiety disorder.* Ashland, OH: Hogrefe & Huber.

Arntz, A., & van Genderen, H. (2009). *Schema therapy for borderline personality disorder.* Chichester: Wiley-Blackwell.

Baars, B. J. (1986). *The cognitive revolution in psychology.* New York, NY: Guilford Press.

Ball, J., & Mitchell, P. (2004). A randomized controlled study of cognitive behavior therapy and behavioral family therapy for anorexia nervosa patients. *Eating Disorders, 12,* 303–314.

Bandura, A. (1978). The self system in reciprocal determinism. *American Psychologist, 33,* 344–358.

Barlow, D. H. (1981). *Behavioral assessment of adult disorders.* New York, NY: Guilford Press.

Barlow, D. H. (2002). *Anxiety and its disorders: The nature and treatment of anxiety and panic* (2nd ed.). New York, NY: Guilford Press.

Barlow, D. H. (Ed.). (2008). *Clinical handbook of psychological disorders: A step-by-step treatment manual.* New York, NY: Guilford Press.

Barlow, D. H., & Craske, M. G. (2006). *Mastery of your anxiety and panic: Patient workbook* (4th ed.). New York, NY: Oxford University Press.

Barlow, D. H., & Hofmann, S. G. (1997). Efficacy and dissemination of psychological treatment. In D. M. Clark & C. G. Fairburn (Eds.), *Science and practice of cognitive behavior therapy* (pp. 95–117). Oxford, UK: Oxford University Press.

Basco, M. R., Kingdon, D. G., Turkington, D., & Wright, J. H. (2009). *Cognitive behavior therapy for severe mental illness: An illustrated manual.* Washington, DC: American Psychological Association.

Baucom, D. H., Shoham, V., Mueser, K. T., Daiuto, A. D., & Stickle, T. R. (1998). Empirically supported couples and family therapies for adult problems. *Journal of Consulting and Clinical Psychology, 66,* 53–88.

Beck, A. T. (1970). Cognitive therapy: Nature and relation to behavior therapy. *Behavior Therapy, 1,* 184–200.

Beck, A. T. (1976). *Cognitive therapy and the emotional disorders.* New York, NY: International Universities Press.

Beck, A. T., & Emery, G. (1985). *Anxiety disorders and phobias: A cognitive perspective.* New York, NY: Basic Books.

Beck, A. T., Freeman, A., & Associates. (1990). *Cognitive therapy of personality disorders.* New York, NY: Guilford Press.

Beck, A. T., Freeman, A., & Davis, D. D. (2003). *Cognitive therapy of personality disorders.* New York, NY: Plenum Press.

Beck, A. T., Rush, A. J., Shaw, B. F., & Emery, G. (1979). *Cognitive therapy of depression.* New York, NY: Guilford Press.

Beck, A. T., Sokol, L., Clark, D. A., Berchick, R. J., & Wright, F. D. (1992). A crossover study of focused cognitive therapy for panic disorder. *American Journal of Psychiatry, 149*(6), 778–783.

Beck, A. T., & Weishaar, M. E. (2008). Cognitive therapy. In R. J. Corsini & D. Wedding (Eds.), *Current psychotherapies* (8th ed., pp. 263–294). Belmont, CA: Thomson.

Beck, A. T., Wright, F. D., & Newman, C. F. (1992). Cocaine abuse. In A. Freeman & F. M. Dattilio (Eds.), *Comprehensive casebook of cognitive therapy* (pp. 185–192). New York, NY: Plenum Press.

Beck, A. T., Wright, F. D., Newman, C. F., & Liese, B. S. (1993). *Cognitive therapy of substance abuse.* New York, NY: Guilford Press.

Beck, J. S. (1995). *Cognitive therapy: Basics and beyond.* New York, NY: Guilford Press.

Beck, J. S. (2005). *Cognitive therapy for challenging problems: What to do when the basics don't work.* New York, NY: Guilford Press.

Beck, R., & Fernandez, E. (1998). Cognitive-behavioral therapy in the treatment of anger: A meta-analysis. *Cognitive Therapy and Research, 22*(1), 63–74.

Bedell, J. R., Archer, R. P., & Marlow, H. A., Jr. (1980). A description and evaluation of a problem solving skills training program. In D. Upper & S. M. Ross (Eds.), *Behavioral group therapy: An annual review* (pp. 83–118). Champaign, IL: Research Press.

Bedrosian, R. C., & Bozicas, G. D. (1994). *Treating family of origin problems: A cognitive approach.* New York, NY: Guilford Press.

Berlin, S. B., & Marsh, J. C. (1993). *Informing practice decisions.* New York, NY: Macmillan.

Bienenfeld, D. (2007). Cognitive therapy of patients with personality disorders. *Psychiatric Annals, 37*(2), 133–139.

Blankstein, K. R., & Segal, Z. V. (2001). Cognitive assessment: Issues and methods. In K. S. Dobson (Ed.), *Handbook of cognitive-behavioral therapies* (2nd ed., pp. 40–85). New York, NY: Guilford Press.

Bohlmeijer, E.T., Fledderus, M., Rokx, T.A., & Pieterse, M.E. (2011). Efficacy of an early intervention based on acceptance and commitment therapy for adults with depressive symptomatology: Evaluation in a randomized controlled trial. *Behavior, Research and Therapy, 49,* 62–67.

Brower, A. M., & Nurius, P. S. (1993). *Social cognition and individual change: Current theory and counseling guidelines.* Newbury Park, CA: Sage.

Burns, D. D. (1980). *Feeling good: The new mood therapy.* New York, NY: Signet.

Cacioppo, J. T., & Petty, R. E. (1981). Social psychological procedures for cognition response assessment. In T. Merluzzi, C. Glass, & M. Genest (Eds.), *Cognitive assessment* (pp. 309–342). New York, NY: Guilford Press.

Chaney, E. F., O'Leary, M. R., & Marlatt, G. A. (1978). Skill training with alcoholics. *Journal of Consulting and Clinical Psychology, 46,* 1092–1104.

Ciminero, A. R., Calhoun, K. S., & Adams, H. E. (Eds.). (1986). *Handbook of behavioral assessment* (2nd ed.). New York, NY: Wiley.

Clark, D. A. (2004a). Cognitive-behavioral theory and treatment of obsessive-compulsive disorder: Past contributions and current developments. In R. L. Leahy (Ed.), *Contemporary cognitive therapy: Theory, research, and practice* (pp. 161–183). New York, NY: Guilford Press.

Clark, D. A. (2004b). *Cognitive-behavioral therapy for OCD.* New York, NY: Guilford Press.

Clark, D. A., Beck, A. T., & Alford, B. A. (1999). *Cognitive theory and therapy of depression.* New York, NY: Wiley.

Clark, D. M., & Ehlers, A. (2004). Posttraumatic stress disorder: From cognitive theory to therapy. In R. L. Leahy (Ed.), *Contemporary cognitive therapy: Theory, research, and practice* (pp. 141–160). New York, NY: Guilford Press.

Clark, D. M., Ehlers, A., Hackmann, A., McManus, F., Fennell, M., Grey, N., et al. (2006). Cognitive therapy versus exposure and applied relaxation in social phobia: A randomized controlled trial. *Journal of Consulting and Clinical Psychology, 74,* 568–578.

Clark, D. M., Ehlers, A., McManus, F., Hackmann, A., Fennel, M., Campbell, H., et al. (2003). Cognitive therapy versus fluoxetine in generalized social phobia: A randomized placebo-controlled trial. *Journal of Consulting and Clinical Psychology, 71,* 1058–1067.

Clark, D. M., Salkovskis, P. M., Hackmann, A., Middleton, H., Anastasiades, P., & Gelder, M. (1994). A comparison of cognitive therapy, applied relaxation and imipramine in the treatment of panic disorder. *British Journal of Psychiatry, 164,* 759–769.

Cloitre, M., & Rosenberg, A. (2006). Sexual revictimization: Risk factors and prevention. In V. M. Follette & J. I. Rusek (Eds.), *Cognitive-behavioral therapies for trauma* (pp. 321–361). New York, NY: Guilford Press.

Cobb, N. (2008). Cognitive-behavioral theory and treatment. In N. Coady & P. Lehmann (Eds.), *Theoretical perspectives in direct social work practice: An eclectic-generalist approach* (2nd ed., pp. 221–248). New York, NY: Springer.

Craighead, L. W., & Agras, W. S. (1991). Mechanisms of action in cognitive-behavioral and pharmacological interventions for obesity and bulimia nervosa. *Journal of Consulting and Clinical Psychology, 59,* 115–125.

Craighead, L. W., Craighead, W. E., Kazdin, A. E., & Mahoney, M. J. (Eds.). (1994). *Cognitive and behavioral interventions: An empirical approach to mental health problems.* Needham Heights, MA: Allyn & Bacon.

Craske, M. G., & Barlow, D. H. (2008). Panic disorder and agoraphobia. In D. H. Barlow (Ed.), *Clinical handbook of psychological disorders: A step-by-step treatment manual* (pp. 1–64). New York, NY: Guilford Press.

Dalrymple, K. L., & Herbert, J. D. (2007). Acceptance and commitment therapy for generalized anxiety disorder: A pilot study. *Behavior Modification, 31*(5), 543–568.

Dancu, C. F., & Foa, E. G. (1992). Posttraumatic stress disorder. In A. Freeman & F. M. Dattilio (Eds.), *Comprehensive casebook of cognitive therapy* (pp. 79–88). New York, NY: Plenum Press.

Dattilio, F. M. (2000). Families in crisis. In F. M. Dattilio & A. Freeman (Eds.), *Cognitive-behavioral strategies in crisis intervention* (2nd ed., pp. 316–338). New York, NY: Guilford Press.

Dattilio, F. M. (2004). Cognitive-behavioral family therapy: A coming of age story. In R. L. Leahy (Ed.), *Contemporary cognitive therapy: Theory, research, and practice* (pp. 389–405). New York, NY: Guilford Press.

Dattilio, F. M., & Epstein, N. B. (2005). Introduction to the special section: The role of cognitive-behavioral interventions in couple and family therapy. *Journal of Marital and Family Therapy, 31,* 7–13.

Dattilio, F. M., & Freeman, A. (Eds.). (2000). *Cognitive-behavioral strategies in crisis intervention* (2nd ed.). New York, Y: Guilford Press.

Dattilio, F. M., & Freeman, A. (Eds). (2007). *Cognitive-behavioral strategies in crisis intervention* (3rd ed.). New York, NY: Guilford Press.

Dattilio, F. M., & Kendall, P. C. (2000). Panic disorder. In F. M. Dattilio & A. Freeman (Eds.), *Cognitive-behavioral strategies in crisis intervention* (2nd ed., pp. 59–83). New York, NY: Guilford Press.

Davidson, K. (2008). *Cognitive therapy for personality disorders: A guide for clinicians* (2nd ed.). New York, NY: Routledge.

Dember, W. N. (1974). Motivation and the cognitive revolution. *American Psychologist, 29,* 161–168.

DeRubeis, R. J., & Beck, A. T. (1988). Cognitive therapy. In K. S. Dobson (Ed.), *Handbook of cognitive-behavioral therapies* (pp. 273–306). New York, NY: Guilford Press.

DeRubeis, R. J., Tang, T. Z., & Beck, A. T. (2001). Cognitive therapy. In K. S. Dobson (Ed.), *Handbook of cognitive-behavioral therapies* (2nd ed., pp. 349–392). New York, NY: Guilford Press.

Dimidjian, S., Hollon, S.D., Dobson, K.S., Schmaling, K.B., Kohlenberg, R.J., Addis, M.E., Gallop, R., . . . Jacobson, N.S. (2006). Randomized trial of behavioral activation, cognitive therapy, and antidepressant medication in the acute treatment of adults with major depression. *Journal of Consulting and Clinical Psychology, 74 (4),* 658–670.

Dimidjian, S., Martell, C. R., Addis, M. E., & Herman-Dunn, R. (2008). Behavioral activation for depression. In D. H. Barlow (Ed.), *Clinical handbook of psychological disorders: A step-by-step treatment manual* (pp. 328–364). New York, NY: Guilford Press.

DiTomasso, R. A., Martin, D. M., & Kovnat, K. D. (2000). Medical patients in crisis. In F. M. Dattilio & A. Freeman (Eds.), *Cognitive-behavioral strategies in crisis intervention* (2nd ed., pp. 409–428). New York, NY: Guilford Press.

Dobson, D. J., & Dobson, K. S. (1981). Problem-solving strategies in depressed and nondepressed college students. *Cognitive Therapy and Research, 5,* 237–249.

Dobson, K. S. (Ed.). (2001). *Handbook of cognitive-behavioral therapies* (2nd ed.). New York, NY: Guilford Press.

Dobson, K.S., Hollon, S.D., Dimidjian, S., Schmaling, K.B., Kohlenberg, R.J., Gallop, R.J., Rizvi, S.L., . . . Jacobson, N.S. (2008). Randomized trial of behavioral activation, cognitive therapy, and antidepressant medication in the prevention of relapse and recurrence in major depression. *Journal of Consulting and Clinical Psychology, 76(3),* 468-477.

Dryden, W., & Ellis, A. (2001). Rational emotive behavior therapy. In K. S. Dobson (Ed.), *Handbook of cognitive-behavioral therapies* (2nd ed., pp. 295–348). New York, NY: Guilford Press.

D'Zurilla, T. J. (1988). Problem-solving therapy. In K. S. Dobson (Ed.), *Handbook of cognitive-behavioral therapies* (pp. 85–135). New York, NY: Guilford Press.

D'Zurilla, T. J., & Goldfried, M. R. (1971). Problem solving and behavior modification. *Journal of Abnormal Psychology, 78,* 107–126.

D'Zurilla, T. J., & Nezu, A. M. (1999). *Problem-solving therapy: A social competence approach to clinical intervention* (2nd ed.). New York, NY: Springer.

D'Zurilla, T. J., & Nezu, A. M. (2001). Problem-solving therapies. In K. S. Dobson (Ed.), *Handbook of cognitive-behavioral therapies* (2nd ed., pp. 211–245). New York, NY: Guilford Press.

D'Zurilla, T. J., Nezu, A. M., & Maydeu-Olivares, A. (2004). Social problem solving: Theory and assessment. In E. C. Chang, T. J. D'Zurilla, & L. J. Sanna (Eds.), *Social problem solving: Theory, research, and training* (pp. 11–27). Washington, DC: American Psychological Association.

Ellis, A. (1962). *Reason and emotion in psychotherapy.* New York, NY: Lyle Stuart.

Ellis, A. (1969). A weekend of rational encounter. *Rational Living, 4,* 1–8.

Ellis, A. (1973). *Humanistic psychotherapy: The rational-emotive approach.* New York, NY: McGraw-Hill.

Ellis, A. (1977a). The basic clinical theory of rational-emotive therapy. In A. Ellis & R. Grieger (Eds.), *Handbook of rational-emotive therapy* (pp. 3–34). New York, NY: Springer.

Ellis, A. (1977b). Psychotherapy and the value of a human being. In A. Ellis & R. Grieger (Eds.), *Handbook of rational-emotive therapy* (pp. 99–112). New York, NY: Springer.

Ellis, A. (1979). The practice of rational-emotive therapy. In A. Ellis & J. M. Whitely (Eds.), *Theoretical and empirical foundations of rational-emotive therapy* (pp. 61–100). Monterey, CA: Brooks/Cole.

Ellis, A. (1984). The essence of RET-1984. *Journal of Rational-Emotive Therapy, 2*(1), 19–25.

Ellis, A. (1989). The history of cognition in psychotherapy. In A. Freeman, K. M. Simon, L. E. Beutler, & H. Arkowitz (Eds.), *Comprehensive handbook of cognitive therapy* (pp. 5–19). New York, NY: Plenum Press.

Ellis, A. (1991). The revised ABC's of rational-emotive therapy (RET). *Journal of Rational-Emotive and Cognitive-Behavior Therapy, 9*(3), 139–172.

Ellis, A. (1993). Changing rational-emotive therapy (RET) to rational emotive behavior therapy (REBT). *Behavior Therapist, 16,* 257–258.

Ellis, A. (1994). *Reason and emotion in psychotherapy: A comprehensive method of treating human disturbances* (Rev. and updated). Secaucus, NJ: Birch Lane Press.

Ellis, A., & Becker, I. (1982). *A guide to personal happiness.* North Hollywood, CA: Wilshire.

Ellis, A., & Bernard, M. E. (1986). What is rational-emotive therapy (RET)? In A. Ellis & M. E. Bernard (Eds.), *Clinical applications of rational-emotive therapy* (pp. 1–30). New York, NY: Plenum Press.

Ellis, A., & Dryden, W. (1987). *The practice of rational-emotive therapy.* New York, NY: Springer.

Ellis, A., Sichel, J. L., Yeager, R. J., DiMattia, D. J., & DiGiuseppe, R. (1989). *Rational-emotive couples therapy.* New York, NY: Pergamon Press.

Emmelkamp, P. M. G., Kuipers, A. C. M., & Eggeraat, J. B. (1978). Cognitive modification versus prolonged exposure in vivo: A comparison with agoraphobics as subjects. *Behavior Research and Therapy, 16,* 33–41.

Epstein, E. M., & Sloan, D. M. (2005). Tailoring cognitive behavioral therapy for individuals diagnosed with bulimia nervosa. *Journal of Contemporary Psychology, 35*(4), 317–330.

Epstein, N. B. (2004). Cognitive-behavioral therapy with couples: Theoretical and empirical status. In R. L. Leahy (Ed.), *Contemporary cognitive therapy: Theory, research, and practice* (pp. 367–388). New York, NY: Guilford Press.

Epstein, N. B., & Baucom, D. H. (2002). *Enhanced cognitive-behavioral therapy for couples: A contextual approach.* Washington, DC: American Psychological Association.

Evers, A. W. M., Kraaimaat, F. W., van Riel, P. L. M. C., & de Jong, A. J. L. (2002). Tailored cognitive-behavioral therapy in early rheumatoid arthritis for patients at risk: A randomized controlled trial. *Pain, 100*(1/2), 141–153.

Ewart, C. K., Burnett, K. F., & Taylor, C. B. (1983). Communication behaviors that affect blood pressure: An A-B-A-B analysis of marital interaction. *Behavior Modification, 7,* 331–344.

Fairburn, C. G., Cooper, Z., Shafran, R., & Wilson, G. T. (2008). Eating disorders: A transdiagnostic protocol. In D. H. Barlow (Ed.), *Clinical handbook of psychological disorders: A step-by-step treatment manual* (pp. 578–614). New York, NY: Guilford Press.

Fairburn, C. G., & Harrison, P. J. (2003). Eating disorders. *Lancet, 361,* 407–416.

Farmer, R. F., & Chapman, A. L. (2008). *Behavioral interventions in cognitive behavior therapy: Practical guidance for putting theory into action.* Washington, DC: American Psychological Association.

Fernandez, E., & Beck, R. (2001). Cognitive-behavioral self-instruction versus self-monitoring of anger: Effects on anger frequency, duration, and intensity. *Behavioural and Cognitive Psychotherapy, 29*(3), 345–356.

Fischer, J., & Corcoran, K. (1994). *Measures for clinical practice: A sourcebook* (Vols. 1 & 2, 2nd ed.). New York, NY: Free Press.

Follette, V. M., & Ruzek, J. I. (Eds.). (2006). *Cognitive-behavioral therapies for trauma.* New York, NY: Guilford Press.

Forman, E. M., Herbert, J. D., Moltra, E., Yeomans, P. D., & Geller, P. A. (2007). A randomized controlled effectiveness trial of acceptance and commitment therapy and cognitive therapy for anxiety and depression. *Behavior Modification, 31*(6), 772–799.

Franklin, C. (1995). Expanding the vision of the social constructionist debates: Creating relevance for practitioners. *Families in Society, 76,* 395–406.

Franklin, C., & Jordan, C. (1999). *Family practice: Brief systems methods for social work.* Pacific Grove, CA: Brooks/Cole.

Franklin, C., & Nurius, P. S. (Eds.). (1998). *Constructivism in practice: Methods, and challenges.* Milwaukee, WI: Families International.

Franklin, M. E., & Foa, E. B. (2008). Obsessive-compulsive disorder. In D. H. Barlow (Ed.), *Clinical handbook of psychological disorders: A step-by-step treatment manual* (pp. 164–215). New York, NY: Guilford Press.

Freeman, A. (1983). Cognitive therapy: An overview. In A. Freeman (Ed.), *Cognitive therapy with couples and groups* (pp. 1–10). New York, NY: Plenum Press.

Freeman, A. (1990). Cognitive therapy. In A. S. Bellack & M. Hersen (Eds.), *Handbook of comparative treatments for adult disorders* (pp. 64–87). New York, NY: Wiley.

Freeman, A., & Dattilio, F. M. (Eds.). (1992). *Comprehensive casebook of cognitive therapy.* New York, NY: Plenum Press.

Freeman, A., Martin, D., & Ronen, T. (2007). Treatment of suicidal behavior. In T. Ronen & A. Freeman (Eds.), *Cognitive behavior therapy in clinical social work practice* (pp. 421–445). New York, NY: Springer.

Freeman, A., Pretzer, J., Fleming, B., & Simon, K. M. (Eds.). (2004). *Clinical applications of cognitive therapy* (2nd ed.). New York, NY: Academic Press.

Freeman, A., & Simon, K. M. (1989). Cognitive therapy of anxiety. In A. Freeman, K. M. Simon, L. E. Beutler, & H. Arkowitz (Eds.), *Comprehensive handbook of cognitive therapy* (pp. 347–365). New York, NY: Plenum Press.

Freeman, S. M., & Storie, M. (2007). Substance misuse and dependence: Crisis as process or outcome. In F. M. Dattilio & A. Freeman (Eds.), *Cognitive-behavioral strategies in crisis intervention* (3rd ed., pp. 175–198). New York, NY: Guilford Press.

Fulton, P. R. (2005). Mindfulness as clinical training. In C. K. Germer, R. D. Siegel, & P. R. Fulton (Eds.), *Mindfulness and psychotherapy* (pp. 55–72). New York, NY: Guilford Press.

Garner, D. M., & Bemis, K. M. (1985). Cognitive therapy for anorexia nervosa. In D. M. Garner & P. E. Garfinkel (Eds.), *Handbook of psychotherapy for anorexia nervosa and bulimia* (pp. 107–146). New York, NY: Guilford Press.

Genest, M., & Turk, D. C. (1981). Think aloud approaches to cognitive assessment. In T. Merluzzi, C. Glass, & M. Genest (Eds.), *Cognitive assessment* (pp. 233–269). New York, NY: Guilford Press.

Gergen, K. J. (1991). *The saturated self: Dilemmas of identity in contemporary life.* New York, NY: Basic Books.

Gergen, K. J. (1994). *Realities and relationships.* Cambridge, MA: Harvard University Press.

Germer, C. K., Siegel, R. D., & Fulton, P. R. (Eds.). (2005). *Mindfulness and psychotherapy.* New York, NY: Guilford Press.

Goodman, D. S., & Maultsby, M. C. (1974). *Emotional well-being through rational behavior training.* Springfield, IL: Charles C Thomas.

Granvold, D. K. (1988). Treating marital couples in conflict and transition. In J. S. McNeil & S. E. Weinstein (Eds.), *Innovations in health care practice* (pp. 68–90). Silver Spring, MD: National Association of Social Workers.

Granvold, D. K. (1989). Postdivorce treatment. In M. R. Textor (Ed.), *The divorce and divorce therapy handbook* (pp. 197–223). Northvale, NJ: Jason Aronson.

Granvold, D. K. (Ed.). (1994a). *Cognitive and behavioral treatment: Methods and applications.* Pacific Grove, CA: Brooks/Cole.

Granvold, D. K. (1994b). Cognitive-behavioral divorce therapy. In D. K. Granvold (Ed.), *Cognitive and behavioral treatment: Methods and applications* (pp. 222–246). Pacific Grove, CA: Brooks/Cole.

Granvold, D. K. (1994c). Concepts and methods of cognitive treatment. In D. K. Granvold (Ed.), *Cognitive and behavioral treatment: Methods and applications* (pp. 3–31). Pacific Grove, CA: Brooks/Cole.

Granvold, D. K. (1996). Constructivist psychotherapy. *Families in Society: The Journal of Contemporary Human Services, 77*(6), 345–357.

Granvold, D. K. (1999). Integrating cognitive and constructivist psychotherapies: A cognitive perspective. In T. B. Northcut & N. R. Heller (Eds.), *Enhancing psychodynamic therapy with cognitive-behavioral techniques* (pp. 53–93). Northvale, NJ: Aronson.

Granvold, D. K. (2000a). The crisis of divorce: Cognitive-behavioral and constructivist assessment and treatment. In A. R. Roberts (Ed.), *Crisis intervention handbook: Assessment, treatment and research* (2nd

ed., pp. 307–336). Oxford, UK: Oxford University Press.

Granvold, D. K. (2000b). Divorce. In F. M. Dattilio & A. Freeman (Eds.), *Cognitive-behavioral strategies in crisis intervention* (2nd ed., pp. 362–384). New York, NY: Guilford Press.

Granvold, D. K. (2007). Working with couples. In T. Ronen & A. Freeman (Eds.), *Cognitive behavior therapy in clinical social work practice* (pp. 303–326). New York, NY: Springer.

Granvold, D. K. (2008a). Constructivist theory and practice. In N. Coady & P. Lehmann (Eds.), *Theoretical perspectives for direct social work practice: A generalist-eclectic approach* (2nd ed., pp. 401–446). New York, NY: Springer.

Granvold, D. K. (2008b). Constructivist treatment of divorce. In J. D. Raskin & S. K. Bridges (Eds.), *Studies in meaning 3: Constructivist psychotherapy in the real world* (pp. 201–226). New York, NY: Pace University Press.

Granvold, D. K. (2009a). Cognitive restructuring. In A. R. Roberts (Ed.), *Social workers' desk reference* (2nd ed., pp. 588–593). New York, NY: Oxford University Press.

Granvold, D. K. (2009b). Divorce therapy: The allocation of cognitive-behavioral and constructivist treatment methods. In A. R. Roberts (Ed.), *Social workers' desk reference* (2nd ed., pp. 732–737). New York, NY: Oxford University Press.

Granvold, D. K., & Jordan, C. (1994). The cognitive-behavioral treatment of marital distress. In D. K. Granvold (Ed.), *Cognitive and behavioral treatment: Methods and applications* (pp. 174–201). Pacific Grove, CA: Brooks/Cole.

Granvold, D. K., & Wodarski, J. S. (1994). Cognitive and behavioral treatment: Clinical issues, transfer of training, and relapse prevention. In D. K. Granvold (Ed.), *Cognitive and behavioral treatment: Methods and applications* (pp. 353–375). Pacific Grove, CA: Brooks/Cole.

Guidano, V. F. (1984). A constructivist outline of cognitive processes. In M. A. Reda & M. J. Mahoney (Eds.), *Cognitive psychotherapies: Recent developments in theory, research, and practice* (pp. 31–45). Cambridge, MA: Ballinger.

Guidano, V. F. (1987). *Complexity of the self: A developmental approach to psychopathology and therapy.* New York, NY: Guilford Press.

Guidano, V. F. (1988). A systems, process-oriented approach to cognitive therapy. In K. S. Dobson

(Ed.), *Handbook of cognitive-behavioral therapies* (pp. 307–356). New York, NY: Guilford Press.

Guidano, V. F. (1991). *The self in process.* New York, NY: Guilford Press.

Guidano, V. F. (1995). Constructivist psychotherapy: A theoretical framework. In R. A. Neimeyer & M. J. Mahoney (Eds.), *Constructivism in psychotherapy* (pp. 93–108). Washington, DC: American Psychological Association.

Guidano, V. F., & Liotti, G. A. (1983). *Cognitive processes and emotional disorders.* New York, NY: Guilford Press.

Guidano, V. F., & Liotti, G. A. (1985). A constructivist foundation for cognitive therapy. In M. J. Mahoney & A. Freeman (Eds.), *Cognition and psychotherapy* (pp. 101–142). New York, NY: Plenum Press.

Hamberger, L. K., & Holtzworth-Munroe, A. (2007). Spousal abuse. In F. M. Dattilio & A. Freeman (Eds.), *Cognitive-behavioral strategies in crisis intervention* (3rd ed., pp. 277–299). New York, NY: Guilford Press.

Hayes, S. C. (2004). Acceptance and commitment therapy, relational frame theory, and the third wave of behavioral and cognitive therapies. *Behavior Therapy, 35,* 639–665.

Hayes, S.C. (2012). *Acceptance and commitment therapy.* Washington, DC: American Psychological Association.

Hayes, S. C., Strosahl, K. D., & Wilson, K. G. (1999). *Acceptance and commitment therapy: An experiential approach to behavior change.* New York, NY: Guilford Press.

Haynes, S. N. (1978). *Principles of behavioral assessment.* New York, NY: Gardner.

Heimberg, R. G., Liebowitz, M. R., Hope, D. A., Schneier, F. R., Holt, C. S., Welkowitz, L. A., et al. (1998). Cognitive behavioral group therapy vs. phenelzine therapy for social phobia: 12-week outcome. *Archives of General Psychiatry, 55,* 1133–1141.

Hersen, M., & Bellack, A. S. (Eds.). (1976). *Behavioral assessment: A practical handbook.* New York, NY: Pergamon Press.

Higgins, S. T., Sigmon, S. C., & Heil, S. H. (2008). Drug abuse and dependence. In D. H. Barlow (Ed.), *Clinical handbook of psychological disorders: A step-by-step treatment manual* (pp. 547–577). New York, NY: Guilford Press.

Hofmann, S. G., & Asmundson, G. J. G. (2008). Acceptance and mindfulness-based therapy: New wave or old hat? *Clinical Psychology Review, 28,* 1–16.

Hollon, S. D., & Beck, A. T. (1986). Cognitive and cognitive-behavioral therapies. In S. L. Garfield & A. E. Bergin (Eds.), *Handbook of psychotherapy and behavior change* (3rd ed.). New York, NY: Wiley.

Hollon, S. D., & Beck, A. T. (1994). Cognitive and cognitive-behavioral therapies. In A. E. Bergin & S. L. Garfield (Eds.), *Handbook of psychotherapy and behavior change: An empirical analysis* (4th ed., pp. 428–466). New York, NY: Wiley.

Hollon, S. D., & DeRubeis, R. J. (2004). Effectiveness of treatment for depression. In R. L. Leahy (Ed.), *Contemporary cognitive therapy: Theory, research, and practice* (pp. 45–61). New York, NY: Guilford Press.

Hollon, S. D., Thase, M. E., & Markowitz, J. C. (2002). Treatment and prevention of depression. *Psychological Science in the Public Interest, 3,* 39–77.

Holtzworth-Munroe, A., Meehan, J. C., Rehman, U., & Marshall, A. D. (2002). Intimate partner violence: An introduction for couple therapists. In A. S. Gurman & N. S. Jacobson (Eds.), *Clinical handbook of couple therapy* (3rd ed., pp. 441–465). New York, NY: Guilford Press.

Hopko, D. R., Armento, M. E., Robertson, S. M., Ryba, M. M., Carvalho, J. P., Colman, L. K., Mullane, C., . . . & Lejuez, C. W. (2011). Brief behavioral activation and problem-solving therapy for depressed breast cancer patients: Randomized trial. *Journal of Consulting and Clinical Psychology, 79*(6), 834-849.

Hudson, W. W. (1990). *The multi-problem screening inventory.* Tempe, AZ: Walmyr.

Ingram, R. E., & Kendall, P. C. (1986). Cognitive clinical psychology: Implications of an information processing perspective. In R. E. Ingram (Ed.), *Information processing approaches to clinical psychology* (pp. 4–21). New York, NY: Academic Press.

Ingram, R. E., & Siegle, G. J. (2001). Cognition and clinical science: From revolution to evolution. In K. S. Dobson (Ed.), *Handbook of cognitive-behavioral therapies* (2nd ed., pp. 111–137). New York, NY: Guilford Press.

Irvin, J. E., Bowers, C. A., Dunn, M. E., & Wong, M. C. (1999). Efficacy of relapse prevention: A meta-analytic review. *Journal of Consulting and Clinical Psychology, 67,* 563–570.

Jacob, T., Ritchey, D., Cvitkovic, J., & Blane, H. (1981). Communication styles of alcoholic and nonalcoholic families when drinking and not drinking. *Journal of Studies on Alcohol, 42,* 466–482.

Jacobson, N. S., & Christensen, A. (1996). *Integrative couple therapy: Promoting acceptance and change.* New York, NY: W. W. Norton.

Jacobson, N. S., & Margolin, G. (1979). *Marital therapy.* New York, NY: Brunner/Mazel.

Jannoun, L., Munby, M., Catalan, J., & Gelder, M. (1980). A home-based treatment program for agoraphobia: Replication and controlled evaluation. *Behavior Therapy, 11,* 294–305.

Kahl, K.G., Winter, L., & Schweiger, U. (2012). The third wave of cognitive behavioural therapies: What is new and what is effective? *Current Opinion in Psychiatry, 25(6),* 522–528.

Kazdin, A. E., Esveldt-Dawson, K., French, N. H., & Unis, A. S. (1987). Problem-solving skills training and relationship therapy in the treatment of antisocial child behavior. *Journal of Consulting and Clinical Psychology, 55,* 76–85.

Keefe, F. J., Caldwell, D. S., Williams, D. A., Gil, K. M., Mitchell, D., Robertson, C., et al. (1990). Pain coping skills training in the management of osteoarthritic knee pain: A comparative study. *Behavior Therapy, 21,* 49–62.

Kelly, G. A. (1955). *The psychology of personal constructs* (Vols. 1 & 2). New York, NY: W. W. Norton.

Kendall, P. C., & Hollon, S. D. (1981). *Assessment strategies for cognitive-behavioral interventions.* New York, NY: Academic Press.

Kingdon, D. G., & Turkington, D. (1994). *Cognitive-behavioral therapy of schizophrenia.* New York, NY: Guilford Press.

Koons, C. R. (2008). Dialectical behavior therapy. *Social Work in Mental Health, 6*(1/2), 109–132.

Kuehlwein, K. T., & Rosen, H. (Eds.). (1993). *Cognitive therapies in action: Evolving innovative practice.* San Francisco, CA: Jossey-Bass.

Lappalainen, R., Lehtonen, T., Skarp, E., Taubert, E., Ojanen, M., & Hayes, S. C. (2007). The impact of CBT and ACT models using psychology trainee therapists: A preliminary controlled effectiveness trial. *Behavior Modification, 31*(4), 488–511.

Leahy, R. L. (2001). *Overcoming resistance in cognitive therapy.* New York, NY: Guilford Press.

Leahy, R. L. (Ed.). (2003). *Roadblocks in cognitive-behavioral therapy: Transforming challenges into opportunities for change.* New York, NY: Guilford Press.

Leahy, R. L. (Ed.). (2004). *Contemporary cognitive therapy: Theory, research, and practice.* New York, NY: Guilford Press.

Linehan, M. M. (1993). *Cognitive-behavioral treatment of borderline personality disorder.* New York, NY: Guilford Press.

Linehan, M. M., & Dexter-Mazza, E. T. (2008). Dialectical behavior therapy for borderline personality disorder. In D. H. Barlow (Ed.), *Clinical handbook of psychological disorders: A step-by-step treatment manual* (pp. 365–420). New York, NY: Guilford Press.

Linehan, M. M., & Koerner, K. (2012). *Doing dialectical behavior therapy.* New York, NY: Guilford Press.

Loerch, B., Graf-Morgenstern, M., Hautzinger, M., Schlegel, S., Hain, C., Snadmann, J., et al. (1999). Randomised placebo-controlled trial of moclobemide, cognitive-behavioural therapy and their combination in panic disorder with agoraphobia. *British Journal of Psychiatry, 174,* 205–212.

Lyddon, W. J. (1990). First-and-second-order change: Implications for rationalist and constructivist cognitive therapies. *Journal of Counseling and Development, 69,* 122–127.

MacPherson, L., Tull., M.T., Matusiewicz, A. K., Rodman, S., Strong, D. R., Kahler, C. W., Hopko, D. R., . . . Lejuez, C.W. (2010). Randomized controlled trial of behavioral activation smoking cessation treatment for smokers with elevated depressive symptoms. *Journal of Consulting and Clinical Psychology, 78*(1), 55–61.

Mahoney, M. J. (1977). Reflection on the cognitive-learning trend in psychotherapy. *American Psychologist, 32,* 5–13.

Mahoney, M. J. (1991). *Human change processes: The scientific foundations of psychotherapy.* New York, NY: Basic Books.

Mahoney, M. J. (1993). Introduction to special section: Theoretical developments in the cognitive psychotherapies. *Journal of Consulting and Clinical Psychology, 61,* 187–193.

Mahoney, M. J. (Ed.). (1995). *Cognitive and constructive psychotherapies.* New York, NY: Springer.

Mahoney, M. J. (2003). *Constructive psychotherapy.* New York, NY: Guilford Press.

Mahoney, M. J., & Granvold, D. K. (2005). Constructivism and psychotherapy. *World Psychiatry, 4*(2), 74–77.

Mahoney, M. J., & Lyddon, W. J. (1988). Recent developments in cognitive approaches to counseling and psychotherapy. *Counseling Psychologist, 16,* 190–234.

Markus, H., & Nurius, P. S. (1986). Possible selves. *American Psychologist, 41,* 954–969.

Marlatt, G. A. (1985). Relapse prevention: Theoretical rationale and overview of the model. In G. A. Marlatt & J. R. Gordon (Eds.), *Relapse prevention* (pp. 3–70). New York, NY: Guilford Press.

Marlatt, G. A., & Gordon, J. R. (Eds.). (1985). *Relapse prevention.* New York, NY: Guilford Press.

Martell, C. R., Dimidjian, S., & Herman-Dunn, R. (2010). *Behavioral activation for depression.* New York, NY: Guilford.

Maultsby, M. C. (1977). Rational-emotive imagery. In A. Ellis & R. Grieger (Eds.), *Handbook of rational-emotive therapy* (pp. 225–230). New York, NY: Springer.

Maultsby, M. C. (1984). *Rational behavior therapy.* Englewood Cliffs, NJ: Prentice Hall.

Maultsby, M. C., & Ellis, A. (1974). *Techniques for using rational-emotive imagery.* New York, NY: Institute for Rational-Emotive Therapy.

McCrady, B. S. (2001). Alcohol use disorders. In D. H. Barlow (Ed.), *Clinical handbook of psychological disorders* (3rd ed., pp. 376–433). New York, NY: Guilford Press.

McDonagh, A., Friedman, M., McHugo, G., Ford, J., Sengupta, A., Mueser, P. P., et al. (2005). Randomized trial of cognitive-behavioral therapy for chronic posttraumatic stress disorder in adult female survivors of childhood sexual abuse. *Journal of Consulting and Clinical Psychology, 73*(3), 515–524.

Meichenbaum, D. (1977). *Cognitive-behavior modification.* New York, NY: Plenum Press.

Meichenbaum, D. H., & Goodman, J. (1971). Training impulsive children to talk to themselves. *Journal of Abnormal Psychology, 77,* 115–126.

Merluzzi, T. V., & Boltwood, M. D. (1989). Cognitive assessment. In A. Freeman, K. M. Simon, L. E. Beutler, & H. Arkowitz (Eds.), *Comprehensive handbook of cognitive therapy* (pp. 249–266). New York, NY: Plenum Press.

Merluzzi, T. V., Glass, C. R., & Genest, M. (Eds.). (1981). *Cognitive assessment.* New York, NY: Guilford Press.

Michelson, L. (1987). Cognitive-behavioral assessment and treatment of agoraphobia. In L. Michelson & L. M. Ascher (Eds.), *Anxiety and stress disorders: Cognitive-behavioral assessment and treatment* (pp. 213–279). New York, NY: Guilford Press.

Michelson, L., & Ascher, L. M. (Eds.). (1987). *Anxiety and stress disorders: Cognitive-behavioral assessment and treatment.* New York, NY: Guilford Press.

Mitchell, J. E., Agras, W. S., Wilson, G. T., Halmi, K., Kraemer, H., & Crow, S. (2004). A trial of a relapse prevention strategy in women with bulimia nervosa who respond to cognitive-behavioral therapy. *International Journal of Eating Disorders, 35*(4), 549–555.

Mueser, K. T., Rosenberg, S. D., Xie, H., Jankowski, M. K., Bolton, E. E., Lu, W., et al. (2008). A randomized controlled trial of cognitive-behavioral treatment for posttraumatic stress disorder in severe mental illness. *Journal of Consulting and Clinical Psychology, 76*(2), 259–271.

Muran, E. (2007). Rape trauma. In F. M. Dattilio & A. Freeman (Eds.), *Cognitive-behavioral strategies in crisis intervention* (3rd ed., pp. 476–493). New York, NY: Guilford Press.

Myers, L. L. (2007). Eating disorders. In T. Ronen & A. Freeman (Eds.), *Cognitive behavior therapy in clinical social work practice* (pp. 551–569). New York, NY: Springer.

Mynors-Wallis, L. M., Gath, D. H., Lloyd-Thomas, A. R., & Tomlinson, D. (1995). Randomized controlled trial comparing problem solving treatment with amitriptyline and placebo for major depression in primary care. *British Medical Journal, 310,* 441–445.

Nay, W. R. (1979). *Multimethod clinical assessment.* New York, NY: Gardner.

Neimeyer, G. J. (Ed.). (1993). *Constructivist assessment: A casebook.* Newbury Park, CA: Sage.

Neimeyer, R. A. (1993a). An appraisal of constructivist psychotherapies. *Journal of Consulting and Clinical Psychology, 61,* 221–234.

Neimeyer, R. A. (1993b). Constructivism and the cognitive psychotherapies: Some conceptual and strategic contrasts. *Journal of Cognitive Psychotherapy: An International Quarterly, 7,* 159–171.

Neimeyer, R. A. (1993c). Constructivist approaches to the measurement of meaning. In G. J. Neimeyer (Ed.), *Constructivist assessment: A casebook* (pp. 188–232). Newbury Park, CA: Sage.

Neimeyer, R. A. (1995). Constructivist psychotherapies: Features, foundations, and future directions. In R. A. Neimeyer & M. J. Mahoney

(Eds.), *Constructivism in psychotherapy* (pp. 11–38). Washington, DC: American Psychological Association.

Neimeyer, R.A. (2009). *Constructivist psychotherapy: Distinctive features.* London, UK: Routledge.

Neimeyer, R. A., & Neimeyer, G. J. (1993). Constructivist assessment: What and when. In G. J. Neimeyer (Ed.), *Constructivist assessment: A casebook* (pp. 206–223). Newbury Park, CA: Sage.

Neimeyer, R. A., & Raskin, J. D. (Eds.). (2000). *Constructions of disorder: Meaning-making frameworks for psychotherapy.* Washington, DC: American Psychological Association.

Neimeyer, R. A., & Raskin, J. D. (2001). Varieties of constructivism in psychotherapy. In K. S. Dobson (Ed.), *Handbook of cognitive-behavioral therapies* (2nd ed., pp. 393–430). New York, NY: Guilford Press.

Newman, C. F. (2004). Substance abuse. In R. L. Leahy (Ed.), *Contemporary cognitive therapy: Theory, research, and practice* (pp. 206–227). New York, NY: Guilford Press.

Nezu, A. M. (1986). Efficacy of a social problem solving therapy approach for unipolar depression. *Journal of Consulting and Clinical Psychology, 54,* 196–202.

Nezu, A. M., & Carnevale, G. J. (1987). Interpersonal problem solving and coping reactions of Vietnam veterans with posttraumatic stress syndrome. *Journal of Abnormal Psychology, 96,* 155–157.

Nezu, C. M., D'Zurilla, T. J., & Nezu, A. M. (2005). Problem solving therapy: Theory, practice, and application to sex offenders. In M. McMurran & J. McGuire (Eds.), *Social problem solving and offending: Evidence, evaluation, and evolution* (pp. 103–123). New York, NY: Wiley.

Nezu, C. M., Nezu, A. M., & Houts, P. S. (1993). Multiple applications of problem-solving principles in clinical practice. In K. T. Kuehlwein & H. Rosen (Eds.), *Cognitive therapies in action: Evolving innovative practice* (pp. 353–378). San Francisco, CA: Jossey-Bass.

Novaco, R. W., & Chemtob, C. M. (1998). Anger and trauma: Conceptualization, assessment, and treatment. In V. M. Folette, J. I. Rusek, & F. R. Abueg (Eds.), *Cognitive-behavioral therapies for trauma* (pp. 162–190). New York, NY: Guilford Press.

Nurius, P. S. (1991). Possible selves and social support: Social cognitive resources for coping and striving. In J. Howard & P. Collero (Eds.), *The self-society dynamic: Cognition, emotion, and action* (pp. 238–258). New York, NY: Cambridge University Press.

Nurius, P. S., & Berlin, S. S. (1994). Treatment of negative self-concept and depression. In D. K. Granvold (Ed.), *Cognitive and behavioral treatment: Methods and applications* (pp. 249–271). Pacific Grove, CA: Brooks/Cole.

Nurius, P. S., & Majerus, D. (1988). Rethinking the self in self-talk: A theoretical note and case example. *Journal of Social and Clinical Psychology, 6,* 335–345.

Ost, L. (2008). Efficacy of the third wave of behavioral therapies: A systematic review and meta-analysis. *Behavior, Research, & Therapy, 46,* 296–321.

Pfammatter, M., Junghan, U. M., & Brenner, H. D. (2006). Efficacy of psychological therapy in schizophrenia: Conclusions from meta-analyses. *Schizophrenia Bulletin, 32*(Suppl. 1), S64–S80.

Popper, K. R. (1972). *Objective knowledge: An evolutionary approach.* London, UK: Oxford University Press.

Premack, D. (1965). Reinforcement theory. In D. Levine (Ed.), *Nebraska symposium on motivation* (pp. 123–180). Lincoln: University of Nebraska Press.

Premack, D. (1971). Catching up with common sense or two sides of a generalization: Reinforcement and punishment. In R. Glaser (Ed.), *The nature of reinforcement* (pp. 121–150). New York, NY: Academic Press.

Pretzer, J., & Beck, J. S. (2004). Cognitive therapy of personality disorders: Twenty years of progress. In R. L. Leahy (Ed.), *Contemporary cognitive therapy: Theory, research, and practice* (pp. 299–318). New York, NY: Guilford Press.

Raskin, J. D., & Bridges, S. K. (2002). *Studies in meaning: Exploring constructivist psychology.* New York, NY: Pace University Press.

Raskin, J. D., & Bridges, S. K. (2004). *Studies in meaning 2: Bridging the personal and social in constructivist psychology.* New York, NY: Pace University Press.

Raskin, J. D., & Bridges, S. K. (2008). *Studies in meaning 3: Constructivist psychotherapy in the real world.* New York, NY: Pace University Press.

Rathod, S., Kingdon, D., Weiden, P., & Turkington, D. (2008). Cognitive-behavioral therapy for medication-resistant schizophrenia: A review. *Journal of Psychiatric Practice, 14*(1), 22–33.

Rector, N. A. (2004). Cognitive theory and therapy of schizophrenia. In R. L. Leahy (Ed.), *Contemporary cognitive therapy: Theory, research, and practice* (pp. 244–265). New York, NY: Guilford Press.

Regehr, C. (2001). Cognitive-behavioral theory. In P. Lehmann & N. Coady (Eds.), *Theoretical perspectives for direct social work practice: A generalist-eclectic approach* (pp. 165–182). New York, NY: Springer.

Reinecke, M. A. (2000). Suicide and depression. In F. M. Dattilio & A. Freeman (Eds.), *Cognitive-behavioral strategies in crisis intervention* (2nd ed., pp. 84–125). New York, NY: Guilford Press.

Reinecke, M. A., Washburn, J. J., & Becker-Weldman, E. (2007). Depression and suicide. In F. M. Dattilio & A. Freeman (Eds.), *Cognitive-behavioral strategies in crisis intervention* (3rd ed., pp. 25–67). New York, NY: Guilford Press.

Resick, P. A., Monson, C. M., & Rizvi, S. L. (2008). Posttraumatic stress disorder. In D. H. Barlow (Ed.), *Clinical handbook of psychological disorders: A step-by-step treatment manual* (pp. 65–122). New York, NY: Guilford Press.

Resick, P. A., Nishith, P., & Griffin, M. G. (2003). How well does cognitive-behavioral therapy treat symptoms of complex PTSD: An examination of child sexual abuse survivors within a clinical trial. *CNS Spectrums, 8*(5), 351–355.

Richey, C. A. (1994). Social support skill training. In D. K. Granvold (Ed.), *Cognitive and behavioral treatment: Methods and applications* (pp. 299–338). Pacific Grove, CA: Brooks/Cole.

Riggs, D. S., Cahill, S. P., & Foa, E. B. (2006). Prolonged exposure treatment of posttraumatic stress disorder. In V. M. Follette & J. I. Rusek (Eds.), *Cognitive-behavioral therapies for trauma* (pp. 65–95). New York, NY: Guilford Press.

Riso, L. P., du Toit, P. L., Stein, D. J., & Young, J. E. (Eds.). (2007). *Cognitive schemas and core beliefs in psychological problems: A scientist-practitioner guide.* Washington, DC: American Psychological Association.

Robins, C. J., Fenwick, C. V., Donnelly, J. E., & Lacy, J. (2008). Borderline personality disorder. In M. A. Whisman (Ed.), *Adapting cognitive therapy for depression: Managing complexity and comorbidity* (pp. 280–305). New York, NY: Guilford Press.

Ronen, T., & Freeman, A. (Eds). (2007). *Cognitive behavior therapy in clinical social work practice.* New York, NY: Springer.

Rosen, H., & Kuehlwein, K. T. (Eds.). (1996). *Constructing realities: Meaning-making perspectives for psychotherapists.* San Francisco, CA: Jossey-Bass.

Rothstein, M. M., & Vallis, T. M. (1991). The application of cognitive therapy to patients with personality disorders. In T. M. Vallis, J. L. Howes, & P. C. Miller (Eds.), *The challenge of cognitive therapy: Applications to non-traditional populations* (pp. 59–84). New York, NY: Plenum Press.

Rush, A. J., & Beck, A. T. (1978). Adults with affective disorders. In M. Hersen & A. S. Bellack (Eds.), *Behavioral therapy in the psychiatric setting* (pp. 69–93). Baltimore, MD: Williams & Wilkins.

Saleebey, D. (Ed.). (2006). *The strengths perspective in social work practice* (4th ed.). New York, NY: Allyn & Bacon.

Schwartz, R. M., & Garamoni, G. L. (1986). A structural model of positive and negative states of mind: Asymmetry in the internal dialogue. In P. C. Kendall (Ed.), *Advances in cognitive behavioral research therapy* (Vol. 5, pp. 1–62). New York, NY: Academic Press.

Scott, J., Williams, J. M. G., & Beck, A. T. (Eds.). (1989). *Cognitive therapy in clinical practice: An illustrative casebook.* New York, NY: Routledge.

Segal, Z. V., & Shaw, B. F. (1988). Cognitive assessment: Issues and methods. In K. S. Dobson (Ed.), *Handbook of cognitive-behavioral therapies* (pp. 39–81). New York, NY: Guilford Press.

Segal, Z. V., Williams, J. M. G., & Teasdale, J. D. (2002). *Mindfulness-based cognitive therapy for depression: A new approach to preventing relapse.* New York, NY: Guilford Press.

Snarski, M., Scogin, F., DiNapoli, E., Presnell, A., McAlpine, J., & Marcinak, J. (2011). The effects of behavioral activation therapy with inpatient geriatric psychiatry patients. *Behavior Therapy, Behavior Therapy, 42*(1), 100–108.

Sperry, L. (1999). *Cognitive behavior therapy of DSM-IV personality disorders: Highly effective interventions for the most common personality disorders.* Philadelphia, PA: Brunner/Mazel.

Stangier, U., Heidenreich, T., Peitz, M., Lauterbach, W., & Clark, D. M. (2003). Cognitive therapy for social phobia: Individual versus group treatment. *Behaviour Research and Therapy, 41,* 991–1007.

Telch, C. F., Agras, W. S., Rossiter, E. M., Wilfley, D., & Kenardy, J. (1990). Group cognitive-behavioral treatment for the nonpurging bulimic: An initial evaluation. *Journal of Consulting and Clinical Psychology, 58,* 629–635.

Thorn, B. E. (2004). *Cognitive therapy for chronic pain: A step-by-step guide.* New York, NY: Guilford Press.

Thorpe, G., & Burns, L. (1983). *The agoraphobia syndrome.* New York, NY: Wiley.

Turk, C. L., Heimberg, R. C., & Magee, L. (2008). Social anxiety disorder. In D. H. Barlow (Ed.), *Clinical handbook of psychological disorders: A step-by-step treatment manual* (pp. 123–163). New York, NY: Guilford Press.

Turk, D. C., & Gatchel, R. J. (Eds.). (2002). *Psychological approaches to pain management: A practitioner's handbook* (2nd ed.). New York, NY: Guilford Press.

Turkington, D., Sensky, T., Scott, J., Barnes, T. R. E., Nur, U., Siddle, R., et al. (2008). A randomized controlled trial of cognitive-behavior therapy for persistent symptoms in schizophrenia: A five-year follow-up. *Schizophrenia Research, 98*(1/3), 1–7.

Vincent, J., Weiss, R., & Birchler, G. (1976). A behavioral analysis of problem solving in distressed and nondistressed married and stranger dyads. *Behavior Therapy, 6,* 475–487.

Vonk, M. E., & Early, T. J. (2009). Cognitive-behavioral therapy. In A. R. Roberts (Ed.), *Social workers' desk reference* (2nd ed., pp. 242–247). New York, NY: Oxford University Press.

Weiss, R. L., & Margolin, G. (1977). Assessment of marital conflict and accord. In A. R. Ciminero, K. S. Calhoun, & H. E. Adams (Eds.), *Handbook of behavioral assessment* (pp. 555–602). New York, NY: Wiley.

Weisz, J. R., Weiss, B., Wasserman, A. A., & Rintoul, B. (1987). Control-related beliefs and depression among clinic-referred children and adolescents. *Journal of Abnormal Psychology, 96,* 58–63.

Wells, A. (1997). *Cognitive therapy of anxiety disorders: A practice manual and conceptual guide.* New York, NY: Wiley.

Whisman, M. A. (Ed.). (2008). *Adapting cognitive therapy for depression: Managing complexity and comorbidity.* New York, NY: Guilford Press.

White, B. (2007). Working with adult survivors of sexual and physical abuse. In T. Ronen & A. Freeman (Eds.), *Cognitive behavior therapy in clinical social work practice* (pp. 467–489). New York, NY: Springer.

Wilson, G. T. (2008). Behavior therapy. In R. J. Corsini & D. Wedding (Eds.), *Current psychotherapies* (8th ed., pp. 223–262). Belmont, CA: Thomson.

Wilson, G. T., Grilo, C. M., & Vitousek, K. M. (2007). Psychological treatment of eating disorders. *American Psychologist, 62*(3), 199–216.

Wilson, G. T., & Pike, K. M. (2001). Eating disorders. In D. H. Barlow (Ed.), *Clinical handbook of psychological disorders* (3rd ed., pp. 332–375). New York, NY: Guilford Press.

Wilson, P. H. (Ed.). (1992). *Principles and practice of relapse prevention.* New York, NY: Guilford Press.

Wright, J. H., Thase, M. E., Beck, A. T., & Ludgate, J. W. (Eds.). (1993). *Cognitive therapy with inpatients: Developing a cognitive milieu.* New York, NY: Guilford Press.

Young, J. E. (1990). *Cognitive therapy for personality disorders: A schema-focused approach.* Sarasota, FL: Professional Resource Press.

Young, J. E., & Brown, G. (1990). *Young schema questionnaire.* New York, NY: Cognitive Therapy Center of New York.

Young, J. E., & Brown, G. (2001). *Young schema questionnaire* (Special ed.). New York, NY: Schema Therapy Institute.

Young, J. E., Klosko, J. S., & Weishaar, M. E. (2003). *Schema therapy: A practitioner's guide.* New York, NY: Guilford Press.

Young, J. E., Rygh, J. L., Weinberger, A. D., & Beck, A. T. (2008). Cognitive therapy for depression. In D. H. Barlow (Ed.), *Clinical handbook of psychological disorders: A step-by-step treatment manual* (pp. 250–305). New York, NY: Guilford Press.

9

PSYCHOANALYTIC PSYCHOTHERAPY WITH ADULTS

FREDRIC T. PERLMAN

Psychoanalytic psychotherapy is a method for the treatment of mental and emotional disorders by means that promote their understanding. By *mental and emotional disorders*, I mean maladaptive patterns of thought, feeling, and behavior that restrict the pursuit of life's pleasures and impose objectively unnecessary suffering. By *understanding*, I refer to both empathic understanding as well as understanding in the psychoanalytic sense. Empathic understanding refers to interpersonal understanding formed on the basis of empathy, the capacity to put oneself in another person's shoes and, in this way, simulate the other person's subjective experience within one's own mind (Akhtar, 2007; Decety, 2012; Goldman, 2006). In the psychoanalytic sense, understanding refers to a discernment of the hidden, unconscious motivations and mental processes that determine subjective experience and behavior and give rise to mental and emotional disorders. Unlike empathy, which is a feature of human nature (Decety & Ickes, 2009; Iacoboni, 2008), psychoanalytic understanding is based on psychoanalytic theories of mental life and is only acquired by study and training. Empathic and psychoanalytic understanding are closely related to each other and are both essential to psychoanalytic therapy. Empathic understanding provides access to the client's mental life, but the application of psychoanalytic understanding is necessary to explain it. Empathic understanding and psychoanalytic understanding are both therapeutic agents. To be accurately understood is calming and soothing. It engenders feelings of being like other people, of being coherent, accepted, and valued as a person (Rogers, 1957, 1961; Truax, 1963; Truax & Carkhuff, 1967). Contemporary research demonstrates that accurate empathy is a therapeutic agent in all forms of therapy (Elliot, Bohart, Watson, and Greenberg, 2011). In psychoanalytic therapy, empathy is a fundamental feature of the therapeutic relationship, but it is not the primary curative agent. The essential curative agent in psychoanalytic therapy is *insight*, the recognition and understanding of hitherto unconscious motivations and how they give rise to maladaptive patterns of living. Psychoanalytic treatment is a contemporary approach to the treatment of human suffering based on the classical Greek ideals of reason and self-knowledge that were central to "the Enlightenment vision" (Eagle, 2012).

Psychoanalytic psychotherapy derives from the theory and technical procedures of psychoanalysis. Psychoanalysis originated with the work of Sigmund Freud (1856–1939), a Viennese physician whose pioneering efforts to help patients suffering from obscure mental disorders led him from the practice of neurology to the field of psychology. Freud discovered that when these patients speak freely about the thoughts that pass through their minds, they regularly express hitherto unconscious wishes, fears, and other painful affects that illuminate the motivational basis of their pathologies. Moreover, he found that when these unconscious motivations were uncovered and exposed to conscious reflection, his patients acquired increased control over their psychological symptoms and problems. The investigation and illumination of the patient's mental life, Freud learned, was thus tantamount to the treatment of his or her mental or emotional problems. The optimal therapeutic process, he concluded, is an individualized investigative procedure that produces self-knowledge, or *insight*. Psychoanalysis aims to modify maladaptive patterns by enabling the client to apprehend, understand, and regulate the psychological forces responsible for symptoms and life problems.

The technical procedures employed in psychoanalytic treatment are intended to promote the freest possible expression of the client's mental life. In a typical psychoanalysis, the analyst and the *analysand* (i.e., the client) meet three to five times per week for 45- or 50-minute sessions. The analysand lies on a couch facing away from the analyst and is asked to say everything that crosses his or her mind, articulating thoughts, images, wishes, fears, memories, dreams, fantasies, fleeting thoughts, sensations—all without editing or censorship. Because the analysand cannot see the analyst, there is less perceptual data to constrain the analysand's subjective experience of the analyst than would be the case in a face-to-face therapy. This sensory deprivation enlarges the role of the fantasy life in shaping the analysand's experience of the analyst, thus opening a unique window into the analysand's mental life. As the analysand

talks, the analyst listens empathically, trying to apprehend the analysand's mental life, and makes timely interventions to promote his or her self-awareness and self-understanding. Among the analyst's techniques for achieving this expanded self-awareness are interventions designed to promote awareness of defensive functioning. As psychological defenses and the emotional forces motivating those defenses are understood, defensive functioning is relaxed and the universe of conscious mental life is enlarged. The analyst does not attempt to influence the analysand's life choices through suggestion, personal influence, or the use of authority. In a model analysis, the analyst steadfastly pursues illumination rather than persuasion. As treatment progresses, the client discovers hitherto hidden and hitherto unconscious childhood strivings, disturbing feelings, and unrealistic ideas that have adversely influenced his or her life and is able to examine and assess them from a mature and realistic perspective.

Freud's discoveries were revolutionary because he demonstrated that our conscious experience is only one aspect of mental life. Freud's work revealed that our conscious thoughts and deliberations are not always decisive in determining the way we think, feel, and act. Unconscious motivations could silently shape our lives in ways that compromise our potential for happiness and mental health. Freud's work attracted wide interest within the general culture as well as among psychiatrists and psychiatric social workers. A large percentage of psychiatrists undertook psychoanalytic training in the 1930s and 1040s, and many social workers sought instruction and supervision from them (Borenzweig, 1971; Grinker, MacGregor, Selan, & Kohrman, 1961; Hellenbrand, 1972; Lubove, 1965; Yelloly, 1980). Psychoanalysis became a premiere treatment modality during these years, reaching an apogee of popularity in the 1950s (Fine, 1979; Kurzweil, 1997; Zaretsky, 2004). While psychoanalysis continued to play an influential role in academic studies and cultural life in the decades that followed (Samuel, 2013), psychoanalysis gradually lost its appeal as a treatment modality. The vast majority of people for whom analysis might have been useful could not afford the time or money that psychoanalysis ordinarily requires. In addition, analysis proved to be unhelpful for many sicker individuals who lacked the psychological capacities needed to make good use of insight. In the years after the Second World War, psychoanalysts introduced new approaches to help those people with limited means as well as those for whom a standard analysis was contraindicated. These efforts gave rise to the new field of psychoanalytic psychotherapy (Wallerstein, 2012).

In the decades since its differentiation from psychoanalysis, psychoanalytic psychotherapy, sometimes referred to as "psychodynamic psychotherapy," has become the more widely practiced form of psychoanalytic treatment. While the popularity of clinical psychoanalysis has waned since its heyday, psychoanalytic therapies have thrived. Many psychoanalytic training institutes now offer advanced courses in psychoanalytic therapy for candidates in psychoanalytic training as well as special training programs for therapists who wish to specialize in psychoanalytic psychotherapy rather than classical psychoanalysis. Psychoanalytic clinics are bustling, not because people are seeking analysis but because they want psychoanalytic therapy. Psychoanalytic psychotherapy is the fulfillment of Freud's dream of a psychoanalytic treatment "for the masses" (Freud, 1919) and may rightfully be regarded as "the enduring legacy of psychoanalysis" (Rangell, 2001).

Psychoanalytic psychotherapy requires substantial time and effort from both the therapist and the client. Other therapies are easier and shorter. Research on the outcomes of psychoanalytic treatment, however, demonstrates the remarkable benefits that are achieved in this form of treatment. While all recognized forms of psychotherapy produce therapeutic effects, meta-analytic outcome studies consistently demonstrate that psychoanalytic psychotherapy produces benefits that continue to accumulate after termination, while the effects of other forms of treatment tend to fade after termination. Reviewing these studies, one researcher observed that "psychodynamic psychotherapy may not only alleviate symptoms but also

develop inner capacities and resources that allow a richer and more fulfilling life" (Shedler, 2010, p. 15). Such outcomes, he notes, may explain why therapists, regardless of their theoretical orientation, generally opt for psychoanalytic therapy when they seek treatment for themselves (Norcross, 2005).

Although I refer to psychoanalytic therapy as one practice or one field of endeavor, psychoanalytic psychotherapy is actually a very diverse enterprise. This diversity reflects the gradual pluralization of psychoanalytic thought and associated approaches to treatment. Although Freud envisioned a unitary discipline of psychoanalysis, many analysts have introduced modifications and, in some instances, radical changes to both theory and practice. This gave rise to different schools of psychoanalytic thought (see "Psychoanalytic Theory," Chapter 3 of this volume). Each of these schools has contributed to a common pool of psychoanalytic ideas while developing its own technical approaches, including its own versions of psychoanalytic psychotherapy. The literature of psychoanalytic psychotherapy has thus come to include textbooks based on a broad mainstream of psychoanalytic ideas (Cabaniss, Cherry, Douglas, & Schwartz, 2011; Elzer & Gerlach, in press; Gabbard, 2010; Huprich, 2009; Lemma, 2003; Luborsky, 1984; Langs, 1973, 1974; McWilliams, 2004; Paolino, 1981; Safran, 2012; Summers & Barber, 2010) as well as texts based on particular schools of psychoanalytic thought, such as *self-psychology* (Elson, 1988; Jackson, 1994; Lee & Martin, 1991; Rowe and MacIsaac, 1993; Wolf, 1988), *intersubjectivity* (Buirski, 2009; Stolorow, Brandschaft, & Atwood, 1987), *object relations* (Cashdan, 1988; Celeni, 2010; Horner, 1991; Waska, 2010; Ogden, 1984; Scharff & Scharff, 2000; Summers, 1999), *interpersonal theory* (Benjamin, 2002, 2003; Frank & Levenson, 2010; Scott & Robertson, 2010; Weissman, Markowitz, & Klerman, 2000, 2007; Markowitz & Weissman, 2012), and *relational psychotherapy* (De Young, 2003; Magnavita, 1999; Wachtel, 2007).

Although psychoanalytic psychotherapy is typically an open-ended treatment, each school of psychoanalytic psychotherapy has introduced short-term versions of their particular treatment approaches (Binder, 2004; Binder & Betan, 2012; Book, 1998; Coren, 2001; Crits-Christ & Barber, 2001; Davanloo, 1977; Della Selva, 1996; Groves, 1996; Have-de Labije & Neborsky, 2012; Lemma, Target, & Fonagy, 2011; Levenson, 2003; Levenson, Butler, Powers, & Beitman, 2002; Rawson, 2002; Sifneos, 1992; Stadter, 2009; Strupp & Binder, 1985; Waska, 2013). In general, short-term treatments are limited to a specified time frame or number of sessions. While the development of these short-term approaches has been largely stimulated by economic pressures and budgetary cuts, short-term treatments often have unique value for clients in crisis and for those with Axis I disorders seeking assistance to alleviate focal pathologies. They also offer an opportunity to taste what treatment is like without making an open-ended commitment or exposing oneself to a situation that might otherwise be too threatening.

When psychoanalytic psychotherapy was first introduced, it was customary to differentiate between two models of treatment, generally referred to as *exploratory* and *supportive* (Knight, 1949). Exploratory therapy, also referred to as "*uncovering, insight-oriented*, or *expressive* therapy, is similar to psychoanalysis in many respects. It is undertaken to explore mental life and expose the unconscious mental factors that give rise to maladaptive functioning. Unlike psychoanalysis, however, exploratory psychotherapy is conducted face-to-face so that the client has a full range of perceptual information with which to form an impression of the therapist. In addition, exploratory therapy is usually conducted on a once or twice a weekly basis, a factor that limits the continuity and intensity of treatment. As in analysis, the client uncovers hitherto unconscious aspects of mental life that, once conscious, can be examined and assessed by the more mature and rational part of his personality. This process of reflection, reality testing, judgment, and understanding facilitates self-regulation and more realistic, mature, and adaptive functioning.

It should be emphasized that the effectiveness of exploratory psychoanalytic therapy rests on successful uncovering as well as successful processing of unconscious contents. Some clients, however, are too frightened of their own feelings and thoughts to participate in a treatment designed to uncover hidden aspects of mental life. These individuals may seek help for problems that trouble them but often attribute their problems to "nerves" or adverse circumstances. Such clients have difficulty imagining that their own motivations contribute to their problems and are typically reluctant to engage in exploratory treatment. They do not want to uncover their feelings. Other clients recognize that their feelings or their lives are out of control and are eager to convey their experience to someone who will help them calm down and organize themselves. Such clients speak very freely about their experiences but often find themselves overwhelmed, confused, or frightened when they open up. Such clients may be able to uncover important mental contents but lack the capacity to process them. In general, exploratory treatment is contraindicated for clients who are too rigidly defensive to participate in an uncovering form of therapy as well as for clients who are unable to productively process what they uncover. These clients may, however, benefit from supportive or suppressive treatment.

Supportive psychotherapy, sometimes called *suppressive therapy*, is intended to improve the client's functioning by providing emotional and psychological support as well as targeted interventions to compensate for specific deficiencies necessary for adequate functioning (such as reality testing, judgment, impulse control, defensive functioning, and frustration tolerance) and to nurture the patient's psychological development. In supportive treatment, the therapist maintains a focus on the realistic adaptive challenges facing the client, while directing the client's attention away from disturbing thoughts or feelings that disrupt organized functioning. Supportive therapy employs techniques such as guidance, advice, reassurance, encouragement, clarification of confusing feelings, help in understanding the environment, and referral for ancillary services, to name a few. We return to the important topic of supportive therapy and supportive techniques later in this chapter.

THEORETICAL FOUNDATIONS

The practice of psychoanalytic therapy requires knowledge of psychoanalytic theory. Psychoanalytic theory has undergone many modifications since its inception. In his own lifetime, Freud repeatedly revised his views to accommodate accumulating clinical data. In the years since his death, psychoanalysts around the world have shaped and reshaped psychoanalytic theory in accordance with their own clinical experience, evolving views, and, less commonly noted, their own local cultures (Kurzweil, 1989). This has resulted in a proliferation of psychoanalytic theories and therapeutic approaches. Naturally, it is impossible to describe each of these approaches in a single chapter. Accordingly, I limit the scope of this introductory exposition to a single representative form of psychoanalytic psychotherapy. In this chapter, I describe open-ended, exploratory psychoanalytic therapy, as developed within the mainstream of contemporary psychoanalytic theory, focusing particularly, though not exclusively, on *modern structural theory.*

Modern structural theory is a contemporary version of the original structural theory, first introduced by Sigmund Freud in the 1920s (Freud, 1920, 1923, 1926). Structural theory introduced a new model of the mind composed of three psychic agencies or structures: *the id, the ego,* and *the superego.* Modern structural theory emerged as Freud's ideas were progressively reviewed (Arlow, 1991; Arlow & Brenner, 1964; Blum, Kramer, Richards, & Richards, 1988; Brenner, 1976, 1982, 1994; Dowling, 1991; Richards & Willick, 1986; Rothstein, 1983). Although this chapter draws on the work of many mainstream theorists, the exposition of psychic conflict and compromise formations is particularly indebted to the later work of Charles Brenner. Brenner (1914–2008) was one of the most influential and creative psychoanalytic theorists of American psychoanalysis (Richards

& Willick, 1986). His work is characterized by the replacement of abstract psychoanalytic constructs with "experience-near" concepts closely linked to clinical data. As a result, Brenner's model of modern structural theory is readily accessible to beginning therapists and is eminently useful for practitioners (Rothstein, 2010; Friedman, 2011).

Let us begin our examination of psychoanalytic theory with a review of its basic and enduring propositions. Briefly stated, psychoanalytic theory posits that mental activity is governed by a fundamental propensity to seek pleasure and avoid pain, termed the *pleasure principle.* Mental activity is motivated by instinctual drives, which acquire psychological representation in the form of specific wishes as a result of "experiences of satisfaction" during development. Since they derive from drives, these wishes are also called *drive derivatives.* Because the gratification of wishes is inherently pleasurable, wishes motivate mental activity. Wishful mental activity becomes complicated as a result of experiences through which the developing child comes to believe that the pursuit of specific wishes will entail calamitous consequences. As the result of such experiences, the arousal of certain wishes elicits contradictory affective signals: affects of pleasure, linked to fantasies of wish fulfillment and affects of unpleasure, linked to the aversive contingencies with which these are associated. These contradictory affective signals instigate an approach-avoidance dilemma characterized as *psychic conflict.*

Wishes are shaped by experiences of satisfaction with human caretakers and bear the imprint of these experiences. Wishes feature mental representations of the specific activities that have been pleasurable and of the persons with whom they were enjoyed. They may be classified as being predominantly sexual or aggressive, according to the character of their aims. In practice, most wishes contain a mixture of sexual and aggressive strivings. (The terms *sexual* and *aggressive* have a broader meaning in psychoanalytic terminology than they do in common parlance.) Affects of unpleasure are shaped by the hurtful experiences of childhood, both real and imagined. These affects are composed of two aspects: (1) bodily sensations of unpleasure and (2) the accompanying mental representations of calamities. These representations of calamity constitute the ideational content of unpleasurable affects. The typical calamities of childhood pertain to loss, especially the loss of parental figures or the loss of their love, and to punishment, including genital mutilation and harsh parental attitudes that induce feelings of shame or guilt. When calamities are anticipated, however unrealistically, the result is anxiety. When calamities are experienced as having already occurred, they produce depressive affect. Most unpleasurable affects contain a mixture of anxiety and depressive affect, and they pertain to a mixture of calamities (Brenner, 1982).

In conditions of psychic conflict, mental activity naturally produces an array of alternative compromise solutions, or compromise formations, each of which permits a limited measure of gratification at a limited cost of unpleasure. Compromise formations are effected through the use of defenses. Defenses are mental activities of any kind that serve to reduce unpleasure. Defenses are deployed in complex ways to alter, disguise, or otherwise distort the experience of wishes and of the unpleasures they arouse. As the result of defenses, childhood wishes and associated affects of unpleasure are typically inaccessible to conscious apprehension as such and can be perceived only through derivative manifestations (Brenner, 1982).

Compromises are not all equally adaptive, however, since each results in a different balance of pleasure and unpleasure. In any condition of psychic conflict, the compromise promoting the best balance of pleasure and unpleasure is naturally preferred over alternatives. This compromise will be repeated whenever the conflictual wish arises. With repetition, compromise formations become enduring programs for the organization of mental activity. Mental activity is construed as a sequence of mental events instigated by the arousal of specific wishes that trigger associated affects of unpleasure, which, in turn, mobilize the

deployment of defenses to reproduce a favored compromise formation. Such sequences of wish-unpleasure-defense are repeated automatically and without conscious deliberation. We are rarely aware that our preferred patterns of living are the end products of such complex activity and often mistakenly regard them as expressions of basic unitary motives. Such programs of mental activity are called *structures*, because they are "processes with a slow rate of change" (Rapaport, 1960). These programs are the structures explained by modern structural theory and illuminated by psychoanalytic therapy.

One of the most remarkable discoveries of psychoanalytic research is that the wishes of childhood, along with the unpleasures and defenses with which they are associated, persist as motivations shaping the mental life of the adult. While the lives of adults differ from those of children in significant ways, adult patterns of thinking, feeling, and behaving derive from those of childhood. Adult patterns are formed as the habitual compromise formations of childhood are progressively reshaped to fit the changing circumstances of life. New compromise formations may be conceptualized as alternative pathways in the sequence of mental events described in the preceding paragraph. All adult compromise formations are developmentally linked to their predecessors, however, and tend to reflect their continuing influence. The extraordinary continuity of psychic conflict and compromise formation in mental life, from childhood through adulthood, is responsible for the fact that we have more or less the same personalities throughout our lives (for an exceptional longitudinal study, see McDevitt, 1997).

At one time, psychoanalysts believed that psychic conflict was a feature of mental illness, while mental health was a state of freedom from psychic conflicts. Psychoanalytic research, however, has demonstrated that mental activity is always characterized by psychic conflicts and compromise formations. Mental health and mental illness are not distinguishable, then, by the absence or presence of psychic conflicts. The difference between normality and pathology lies in the character of the compromise formations to which they give rise. Healthy compromise formations promote adaptive functioning, characterized by a favorable balance of pleasure over unpleasure, while pathological compromise formations promote maladaptive functioning, with an unfavorable balance of pleasure and unpleasure.

Analysis of the healthy aspects of any individual's mental functioning, such as a happy vocational choice or the pursuit of a pleasurable hobby, regularly reveals the influence of the same desires and conflicts that determine their psychopathology. This may be illustrated by the following examples.

Mr. A was an actor who sought help with crippling bouts of stage fright that had caused him to miss several performances. Although he had always been nervous about performing, he had never before been so paralyzed that he could not go on stage. He was frustrated and furious at himself, especially since his stage fright appeared just when he was playing a leading role in a play that could make him a star. His stage fright felt like some cosmic punishment for a crime he could not remember committing.

Mr. A had grown up in an inner-city slum, one of many children in a marginally intact family, headed by an alcoholic father who was chronically aloof and contemptuous. As a child, Mr. A secretly nurtured fantasies of great wealth and fame. He imagined that he would use his success to inspire others. He began to act in plays at school and studied acting at a teen center. Later, he attended a professional acting school. He experienced intense feelings of personal triumph whenever he performed well and had pursued his career with intense zeal despite the many painful sacrifices, including years of menial work and professional insignificance.

In the course of a lengthy therapy, we discovered that Mr. A's ambitions were motivated, in part, by unconscious wishes to hurt his father, to make him burn with envy at his son's prestige and status. These vengeful wishes triggered little recognizable anxiety or guilt, because they were disguised as artistic dreams and masked by altruistic concerns for others. If he felt any residual guilt, his sacrifices were ample atonement.

When Mr. A landed a leading role in a Broadway play, however, his long-simmering desire to torment his father was stimulated by the prospect of his imminent stardom. At the same time, the chronic deprivation that permitted him to atone through sacrifices for his art was about to be ameliorated. As a result, he became increasingly panicked and guilt ridden. Consciously, he was terrified that the audience would hate him, and the critics would ridicule him as a pompous fraud. His stage fright and his missed performances were a pathological compromise formation, fueled by vengeful wishes to hurt his father (by being a star), fear of his father's retaliation (the audience and critics despising and ridiculing him), and guilt (his stage fright is a cosmic punishment). Mr. A kept his panic within limits by periodically missing performances, a symptom that undermined his success (i.e., inhibited his aggression) and thereby diminished his feelings of anxiety and guilt.

Similar motivations are apparent in a healthy aspect of Mr. A's life. Mr. A volunteered to teach acting to inner-city youths at the teen center where he first took acting lessons. He took great pleasure in

(Continued)

(Continued)

this work, which won him praise from other actors, as well as gratitude from the community center staff, and enabled him to enjoy the admiration of the boys he taught. All these experiences gratified unconscious desires to supersede his father in social importance and success. The fulfillment of these wishes was highly disguised, and any guilt he may have experienced was balanced by the obvious generosity and social virtue of his efforts. These activities are clearly a successful compromise formation, forged of the same psychic conflicts that gave rise to his painfully disrupted career.

Ms. B was a 29-year-old nurse who entered therapy complaining of failed relationships, feelings of inadequacy, and a painful sexual inhibition. She was inclined to become romantically "enchanted" by sophisticated and worldly men. She enjoyed being wined and dined and could be coaxed into bed if the man were sufficiently aggressive. Once lovemaking commenced, however, she typically became nauseated and disgusted by any further thoughts of sex. She believed that her inhibition was due to guilt over sex, for which she blamed her strict Catholic upbringing.

Ms. B was the first of four children. Her mother was a cold and bitter woman who offered little warmth or nurturance. Ms. B was always her father's favorite. Her father was an "enchanting" man, who was always loving, kind, and nurturing to her. Analytic treatment revealed that her sexual problems were caused by the persistent influence of unconscious sexual desires for her father. Although she was aware of loving her father a great deal, she was not aware of her sexual desires for him, nor was she aware that she chose her sexual partners on the basis of their similarities to him. Her lovemaking with "enchanting" men thus represented the fulfillment of unconscious incestuous desires, as a result of which sex had become morally abhorrent and disgusting. Her sexual relationships were a compromise formation, in which her incestuous sexuality was partially gratified in a disguised form at the cost of anxiety, guilt, and disgust, which she minimized by attributing them to her Catholic upbringing. Her nausea was the somatic equivalent of moral disgust.

While Ms. B suffered in her love life, she derived great pleasure from her work as a nurse. She was devoted to her clients and enjoyed the feeling of intimacy she experienced from caring for their bodily needs. She was especially moved by feelings of tenderness toward her elderly male clients and felt "privileged" to care for them. These professional activities were highly pleasurable because they permitted her to gratify her wishes for greater intimacy with her father without arousing the feelings of guilt and disgust associated with sexual desires. Her professional life was a successful compromise formation.

Compromise formations are fueled by psychological forces of which we have only partial awareness. Mr. A, for example, knew that he was ambitious and fearful of the audience's criticism, but he did not know that his theatrical ambitions were intended to achieve a triumphant revenge against his father or that he feared his father's retaliatory attack. Ms. B knew she was "enchanted" by men of a certain type and that she felt guilty and disgusted when trying to make love to them. She did not know that she yearned for a sexual union with her father, or that she felt frightened, guilty, and disgusted by this fantasy. Although Mr. A and

Ms. B are intelligent and reasonable persons, neither could exercise control over the pathological aspects of their lives. Both were encouraged by their friends to "straighten up and fly right," but neither could. Both felt that they were in the grip of something, something alien to themselves that they could neither understand nor control. In each case, what was experienced as alien was nothing other than disowned aspects of themselves, which had acquired the status of being alien as a result of defensive activities, exercised over a lifetime. Because these clients had little understanding or sense of ownership in relation to their own unconscious wishes, their ability to regulate their mental functioning was severely handicapped.

The therapist who treats clients such as Mr. A or Ms. B may endeavor to change their maladaptive patterns of thought or behavior through guidance, advice, or other prescriptive measures. Psychoanalytic psychotherapy differs from other therapies because it does not attempt to modify maladaptive patterns by any direct means. It is a radical (from *radex*, Latin for *root*) form of treatment because it attempts to illuminate the motivational roots of the client's problems. While other therapists endeavor to modify pathological patterns by direct means, the psychoanalytic therapist seeks only to understand his or her clients and to help them understand themselves.

With a deepening understanding of the emotional forces by which they are motivated, clients are able to forge new and more adaptive solutions for their psychic conflicts and to replace habitual pathological compromise formations with healthier and more gratifying ones. As the client becomes familiar with his or her inner conflicts, the client is able to think about them with the most mature aspects of his or her personality. This process of reflection enables the client to appreciate the childhood character of his or her wishes and unpleasures, to contemplate the circumstances in which they formed, and to weigh their present significance and importance—in brief, to reconsider them from the vantage point of mature judgment (Loewald, 1971). This process facilitates their

gradual transformation. Mr. A, for instance, recognized that his wish for vengeance was a plan he had made as a child, when he had no better means to cope with the suffering he experienced on a daily basis at his father's hands. Although his vengeful fantasies enabled him to endure the pain of his father's contemptuous attitude, he recognized that he was no longer subject to these indignities. Of course, he still felt the sting of these childhood injuries, such as feelings of helpless indignation and humiliation. On reflection, however, these feelings became less painful as he reviewed them from his adult perspective. His father was, after all, an unhappy and frustrated man. He should not have taken out his frustration on his son, but his nasty and denigrating attitude carried less weight when viewed from this present vantage point. Mr. A's feelings of helplessness and inadequacy were recontextualized as the psychic reality of a small boy that no longer applies to Mr. A, the man. Other significant aspects of Mr. A's conflicts, such as his fear of punishment and his feelings of guilt, were also progressively modified as they became accessible to his mature reflection and judgment. Similar observations can be made about Ms. B, who eventually came to accept her incestuous desires as an aspect of her fantasy life, to recognize the wish-fulfilling confusion that enabled her to identify her "enchanting" lovers with her father, and, finally, to differentiate consciously between her lovers and her father.

With progressive understanding, clients can alter their maladaptive patterns of living and replace them with more adaptive patterns. This process occurs spontaneously as the result of shifts in the organization of wishes, unpleasures, and defenses brought about by the client's understanding and reflection. The new patterns are also compromise formations, and they too are subject to continuing analysis and reorganization, a process that permits the creation of ever more adaptive compromises. Therapeutic change in psychoanalytic psychotherapy may be understood as a beneficial reorganization of compromise formations.

Mr. A began approaching his theatrical career more realistically. He felt less exalted and triumphant when the audience applauded, and his stage fright gradually dissipated. He took greater pleasure in the perfection of his craft and eventually began directing theatrical productions, activities that permitted the satisfaction of other desires he had previously ignored. As he reflected on his vengeful fantasies, Mr. A sought a more mature resolution of his problems with his father, which prompted him to initiate a dialogue in which he aggressively confronted his father for his myriad failings. As his persistent wish to humiliate his father was repeatedly observed and explored, Mr. A slowly adopted a more realistic attitude, which permitted him to establish a limited but happier relationship with his father.

As Ms. B came to recognize the incestuous fantasies that motivated her love life, she was able to better discriminate between reality and fantasy and began enjoying full sexual relations without nausea or other impairments. As a result, she was able to form more lasting relationships. Her behavior in these relationships, however, reflected an attitude of dependency and entitlement, which had characterized her relationship to her father. As these features of her continuing yearning for her father's love were analyzed, Ms. B slowly came to recognize both the power and the futility of her wishes to relive her childhood relationship with her father and, through this, to compensate herself for the painful feelings of rejection she experienced in relation to her mother. Her emerging desire for a partner with whom she could feel more adult and competent gradually superseded her desire for a father figure. Her new relationships were less enchanting (she was not refinding Daddy) but permitted her to experience new forms of intimacy, which eventually included marriage and motherhood.

As the client's compromise formations become healthier, permitting greater pleasure at less psychic cost, they cease to attract the client's attention, and the focus of the therapeutic work shifts. When the client has achieved sufficient mastery over his or her conflicts, the motivation for treatment often gradually dissipates, and therapy comes to a natural conclusion. Many clients who are excited by their emotional growth wish to continue in therapy to achieve further self-knowledge, often to pursue more ambitious therapeutic goals. Since self-knowledge is never total, every therapy is in a sense incomplete. There is no fixed point at which psychoanalytic therapy should come to an end. Termination never implies perfect health or the absence of conflicts.

THE PROCESS OF PSYCHOANALYTIC PSYCHOTHERAPY

Psychoanalytic psychotherapy is a collaborative undertaking. It cannot be administered to a passive or uninvolved client. The therapist cannot directly observe the client's inner life. Only the client has access to knowledge of his or her inner world. The therapist cannot reliably infer the nature of the client's psychic conflicts from knowledge of the client's symptoms, psychiatric diagnosis, lifestyle, social relations, work history, culture, socioeconomic status, family background, or any source other than the client's most private thoughts and musings. Psychoanalytic therapy, then, must be a collaborative undertaking, or it cannot be undertaken at all.

Psychoanalytic psychotherapy is a difficult and demanding form of therapy. It requires sustained effort over a protracted period of time, often many years. The client must be willing to expose his or her innermost thoughts and feelings to another person, a stranger, about whose attitudes and feelings he or she can have little knowledge. The client must be willing to tolerate the emotional discomforts this exposure evokes and to persist in the process even when it is painful. The therapist must have the skills, confidence, and emotional fortitude to accept the responsibilities this entails. The therapist presides over the entire therapeutic process. He or she is responsible for providing a safe and supportive context in which to explore buried feelings and for offering the client a coherent understanding of those feelings. The therapist is also responsible for protecting the client and the therapy from the emotional turbulence the process unleashes.

It is sometimes said that therapy begins with the first contact between the therapist and the client. While the first contact ought to be therapeutic in a general sense, psychoanalytic therapy per se can be initiated only after both parties have met and come to a mutual understanding and agreement about the nature of the treatment and the procedures to be employed. This agreement or *therapeutic contract* (Menninger, 1958) is the rational basis of all further interactions between client and therapist. In psychoanalytic therapy, the roles of client and therapist are clearly defined. The client's task is to communicate his or her thoughts to the therapist. Most psychoanalytic therapists invite the client to free-associate—to say aloud all the thoughts that come to mind, without censorship or conscious deliberation, thus enabling the therapist to sample the client's mental life. The therapist's primary task is to listen to the client's thoughts, understand the client's mental life and behavior, and communicate this understanding to the client in the form of interpretations or comments that increase the client's self-knowledge.

The client will naturally talk about many things, including his or her problems, current interpersonal relationships, relationships with family members, childhood memories, and dreams. Over time, the therapist will become increasingly familiar with the client's mental life. The client's communications enable the therapist to empathize, to form a picture of the client's subjective experience. Although the client may report every aspect of his or her thoughts and conduct faithfully and without reserve, the client cannot intentionally report the unconscious aspects of mental life. This is due to the fact that self-awareness is restricted by the operation of defenses. These unconscious aspects, especially the wishes, unpleasures, and defenses that constitute the client's pathogenic psychic conflicts, can be discovered only over time, through the application of the psychoanalytic method.

Freud employed an archaeological metaphor to describe the psychoanalytic process. The archaeologist observes a particular terrain, studies it carefully, and begins to excavate at selected sites. The process of excavation is conducted in a methodical fashion, starting at the geological surface and proceeding layer by layer to an uncovering of artifacts and objects at successively lower levels. Although psychoanalytic treatment is not archaeology, the metaphor highlights certain meaningful parallels. Like an archaeological dig, a psychoanalytic investigation proceeds from the surface to the depth—from facts and feelings that are on the surface to those aspects of mental life that are hidden and can be observed only when they are uncovered. Although analysts vary somewhat in their usage of the term, most writers use the term *surface* to characterize the observable or manifest aspects of the client's mental life (Freud, 1905a; Levy & Inderbitzen, 1990; Paniagua, 1985, 1991; Poland, 1992).

A therapy session is composed of innumerable surfaces, some of which are allowed to pass by without particular attention, while others become focal points for exploration. The surfaces selected for "excavation" may be determined by the client, whose attention is drawn to those life events and experiences that are emotionally meaningful in one way or another. Some surfaces are selected by the therapist, who notices loaded comments, pregnant pauses, incongruent gestures, or various discontinuities in the client's thoughts and brings them to the client's attention. Since the process of psychoanalytic therapy is a collaborative venture, the selection of any surface for exploration should be consensual (Paniagua, 1991; Poland, 1992). Any selected surface is progressively uncovered as the client verbalizes the thoughts that come to mind in connection with it. These associations reveal the network of feelings and thoughts within which the particular experience is embedded. They provide clues to the emotional meanings of the manifest experience. When the client follows these associated thoughts and feelings, they link up with other trains of thought that help explain the meaning of an experience by connecting the surface to deeper and deeper levels of mental activity.

In an actual archaeological site of any size, excavation proceeds at a number of specific areas simultaneously. The process of digging begins more or less simultaneously at each of these selected surfaces, with new surfaces selected for excavation as the dig proceeds. As selected areas are unearthed and their contents identified, the archaeologist's understanding of the other areas under excavation is enhanced. Similarly, psychoanalytic exploration entails the concurrent investigation of an expanding number of surfaces. As each individual surface is explored, the therapist comes to understand the specific conflicts that have given rise to the features of that particular surface. As numerous surfaces are explored, the therapist discovers that similar conflicts determine many different surfaces. These conflicts are called *core conflicts* (or *nuclear* conflicts) because they lie at the core (or nucleus) of many different aspects of mental life. A familiarity with the client's core conflicts can come about only when they are discovered over and over again as numerous individual surfaces are explored. The unique power of psychoanalytic therapy derives from the fact that the exposure and progressive mastery of core conflicts permits the client to alter a very wide range of problematic behaviors.

Freud's archaeological metaphor also provides a model for the therapeutic action of insight. The buried relics that archaeologists discover are often in states of remarkable preservation. As a result of being buried, these artifacts have been protected from the destructive effects of exposure to the elements. Buried, they have existed in a timeless universe, unaffected by the passage of the years. The tragic aspect of archaeology lies in the fact that the process of discovery is inherently destructive. When these

precious artifacts are uncovered, they are once again exposed to the corrosive effects of the elements and thus returned to the realm of passing time. Freud discovered that unconscious wishes and fears are similarly protected from the effects of time. Because they are unconscious, they do not partake in developmental processes. They are not transformed by learning or by the individual's developing capacities for judgment and reality testing. Freud characterized the unconscious sector of the mind as timeless because unconscious contents, like buried relics, are isolated from the effects of passing time. When "buried" wishes and fears are uncovered in psychoanalytic therapy, however, they are exposed to the "psychic elements"—the impact of the client's own mature mental functions (Freud, 1909; see also Loewald, 1971).

Although the archaeological metaphor is useful, it should not be taken too far. Psychoanalytic treatment does not follow a simple course of progressive uncovering as the archaeological metaphor might appear to suggest. The client is a living person, not an archaeological site. The therapist cannot simply dig through the client's psyche, shoveling through the layers of the client's mental life as though the client were an inanimate field. Unconscious wishes, thoughts, feelings, and memories are not merely buried by the psychic debris of passing time. They were intentionally buried because, when experienced, they were painful. As these contents are revealed, the client feels these old and forgotten pains anew, and the old defensive methods, by which the painful contents were buried in the first place, are once again set in motion. The client inevitably comes to see the therapy as a hazard and the therapist as a menacing figure who imperils the client's precarious stability and well-being. The therapeutic process and the collaborative relationship between the therapist and the client are thus inexorably complicated by the client's suffering and defensiveness. This inner turbulence gives rise to resistance.

Resistance may be defined as the client's paradoxical opposition to the process of psychoanalytic therapy. Resistance is a manifestation of the client's defensive functioning as it is mobilized in the context of psychoanalytic therapy. It reflects the client's feeling of being endangered by therapy and gives rise to efforts, large and small, to retard or disrupt the treatment. Resistance is evident in curious discontinuities of thought, abrupt shifts of content, odd circumlocutions, ellipses, non sequiturs, unproductive silences, and other such signs of a derailed train of thought. Sometimes the client's resistance will manifest as a feeling of resignation about the treatment, doubts about its efficacy, lateness and missed appointments, problems in paying or scheduling, and other disruptive actions. In more extreme cases, the client may attempt to abandon treatment entirely, sometimes through a determined effort to "get it together" and a concomitant improvement in mood, which the client mistakes for a cure (the so-called flight into health). More destructive clients may unconsciously seek to derail the treatment by proving its worthlessness: by getting worse, engaging in self-destructive activity, adopting a combative attitude, or trying to seduce the therapist into a sexual or criminal partnership.

Resistance is an inevitable feature of every psychoanalytic therapy, from the very beginning of treatment to the very end. The success of therapy depends in large part on the therapist's capacity to deal productively with the client's resistance. Psychoanalytic technique aims to modify the client's resistance by exposing and exploring it, so that the client may understand the unsettling feelings that motivate it. As the client recognizes and grapples with these painful feelings, they are gradually reduced, and defenses relax. As a result, previously warded-off contents can emerge and be assimilated into the client's conscious mental life (Weiss, 1971, 1993; Weiss & Sampson, 1986). This process continues throughout the course of treatment. It is the basic method by which unconscious contents are uncovered (Brenner, 1976; Busch, 1995; Gray, 1994).

The process of psychoanalytic therapy differs from archaeology in another profound way. Archaeological artifacts do not arise from their place of burial on their own accord. The same

cannot be said of buried wishes, fears, grief, or memories. When buried feelings are stirred up, they return to life, like the mummies in old horror films. Repressed contents spontaneously arise because they are buoyed up by unconscious wishes seeking gratification. This tendency to return is facilitated whenever resistance is reduced. This is why the interpretation of resistance promotes the process of uncovering. The mobilization of archaic wishes can be a source of great emotional turbulence. In some instances, for example, the client may be unable to tolerate the arousal of these wishes without also taking some action to gratify them. In other instances, the arousal of repressed wishes is so threatening that the client is driven to deny, suppress, disguise, or otherwise defend against their emergence or expression.

Unconscious wishes are aroused by temptations—enticing prospects for the fulfillment of longings and desires. The therapist—who listens empathically and attentively for many hours—provides acceptance, support, and understanding and makes no demands for reciprocation—often comes to represent such a temptation. Because the therapist does not divulge personal information or engage the client socially, the client has no clear picture of the therapist's personality or life circumstances. As a result, the client's perception of the therapist, to a large extent, comes to reflect the influence of the client's fantasy life. This phenomenon is called *transference.* Transference is fueled by unconscious wishes and the unpleasures and defenses with which they are associated. Because these conflicts derive from childhood relationships with parents and other significant figures, the transference tends to replicate aspects of these childhood relationships.

Transference presents the psychoanalytic therapist with a major challenge as well as an unparalleled opportunity. Because transference is a distortion, the presence of transference is an inevitable source of confusion for the client. Sometimes the client is very pleased by the appearance of transference feelings, as occurs, for example, in cases where the client feels the therapist to be very loving, nurturing, or protective.

Sometimes the client is frightened or upset by transference experiences, as when the client feels that the therapist is dismissive, angry, or condemning. In both cases, the client is likely to experience the therapist as *really* loving or *really* hostile. These experiences are of potentially great value because they bring aspects of the client's emotional life to light in a manner that both therapist and client can observe together. On the other hand, if transference feelings are too intense or too readily taken for reality, they can derail the therapy entirely. Where the client is intent on gratifying transference wishes, the demand for gratification can supplant the goal of understanding. Where the client feels endangered by the therapist, this fear may engender a total disruption of treatment. Transference presents a challenge that the psychoanalytic therapist attempts to manage interpretively. The therapist maintains a therapeutic attitude of interest toward the client's transference feelings and attempts to engage the client in a collaborative effort to explore them. This process helps the client recognize the transference as an expression of his or her own psychology rather than as a veridical perception of reality.

Resistance and transference are closely related. Resistance is often triggered by fears that are aroused within the transference. At the same time, transference may be used as a means of resisting the process of treatment by changing the agenda from the understanding of conflicts to the pursuit of gratifications. At the beginning of his career, Freud saw both transference and resistance as unfortunate impediments to the exploration of the client's mental life. It is a credit to Freud's genius that he discovered a means to exploit these phenomena for therapeutic purposes, turning them from mere obstacles into unique opportunities. In a famous passage, Freud (1914a) defined psychoanalysis as the therapeutic method that takes the facts of transference and resistance as its starting point. Many of the procedures of psychoanalytic therapy, in fact, may be best understood as techniques designed to protect the treatment from the disruptive effects of transference and resistance

and to ensure that they will be exploited to their fullest potential.

THE TECHNIQUE OF PSYCHOANALYTIC THERAPY

The goal of psychoanalytic therapy is the promotion of the client's self-knowledge or insight. Psychoanalytic technique is the method by which this is accomplished. This technique is best understood if the practitioner has a clear appreciation of what is meant by insight or self-knowledge. The philosopher Bertrand Russell differentiated between *knowledge by description* and *knowledge by acquaintance.* Knowledge by description refers to information about phenomena that have not personally been experienced. Knowledge by description is composed of ideas without any actual experiential referents. As a result, such knowledge lacks the personal and compelling quality of knowledge that derives from actual experience. Knowledge by acquaintance, on the other hand, is information acquired by the individual through direct contact with the phenomena in question. The goal of psychoanalytic therapy is self-knowledge of this personal and authentic kind. In a classic essay, Richfield (1954), citing Russell, introduced the term *ostensive insight* to describe insights that are subjectively meaningful because they "incorporate the actual, conscious experience of their referents" (p. 404).

Ostensive insight can be achieved only through a conjoining of actual experience, on the one hand, and observation, on the other. Accordingly, a fundamental aim of psychoanalytic technique is to promote the client's experience of mental life as well as his or her observation of this experience. To experience mental life is to encounter directly the urges, desires, emotions, images, and other events that constitute mental life as specific realities with perceptible qualities and intensities. To observe mental life is to apprehend and describe the particularities of what is experienced and to reflect thoughtfully on these observed particularities from the perspective of one's mature sensibility and with the participation of one's best judgment and highest mental faculties. Without experiencing the events of mental life, the client has nothing to observe or reflect on. Without observation and reflection, nothing can be learned from experience. Accordingly, the technique of psychoanalytic psychotherapy is designed to promote an expanding experience of mental life in the context of ongoing self-observation and reflection. In a seminal essay, the psychoanalyst Richard Sterba (1934) wrote that psychoanalytic treatment must facilitate a "therapeutic split" in the client's mind, thus enabling the client to take his or her own experience as the object of observation. To acquire insight, he reasoned, the client must be able to "oscillate" between the "experiencing" and "observing" sectors of his or her mind. These ideas are still central to contemporary psychoanalytic technique.

The technique of psychoanalytic therapy may be understood as a complex system of interdependent parts, which function in concert to promote insight by facilitating the expansion of inner experience in conjunction with self-observation and reflection. The main elements of psychoanalytic technique include the creation of a *therapeutic situation* within which a *therapeutic relationship* and a *therapeutic dialogue* can be initiated. The *therapeutic situation* is the basic setup of the treatment, which includes the working agreements and ground rules, by which the treatment is conducted and the interpersonal conditions created by the therapist's attitude of acceptance, respect, and dedication to the goal of understanding. The *therapeutic relationship* is a unique human relationship, intentionally structured to permit the unfolding of intimate longings in an interpersonal context in which they will be studied rather than gratified. The therapeutic dialogue refers to the communications through which the client reveals his or her inner life to the therapist and to the therapist's efforts to understand the client's experience and to communicate this understanding to the client in a useful manner. Together, the three components of psychoanalytic technique create a safe and permissive interpersonal context for the mobilization of unconscious wishes and associated affects while simultaneously establishing controlled conditions for these experiences to be communicated, studied, and understood.

The Therapeutic Situation

The therapeutic situation is initiated when the therapist and the client each agree to work together in a specified manner toward the achievement of specified goals, according to the terms of an explicit *therapeutic contract* (Menninger, 1958). The therapeutic contract is the indispensable basis for the formation of the therapeutic situation. It is a rational agreement between equal adults, designed to serve the needs of both parties. The terms of the contract are the basis for the working relationship between the client and the therapist. The therapeutic contract includes an explicit explanation of the roles and responsibilities of each party, the frequency and duration of therapy sessions, and the basic ground rules of the treatment, including arrangements regarding the fee, missed sessions, vacations, and so on. These structures constitute the *frame* of the therapy, a metaphor suggesting boundaries that contain the therapeutic process (Langs, 1973, 1974).

Psychoanalytic therapy can proceed only within the context of fixed and stable arrangements. These ensure the continuity of the therapeutic process and the intelligibility of the client's responses to it. Fixed routines are a baseline from which potentially meaningful deviations are discernible. Lateness in attending sessions or paying bills, for example, cannot be observed if the scheduled times for appointments and for paying bills are overly vague. An anxious client will often feel the urge to avoid or cancel therapy sessions. If the schedule is overly flexible, the client will feel freer to act on this impulse than if the schedule were fixed. Such acting out permits the client to avoid dealing with the distressing affects that have been aroused. The therapist can address such problems only if he or she can recognize them. The frame helps ensure that the client's emotional reactions are recognized and addressed within the context of the therapy.

The fixed arrangements of the therapy always include regular times for therapy sessions. A minimum of at least one session per week is generally required, and more frequent sessions are often preferable. Sessions should be scheduled for a fixed length of time, usually 45 to 50 minutes. The relationship between the therapist and the client is strictly limited to verbal interactions within the context of scheduled appointments (except in the case of emergencies, of course). Beyond attendance and payment for services, the client's principal responsibility is to observe and express, as openly as possible, the feelings, thoughts, and ideas that pass through his or her mind during the course of the session and, at times, to reflect on the therapist's communications. The therapist's principal responsibilities are to listen attentively, to help the client speak freely through the investigation of resistances, to form conjectures about significant aspects of the client's mental life, and, at appropriate times, to communicate this understanding to the client.

The psychoanalytic situation is also shaped by the therapist's professional manner and attitude toward the client. The therapist should be professional and courteous in manner, empathic, reasonable, and consistent in routines and habits. This, of course, applies to all therapists. The psychoanalytic therapist, however, also strives to maintain a specialized "analytic attitude" (Brenner, 1976; Schafer, 1983). The analytic attitude is a natural expression of the therapist's basic intent to help the client by understanding his or her psychic conflicts. It is an attitude of acceptance, empathy, respect, and benevolent curiosity about all the client's experiences. Brenner observes that the analytic therapist should behave "naturally" with the client. For the psychoanalytic therapist, *naturally* means in a manner that is in accord with the therapist's intent to understand psychic conflicts. It is natural for the psychoanalytic therapist to be curious about the client's fantasy life, to listen for latent content, and to refrain from social chitchat with clients. It might be just as natural for therapists of another stripe to hug their clients, socialize with them, and so on. These forms of interaction

would be quite unnatural for the analytic therapist, who is intent on helping through understanding (Brenner, 1976).

The analytic attitude is one of profound respect for the client's individuality and autonomy. This respect is often conveyed by the term *neutrality.* Neutrality is manifested in many forms. The therapist's respect for the client's individuality manifests as neutrality with regard to the client's life decisions. The psychoanalytic therapist imposes no private ideals on the client and refrains from the use of personal influence or authority to shape the client's attitudes or to direct the client's life. As Freud (1919) wrote,

> We refused most emphatically to turn a client who puts himself in our hands in search of help into our private property, to decide his fate for him, to force our own ideals upon him, and with the pride of a Creator to form him in our own image and to see that it is good. (p. 164)

The therapist's neutrality is manifested in the therapy as an attitude of impartial and nonjudgmental receptivity to all the client's communications. This is operationally reflected in the dictum that the client determines the content of the hour. With regard to the client's psychic conflicts, the therapist's respect for the client's individuality is manifested by neutrality in relation to all sides of the conflict. Anna Freud (1936) characterized this as a position of "equidistance" from each side. Neutrality should not be confused with personal indifference, unfriendliness, or disinterest with regard to the client's welfare. Neutrality is not an attitude of uncaring. On the contrary, it is the analytic therapist's way of caring (Dorpat, 1977; Gitelson, 1952; Hoffer, 1985; Kris, 1982; Poland, 1984; Shapiro, 1984; Wallerstein, 1965). True neutrality should be differentiated from a "pseudo-neutral" disregard for the client's welfare, especially in the context of dangerous acting out (Dorpat, 1977; Menninger, 1958; Poland, 1984).

Abstinence and *anonymity* are principles that derive from the attitude of neutrality and serve to ensure that the therapeutic "process proceeds on the basis of what the client brings to it" (Gitelson, 1952). The *principle of anonymity* directs the therapist to refrain from self-disclosures—from expressing personal points of view, life experiences, suggestions, values, and so on. It protects the treatment from intrusions of the therapist's personality, which may "confound the discovery process" (Shapiro, 1984). Self-disclosure may suggest to the client that cure can be achieved through intimacy, love, or lessons from the life of the therapist rather than through self-understanding. Equally important, self-disclosures introduce personal facts, which may complicate the transference. It should be emphasized that anonymity is appropriate only in the context of a treatment designed to promote the uncovering of unconscious fantasies and psychic conflict. It would make no sense in a therapy whose curative properties were unrelated to the therapeutic relationship or whose therapeutic action resulted from experiences of intimacy or identification with the therapist (see Goldstein, 1994).

The *principle of abstinence* directs the therapist to conduct the treatment in a manner that does not gratify the client's demands for emotional relief through any means that might undermine the goal of understanding. Abstinence entails "the inhibition of short-term helpfulness" to promote "substantial long-term analytic goals" (Poland, 1984), even when the client explicitly requests such help. The abstinent therapist will not try to help the client through advice, guidance, reassurance, sympathy, love, or any form of special affection that may relieve emotional pain without illuminating its meaning. The abstinent therapist also declines to gratify wishes extraneous to the treatment contract or to take on special roles that the client consciously or unconsciously strives to impose or induce. Most important, abstinence provides a vital measure of safety by assuring the client that, no matter what he or she wishes and no matter how he or she strives to induce, seduce, or provoke the therapist into gratifying those wishes, the therapist's attitude and conduct will be predictably and routinely geared toward the pursuit of understanding.

The structure of the therapeutic situation, the consistency of the frame, and the reliability of the therapist's benign and disciplined responsiveness provide a context of safety, within which the client may express himself or herself freely without being rejected, criticized, or exploited. Of course, every client will experience the basic structures of the therapeutic situation according to his or her unique psychology. Many clients will experience the therapeutic situation as a source of security or as a "holding environment" (Cabaniss et al., 2011; Modell, 1976). Sometimes the client will experience the therapeutic situation as a source of frustration, danger, or injury. However the client perceives it, the consistent and unchanging features of the therapeutic situation provide an optimal backdrop for the exploration of the client's mental life and psychic conflicts.

The Therapeutic Relationship

The therapeutic relationship is the interpersonal context for the activities constituting the therapeutic process. In all forms of therapy, as in all forms of social work treatment, the social worker approaches the client with an attitude of understanding, including the key elements that constitute this understanding: empathy, respect, acceptance, and positive regard. The affirmative qualities of the therapeutic relationship facilitate the client's participation in the treatment and generally promote a sense of safety and well-being in relation to the therapist. As discussed in the opening section of this chapter, it is widely recognized that these elements of empathic understanding engender therapeutic effects that are independent of those produced by the therapist's specific techniques (Elliot et al., 2011). Carl Rogers and his associates, for example, identified the therapist's empathy, genuineness, and unconditional positive regard as independent curative agents in psychotherapy (Rogers, 1957, 1961; Truax, 1963; Truax & Carkhuff, 1967). Within psychoanalytic circles, it has long been recognized that the therapist's benevolent attitude toward the client may soften the client's harsh self-criticism (Alexander, 1925; Kris, 1982, 1995; Strachey, 1934). Alexander and French (1948) held that the therapist's conduct, if different from that of the pathogenic parent, provides a "corrective emotional experience," which disrupts the client's expectations of hurtful responsiveness. Kohut (1984) and other self-psychologically oriented therapists have cited empathy as an essential curative feature in psychotherapy (Rowe & MacIsaac, 1993; Wolf, 1988).

Traditional psychoanalytic therapists affirm the importance of the therapeutic relationship without regarding relational factors as the primary agents of therapeutic change. Most analysts distinguish between the curative effects of insight and those of relational factors (e.g., Oremland, 1991). Self-knowledge and the capacity for continuing self-inquiry, which develop in the course of psychoanalytic therapy, are qualitatively different, at least conceptually, from changes that accrue as a result of identifications with another person or internalizations of another's positive regard for oneself.

This is not to elevate the former at the expense of the latter. There is good evidence that supportive therapeutic relationships can have an enduring positive influence (Wallerstein, 1986). But a naive reliance on relational factors to alleviate complicated psychological problems does not always lead to optimal outcomes. Most clients, for instance, suffer from low self-esteem as a result of their psychic conflicts and maladaptive compromise formations. Recall, for example, that Mr. A was intensely self-critical with regard to his stage fright and that Ms. B always felt inadequate. While the client's feelings of self-doubt, shame, or guilt may be alleviated to some degree by the therapist's benign attitudes, this not quite the same as the results attained through a psychoanalytic exploration of the client's problems. One may imaginatively compare the actual outcomes in the cases of Mr. A and Ms. B with the results that might have been achieved had they been treated by a warm and empathic therapist who did not uncover their psychic conflicts. This contrast may be observed in the following case.

Mr. C was a 28-year-old social worker who sought therapy because he was unable to approach women he found attractive. These women were invariably of a "classy type," and he felt sure that they would reject him. He felt painfully inadequate and inferior in relation to other men and was particularly ashamed of his penis, which he felt was too small. He had been successfully treated for this problem for 3 years while in college. His therapist was a humanistic social worker, an older man whose attitude of support and friendship had boosted his confidence sufficiently to enable him to begin dating.

Mr. C hoped that I would help him, as his former therapist had, by providing him encouragement and support. I articulated my understanding of Mr. C's wish, adding my own suggestion that we try to discover why he feels so badly about himself. Mr. C was skeptical (he had read that psychoanalytic therapy was "obsolete"), but he agreed to give it a try, and we contracted for twice-weekly therapy. I soon discovered that Mr. C was reluctant to describe his romantic yearnings to me unless I explicitly assured him of my support. Further exploration of his need for my support revealed that Mr. C feared that I would disapprove of his sexual desires for "classy" women, that we were rivals for the love of the same woman, and that I would humiliate him for daring to poach on my turf.

Mr. C's emotional problems were the consequence of persistent oedipal conflicts. His feelings of inadequacy and low self-esteem represented, in a condensed and disguised form, his feelings of being small and inferior in relation to his father, especially regarding the size of his penis; misery about his inability to become his mother's exclusive love object; guilt over trying to displace his father in his mother's affections; and a defensively motivated stance of self-effacement and self-criticism, employed to ward off his father's punishment ("I am so inadequate, and my penis is so small that I am no threat to you; I suffer so greatly already that no further punishment is needed").

Mr. C sought a nurturing, supportive therapeutic relationship to counteract his feelings of guilt and fear of punishment. Had I attempted to help him by providing him support, as his former therapist had done, he might have been sufficiently emboldened to begin dating "classy" women again, as he had after his first therapy. Such help would not, however, have enabled him to understand why he desired "classy" women or why he felt so inadequate when he tried to woo them. In all probability, his problems with women would have recurred, as they had after his first treatment. The use of the therapeutic relationship to reduce Mr. C's guilt and anxiety would have fostered his reliance on my support as a defense, an outcome that would promote his dependency on me and might inspire otherwise unnecessary identifications with me. While such identifications may be therapeutic in some ways, they may also complicate the client's life. Mr. C had gone to college to study journalism, a field in which he majored and in which he excelled. His decision to become a social worker was an identification motivated by his dependence on his therapist's support. The therapeutic relationship had enabled Mr. C to date classy women but had saddled him with a career to which he had never aspired.

To summarize, the therapeutic relationship is central to the conduct of psychoanalytic therapy. While the therapeutic relationship may produce beneficial effects, the aim of psychoanalytic psychotherapy is the attainment of self-knowledge, not merely the improvement of attitudes, feelings, or behavior (Eissler, 1963).

Psychoanalytic therapists traditionally regard the therapeutic relationship as the interpersonal context for all therapeutic procedures. As such, it serves two essential functions. As in any other form of psychotherapy, the therapeutic relationship is a safe and supportive interpersonal context for the specialized activities constituting the therapeutic method. In psychoanalytic treatment, the therapeutic relationship also serves as an interpersonal medium for the emergence and expression of the client's psychic conflicts. This specialized use of the therapeutic relationship as a vehicle for the study of the client's mental life is unique to psychoanalytic treatment. These two dimensions of the therapeutic relationship are referred to as the helping alliance and the transference.

The Helping Alliance

Psychoanalytic therapy is a collaborative process that requires the client and the therapist to work together as partners in the therapeutic enterprise. This partnership is predicated on a shared understanding of the aims and methods of the treatment. The introduction and explanation of the therapeutic contract inaugurates this partnership. The therapist's conduct, including the therapist's attitude of concern and empathy; the therapist's recognizable intent to understand rather than to change or manipulate the client; the therapist's attitude of neutrality and respect for the client's autonomy and self-determination; and the therapist's abstinence and anonymity all contribute to the formation of a productive partnership.

The idea that psychoanalytic treatment proceeds on the basis of a collaborative relationship between therapist and client is as old as psychoanalysis itself. In 1895, Freud wrote that, by explaining the analytic procedure and discoveries of psychoanalysis, we recruit the client as "a collaborator" and "induce him to regard himself with the objective interest of an investigator" (Breuer & Freud, 1895, p. 282). In his 1912 paper, "On Beginning Treatment," Freud writes that treatment requires that the therapist establish a "rapport" with the patient by taking a "serious interest in him" and adopting an attitude of "sympathetic understanding" (Freud, 1913).[1] In later writings Freud cites the patient's "ego" (or conscious self) as a "collaborator" in the psychoanalytic process (1916–1917, p. 437), and elsewhere, notes that the analyst "allies" himself with the client's ego, referring to this alliance as a "pact" (Freud, 1937, p. 235). In the posthumously published "Outline of Psychoanalysis" Freud writes that the analyst and the patient's struggling egos "band themselves into a party" to master the patient's conflicts (1940, p. 173). The idea of an "alliance" was further developed in signal contributions by Richard Sterba (1934) and Edward Bibring (1937). Although the collaborative dimension of the therapeutic procedure was well established, the notion of the alliance between therapist and client acquired special importance following signal contributions by Zetzel (1956) and Greenson (1965).

Zetzel (1956) emphasized the importance of the client's experience of the therapist as a benevolent figure on whom he or she can safely depend for emotional nurture and support as well as therapeutic help. She characterized this dimension of the client's relationship to the therapist as the "therapeutic alliance." In her view, special efforts are needed to promote the development of the therapeutic alliance, especially when working with clients whose capacity for sustained, stable, and meaningful relationships is compromised. Zetzel believed that the therapeutic alliance is promoted by the therapist's nurturing attitude and fueled by the revival of the client's love for the nurturing figures of childhood. Some years later, Greenson (1965) introduced the concept of the "working alliance." Like Zetzel, Greenson believed that it was important to promote a productive working partnership with the client, especially where the client's capacities to cooperate in the treatment process were limited or prone to disruption. In contrast to Zetzel's thinking, however, Greenson envisioned the working alliance as a rational partnership, motivated by a reasonable desire to achieve realistic goals.

Luborsky (1976), employing empirical research methods, discovered the existence of two kinds of alliances, which he characterized as helping alliances. Type 1 alliances are based on the client's experience of the therapist as "supportive and helpful with himself as the recipient." Type 2 alliances are based on a sense of "working together in joint struggle against what is impeding the patient" and are characterized by a feeling of shared responsibility for the therapeutic process along with a sense of "we-ness" in relation to the therapist (p. 94). Both types of alliances coexist, with a shift to the second type typically occurring as treatment progresses (Luborsky, 1984). Luborsky's Type 1 and Type 2 alliances correspond closely to those described by Zetzel and Greenson, respectively.

The concept of the alliance has become a mainstay in the theory of psychoanalytic therapy as well as in wider field of psychotherapy (Hilsenroth, Cromr, & Ackerman, 2011; Horvath, Del Re, Fluckiger, & Symonds, 2011; Muran & Barber). Virtually every contemporary textbook in psychoanalytic psychotherapy highlights the role of the helping alliance in treatment (Cabaniss et al., 2011; Gabbard, 2010; Huprich, 2009; Langs, 1973, 1974; Lemma, 2003: Luborsky, 1984; McWilliams, 2004; Paolino, 1981; Safran, 2012; Summers & Barber, 2010). Empirical studies demonstrate that a helping alliance is

---

[1] "Sympathetic understanding" is actually a mistranslation of the German *einfuhlung*, which means *empathy* or *empathic understanding*

consistently correlated with good outcomes in psychoanalytic treatment (Luborsky, 1994; Luborsky, Crits-Christoph, Mintz, & Auerbach, 1988; Nuetzel, Larson, & Prizmic, 2007) as well as in other forms of psychological treatment (Horvath & Symonds, 1991; Horvath et al., 2011; Hilsenroth et al., 2011; Martin, Garske, & Davis, 2000; Wampold, 2001). In fact, the alliance, defined as the collaborative dimension of the therapeutic relationship, "has been found to be one of the most robust predictors of positive psychotherapy outcome regardless of the type of therapy utilized" (Hilsenroth et al., 2011, p. 361).

In both exploratory and supportive forms of psychoanalytic psychotherapy, the therapist sets the stage for the development of a helping alliance at the initial consultation by demonstrating interest and empathic attunement with the client's feelings and by offering some initial understanding of the client's problems. Gabbard (2010) notes that the therapist's empathic and attentive presence and attitude of acceptance encourages clients to collaborate in treatment by conveying that their lives have meaning and value and that they will be heard and understood, perhaps for the first time. Some clients, he notes, are motivated to collaborate because they yearn for a witness to their lives. In addition to these initial efforts at emotional engagement, it is also important that the therapist provide the client with an explanation of the treatment process and a description of the tasks that client and therapist each undertake to make treatment work. These explanations provide a cognitive map of the treatment and a guide to collaboration.

The initial consultation phase is critical to the development of a good alliance because it is an opportunity for therapist and client to begin collaborating on the tasks of problem identification, assessment, and treatment planning. If the therapist's approach is collaborative, the consultation process offers the client a taste of the collaborative nature of the work ahead. Hilsenroth et al. (2011) cites a number of psychotherapy research studies demonstrating that a therapeutic approach to the initial consultation and assessment promotes a stronger alliance than a traditional information

gathering approach. They recommend that therapists adopt an empathic mode of relating to clients when assessing their problems, employ a collaborative approach to defining individualized treatment goals, and engage clients in an exploratory discussion of their initial impressions and assessments before embarking on treatment. In a meta-analytic study of the alliance in different forms of therapy, Tryon and Winograd (2011) found that "goal consensus" at the outset of treatment is predictive of both a strong treatment alliance and a good therapeutic outcome. Horvath et al., 2011) make similar recommendations based on their review of the literature, concluding that "the development of a 'good enough' alliance early in therapy is vital for therapy success" (p. 56).

While the successful establishment of a helping alliance is a good prognostic sign, difficulty in forming an alliance in the early phases of treatment should not be regarded as predictive of failure. The client who attends sessions has some hope of getting help, and this hope often grows over time. Where the client's attitude toward the treatment of the therapist is hostile or uncooperative, the therapist may gently observe these attitudes and invite the client to participate in a joint effort to examine their emotional meaning or purpose. This invitation signals the therapist's interest, emphasizes the importance of collaboration, and keeps the treatment on course by enabling the therapist to apply the instruments of analytic helping (i.e., listening and understanding) to the client's experience of the therapy and the therapist. To the extent that client's adverse attitudes toward treatment are respected, accepted, and empathically understood by the therapist, the alliance and the treatment are both likely to be promoted.

Sometimes, often with more disturbed clients, the helping alliance is better promoted by noninterpretive or supportive methods. Luborsky (1984) recommends specific techniques to promote both Type 1 and Type 2 alliances. To encourage a Type 1 alliance, he suggests that the therapist "develop a liking" for the client, convey understanding and acceptance of the client as a person, communicate support for the client's desire to achieve therapeutic goals, express a realistically hopeful attitude about attaining those goals, and provide recognition for any progress the client has achieved. He also recommends providing direct support for the client's defenses and psychosocial functioning. To promote Type 2 alliances, Luborsky suggests that the therapist encourage a "we bond," convey respect for the client, recognize the client's growing ability to "use the basic tools of treatment," and refer to the experiences that the therapist and client have already been through together.

It should be emphasized that the helping alliance is not a fixed structure. The client's capacity to collaborate will ebb and flow with the stresses and challenges of the therapeutic process. Under certain conditions, the client's experience of the therapist may undergo disturbing shifts, leaving the client unsure of the therapist's understanding, good will, or competence. Such experiences, sometimes called *ruptures*, can endanger the treatment. Ruptures must be constructively addressed in order to restore the partnership on which the treatment depends. Heinz Kohut (1984) observed that ruptures can occur when clients experience the therapist's empathy to be inadequate or inaccurate. At such times, some clients are prone to feel alone, frightened, or enraged. Kohut believed that such ruptures can be repaired by recognizing that the rupture has occurred, trying to understand how it occurred, and empathizing with the client's experience of the rupture and the ensuing state of disconnectedness (see also Elson, 1988; Rowe & MacIsaac, 1993; Wolf, 1988). Safran and his collaborators, who define a rupture as "tension or breakdown in the collaborative relationship between patient and therapist" (Safran, Muran, & Eubanks-Carter, 2011, p. 224), cite a growing body of empirical studies demonstrating that the repair of ruptures is associated with positive therapy outcomes in a variety of psychotherapies. Some of the specific repair techniques that Safran and his collaborators recommend echo Kohut's approach to ruptures, including the maintenance of an attitude of nondefensive openness, acceptance, curiosity, and empathy with regard to the client's negative feelings, and an effort to engage in a collaborative effort to identify the factors that produced the rupture.

While the concept of the alliance has become very well established in the literature of psychoanalytic treatment, as well as in the wider literature of psychotherapy, it is not universally accepted among analysts. Some analysts, including Brenner (1979) observe that the helping alliance is inevitably fueled by unconscious wishes of childhood origin, and that efforts to promote the therapeutic alliance may gratify unconscious wishes that need to be interpreted. While rational considerations, including the expectation of benefits, contribute to the client's collaborative participation in treatment, every client's participation in treatment is inevitably motivated, to one degree or another, by unconscious wishes and fantasies that, in time, may need to be recognized and understood. For example, excessive dependency, compliance, idealization, and other attitudes of childhood origin may promote a Type I helping alliance while simultaneously constituting the personality problems that need to be addressed. This does not negate the value of the alliance to which they contribute nor does it preclude their interpretation over time. As the therapeutic process proceeds, and the client's understanding gradually comes to sustain the client's functioning, the client's childlike attitudes may be examined, interpreted, and eventually supplanted by a more mature attitudes and a more realistic alliance (Gitelson, 1962). This view of the changing nature of the therapeutic alliance is supported by Luborsky's finding that Type I alliances typically predominate early in treatment, while Type II alliances crystallize later in treatment.

The Transference

While the helping alliance is the central and enduring basis of the client's relationship with the therapist, the client's attitude toward the therapist will take on progressive complexity as the therapy proceeds. In fact, the client normally develops multiple concurrent relationships with the therapist. Each reflects a different organization of motivations and mental representations of the self and of the therapist, and each is manifested by different patterns of interpersonal behavior. Mr. A, for example, began to view me as a dismissive authority whom he wished to hurt. This was manifested in the treatment situation by enthusiastic reports of his theatrical triumphs and by his occasional remarks about my ignorance about theatrical events or about my inability to help or understand him (e.g., "It's too bad you can't know what it's like to receive a standing ovation so that you could understand my feelings"). Ms. B grew to fear me as a sexual predator who would use my great powers of persuasion to seduce her. This fantasy first showed itself by expressions of anxiety about my emotional power over her. Later, she expressed concern that I might suggest that we have a session over dinner, in which case she would "have" to invite me to her home for cocktails, after which she would be powerless to resist my sexual intentions. Mr. C feared that I wished to punish him for sexually approaching "classy" women and thereby "poaching" on my turf.

In these examples, the client's view of the therapist did not fit the objective reality of the relationship actually existing between them. When asked, "What is it that gives you the feeling that I am dismissive toward you?" Mr. A angrily noted that I never attend his plays or admire his success. In response to a similar inquiry, Ms. B protested that I am too empathic, a sure sign of my sexual designs. Mr. C complained that I offer no explicit endorsement for his desires to date "classy" women, evidence of my opposition to his romantic wishes. Although these clients accurately perceived certain objective features of my behavior, they interpreted these features in a highly unrealistic way. The meanings they ascribed to my behavior reflected their own particular hopes and fears. Put simply, these clients confused me with fantasy figures, persons with whom they interact in their imaginations. This fascinating phenomenon is called *transference.*

The concept of transference was introduced by Freud when he discovered that clients often confuse the therapist with the significant figures of childhood, unconsciously attributing to the therapist various characteristics that belonged to those childhood figures. As a result of this confusion, Freud observed, the client re-experiences feelings and attitudes that originated in his or her childhood relationships as if they were aspects of the current relationship with the therapist. These feelings and attitudes are unconsciously *transferred* from the mental representations of childhood figures to the representation of the therapist. In an early paper, Freud (1912a) characterized transference as a "new edition of an old object relationship," forged under the pressure of drives seeking gratification. Transference relationships, he observed, are highly stereotypical because each new transference relationship is modeled on the same "stereotype plate" or "template." In a more recent contribution, Greenson (1967) defined transference as the

> experiencing of feelings, drives, attitudes, fantasies, and defenses toward a person in the present which do not befit that person but are a repetition of reactions originating in regard to significant persons of early childhood, unconsciously displaced onto figures in the present. The two outstanding characteristics of a transference reaction are: it is a repetition and it is inappropriate. (p. 155)

These definitions correctly emphasize the confusion of past and present relationships. Transferences, however, need not reproduce the actual interpersonal relationships of childhood. These relationships, construed through the eyes of the child, are inevitably distorted as the result of the child's immature mental functioning. An important aspect of the child's relationship to parents and other significant caretakers consists of the fantasies he or she elaborates about them. These include sexual fantasies, such as Ms. B's oedipal desires for her father, as well as aggressive fantasies, such as Mr. A's fantasy of humiliating his father. Transference is best viewed as a reproduction in current life, especially in relation to the analyst or therapist, of archaic thoughts, feelings, and behavior originating in the context of significant conflictual childhood relationships and the fantasies to which these relationships gave rise.

Although transference was discovered in the context of the therapeutic relationship, it is actually a feature of all our interpersonal relationships (Bird, 1972; Brenner, 1976, 1982; Freud, 1912a). Whenever we encounter new people, we approach them with our own unique interpersonal agendas. Although we have realistic wishes, goals, or concerns that are appropriate to current lives, our feelings about the new person are also determined by unconscious wishes and fears of childhood origin. Even as adults, we remain unconsciously attached to the love objects of childhood and unconsciously seek to relive these relationships. This is most evident in the sphere of romantic love. In romantic love, the lover's image of the beloved is formed by merging realistic perceptions of the beloved with preexisting mental representations of childhood love objects or fantasied versions of such persons. Freud (1905b) described the experience of falling in love as the process of "refinding" childhood love objects in the persons of adulthood. Transference effects this "refinding," permitting us to experience feelings of intense intimacy and familiarity with people who are actually newcomers in our lives. The exhilaration of romance is due, in part, to the unexpected joy of "refinding" these lost love objects, just as the pain of romantic disillusionment or loss is often profound grief at the "relosing" of them. This effort to refind childhood love objects explains Ms. B's love for "enchanting" men and Mr. C's fascination with "classy" women (as well as the conflicts each experienced in connection with these wishes). As illustrated in the case of Mr. A, transference may also be driven by hostile wishes, such as the wish to avenge injuries inflicted in childhood by a powerful aggressor.

Transference is sometimes conceptualized as a cognitive distortion that occurs when new persons or situations are classified according to existing categories or prototypes formed during the course of development. While this view is accurate, it does not explain the driving power of transference. Transferences are not merely automatic assumptions that are operative until proven otherwise. Transferences may have extraordinary power over the individual's mental functioning. It is often observed, for instance, that "love is blind"—that lovers often idealize the objects of their romantic passion in flagrant disregard of the beloved's realistic attributes. This is not simply the result of cognitive error. It is a motivated distortion, fueled by unconscious motivations, such as longings for reunion with the love objects of childhood. All transferences may be understood as attempts to gratify unconscious fantasies in the context of real life. Transference reflects the operation of the pleasure principle, which seeks to transform fantasies into actualities, to experience fantasied relationships as real interpersonal events.

Analysts have traditionally categorized transferences to the therapist as either *positive* or *negative*. *Positive transferences* are characterized by warm, friendly, or loving feelings. *Negative transferences* are characterized by hostile, rivalrous, or sadistic feelings. Anna Freud (1936) introduced the concept of the *transference of defense* to refer to the tendency to treat others defensively, as though they were potentially hurtful. It is also common to classify transferences according to the primary object in relation to whom the transference feelings originated (e.g., *mother transference, father transference*) or according to the developmental level at which the transferred feelings originated (e.g., *pre-oedipal transference, oedipal transference*). These classifications are a useful shorthand for describing the prominent features of any given transference, but they fail to convey the actual complexity of transference phenomena. No transference is purely positive or purely negative, although it may appear that way at any given moment. All transferences, like all relationships, are ultimately ambivalent. They are constituted by complex configurations of wishes, anxieties, depressive affects, and defenses, forged in the process of development in relation to the significant figures of childhood. Transferences, in other words, are compromise formations (Brenner, 1982).

This is also illustrated by the phenomenon of romantic love. The capacity for feelings of romance originates with the Oedipus complex. Most children develop a feeling of romantic love for one or both parents during the oedipal years (see Chapter 3, "Psychoanalytic Theory," this volume). This love is normally doomed to defeat. Under normal circumstances, the child is dissuaded from his or her romantic quest by an inability to win exclusive possession of the desired parent and by feelings of guilt and fear of retaliation from the rival parent. This is a very bitter defeat for some children, leaving emotional scars, such as feelings of inferiority, fear of rejection, fear of hostile or dangerous rivals, and so on. When love is aroused in adult life, it is associated with these affects of unpleasure, along with the psychological defenses habitually employed to ward them off. The adult experience of falling in love, then, cannot be described as a transference of love alone but, rather, as a transference of a whole configuration of emotional forces (Bergmann, 1987). Ms. B's love for "enchanting" men, which represented her oedipal wish for a tryst with her father, aroused feelings of anxiety, guilt, and revulsion, which she managed in adult life, as she did in childhood, by suppressing genital feelings. Mr. C's love of "classy" women, which represented an oedipal love of his mother, triggered guilt and fears of punishment, which he warded off in adult life, much as he did in childhood, by restricting his sexual desires and by adopting a placating and subordinate stance to father figures to elicit their pity and protection.

From the clinical perspective, the most significant distinctions to be drawn with regard to the classification of transferences pertain to the subjective context in which they are experienced and understood by the client. Tarachow (1963) introduced the useful distinction between transferences that are apprehended as real and those that are experienced *as if* they were real. *As-if* transferences are relational experiences of great affective power and immediacy, but they are bounded or framed within a realistic perspective. The client recognizes the transference feelings as inappropriate to the actual character of the therapeutic relationship and thus experiences them with an attitude of reflection and curiosity. When the client experiences the transference *as if* it were real while retaining a realistic perspective, the "experiencing" and "observing" parts of the client's personality are in a state of balance and cooperation. This is optimal for therapeutic exploration and insight.

When transference is consistently mistaken for reality, however, it may be disruptive to the therapeutic relationship and refractory to the therapist's efforts to interpret it. When a transference is experienced as a taken-for-granted reality, the client can experience the therapist only from within the transferential frame of reference. Such a transference is called *unanalyzable* or, in extreme cases, a *transference psychosis*. If Mr. A had been convinced that I really was contemptuous of him or if Ms. B had been certain that I really intended to seduce her, it might have been impossible for me to help them. The occurrence of an intractable and unanalyzable transference may indicate that the client requires a more supportive and reality-oriented form of therapy. Sometimes, however, an unanalyzable transference crystallizes as a consequence of subtle or unconscious aspects of the client-therapist interaction. An unanalyzable transference may be provoked or reinforced by the therapist's eccentric, inconsistent, or irrational responsiveness to the client. This may occur when the therapist is overwhelmed by the client's transference or when the therapist is caught up in his own transference to the client. This phenomenon is called *countertransference*. When the therapist's functioning is impaired by his or her emotional reactions to the client, an improvement in the therapist's understanding through supervision or therapy may restore the prospects for a better outcome. Sometimes, however, it is in the client's best interest to refer the client to another therapist for continued treatment.

To summarize, the helping alliance and the transference coexist as aspects of the therapeutic relationship. It is optimal for the transference to be nested within the realistic context of the helping alliance. The transference is a potentially invaluable vehicle for the communication of inner life, but it can disrupt the therapeutic enterprise if it becomes a dominant reality.

The Therapeutic Dialogue

The therapeutic dialogue is a unique form of discourse, structured to promote the exploration of the client's mental life and the discovery of the psychic conflicts that cause his or her problems. In brief, the client is invited to express, as freely as possible, all the thoughts that pass through his or her mind in the course of the session, thus giving voice to his or her stream of consciousness. This process is known as *free association.* The therapist, in turn, listens to the client's associations and forms hypotheses, or conjectures, about the psychological conflicts they reveal. When he or she has understood something that may help the client, the therapist communicates this understanding in a statement or a series of statements, sometimes referred to as *interpretations.* Once the therapist has spoken, the therapist returns to listening, now with a special ear for the client's response to the interpretation. The client's reactions help the therapist to judge the accuracy of the interpretation and to refine it in accordance with accumulating evidence.

Once the therapeutic situation has been initiated, the therapeutic dialogue assumes a characteristic form, determined by the aims of exploration and discovery. A basic principle is that the therapy hour belongs to the client. As a rule, the therapist does not open the session by selecting or suggesting a topic or in any other way influencing the client's first communications. The client begins the hour with whatever thoughts or feelings are passing through his or her mind at that particular moment. The therapist gives the client room to settle into his or her musings, to shift from topic to topic as his or her attention is spontaneously drawn from one mental content to another. The therapist listens to the client's associations in a state of open receptivity, tuning in to the client's feelings and thoughts, as well as to his or her own reactions and intuitions.

In keeping with the goal of discovery, the therapist will not interfere with the unfolding of the client's thoughts by encouraging the client to talk about one thing at a time or trying to help the client stay focused on the main point, or in any other fashion that might be natural in another context. Most therapists listen quietly for long stretches of time, intervening only when the client encounters obstacles to the free flow of his or her thoughts or when the client is attempting to clarify the feelings or reactions that have already been produced. Although the therapeutic dialogue entails multiple exchanges between the client and the therapist, they do not occur in the same manner or rhythm as social interactions. The therapeutic interaction is not less natural than social dialogue. It is a natural expression of the unique aims of psychoanalytic therapy.

For the purpose of clear exposition, I will discuss the client's communications first, followed by a description and explanation of the therapist's communicative tasks. Although I discuss the communications of each party separately for the purposes of presentation, it should be recognized that I am actually describing a dialogue, albeit a most unusual one (see Kaplan, 1968).

The Client's Communications

In psychoanalytic psychotherapy, the client is invited to participate in an unusual procedure called *free association.* Free association is a method for the exploration of mental life. Although psychoanalytic therapists differ in the way they introduce and explain the task of free association (Lichtenberg & Caller, 1987), most therapists instruct or, preferably, invite their clients to say whatever passes through their mind, to speak freely without regard to any agenda or goal, and to give voice not only to their thoughts but also to their feelings, even their bodily sensations. Free association is not merely an exhortation to extreme honesty; it is a method for promoting an altered state of mind in which the client's attention may shift quite freely, without the organizing influence of realistic concerns or agendas. The mental activity involved in free association is characterized by the flow of thoughts from one idea to the next and resembles the apparently aimless thought that naturally occurs when one is daydreaming.

Free association is employed as an investigative tool because it facilitates the expression of unconscious activity. Free association reduces the organizing influence of purposeful thought and suspends the rules of normal conversation. Purposeful thought concentrates attention on a limited number of focal concerns. When purposeful thought is suspended, this concentration of attention is relaxed, and mental contents that were previously marginal or disregarded may attract notice. A second characteristic of free association is the verbalization of thoughts while they are forming. In everyday life, we think before we speak. We normally edit our thoughts for coherence, relevance, consistency, and social desirability before we communicate them. As a result, our spoken words do not readily reveal the multiple or conflicting trains of thought from which they are derived. In free association, however, the client speaks while he or she thinks. Free association thus reveals much of the raw material typically edited out in the fashioning of our normal discourse. Free association permits the client to verbalize the inner dialogue that occurs between the different sides of his or her personality. Citing Freud's structural model, Bergmann (1968) characterized free association as a "trialogue" in which the voices of the id, ego, and superego may be heard.

The rationale for the technique of free association derives from the discovery that mental life is regulated by the tendency to seek pleasure and to avoid unpleasure. Unconscious wishes exert a more or less continuous pressure on all mental activity. Unconscious wishes prompt us to recall and relive past experiences of gratification and to imagine new scenes in which our wishes are satisfied. Mr. A, for instance, frequently thought about

being a star, Ms. B about "enchanting" men, and Mr. C about "classy" women. If free association simply facilitated the unfettered expression of wishes, however, psychoanalysts would never have learned about psychic conflicts. The fact is that many of the client's wishes do not emerge in comfort but in the context of unpleasurable affects. When Mr. A reported his fantasies about being a star, he was often quite anxious. When Ms. B talked about her sexual feelings toward "enchanting" men, she felt nauseated and often, for no apparent reason, also talked about women whom she felt were hostile to her. When Mr. C described his wish to date "classy" women, he felt "inadequate" and fearful of my criticism. These recurring, patterned associations between wishes and unpleasures reveal the influence of psychic conflict. Of course, the meaning of these recurring associations is rarely apparent at the outset of the treatment. Mr. A's wish to be a star was not explicitly expressed as a wish to humiliate his father, and his anxiety initially had no recognizable meaning as a fear of retribution. Ms. B's excitement about "enchanting" men, her nausea, and her concerns about the enmities of various women friends had no overtly meaningful relationship. The same may be said about Mr. C's idealized view of "classy" women, his manifest feelings of "inadequacy," and his fear of my criticism. When wishes and unpleasures repeatedly occur in the same trains of thought, however, it may be assumed that they are both aspects of an unconscious psychic conflict.

Free association, as Loewenstein (1963), Eissler (1963), and others have emphasized, is a most difficult challenge precisely because it facilitates the experience of psychic conflict. The arousal of the client's repressed wishes inevitably triggers feelings of unpleasure, which engage the client's defenses. No client can speak without restraint or inhibition, especially at the outset of treatment. Even the prospect of free association typically stirs up feelings of embarrassment, shame, guilt, exposure, suspicion, and so on. These feelings are usually connected with the client's central conflicts. The exploration of these feelings is thus not merely preparatory to the therapeutic process; it is an essential aspect of it. It is therefore important to introduce the technique of free association in a manner that will encourage the client to discuss his or her feelings and questions about it. I generally invite the client to free-associate (rather than instruct the client). I also explain to the client that free association is naturally difficult and discomforting and that it is just as important for us to work together to understand these discomforts as it is for us to understand anything else that free association may enable him or her to express (Busch, 1994; Gray, 1986; Loewenstein, 1963). (With clients who are unusually threatened or psychologically vulnerable, I suggest that they speak as freely as they wish. This contributes to a feeling of safety and control and enables them to cooperate with a level of openness they can handle.)

As the client expresses the various concerns and hesitations that the invitation to free-associate stirs up, the therapeutic dialogue usually gets under way. Most clients eventually try to associate as freely as they can, observing and discussing feelings of reluctance that crop up along the way. As their discomforts are reduced, their associations become freer and freer. Even when the client speaks with minimal reluctance and restraint, however, the freedom of the client's associations is restricted by unconscious defenses. The technique of free association is intended to suspend, or at least reduce, the client's conscious reluctance, but free association is never totally free because the expression of warded-off wishes (itself a signal of increased associative freedom) arouses associated unpleasures, which mobilize defenses that curtail or disrupt the client's ongoing associations. This sequence of wish, unpleasure, and defense may sometimes be quite obvious, as when a client expresses a wishful fancy or musing, becomes visibly agitated or uncomfortable, and then issues another statement that undoes or modifies the meaning of the wishful communication. An obsessional client, for example, will often make a snide or hostile remark ("He's such a pain in the neck"), express discomfort ("Please don't get me wrong"), and then retract it ("He's really a good guy; he's just doing his job"). Some overt behaviors may also be recognized as serving defensive purposes. When he expressed fantasies of stardom, Mr. A not only became anxious; he also became self-critical, often severely so. For a time, Ms. B became so upset by her nausea that she had to stop speaking. Mr. C insisted on hearing expressions of support. Such sequences of mental activity are meaningful expressions of the client's psychic conflicts.

This sequence of wish, unpleasure, and defense is not always readily recognizable. Defenses are often automatically engaged with such remarkable rapidity that no recognizable trace of the briefly aroused wish and associated unpleasure is evident in the client's communications. Fortunately, however, free association is a sensitive instrument for the detection of such defensive functioning. When defenses have eliminated or disguised distressing contents, the associative process often betrays the subtle effects of defensive tampering. This is evident as discontinuities in the flow, pauses, shifts of posture or facial expression, subtle shifts of attention to other material or environmental distractions, abrupt transitions to "more important" matters, curious non sequiturs or illogical conclusions expressed with blithe conviction, vague references or omissions in a story that may leave the therapist feeling as though he or she has missed something, and so on. The meaning of such discontinuities can often be discerned through attention to the associative context in which they occur. An associative context is the network of associations within which a particular thought, affect, or other event occurs. It may be defined as the thoughts that precede and follow a particular event. Discontinuities often occur regularly in the same associative contexts, that is, when the client's associations reflect a particular theme, such as rivalry with powerful men or dependency on uncaring authorities. In such instances, the discontinuities probably reflect defensive functioning mobilized by wishes and unpleasures connected with that theme.

To summarize, unconscious wishes exert a continuous pressure on mental life. As a result, the client's associations are shaped, in part, by the influence of his or her unconscious wishes.

Unconscious wishes, however, are conflictually entangled in affects of unpleasure. This entanglement is also reflected in the client's associations. When unconscious wishes are aroused, they emerge in association with the specific affect of unpleasure. These affects habitually mobilize specific defensive operations that reduce this unpleasure. Free association reveals that specific wishes, specific unpleasures, and specific defensive operations cluster together in the same associative contexts. By systematically charting these recurring clusters of wish, unpleasure, and defense in the client's free associations, the client and the therapist are able to discern the unconscious conflicts that underlie the client's pathology.

We turn now to a discussion of the natural flow of a client's thoughts during the course of an hour. The client's free associations naturally begin at the surface of his or her thoughts and proceed, metaphorically, in both *vertical* and *horizontal* directions. Horizontal associations are thoughts about other surfaces that are, in one way or another, connected with the first. Vertical associations expose progressively deeper aspects of an event or experience. This is illustrated by the following example, drawn from the treatment of Ms. D.

Ms. D was a depressed 44-year-old woman, a computer programmer, who was emotionally inhibited and frustrated in all her relationships. Although she had a few good women friends, her romances were all unfulfilling and painful, due to the egocentrism of the "macho" men she chose and to her own "mousiness" with them. Ms. D opened one session in the first year of her therapy by describing a dream in which she could not get a taxi in a snowstorm. With no further thoughts about the dream, she went on to describe a recurring plumbing problem that her landlord would not fix, an incident in which her boyfriend Mark arrived late for a dinner date, and, finally, a childhood incident in which her father did not pick her up from school. The dream, the landlord, Mark's lateness, and the childhood memory all evoke a similar feeling of being neglected. The data suggest that a feeling of neglect has organized the constellation of the client's associations. Ms. D continued,

> I am still bugged about the dream. It's the same feeling. The cab drivers don't care. I'm standing out there in the cold, and no one cares. That's the feeling: No one cares. It's so painful, really, to feel so unimportant. I've felt this way so much. Other people are just so into their own things. I get so angry. You have to be a squeaky wheel to get oiled in this world . . . but you can't get too squeaky or people think you're a crank. You always have to be nice about every damned thing. Do you know, my toilet's been leaking for four months, and I leave a million mousy little messages on the landlord's machine. I'm afraid to piss him off! I should have him thrown in jail! I'm also sick and tired of being so mousy around Mark. I'm sick of this Minnie Mouse and Macho Mark shit.

In this sequence, Ms. D's associations revealed a good deal more about her state of mind and psychic conflicts. She expressed wishes to be cared for, feelings of frustration and helplessness, aggressive wishes to fight back, anxieties about being ignored or dismissed if she does fight back, and descriptions of the "mousy" attitude with which she reduces her acute feeling of endangerment.

(Continued)

(Continued)

Where the first series of associations was largely horizontal in character, these latter associations also took a vertical direction. They add to our depth of understanding. They also continued in a horizontal direction, as Ms. D linked the various episodes at deeper levels. Her anger and mousiness in relation to her landlord, for example, prompted an association with Mark. In later sessions, similar feelings emerged in connection to her father and toward the therapist. As it turned out, unspoken transference feelings were the organizing impetus behind the whole sequence of Ms. D's thoughts in this session.

The client's free associations often take the form of stories or narratives about significant relationships and situations. This reflects the centrality of interpersonal relationships in human life. Our sexual and aggressive wishes always engage us with other people. This is true even when anxieties and depressive affects disrupt relationships in extreme ways, as occurs in schizoid characters or schizophrenics. Even among those very sick individuals in whom outward relatedness is dramatically interrupted, fantasy life reflects a continuing, albeit imaginary, involvement with other people (Arlow & Brenner, 1964). Our relationships with other people may be seen as compromise formations, formed to gratify our wishes despite our unpleasures. Of course, each of our actual interpersonal relationships is unique because each of our partners brings a different personality to the encounter. Even so, certain relatively invariant relationship patterns are usually evident in all the significant relationships of an individual (see Luborsky & Crits-Christoph, 1990). Where the individual suffers from emotional conflicts, these will generally be apparent in his or her relationships. It is not surprising that relationship problems are the most common complaint of clients seeking psychotherapy.

The client's stories about his or her relationships are important surfaces to be explored. They permit the therapist to identify the client's maladaptive patterns of living and to explore the psychic conflicts that shape them.

In describing any one interpersonal episode, the client will typically be reminded of others in which a similar conflict or feeling is present. These associated episodes will come to include a growing number of childhood memories in which the client recalls significant experiences with parents and other childhood figures. The client's associations will also come to reflect the client's experience of the therapist. If the client is engaged in the treatment, the therapist will naturally become a person of growing importance to the client. The client may see the therapist as a person who might fulfill abandoned hopes or as one who might repeat past hurts and injuries. As the client's psychic conflicts influence his or her experience of the therapist, the transferential dimension of the therapeutic relationship will become increasingly salient.

Transference typically begins to develop unconsciously and initially appears to the client as an aspect of reality. The therapist's yawn is taken as an obvious sign of boredom, his beard as a self-evident sign of religiosity, and a cough as a clear expression of irritation. As the transference is forming, the client's free associations begin to reflect the client's emerging experience of the therapist, often in the form of indirect allusions, such as references to other figures toward whom the client harbors a similar feeling (e.g., authority figures such as teachers or coaches, service providers, such as the taxi driver in Ms. D's dream, and so on; see Gill & Hoffman, 1982) or as expressions of interest about the therapist's life or professional activities. The client's first expressions of transference may seem trivial. On one occasion early in his treatment, Mr. A interrupted his enthusiastic description of a theatrical "triumph" to ask if I took notes. He was "just curious," he said, brushing off my inquiry about what prompted the question. He returned to his narrative, and again, as he described the audience's thunderous ovation, he paused to ask if I took notes. In a state of mounting anxiety (much like his stage fright), he expressed a fear that I might envy his "triumphs," feel humiliated to be a mere therapist while he is a "star," and sell my notes about him to disgrace him in the eyes of his admirers. His "confession" was offered amid a flurry of self-recriminations and apologies. This intense and most revealing transference first manifested as a "simple" question— ostensibly nothing more than idle curiosity. Mr. A's deepening associations, however, provided our first glimpse of the conflict that had given rise to his stage fright: aggressive wishes to cause me (his father) to suffer from feelings of envy, coupled with fears of retribution, and a defensive attitude of self-criticism and self-denigration. Over time, the same wish, unpleasure, and defense appeared repeatedly in relation to his father, in relation to other men, in relation to the audience, and elsewhere.

To recapitulate, the client's associations expand horizontally and vertically. Horizontal associations link interpersonal episodes or life situations that share subjectively significant characteristics. Vertical associations expose the psychic conflicts that are significant in those situations. Most of the client's narratives will pertain to the client's current or recent relationships, to the client's childhood relationship with parents and caretakers, and to the client's ongoing relationship with the therapist. Each of these domains offers numerous surfaces for the exploration of psychic conflict.

I close this discussion with a few observations about the role of the client's nonverbal material in the therapeutic dialogue. These include *paraverbal communications*, *enactments*, and *symptoms.* Although communication in psychoanalytic therapy is predominantly verbal, the client's associations are always accompanied by paraverbal features, including the pitch, tempo, and tone of the client's voice; various facial expressions and bodily postures; and small movements of the hands or feet. These behaviors often express aspects of subjective experience of which the client is unaware or that the client is unable to express. Paraverbal behavior often expresses affects associated with the client's thoughts. Affects always accompany subjectively meaningful trains of thought. They can be metaphorically described as the music that accompanies the client's words. Expressions of affect are particularly notable when the words and the music do not go together. A client may announce his great joy at finally getting his divorce, while looking sad and wringing his hands. Another may dolefully report the same event while smiling or tapping out a tune with her fingers. When affects are incongruent with the client's manifest thoughts, they are usually appropriate to latent trains of thought. The appearance of the affect in such instances reflects the fact that affects are often harder to ward off than thoughts. These latent thoughts may be discovered by following the affective track, that is, by asking the client to note the feeling and listening for the client's associations.

Transference is sometimes expressed through enactments. In the preceding discussion, transference has been described as an aspect of fantasy life that becomes manifest in the client's free associations. Because transference is driven by unconscious wishes, the client is motivated to confuse the transference fantasy with social reality so that transference wishes may be actualized in the relationship with the therapist. As a result, transference is sometimes expressed as social behaviors, often very subtle, intended to induce the therapist to adopt the role he or she plays in the client's fantasy life (Boesky, 1982, 1989; Jacobs, 1991; McLaughlin, 1987, 1991; Sandler, 1976). Enactments may be regarded as expressions of the client's efforts to live out the transference with the therapist rather than to achieve insight into it (Freud, 1914b). For a period of time, Mr. A made a series of curious requests. He asked me to get him a glass of water, pass him the tissues when he was no farther from the box of tissues than I was, jot down a few key comments I had made so that he could refer to them later, and save a review of his play, which he knew would appear in the particular newspaper I read. Over time, I recognized that he wished me to assume the role of a subordinate assistant, a derivative of his wish to tower over me. The following incident, taken from the case of Ms. B, is a more dramatic example of enactment.

On one occasion, Ms. B arrived at my office with her grocery shopping. While waiting for her session to begin, she put the groceries in the refrigerator of a private kitchen, located behind a closed door in the waiting room. I learned of this when she thanked me at the end of the session for having a refrigerator handy. Having been thanked, the impulse was naturally to say, "You're welcome," a comment that would have signaled participation in the intimate arrangement Ms. B had engineered. Fortunately, I refrained from such reciprocation. In the next session, I suggested to Ms. B that we examine the thoughts that prompted her to use my refrigerator. After initially protesting that the kitchen is no more private than the bathroom, she acknowledged having viewed the kitchen as "our" kitchen, a thought that spontaneously reminded her of a recent dream in which she was living with me in the office suite. She had had no recognition of the fact that she was acting inappropriately when she blithely entered my closed-off kitchen.

These examples demonstrate that enactments have important potential communicative value. If the therapist can recognize an enactment and understand it as the behavioral expression of transference desires, he or she can help the client verbalize and explore its emotional meaning. Enactments may thus augment the client's associations as communications of inner life.

Finally, I turn to a most fascinating phenomenon that has important communicative potential, although it is not an intentional communication. One of the most interesting events that occurs in psychotherapy is the spontaneous appearance of a symptom during a session. This is by no means rare. Mr. A often became acutely anxious during his sessions, Ms. B sometimes experienced nausea, and Ms. D frequently felt intense waves of depressive affect. Symptoms crystallize when psychic conflicts become too intense to be managed by ordinary means. The conflicts determining the symptom may be discovered by reconstructing the thoughts and feelings with which the client was struggling at the time the symptom emerged. When a symptom crystallizes during a therapy session, the therapist has an unusual opportunity to observe the thoughts that preceded and followed the onset of the symptom, that is, to study the associative context in which it has appeared. When symptoms occur frequently enough in therapy sessions, the psychic conflicts that determine them may be discerned by identifying the invariant aspects of the associative contexts in which they repeatedly occur. The study of associative contexts is a most valuable method by which a great many recurrent phenomena, including symptoms, mysterious affects, and defensive disruptions of thought (described earlier), may be investigated (see Luborsky & Auerbach, 1969). This is illustrated by the following example:

Ms. E was a 41-year-old woman, a child of Holocaust survivors, who entered therapy to overcome anxieties about marrying her boyfriend of long standing. Shortly after her wedding, she developed a mysterious dermatitis, which flared up only in the company of her mother-in-law. Although prone to allergies as a child, she had never suffered from them as an adult. At first, she thought she was allergic to something in her mother-in-law's house, but she soon discovered that the worst bouts occurred when the mother-in-law visited at Ms. E's home. Neither Ms. E nor her doctor could identify the responsible allergen. Ms. E concluded that she must be allergic to something her mother-in-law wears, perhaps her perfume.

In succeeding weeks, Ms. E rarely talked about her mother-in-law and showed no interest in doing so. The subject was raised again, however, when she suffered a particularly miserable dermatitis during an impromptu weekend visit by her mother-in-law. It seemed her mother-in-law was taking over her life, prying into her personal business, reorganizing the kitchen, and insinuating herself into private aspects of her marital life. As she spoke, Ms. E felt a mounting rage that she tried to control, saying that she did not want to hurt her mother-in-law's feelings. "But she's constantly getting under my skin," she muttered, scratching her arms and face. To my astonishment, her skin had broken out in large red splotches! The associative context of this and several later episodes revealed that the allergen was a state of mind in which she felt "invaded" and unable to maintain social boundaries. Although she wished to assert herself, she felt guilty about hurting a needy parent. Over time, I discovered that this dilemma recapitulated a conflict she had experienced with both her parents that had caused her anxiety about forming intimate relationships.

While psychoanalytic therapy is a method of treatment that is primarily verbal, paraverbal communications, enactments, and symptoms are important expressions of the client's inner life. Their value, however, depends on the elucidation of their meaning through the free association method. Just as the value of the transference depends on its containment within the subjective context of the therapeutic alliance, the communicative potential of nonverbal behavior is fulfilled only when its meaning is illuminated by the client's verbalized associations.

Therapeutic Listening

The psychoanalytic therapist listens to the client's free associations to understand the client's mental life. The client's conscious thoughts are referred to as the *manifest content* or, metaphorically, as the surface of the client's mental life. The unconscious undercurrents are referred to as *latent contents* and are metaphorically located at some depth below the surface. The therapist's goal when listening to the client's associations is to hear or infer the latent contents of the client's communications. The listening process by which the therapist apprehends the latent content is highly complex and differs from therapist to therapist. Freud (1912b) suggested a listening attitude of unfocused receptivity in which all conscious puzzle solving is suspended. He termed this listening stance "evenly hovering attention" and likened it to the client's free association. By suspending the therapist's inclination to conscious "figuring," evenly hovering attention diminishes the therapist's propensity to focus on contents that fit preconceived expectations or ideas about what is important. Evenly hovering attention thus enables the therapist to hear unanticipated themes and patterns in the client's associations, much as it would enable a music lover to recognize subtle themes in a complex musical composition.

Freud discovered that the client's associations elicit emotional reactions in the therapist, which provide clues to latent aspects of the client's mental state. These include resonating affects or memories from the therapist's own mental life, as well as complementary reactions to the interpersonal pressures the client is exerting in the therapeutic relationship (sometimes called the *induced countertransference*). The therapist's own associations to the client's material will often illuminate important connections by recalling the contents of previous sessions, experiences with other clients, literary themes or figures, and so on (Arlow, 1980; Freud, 1912b). These reactions in the therapist do not reveal the client's unconscious, but they may alert the therapist to unnoticed aspects of the client's communications or enable the therapist to recognize subtle connections, patterns, or parallels between one set of observations and another.

Many analytic thinkers place special emphasis on empathy as a method for understanding the client's mental life (Fliess, 1942; Fromm-Reichmann, 1950; Greenson, 1960; Kohut, 1959, 1984; Rowe & MacIsaac, 1993; Schafer, 1959; Schwaber, 1995). Empathy is an aspect of evenly hovering attention. It may be described as an imaginative process of putting oneself in the client's shoes through "transient trial identifications" (Fliess, 1942). The therapist imagines what it is like to be the client and then examines this empathically constructed experience to understand the client, a process characterized as "vicarious introspection" (Kohut, 1959). Through repeated empathic experiences, the therapist builds up a "working model" (Greenson, 1960) of the client's mental life, a model that is accessed and refined with each successive therapeutic encounter.

While evenly hovering attention and empathic listening prompt the therapist to form numerous impressions of the client's mental life, these processes are not sufficient to guide the therapist's interpretive activity. The therapist's impressions must be tested and refined through systematic observations of repetitive patterns in the client's thoughts and behavior, and they must be logically organized to form coherent conjectures about the client's mental functioning and psychic conflicts. These logical activities augment the unfocused receptivity and empathic attunement described above. In practice, then, the therapist oscillates between alternative states of mind, shifting back and forth between unfocused receptivity and empathy, on the one hand, and objective observation and logical analysis of the data, on the other (Arlow, 1980; Fenichel, 1941; Ferenczi, 1919/1951; Spencer & Balter, 1990). This shifting of perspectives parallels the client's oscillation between experiencing and observing (Sterba, 1934).

Conjectures

Conjectures are the therapist's hypotheses about the client's mental life (Brenner, 1976). They are formed through the various modes of therapeutic listening and reflect the therapist's efforts to understand the client and the client's problems. The formation and refinement of conjectures is preliminary to the activity of interpretation. Conjectures vary with regard to their depth and their breadth, in accordance with the stage of the treatment and the extent of the therapist's understanding. Some conjectures pertain to the particularities of a specific moment, such as the client's reaction to a particular event, while others pertain to wider patterns of thought and behavior. Some conjectures pertain to contents that are relatively accessible to introspection, such as a lurking feeling of sadness or a passing thought about the therapist's appearance. Others pertain to the deeper unconscious determinants of such feelings and thoughts.

Although therapists vary in the ways they arrive at conjectures, once conjectures are formed, they must be tested empirically. The therapist's formulations should correspond to the actual facts. They should accord with the contents of the client's associations, paraverbal communications, enactments, and so on. The therapist can often test the validity of a conjecture by using it to predict future behavior or associations. A schoolteacher, Mr. F, described an episode in which his girlfriend acted in an obviously careless and selfish manner. After only the briefest pause, he went on to speak about her kindness and decency with unusual softness and gratitude. I conjectured that Mr. F was warding off angry feelings by adopting the attitude of a contrary character. Some moments later, he became quite agitated about the selfishness of a school secretary who simply refuses to take telephone messages because "she's too damned busy doing her nails!" This outburst provided initial confirmation, since the feelings expressed toward the secretary corresponded to those I imagined he might feel in relation to his girlfriend. I tested my conjecture further by predicting that Mr. F would again express especially loving attitudes in situations where his girlfriend behaves in a hurtful way. The repetition of the predicted pattern over a course of several months further confirmed the conjecture.

The Interpretive Process

Interpretations are statements a therapist makes to the client, by which he or she communicates an understanding of the client's mental life. The therapist may schematically organize the interpretive task by reference to Malan's (1979) two triangles, the triangle of conflict and the triangle of persons. Malan represents psychic conflict as an inverted triangle. The three points of the triangle represent the three components of conflict: (1) a conflictual wish, (2) an associated unpleasure, and (3) a defense. The wish is represented at the bottom of the pyramid to indicate that it lies at the metaphoric root of the conflictual configuration, and the unpleasure and defense are located at the upper corners. To interpret a symptom, character trait, or any other compromise formation, the therapist must illuminate the wishes, unpleasures, and defenses that give rise to that

compromise formation and elucidate the way these components are functionally connected. Such interpretations are called *dynamic* because they illuminate the dynamic forces (wishes, unpleasures, and defenses) that determine any given expression of mental activity.

Dynamic interpretations, or interpretations of the triangle of conflict, always link an observable surface, that is, a conscious aspect of mental life or behavior, with its unconscious roots. Dynamic interpretations can only be made, then, from a manifest point of departure. This is another way of saying that interpretation can only lead to ostensive insight when the client is in direct contact with the phenomenon being explored. It follows that psychic conflict should be interpreted when the client is struggling with some real manifestation of it, such as a problem or relationship, during the therapy session. Any important psychic conflict will be discernible in three separate spheres of the client's life: (1) the client's current social relationships, (2) the history of a client's childhood relationships with parents and caretakers, and (3) the client's transference to the therapist. These three spheres may be represented by another inverted triangle, which Malan (1976) calls the *triangle of persons.* Childhood relationships are represented at the bottom, with current relationships and transference at the upper corners, to signify that childhood relationships influence the shape of later relationships, including the client's current relationships and the transference. A complete interpretation of any significant psychic conflict is achieved when it has been interpreted in all three spheres. Malan describes the linking of the three corners of the triangle of conflict and the three corners of the triangle of persons and the completion of these two triangles. The completion of the triangles enables the client to recognize maladaptive patterns of living as they occur in his or her life, the psychic conflicts that fuel them, and their origin in the significant relationships of childhood.

The interpretive process unfolds in a natural and systematic manner, normally proceeding in "installments" over the course of many interactions (Loewenstein, 1951). Because interpretations are intended to connect manifest aspects of mental life with their latent determinants, effective interpretations begin with a surface that the client can directly experience. This surface, a particular state of mind, let us say, serves as a point of departure for the client's continuing associations. As the client mulls over the manifest experience, its marginal and shadowy features come into better focus. The therapist's interventions help the client attend to these aspects or elucidate them. As the details of experience become salient, associated contents, such as fleeting thoughts that the client had previously ignored or brushed aside, now draw the client's attention and become new focal points of experience. These previously dismissed thoughts are themselves now manifest contents and serve as points of departure for further clarification and elucidation. The client's deepening associations provide a continuing source of new surfaces for exploration and interpretation. The interpretation proceeds in a step-by-step advance, from one newly emergent set of contents to the next.

Of course, the associative process does not proceed in complete freedom. The client's associations inevitably arouse feelings of unpleasure and defensiveness. As a result, resistances repeatedly impede the flow of the client's associations. Whenever this occurs, the resistance itself becomes an important surface for interpretive work. The successful interpretation of resistance permits the resumption of the flow. Interpretations may be schematically classified as *interpretations of content*, intended to illuminate warded-off or latent contents, such as hidden feelings or impulses, or *interpretations of resistance*, intended to illuminate the interference of the client's defenses in the associative process, as well as the unpleasures that motivate it.

Greenson (1967) described the interpretive process as a natural progression in which four different types of interventions are employed:

1. *Confrontations* (I prefer the word *observations*), comments intended to draw the client's attention to a particular surface: They may be as subtle as the thoughtful repetition of a phrase the client has spoken, or they may be more explicit requests to focus on the phenomenon in question. Once a phenomenon is in focus, it must be clarified.

2. *Clarifications*, which bring out the details of a particular experience: Confrontations and clarifications help the client apprehend experience better, but they do not expose its unconscious aspects.

3. *Interpretations*, which are communications intended to illuminate unconscious contents, such as unconscious wishes, affects, or defensive activities: Although all interventions that enhance the intelligibility of mental life may be called *interpretations*, some authors, like Greenson, employ this term more restrictively, to denote only interventions that "make the unconscious conscious." (According to this convention, confrontations and clarifications are classified as interventions preparatory to interpretation.)

4. *Working through*, the continuing repetition of interpretations of a conflict as it appears over and over again in the client's history, in the client's current life outside the treatment, and in the transference (Freud, 1914b; Greenson, 1967; Luborsky, 1984; Malan, 1979; Menninger, 1958).

The course of any therapy session presents the therapist with an extraordinary array of potential surfaces to explore. The therapist must decide what to interpret, when to interpret, at what level to interpret, and how to interpret. Therapists differ in their preferences for various types of surface. Some therapists prefer to interpret transference material, others prefer to begin with discontinuities in the associative process, and so on (see Levy & Inderbitzen, 1990). The choice of surface may be inconsequential since the same core conflicts lie beneath many different surfaces. What is most important, however, is the process by which the client's conflicts are explored and interpreted. The therapist's choices should be guided by a few basic principles:

1. The interpretive process always begins at the surface with a manifest content to which both the therapist and the client can attend.

2. Interpret at the point of urgency. The surface selected for interpretive work should be

affectively charged, experientially immediate, and important to the client. The importance of transference interpretations derives, in part, from the affective immediacy of the transference. (Of course, transference is not always the point of urgency.)

3. Resistance should always be interpreted before warded-off contents. Any given content is warded off because it arouses intolerable unpleasures. To interpret a content that arouses intolerable unpleasures is overwhelming, perhaps even traumatizing to the client. Imagine if Ms. B were told early in treatment that her nausea is a symptom of her conflict over her desire to have sexual relations with her father. In vulnerable individuals, such "wild" or premature interpretations may produce pathological states of disorganization or trigger crises in the therapeutic alliance. Even where no such crisis occurs, premature interpretations of warded-off contents usually instigate further defensiveness, which retards the therapeutic process. The timely interpretation of resistance helps the client process the unpleasure aroused by the warded-off content in manageable doses and thus prepares the client to manage the unpleasure stimulated by the later interpretation of the warded-off content itself.

4. Interpretations should always be in the neighborhood of the client's thoughts, so that the client can readily connect the therapist's communications with his or her own immediate thoughts and feelings (Busch, 1995; Freud, 1910). Interpretations should be formulated at a depth consistent with the client's subjective experience. Interpretations of warded-off contents should be offered only when those contents are sufficiently close to the client's awareness to be recognized when the therapist interprets them.

In general, negative transference or other potential disruptions of the therapeutic alliance should be an interpretive priority. Many therapists, in fact, caution that the interpretation of distressing contents should be offered only in the context of a reliable helping alliance. While this seems desirable, it is often impossible. In fact, the interpretation of distressing contents (after the interpretation of resistance, of course) often

serves to enhance the alliance. On one occasion, a very disgruntled client first experienced a feeling of alliance when I, in a state of exasperation, offered a relatively deep interpretation that, in his words, "lanced the boil" of his confusion.

A few additional comments about the form and delivery of interpretations may be helpful. Interpretations should always be offered in the spirit of collaboration. They should always be somewhat tentative, since the therapist can never be absolutely certain of their accuracy. Incorrect interpretations are unlikely to be harmful when the client feels free to reject them. They may even prompt the client to offer a more accurate interpretation of his or her own. Interpretations should usually be short and simple, so that the client may hear them without losing contact with the subjective experiences being examined. If the client is drawn into protracted listening or intellectual processing, the experiential aspect of the process is disrupted. (Excellent discussions of these and other clinical rules of thumb may be found in Brenner, 1976; Greenson, 1967; Lasky, 1993; Levy, 1984; Loewenstein, 1951; and many other basic texts.)

I turn now to a more detailed discussion of interpretation of transference and resistance, the two hallmarks of the psychoanalytic approach (Freud, 1914a).

Interpretation of Transference

The interpretation of transference, like all other interpretive activity, begins at the surface with communications or behaviors that indicate transference. Transference manifestations may be subtle, fleeting, and disguised, especially when the transference is disagreeable or distressing. Transference is often expressed by paraverbal behaviors, enactments, and indirect allusions to other individuals (e.g., "My accountant is so irritating. I give him all the figures, and he gives me gobbledygook that I can't understand!"). When transference is unacknowledged, gentle confrontations may draw the client's attention to surface phenomena that suggest its existence. Depending on the client's response, the therapist can comment that the client seems to be experiencing the therapist in a particular way (e.g., "I sense that you may be feeling a bit irritated with me"). The therapist might explain that feelings about other persons might come to mind during the session because they pertain to the therapist. ("Perhaps your comments about your accountant could also pertain to me. Is it possible that you might be feeling irritated at me for taking your thoughts and giving you back gobbledygook you can't use?") Sometimes the client will not recognize any such feeling toward the therapist or will aggressively disavow any such feeling even though the evidence for it is strong. These reactions suggest that the client is warding off the transference feelings because they are discomforting (Gill, 1979). In such cases, the therapist should address the client's resistance.

Once the client acknowledges the transference, it can be explored. All the attitudes, perceptions, and strands of feeling that constitute the transference should be followed and carefully clarified, so that the details of the transference experience may be accurately perceived and felt. The therapist should maintain a consistent analytic attitude during this process. The therapist should be curious and empathic, without becoming reactive or overly responsive in any unusual way (e.g., to Mr. A: "It seems you are very uneasy talking about your exciting reviews with me because you worry that while I *seem* okay, I am wounded and crying inside, because I am not having as great a life as you are"). The therapist should not "correct" the client's transference by emphasizing how he or she *really* feels or behaves ("I understand how you feel, but let me assure you, I feel really fine. Let's get back to the therapy now."). Similarly, the therapist should not inform the client that his or her transference feelings really pertain to someone else ("I think this anger really belongs with your father"). Such comments prematurely dispel the transference, thus precluding its exploration. Such corrections, moreover, may strike the client as defensive and may thus complicate the interpretive exploration of the transference.

It is often helpful to inquire about the actual experiences on which the client bases his or her transference feelings. The client may point to specific aspects of the therapist's manner or conduct. While these perceptions are often accurate, the client's interpretation of them will reflect the influence of his or her fantasies. Transference is always connected to current reality. The fact that the client accurately perceives certain aspects of the therapist's personality does not mean that his or her reactions are not transferential. A client who feared that I might be as crazy as his psychotic mother panicked on one occasion when he saw that I was somewhat on edge. This perception of the therapist's edginess may be accurate. The client did not know the intensity or meaning of my tension, although he was quite certain that he did. When the missing data were unwittingly supplied by the client's fantasy life, he observed that I was "having a nervous breakdown."

Some clients need the therapist to acknowledge the facts to which the transference is connected in order to proceed without feeling that they are "crazy" or that their therapist is lying to them. This acknowledgment often enables the client to relax enough to realize that the facts do not speak for themselves, and that other interpretations of the therapist's behavior are possible. The client's ensuing capacity to disentangle realistic perceptions from their transferential elaboration helps protect the client's reality testing and thus enables transference to be experienced and explored *as if* it were real. The client's understanding that transference feelings may be safely communicated and jointly studied with the therapist is also promoted by the unflappable consistency of the therapist's manner and analytic attitude.

The client's experience and understanding of the transference may be furthered whenever transference feelings are explored. While this is often difficult for the client (and for the therapist), the affective immediacy of the experience makes it a most productive undertaking. The intensity of the client's transference feelings often enables them to emerge with unusual lucidity. As the client is able to describe his or her transference feelings with progressive freedom, depth, and detail, the therapist is able to interpret specific unconscious aspects of the transference. As a result, psychic conflicts are often first illuminated in the context of transference. In Malan's (1976) terminology, the triangle of conflict is often completed in relation to the therapist before it is completed in relation to the other spheres. As transference is understood, this knowledge helps illuminate the unconscious conflicts that have shaped the client's other relationships, including those of childhood.

Transference interpretation, then, is central to analytic treatment. Transference is a richly textured experience, formed of multiple developmentally stratified layers of psychic conflict and compromise formation. Because transference experience is often vivid and immediate, it offers an unusually productive surface. There is another aspect of transference, however, that makes its interpretation uniquely mutative (Strachey, 1934). Transference is a psychic reality that is subjectively immediate. It pertains to a social reality that is objectively immediate. When transference is explored in the context of the therapeutic interaction, psychic reality and social reality meet. This is uniquely mutative because it enables the client to experience the therapist as fantasized while perceiving the therapist as he or she actually behaves. The immediacy of this contrast helps the client appreciate the distorting effect of transference on the experience of the therapist and prompts the client to consider the possibility of distortions in other relationships. Many therapists believe that the collaborative study of the transference is the most powerful technical procedure of psychoanalytic treatment (Gill, 1979; Malan, 1976, 1979; Strachey, 1934).

Interpretation of Resistance

Psychoanalytic psychotherapy is painful because it stirs up affects of unpleasure. The arousal of these feelings mobilizes resistance. This process is largely involuntary and unconscious and results in an infinite variety of obstacles to the progress of the treatment. Resistance is a manifestation of defenses in the context of psychoanalytic therapy. The appearance of resistance signals the client's active engagement in a psychic conflict. Resistance is thus a most promising surface for exploration. The skillful interpretation of resistance enables the client to understand and reconsider the motives for his or her defensiveness. This deepens the therapeutic process by permitting the expression of previously warded-off contents. The psychoanalytic approach to resistance is purely interpretive. The interpretation of resistance may be conceptualized as a series of steps. Schematically rendered, the therapist must demonstrate to the client *that* he or she is resisting, *how* he or she is resisting, *why* he or she is resisting, and *against what* he or she is resisting. This is a natural sequence, which begins at the surface and proceeds, in stepwise fashion, to illuminate deeper determinants. In any given instance, this process may extend over numerous sessions or may be completed by a few terse comments.

Like all other interpretive processes, the interpretation of resistance begins with confrontations that direct the client's attention to the most recognizable manifestations of the resistance. The demonstration to the client that he or she is resisting reorients the client's attitude toward the manifestations of resistance. It alerts the client that these aspects of his or her functioning thwart the treatment and communicates to the client that this paradoxical functioning is meaningful and subject to exploration. A confrontation of resistance should be offered in the spirit of analytic inquiry, with the clear intent to engage the client's curiosity and self-observation. A confrontation of resistance should never be accusatory, indignant, or critical. Such attitudes communicate that the therapist thinks that the resistance is conscious, that it is willful, and that it is not allowed. Naturally, such communications are utterly antithetical to psychoanalytic therapy.

The exploration of how the client resists reveals the character of the client's defenses, especially in the context of therapy. This is valuable information, because it equips the client to recognize defensive behavior and eventually to control it. A client who subjects the therapist's comments to insistent, incessant, and pointless intellectual dissection whenever the therapist's utterances strike a vulnerable nerve will be able to participate more productively when he or she understands that this habit is a means of disrupting the treatment. A client who gets sleepy whenever certain distressing thoughts arise in therapy sessions may learn to recognize this sleepiness as a resistance and to bring it to the therapist's attention so that they may work in partnership to discover the source of the client's uneasiness.

When the client recognizes how he or she thwarts the treatment, the therapist can invite the client to explore why he or she thwarts the treatment. If the client does not spontaneously address his or her discomforts, the therapist may note the evidence of the client's distress. This facilitates progressive clarification of the specific affects of unpleasure that appear in the associative context of the resistance. As these unpleasures are addressed, they usually become more tolerable. This is in part due to the influence of the client's mature judgment and reality testing, the supportive presence of the therapist, and the general ambience of safety existing in the therapeutic situation. Feelings that could not be endured in childhood, such as grief or guilt at the death of a sibling or fears of castration by an angry parent, may be tolerated when reexperienced in adult life, especially in the context of therapy. The uncovering of these painful affects thus reduces the client's defensiveness. As defenses are relaxed, the mental contents against which they had previously been deployed become accessible to exploration (Weiss, 1971).

When previously warded-off contents are recognizable to the therapist and are believed to be sufficiently close to the client's awareness to be recognizable, the therapist can interpret the mental content against which the client has been resisting. Although these contents will still trigger affects of unpleasure, these affects are now tolerable; and although they may still stimulate habitual defensive activity, this activity can now be inhibited because it is recognizable (the client knows how he or she resisted) and because it is no longer needed (the client knows why he or she resisted and no longer needs to). When the interpretation of resistance permits the disclosure of the contents that the client has been resisting, it becomes synonymous with the interpretation of warded-off contents.

The manifestations of resistance are often rather dramatic, as in the case of clients who attempt to overturn the whole therapeutic endeavor by "proving" that the therapist is incompetent, trying to engage the therapist in criminal activity (one client suggested that we sell illicit drugs together), or attempting to seduce the therapist sexually. More common signs of resistance are lateness or missed appointments, rigid routines, monotonous or affectless speech, repetitive material, perseveration about trivia, avoidance of particular topics, expressions of boredom with the treatment, silences, and subtle discontinuities of associative flow. The therapist's basic approach to resistance is the same in every case. It is always interpretive, starting with a manifest surface and proceeding in the manner described above. Let us return to Ms. D, the emotionally inhibited computer programmer.

One day during the third year of her therapy, Ms. D made an uncharacteristically affectionate comment to me. The following week, she forgot her therapy appointment. Recalling her unusual expression of affection, I conjectured that the forgotten appointment was a manifestation of resistance triggered by her affectionate feelings. In the absence of confirmatory associations by the client in her next session, I waited and tested my conjecture by predicting that future expressions of affection would be followed by similar behavior or by associations suggesting discomfort and a desire to withdraw.

Ms. D was rather cool in the weeks after the missed appointment but gradually warmed up again after a while. Two months later, she made another affectionate comment, and again, she forgot the next appointment. As the resistance was now demonstrable, I drew Ms. D's attention to the missed appointments and asked for her thoughts about it. She acknowledged that it was indeed curious. On reflection, she noted that she had felt vaguely uncomfortable after the previous session. As she mulled over this experience, she recalled having been confused about the schedule. She had had a fleeting thought that I had canceled the appointment due to vacation plans (in fact, I had canceled a session for the following month). She'd also thought of cutting back to one session every other week.

"Well," I said, "let's think this over together. You felt uncomfortable in the last session. Then, during the week you had the idea that I'd canceled, and then you thought about cutting back, and then you actually did sort of cut back." I was prepared to suggest that she might be trying to get away from therapy because something upset her, when she shook her head in bewilderment. "I don't know how this happened. I mean, I guess I was more upset than I realize. I don't know, but I guess I somehow avoided the session."

"Yes, somehow," I mulled aloud, inviting Ms. D to explore how she had arranged to forget the session. She said, "I remember thinking, 'Don't forget your appointment, tonight' and then . . . Actually, I called Mark—do you remember him? Macho Mark? My 'ex.' Anyway I called him that evening and we got into a big fight about why it never worked out, about why he was always so cold to me. It just riled me so. You know, that's funny. The last time I forgot an appointment, it was the same thing. I'd had another fight with Mark."

I noted that she had twice avoided the therapy session by picking a fight with Mark. "Could this all have something to do with how you were feeling after the last session? You said you were uncomfortable. Can you get back to that feeling?" Here Ms. D became irritated and said she preferred to talk about Mark. She lambasted him for his coldness, for leading her on, for taking advantage of her sexually, and finally for humiliating her. At the end of a long tirade, she commented, "I'm so stupid. I should have seen it coming."

In the ensuing sessions, Ms. D spoke about Mark, about how hurt she had been by him, and how she wished she had protected herself by holding herself back from loving him. Since these feelings had come up as we tried to make sense of two forgotten sessions, each preceded by sessions in which she had expressed affection for me, and each forgotten by means of a telephone call and a fight with Mark, it seemed reasonable to make the following interpretation: "You've been very agitated about Mark lately, and I've been wondering what brought that up. We were trying to figure out what caused you to 'forget' those two appointments, and since then, you've been thinking a lot about Mark and how much he hurt you and how you should have pulled back. I wonder if all this might be your way of answering the question about what prompted the 'forgotten' appointment?"

"I don't understand," she said, looking a bit frightened.

"Perhaps you are afraid of being hurt by me, too?" I said softly.

As her tears began to fall, she admitted, "I'm terrified of . . . terrified of becoming attached to you."

It is most useful to interpret resistance as it is occurring, so that the client may observe the rising affects of unpleasure and the defensive activities employed to dispel them. Paul Gray and his associates have developed a method for interpreting resistance as it manifests in the client's associations, called *close process monitoring* (Busch, 1995; Goldberger, 1996; Gray, 1994; Pray, 1994). Gray has likened close process monitoring to the work of an apple picker watching a conveyor belt for bad apples. The therapist listens to the flow of the client's material with an ear to discontinuities suggesting that the flow has been blocked by resistance. Such discontinuities may be blatant, as a massive derailment of the narrative, accompanied by paraverbal signals of distress and followed by a change of topic, or they may be quite subtle—a fleeting pause, shift of posture, and change in the affective tone with which a narrative is reported. Gray (1986) characterizes these moments as "breaking points." Breaking points indicate that the client has encountered a conflict. Most important, a breaking point is an accessible manifestation of resistance that can be brought to the client's awareness.

The therapist who monitors the process with an eye to such discontinuities will listen for the moment when a resistance is evident and then draw the client's attention to it (a familiar confrontation). Gray (1986) regards as an

> optimum surface for interpretive interventions a selection of those elements in the material that may successfully illustrate [for the clients] that when they were speaking, they encountered a conflict over something being revealed, which caused them involuntarily and unknowingly to react in identifiable ways. (p. 253)

In Gray's view, resistance is usually prompted by feelings of guilt, which derive from the internalization of parental criticism and which the client re-externalizes onto the therapist. In his discussion of Gray's work, Busch (1995) adds that a wider range of unpleasure may stimulate resistance in the session. Busch's perspective is thus more in line with the views presented in this chapter, which in large measure derive from Brenner (1982).

Close process monitoring is a particularly useful approach to the exploration and interpretation of resistances because the breaking point is an immediate experience of conflict to which the client usually has access. Close process monitoring enables the client to participate actively in the therapeutic work. This strengthens the client's sense of ownership and responsibility for the treatment and promotes a robust helping alliance (a Type 2 alliance). It also provides the client with the means to observe his or her own mental life independently. The client who becomes familiar with the defensive disruptions of his or her thoughts will be able to take note of these experiences as they occur in life. The client need not rely on the therapist's unconscious processes, intuition, or empathy. Put simply, close process monitoring is a rational procedure, based on an empirical method, that can be practiced by any trained observer.

The Validation of Interpretations

The client's response to the therapist's communications provides an important source of data by which the therapist can assess the accuracy of his or her understanding. The therapist's interpretations may (or may not) have some impact on the client, and the client's responses may be employed to study the nature of that impact. An interpretation to the client may be viewed as an experiment whose outcome may help confirm or disconfirm the understanding on which it is based. For example, if a therapist suggests that the client may fear a particular calamity, the client's response may help the therapist determine if the interpretation is true. On one occasion, I was treating a very profoundly disturbed individual who suffered from an itch in his perineum. The itch was particularly tormenting because he believed that scratching it would cause his legs to fall off. After listening to his thoughts for many weeks, I formed the opinion that this symptom represented a conflict over masturbation, which featured a prominent fear that his penis would be harmed. At an appropriate moment in his associations, I suggested that he might be worried about his penis falling off. "No," he said thoughtfully. "I don't worry about that at all. But I *do* worry that someone will come and chop it off."

Such a response to an interpretation is very convincing because it includes the spontaneous expression of the inferred content that I had only begun to approach interpretively. The interpretation about his penis falling off was in the neighborhood of the client's fears, and this prompted a series of private thoughts that enabled the client to recognize and express his fear more accurately. Clients are often able to recognize a content about which they have been reminded before being able to evoke that content independently (Kris, 1956/1975). In the case reported above, the client's capacity to experience and verbalize the warded-off fear was prepared by numerous preceding interactions that reduced the client's anxiety and heightened his feeling of safety with me, including similar episodes about other terrifying fears.

In general, the client's response to the therapist's interpretation favors the confirmation of the interpretation when it includes the expression of new material congruent with the interpretation. Other typical confirmatory responses are the spontaneous recall of forgotten events or dreams, a subjective sense that an interpretation clicks, feelings of recognition or familiarity about the contents of the interpretation, or an emotional reaction such as laughter, crying, or anger, which suggests the release of a pent-up feeling. All these reactions suggest that the interpretation has altered the balance of psychic forces, so that warded-off contents can emerge with progressive freedom from the disguises and encumbrances imposed by defenses. A single verbalization of an interpretation does not constitute a valid test of its accuracy, since no single interpretation is likely to alter this balance of forces appreciably (Brenner, 1976).

The client's assent to an interpretation is not necessarily confirmatory, since assent by itself may be motivated by numerous possible factors, such as a need to comply, relief that the therapist is off the mark, and so on. By the same token, symptomatic improvement does not confirm an interpretation. Symptoms improve for many reasons, including the relational factors described earlier, intercurrent events in the client's life, and so on. Symptoms also improve in response to "inexact interpretations" that provide a soothing and palatable explanation for the client's anxieties or problems (Glover, 1931). However, if a particular interpretation is repeated many times and in many different contexts with no discernible impact on the client's symptoms or problems, this *does* suggest that the interpretation may be inaccurate (Brenner, 1976). (Further discussions of the validating process in psychoanalytic therapy will be found in most good textbooks, including Brenner, 1976; Fenichel, 1941; Greenson, 1967; and Langs, 1974, 1977, to name but a few.)

PSYCHOANALYTIC THERAPY AND ITS MODIFICATIONS

Exploratory psychoanalytic psychotherapy is a difficult undertaking. It is intended to uncover wishes, feelings, ideas, memories, and fantasies that are ordinarily painful, disruptive, and confusing. Naturally, this process is productive only if the client can tolerate these contents as well as the turbulent emotional states they engender and reflect on them productively. Exploratory therapy may be damaging if the client is overwhelmed by emotional experiences that he or she cannot psychologically digest. It follows that this form of therapy is not for everyone, and that the therapist must assess the client's capacity to benefit from this treatment before recommending it.

In brief, psychoanalytic therapy requires that the client possess adequate ego strengths to benefit from the process of uncovering. The client must be able to tolerate significant anxiety and depressive affect and to manage potentially harmful impulses safely. Since the curative process rests upon the client's ability to view his or her mental life from a mature perspective, the treatment will falter unless the client has at least some capacity for mature judgment and reality testing. Participation in psychoanalytic therapy is enhanced by psychological-mindedness, a capacity for sustained and cooperative interpersonal relations, and adequate motivation for this form of therapy. Psychological mindedness refers to the "ability to see relationships among thoughts, feelings and actions with the goal of learning the meanings and causes of experience and behavior" (Appelbaum, 1973, p. 36). To engage productively in treatment, the client must also be able to sustain a collaborative therapeutic relationship, even during periods of negative transference, frustration, or disappointment. The client will also need to be sufficiently motivated by long-term goals to tolerate the gradual character of therapeutic change.

For clients who do not possess these attributes, alternative approaches may be indicated. For instance, if the client lacks sufficient motivation for a sustained course of psychoanalytic therapy, is fearful of an open-ended commitment, or has trouble sustaining relationships, short-term treatment may provide adequate relief without foreclosing opportunities for an open-ended therapy at a later time. As noted earlier, short-term therapies are also very useful with clients seeking help with Axis I pathology or limited focal complaints. I have found that "time-limited dynamic psychotherapy" (Strupp & Binder, 1984) is a serviceable, flexible, and theoretically congenial approach, which permits conversion to longer-term therapy if this is later indicated.

Supportive psychotherapy is another good treatment option when exploratory psychotherapy is contraindicated. Although supportive psychoanalytic therapies are informed by psychoanalytic theory, they are employed to achieve goals other than insight. Supportive interventions are designed to improve mental life and social functioning by suppressing painful affects, redirecting the client's attention from inner life to real life, and by providing necessary emotional and cognitive supplies to enable clients to adequately understand and meet the adaptive demands of life. A major objective in

supportive therapy is to strengthen the client's defenses, rather than to analyze them as in exploratory treatment. Supportive therapy is called *supportive* because it is designed to support the client's ability to function adaptively when the client lacks the necessary psychological capacities necessary or is unable to recruit those capacities in particular context. In supportive therapy, the therapist can compensate for absent or deficient functions, buttress the client's existing capacities, and cultivate the development of needed functions.

As noted in the introductory section of this chapter, supportive therapy was first introduced in the midcentury years to provide help for clients who could not use exploratory treatment (Alexander, 1961; Bibring, 1954; Dewald, 1964; Gill, 1951, 1954; Glover, 1931; Knight, 1954; Tarachow, 1963). At the time of its introduction, supportive therapy featured measures such as the use of suggestion to induce adaptive attitudes, abreaction to relieve emotional tension, reassurance to relieve anxieties, advice and guidance to help foster adaptive functioning, praise and encouragement to reinforce adaptive behavior, along with interventions to discourage maladaptive behavior, such as reminders of reality and of the possible consequences of such behavior. In supportive therapy, the therapist takes an active role in directing the treatment, focusing the client's attention toward reality, and guiding the client through life choices. One of the most interesting and sophisticated supportive techniques was introduced very early in psychoanalytic history to help clients manage frightening and disruptive aspects of subjective experience. Glover (1931) recommended the use of "inexact interpretations" to provide the client with a credible but not altogether accurate explanation for his or her feelings or symptoms. A good inexact interpretation helps the client form a relatively benign understanding of his or her subjective experience; reduces the tendency to internal preoccupations, panic, and other disruptive or painful affects; and thus facilitates more realistic and adaptive functioning. Each of these supportive techniques has contributed to the expanding toolkit of supportive psychotherapy.

The therapeutic relationship in supportive therapy differs from that in exploratory psychotherapy. While the therapist in exploratory psychotherapy maintains a position of neutrality, abstinence, and anonymity, the therapist conducting supportive therapy must be more real. The effective supportive therapist cannot be neutral with regard to the client's life choices if the client is not capable of making adaptive decisions and cannot be abstinent if the client depends on the therapist's care and nurture to function. Naturally, the therapist cannot be anonymous in a treatment relationship that is based on the therapist's provision of guidance, care, and emotional sustainment. Oremland (1991) has suggested the term *interactional therapy* to describe this form of treatment because the therapist uses the relationship, including its transference components, to engender more adaptive ways of relating, thinking, and behaving. This is in contrast to exploratory therapy, in which the transference is collaboratively examined rather than exploited as an agent of influence without such examination.

Supportive therapy has undergone considerable development and refinement since it was first introduced. Even at the time of its introduction, many recognized the need for refinement. Many of the major ideas were somewhat impressionistic and general. For example, one early contributor observed: "The expression 'strengthening of defenses' has come into quite general use in the literature of psychotherapy, but the techniques to be used for this purpose are not sufficiently specified, and the theory of these techniques, from the point of view of our knowledge of the structure of the ego, insufficiently systematized." In the decades that followed its introduction, in fact, supportive therapy received little attention among psychoanalysts and was widely regarded as a second-class treatment. The classification of supportive measures first spelled out by Gill (1951), Bibring (1954) and others changed little over these years. For many years, supportive therapy was regarded as an afterthought among psychoanalysts (Rockland, L. H., 1989).

Attitudes toward supportive therapy began to change following publication of the first full-length textbook treatment of supportive therapy (Werman, 1984), and two years later, the release of Robert Wallerstein's *Forty-Two Lives in Treatment* (1986). In the first of these volumes, Werman expanded the theory of supportive treatment, recapitulating established techniques in a more sophisticated and detailed fashion, and introducing new approaches utilizing the client's strengths. Among the new techniques were methods to remodel defenses and channel sexual and aggressive wishes into socially adaptive forms. Wallerstein's book detailed the findings of a longitudinal research project conducted at the Menninger Clinic. Patients were assigned to exploratory or supportive therapy based on clinical assessments of their levels of psychological functioning. The findings were surprising. Outcomes of supportive psychotherapy rivaled those of traditional exploratory treatment.

These events stimulated new interest in supportive treatment. Since Werman's volume in 1984, several new major textbooks have now been devoted to supportive psychotherapy (Pinsker, 2003; Rockland, 1989; Werman, 1984; Winston, Rosenthal, & Pinsker, 2012). Each of these volumes offers a very readable and comprehensive exposition of the principles and practices of this form of treatment. Interest in supportive therapy has also been stimulated by expanding knowledge of childhood development and increasing recognition of the role of interpersonal relationships in the acquisition and development of ego functions. In a most valuable series of papers, De Jonghe, Rijnierse, and Janssen (1991, 1992, 1994) introduced *psychoanalytic supportive psychotherapy* (PSP), a sophisticated supportive treatment that employs traditional supportive techniques but places primary emphasis on the creation of a nurturing therapeutic relationship to promote emotional growth and the development of healthy psychic structures.

Nancy McWilliams (1994, pp. 72–80) offers a series of valuable recommendations for supportive work with clients who have fragile, psychotic-level character organizations. She emphasizes that the therapist working with such fragile clients must provide a condition of psychological safety by demonstrating trustworthiness. She recommends a deliberate effort to act in a manner that is consistently different from the client's most frightening expectations, to behave with "unwavering honesty," to openly explain the treatment approach and its rationale, and, in some instances, to demonstrate care by offering advice and self-disclosures (p. 73). A second recommendation is to provide psychological education to help the client recognize his or her feelings, to differentiate feelings and fantasies from reality, and, where possible, to "normalize" disturbing experiences and reactions by "reframing" them as variations of normal experience. The latter suggestion to "reframe" disturbing experiences is an example of an "inexact interpretation" (Glover, 1931), sometimes referred to in contemporary psychiatric and psychoanalytic literature as *interpretation upward*, that is, interpreting experience as the product of higher-order or normal functioning. A third recommendation is to relate emotional upsets to specific events and stresses. This recommendation is similar to recommendations offered by Kohut (1984) in work with narcissistically fragile individuals whose sense of coherence and intactness is protected when episodes of disorganization can be related to particular events, such as disturbances in the therapist's empathic attunement or disruptions in relationships with others.

Although exploratory and supportive therapies differ with regard to their aims, their techniques, and the nature of the therapeutic relationship formed in each modality, in actual practice, no single course of psychotherapy is either exclusively exploratory or exclusively supportive. Clients in predominantly supportive therapy often benefit from the exploration of some thoughts and feelings. At the same time, clients in exploratory psychotherapy sometimes need substantial support at particular times or with regard to particularly difficult issues. Psychoanalytic therapists today commonly think of psychoanalytic

therapy as a continuum of treatment approaches with exploratory and supportive therapies constituting its opposite endpoints. Exploratory therapy may be undertaken with modifications intended to provide additional support. Similarly, supportive therapy may be undertaken with limited uncovering objectives or with a long-term goal of exploring pathogenic factors when the client is better equipped to do so.

Many very disturbed clients can do surprisingly well in long-term exploratory psychoanalytic therapy if the treatment is sensitively conducted and modified to provide sufficient psychological support as needed. It should be emphasized that even the most stringently exploratory treatment has built-in supports. Perhaps the most important of these supports is the therapeutic relationship, especially its collaborative aspect, the helping alliance. The therapeutic relationship in both exploratory and supportive therapy is characterized by the analyst's empathic understanding, acceptance, warmth, and respect for the client, as well as a commitment to work together to promote the client's well-being. It has long been known that empathy, positive regard, and genuineness reduce anxiety (Truax & Carkhuff, 1967). A helping alliance promotes hope and relieves painful and frightening feelings of isolation and aloneness in the face of one's problems. These factors and the reliable consistency and steadiness of the therapist's adherence to this therapeutic stance, especially in the face of rage, contempt, or other provocative attitudes, constitutes a basic therapeutic "holding environment" that makes exploration possible (Cabaniss et al., 2011; see also Modell, 1976; see also Winnicott, 1965).

Exploratory therapy with more disturbed clients may require greater attention to the promotion and preservation of the therapeutic relationship and the helping alliance. Zetzel (1956), Gitelson (1962), and others have recommended adoption of a warm and nurturing approach to promote a therapeutic alliance. As discussed above, Luborsky has identified this form of alliance as a Type I alliance and recommended interventions to promote its development. Also noted above, such interventions include developing a liking for the client, communicating understanding and a deep attitude of acceptance, expressing support and realistic hope with regard to the client's desire to achieve therapeutic goals, and explicitly recognizing the client's progress toward those goals. Since more disturbed clients frequently suffer from disturbances in their relationships, it is especially important to attend to subtle fluctuations in the client's attitude and emotional stance toward the therapist. However outwardly innocuous or unobtrusive, such fluctuations may reflect important reactions to the therapist or to the therapist's interventions. A failure to explore such manifestations may leave the client feeling alone and disconnected from the therapist. Consistent attentiveness to the client's experience of the therapist promotes rapid interventions to address negative transferences and emerging ruptures in the alliance. Ruptures and their effective repair are features of every exploratory therapy but are apt to be prominent and critical features of exploratory therapy with more disturbed clients.

Similarly, tact, timing, and dosage are important considerations in every exploratory treatment. Interventions should always be offered with adequate regard to the client's vulnerabilities, sensitivities, and readiness to grapple productively with emerging material. The therapist in exploratory therapy is always attentive to the state of the helping alliance, the client's state of mind, receptivity to interventions, and his or her digestive capacity when considering an intervention. Again, this is particularly important when working interpretively with emotionally unstable persons, especially those who are prone to disorganization or panic (Hurvich, 2011; in press). In such treatment, attention to the client's capacity to tolerate and use interpretations is critical. A carefully regulated pace and a gingerly approach can be critical in exploratory treatment with such clients. This may entail a very deliberate bit by bit interpretative process, with generous allowance of time to process interpretations and as-needed support to process each bit. In a classic contribution, Pine (1984) introduced a series of technical modifications designed to facilitate a productive interpretive process with psychologically vulnerable clients. He suggests, for example, that interpretations of disturbing contents be offered when the client has some emotional distance from those contents ("Strike while the iron is *cold*"). Sometimes the therapist may reduce the potential anxiety aroused by an interpretation by assuring the client that he or she is *not* expected to respond to an interpretation at the time it is offered. The therapist can also prepare fragile clients for upsetting interpretations by alerting them that they may be upset by what the therapist is about to say.

Many technical procedures described in connection with supportive therapy can also be used to provide support in exploratory treatment. Therapists conducting exploratory therapy, for example, can be reassuring, soothing, or encouraging when the client is in need of extra help. When using supportive measures, however, it is important to calibrate the level of support to the client's actual need. This is true in supportive therapy as well as in exploratory therapy. When support exceeds the client's actual need, the provision of unnecessary support can convey an unrealistically low appraisal of the client's capacities and thereby undermine the client's perception of his or her actual strengths. The provision of inadequate support may convey unrealistically high expectations, exposing the client to experiences of failure that obscure actual strengths and discourage the client. Since a client's capacity may fluctuate, as occurs in the face of stress or in response to treatment, it is vital to keep track of the client's capacities and to match supportive measures to client's shifting capacities. In some instances, a collaborative approach to the identification of needs and strengths and to the selection of supportive measures can promote the treatment as well as the alliance on which treatment depends.

Cabaniss et al. (2011) have recently introduced a sophisticated and nuanced classification of supportive measures to facilitate this matching process. These authors identify two levels of support, each commensurate with different levels of client need. They recommend *supplying* interventions to compensate for functional deficits and *assisting* interventions to help clients utilize existing capabilities that they cannot employ on their own. They identify 10 categories of supplying interventions and three categories of assisting intervention. Each category includes a cluster of related interventions, examples of which are cited here. Supplying interventions include "encouragement" (inspiring, motivating, reminding clients of their capacities), "naming" (providing words for feelings or experiences), "redirecting" (providing "inexact" or "upwards" interpretations, bypassing disturbing material), "soothing" (reassuring, calming, empathizing), "protecting" (setting limits, providing advice), "structuring" (slowing the client down, helping the client organize his or her life, partializing tasks and problems), "supplying perspective" (correcting misperceptions, validating experience), and, finally, "providing practical support outside the therapeutic relationship" (arranging for hospitalization or other services). Assisting interventions include "modeling" (modeling more adaptive ways of behaving and thinking), "instructing" (teaching clients how to relax, soothe themselves, problem-solve, organize tasks), and "collaborating" (explicitly recruiting the client to a "joint" exercise of weak or fledgling capacities, such as "joint goal setting," "joint inquiry," "joint reality testing," and so on).

It will be evident on reflection that supplying and assisting interventions address similar tasks, each in accordance with different client capabilities. A therapist, for example, can *supply perspective* or invite the client to a *joint inquiry* into the nature of an event or situation. Similarly, a therapist can supply *structure* by directing the client to take one specific step after another in order to address a problem or can teach the client to partialize tasks independently. The classification offered by Cabaniss and her collaborators can be used as a model for creative thinking about how to provide the appropriate level of targeted support to match the client's shifting capacities and needs.

The application of psychoanalytic techniques to treatment of more disturbed clients is one of the great challenges of psychoanalytic psychotherapy. For the individual psychotherapist, such work demands a high degree of sensitivity and empathic attunement to the client's mental life, as well as a sophisticated capacity to use both exploratory and supportive approaches in a flexible and nuanced manner to meet the client's fluctuating needs. For those therapists who accept this challenge, the effort will contribute very significantly to the development of a mature clinical capability and will permit a privileged perspective on our resilience and enduring potential for growth and development in an understanding and supportive therapeutic context.

CONCLUSION

The client who consults a social worker for help with his or her problems often anticipates that the social worker will prescribe solutions in the form of things to do or ways to think. If the client has consulted a social worker who is a behavioral therapist, a cognitive therapist, or a problem-solving therapist, the client may receive a form of therapy that is more or less in keeping with those expectations. If the client has consulted a psychoanalytic therapist, however, he or she is likely to get the most astonishing response. If the social worker has decided that a course of psychoanalytic therapy is indicated, he or she will inform the client that there is far more to be understood about the client's problems than can be learned in a single discussion or even in a single series of discussions. The client will probably be surprised to hear from the social worker that the best way to overcome his or her problems is to understand himself or herself as a person, as an individual with a unique life story.

The psychoanalytic therapist extends to the client a remarkable invitation to explore the innermost realms of his or her private self for the purpose of self-understanding in the service of a freer and more authentic selfhood. It is probably unlike any other invitation the client has ever received. It is certainly unlike anything the client had in mind when he or she first consulted the therapist. The client who accepts this invitation may encounter many surprises about his or her own inner life. Many of these discoveries are disturbing, especially at first. Over time, other discoveries may occasion joy, often an indescribable joy, as when the client conquers a fear, recognizes a self-defeating habit and masters it, or rediscovers a capacity to love, laugh, or think independently. Psychoanalytic therapy is an extraordinary experience for many clients. But it is rarely what they expected.

The reader of this chapter may similarly discover that psychoanalytic therapy is not like any other form of treatment that he or she has studied before. To be sure, psychoanalytic therapy is not a simple form of treatment for the alteration of specific or delimited problems. It is not a method of modifying the client's behavior or social functioning in any particular direction. It is a treatment for the psyche, a therapy for the soul. To the reader who finds these ideas intriguing, who would like to help disturbed clients in a profound and private way, this chapter is an invitation to explore the universe of psychoanalytic ideas.

REFERENCES

Akhtar, S. (Ed.). (2007). *Listening to others: Developmental and clinical aspects of empathy and attunement.* New York, NY: Jason Aronson.

Alexander, F. (1925). A metapsychological description of the process of cure. *International Journal of Psychoanalysis, 6,* 13–34.

Alexander, F. (1961). *The scope of psychoanalysis.* New York, NY: Basic Books.

Alexander, F., & French, T. M. (1948). *Psychoanalytic therapy: Principles and applications.* New York, NY: Ronald Press.

Appelbaum, S. A. (1973). Psychological mindedness: Word, concept and essence. *International Journal of Psychoanalysis, 54,* 35–46.

Arlow, J. (1980). The genesis of interpretation. In H. Blum (Ed.), *Psychoanalytic explorations in technique: Discourse on the theory of therapy* (pp. 193–206). New York, NY: International Universities Press.

Arlow, J. (1991). *Psychoanalysis: Clinical theory and practice.* New York, NY: International Universities Press.

Arlow, J., & Brenner, C. (1964). *Psychoanalytic concepts and the structural theory.* New York, NY: International Universities Press.

Benjamin, L. S. (2002). *Interpersonal diagnosis and treatment of personality disorders (2nd edition).* New York, NY: Guilford Press.

Benjamin, L. S. (2003). *Interpersonal reconstructive psychotherapy: An integrative, personality-based treatment.* New York, NY: Guilford Press.

Bergmann, M. (1968). Free association and the interpretation of dreams. In J. E. Hammer (Ed.), *The use of interpretation in treatment* (pp. 270–279). New York, NY: Grupe & Stratton.

Bergmann, M. (1987). *The anatomy of loving.* New York, NY: Columbia University Press.

Bibring, E. (1937). Symposium on the theory of the therapeutic results of psychoanalysis. *International Journal of Psychoanalysis, 18:*170–189.

Bibring, E. (1954). Psychoanalysis and the dynamic therapies. *Journal of the American Psychoanalytic Association, 2,* 745–770.

Binder, J. L. (2004). *Key competencies in brief dynamic psychotherapy: Clinical practice beyond the manual.* New York: Guilford Press.

Binder, J. L., & Betan, E. J. (2012). *Core competencies in brief dynamic psychotherapy: Becoming a highly effective and competent brief psychodynamic therapist.* London, UK: Routledge.

Bird, B. (1972). Notes on transference: Universal phenomenon and the hardest part of analysis. *Journal of the American Psychoanalytic Association, 20,* 267–301.

Blum, H. P., Kramer, Y., Richards, A. K., & Richards, A. D. (eds.). (1988). *Fantasy, myth and reality: Essays in honor of Jacob Arlow.* Madison, CT: International Universities Press.

Boesky, D. (1982). Acting out: A reconsideration of the concept. *International Journal of Psychoanalysis, 63,* 39–55.

Boesky, D. (1989, May). *Enactments, acting out, and considerations of reality.* Paper presented on the Panel on Enactments at the annual meeting of the American Psychoanalytic Association, San Francisco. (Reported in Panel on Enactments in Psychoanalysis by M. Johan. *Journal of the American Psychoanalytic Association, 40,* 827–841.)

Book, H. (1998). *How to practice brief psychodynamic therapy: The core conflictual relationship theme method.* Washington, DC: American Psychological Association.

Borenzweig. (1971). Social work and psychoanalytic theory: A historical analysis. *Social Work, 16:* 7–16.

Brenner, C. (1976). *Psychic conflict and psychoanalytic technique.* New York, NY: International Universities Press.

Brenner, C. (1979). Working alliance, therapeutic alliance, and transference. *Journal of the American Psychoanalytic Association, 27 (Supplement):*137–157.

Brenner, C. (1982). *The mind in conflict.* New York, NY: International Universities Press.

Brenner, C. (1994). The mind as conflict and compromise formation. *Journal of Clinical Psychoanalysis, 3,* 473–488.

Breuer, J., & Freud, S. (1895). *Studies on hysteria. Standard Edition*: II.

Buirski, P. (2009). *Making sense together.* New York, NY: Jason Aronson.

Busch, F. (1994). Some ambiguities in the method of free association and their implications for technique. *Journal of the American Psychoanalytic Association, 42,* 363–384.

Busch, F. (1995). *The ego at the center.* Northvale, NJ: Jason Aronson.

Cabaniss, D. L., Cherry, S., Douglas, C.J., & Schwartz, A. R. (2011). *Psychodynamic psychotherapy: A clinical manual.* New York, NY: Wiley.

Cashdan, S. (1988). *Object relations therapy: Using the relationship.* New York, NY: W. W. Norton.

Celeni, C.P. (2010). *Fairbairn's object relations theory in the clinical setting.* New York, NY: Columbia University Press.

Coren, A. (2001). *Short term psychotherapy: A psychodynamic approach.* New York, NY: Other Press.

Crits-Christ, P., & Barber, J. P. (2001). *Handbook of short-term dynamic psychotherapy.* New York, NY: Basic Books.

Davanloo, H. (1977). *Short term dynamic therapy.* New York, NY: Jason Aronson.

De Jonghe, F., Rijnierse, P., & Janssen, R. (1991). Aspects of the analytic relationship. *International Journal of Psychoanalysis, 72,* 693–707.

De Jonghe, F., Rijnierse, P., & Janssen, R. (1992). The role of support in psychoanalysis. *Journal of the American Psychoanalytic Association, 40,* 475–500.

De Jonghe, F., Rijnierse, P., & Janssen, R. (1994). Psychoanalytic supportive psychotherapy. *Journal of the American Psychoanalytic Association, 42,* 421–446.

De Young, P. (2003). *Relational Psychotherapy: A primer.* London, UK: Routledge.

Decety, J. (Ed.). (2012). *Empathy: From bench to bedside.* Cambridge, MA: MIT Press.

Decety, J., & Ickes, W. (Eds.). (2009). *The social neuroscience of empathy.* Cambridge, MA: MIT Press.

Della Selva, P.C. (1996). *Intensive short-term dynamic psychotherapy: Technique and synopsis.* New York, NY: Wiley.

Dewald, P. (1964). *Psychotherapy: A dynamic approach.* New York, NY: Basic Books.

Dorpat, T. (1977). On neutrality. *International Journal of Psychoanalytic Psychotherapy, 6,* 39–64.

Dowling, S. (Ed.). (1991). *Conflict and compromise: Therapeutic implications.* New York, NY: International Universities Press.

Eagle, M. (2012). Classical theory, the enlightenment vision, and contemporary psychoanalysis. In M. J. Diamond & C. Christian (Eds.), *The second century of psychoanalysis: Evolving perspectives on therapeutic action* (pp. 41–67). London, UK: Karnac.

Elliot, R., Bohart, A. C., Watson, J. C., & Greenberg, L. S. (2011). Empathy. In J. C. Norcross (Ed.), *Psychotherapy relationships that work* (2nd ed., pp. 132–152). New York, NY: Oxford University Press, 2011.

Elson, M. (1988). *Self-psychology in clinical social work.* New York, NY: W. W. Norton.

Elzer, E., & Gerlach, A. (in press). *Psychoanalytic psychotherapy: A handbook.* London, UK: Karnac Press.

Eissler, K. (1963). Notes on the psychoanalytic concept of cure. *Psychoanalytic Study of the Child, 18,* 424–463.

Fenichel, O. (1941). *Problems of psychoanalytic technique.* New York, NY: Psychoanalytic Quarterly.

Ferenczi, S. (1951). On the technique of psychoanalysis. In J. Rickman (Ed.) & J. I. Suttie (Trans.), *Further contributions to the theory and technique of psychoanalysis* (pp. 177–189). London, UK: Hogarth Press. (Original work published 1919)

Fine, R. (1979). *A history of psychoanalysis.* New York, NY: Columbia University Press.

Fliess, R. (1942). The metapsychology of the analyst. *Psychoanalytic Quarterly, 11,* 211–227.

Frank, E., & Levenson, J. C. (2010). *Interpersonal psychotherapy.* Washington, DC: American Psychological Association.

Freud, A. (1936). *The ego and the mechanisms of defense.* New York, NY: International Universities Press.

Freud, S. (1905a). Fragment of an analysis of a case of hysteria: Prefatory remarks. In J. Strachey (Ed. & Trans.), *The standard edition of the complete psychological works of Sigmund Freud* (Vol. 7, pp. 3–122). London, UK: Hogarth Press.

Freud, S. (1905b). Three essays on the theory of sexuality. In J. Strachey (Ed. & Trans.), *The standard edition of the complete psychological works of Sigmund Freud* (Vol. 7, pp. 125–243). London, UK: Hogarth Press.

Freud, S. (1909). Notes upon a case of obsessional neurosis. In J. Strachey (Ed. & Trans.), *The standard edition of the complete psychological works of Sigmund Freud* (Vol. 10, pp. 153–318). London, UK: Hogarth Press.

Freud, S. (1910). "Wild" psycho-analysis. In J. Strachey (Ed. & Trans.), *The standard edition of the complete psychological works of Sigmund Freud* (Vol. 11, pp. 219–230). London, UK: Hogarth Press.

Freud, S. (1912a). The dynamics of the transference. In J. Strachey (Ed. & Trans.), *The standard edition of the complete psychological works of Sigmund Freud* (Vol. 12, pp. 97–108). London, UK: Hogarth Press.

Freud, S. (1912b). Recommendations to physicians practicing psycho-analysis. In J. Strachey (Ed. & Trans.), *The standard edition of the complete psychological works of Sigmund Freud* (Vol. 12, pp. 109–120). London, U: Hogarth Press.

Freud, S. (1913). On beginning the treatment. In J. Strachey (Ed. & Trans.), *The standard edition of the complete psychological works of Sigmund Freud* (Vol. 12, pp. 123–144). London, UK: Hogarth Press.

Freud, S. (1914a). On the history of the psychoanalytic movement. In J. Strachey (Ed. & Trans.), *The standard edition of the complete psychological works of Sigmund Freud* (Vol. 14, pp. 7–66). London, UK: Hogarth Press.

Freud, S. (1914b). Remembering, repeating and working through. In J. Strachey (Ed. & Trans.), *The standard edition of the complete psychological works of Sigmund Freud* (Vol. 12, pp. 145–156). London, UK: Hogarth Press.

Freud, S. (1916–1917). *Introductory Lectures on Psychoanalysis.* Standard Edition: Volume XV and Volume XVI.

Freud, S. (1919). Lines of advance in psycho-analytic therapy. In J. Strachey (Ed. & Trans.), *The standard edition of the complete psychological works of Sigmund Freud* (Vol. 17, pp. 157–168). London, UK: Hogarth Press.

Freud, S. (1920). *Beyond the pleasure principle.* In J. Strachey (Ed. & Trans.), *The standard edition of the complete psychological works of Sigmund Freud* (Vol. 18, pp. 3–64). London, UK: Hogarth Press.

Freud, S. (1923). *The ego and the id.* In J. Strachey (Ed. & Trans.), *The standard edition of the complete psychological works of Sigmund Freud* (Vol. 19, pp. 3–66). London, UK: Hogarth Press.

Freud, S. (1926). *Inhibitions, symptoms and anxiety.* In J. Strachey (Ed. & Trans.), *The standard edition of the complete psychological works of Sigmund Freud* (Vol. 20, pp. 77–174). London, UK: Hogarth Press.

Freud, S. (1937). *Analysis: Terminable and interminable.* Standard Edition, XXII.

Freud, S. (1940). *An outline of psychoanalysis.* Standard Edition, Vol. XXII.

Friedman, L. (2011). Charles Brenner: A practitioner's theorist. *Journal of the American Psychoanalytic Association, 59:* 679–700.

Fromm-Reichmann, F. (1950). *Principles of intensive psychotherapy.* Chicago, IL: University of Chicago Press.

Gabbard, G. O. (2010). *Long term psychodynamic psychotherapy: A basic text (Core competencies in pychotherapy).* Washington, DC, American Psychiatric Publishing.

Gill, M. M. (1951). Ego psychology and psychotherapy. *Psychoanalytic Quarterly, 20,* 62–71.

Gill, M. M. (1954). Psychoanalysis and exploratory psychotherapy. *Journal of the American Psychoanalytic Association, 2,* 771–797.

Gill, M. M. (1979). The analysis of transference. *Journal of the American Psychoanalytic Association, 27*(Suppl.), 263–289.

Gill, M. M., & Hoffman, I. Z. (1982). A method for studying the analysis of aspects of the patient's experience of the relationship in psychotherapy and psychoanalysis. *Journal of the American Psychoanalytic Association, 30,* 137–167.

Gitelson, M. (1952). The emotional position of the analyst in the psychoanalytic situation. *International Journal of Psychoanalysis, 33,* 1–10.

Gitelson, M. (1962). The curative factors in psychoanalysis. *International Journal of Psychoanalysis, 43:* 194–205.

Glover, E. (1931). The therapeutic effect of inexact interpretations: A contribution to the theory of suggestion. *International Journal of Psychoanalysis, 12,* 397–411.

Goldberger, M. (Ed.). (1996). *Danger and defense: The technique of close process attention.* Northvale, NJ: Jason Aronson.

Goldman. A. I. (2006). *Simulating minds: The philosophy, psychology and neuroscience of mindreading.* New York, NY: Oxford University Press.

Goldstein, E. (1994). Self-disclosure in treatment: What therapists do and don't talk about. *Clinical Social Work Journal, 22,* 417–433.

Gray, P. (1986). On helping analysands to observe intrapsychic activity. In A. B. Richards & M. S. Willick (Eds.), *Psychoanalysis: A science of mental conflict* (pp. 245–262). Hillsdale, NJ: Analytic Press.

Gray, P. (1994). *The ego and the analysis of defense.* Northvale, NJ: Jason Aronson.

Greenson, R. R. (1960). Empathy and its vicissitudes. *International Journal of Psychoanalysis, 41,* 418–424.

Greenson, R. R. (1965). The working alliance and the transference neurosis. *Psychoanalytic Quarterly, 34,* 158–181.

Greenson, R. R. (1967). *The technique of psychoanalysis.* New York, NY: International Universities Press.

Grinker, R. M., MacGregor, H., Selan, K., & Kohrman, J. (1961). The early years of psychiatric social work. *Social Service Review, 35:* 44–55.

Groves, M.D. (Ed.). (1996*). Essential papers on short-term dynamic therapy.* New York: NYU Press.

Have-de Labije, J., & Neborsky, R.J. (2012). *Mastering intensive short-term dynamic psychotherapy: A roadmap to the unconscious.* London, UK: Karnac Books.

Hellenbrand, A. (1972). Freud's influence on social casework. *Bulletin of the Menniger Clinic, 36:* 169–181.

Hilsenroth, M. J., Cromer, T. D., & Ackerman, S. J. (2011). How to make practical use of therapeutic alliance research in your clinical work. In R. A. Levy, J. Stuart Ablon, & H. Kachele (Eds.), *Psychodynamic psychotherapy research* (pp. 361–380). New York, NY: Humana Press.

Hoffer, A. (1985). Toward a definition of psychoanalytic neutrality. *Journal of the American Psychoanalytic Association, 33,* 771–796.

Horner, A. (1991). *Psychoanalytic object relations therapy.* New York, NY: Jason Aronson.

Horvath, A. D., & Symonds, B. D. (1991). Relations between working alliance and outcome in psychotherapy: A meta-analysis. *Journal of Counseling and Psychology, 38:* 139–149.

Horvath, A.O., Del Re, A.C., Fluckiger, C., & Symonds, D. (2011). Alliance in individual psychotherapy. In J. C. Norcross (Ed.), *Psychotherapy relationships that work* (2nd ed., pp. 25–69). New York, NY: Oxford University Press.

Huprich, S. K. (2009). *Psychodynamic therapy: Conceptual and empirical foundations.* New York, NY: Routledge.

Hurvich, M. (2011). New developments in the theory and clinical application of the annihilation anxiety concept. In A. B. Druck, C. Ellman, N. Freedman, & A. Thaler (Eds.), *A new Freudian synthesis: Clinical process in the next generation.* London, UK: Karnac.

Hurvich, M. (in press). *Annihilation anxiety: Clinical, theoretical and empirical implications.* London, UK: Karnac Press.

Iacoboni, M. (2008). *Mirroring people: The new science of how we connect with others.* New York, NY: Farrar, Strauss & Giroux.

Jackson, H. (ed.). (1994). *Using self-psychology in psychotherapy.* New York, NY: Jason Aronson.

Jacobs, T. (1991). *The use of the self: Countertransference and communication in the analytic situation.* Madison, CT: International Universities Press.

Kaplan, D. (1968). Dialogue in classical psychoanalysis. In E. Hammer (Ed.), *Use of interpretation in treatment* (pp. 129–140). New York, NY: Grune & Stratton.

Knight, R. (1949). A critique of the present status of the psychotherapies. *Bulletin of the New York Academy of Medicine, 25,* 100–114.

Knight, R. P. (1954). Evaluation of psychotherapeutic techniques. In R. P. Knight & C. R. Friedman (Eds.), *Psychoanalytic psychiatry and psychology* (pp. 65–76). New York, NY: International Universities Press.

Kohut, H. (1959). Introspection, empathy, and psychoanalysis. *Journal of the American Psychoanalytic Association, 7,* 459–483.

Kohut, H. (1984). *How does analysis cure?* Chicago, IL: University of Chicago Press.

Kris, A. (1982). *Free association: Method and process.* New Haven, CT: Yale University Press.

Kris, A. (1995). Support and psychic structural change. In M. J. Horowitz, O. F. Kemberg, &

E. J. Weinshel (Eds.), *Psychic structure and psychic change: Essays in honor of Robert Wallerstein* (pp. 95–115). Madison, CT: International Universities Press.

Kris, E. (1975). The recovery of childhood memories in psychoanalysis. In *The selected papers of Ernst Kris.* New Haven, CT: Yale University Press. (Original work published 1956)

Kurzweil, E. (1989). *The Freudians: A comparative perspective.* New Haven, CT: Yale University Press.

Kurzweil, E. (1997). *The Freudians: A comparative perspective* (2nd ed). New Brunswick, NJ: Transaction Books.

Langs, R. (1973). *The technique of psychoanalytic psychotherapy* (Vol. 1). New York, NY: Jason Aronson.

Langs, R. (1974). *The technique of psychoanalytic psychotherapy* (Vol. 2). New York, NY: Jason Aronson.

Langs, R. (1977). *The therapeutic interaction: A synthesis.* New York, NY: Jason Aronson.

Lasky, R. (1993). *The development and dynamics of the psychoanalytic process.* Northvale, NJ: Jason Aronson.

Lee, R. L., & Martin, J. C. (1991). *Psychotherapy after Kohut.* London, UK: Routledge.

Lemma, A. (2003). *Introduction to the practice of psychoanalytic psychotherapy.* New York, NY: Wiley.

Lemma, A., Target, M., & Fonagy, P. (2011). *Brief dynamic interpersonal psychotherapy.* Oxford, UK: Oxford University Press.

Levenson, H. (2003). *Brief dynamic psychotherapy.* Washington, DC: American Psychological Association.

Levenson, H., Butler, S. F., Powers, T. A., & Beitman, B.D. (2002). *Concise guide to brief dynamic and interpersonal therapy.* Washington, DC: American Psychiatric Publishing.

Levy, S. T. (1984). *Principles of interpretation.* New York, NY: Jason Aronson.

Levy, S. T., & Inderbitzen, C. B. (1990). The analytic surface and the theory of technique. *Journal of the American Psychoanalytic Association, 38,* 371–392.

Lichtenberg, J. D., & Caller, F. (1987). The fundamental rule: A study of current usage. *Journal of the American Psychoanalytic Association, 35,* 47–76.

Loewald, H. (1971). Some considerations on repetition and the repetition compulsion. *International Journal of Psychoanalysis, 52,* 59–66.

Loewenstein, R. (1951). The problem of interpretation. *Psychoanalytic Quarterly, 20,* 1–14.

Loewenstein, R. (1963). Some considerations on free association. *Journal of the American Psychoanalytic Association, 11,* 451–473.

Luborsky, L. (1976). Helping alliances in psychotherapy: The groundwork for a study of their relationship to outcome. In J. L. Claghom (Ed.), *Successful psychotherapy* (pp. 92–116). New York, NY: Brunner/Mazel.

Luborsky, L. (1984). *Principles of psychoanalytic psychotherapy: A manual for supportive-expressive treatment.* New York, NY: Basic Books.

Luborsky, L. (1994). Therapeutic alliances as predictors of psychotherapy outcomes: Factors explaining the predictive success. In A. Horvath & L. Greenberg (Eds.), *The working alliance: Therapy, research and practice* (pp. 38–50). New York, NY: Wiley.

Luborsky, L., & Auerbach, A. H. (1969). The symptom-context method: Quantitative studies of symptom formation in psychotherapy. *Journal of the American Psychoanalytic Association, 17,* 68–99.

Luborsky, L., & Crits-Christoph, P. (1990). *Understanding transference: The CCRT method.* New York, NY: Basic Books.

Luborsky, L., Crits-Christoph, P., Mintz, J., & Auerbach, A. (1988). *Who will benefit from psychotherapy? Predicting therapeutic outcomes.* New York, NY: Basic Books.

Lubove, R. (1965). *The professional altruist.* Cambridge, MA: Harvard University Press.

Magnavita, J. J. (1999). *Relational therapy for personality disorders.* New York, NY: Wiley.

Malan, D. (1976). *Toward the validation of dynamic psychotherapy.* New York, NY: Plenum Press.

Malan, D. (1979). *Individual psychotherapy and the science of psychodynamics.* London, UK: Butterworth-Heinemann.

Markowitz, J. C., & Weissman, M. M. (2012). *Casebook of interpersonal psychotherapy.* Oxford, UK: Oxford University Press..

Martin, D. J., Garske, J. P., & Davis, K. K. (2000). Review of the therapeutic alliance with outcome and other variables: A meta-analytic review. *Journal of Consulting and Clinical Psychology, 68:* 438–450.

McDevitt, J. (1997). The continuity of conflict and compromise formation from infancy to adulthood: A 25 year follow-up. *Journal of the American Psychoanalytic Association, 45,* 106–126.

McLaughlin, J. T. (1987). The play of transference: Some reflections on enactment in the psychoanalytic situation. *Journal of the American Psychoanalytic Association, 35,* 557–582.

McLaughlin, J. T. (1991). Clinical and theoretical aspects of enactment. *Journal of the American Psychoanalytic Association, 39,* 595–614.

McWilliams, N. (1994). *Psychoanalytic diagnosis: Understanding personality structure in the clinical process.* New York, NY: Guilford Press.

McWilliams, N. (2004). *Psychoanalytic psychotherapy: A practitioner's guide.* New York, NY: Guilford Press.

Menninger, K. (1958). *The theory of psychoanalytic technique.* New York, NY: Basic Books.

Modell, A. (1976). "The holding environment" and the therapeutic action of psychoanalysis. *Journal of the American Psychoanalytic Association, 4,* 285–307.

Modell, A. H. (1976). "The holding environment" and the therapeutic action of psychoanalysis. *Journal of the American Psychoanalytic Association, 23:* 285–307.

Muran, C. J., & Barber, J.P. (2010). *The therapeutic alliance: An evidence-based guide to practice.* New York, NY: Guilford Press.

Nuetzel, E. H., Larson, R. J., & Prizmic Z. (2007). The dynamics of empirically derived factors in the therapeutic relationship. *Journal of the American Psychoanalytic Association, 55:* 1321–1353.

Norcross, J. C. (2005). The psychotherapist's own psychotherapy: Educating and developing psychologists. *American Psychologist,* 60, 840–850.

Ogden, T. H. (1984). *The matrix of the mind: Object relations and the psychoanalytic dialogue.* New York, NY: Jason Aronson.

Oremland, J. (1991). *Interpretation and interaction: Psychoanalysis or psychotherapy.* Hillsdale, NJ: Analytic Press.

Paniagua, C. (1985). A methodological approach to surface material. *International Review of Psychoanalysis, 12,* 311–325.

Paniagua, C. (1991). Patient's surface, clinical surface and workable surface. *Journal of the American Psychoanalytic Association, 39,* 669–685.

Paolino, T. J. (1981). *Psychoanalytic psychotherapy: Theory, technique, therapeutic relationship and treatability.* New York, NY: Brunner/Mazel.

Pine, F. (1984). The interpretive moment. *Bulletin of the Menninger Clinic, 48,* 54–71.

Pinsker, H. (2003). *A primer in supportive psychotherapy.* London, UK: Routledge.

Poland, W. (1984). On the analyst's neutrality. *Journal of the American Psychoanalytic Association, 32,* 283–299.

Poland, W. (1992). From analytic surface to analytic space. *Journal of the American Psychoanalytic Association, 40,* 349–380.

Pray, M. (1994). Analyzing defenses: Two different methods. *Journal of Clinical Psychoanalysis, 3,* 87–126.

Rangell, L. (2001). Psychoanalytic psychotherapy: The enduring legacy of psychoanalysis. *Psychoanalytic Review, 88:*1–14.

Rapaport, D. (1960). *The structure of psychoanalytic theory: A systematizing attempt.* New York, NY: International Universities Press.

Rawson, P. (2002). *Short-term psychodynamic psychotherapy: An analysis of the key principles.* London, UK: Karnac Books.

Richards, A. D., & Willick, M. S. (1986). *Psychoanalysis: The science of mental conflict. Essays in honor of Charles Brenner.* Hillsdale, New Jersey: Analytic Press.

Richfield, J. (1954). An analysis of the concept of insight. *Psychoanalytic Quarterly, 23,* 390–408.

Rockland, L. (1989). *Supportive therapy: A psychoanalytic approach.* New York, NY: Basic Books.

Rockland, L. H. (1989). Psychoanalytically oriented supportive therapy. *Journal of the American Academy of Psychoanalysis and Dynamic Psychiatry, 17:* 451–462

Rogers, C. (1957). The necessary and sufficient conditions of therapeutic personality change. *Journal of Consulting Psychology, 21,* 95–103.

Rogers, C. (1961). *On becoming a person.* Boston, MA: Houghton Mifflin.

Rothstein, A. (1983). *The structural hypothesis.* New York, NY: International Universities Press.

Rothstein, A. (2010). *Making Freud more Freudian.* London, UK: Karnac.

Rowe, C., & MacIsaac, D. (1993). *Empathic attunement: The technique of self-psychology.* New York, NY: Jason Aronson.

Safran, J., Muran, C., & Eubanks-Carter, C. (2011). Repairing alliance ruptures. In J. C. Norcross (ed.), *Psychotherapy relationships that work* (2nd ed., pp. 224–238). New York, NY: Oxford University Press.

Safran, J. D. (2012). *Psychoanalysis and psychoanalytic therapies.* Washington, DC: American Psychological Association.

Samuel, L. R. (2013). *Shrink: A cultural history of psychoanalysis in America.* Lincoln: University of Nebraska press.

Sandler, J. (1976). Countertransference and role-responsiveness. *International Review of Psychoanalysis, 3,* 43–47.

Schafer, R. (1959). Generative empathy in the treatment situation. *Psychoanalytic Quarterly, 28,* 342–373.

Schafer, R. (1983). *The analytic attitude.* New York, NY: Basic Books.

Scharff, D. E., & Scharf, J. S. (2000). *Object relations individual therapy.* New York, NY: Jason Aronson.

Schwaber, E. A. (1995). The psychoanalyst's mind: From listening to interpretation—a clinical report. *International Journal of Psychoanalysis, 76,* 271–281.

Scott, S., & Robertson, M. (2003). *Interpersonal psychotherapy: A clinician's guide* (2nd Ed.). London, UK: Arnold Press.

Shapiro, T. (1984). On neutrality. *Journal of the American Psychoanalytic Association, 32,* 269–282.

Shedler, J. (2010). The efficacy of psychodynamic psychotherapy. *American Psychologist, 65:* 2, 98–109. Also in R. A. Levy, J. Stuart Ablon, & H. Kachele (Eds.), *Psychodynamic psychotherapy research* (pp. 9–25). New York, NY: Humana Press.

Sifneos, P. (1992). *Short-term anxiety provoking psychotherapy: A treatment manual.* New York, NY: Basic Books.

Spencer, J., & Balter, L. (1990). Psychoanalytic observation. *Journal of the American Psychoanalytic Association, 38,* 393–421.

Stadter, M. (2009). *Object relations brief therapy: The therapy relationship in short term work.* New York, NY: Jason Aronson.

Sterba, R. (1934). The fate of the ego in psychoanalytic therapy. *International Journal of Psychoanalysis, 15,* 117–126.

Stolorow, R., Brandschaft, B., & Atwood, G. (1987). *Psychoanalytic treatment. An intersubjective approach.* Hillsdale, NJ: Analytic Press.

Strachey, J. (1934). The therapeutic action of psychoanalysis. *International Journal of Psychoanalysis, 15,* 127–159.

Strupp, H., & Binder, J. (1984). *Psychotherapy in a new key: A guide to time limited dynamic psychotherapy.* New York, NY: Basic Books.

Strupp, H., & Binder, J. L. (1985). *Psychotherapy in a new key: A guide to time-limited dynamic psychotherapy.* New York, NY: Basic Books.

Summers, F. (1999). *Transcending the self: An object relations model of psychotherapy.* New York, NY: Routledge.

Summers, R. F., & Barber, J. P. (2010). *Psychodynamic therapy: A guide to evidence-based practice.* New York, NY: Guilford Press.

Tarachow, S. (1963). *An introduction to psychotherapy.* New York, NY: International Universities Press.

Truax, C. B. (1963). Effective ingredients in psychotherapy: An approach to unraveling the patient-therapist interaction. *Journal of Counseling Psychology, 19,* 256–263.

Truax, C. B., & Carkhuff, R. (1967). *Toward effective counseling and psychotherapy: Training and practice.* Chicago, IL: Aldine.

Tryon, G.S., & Winograd, G. (2011). Goal consensus and collaboration. In J. C. Norcross (Ed.), *Psychotherapy relationships that work* (2nd ed., pp. 153–167). New York, NY: Oxford University Press.

Wachtel, P. (2007). *Relational theory and the practice of psychotherapy.* New York, NY: Guilford Press.

Wallerstein, R. (2012). Psychoanalysis and psychodynamic psychotherapy: Historical developments and present relationship. In G.O. Gabbard, B. E. Litowitz, & R. Williams (Eds.), *Textbook of psychoanalysis* (pp. 367–382). New York, NY: American Psychoanalytic Association.

Wallerstein, R. S. (1965). The goals of psychoanalysis: A survey of analytic viewpoints. *Journal of the American Psychoanalytic Association, 13,* 748–770.

Wallerstein, R. S. (1986). *Forty-two lives in treatment: A study of psychoanalysis and psychotherapy.* New York, NY: Guilford Press.

Wampold, B. E. (2001). *The great therapy debate: Models, methods, and findings.* Mahwah, NJ: Lawrence Erlbaum.

Waska, R. (2010). *Psychoanalytic psychotherapy: A modern Kleinian approach.* Hauppauge, NY: Nova Science Publishers.

Waska, R. (2013*). A practical casebook of time-limited psychoanalytic work. A modern Kleinian approach.* London, UK: Routledge.

Weiss, J. (1971). The emergence of new themes: A contribution to the psychoanalytic theory of therapy. *International Journal of Psychoanalysis, 52,* 459–467.

Weiss, J. (1993). Empirical studies of the psychoanalytic process. *Journal of the American Psychoanalytic Association, 41*(Suppl.), 7–29.

Weiss, J., & Sampson, H. (1986). *The psychoanalytic process: Theory, clinical observation and empirical research.* New York, NY: Guilford Press.

Weissman, M., Markowitz, J., & Klerman, G. (2000). *Comprehensive guide to interpersonal psychotherapy.* New York, NY: Basic Books.

Weissman, M., Markowitz, J., & Klerman, G. (2007). *Clinician's quick guide to interpersonal psychotherapy.* New York, NY: Oxford University Press.

Werman, D. S. (1984). *The practice of supportive psychotherapy.* New York, NY: Brunner/Mazel.

Winnicott, D. (1965). *The maturational process and the facilitating environment.* New York, NY: International Universities Press.

Winston, A., Rosenthal, R. N., & Pinsker, H. (2012). *Learning supportive psychotherapy (Core competencies in psychotherapy).* Washington, DC: American Psychiatric Publishing.

Wolf, E. (1988). *Treating the self.* New York, NY: Guilford Press.

Yelloly, M.A. 1980). *Social work theory and psychoanalysis.* New York, NY: Van Nostrand Reinhold.

Zaretsky, E. (2004). *Secrets of the soul: A social and cultural history of psychoanalysis.* New York, NY: Alfred A. Knopf.

Zetzel, E. (1956). Current concepts of transference. *International Journal of Psychoanalysis, 37,* 369–376.

10

GROUP TREATMENT WITH CHILDREN AND ADOLESCENTS

JOAN GRANUCCI LESSER[1]

A *group* is a "small face-to-face collection of persons who interact to accomplish some purpose" (Brown, 1991, p. 3). Most children are born into their first group—the family—which Germain (1991) refers to as a *community subsystem.* As children develop and grow, they move into many other groups, including peer, recreational, and organizational groups such as school. The term *treatment* is used to signify a group "whose major purpose is to meet members' socioemotional needs . . . for support education, therapy, growth and socialization" (Toseland & Rivas, 2001, p. 15). Stewart, Christner, and Freeman (2007) refer to the group therapy setting as "a natural laboratory in which members can 'test out' their beliefs, as well as newly acquired skills" (p. 8). The benchmark of a group is the mutual aid that develops among group members (Schwartz, 1986; Shulman, 1985, 1992). This happens when group members reflect on themselves and on the other person's situation, a process that benefits both the giver and the receiver. Tijhuis (1998), discussing the supportive help children and adolescents give each other in

certain types of treatment groups, refers to peers as the "guardian angels" of the individual group members. Jagendorf and Malekoff (2000) and Malekoff (2004) capture the concept of mutual aid with "groups on the go"—spontaneously formed mutual aid groups for adolescents in distress. One group took place when the school counselor met with an unhappy student who did not want to go to a party because he could not dance. The counselor skillfully negotiated the interruptions of a counseling session at a busy school to recruit and engage the students in a process of mutual aid—a group on the go. Excerpts from an impromptu group of five adolescents who were invited to assist this student illustrate the dynamics of mutual aid: discussing a taboo subject ("I can't dance"), mutual support ("You're doing the meringue, how do you know how to do that?"), mutual demand ("Don't forget, we're here to help Jay"), rehearsal ("And then magically in the moment with the music, the group was dancing together"), sharing data ("Jerold walked over to Jay and started to systematically show him how to do a reggae step").

[1]*Author's Note:* The author wishes to thank Dr. Heidi Haas, PhD, and Jana Jagendorf, MSW, for the case material each contributed to this chapter.

Mishna and Muskat (2004) describe mutual aid in a therapy group for adolescents with learning disorders (LD), where members have the chance to feel that others are "in the same boat" and to experience "strength in numbers" as they often struggle with isolation and stigma in the larger school environment. The authors also discuss the importance of the group leader, who is needed to help activate the group's power to assist an individual member, an example of "mutual aid in action" (p. 461).

Anna spoke incessantly, without pausing or noticing the others' responses to her. She leaned forward in her chair and stared at one of the leaders, at no time making eye contact with the girls. The other members stopped paying attention, became restless, and began to whisper to one another. As Anna did not cue in, one of the leaders gently interrupted Anna and asked the other members if there was a way the group could help Anna talk to the whole group rather than just to the leader. The girls said they could and with encouragement told Anna to turn and look at them. (p. 465)

HISTORY OF GROUP WORK WITH CHILDREN AND ADOLESCENTS

In 1934, Slavson shifted the focus from group work with adults to group work with children. His goals in group work were consistent with his psychoanalytic treatment of individual patients— namely, the resolution of unconscious conflict that was blocking the functioning and productivity of children in home and school settings. He both worked with children who were considered to be disturbed and ran child-focused group treatment for the parents of these children. With the publication of his book *An Introduction to Group Therapy,* Slavson (1943) introduced activity-group therapy (AGT) for children. Slavson's work emphasized the importance of understanding the differences among age and developmental trends in childhood in play therapy. He felt that children benefit most from being with peers who

have skills that are compatible with their own and by being challenged in ways that allow them to be successful (Stewart et al., 2007, p. 5). Slavson (1943) and Axline (1947) recognized the importance of the group as a "holding environment" that promoted corrective peer interaction (Connors, Schamess, & Strieder, 1997, p. 290). The *holding environment* refers to the supportive continuity provided by the therapeutic situation, as well as the underlying empathy and reliability of the object and attunement to developmental processes that contain potentially disruptive and disorganizing early wishes and fears (Winnicott, 1965, cited in Connors et al., 1997, p. 291). The group environment provides the opportunity for members to express feelings through participation in games, crafts, and other activities of interest to their particular age group (Johnson et al., 1998; Schaefer & Reid, 2001). Webb (1999) cautions that as the group activity is also therapeutic, before choosing an activity, the leader must consider 10 factors: (1) the purpose that the activity will achieve; (2) intimacy versus distance, sharing versus competition, and cooperation versus conflict; (3) focus—individual, group, or both; (4) required skills; (5) decision-making opportunities for the individual and the group; (6) appropriateness to members' life situations; (7) cultural sensitivity; (8) impact on behavioral expression; (9) timing within the session and the stage of development of the group; and (10) availability of resources (pp. 76–77). The group leader should also consider the allocated group space and degree of "mess" that the space and the group members can handle. As Malekoff (2004) writes, "group work with kids is rarely neat" (p. 19).

DeGangi and Nemiroff (2011) discuss the narrative tool of letter writing as an approach to stimulating dialogue in therapy groups for children and adolescents. The leader introduces a phantom child or adolescent letter writer into the group who seeks advice from the group related to a particular problem. This approach facilitates discussion of uncomfortable topics as the adolescent group members are able to express their thoughts and feelings on the topic with some emotional distance.

LeCroy and Archer (2001) also write about the significance of a chosen activity in group work with children. They introduce the social skills game board as a tool to use when working with children in social skills training groups. These are strengths-based groups focused on building up the child's repertoires of skills rather than on eliminating pathological behavior. The targeted skills include creating positive interactions, starting conversations, making requests, expressing feelings directly, saying no, asserting rights, empathy, dealing with those in authority, responsible decision making, negotiation and conflict resolution, and asking for help. The playing cards cover four different areas: situations the children might encounter in life, feelings, role plays, and fun activities. As they move around the game board, the children are asked to pick a card, respond to a question, or initiate a prosocial behavior (LeCroy & Archer, 2001). The activity facilitates interpersonal interaction and uses a board game to help children develop interpersonal behaviors both indirectly, by watching other children repeating and practicing new behaviors, and directly, by repeating and practicing new behaviors (Toseland & Rivas, 2001, p. 294).

The following example provides a snapshot of a group where the combined importance of the holding environment and the importance of the chosen activity are demonstrated.

Group Example: Expressing Feeling Through Art: Group Treatment for Traumatized Children

This group took place in Kingston, Jamaica, with children of ages 7 to 10 who had been sexually abused and were now living in a small, protected house. Two therapists worked with a group of six children over 4 weeks, using expressive arts to help the children communicate their feelings. The leaders engaged the children in decorating white T-shirts, offering a range of art materials, such as different-colored markers, feathers, beads, and sequins. The therapists remained emotionally present to the children as they worked on their projects, offering encouragement or helping a child choose a particular art medium. They would make simple verbal interactions as the children worked: "I can see you are showing how you feel with the colors you are choosing." or "That's a strong color you are using—maybe it tells about your anger." Buoyed by the therapists, the children turned and made encouraging comments to each other: "I like where you put that feather." This was a purposeful group treatment approach, focused on helping the children feel less isolated in their suffering with the provision of successful peer relationships, a trusting relationship with two adults, and a safe place—a holding environment—to share their feelings in relation to the trauma each had suffered (Weber & Haen, 2005). As Shelby (1997) writes, "Traumatized children need to be heard in the presence of another who is not afraid to grieve with them" (p. 149). As the project progressed, some of the children moved from grief to anger, from decorating T-shirts with designs to writing messages of empowerment on their shirts: "You can't hurt me anymore." and "I'm not afraid of you." At the end of the group, the children and the therapists hung the shirts on a long clothesline between two trees, right outside the protected house—a display of their resiliency to the community. The leaders of this particular group wove process and content with a group termination that demonstrates what Cattanach (1996) calls "powerful endings."

Group Play Therapy

A historical parallel occurred between the history of group activity therapy and that of play therapy and led to the development of group play therapy (O'Connor, 2000). The Association for Play Therapy (APA) (2008) defines *play therapy* as "the systematic use of a theoretical model to establish an interpersonal process wherein trained play therapists use the therapeutic powers of play to help clients prevent or resolve psychosocial difficulties and achieve optimal growth and development." O'Connor (2000, p. 414) identifies seven benefits of group play therapy with children:

1. Groups tend to promote more spontaneity than the child might show when alone with the therapist.

2. The group modality provides the opportunity to address both intrapsychic and interpersonal issues.

3. Vicarious learning and catharsis take place in the group.

4. Children have the opportunity to receive and reflect on feedback from their peers.

5. The presence of peers tends to anchor the session more solidly in reality. The child is less likely to engage in repetitive behavior or to withdraw into fantasy.

6. The pattern of the child's interaction in the group provides the therapist an opportunity to observe a sample of the child's "real-life" behavior.

7. Children have the opportunity to practice new behaviors and social skills.

Slavson (1999) notes that in group play therapy, there is a "catalytic effect"—both positive and negative—that results from the "interstimulation and the various types of interaction . . . that inevitably arise from the concurrent activity of several children" (p. 25). The therapist must be aware of the significance of the children's play, including traumatic fixations, conflicts, hostilities, communication, abreaction, and sublimation of primary instinctual drives. The fundamental dynamics present in play groups include (a) relationship, (b) catharsis, (c) insight and/or ego strengthening, (d) reality testing, and (e) sublimation (p. 27). Relationships are multilateral among the members and serve to neutralize the transference toward the therapist.

The group play therapist responds to the acts of the children in the group to help them acquire insight. Play is the means through which children communicate the contents of the unconscious and the distress that pressures from the environment create. Participation in play therapy groups helps the executive function of the ego as a controller of impulses and as the mediator between the self and the outer realities. Play activity becomes a measure of the child's self in relation to the reality of the play group. The acceptance of the child by the therapist and the other children assures the child that he or she is loved and accepted. Finally, within the context of the play therapy group, children are able to sublimate their drives into controlled, socially approved patterns of behavior and more adequate adaptations to reality (Slavson, 1999, pp. 28–29).

DEVELOPMENTAL ASSESSMENT

There are various developmental frameworks that can be used to provide diagnostic screening templates for the cognitive, linguistic, physical, emotional, social, and play development of children within their environmental context. These models include Erikson's (1950, 1959) psychosocial model, Freud's (1905) psychosexual model, Kail's (2001) model of emotional development, Stern's (1977, 1985) self-development model, Kohlberg's (1984) model of moral development, Vygotsky's (1978) sociocultural-cognitive constructivist model, and Piaget's (1936/1952) model of cognitive development. There are also a number of feminist and multicultural developmental models that address gay, lesbian, bisexual, and transgender identity development; children with a number of ethnic identities; and children whose primary identity may be different from that of the dominant culture in which they reside (Butler,

1999; Calhoun, 2000; Cass, 1979, 1984, 1990; Chodorow, 1973; Gilligan, 1982; Sue & Sue, 2003). In addition, concepts such as equifinality, multifinality, and heterotypic continuity provide further guides to assess and screen children for appropriate placement in treatment groups. *Equifinality* means that a single disorder (such as a child's anxiety) can be produced via different developmental pathways (perhaps as a result of having an undiagnosed LD or in reaction to a stress in the family). *Multifinality* suggests that the same developmental events may lead to different adaptive and/or maladaptive outcomes. For example, a teenager with attention deficit hyperactivity disorder (ADHD) may have different ways of coping: withdraw and become depressed, become oppositional, or give up and look disengaged from school and family. Heterotypic continuity implies that a given pathological process will be exhibited differently with continued development (Cooper & Lesser, 2008, p. 211). These developmental concepts are significant when the leader is assessing the group members' capacity to provide mutual aid and support to each other.

O'Connor (2000) offers a typology grouped according to "levels of development," a concise, useful guide to group leaders. Group work is best conducted with children who have achieved Level II development, approximately 2 to 6 years of age. Children at this stage have acquired language skills, are physically more capable, and have achieved some object constancy. Play behavior makes the transition from parallel to interactive during these years. Preschool children have a limited understanding of emotions and a limited awareness of their own and others' affect. Children at this age are just learning what emotions are in themselves and others. They therefore have a limited capacity for empathy, and groups for this age group should be structured and rely on guided social time for both free and structured play (Indiana University, n.d.).

Level III children, ages 6 to 12, are developing executive functions during these years, including the following: (1) the ability to articulate a problem and generate ideas about how to solve it, (2) knowledge of cognitive strategies that help in problem solving and when to use them, (3) a more flexible approach to problem solving, (4) a longer attention span, (5) better control of anxiety, (6) the ability to monitor one's own performance, (7) faith in one's ability to think about problems, and (8) awareness of one's shortcomings in thinking about problem solving (Kagan, 1984, cited in Davies, 2004, pp. 365–366). During these years, children are beginning to acquire the skills of empathy and to master increasing levels of impulse control. They are ideally suited for activity-oriented group therapy because they have strong attachments to their peers and are able to see themselves as part of a group without losing a sense of their own individuality (O'Connor, 2000).

ADOLESCENT GROUPS

Dies (1996) writes that "the adolescent group has its own special place in therapy. It is not quite a children's or an adult group" (p. 35). As children enter Level IV, from age 12 to age 17 or 18, they are less interested in a highly structured group (O'Connor, 2000). Children in middle school, and often the first 2 years of high school, have generally acquired a good cognitive grasp of what emotions are and the ability to distinguish subtle differences in feelings. They are concurrently acquiring the ability to think in the abstract, to engage in metacognition, and to struggle with conflicting feelings. Wood (2000) sees the group as a natural setting for adolescents, since "they are taught in groups, live in groups, and often play in groups" (p. 1). The developmental questions of this life phase can appropriately be explored: Who am I? With whom do I identify? What do I believe in? and Where am I going? (p. 1). Despite the benefits, adolescents are often reluctant to participate in certain kinds of groups, particularly therapy groups.

Feldstein Ewing, Walters, and Baer (2013) write about "motivational interviewing" (MI) as a "promising approach" in working with adolescents in groups. Motivational interviewing is a "collaborative, person-centered form of guiding to elicit and strengthen motivation for change" (Naar-King & Suarez, 2011, p. 5). MI groups provide a safe, nonjudgmental atmosphere where teen members can explore their ideas and intentions around behavior change. This is done through the use of an "elicit-provide-elicit" approach that invites discussion, reflects back on the responses, and waits for any continued discussion to emerge. The group leader is focused on broadening the adolescent members' perspectives by developing discrepancies between current behaviors and future goals. The emphasis is on personal choice and control. Participation and open exchange are encouraged while the leader rolls with the arguments against change, avoiding taking an expert stance (Wagner & Ingersoll, 2013, p. 54). One of the techniques used in MI groups is eliciting change success stories by encouraging discussion of a time they did something they thought they could not do. The focus remains on what a person could do if he or she wanted to make behavior changes (Feldstein Ewing, Walters, & Baer, 2013).

Malekoff (2004, pp. 36–37) introduces "strengths-based group work" as a conceptual frame when planning groups for adolescents. He identifies seven practice principles that can also be applied to group work with younger children:

1. Form groups based on members' felt needs and wants, not diagnoses.

2. Select groups to welcome the whole person, not just the troubled parts.

3. Integrate verbal and nonverbal activities.

4. Develop alliances with relevant other people in group members' lives.

5. Decentralize authority and turn control over to group members.

6. Maintain a dual focus on individual change and social reform.

7. Understand and respect group development as a key to promoting change.

Dies (1996, pp. 35–51) defines five stages an adolescent group undergoes:

1. *Stage 1: Initial relatedness.* This stage centers on the clarification of expectations, education around group process, and issues of engagement with the leader and each other. The therapist is active so as to build a safe, supportive environment and to model an appropriate level of openness and self-disclosure, but he or she should be careful not to overwhelm or threaten those teens who may be cautious about beginning.

2. *Stage 2: Testing of limits.* In this stage, the group process approximates the adolescent's developmental struggles related to separation, individuation, and identity formation. The leader plays a pivotal role in creating a climate where differences may emerge and be accepted. This is done by modeling acceptance and validation as the group members are trying on and discarding different aspects of their personality. The testing centers on the group leader's commitment to the group and to the group process.

3. *Stage 3: Resolving authority issues.* This generally occurs after the group members have accepted the leader's ability to tolerate the challenges of the individual group members and the group as a whole. The rules or contract may be directly challenged at this point. It is important to maintain the boundaries established in the negotiated contract but to allow open discussion and acknowledgment of individual and group feelings.

4. *Stage 4:* The leader takes a less active role, and the group members assume greater responsibility. The adolescents have now gained greater comfort with each other in the group. It is often helpful for the leader to share with the teens that he or she is going to decrease involvement so that actions are not misunderstood. Member-to-member activity increases, focused on interpersonal skill development. The leader's interventions focus on generalizing from the group to members' lives outside the group.

5. *Stage 5:* This is the termination stage, when the members process what the group has meant to them with their feelings about the group ending. Adolescents may resort to denial to avoid confronting these feelings; reunions and get-togethers

are often planned during this time. It is important for the group leader to share his or her own feelings about what the group has meant and about its end. An appropriate termination helps the adolescents learn how to move on in the future, as they will have to do many times in their lives as they continue to grow.

An important issue for leaders of adolescent groups to consider is self-disclosure related to different topics. The handling of self-disclosure is a function of both the theoretical model being used as well as the leader's personal comfort. Many adolescents will ask the group leader questions to test the authenticity of the leader. It is important to thoughtfully consider how to respond to personal questions without becoming defensive or overly revealing in a way that may not be helpful to the group members (Schneider Cory, Corey, & Corey, 2013).

DRAMA GROUPS

Drama and therapy have been historical partners in the use of emotional reflection, expression, and language (Gallo-Lopez & Schaefer, 2010). Drama groups provide a conduit to facilitate the skills of emotional intelligence, "the ability to perceive emotions, to access and generate emotions so as to assist thought, to understand emotions and emotional knowledge, and to reflectively regulate emotions in order to promote emotional

and intellectual growth" (Salovey & Sluyter, 1997, p. 5). They can also assist with feelings of depression, anxiety, and oppositional behavioral disorders that result from unmanageable or uncontrolled feelings of sadness, fear, and anger. Children and adolescents may then be less likely to act out these emotions in a dysfunctional manner against themselves, others, and their environments (Weber & Haen, 2005, p. 157). The dramatic element of distancing facilitates the group member's movement between real and fictional experience and between cognitive and affective experience, integrating subjective emotional feelings with objective understanding and resulting in healthier functioning. The projective technique of theater helps group members balance feelings, thoughts, and behaviors. Creating scenes to demonstrate and act out problem-ridden life narratives helps the adolescents "dis-identify from and reflect on the effects of these meanings and rules in their lives" (Strong, 2002, p. 224). The teens then unite with each other and with the group leader or facilitator in challenging the problem, rather than fighting and blaming each other, and this results in conversational accomplishment. Theater improvisation provides distancing, offering these students the chance to trust themselves and their peers (scene partners), to be spontaneous with editing themselves or being edited by adults outside the group, and to be playful in their lives, which are often stressful.

Group Example

A group leader uses drama in her work with a group of eight adolescents at an alternative high school. These youths demonstrate emotional and behavioral problems that hindered their participation in the public high school. They are not always able to talk about their feelings or their goals in life. The leader engages the students in creating their own theater game: High School Reunion. This provides the distancing that enables them to demonstrate some of their thoughts about the future and the challenges they are coping with.

(Continued)

(Continued)

Leader: I want to welcome all of you back after 10 years. I am so pleased with the turnout. I hope you all get a chance to share what you have been up to.

Amid the giggles, one student, Nina, pretends to rock a baby in her arms. Two other students are greeting each other enthusiastically as if this were the first time they were seeing each other since graduation. There are hugs and kisses.

Nina: (*smiling and introducing her husband, her baby, and her toddler*) I have another on the way. I am so happy. I am working as a dental hygienist finally married the man I have loved for years.

Martina: (*getting up and strutting about a bit*) I am a dentist, living in Texas. I was also a chef for a few years.

Rose: Hey Martina, did you get into the Marines? And did you get the tattoo you wanted?

Martina: You bet, girl. I was in the Marines for a few years. And the tattoo is on my thigh like I wanted—I can't show you that (*laughs*).

Shawnika: I became the Queen as I knew I would (*lots of laughter from the others*). And then I bought my auto body shop and got married. I am doing real good!

Rose (to Kenya): Whatever happened to you and Luc?

Kenya: You didn't hear? Luc got a sex change after being on an NFL football team. He has some great boobs now. We broke up. I could not live with him as a woman. He—I mean she—was busy flirting with all the guys!

Nina: Hey Sam, you still so quiet? (*everyone looks over at Sam*)

Sam: (*stirring a bit and almost inaudible*) I went into the army, and I am now an auto mechanic.

Rose: Well, Sam, did you get married? Hook with anyone?

Sam: Just Luc, I mean Lucy, but not anymore. No, I like living alone.

The group members suddenly notice Luc/Lucy walking in and shout out his name: "Hey Luc, is it true? You played for the NFL? Are those boobs for real?"

Luc/Lucy: Yeah! Don't they look good? (*turning to Kenya*) Sorry it didn't work out. I couldn't keep my eyes off the guys.

Nina (to Rose): What about you, girl? You look good.

Rose (very proudly): I am a pharmacist, and me and my husband just put a down payment on a house.

Everyone whoops for her!

GROUP COMPONENTS

The first component of any group is *pregroup planning.* Kurland (1978) refers to planning as "the neglected component of group development" (p. 173). She constructed the following framework as a guide for the group leader to use during the planning stage of development, before the start of the group. The other components of Kurland's group typology include social context, agency context, need, purpose, composition, structure, content, and pregroup planning and contact. I have added the additional component of theoretical framework, another often neglected component of group development. The following section will describe each of these group components and apply them to the "good-enough group"—adolescents preparing to take a test for the General Equivalency Diploma (GED)—the "good-enough degree." This model is not intended to be a checklist but a conceptual framework that provides venues to consider and reflect on. It is to be used flexibly insofar as different components may be more or less important depending on the type of group and the setting in which it takes place.

Social Context

Social context includes attention to the political environment, the geographic community, the agency climate, and any cultural attitudes toward participation in groups. The personal and historical experiences that individuals bring to the group are also important. The impact of oppression or racism, for example, is going to influence the participation of the individual in the group. It is the interplay between the group members and what occurs in the political, economic, social, and racial climates in which they live that contributes to an understanding of their needs (Walsh, 1996).

Example: The Good-Enough Group

This is a group of African American and Latino adolescents attending a school in Queens, New York, and preparing to take a state-wide test for a GED. The adolescents range in age from 16 to 18, and all dropped out of high school. Over 80% of the students in the program come from single-parent, low-socioeconomic-status households. Many have witnessed domestic violence and have parents who are incarcerated or addicted to drugs.

Some of the students were on probation or parole for use and distribution of drugs, and others have been in gangs. According to the group leader, "These adolescents were traumatized, depressed, strong, resilient, sad, funny, smart, quick, savvy, hip, old, and young at the same time" (personal interview with J. Jagendorf, January 2009).

Agency Context and Sponsorship

The purpose of the organization sponsoring the group, the problems and people that the agency services, the resources that are allocated to the formation of the group, and the policies regarding confidentiality, informed consent, eligibility, fees, and accountability are all significant.

It is also important to consider the relationship of the agency to the surrounding community and how the agency's place and reputation in the community act on the group.

Example: The Good-Enough Group

The GED school is the sister agency of a large, traditional, nonprofit, faith-based social service organization that enjoys a good reputation in the community. The program includes both an educational and a counseling component. The school consists of 90 students, six teachers, and seven counselors. The students must be officially withdrawn from high school to be eligible to attend this program, and any student under the age of 18 must have parental approval for attending. The students attend classes, and when they and their teachers feel they are ready, they study for and take a predictor test. Those who pass this test are eligible to take the statewide examination they must pass to get a GED.

Need

This is the reason why the group was formed, as perceived by the group leader, agency administrators, potential group members, and any other relevant persons. There can sometimes be differences as well as commonalities between and among these persons. When developing a group within a school setting, it is important to clearly state how the group complements the mission of the school and will help the members achieve both academically and socially (Steen, Bauman, & Smith, 2008). The developmental stage of the members, values, socioeconomic conditions, race, culture, and ability to meet the needs of the members through participation in this group are all important factors. Need may be determined both formally, through individual interviews and testing, and by more informal methods such as hanging out and listening to what young people talk about among themselves and learning what is important to them.

Example: The Good-Enough Group

There was a 12-week wait between the time the students passed the predictor test and the day they would actually take the test. Through informal conversations with the teens and also with their teachers, the counselor at the school recognized this as a challenging time for these kids. They were relieved that they were going to be able to take the test, worried about passing it, and concerned about their future goals. They felt bruised and stigmatized from the experiences they had had in high school, which resulted in their dropping out and now getting what they disparagingly referred to as a "good-enough" degree. The counselor initiated a 12-week group for students waiting to take the GED test. A brief exchange from the first group illustrates how discussing some of these feelings resulted in the name of the group.

Leader: And so, here we are. We all know each other, and so I am going to skip the introductions and get right down to business *(smiling and making eye contact with each of the kids)*. I'm glad we're together today and that we are going to be together until you take your test. Let's talk about how we are going to use this time.

Jay: Oh, yeah, some big day. My mother is still pissed at me for dropping out of school . . . she doesn't think getting a GED is any big deal.

Jose: Right, man, like who really gives a s about a GED?

Rose: Somebody I know said it was like a second-class degree, you know, just "good enough."

Leader: "Good enough." Hmmm, what does *good enough* mean?

Jay: It means we ain't getting the real degree—the high school diploma—and that we're losers.

Leader: Do you feel like losers?

Malcolm: I ain't no loser, man. I'm proud of myself for being here. I hated school, but now I'm coming back to get my high school diploma. I don't care what anybody says.

Leader: Anybody else have anything to say about this, because I'm thinking that maybe a lot of people who think you guys are getting a second-class degree don't really get what it takes to go back to school and get a GED.

Carla: Yeah, and I don't like the word "drop out" either. I feel like I was forced out. I didn't do good in school—all right, I know I had an attitude, but I don't think there was any place for me in that school. It's different here, you know, people really get who you are and want to help you.

Leader: And so maybe the degree you are getting really is good enough.

Shequan: Yeah, like we are getting the good-enough degree so that makes us the "good-enough group."

Leader: What a great name for our group! What do you think, men and women? Are we good enough?

Members: *(laughing and joining in, including those who have not spoken)* Yeah, "good enough," that's it.

Purpose and Theoretical Framework

The purpose of the group is what it is hoping to accomplish collectively. It flows from the need and involves collaboration on the part of the leader and the members in meeting that need. Purpose is synonymous with group content, which is how the group will work together to achieve its goal.

The theoretical framework of the group forms the conceptual rationale for the purpose and how the purpose will be implemented. The number of theoretical models of therapy has expanded in recent years. Some of the major theoretical models include psychodynamic models such as ego supportive, self psychology, and object relations; cognitive behavioral models; dialectical behavioral therapy; eco-systemic theory; narrative therapy; solution focused brief therapy; multicultural and social justice models; and integrative approaches (Comas-Diaz, 2011; Corsini & Wedding, 2011; Farber, 2002; Hays, Arredonto, Gladding, & Toporek, 2010; Sharf, 2012). The choice of a theoretical model is a complex one, and attention must be given to the group members' developmental, sociohistorical, organizational, political, and cultural contexts, in addition to the purpose of the group. Multicultural theory has provided a conceptual framework to assist the practitioner in selecting and using the theoretical approach most consistent with the life experiences and cultural perspectives of clients. Group workers facilitating groups with children and adolescents from other cultures should be engaged in a process of cultural identity development and committed to learning multicultural group skills. These include understanding whether a problem stems from racism or bias; the ability to engage in a variety of verbal and nonverbal group-counseling methods; awareness of limitations of diagnostic screening tests that may be culture bound; showing sensitivity to issues of sexism, elitism, and racism when conducting evaluations and screening interviews; and assuming responsibility for educating group members, and their parents, about the counselor's theoretical orientation and about alternative methods of counseling that may be available in the community (Lesser & Pope, 2007, pp. 46–47). Schneider et al. (2013) remind us that "the values leaders bring to the group process must consciously acknowledge the reality of human diversity in our society (p. 76). Malekoff (2004, pp. 208–209) outlines several practice principles for addressing diversity in group work with adolescents, which can be applied to group work with younger children with modification that is appropriate to their age:

1. Address diversity as a normative adolescent identity issue and not only in reaction to emergent conflicts.

2. Help the group tune in to ethnically and racially charged local, national, and international events.

3. Confront prejudice, stereotyping, and oppression in the here-and-now of the group, as it relates to use of racial-ethnic slurs.

4. Use cultural self-awareness to model effective cross-cultural relationships.

5. Promote understanding and respect for the worldviews and values of culturally different group members.

6. Tune in to the differential experiences of ethnic group members within their own particular culture, addressing stereotyping.

7. Open pathways for intercultural communication and socialization that draw attention to the commonalities culturally different group members may show.

Example: The Good-Enough Group

The leader chose to work within the framework of intersubjectivity. *Intersubjectivity* is a metatheory that "examines the field—two subjectivities in the system they create and from which they emerge—in any form of psychoanalytic treatment" (Orange, Atwood, & Stolorow, 1997, p. 3). The therapist and the patient join each other in an intersubjective space where each participant brings an emotional history and psychological organization that is equally important to the understanding of the clinical exchange (Stolorow, 1994a, 1994b; Stolorow & Atwood, 1992). In other words, "What we inquire about or interpret or leave alone depends on who we are" (Orange et al., 1997, p. 3). For example when the group leader picks up on the words *good enough*, she brings her own history to the exchange; something in her own historical unconscious has been triggered. We will see later how she draws on this in discussing racism with the members.

The group met for 1½ hours per week for 12 weeks. The purpose of the group was to foster a sense of belonging where personal pride and a sense of accomplishment could be shared, just as happens in high school when students graduate. It would also provide a place to address the students' fears and anxieties related to taking the test as well as their questions, concerns, and options for future schooling, jobs, and careers. And it would be a group where the traumatic experiences that led these students to become high school dropouts would be talked about and understood.

Composition

The composition of the group refers to both the members and the leaders. The characteristics of the members include the degree of homogeneity or heterogeneity regarding age, sex, racial, ethnic, and religious background, socioeconomic level, behavioral characteristics, previous group experience, mental status, nature of the problem, and any other issues that may affect a member's ability to share with others in the group. Generally speaking, there should not be more than 5 or 6 children in a group with one adult leader; and no more than 6 to 10 children in a group with two adult leaders. Groups with adolescents over the age of 14 can be larger, with 6 to 8 children and one leader but not more than 10 or 12 children if there are two leaders. This also depends on the type of group and the setting it is taking place in. The age spread among the group members should not exceed 3 years, especially among younger children. The children should all be within 15 IQ points of one another. There is no fixed rule on including boys and girls within a group; this varies with the age of the children, the type of group, and the goals (O'Connor, 2000, p. 417). Too much heterogeneity makes it very difficult, if not impossible, for the group to develop a cohesive identity separate from that of its individual members. Generally, the more distinct the problem the members have in common, the more heterogeneity can be accommodated.

Example: The Good-Enough Group

The group under discussion consisted of 10 adolescents ranging in age from 16 to 18; included among these were four girls and six boys; two of the boys were African American, and the rest of the students were Latina/Latino. All the Latino teens were the first generation to be born in the United States. Their parents had immigrated from Puerto Rico and the Dominican Republic. As minority youth, these adolescents deal with the double crisis of normal developmental stress and society's reaction to their ascribed status. The group leader, a married, Caucasian, Jewish woman in her late 30s, must consider the racial and cultural divide between herself and her group members. She knows that while they have many differences, they share the complexity of belonging to two cultures—hers, as a Jewish person, is a "hidden diversity" (Naumburg, 2007, p. 79). The leader has some appreciation for the socialization that occurs in a minority culture as well as the difficulties involved in moving between two cultures. She also recognizes that when otherness is more hidden, it provides safety that may not be available to those whose diversity is not hidden. As a White woman she belongs to the majority U.S. culture, but as a Jewish woman she does not. Nonetheless, she recognizes that the difference in skin color between herself and the group members is a presence in the room that speaks to their differences in history, culture, worldview, and privilege (Naumburg, 2007). Working intersubjectively, she hopes to create the space to talk about these racially charged topics.

Structure

This component refers to the arrangements that are made to facilitate the group, such as how often and for how long the group will meet and whether new members will be able to join once the group begins. It also includes the meeting place, the size of the meeting room, the physical arrangements in the meeting room, program supplies and equipment, fees, and confidentiality concerns.

Content

The content of a group includes what will actually take place when the group meets. It might include arts and crafts, role plays, discussion, media, dance, and many other activities. Brandler and Roman (1999) include suggestions of group games and exercises for children and adolescents that can be used at different phases of group development. Developmentally appropriate rules must be established from the beginning, and the group leader must take the initiative in introducing them. These include rules regarding safety and confidentiality. Other rules are best negotiated between and among the leader and the group members. These group rules can then be incorporated into a group contract that is signed by the leader and each member.

Example: The Good-Enough Group

The group was closed-ended to provide a safe, consistent place for the students to talk about their feelings and gain a sense of emotional mastery related to the upcoming test, especially significant given their history of academic challenges and perceived failures. The meeting room was comfortable and decorated in lounge fashion, with low couches and chairs that the kids could slouch into. This was meant to create an air of informality, different from the structure of the classes the students attended outside the group.

Example: The Good-Enough Group

An excerpt from one group illustrates the leader working intersubjectively with the group members regarding racism and stereotyping. The leader uses her own cultural awareness to model effective cross-cultural/racial dialogue (Malekoff, 204, pp. 208–209).

Shequan: Why are most of the kids in this school Black and Latino? What's up with that, man? I can tell you what's up . . . because we're the ones livin' in the hood . . . too many distractions, do you know what I mean?

Jose: Yeah, I know what you mean. These White people, they don't get it. They don't have to deal with people crossin' the street when they see you walk by.

Carla: It's like I said before. I feel like I was forced out of school . . . maybe lots of kids here were forced out, or just felt like they didn't fit in.

Leader: Well, I can't help but notice that you guys are talking about things that don't really include me because I'm one of those White people.

Malcolm: You're chill, man . . . but you can't really get what we're talking about.

Leader: This is true. You're talking about racism, something I have not experienced, but I have felt something else. Do you know what I am talking about?

The kids look confused.

Leader:	Anti-Semitism is what I am talking about. That basically means people who don't like Jews. In America, Jews are also a minority group.
Malcolm:	Really, I didn't know that. Did anyone else know that?
Carla:	I did, but I never thought about it like that, because Jews are White people.
Leader:	Right. And it's not the same because people can't see that you are Jewish the way they can see if you have dark skin. And by the way, not all Jews are White—there are many Black Jews as well. Some live in Africa, and many live in Spanish-speaking countries like Equador. Jews even live in China. And wherever they live, they look like the other people who live in those countries, only they are Jewish.
Shequan:	I didn't really know that.
Jose:	So how come all the kids here are Black and Latin? I don't see no White Jews and I don't see no Black Jews either, man, so what is the point?
Leader:	I don't know if there is a point. There's racism. Maybe that's why the kids are all Black and Latino. So in some ways we are very different, but I guess I wanted you to think about some ways in which we may share something. That's all.
Maria (who has been quiet during this conversation):	I think you are also trying to tell us not to only think about people shutting us out, because maybe there are some people who don't shut us out, like here in this school, like we just have to do it another way if the first way doesn't work.
Shequan:	Yeah, and like even though bad things happen to us, like maybe we ain't perfect either. Maybe we say things that hurt other people. Maybe we have to watch that.
Leader:	That's a really brave thing you just said, Shequan. I do think racism is a bad thing and it does bad things to people, and you guys are telling me the ways in which it hurt you, but I think maybe this whole thing got started because I don't want you to feel stuck in anger. I want you to pass that GED test and go to college if that is what you want to do, and be whatever you want to be. That's my point.

THEORETICAL ORIENTATION: STAGES OF GROUP DEVELOPMENT AND THE ROLE OF THE GROUP LEADER

The theoretical framework selected by the group leader guides the four stages of development that most groups pass through. It also influences how the group leader uses himself or herself differently and facilitates interaction differently during each stage. Conceptualizing group practice in this way can also help the group leader anticipate the thematic behaviors characteristic of each stage, recognize them when they occur, know how to intervene when they do, and evaluate whether this approach is working. The following examples demonstrate the application of two different theoretical models to group work with children and adolescents during the four stages of group development. Although the stages of group development form the conceptual background (general themes), the theory guides how these will be understood and implemented. The theories in these two examples are selected based on a rationale the leader explains from her understanding of the literature related to the problems and the challenges she is hoping to address with the children. These theories will also provide the background against which the leader will evaluate whether the goals of the group have been met. As Northern and Kurland (2001) write, "The practitioner has an ethical responsibility to practice within the realm of the accumulated theoretical base and tested interventions" (p. 448).

Example: The Detectives Club: A Narrative Approach to Group Work With Middle School Children

This is a group of children ages 10 to 12 who are having difficulties in school, in meeting classroom behavioral expectations, and in social interactions with peers. The children have been diagnosed with ADHD and referred to the group by school guidance counselors and physicians and therapists practicing in the community. The *Diagnostic and Statistical Manual of Mental Disorders,* fourth edition (*DSM-IV;* American Psychiatric Association, 1994) lists three types of ADHD—inattentive type, impulsive type, and combined type—and describes the disorder "as a discrete set of symptoms or behaviors that...ought to be distinguishable from normal childhood behavior." (See *DSM-IV* for a complete description of the characteristics for each of these conditions.) These symptoms manifest differently in each child (Barkley, 1997, 2012, 2013). (For example, girls tend to have more problems with attention and may engage in daydreaming, may have difficulty processing information and following directions, or may be shy and withdrawn. Girls with hyperactivity can generally be hyper-talkative, cry a lot, and slam doors, all behaviors that may not typically be associated with ADHD; About.com, n.d.)

The group leader uses narrative therapy as the theoretical model with this group. Narrative therapy is based on a postmodern, constructivist framework in which the therapist facilitates the deconstructing of problem-saturated stories and the reauthoring of new, empowering stories (Cooper & Lesser, 2008, p. 177). The goal of narrative therapy is to take apart the dominant story that is filled with problems and devise new stories that focus on the entire life experience of the person (Polkinghorne, 2004). Children referred for therapy with diagnoses of ADHD often arrive with self-esteem problems related to difficulties they have experienced at home, in school, and with peers and recount "dominant stories" about themselves that are not positive. Therefore, when narrative therapy is used as a framework for group work with children diagnosed with ADHD, the group leader seeks to promote conversations with the children that "emphasize the client's own knowledge, experience, and ideas for solutions" (Nylund, 2000, p. 46). According to Cattanach (1996), Waters (2011), and White (2007), the narrative therapist will encourage the children in the group to develop alternative and preferred stories about their lives.

The therapist combines the work of Debra Brooks (1998, as cited in Nylund, 2000), who coined the clever title of "The Detective Club" in her work with families of children diagnosed with ADHD, and Nylund's (2000, p. 50) five-step SMART approach to treating these children:

1. Separating the problem of ADHD from the child through the use of externalizing conversations

2. Mapping the influence of ADHD on the child and the family: A series of questions is designed to explore the strength of the problem relative to the strength of the child.

3. Attending to the exceptions to the ADHD story: The therapist looks for unique outcomes, or "sparkling moments," when the problem story is not the dominant one.

4. Reclaiming special abilities of children diagnosed with ADHD: The exceptions to the dominant story become the entry point to a new story, one of competence and ability. Questions are now asked to detail the child's history of hidden talents and successes.

5. Telling and celebrating the new story: The therapist engages the child in seeking out people in his life to corroborate and highlight the new story, "reworking the child's reputation."

Example: The Girls-Only Group: Self Psychology as a Framework in Group Therapy With Adolescent Girls Who Self-Injure

The group leader uses self psychology as a theoretical framework in a 12-week group for adolescent girls who self-injure through cutting behaviors. Self psychology theory is based on the centrality of empathy. Kohut (1984) defined empathy as "the capacity to think and feel oneself into the inner life of another person" (p. 82). Kohut felt that parents' failure to empathize with their children and the response of the children to these failures was at the core of all psychopathology. He also saw empathy as the scientific tool through which the therapist vicariously introspects his way into a patient's experience (Kohut, 1959/1978). The other central tenet of self psychology is the significance of selfobjects, or one's experience of interpersonal functions provided by another person as part of the self. Kohut (1971, 1977) defined three basic selfobject needs: (1) the mirroring selfobject recognizes a child's unique capabilities; (2) the idealizing selfobject links the child with admired caregivers; and (3) the twinship selfobject (also called alter ego or partnering selfobject) experience provides a sense of sameness with the selfobject that is essential to psychic growth, attainment of skills, and a sense of competence (Cooper & Lesser, 2008, p. 106). Palombo (2001) writes about the emergence of the self as revealing the child's experiences with significant others and the emergence of the self narrative as the child's integration of those experiences. He defines self narrative as "the broad set of communications through which children tell us about themselves that reflect the organization of their experiences" (p. 43). Persistent failures in phase-specific responses to the child's selfobject needs by caretakers can result in compulsive efforts by the adolescent to fill in missing psychological and self-regulatory functions. From a self-psychological perspective, self-injury behaviors such as cutting—deliberate and self-inflicted harm done without suicidal intent—can serve as a substitute for internal regulatory functions (Deiter, Nicholls, & Pearlman, 2000). When situations or feelings become intolerable and a youngster's distress exceeds his or her ability to cope, self-injury may reduce the extent and intensity of the feelings and provide "self-soothing" and a distraction from unacceptable feelings and anger (Connors, 2000; McAllister, 2003; Hollander, 2008; Strong, 1999). Straker (2006, p. 95) suggests that self-injury is an attempt to put together the different parts involved in the building of

(Continued)

(Continued)

self-identity. She also feels that cutting represents a means of communication when there are deficits in the capacity to process feelings through language. Farber (2002) agrees:

It is a salient voice and it is bodily language that must be decoded...there will be no sound...only unfelt and silent pain which makes its appearance in another pain, self inflicted, and when that second, collateral pain emerges it will articulate in blood or blisters the open definition you desire, although it may not be in a language you care to see. This, it says, is pain, and this is real in any language you care to speak. (p. 91)

Pregroup Contact

Recruitment for groups is a very important function and one that requires a great deal of thought. Whenever possible, the group leader should personally conduct an interview with potential group members. The purpose of this screening interview is to assess the particular needs of the child or adolescent, to determine his or her suitability for the group, to develop a beginning relationship or alliance with the prospective member and parents, to provide information about the group and how it might be beneficial to the youngster, and to clarify the goals and expectations of the leader and the members as well as the parents. It is important to address any potential fears or anxieties the children may have about joining a group, such as the following: Will I have to talk? What if I don't fit in? What if no one likes me? These may be some of the very issues that these potential group members have faced in their young lives. Another important issue to discuss with both children and parents is attendance and confidentiality, including the fact that you may not release any names of potential group members, and until the group actually meets they will not know

whether or not their attendance will be totally anonymous; in other words, the child or parent may know another child in the group (Smead, 2000). It is also important to remember that it may be more difficult to maintain confidentiality in a school setting where teachers and administrators will know who is participating in a group than, for example, in a private practice or mental health setting (Schneider Corey et al., 2013).

Legal and ethical constraints, such as what you can and cannot keep confidential, must be reviewed with potential group members and their parents or guardians. It is important to have both parents and older children and adolescents sign a written group contract that includes their understanding of these principles. An assessment interview should take place with each child, adolescent, and parent prior to joining the group, ending in a joint child/parent meeting during which the group contract may be introduced and signed. If the leader is accepting referrals from different sources, these sources must be acquainted with the purpose and structure of the group and the type of members the leader is interested in including (Smead, 2000; Bertram, 2011; Schneider Corey et al., 2013).

Example: The Detectives Club

The eight children in this group were recommended by school counselors, physicians, and other therapists in the community. The group included five girls and three boys between the ages of 9 and 11, all Caucasian, from working and lower- to middle-income families. All of the children carried a diagnosis of ADHD, and each was having significant academic, behavioral, and social problems. The leader scheduled a meeting with the parent(s) of each of the children to talk about the way in which the group would be run and to introduce the parent(s) to how narrative therapy works. She also met with each of the children to establish an initial therapeutic bond and to introduce them to narrative therapy. An excerpt from the screening interview with one of the children follows:

Dr. J: Hello Jane, I am Dr. J, and I am so happy to meet you. Your school counselor, Mr. P, thought you might be interested in a group I am starting. It's really kind of a club for kids. I'd like to tell you a little about it. But first let me ask you something, okay?

Jane: *(smiles, relaxing a bit in her seat)* Okay.

Dr. J: Since we are starting with names *(smiles also)* I want to ask you about a name that has been given to a problem your counselor tells me has been giving you some trouble in school. The name of this problem is ADHD. What do you know about this name?

Jane: It means that sometimes I get hyper.

Dr. J: Okay, so tell me, Jane, when did ADHD show up in your life and get you to act hyper?

Jane: I don't remember. I think maybe it was always in my life, but you know I am older now, and it gets in the way more because I am supposed to be doing my work and stuff in school and sometimes it's hard for me to sit still. I think, like when is this class going to be over.

Dr. J: I think I know what you mean, and that's exactly why I am starting this group. I call it the Detectives Club because I am hoping when we get together we can all figure out the ways that ADHD is showing up in kids' lives and figure out how to make it slow down or even stop when you don't want it showing up. What do you think? Would you be willing to come to a meeting and see how it goes? Would you like to join the Detectives Club?

Jane: Okay, sure, that sounds like fun.

Example: The Girls-Only Group

The seven girls selected for this group were all known to the group therapist, who had been working with each girl individually, weekly, for between 6 and 8 months. The girls were between the ages of 13 and 15 and included first-generation Caucasian and Latina teens whose parents had emigrated from another country. Kroger (2000) writes of the significance of sociohistorical events during an adolescent's identity formation. All the girls faced the pressure of acculturation into the majority culture, which conflicted with their parental values and expectations. They experienced internal conflicts related to beliefs about identity, guilt, betrayal of their parents' culture, and isolation when perceiving that they did not fit into either culture. The challenges and ability to cross back and forth between the conflicting worlds of family, peers, and school may not be easily negotiated by girls who self-injure. Isolation and alienation then become imposed from both sides of the cultural divide and can result in distorted perceptions and feelings that

(Continued)

(Continued)

they are not able to identify, understand, or verbalize (Stewart & Christner, 2007). These girls did not fit the profile of self-injurers who have a history of childhood trauma (see Farber, 2002). They were, however, experiencing significant attachment rupture with parental figures, particularly their mothers, and a profound sense of loss during an important developmental stage of life. Children of immigrants often assimilate into American culture more fully and faster than their parents. Acculturative stress results as these two generations face conflicts on issues such as sex roles, peer relations, and dating. These acculturative stresses are considered to be the key factors triggering psychosocial problems among immigrants and refugees. Rumbault (1994), in a large multiethnic study of over 5,000 second-generation students, found that the strongest predictor associated with lower self-esteem and higher depression in second-generation adolescents was parent-child conflict. Daughters struggled the most during the acculturation process. This may be due to the traditional parental attitudes about sex roles and dating contributing to the adolescent girl's identity crisis as she assimilates to the American teen culture. Girls' relationships with their mothers are particularly important during adolescence, as their fundamental gender identity develops in relation to their mothers. When such relational conflicts ensue and escalate, self-development and cultural identity can become divided, creating a division of loyalties (de las Fuentes & Vasquez, 1999).

Beginnings (Inclusion/Orientation)

The norms, values and purpose, and tone of the group are established during this time. Commonalities must be highlighted to establish the basis for communication and team building. Smead (1995, 2000) cautions about the formation of cliques, girls who come into the group already having a special connection or who develop connections within the group. During the initial phase of the group, this can inadvertently happen as members try to identify with members of the group who are perceived as being high status.

This jockeying for position is particularly powerful among middle school–age children who are anxious to be accepted in their social role. The leader must be sensitive to both verbal and nonverbal forms of communication, such as body language, tension, or affect that seems inappropriate to the content. The leader must also follow the manifest content of the group discussion as well as understand the latent content. "The manifest content consists of the literal and obvious meanings of the verbal messages; the latent content is what is below the threshold of superficial observation" (Northern & Kurland, 2001, p. 319).

Example: The Detectives Club

During the beginning sessions, the leader of the Detectives Club relies on externalizing to "consult the problem" (Nylund, 2000, p. 76; Roth & Epston, 1996). The following group exchange illustrates this technique.

Leader: Okay, guys, let's open this club's group meeting . . . how is everyone doing?

Children: *(shuffling of feet, giggling, glances at each other and at the leader)* Okay.

Leader: Well, let me tell you how happy I am to be here with all of you today. I know every one of you, but you don't know each other, and so we are going to introduce everybody to each other.

The leader gets a small ball from a basket in the corner of the room and asks the children to stand up in a circle.

Leader: When you get the ball the first time it comes around the circle, please say your name. The next time you get the ball you say where you go to school. The third time you can let me know what things you would like to know about each other. I will repeat these directions each time the ball is ready to start around the room, so you don't need to remember everything I am saying right now. Okay, I will start. I am Dr. Joan Lesser *(gently throwing the ball to the girl on her left)*. Say your name when you get the ball.

This continues until all the girls have said their names.

Leader: Okay, now that we all know each other I am going to ask you to help me out with understanding something. I put this club together because others have told me and you also have told me when I met with each of you that something called ADHD is causing some problems in your lives. Can you become detectives along with me to figure out a few things about ADHD? Let's get started. Oh, I have something for each of you.

The leader gives each girl a gold handmade detective badge printed with the girl's name. The children look interested and happy about the badges. They put them on, looking anticipatory and a little nervous, seeing how the badges look on each other.

Leader: Okay then, I also have a badge (puts on a badge with her name printed on it). First question for our detective club: "How does ADHD get in the way in your life?"

Melissa: I can go first. It gets in my way when I start fighting with my sister and I can't stop. The other night I threw something at her and had to go to my room.

Jennifer: Yeah, that happens to me too. And it also gets in my way at school sometimes because I get really bored and then I start tapping my pencil or my foot, and the teacher walks by my desk and puts her hand on it to remind me to stop, but I can't always stop.

Leader: These are great examples of how ADHD gets in your way. Anybody have any other examples to share?

Ashley: Yeah, ADHD gets in my way during recess sometimes when I get a time out from the monitor because she says I am getting "too wild." That really makes me mad because this is the time we are supposed to be free, right?

Leader: Well, what do some of you other girls think about this. Ashley is describing a way that ADHD gets in the way of her having fun. Does that happen to anyone else?

Emily: Well, I think it gets in the way sometimes when I am with my friends. I don't know. My mom tells me that sometimes I get bossy when I am with my friends or don't always listen to what they want to do.

(Continued)

(Continued)

Leader: Okay, now it sounds like your mom is thinking ADHD is getting in the way of your having fun with your friends. Let me ask if any of you other girls have moms or dads or even teachers telling you that ADHD is getting in the way of your having fun with your friends?

Jamie: Yeah, my mom tells me that sometimes too. Sometimes I get angry at her when she says it, though, and tell her that my friends are just making me mad.

Emily: I get angry at my mom too. It makes me feel like she is taking my friends' side over her own daughter when she says things like that.

Leader: Hmmm. I can see how you might feel that way. It's hard to be told by someone—even your mom—that you are doing something that maybe you don't agree with. And so let me ask you this: Is there any time when you yourself feel that ADHD is getting in the way of your having fun with your friends, Emily or Jamie or anyone else?

Carly: Well, I just had a big fight with my best friend, and I think ADHD got in the way. She wanted to do one thing, and I wanted to do something else, and I was just getting so frustrated because we started to do what she wanted, which was one computer game, and then I wanted to switch to my choice, but she wouldn't, and I started yelling at her and telling her to go home, that I didn't want her at my house anymore.

Jamie: Yeah, I guess that is ADHD getting in the way. Sometimes I think my friends are just making me mad, but maybe ADHD makes me too mad and I can't seem to stop myself.

Leader: Well now, how does ADHD convince you that you can't do anything to stop yourself? I mean that you can't do anything about it when it is making you get too mad?

Jamie: I don't know, it just comes over me.

Emily: Me too. My dad says that sometimes I just change into another person.

Leader: Well, it sounds to me like ADHD is making you sometimes do things that you might not want to be doing, but I think as detectives we can figure out a way to show ADHD that it can't just do things to you that you can't do anything about. What do you think? Shall we try to figure out some ways to fight back at ADHD?

Example: The Girls-Only Group

The major theme of the beginning stage (first two sessions) of this group was trust. The girls were concerned about being accepted by the other group members and focused on trying to figure out what behaviors were acceptable to their group peers. The leader took an active role by using and role modeling herself as a selfobject, helping the girls recognize similarities and differences in each other, and helping them find common ground. Elson (1986, p. 106) writes about the intense need adolescents have for selfobject peers, as alter egos—partners in the process of sharing their anxiety about changing body structure, as well as of defining and experiencing pleasure in their new freedom and power. From a self-psychological perspective, the group provides a safe space in which the girls can learn to understand each other and deal with relationships, meet selfobject needs, and promote self-understanding, especially when empathic failures are experienced and worked through (Levine & Mishna, 2007, p. 174).

A second theme during this early phase (Weeks 3 and 4) was the issue of shame about the cutting behaviors. The therapist uses herself as a selfobject, recognizing that the girls have not received much, if any, understanding from family and friends about why they cut. The leader's depth of understanding is related to her knowledge about cutting behaviors and their impact on relationships with others. The leader maintains an empathic stance that sets the relational tone for the group and mitigates the shame associated with the self-injurious behaviors (Shapiro, 1999).

The leader has just greeted the girls in the waiting room, where they were sitting in silence, not quite looking at each other, and invited them to follow her into the "room where we will be meeting."

Group therapist: Hello girls. I am so glad to see you are all here. I know you must be feeling a little weird since I know all of you and none of you know each other, but I will help with that. I just wanted to say a few words first. I have known each of you for some time and some of the struggles you have had that have resulted in your hurting yourself in some way—usually by cutting your leg or your arm. You all have that in common, as I shared with each of you when I told you about the group. That's the whole point—to give you all a place to talk about this with people your own age, not just with me. I think you will be able to help each other because you understand what cutting yourself is all about. And so now, let's just begin slowly. It will seem a little strange, but I am here to help. Let's just go around the room and say your name and one wish you have—nothing about money or clothes, okay. You know what I mean.

The girls smile, but their responses reflect their caution and some feelings of shame related to cutting themselves:

Carrie: I am Carrie, and I am feeling really scared right now. My wish is that I could stop thinking about cutting myself. Sometimes I just can't get it out of my mind.

Meg: I'm Meg. I really want to stop cutting myself also, and sometimes I do, but then I get so frustrated, and I start up again. I actually haven't cut myself in 3 months.

Anna: I'm Anna. Wow, that's a long time. I wish I could have a better relationship with my mom. We fight a lot, and then I get angry or I feel bad.

Susan: I'm Susan, and I wish my father wasn't such a big jerk. He makes promises to see me, and then he doesn't, and it makes me mad.

Patty: I'm Patty. I just wish I had cooler parents, period. They don't let me do anything. They don't trust me. Yeah, that's it, I wish they trusted me.

Jessica: I'm Jessica. Hi. I feel a little weird talking about what I do. I mean I know everyone does it too, but I still feel weird. I wish I didn't feel so weird.

(Continued)

(Continued)

Mary:	I'm Mary, and I just wish I could go to a different school where people didn't know all about me. They talk about me, you know, she's the one who cuts herself, she's strange.
Group therapist:	Thanks so much, girls. That was great. I know it isn't easy to meet new people and talk about something so personal, but I really think it is going to help, and I just want to say that I don't think any of you are weird, or strange. I think you are wonderful and brave to be here and learn a little more about what cutting yourself is all about. Maybe figure out a way to help your parents and other people get it and then, of course, because you have each heard me say this many times, to stop it because I don't want to see you hurt yourselves this way.

Middles (Uncertainty/Exploration)

There is an intensification of involvement during this phase, Weeks 4 through 9, both personally and as a group. This includes empathy, mutual acceptance, self-disclosure, and respect for differences. Conflict sometimes emerges during this stage in relation to the authority of the leader and to each other. Children and some adolescents do not have the verbal skills to deal with conflicts, and arguments can erupt during this phase of the group. Strong emotions, if handled correctly, can also help the youngsters feel a greater sense of connection to each other and to the group. Arguments must never be allowed to escalate into physical fighting. Facilitating group arguments and disagreements can help bring out different points of view and help the group members learn to tolerate differences.

Example: The Detectives Club

In the next illustration, the leader has moved to engaging the children in conversations about what is happening when ADHD is not causing them problems.

Leader:	Okay then, we have been spending a lot of time talking about when ADHD gets in the way. I would like us to be detectives in a different way now. When does ADHD have a really hard time getting to you? And what has been helping you in your fight against ADHD?
Abby:	Well, my teacher tells me that I am really funny and I make her laugh with my jokes. As long as I don't tell too many jokes, especially when we are not supposed to be talking.
Leader:	Okay then, that's a great example, Detective Abby. Anyone else?
Jessica:	Well, I know my friends think I am a lot of fun because I like to do different things and I'm really good at running. People usually want me to be on their teams.
Jane:	Me too. I get picked a lot for teams. That makes me feel good.
Sam:	So what you are saying is that these are times when it is okay for ADHD to be around, like it's okay to be a little hyper, or something like that.
Leader:	Exactly, Detective Sam. The reason I am asking about this is because I am wondering what ADHD gets you to think about yourselves?

Rachel: Well, sometimes it makes me feel bad, like people don't really like me because I get angry too fast or I don't listen when my mom tells me to do something.

Paul: Yeah, ADHD makes me think bad things about myself too, especially when other people call me a troublemaker and stuff like that and don't want to play with me.

Leader: Yeah, ADHD can be rough on kids sometimes and make you guys think bad things about yourself. That's why I think it is important to make sure you don't let ADHD convince you that it's always the boss or convince you that you can't do anything about it. I think we may need some help from some other people in your lives to let you know when ADHD is not in the way. I want to make sure that ADHD is not going to convince you that you can't do anything about it, and I bet there are times when you don't even know you are the one in charge of ADHD.

The group leader engages the children in writing letters to parents and teachers. The letter below has been adapted from one written by Nylund (2000, p. 127) in individual work with a child and his family.

Dear Mom and Dad/Teacher,

(Name of child) is working with me in a group with other children to get free of Trouble and its friend ADHD. *(Name of child)* sees that ADHD and its friend Trouble are making problems in his/her life. It may be hard for *(name of child)* to get rid of Trouble quickly. We would like your help in noticing and letting *(name of child)* know any time Trouble has given him/her the slip and not made a problem. Would you be willing to join *(name of child's)* team and notice any efforts he/she is making to get Trouble out of his/her life? These efforts may include handing in homework on time, listening in class, staying out of fights, not talking back to adults.

Many thanks for helping *(name of child)* and me.

Sincerely,

Joan Lesser, PhD

Example: The Girls-Only Group

The leader is focused in Sessions 4 through 9 on helping the girls stay attuned to each other, and she validates their experiences, helping them validate each other's. She also helps them recognize each girl's uniqueness, beginning the process of restoring damaged self-esteem. Issues related to

(Continued)

(Continued)

diversity emerge more clearly during this phase of the group. All the girls are engaged in a developmental process of separation and individuation that has become derailed. They face challenges as girls, such as feeling that boys only wanted to "hook up with them." The therapist uses the language of twinship (Kohut, 1971, 1977) to provide the context for a common human bond among the group members.

Group therapist:	Okay then, welcome to group meeting number five. Let's see, who might like to begin tonight. Anyone?
Carrie:	I had a really rough week. I broke up with my boyfriend because basically I found out he has been hooking up with other girls and lying to me. But then I got kind of scared and called him. He said it was probably good that we chill for a while. I felt horrible. I really wanted to cut myself. I used the ice cube instead like we talked about. That helped a little, but it's not the same.
Susan:	But that's great. You didn't cut yourself. I don't know I could be that strong if something like that happened to me.
Anna:	I feel the same way. I think what you did was great, Carrie. But can I ask you something. Why did you call him? Why did you want to go back with him? He sounds like a jerk.
Carrie (defensively):	He's not a jerk. He said he was sorry and everybody makes mistakes.
Patty:	Yeah, well I sort of agree with Anna. I'm sorry, Carrie, but he sounds like one of those guys who just wants to hook up with as many girls as he can, and maybe have a girlfriend too.
Group therapist:	Okay, girls, let's take a look at this together. I know you are all looking out for Carrie and want her to be happy and not get taken advantage of, but let's check in with her and see how she's feeling right now. Carrie?
Carrie (looking up cautiously):	I'm okay. *(looking down)* I feel kinda bad, like I have to defend Jay or maybe that you all think I'm stupid or something. It's just so hard to end this relationship. I really don't want to be alone, without a boyfriend.
Jessica:	I know how you feel, Carrie. Sometimes it just isn't so easy. I went out with a guy like Jay, and my mother and everyone else was so mad at me for not seeing that he wasn't treating me right. But I couldn't see it, and it just made me feel worse when everybody got mad at me. That was one of the times I cut myself really bad. I just took a razor and cut my leg until it started bleeding.
Patty:	I'm sorry, Carrie. I'm not mad at you. Maybe I came on too strong.
Group therapist:	You girls care about each other. I can see that, but it's hard sometimes to figure out the best way to show someone we care about them, especially when they won't listen to us *(said with some laughter)*. What do you think?
	The girls laugh together, and the tension lifts.

Group therapist:	But I do want to get back to what Jessica and Carrie were talking about because it is very, very important and we have talked about this before. Somehow when you feel bad and maybe feel people think you are bad or not doing the right thing . . . you hurt yourself.
Patty:	Yeah, but that doesn't work either because then they just think we are crazy.
Group therapist:	I understand. It creates another problem that you didn't really want to happen. But what I worry a lot about is that cutting yourself makes you feel better? Is that right?
	Several of the girls answer, "Yes, that's right. You got it."
	Group therapist (in a questioning tone): And that means that hurting yourself makes you feel better?
Patty:	Well, I never thought of it that way, but yes, I guess it does.
Carrie:	Yes, it definitely does.
	The other girls are silent but nod their heads affirmatively.
Group therapist:	So stay with me here, okay? I am wondering if hurting yourself makes you feel better, if you might feel that you deserve some sort of punishment. Usually, people feel they deserve punishment if they feel they have done something bad or sometimes even that they themselves are bad. Anybody ever feel that way?
	The girls are looking at the therapist intently now.
Anna:	That's it. Wow, it kind of all fits together.
Susan:	It kind of goes in a circle. Maybe that's why the ice cube doesn't always help. It doesn't really hurt as much as cutting does.
	Meg (who has been a more silent member of the group): You know. I do feel bad about myself a lot, especially when my parents don'tunderstand and think I am acting like I hate my family.
Mary:	I know. Me too, but I never really understood myself why I was cutting myself. To tell you the truth, it seemed weird even to me. But I just knew that I couldn't stop. I think I get it now.

Endings (Separation/Termination)

The leader and the group members may have conflicting feelings about the ending of the group. Questions that might be discussed during the termination phase of the group and used as a basis for evaluation of whether or not the group met its intended purpose include (1) whether the members and leader feel that the group served the purpose for which it was designed; (2) the special topics or experiences or problems the group may have faced during its tenure; (3) whether the group served any purpose in connecting to others in the environment or making an impact on a sponsoring agency; (4) what kinds of things might be done differently with future groups; and (5) what changes happened for individual members and with the group as a whole (Phillips & Markowitz, 1989, p. 89, cited in Malekoff, 2004, p. 70).

Example: The Detectives Club

During the final weeks of the group, the leader focuses on helping the children reclaim their special abilities from ADHD. Many children diagnosed with ADHD have creative abilities that fall outside the narrow ones that our society values most. Deficit descriptions need to be reevaluated and seen as creativity, imagination, a powerful intuitive sense, courage, and an ability to do many things at once. The following dialogue shows the group leader engaging the children in designing a school that would stand up to ADHD and bring the children's best talents into the classroom.

Leader: You know, I would really love to have your help in designing a school that you guys think would really bring your best talents into the classroom. Can you help me out with that? Let's figure it out a little, and then it might be fun if we drew this school. I have a very long roll of paper that would give everyone room to take part when we are ready. Okay, let's go, then. What would this school be like?

Sam: Well, first of all there would be more time for recess, and we would be able to go out and play even when it is cold or bad weather.

Jessica: I would like more time for art projects. Just when I am getting into something, it is time to stop.

Jane: I don't think we should have the kids sitting so much of the time. Maybe we could do some exercises or take a walk or something like that. Not at recess, but sometimes during a boring class.

Abby: I would never have mean teachers in a school like this. I would only have teachers who are nice to the kids, even when the kids are being bad.

Leader: Well these are all very good ideas. Let's take some markers and try to draw what this school would look like, shall we?

The leader rolls out a long sheet of white paper, and the children take their places lying on the floor in front of the paper and begin to draw.

In the final group meeting, the leader ends with a game called Magic Glasses (Brandler & Roman, 1999, p. 320). The group leader brings in a decorated, nonsensical pair of large eyeglasses that look magical. All the children get a chance to put on the glasses and share with the other group members what they learned that was pretty magical or wonderful about themselves. Some of their sharing follows:

Jane: I learned that I am a good friend because I never ever say mean things about anybody!

Bobby: I am a lot of fun to be around!

Jessica: I am a really good artist!

Jennifer: I am a good friend too. Oh, and I also learned that I can do my homework really fast—sometimes.

Example: The Girls-Only Group

In this last stage of the group, Weeks 10, 11, and 12, the girls began to show signs of autonomy, giving each other constructive feedback regarding how to handle their feelings and stop cutting. At this stage of the group, the leader encourages the girls to talk about how they will carry what they learned in the group to their relationships outside the group. The girls engage in identifying triggers to their cutting behaviors. Interpersonal challenges, such as inability to express anger, are now more openly handled by the group members but within a context of empathic connection. The leader ends the group with the farewell circle (Malekoff, 2004, p. 197).

Group therapist: And so we were talking about how when other people let you down or you feel they don't like you, you think the reason may be because you aren't such a good friend or a good person or maybe you just feel lonely and scared. What will you do the next time something like this happens?

Carrie: Well, the first thing I am going to do is to remember what we said here—that it doesn't mean I did anything wrong.

Patty: I am going to try to talk with my mom more. I know she is trying too.

Anna: I think I am going to try to tell my mom before I do anything like cutting myself or anything like that. Maybe I will also run around the block a few times.

The leader invites the girls to stand and form a circle with their backs to one another. She says, "Remember how you first felt when you came into the group." She then asks the girls to take a step forward, and she says, "As time went by, and you got to know one another, it was not so scary." The leader asks the girls to take another step forward and says, "Then you became closer still." Some of the girls are crying. The leader asks them now to take a step backward: "Now that the group is ending, you will be moving away." She asks them to take another step back. "You will have a chance to take what you have learned from here." She asks them to take another step back. "The time together and the relationships won't be forgotten." The leader asks the group members to take one last step back and then to turn and face each other. All the girls are now crying. There is a silence, giving the girls time to reflect.

Group therapist: I would like anyone who wants to share what the group has meant to them or what they learned about themselves or each other. I would like to begin *(looking around at each girl and smiling)*. Thank you so much for coming to this group and sharing with me and with each other. It has meant a lot to me to be able to work with each and every one of you. I think you are wonderful girls who have so much to offer the world, and I am so glad to have been a part of your lives for the time we shared in this group.

Anna: I learned that other people feel the same way that I do, and that makes me feel more normal.

Susan: I learned that I can help other girls like me, and that means a lot.

Patty: I feel really sad to be ending this group, but it helped me a lot. Sometimes I just think about the things we talked about here every week, and it makes me feel better when I am down.

GROUPS FOR PARENTS AND CAREGIVERS OF CHILDREN AND ADOLESCENTS

Therapists who work with children and adolescents in groups may want to consider concurrent parent education groups, as these are an important adjunct to group work with children and adolescents. The first formal parent education program—Systematic Training in Effective Parenting (STEP)—was based on Adlerian theory and methods. These generally combine psychological education about child development and basic behavioral techniques that focus on praise to encourage prosocial behavior and the consequences for misbehavior (Dinkmeyer, McKay, & Dinkmeyer, 1973). Communication and active listening skills are also popular components of parent groups (Gordon, 2000). "The general goals of most parent education programs is to improve parents' knowledge, alter the way they think about themselves and their children, build skills and expand behavioral repertoires" (Christner, Stewart, & Freeman, 2007, p. 469). There are times, however, when skills training for parents is not enough, and parents may need help to use the skill. Therefore, the leader of the Girls-Only Group ran a simultaneous group for the mothers of these girls—the Moms Group.

Group Example: The Moms Group

Elson (1986, p. 93) writes about the "unique significance of the ongoing process of the experience of self and other in parents and children." Parents as selfobjects during the developmental phase of adolescence have the greatest need for flexibility and strength in reviewing and expanding their own values. They go through upheaval along with their adolescent children during this time. Immigrant parents are challenged to examine the validity and importance of values and beliefs that have been intrinsic to their own cohesive functioning. For example, parents may be excessively punitive and counterproductive to the adolescent's development or unrealistic in relation to the adolescent's interests. One Latina mother described how confused she felt when her daughter wanted to celebrate her sweet 16 birthday rather than her *quinceañera,* which in their Dominican culture was a very important milestone for a girl.

Consistent with self psychological principles, the purpose of the group was to strengthen the parents through empathic understanding of their experience and to promote the parents' empathy for the child's experience, which is informed by knowledge of the cutting behaviors (Amerogen & Mishna, 2004; Palombo, 2001). Leone (2001) writes, "Educating interventions are indicated only if they constitute an empathically attuned response to the parents' selfobject needs at the moment" (p. 278). The parents were eager to participate and learn ways in which they could help their children "stop cutting themselves," and over the 12 weeks the group met, the parents talked about their own teenage experiences, their hopes and dreams for their children, and the ways they perhaps needed to listen more to the struggles their adolescents faced in today's world. These parents were well-meaning but not able to provide their adolescent daughters with the selfobject experiences they needed, especially from their mothers, during this stage of their development. The mothers, understandably struggling with their own fears about raising their daughters in a society they did not grow up in and felt disconnected from, inadvertently were putting a wedge in their relationships with their daughters at a crucial developmental juncture. The leader uses herself as a selfobject for the parents, providing an opportunity for them to share their own adolescent experiences and then moving them toward an appreciation of what their children are facing as first-generation Americans. Finally, the group leader uses informed empathy (Palombo, 2001) to educate the parents about the cutting behaviors.

Mrs. A: (in an angry, frustrated voice): I don't understand this type of behavior *(referring to her daughter's cutting her leg with a sharp knife until she draws blood)*. It is not normal.

Mrs. J: I don't understand it either. It makes me feel angry and sad at the same time. She has so much that I didn't have in my life. I never knew anyone who did this type of thing.

Mrs. R: I know, but the girls today—they have too much time on their hands, and they want too many things. I don't think it is good for them.

Mrs. T (crying softly):   I feel like a bad mother, that my daughter is doing this to herself. People will think she comes from a bad home. We came to this country to give our children a better life, and instead, we have our daughter hurting herself like this. I want her to be happy, but I don't know how to make her happy.

Group therapist (looking around the room):   I can hear how sad and confused and angry you are. This is very hard, I can see that. I also hear that your own experiences as teenagers in your countries have been very different from your daughters'. Would it be helpful to talk about those experiences? What was it like when you were 15 where you grew up?

The women share some of their experiences as teenagers in their respective countries.

Group therapist: I can see that it was very different for you. It is understandable that you would wonder what is making your daughters so upset when they seem to have a much easier life than you had. I think maybe your girls are struggling because their life is so different from their mothers', from yours. What I mean by this is that they love you, even though right now it does not seem that way, but they may feel that you cannot completely understand what they are dealing with as American teenagers. Do you think this makes any sense?

Mrs. A: I don't know, maybe. I know my daughter doesn't think I know anything anymore. All she cares about is going out with her friends.

Mrs. J: But I know it is hard for my daughter. She tells me that other kids can do things she is not allowed to do; they stay out later than she does, go to parties. She wants to do this too, and then we fight.

Mrs. P: Our values are our values. We are different from American parents, and I am not going to change my values. She has to understand that.

Group therapist: I can see what a struggle this is for all of you as parents, and for your daughters also. You grew up in one world. They are growing up in another world. I am wondering if we

(Continued)

(Continued)

	can figure out a way that you can all talk with your daughters about what life is like for them—as teenagers here in America—with parents who did not grow up in America. What do you think? It doesn't mean you have to change your values or the way you parent, but maybe it will help.
Mrs. T:	I think sometimes I am quick to say no to things because I am afraid, and then my daughter, she gets angry with me, and then we fight.
Group therapist:	And I know that is hard for both of you, and for the rest of you parents when that sort of thing happens with your daughters. I think it may also be hard for the girls, again, because I believe they love their mothers very much, and they need you to understand their struggles as kids growing up and trying to find their way. They are first-generation Americans and that means in some ways they are pathfinders. You gave them that opportunity, but it means they will do some things differently from what you did, and maybe from what you would like. Can we talk more about that?

CONCLUSION

This chapter discussed group work with children and adolescents, reviewing salient group work principles and offering select examples. It seems important to end the chapter with some commentary about group leaders, who they are, and what makes them want to and be able to do this type of work. In 1992, Middleman wrote this about group workers:

> Group workers were different, often were thought of as unprofessional by the caseworkers. They were workers who enjoyed having a meal or a party with their people, who used activities like singing and dancing, who weren't neutral but shared their beliefs. (p. 26)

Kurland and Salmon (2006, pp. 78–83) describe several characteristics of social workers who are drawn to group work and hold these to be intrinsic to their worldview:

1. A belief in the strength of the group members

2. A belief in the importance of mutual aid

3. Excitement in the unpredictability of the group

4. An acceptance of their own fallibility, a corollary to sharing control

5. A view of conflict and differences of opinion as natural, not threatening

6. An appreciation for the commonalities of the human experience, despite differences

7. Comfort with their own authority

8. Creativity

Therapists who conduct treatment groups with children and adolescents must also be able to form a relationship with clients who are in a developmental stage of life they may have left behind. Toffel (2005) suggests that those working with youth learn "a lot about the pop culture world that adolescents inhabit" (p. 36). I would add that the same is true of younger children, who smile with glee when you are able to draw on current television shows, books, sports, or movie star icons in group conversation and activities. This involves seeing movies you might avoid, reading books you have outgrown, and listening to music you may dislike. This should not be done to portray a false sense of being cool but to try to understand the world that children and adolescents are exposed to and live in and to be able to engage with them about that world. Group therapists who work with children and adolescents must also be prepared to provide adult guidance so that "your voice and advice become an ongoing presence in a teen's psyche" (p. 27). It helps therapists to reflect on their own experiences as children and adolescents. This includes memories of groups they belonged to, beginning of course with membership in their own families. Group therapists must also reflect on the nature and quality of their relationship with each member of the group as well as with the group as a collective. They must consider the qualities of empathy, acceptance, genuineness, adherence to ethical principles, and the ability to accept and respond to both positive and negative feelings expressed toward themselves and between the members. They must also consider their role as leaders and the extent to which they use this role to provide emotional support and to help members support each other. The leader must be willing to engage with the members in a collaborative evaluation of their experience. This process leads to competence, which is "the performance of roles with integrity, knowledge and skill" (Northern & Kurland, 2001, p. 447). Schneider Corey et al. (2013) offer the following competencies for conducting groups with children and adolescents:

(1) A thorough understanding of developmental stages and tasks; (2) good understanding of group process as it pertains to working with children and adolescents; (3) awareness and skills to work effectively with children and adolescents within a multicultural framework; (4) supervised training in working with children and adolescents in groups before leading a group alone; (5) knowledge of research related to group counseling with children and adolescents; and (6) a clear understanding of expectation from the school or organization where the groups are being conducted. (p. 334)

In summary,

Group leaders need to appreciate both the science and the art of group work practice: a combination of professional knowledge based on literature and research and heartfelt practice that is open to the creative possibilities that are created when people come together. (Steinberg, 2006, p. 26)

REFERENCES

About.com. (n.d.). *ADD/ADHD.* Retrieved March 10, 2009, from http://add.about.com/od/adhdthebasics/a/Inherited-ADHD.htm

American Psychiatric Association. (1994). *Diagnostic and statistical manual of mental disorders* (4th ed.). Washington, DC: Author.

Amerogen, M., & Mishna, F. (2004). Learning disabilities and behavior problems: A self psychological approach to working with parents. *Psychoanalytic Social Work, 11*(2), 33–53.

Association for Play Therapy (2008), Retrieved from http://www.a4pt.org

Axline, V. (1947). *Play therapy.* Boston, MA: Houghton Mifflin.

Barkley, R. A. (1997). Behavioral inhibition, sustained attention, and executive function: Constructing a unifying theory of ADHD. *Psychological Bulletin, 121,* 65–94.

Barkley, R. A. (2012). *Deficits in executive functioning scale–children and adolescents (BDEFS-CA).* New York, NY: Guilford Press.

Barkley, R. A. (2013). *Taking charge of ADHD, Revised edition: The complete, authoritative guide for parents.* New York, NY: Guilford Press.

Bertram, B. (2011). Ethics and légal issues for group work. In T. Fitch & J. L. Mashall (Eds.) *Group work and outreach plans for collège counselors* (pp. 9–17). Alexandria, VA : American Counseling Association.

Brandler, S., & Roman, C. (1999). *Group work: Skills and strategies for effective interventions* (2nd ed.). New York, NY: Haworth Press.

Brown, L. (1991). *Groups for growth and change.* New York, NY: Longman.

Butler, J. (1999). *Gender trouble: Feminism and subversion of identity.* New York, NY: Routledge.

Calhoun, C. (2000). *Feminism, the family and the politics of the closet: Lesbian and gay displacement.* New York, NY: Oxford University Press.

Cass, V. (1979). Homosexual identity formation: A theoretical model. *Journal of Homosexuality, 4,* 219–235.

Cass, V. (1984). Homosexual identity formation: Testing a theoretical model. *Journal of Sex Research, 20,* 143–167.

Cass, V. (1990). The implications of homosexual identity formation for the Kinsey model and scale of sexual preference. In D. McWhirter, S. Sanders, & J. Reinish (Eds.), *Homosexuality/heterosexuality: Concepts of sexual orientation* (pp. 23–66). New York, NY: Oxford University Press.

Cattanach, A. (1996). The use of drama therapy and play therapy to help de-brief children after the trauma of sexual abuse. In A. Gersie (Ed.), *Dramatic approaches to brief therapy* (pp. 177–187). London, UK: Jessica Kingsley.

Chodorow, N. (1973). *The reproduction of mothering.* Berkeley: University of California Press.

Christner, R. W., Stewart, J. L., & Freeman, A. (Eds.). (2007). *Handbook of cognitive-behavior group therapy with children and adolescents.* New York, NY: Routledge.

Comas-Diaz, L. (2011). Mulitcultrual theories of psychotherapy. In R. Corsini & D. Wedding (Eds.) *Current psychotherapies* (9th ed.). (pp. 536–567). Belmont, CA: Brooks/Cole, Cengage Learning.

Connors, K. M., Schamess, G., & Strieder, F. H. (1997). Children's treatment groups. In J. R. Brandell (Ed.), *Theory and practice in clinical social work* (pp. 288–314). New York, NY: Free Press.

Connors, R. (2000). *Self-injury: Psychotherapy with people who engage in self-inflicted violence.* Northvale, NJ: Jason Aronson.

Cooper, M., & Lesser, J. G. (2008). *Clinical social work practice* (3rd ed.). Boston, MA: Allyn & Bacon.

Corsini, R. L., & Wedding, D. (Eds). (2011). Current psychotherapies (9th ed.). Belmont, CA: Brooks/Cole, Cengage Learning.

Davies, D. (2004). *Child development: A practitioner's guide* (2nd ed.). New York, NY: Guilford Press.

DeGangi, G.A., & Nemiroff, M. (2011). *Kids' club letters: Narrative tools for stimulating process and dialogue in therapy groups for children and adolescents.* New York, NY: Taylor & Francis Books.

Deiter, P. J., Nicholls, S. S., & Pearlman, L. A. (2000). Self-injury and self-capacities: Assisting an individual in crisis. *Journal of Clinical Psychology, 56*(9), 1173–1191.

de las Fuentes, C., & Vasquez, M. J. T. (1999). Immigrant adolescent girls of color: Facing American challenges. In N. G. Johnson, M. C. Roberts, & J. Worell (Eds.), *Beyond appearance: A new look at adolescent girls* (pp. 151–175). Washington, DC: American Psychological Association.

Dies, D. R. (1996). The unfolding of adolescent groups: A five phase model of development. In P. Kymissis & D. A. Halperin (Eds.), *Group therapy with children and adolescents* (pp. 35–53). Washington, DC: American Psychiatric Press.

Dinkmeyer, D., McKay, G. D., & Dinkmeyer, D. (1973). *Systematic training for effective parenting.* Lebanon, IN: Pearson.

Elson, M. (1986). *Self psychology in clinical social work.* New York, NY: W. W. Norton.

Erikson, E. (1950). *Childhood and society* New York, NY: W. W. Norton.

Erikson, E. (1959). *Identity and the life cycle: Vol. 1. Selected papers, psychologial issues.* New York, NY: International Universities Press.

Farber, S. K. (2002). *When the body is the target: Self-harm, pain, traumatic attachments.* Northvale, NJ: Jason Aronson.

Feldstein Ewing, S.W., Walters, S.T., & Baer, J.S. (2013). Motivational interviewing for adolescents and emerging adults. In C. C. Wagner & K. S. Ingersoll (Eds.). *Motivational interviewing in groups.* (pp. 387–406). New York, NY: Guilford Press.

Freud, S. (1905). *Three essays on the theory of sexuality* (J. Strachey, Trans.). London, UK: Imago Publishing.

Gallo-Lopez, L., & Schaefer, C. (2010). *Play therapy with adolescents.* Northvale, NJ: Jason Aronson.

Germain, C. (1991). *Human behavior and the social environment.* New York, NY: Columbia University Press.

Gilligan, C. (1982). *In a different voice: Psychological theory and women's development.* Cambridge, MA: Harvard University Press.

Gordon, T. (2000). *Parent effectiveness training: The proven program for raising responsible children.* New York, NY: Crown.

Hays, D.G., Arredonto, P., Gladding, S.T., & Toporek, R.L. (2010). Integrating social justice in group work: The next decade. *Journal for Specialists in Group Work, 35*(2), 177–206.

Hollander, M. (2008). *Helping teens who cut: Understanding and ending self-injury.* New York, NY: Guilford Press.

Indiana University. (n.d.). *G532: Introduction to group counseling.* Retrieved November 10, 2008, from www.iupui.edu/~flip/g532kids.html

Jagendorf, J., & Malekoff, A. (2000). Groups-on-the-go: Spontaneously formed mutual aid groups for adolescents in distress. *Social Work With Groups, 22*(4), 15–32.

Johnson, C. V., Riester, A. E., Corbett, C., Buehler, A., Huffaker, L., Levich, K., et al. (1998). Group activities for children and adolescents: An activity group therapy approach. *Journal of Child and Adolescent Group Therapy, 8*(2), 71–88.

Kail, R. V. (2001). *Children and their development* (4th ed.). New York, NY: Prentice Hall.

Kohlberg, L. (1984). *The psychology of moral development: The nature and validity of moral stages* (Essays on Moral Development, Vol. 2). New York, NY: Harper & Row.

Kohut, H. (1971). *The analysis of the self.* New York, NY: International Universities Press.

Kohut, H. (1977). *The restoration of the self.* New York, NY: International Universities Press.

Kohut, H. (1978). Introspection, empathy and psychoanalysis: An examination of the relationship between mode of observation and theory. In P. Ornstein (Ed.), *The search for the self: Selected writings of Heinz Kohut, 1950–1978* (Vol. 1, pp. 205–232). New York, NY: International Universities Press. (Original work published 1959)

Kohut, H. (1984). *How does analysis cure?* Chicago, IL: University of Chicago Press.

Kroger, J. (2000). *Identity development: Adolescence through adulthood.* Thousand Oaks, CA: Sage.

Kurland, R. (1978). Planning: The neglected component of group development. *Social Work With Groups, 1*(2), 173–178.

Kurland, R., & Salmon, R. (2006). Making joyful noise: Presenting, promoting, and portraying group work to and for the profession. In A. Malekoff, R. Salmon, & D. M. Steinberg (Eds.), *Making joyful noise: The art, science and soul of group work* (pp. 73–90). Binghamton, NY: Haworth Press.

LeCroy, C. W., & Archer, J. C. (2001). Teaching social skills: A board game approach. In C. E. Schaefer & S. E. Reid (Eds.), *Game play: Therapeutic use of childhood games* (pp. 331–345). New York, NY: Wiley.

Leone, C. (2001). Toward a more optimal selfobject milieu: Family psychotherapy from the perspective of self psychology. *Clinical Social Work Journal, 29*(3), 269–289.

Lesser, J. G., & Pope, D. S. (2007). *Human behavior and the social environment: Theory and practice.* Boston, MA: Allyn & Bacon.

Levine, D., & Mishna, F. (2007). A self psychological and relational approach to group therapy for university students with bulimia. *International Journal of Group Psychotherapy, 57*(2), 167–185.

Malekoff, A. (2004). *Group work with adolescents: Principles and practice* (2nd ed.). New York, NY: Guilford Press.

McAllister, M. (2003). Multiple meanings of self harm: A critical review. *International Journal of Mental Health Nursing, 12*(3), 177–185.

Middleman, R. (1992). Group work and the Heimlich maneuver: Unchoking social work education. In D. Fike & B. Rittner (Eds.), *Working from strengths: The essence of group work* (pp. 16–39). Miami, FL: Center for Group Work Studies.

Mishna, F., & Muskat, B. (2004). "I'm not the only one!" Group therapy with older children and adolescents who have learning disabilities. *International Journal of Group Psychotherapy, 54*(4), 455–476.

Naar-King, S., & Suarez, M. (2011). *Motivational interviewing with adolescents and young adults.* New York, NY: Guilford Press.

Naumburg, C. (2007). Judaism: A hidden diversity. *Smith College Studies in Social Work, 77*(2/3), 79–99.

Northern, H., & Kurland, R. (2001). *Social work with groups* (3rd ed.). New York, NY: Columbia University Press.

Nylund, D. (2000). *Treating Huckleberry Finn: A new narrative approach to working with kids diagnosed with ADD/ADHD.* San Francisco, CA: Jossey-Bass.

O'Connor, K. (2000). *The play therapy primer* (2nd ed.). New York, NY: Wiley.

Orange, D. M., Atwood, G. E., & Stolorow, R. D. (1997). *Working intersubjectively: Contextualism in psychoanalytic practice.* New York, NY: Analytic Press.

Palombo, J. (2001). *Learning disorders and disorders of the self in children and adolescents.* New York, NY: W. W. Norton.

Piaget, J. (1952). *The origins of intelligence in children.* New York, NY: International Universities Press. (Original work published 1936)

Polkinghorne, D.E. (2004). Narrative therapy and postmodernism. In L.E. Angus & J. McLeod (Eds.). *The handbook of narrative and psychotherapy* (pp. 53–67). Thousand Oaks, CA: Sage.

Roth, S., & Epston, D. (1996). Consulting the problem about the problematic relationship: An exercise for experiencing a relationship with an externalized problem. In M. F. Hoyt (Ed.), *Constructive therapies* (Vol. 2, pp. 148–162). New York, NY: Guilford Press.

Rumbault, R. G. (1994). The crucible within: Ethnic identity, self esteem, and segmented assimilation among children of immigrants. *International Migration Review, 28,* 748–794.

Salovey, P., & Sluyter, D. J. (Eds.). (1997). *Emotional development and emotional intelligence: Educational implications.* New York, NY: Basic Books.

Schaefer, D. E., & Reid, S. E. (Eds.). (2001). *Game play: Therapeutic use of childhood games.* New York, NY: Wiley.

Schneider Corey, M., Corey, G., & Corey, C. (2013). *Groups: Process and practice.* Belmont, CA: Brooks/Cole.

Schwartz, W. (1986). Between client and system: The mediating function. In R. Roberts & H. Northern (Eds.), *Theories of social work with groups* (pp. 171–197). New York, NY: Columbia University Press.

Shapiro, E. (1999). Trauma, shame and group psychotherapy: A self psychology perspective. *Group, 23,* 51–65.

Sharf, R.S. (2012). *Theories of psychotherapy and counseling: Concepts and cases* (5th ed.). Belmont, CA: Brooks/Cole, Cengage Learning.

Shelby, J. S. (1997). Rubble, disruption, and tears: Helping young survivors of natural disaster. In H. G. Kaduson, D. M. Cangelosi, & C. E. Schaefer (Eds.), *The playing cure: Individualized play therapy for specific childhood problems* (pp. 143–169). Northvale, NJ: Jason Aronson.

Shulman, L. (1985). The dynamics of mutual aid. *Social Work With Groups, 8*(4), 51–60.

Shulman, L. (1992). *The skills of helping: Individuals, families and groups* (3rd ed.). Itasca, IL: F. E. Peacock.

Slavson, S. R. (1943). *An introduction to group therapy.* New York, NY: International Universities Press.

Slavson, S. R. (1999). Play group therapy for young children. In D. S. Sweeney & L. E. Homeyer (Eds.), *The handbook of group play therapy: How to do it, how it works and whom it's best for* (pp. 24–35). San Francisco, CA: Jossey-Bass.

Smead, R. (1995). *Skills and techniques for group work with children and adolescents.* Champaign, IL: Research Press.

Smead, R. (2000). *Skills and techniques for group work with children and adolescents* (2nd ed.). Champaign, IL: Research Press.

Steen, S., Bauman. S., & Smith, J. (2008). The preparation of professional school counselors for group work. *Journal for Specialists in Group Work, 33*(4), 335–350.

Steinberg, D. M. (2006). The art, science, heart and ethics of social group work: Lessons from a great teacher. In A. Malekoff, R. Salmon, & D. M. Steinberg (Eds.), *Making joyful noise: The art, science and soul of group work* (pp. 3–47). Binghamton, NY: Haworth Press.

Stern, D. N. (1977). *The first relationship: Mother and infant.* Cambridge, MA: Harvard University Press.

Stern, D. N. (1985). *The interpersonal world of the infant.* New York, NY: Basic Books.

Stewart, J. L., & Christner, R. W. (2007). Future directions in CBT group treatments. In R. W. Christner, J. L. Stewart, & A. Freeman (Eds.), *Handbook of cognitive-behavior group therapy with children and adolescents* (pp. 509–513). New York, NY: Routledge.

Stewart, J. L., Christner, R. W., & Freeman, A. (Eds.). (2007). *Handbook of cognitive-behavioral group therapy with children and adolescents.* New York, NY: Routledge.

Stolorow, R. D. (1994a). The nature and therapeutic action of psychoanalytic interpretation. In R. D. Stolorow & G. E. Atwood (Eds.), *The intersubjective perspective* (pp. 43–55). Northvale, NJ: Jason Aronson.

Stolorow, R. D. (1994b). Subjectivity and self psychology. In R. D. Stolorow & G. E. Atwood (Eds.), *The intersubjective perspective* (pp. 31–42). Northvale, NJ: Jason Aronson.

Stolorow, R. D., & Atwood, G. D. (1992). *Contexts of being: The intersubjective foundations of psychological life.* Hillsdale, NJ: Analytic Press.

Straker, G. (2006). Signing with a scar: Understanding self-harm. *Psychoanalytic Dialogues, 16,* 93–112.

Strong, M. (1999). *A bright red scream: Self-mutilation and the language of pain.* New York, NY: Penguin.

Strong, T. (2002). Collaborative "expertise" after the discursive turn. *Journal of Psychotherapy Integration, 12*(2), 218–232.

Sue, D. W., & Sue, D. (2003). *Counseling the culturally different* (4th ed.). New York, NY: Wiley.

Tijhuis, L. (1998). Peers as the "guardian angels" of individuation in the therapy group: Ego supportive group therapy for children and adolescents. *Journal of Group Analytic Psychotherapy, 31*(1), 547–564.

Toffel, R. (2005). *Breaking through to teens: A new psychotherapy for the new adolescence.* New York, NY: Guilford Press.

Toseland, R. W., & Rivas, R. F. (2001). *An introduction to group work practice* (2nd ed.). Needham Heights, MA: Allyn & Bacon.

Vygotsky, L. S. (1978). *Mind in society: The development of higher mental processes.* Cambridge, MA: MIT Press.

Wagner, C.C., & Ingersoll, K.S. (2013). *Motivational interviewing in groups.* New York, NY: Guilford Press.

Walsh, F. (1996). The concept of family resilience: Crisis and challenge. *Family Process, 35,* 261–281.

Waters, K.R. (2011). The hungry-for-attention metaphor: Integrating narrative and behavioral therapy for families with attention seeking children. *The Australian and New Zealand Journal of Family Therapy, 32*(3).

Webb, N. B. (Ed.). (1999). *Play therapy with children in crisis* (2nd ed.). New York, NY: Guilford Press.

Weber, A. M., & Haen, C. (Eds.). (2005). *Clinical applications of drama therapy in child and adolescent treatment.* New York, NY: Brunner/ Routledge.

White M. (2007). *Maps of narrative practice.* New York, NY: W.W. Norton.

Wood, D. (2000). *Group therapy for adolescents.* Retrieved January 29, 2009, from www.healersoul .org/comments

11

GROUP TREATMENT WITH ADULTS

CHARLES D. GARVIN

A variety of approaches are currently employed for group treatment of adults by social workers. Some workers have a preferred approach, while others draw on several approaches depending on the purpose of the group. The ways in which these workers act differ depending on the approach they have chosen, but there are also common elements.

PRACTICE MODELS FOR GROUP TREATMENT WITH ADULTS

Group work in social work did not start with a variety of models but rather started when people who were developing practice in certain community institutions in the latter part of the 19th and early 20th centuries began to share their ideas with each other. Examples of these institutions were settlement houses, Jewish community centers, and Young Men's and Young Women's Christian Associations (YM/YWCAs), and some of these people were Jane Addams, Grace Coyle, Gertrude Wilson, and Clara Kaiser. The ideas of these group work

pioneers related to how to help people, primarily in the inner city, through the processes of mutual aid. These group work pioneers were also interested in helping people learn and use democratic processes in groups to enable them to cope with their circumstances as well as to achieve changes in their environments.

These pioneers did not think of their method as group therapy, but in the 1950s and early 1960s, a number of group workers in social work began to test the use of the group work method in psychotherapy settings (Konopka, 1949; National Association of Social Workers, 1960). This type of application rapidly spread to other institutions such as prisons, schools, hospitals, family agencies, and child welfare organizations, in which social workers offered various forms of treatment. This expansion of the settings in which group work methods were employed was associated with an expansion in the therapeutic approaches employed.

The Mediational Model

The creation of this model is usually attributed to William Schwartz (1994), although it has undergone considerable development by Alex Gitterman and Lawrence Shulman (Gitterman, 2004; Gitterman & Shulman, 1994; Steinberg, 2010). These authors pay great attention to the processes that occur among group members and between members and social workers as these people seek to develop authentic and mutually beneficial relationships. Serious attention is paid to the feelings members and workers experience in this process. This approach seeks to be systemic in that the various relevant systems are taken into consideration by the worker, who acts as a mediator between these systems. As Schwartz (1994) states,

> We would suggest that the general assignment for the social work profession is to mediate the process through which the individual and his society reach out for each other through a mutual need for self-fulfillment. This presupposes a relationship between the individual and his nurturing group which we would describe as "symbiotic"—each needing the other for its own life and growth, and each reaching out to the other with all the strength it can command at a given moment. The social worker's field of intervention lies at the point where two forces meet: the individual's impetus toward health, growth, and belonging; and the organized efforts of society to integrate its parts into a productive and dynamic whole. (pp. 263–264)

The Remedial Model

This model developed out of the work of Robert Vinter and his colleagues at the University of Michigan. The collection of articles edited by Sundel, Glasser, Sarri, and Vinter (1985) presents a comprehensive view of this model. The model is directed at situations in which the individual member is the focus of change; the group is described as the "means and context" of such change. This approach sharply contrasts with that of Schwartz (1994) in its strong emphasis on the establishment of individual treatment goals with each member. These goals are to be precise and operational as the worker helps the members use the group processes most likely to help them achieve these goals.

This model also requires that workers seek evidence of effectiveness of the interventions they use through a search of the research literature, as well as through an examination of their own practice outcomes. In their search for validation of the model, writers have explored phases of group development (Sarri & Galinsky, 1985), the operation of different group processes (Garvin, 1985), the differential use of program activities (Vinter, 1985), and the worker's intervention in the social environment (Garvin, Glasser, Carter, English, & Wolfson, 1985). In addition, such recent works such as that of Macgowan (2008b) on evidence-based group work can be considered to be highly related to this model. Macgowan has also utilized the group work standards developed by the International Association for Social Work with Groups (Toseland and Rivas, 2012; 452-463) to develop an instrument to determine competencies in group work practice (Macgowan, 2012).

The Task-Centered Model

This model of social work practice was originally developed by Reid and Epstein (1972), although the group application was first presented by Garvin (1974). Subsequent to this early paper, a number of articles have reported developments in task-centered group work. Some of the latest and most detailed of these may be found in Tolson, Reid, and Garvin (2003) and in Garvin (2009).

The task-centered approach sees the group as helping members select and carry out activities to reach their goals. These activities, referred to as tasks, are created by each group member by drawing on other group members for assistance. The group members subsequently help one another carry out their tasks. This help may be offered in the form of group problem solving to assist members in overcoming barriers to task accomplishment, providing support to members in accomplishing tasks, and offering members an opportunity to practice their tasks in the group through role plays and other simulations.

FEMINIST, SOCIAL JUSTICE, AND OTHER MODELS FOR MEMBER EMPOWERMENT

The field of social work has recently introduced the goal of empowerment as one that should be considered in all social work practice, including clinical practice. This goal is particularly relevant when the group members are oppressed by social conditions. People of color; women; gay men, lesbians, or transsexuals; and people with disabilities are likely to fall into this category. Several writers have described models for this kind of practice (Finn & Jacobson, 2008, pp. 252–258; Gutiérrez, 1990; Reed, Ortega, & Garvin, 2009).

Empowerment and social justice models in group work stress the following:

1. Workers and members should consider whether the issues or problems of the members are related to forms of oppression (e.g., racism, sexism, ageism, homophobia) or powerlessness.

2. Members must have an opportunity to exercise significant influence on all phases of the group work process. This influence must start with the decision as to the kinds of groups that agencies will offer and who will be recruited as members and workers. Also included are the ways in which the group will be facilitated, how the group experience will be evaluated, and when the group will end.

3. Members should be helped not only to work to change themselves but also to change their oppressive circumstances.

4. Members may have difficulty deciding on group conditions, change goals, and change methods unless they are helped to attain a critical consciousness (Freire, 1973). This means that they are helped to understand the forces that maintain their oppressive social circumstances and also whether these forces occur in their own situations.

Work has been done to develop feminist models of group work, and these are relevant to empowerment objectives (Garvin & Reed, 1995; Dass-Brailsford, 2012; Hall, 2011). Feminist group work models draw on feminist theories that deal with how societies deny power to women as compared with men, how the needs and views of women are not represented in social work models, and how many concepts are gendered in the sense that women are depreciated, often subtly, by theories and terms that are widely employed. Feminist group work models identify ways in which members of groups are oppressed because of their gender and how workers and members can help each other identify and seek to change the sources of such oppression.

Group Psychotherapy Models

The group psychotherapy model emphasizes group procedures that facilitate the development of members' self-understanding. This understanding includes how their behavior is experienced by others as well as how their thoughts and actions are determined by unconscious elements. The members are helped to use this understanding in order to explore ways of altering the way they behave within as well as outside the group. An important set of such procedures enables the members to examine processes occurring among each other as well as in the group as a whole. The focus in such an examination is on the relationship implications of interactions. An example is the feedback a member received when he offered advice to another member who saw him as seeking to control her.

The member's new self-understanding may be in areas of thought or feeling of which the member was not previously conscious; workers and members may make interpretations to each other of the meaning of behaviors to help bring this kind of understanding about. While social workers generally draw on the work of Yalom and Leszcz (2005) and Rutan, Stone, and Shay (2007) in their practice of group psychotherapy, there are also other social work writers who have contributed to the understanding of group psychotherapy (Levine, 1979).

CHANGE THEORIES RELEVANT TO GROUP TREATMENT OF ADULTS

Group workers draw on one or more theories of change in considering how to engage in group treatment of adults.

Psychodynamic Theory

A number of theorists have written about group phenomena from a psychoanalytic perspective (Bion, 1959; Ezriel, 1973; Foulkes, 1965; Whitaker & Lieberman, 1965). Some of the ideas of these writers are summarized below:

1. Members of groups will identify common ideational and emotional reactions among themselves and direct their discussion to them. These reactions often relate to individual drives and psychological states.

2. Reactions to therapists include both realistic elements and distortions determined by members' past experiences (i.e., transference).

3. Conflicts occur when a desire to fulfill individual needs gives rise to a fear of the consequences of striving to meet these needs, and these are often shared by members. The consensus reached as to the resolution of such conflicts may be compatible with the goals of group therapy or may hinder the resolution of both individual and group problems.

The task of the group worker operating within a psychodynamic framework is to promote an examination of these phenomena. Such an examination should help the worker to offer interpretations that enable the members to overcome barriers to change. These barriers come from the ideational and emotional reactions, transferences, and conflicts.

The work of Bion (1959) deserves special mention because of its widespread influence on psychodynamic group therapy, especially at the Tavistock Institute in London. Bion was psychoanalytically trained and then became interested in groups. One of his central propositions was

that groups often avoid "work" through a set of processes he called "basic assumptions." These consist of dependence on the leader, fight-flight reactions, and some members pairing off. These states and Bion's analysis of how they occur may be useful in determining why groups at times become mired in unproductive activities.

Cognitive-Behavioral Theory

Behavioral theory seeks to add to our understanding of how external events (referred to as stimuli) create, maintain, or diminish individual behaviors (for a detailed discussion of this theory, see Martin & Pear, 1999). Cognitive-behavioral theory focuses on how thought processes play a role in the association between external events and behaviors. Cognitive-behavioral theorists insist that the validation of their theories should not depend on untested assumptions about people's thoughts and feelings but that these should be carefully identified through observations and measurements of observable phenomena.

Investigators interested in the application of cognitive-behavioral theory to group situations, such as Rose (1998), pay attention to how group processes affect behaviors and cognitions. For example, group members imitate each other, and this process can be employed to help members acquire new behaviors. Members can also help each other identify thoughts that hinder the acquisition of new behaviors, such as the idea that one can never change or that one can never be liked by others. Members can also reinforce behaviors of others in the group who are trying to learn these behaviors.

Social-Psychological and Small-Group Theories

Undoubtedly, the theories that are most universally drawn on by group workers are theories about how behavior is affected by interaction with others, especially in small groups. The broad behavioral science area into which these theories fall is that of social psychology. An important social-psychological field of inquiry is role theory (Garvin, 1991). This field helps us understand how people act in social positions (e.g., as student, parent, or drug user) in response to the views others hold of such positions. Other important social-psychological theories of relevance to group work are attribution theory, social cognition theory (Nurius & Brower, 1993), and theories of interpersonal influence.

Small-group theory itself illuminates many aspects of groups, such as group development, group structures, group processes, leadership, decision making, the evolution of norms in groups, scapegoating, the allocation of power in groups, and the relationship between group tasks and other group processes. Social workers have contributed a great deal to the development of small-group theory (Garvin, 1987; Macgowan, 2008a). Group workers also draw on many excellent texts written by social psychologists, such as Forsyth (2010), Napier and Gershenfeld (1987), and Nixon (1979).

Ecological Theories

Group workers, like all other social workers, have largely come to think of their practice as informed by an ecological perspective, in which the interdependence of individuals, groups, and larger social systems, such as the organization and community, is understood as the basis of practice (Germain & Gitterman, 2008). As Germain and Gitterman (2008) state,

> Ecological thinking focuses on the reciprocity of person-environment exchanges, in which each shapes and influences the other over time. This mode of thought differs markedly from the simple cause-and-effect linear thinking that now pervades our language, culture, education, systems of ideas, and practice research. . . . [E]cological thinking explains more complex phenomena, such as those encountered every day in social work practice. (p. 53)

Therapeutic Factors

An important understanding of how groups benefit members stems from the idea of therapeutic factors—for example, instilling hope, universality (others are in the same boat), guidance from others, altruism (I can help others), learning from interpersonal action, vicarious learning (learning from the experiences of others), insight (learning important things about one's self), acceptance (accepting others in the group and being accepted by them), catharsis (release of emotions within the group), and self-disclosure. These factors have evolved out of the writing of several authors who have used a variety of research tools to ascertain the sources of therapeutic change in groups (Bloch & Crouch, 1985; Yalom & Leszcz, 2005). Elsewhere, I have written about these factors as they apply to social work groups (Garvin, 1997).

THE ASSESSMENT PHASE

The term *assessment* rather than *diagnosis* is used because the group worker seeks an understanding of the nature of the client's problems and the conditions that either maintain these problems or can be drawn on to ameliorate them. The term *diagnosis* is often more narrowly used to categorize the problem using some set of categories such as those defined in the *Diagnostic and Statistical Manual of Mental Disorders,* fourth edition (American Psychiatric Association, 1994). Social workers with groups sometimes use such typologies in composing groups but find that an assessment process is most useful for group treatment aims such as the following:

1. To determine whether to recommend group treatment

2. To determine, if group treatment is appropriate, the type of group to which the person should be referred

3. To help the practitioner decide how to compose the group

4. To help the practitioner and members select appropriate treatment goals

Whether to Recommend Group Treatment

Burlingame, MacKenzie, and Strauss (2004) examined a number of studies as well as meta-analyses of the comparative effectiveness of individual and group therapy. They concluded the following:

> At face value, the findings from multiple meta-analytic studies portray a very persuasive argument regarding the general equivalence of the two formats. In short, the aggregate message is that the literature does not support differential effectiveness between the two formats. On the other hand, the meta-analyses cited above often do not separately test for differential effectiveness of format by patient diagnosis. Even when these tests are conducted) the findings are limited since the number of studies of the most frequent categories seldom rises above three or four (e.g., chemical dependency and depression). Small sample sizes limit the power of a statistic to detect real differences, leading us to conclude that it is premature to accept the equivalence finding at the individual diagnosis level. (pp. 651–652)

Nevertheless, there are situations where groups have advantages: For instance, clients may be helped to realize that they are not unique in their problems; clients who wish to experiment with better ways of improving their relationships, who seek to test their views of reality against the views of others, who seek a place to practice behaviors, or who wish to interact with peers in nonverbal ways by participating in activities may also benefit from group treatment. Toseland and Rivas (2012) sum up the circumstances for referring people to groups as follows:

> Overall, findings from both the clinical and the empirical literature suggest that social workers should consider recommending group treatment for individuals who suffer from isolation or who have other difficulties with interpersonal relationships, and individual treatment for those with highly personal psychological problems. (p. 18)

I disagree with Toseland and Rivas (2012) on the issue of people with highly personal problems since group work with such people has been effective when this is what they desire. Thus, a major factor in recommending group treatment is that the individual accepts the idea of working on problems in a group. Groups, moreover, have been useful for individuals with the same range of problems dealt with in individual treatment.

The same view does not apply to family treatment because some family problems stem from current dysfunctional patterns best altered when workers interact with several or all family members simultaneously. Sometimes the other family members are not available. The group can be experienced by the individual in ways that are analogous to how he or she experiences the family. The group consequently becomes a place where family issues are identified and worked on. (It is also possible to form a group composed of some or all members of several families.)

Type of Group

There are many types of groups used for group treatment, and the worker must determine which is best for the client. However, it is not likely that all these types will be available, so the worker may choose one that is second best or even decide that it is not possible to offer group treatment at all.

Short Term (Time Limited) Versus Long Term

A group might be scheduled to meet for a specified number of sessions over anywhere from 1 to 3 months. Alternatively, the group might meet for 1 or more years. The time-limited, short-term group usually focuses on a specific skill or problem, such as parenting skills, preparing for retirement, planning for discharge from an institution, or learning how to relate to a family member recently diagnosed as suffering from a severe mental illness. The short-term group will often have an assigned topic for each meeting and a structured plan for the session itself. Clients who are not motivated to remain in the group for a long period of time or who see themselves as learning to cope with a specific issue often prefer such a group. In the current managed-care environment, insurance companies and other providers often prefer this type of service.

A long-term group may meet for 1 or more years. Members often seek such an experience when they recognize that their problems in relating to others are deep-seated and even obscure, and they wish to have the opportunity for a great deal of self-exploration based on the feedback they receive in the group. Another form of long-term group is very different, in that it has been designed to provide support to people who are severely disabled by their emotional problems and can remain in the community only when they receive such support. Sometimes, such a group is even offered on a self-help basis in which the members themselves are in charge of all or most aspects of the group.

Open Versus Closed

In some groups, the members begin and end the group at the same time, and these are referred to as closed groups. In other groups, members may enter and leave at different times, and these are open. A group with a structured program will often be closed, while a group in which members work on relationship issues through examination of interpersonal processes may be an open one. Clients who are referred to a closed group must wait until a group begins, and this can be a disadvantage to certain individuals who should have a group made immediately available to them.

Support Versus Therapy

A distinction is often made between support groups and therapy groups. In support groups, members with similar issues provide empathy and encouragement to one another, as well as help in problem solving. In therapy groups, members explore thoughts and feelings (which may be beyond their awareness) to alter well-established patterns of behavior. A decision as to whether to refer a person to a support or a therapy group is based on the client's goals, motivation, and capacity for in-depth exploration, as well as the nature of the problem.

The distinction between support groups and therapy groups may not be as meaningful as some writers contend. This is because workers are often unclear themselves as to what they mean when they advertise a group as support or therapy. It is also true that some inexperienced workers may call their groups *support* because they have not been adequately trained to offer group therapy. In addition, there are many examples of therapy in support groups and many elements of support in therapy groups.

Assessment Approaches

The assessment of group members typically begins with an individual interview scheduled before the client enters the group. There is now a considerable body of evidence that such an interview will make it more likely that the clients will remain in the group for the designated period of time and will benefit from the group experience (Garvin, 1987, p. 66; Toseland & Rivas, 2012, pp. 179–180). This interview should include information on the value of group treatment, the difficulties groups have in their formation stage, and the need for members to be open with one another. The clients, in turn, express their expectations for the group, their ideas as to how they will use the group, their reasons for joining, their reservations about affiliating, and what they anticipate will be forthcoming from the worker and other members.

In more formally assessing group members, workers may use the same instruments employed in individual treatment. In addition, however, there are assessment tools that make use of the group context itself. One of these is the opportunity the group offers to observe how the member interacts with peers, which in other forms of treatment can be known only through self-report.

The following are some of the interactional behaviors that become evident in groups:

1. *How the member initiates or fails to initiate relationships:* The member may approach others in an aggressive fashion or in a submissive and self-effacing manner. The member may be open or closed to efforts made by others to form a relationship.

2. *How the member responds to feedback from others:* The member may give serious consideration to what others say or may find ways of rejecting this type of information without any thought.

3. *How the member responds to the emotions expressed by others:* The member may respond in an empathic and caring way or in a cold and rejecting manner.

Because the group offers such an excellent opportunity to gather information about members' typical behavior in interpersonal situations, some workers invite the potential member to participate for a session or two in a pregroup experience. This experience can have the twofold purpose of orienting the client to a group experience while giving the worker information that can be used in planning the subsequent, longer-term group.

When it is not possible to observe the client in a group situation, the worker will use self-report to obtain this type of information during a pregroup screening interview. The worker will ask the clients about the groups in which they have participated, how they felt about the group experience and the other members, how they interacted with others in the group, and what benefits or difficulties resulted from being in the group.

Another assessment device used in some groups is to ask the members to tell their life story to each other. A good example was reported by Adolph (1983) in her work with a women's group in a partial hospitalization program. In the beginning of the group, the women told "herstory" of "growing up female." The women who wished to participate in this experience were given the "herstory outline" a week in advance. The following is an example of how a member used this experience.

Helene, 60 years old, widow: Helene had been a professional actress doing monologues throughout the United States during her younger years. She felt depleted, alone, isolated, and impoverished, living on Public Aid when in the past she had been married to a physician and lived in comparative luxury. Helene's "herstory" was an exciting oral document presented as a dramatic musical event like her former theatrical monologues. She was enthusiastically applauded by the group and encouraged to resume her theatrical life by entertaining senior citizen groups. Helene seemed pleased with that suggestion and did follow through following discharge from the Alternative Hospital Program. (Adolph, 1983, p. 126)

When approaches using instruments originally developed for assessment in one-to-one treatment are employed, there may be advantages in bringing these instruments into the group to obtain the reactions of other members. An example is a chart on which a member recorded how often he initiated conversations with other employees at his place of work. At first, he had been reluctant to keep the chart, but the interest of other group members encouraged him to do so. He was also able to tell the other members what his feelings were as he contemplated making such social contacts, and this gave him new insights into the nature of his difficulties.

Members should be helped to formulate goals regarding what they would like to see occur as a result of their group participation. These goals are usually expressed in terms of an improvement in the problem for which the individual sought group treatment. The member may have discussed goals during the pregroup interview yet may want to modify these as he or she experiences the reality of the group and listens to the goals of others. The member may decide that he or she is not comfortable working on some goals with these particular people; the opposite may also be true, and the member may be encouraged to work on a problem that he or she was fearful to divulge until others acknowledged similar difficulties.

It is difficult for some people to think in terms of personal goals. The group context is a place where they can be helped through examples provided by the worker or other members to express personal aspirations in clear and realistic ways. In one group, for example, a member stated that her goal was to get along better with her son. Other members asked her what she meant by "get along better." She explained that if she could have conversations with him about his efforts to cope with his psychiatric disability, she would be able without feeling guilty to set limits on him, such as what time he had to come home. Members are often very useful to one another in developing specific goals because of the similarities in their situations.

CREATING GROUPS

At times, the worker begins to conduct a group that is already in existence—for example, one composed of adults who live in the same unit of a residential facility. Under other circumstances, the worker secures a list of potential members from colleagues or from advertising the group in the community or agency. Sometimes, the worker will receive the names of a small number of potential members and must begin with all (or almost all) these people or abandon plans for the group.

The question facing the worker who will have little or nothing to say in the selection of members is, "Given this set of people, what purposes might the group accomplish?" When the worker is able to select members from a pool of possible members, the question is, "Given the agency's purpose for the group, which combination of people is most likely to achieve the purpose?" In the first circumstance, the implication is not that the worker determines the purpose and foists it on the members but rather that this is an issue for the worker and members to resolve together.

The process of composing groups is not usually one that the member shares with other clients. It is possible, however, to bring an empowerment perspective to this task by asking potential members what attributes they think should be present in people who will be able to work well together in the proposed group. Workers may be surprised to learn that their cherished ideas about group composition are rejected by those who are most affected by the group's composition.

Some workers have been concerned that if group members are too similar to one another, they will likely reinforce rather than resolve their problems. In practice, this is rarely, if ever, the case since there are always sufficient differences among the experiences of group members to provide for different perspectives on a situation. The worker also is in a position to challenge too much conformity if this should become a problem.

On the other hand, members must come to care enough for one another to sustain their commitment to the group, to support one another when the going gets rough, and to become the system of mutual aid envisioned by most group workers. This is likely to occur when members see some similarities in one another, even though they may also see glaring differences. Workers are advised to make a list of the attributes that are most likely to matter when members meet and look each other over (Garvin, 1997, pp. 54–60). The member who sees nothing in common with other members is most likely to discontinue the group, and reciprocally, the other members are not likely to act in an accepting manner toward him or her.

An example is a group established to help members deal with their ability to sustain intimate relationships. The worker hypothesized that the most critical attributes affecting the ways these members identified with each other would be age, gender, marital status, ways they had used to develop intimacy, education, and occupation. Rather than seeking members who were alike on all these attributes, the worker composed groups such that no two members would be different on all these criteria. It was anticipated that each member would be similar to other members in at least a few ways. This proved to be the case as the members introduced themselves to the others. Some men were pleased that there were other men present, for example, and others liked the idea that women were in the group. The women felt similarly. A divorced person was pleased to see that he was not the only person in that category.

There are occasions when the purpose of the group requires that all the members be alike on one attribute—for example, men's and women's consciousness-raising and support groups, groups for women who have experienced an assault from a man, groups of assaultive men, groups to enhance ethnic identity or to help people who have experienced loss, and coming-out groups for gay men and lesbians.

An issue that has received much attention is the gender and ethnic composition of the group, especially when the latter involves people of color. Garvin and Reed (1983) have written that there is a tendency in many groups for men to dominate the discussion and to compete with other men. They also note that women are likely to be depreciated by men when they assume positions of leadership, and that women's groups are likely to have different developmental patterns from men's groups (Schiller, 1997).

The ethnicity of group members is also important to consider in composing groups. Davis (1984), for example, reported instances when Black group members had questioned the legitimacy of all Black treatment groups, although this concern shortly disappeared. Black members have also questioned the legitimacy of having a White worker assigned to a predominantly Black group. Davis (1984) has done pioneering work on how Black-White proportions are perceived

differently by Black and White members and reports the following:

> Blacks, it appears, prefer groups that are 50 percent black and 50 percent white—numerical equality. Whites, on the other hand, appear to prefer groups that are approximately 20 percent black and 80 percent white, societal ratios of blacks and whites. Needless to say, the preferences of both groups cannot be simultaneously met. The difference in preference for racial balance has the potential to lead to member dissatisfaction, discomfort, and withdrawal. (p. 102)

Chu and Sue (1984) provide information on compositional issues related to Asian American members as follows:

> In a group of very verbose, articulate and aggressive non-Asians, the Asian member may be hesitant to speak up. In a confrontation, which inevitably happens at some point in a long-term group, the Asian may not know what to say, not being used to such interaction. (p. 30)

These are only a few examples from a growing literature on the ethnic composition of groups. This type of inquiry must be ongoing in view of the many changes occurring in American and other societies regarding the interactions among various ethnic groups.

GROUP FORMATION

All groups in which the members do not know one another prior to the group (although there may be a few who have previously met) go through a period of formation. Workers should understand this phase because they can be very helpful to members in accomplishing formation tasks. If these tasks are not undertaken appropriately, the future of the group may be in jeopardy. During formation, the members agree on group purpose and individual goals, establish group norms, develop initial relationships with each other and with the group worker, determine the kinds of activities in which they will engage, deal with their feelings about the group, and decide how the success of the group will be evaluated. These agreements may be thought of as a contract the members have with each other and with the worker, which may be either implicit or in the form of a written document.

Agreement on Group Purpose

The members discuss the group purpose with the worker in their pregroup interviews. The worker, however, should discuss group purpose again when the group begins. As members gain first impressions of one another, they may wish to reconsider or modify that statement of purpose. An example was a group of adults who had recently been divorced. The original stated purpose was to help members deal with their feelings about the divorce. As the members told their divorce stories, however, they discovered how lonely they now were. They insisted that the group purpose include learning ways of dealing with loneliness, especially on weekends and holidays.

Individual Goals

Members may also have considered individual goals during the pregroup interview but should be asked to clarify these for themselves and other group members when the group begins. We recognize that members may reformulate their goals as the group proceeds, and their individual situations may change too. In a treatment group of five men on probation, the following goals were arrived at by the third meeting:

- Ed's goal was to find a job.
- Sam's goal was to enroll in an educational program for people who want to be electricians.
- Phil wanted to find ways to decrease his use of alcohol.
- Rick wanted to reestablish his relationship with his wife, who had left him because he verbally abused her.
- Dick wanted to cut off his relationships with others who broke the law and to develop a new set of friends.

Establishing Group Norms

During the formation period, norms are established that may help the group in (or hinder it from) accomplishing its purposes. Some of these are explicitly proposed by the group worker—for example, that members will not inform anyone outside the group about other members of the group (confidentiality). Another norm proposed in most treatment groups is that when members meet outside group sessions, they will report on this at the next group meeting. This norm helps prevent members from hindering the treatment process by forming cliques. A positive consequence of this norm is that the content of discussions outside the group can enhance the content of discussions within the group. Another important norm is that when members are experienced as difficult, this will be discussed at a meeting, and members will not attempt to expel a fellow member.

Workers also seek to promote a norm related to the democratic functioning of the group. This is a complex issue in treatment groups since decisions are not normally made by taking votes; nevertheless, the principle should be that workers help groups develop as great a measure of democratic decision making as is feasible.

Such decision making may be called on, for example, when the group is considering a change in meeting times. The worker will always try to help members move to a high level of participation in decision making. Examples are group discussions on fees, group size, and composition principles (although not on specific individuals to be included).

Finally, groups should develop norms for attendance and promptness. When these are not explicit and regularly monitored, it is likely that members will begin to come late and fail to notify anyone when they miss a session. Apart from the disorganization that can ensue under such circumstances, these conditions convey to members that they are not valued and that no one cares when or if they come to the group.

Developing Relationships Among Members

For group members to invest themselves fully in the group in order to accomplish their goals, they must develop relationships with each other. These relationships are likely to continue to deepen as long as the group is in existence. Important aspects of such relationships are that members will trust each other, which means that they will assume that others in the group consciously wish to be of help; they will believe that they are basically liked and accepted by others in the group; and when this is not true, members will be committed to working so that obstacles to this state can be removed.

To establish relationships during the formation stage, workers should do the following:

- Help members identify similarities between themselves and other members of the group. For example, if several women speak of ways they have been harassed by men, the worker points out this commonality.
- Help members talk with each other rather than addressing their comments to the worker. For example, the worker points out to group members that they are asking him questions rather than asking questions of each other (on issues about which the members had the most experience).
- Help members listen to each other. For example, the worker notes that members are ignoring each other's contributions and suggests that, for a short period, each member should summarize the previous comment before speaking.
- Help members reduce distortions in their perceptions of each other. For example, members are asked to select a member who reminds them of someone outside the group. The members are then asked to discuss these perceptions with the member to see how far this resemblance goes.

Developing Relationships With the Group Worker

The worker should find ways of developing relationships with all group members. This can be done by making eye contact with members when they speak, allowing one's eyes to shift from member to member during the course of the meeting, and responding empathically to members when they express their feelings. The worker should address members by name and be sure to single out each member during the course of the meeting for a comment, a question, or an encouraging remark.

Planning Group Activities

The worker and members should suggest specific activities as the group evolves that will help the group accomplish its purposes. These activities cannot all be planned in advance because it is impossible to anticipate all the events that will occur over time. Nevertheless, as the group begins, the members have a right to be told about the worker's approach to helping the group accomplish its purposes. Does the worker anticipate that the members will primarily use discussion and verbal problem-solving methods? Does the worker expect the members to analyze processes occurring in the group and their roles in these processes? Does the worker anticipate introducing other types of activities, such as role-playing, art, guided imagery, or trips? An understanding of the way the members will be helped in the group and a consensus on this is necessary for the group to enter the middle stages of group development (in which the members are actively at work to attain their goals). The topic of group development is an important one that goes beyond the scope of this chapter. For a detailed discussion of this concept, see Toseland and Rivas (2012, pp. 90–93).

Dealing With Feelings About the Group

Members often have contradictory feelings about the group. Some of these feelings are positive and are tied in with the reasons why the members have joined the group and the likelihood that their hopes will be realized. Other feelings are negative as members fear that their efforts in the group will come to naught, that other members will be rejecting and unsympathetic, and that they will leave the group worse off than when they entered. The job of the worker is to strengthen the positive feelings and diminish the negative ones by encouraging members to express their aspirations and fears. The worker can help members examine their fears in light of the reality of the group as they perceive it, and bringing these fears into the open will contribute to this goal.

An example of this occurred in a group of parents working on their parenting skills. One father said he was fearful that other members would be very critical of how he was raising his children. Other members expressed similar concerns, and this recognition of commonality was reassuring. Several members reiterated the idea that they were there to help each other, not to make one another miserable. The worker also encouraged the members to tell the group if they felt they were being criticized excessively.

Evaluation

Being an accountable practitioner requires the worker to help the members evaluate the group experience and their individual progress toward attaining their goals. This process aids the worker in his or her growth as a practitioner by providing feedback as to the effects of his or her practice with the group. It also enables the members to know if they have achieved their objectives and further work that they may have after they leave the group. The agency too has a right to know whether its expenditure of resources on the group has accomplished agency purposes. Members should be told this when the group begins, and the means the worker and the members agree to use for evaluation should be clarified in the beginning. An extensive discussion of evaluation in groups may be found in Gant (2004).

The formation period ends when the membership of the group has stabilized, the purposes of the group have been clarified and agreed to, initial relationships have developed both among members and between members and the worker, and norms are established.

CHANGE PROCESSES DURING THE MIDDLE PHASE

During the middle phase, group workers have three major focuses. The first is to enhance the ways in which members relate to one another so that their feelings of trust, closeness, and caring are strengthened. The second is to help members accomplish group purposes, such as problem solving, acquisition of skills, increased self-awareness, and improved ability to cope with feelings. These processes are not consistent. Most theorists of group development note the likelihood that there will be alternative phases—one in which the group members are actively at work on their relationships and their tasks, the other in which conflict emerges among members or between members and the worker.

Such conflicts are likely to result from inevitable differences among members, the competition for leadership that might emerge, and the changing roles that evolve as different group processes are brought into play. Thus, a third worker task is to help sustain the group during periods of tension and conflict. This is done through reassuring the group that conflict is an inevitable consequence of development, albeit a difficult and sometimes painful one. The worker can help mediate between conflicting parties, help members learn the process of negotiation, and help members establish ground rules so that conflict resolution is experienced as manageable and not destructive to any of the parties.

An important issue at all phases is that of power. Some power accrues to the workers by virtue of their position in the group and their presumed expertise. This can at times be dysfunctional as members may defer to the workers even when their judgments are faulty. Other sources of power may relate to gender, ethnicity, social class, and so forth. These are likely to hinder the group's achievement of its goals and therefore should be analyzed and confronted by the worker and the members.

There are a number of approaches that workers use in group treatment with adults. Some workers emphasize one or another of these, while others employ them in some combination. In the discussion, these approaches are described, and the client populations and group circumstances for which the approach is the best fit are noted.

Problem Solving

A problem-solving process will be used in virtually all treatment groups. Sometimes this process is employed to help individual members determine how they will cope with a situation in their lives outside the group; at other times the group uses problem solving to resolve a group issue, such as how to deal with members' low rate of participation in discussions. When the problem relates to the situation of only an individual member, the group should not impose a group solution on that person. On the other hand, when the problem relates to the group as a whole, a solution can be adopted to which the group agrees.

No problem-solving approach should be rigidly followed in a group since circumstances vary widely. Sometimes problem solving occurs as soon as a member becomes aware of the alternatives; at other times, it occurs when the member develops insight into an emotional barrier that prevents him or her from carrying out an action. An example of the latter was a member who asked the group for help in identifying ways in which she could ask a coworker out on a date with her. Discussion of this issue made it obvious that she knew the ways in which this might be accomplished, but any option she considered led to her fear of rejection. The discussion quickly turned from the skills of starting a relationship to the sources of her fear of rejection and how she might deal with that fear.

At times, the worker will employ a more systematic problem-solving process. The process begins with specifying the problem in detail, such as who does what to whom, under what conditions, and with what response. The frequency with which the problem occurs should also be examined. The next stage is to determine the goals that will be attained as a result of problem solving.

The group then seeks information that will help it to generate alternative solutions to the problem. This information might include what actions the member has used in the past, what actions the person would have liked to use but did not, and the reasons. It is useful to propose more than a single solution. Some groups stop with one and devote time to discussing the pros and cons of that solution as if no alternative is possible, a process that can be unnecessarily restrictive. When groups consider multiple solutions, the alternatives are evaluated for their feasibility with respect to the internal and external resources available to the member and their benefits to that member and to others. There may be undesirable consequences also, and these too should be considered.

On the basis of this evaluation, the member chooses one alternative with the help of the group. The group must then help the member carry out the action. The activities that may be used for this include rehearsing the action through a role play, dividing the solution into a series of actions or tasks and discussing each separately, or considering ways of removing barriers to implementing the solution.

An example of problem solving took place in a group of college students who had been experiencing difficulties in making friends, especially of the other gender, in the college setting: They all were now living some distance away from the communities in which they had been raised.

The third session of the group began with Sam discussing his recent experience at a party in his dorm. Almost everyone he approached soon wandered away shortly after he sought to begin

(Continued)

(Continued)

conversation. Bill asked Sam for more details as to what happened. Sam said he walked up to two men who were talking to each other. He injected the comment that he hoped the college basketball team would win its next game. The men, he thought, looked at him kind of strangely and soon departed. Frank asked him why he thought they did so, and he said he couldn't tell. Bill wondered if they were talking about something else and didn't want to change the subject. Alice added that maybe they weren't interested in sports.

Sam thought that that might have been the case, and Alice asked him what else he could have done. Sam said he guessed that he might have first asked if they were talking about something personal. Bill said that might have been a good start and added that he could have introduced himself and said that he lived in this dorm. Alice commented that he might then have listened to what they were already discussing and, assuming it was okay to join them, tried to contribute to that topic. Sam said he hadn't, of course, gotten that far but he thought these were good ideas. He wouldn't have added that he lived in the dorm but might have asked them if they did. Ed suggested that he and Bill might role-play a situation that could be something like what had actually happened.

As the role play began, Ed and Bill were talking softly. Sam got up, walked over to them, and asked if he might join in. Ed and Bill said he could and then resumed their conversation. They were talking about how Barack Obama was doing in his first months as president. After a while, Sam interjected that he liked the way he had pressed for government support of the auto industry. Ed and Bill said they agreed, and the conversation moved in such a way as to include Sam in their conversation.

Sam asked how he had done. Bill said he thought he had done well but might have made more eye contact with Ed and Bill. Alice added that he seemed to be talking a little more loudly than he needed to even though the room was noisy.

Cognitive-Behavioral Approaches

These approaches are used in groups when members wish to learn specific ways of behaving and also to acquire ways of thinking that support such actions. Examples of such situations are those in which members wish to act assertively, cope with stress, or handle specific types of interpersonal situations more effectively. The approach is initiated with the member's specifying the problem situation. It is especially important for the member to describe in detail his or her own behavior and the responses of the other person. Members will often ask the individual questions to help in this process.

The group then helps the member to determine the way he or she would like to behave in the situation. When this is accomplished, it is helpful for the member to have the opportunity to observe what it is like to act in this manner. Therefore, another member who has made progress in attaining this skill role-plays the desired behavior, together with other members who act as other people in the individual's situation.

The members then have an opportunity to comment on the role play. The individual also may ask questions. Subsequently, the individual role-plays himself or herself and also receives feedback from the group, especially on the positive aspects of the role play.

At times, it is difficult for the individual to act effectively in the role play. One major reason is that he or she may have thoughts that are detrimental, such as "Nothing I do works" or "No matter what I do, I will not be liked." The worker, together with the group, helps the member to identify such thoughts and to replace them with more functional ones. Another source of difficulty is that the member may experience overwhelming anxiety in the simulated (as well as real) situation.

The worker, if he or she has not already done so, may have to teach the group members ways of relaxing in situations that normally make them tense. One means of doing this is to employ progressive muscle relaxation (Toseland & Rivas, 2012, pp. 304-305), in which members learn how they may induce relaxation by systematically relaxing each muscle group in the body. When

this skill is acquired, the member is often able to relax without going through each step of this procedure. Other means of relaxation are yoga exercises, meditation, and imagining peaceful scenes.

After the role play, the member is asked to discuss when he or she will try out this behavior in the actual life situation. The member is also asked to report back to the group as to how it went. If at the next meeting the member reports some difficulty, the process might begin again at an appropriate point depending on whether the behavior was entirely wrong for the situation or if the member needs more practice or encouragement.

An example of this process took place in the same group of college students referred to in the example of problem solving described above. At the following meeting, Sam said that he went to another party and used what he had learned to try and join in a conversation. The group worker asked him to describe that situation. When Sam described it, the group worker noticed that he presented it with a lot of anxiety in his voice. He asked Sam if he was feeling anxious in the situation, and Sam said that he was. The worker wondered what Sam could have done to reduce that feeling. He prompted Sam by mentioning that at one of the first sessions of the group they had practiced progressive muscle relaxation. Sam remembered this but said he had not tried this when he approached the other students. The worker asked if he was aware of any tension in his body in that situation. Sam said that he felt a lot of tension in his shoulders. The worker suggested that he might have sought to reduce that tension, using the techniques they had learned earlier. Sam agreed with this, and the worker then suggested that he try this out now in the group. (This occurred, and then the meeting progressed.)

The worker asked Sam what he might have begun thinking at that time. Sam said he had said to himself that he was never going to make any friends and that what was then happening proved this. The worker asked other members what dysfunctional thoughts were being expressed here. Bill said that what was happening at this party was not a "never" situation. He added that Sam might have said to himself that there were a lot of other people at the party and thus many other opportunities to try and make friends; furthermore, no one can be friends with everyone. Alice said she thought Sam was really a "good guy," and he should hold onto that view of himself.

Process and Process Illumination

This approach seeks to clarify for members the interpersonal meanings attached to communications among them. For example, if one

member asks another to move her chair, this can have a variety of meanings to each of the members (e.g., superiority, caring, or hostility). The improvement of relationships depends in part on knowing how to communicate what one means to say and knowing how other people receive the message. The group offers an opportunity to learn about these issues, acquire ways of improving communication, and testing these ways outside the group.

Listed below are some statements that can help members examine processes (Garvin, 1997):

"How did you feel when X said that to you?"

"What did you think Y was saying?"

"What did X remind you of when he said that?"

"Why did X attack Y?"

"Why was X attacked when he said that?"

"Why are you not saying anything now?"

"Why did you laugh when X said that?"

"Each time I said something tonight, you disagreed with me."

"Even though you argue with me, you always sit next to me." (p. 164)

The Use of a Program

A major contribution to group treatment made by social workers involves the use of activities, usually collectively referred to as a *program,* for group treatment purposes. Discussion, of course, is one type of activity, but other types include the use of media such as art, drama, games, trips, and music, which allow members to communicate information to one another that is not conveyed by words alone while opening up new possibilities for creative problem solving as well as expanded levels of awareness of self and others (Middleman, 1968; Wilson & Ryland, 1949).

An important contribution to an understanding of the program was made by Vinter (1985), who identified a series of program dimensions. He pointed out that all activities occur in a physical field, which he defined as "the physical space and terrain, and the physical and social objects characteristic of each activity," and all activities consist of *constituent performances,* which are "behaviors that are essential to the activity and thus are required of the participants"

(p. 227). The physical field and the constituent performance compose the activity setting, which produces respondent behaviors. These respondent behaviors are essentially the treatment outcomes for that activity.

An example of an analysis using this model was the use a worker made of a program in a group of clients suffering from severe mental illnesses who regularly met in a community mental health center. The members had difficulty experiencing themselves as a group. The worker noted that there was a guitar in the room as well as some other instruments, such as small drums and cymbals (parts of the *physical field*). She knew how to play the guitar and began to play some well-known tunes. She invited the members to make use of the other instruments to keep time with her (*constituent performance*). After a few songs, some of the less expressive members began to smile, and all the members pulled their chairs a little closer together, indicating a greater sense of being in a group (*respondent behaviors*).

Vinter (1985) has also provided a way of analyzing the activity setting so that workers can help group members make modifications in the activity to increase the likelihood of desired outcomes. The following are six dimensions of this analysis, together with examples of how these might be employed to enhance the musical activity just described:

1. *Prescriptiveness of the pattern of constituent performances:* This is the extent of the rules that guide the activity. The worker implied a rule when she urged the members to try and keep the same rhythm she used in her playing of the guitar.

2. *Institutionalized controls governing participant activity:* This deals with whether behavior is controlled during an activity by some members, by the worker, or by norms that all the members have internalized. In the musical activity, some members pointed out to other members when they were not following the rhythm.

3. *Provision for physical movement:* This refers to the degree to which members are required to or permitted to engage in physical movement as

part of the activity. In the example, the worker encouraged a restless member to dance to the music if she wished to do so.

4. *Competence required for performance:* This refers to the least amount of ability required of members to participate. In this musical activity, if the worker thought that the members were having too much difficulty in keeping the rhythm, she could have asked one of the musically knowledgeable members to conduct by standing in front of the group and moving his or her arms in time to the music.

5. *Provision for participant interactiveness:* This refers to the amount of interaction among members that is permitted or elicited by the activity. In the musical example, if some members had begun to dance with each other, the amount of interaction would have increased.

6. *Reward structure:* This consists of the rewards that are made available during the activity and how these are distributed among the members. In this musical activity, the members all seemed to be having fun, and this reward was distributed among everyone. The worker also entertained the group after this event by playing and singing a few popular songs. This was also a source of gratification that was highly associated with the musical activity in which the group members had just participated.

The Use of Structure and Role Assignments

One of the advantages of working with groups is the opportunity for the worker and the members to alter the group structure so that the group can help its members better attain its purposes. Group structure refers to the ways in which relationships among the members are patterned. I have categorized aspects of the group's structure elsewhere (Garvin, 1997, pp. 103–104) and shall now describe how these various aspects of structure can be modified for treatment purposes.

Communications Structure

This refers to who in the group speaks to whom and about what. In one group, for example, the members had a problem indicating when they wished to say something, and even then, the members frequently interrupted one another. The members acknowledged this problem, and the worker suggested that they try a device used in some Native American groups— a *talking stick.* A member who wished to speak would ask the member who was speaking for the stick. No one was permitted to interrupt the speaker until the stick was relinquished by him or her.

Sociometric (Affectional) Structure

This refers to the existence of subgroups in which members are closer to each other than to members not a part of the subgroup. In one group, the members noted the existence of a few people who gave more support to each other than to others who were not in the subgroup. They also avoided confronting one another, which they freely did with people outside their clique. The worker spent a considerable amount of time helping the group to analyze this condition. It became evident that the members of this subgroup thought that they had more education than the other group members. Further discussion led to the awareness of these members that they used this fact to avoid facing certain defenses against intimacy that members outside their clique had tried to bring to their attention.

Power Structure

This refers to who in the group influences whom and how this is done. In a group of men and women working on relationship issues, one of the men maintained that his wife was totally to blame for their difficulties. The other men supported him in this view. The worker helped these other men realize that they feared that this member would question whether they were "true men" if they failed to support him.

Leadership Structure

This refers to who contributes the most to the determination and accomplishment of group tasks and to enhancing the quality of relationships in the group. In one group, every time a conflict emerged, one member sought to help mediate the conflict, which precluded other members from playing a role in this process. The worker subsequently initiated a discussion of this topic in the group, and the group learned that this member did the same thing in his family, largely owing to his parents' insistence that he play this role in family conflicts.

Role Structure

In treatment groups where formal roles such as chairperson and secretary seldom exist, the important roles are informal ones, for example, *the mediator*, *the clown*, *the devil's advocate*, and *the rebel*. In one treatment group, the worker believed that such roles had emerged, and to confirm her thinking, she listed them on a large sheet of paper and then engaged the group in a discussion of who filled each role. The group quickly agreed on who fit which position. This led to an animated discussion that lasted several weeks as to whether the members wanted to fill the roles they were in or wished to be in different roles and how this related to the way the members were cast in their situations outside the group.

The Use of Interpretation

The worker's role in the discussions of process represents one type of interpretation. There are other types as well. For example, the worker notes a pattern in the responses of the individual ("Each time you began to drink, it was after you had been turned down when you asked for a date"), or the worker suspects that there is an underlying issue of which the member is unaware ("I wonder if your wife at times reminds you of your sister").

Another very important type of interpretation in groups is made to draw a member's attention to transference phenomena occurring in the group. As Yalom and Leszcz (2005) state,

> Every patient, to a greater or lesser degree, perceives the therapist incorrectly because of transference distortions. Few patients are entirely conflict-free in their attitudes towards such issues as parental authority, dependency, God, autonomy, and rebellion—all of which are often personified in the person of the therapist. These distortions are continually at play under the surface of the group discourse. Indeed, hardly a meeting passes without some clear token of the powerful feelings evoked by the therapist. (pp. 205–206)

Transference phenomena also occur in the reactions of members to each other. This can be one of the richest sources of therapeutic gain in groups as members learn about transference phenomena in the group and then apply this learning to create a reality-oriented basis for their relationships outside the group. Workers should also take note of their own countertransference issues, which may be evoked when the worker displaces affects, attitudes, and conflicts that have their origins in the worker's relationships with parents, children, and siblings onto the group member(s).

Several countertransference manifestations frequently occur in groups. A major one is when the worker needs to remain in a central position in the group and receive an inordinate amount of attention from group members. An example of this is a worker who responded to virtually all member comments with one of his own, and this precluded members from giving feedback to one another. Another countertransference manifestation is when workers assume that most member comments, particularly critical comments, represent their transferential reactions and fail to recognize the reality basis of such criticisms. Still another is when workers devalue their own contributions and are unduly passive during group discussions.

TERMINATION

There are a number of occasions when the worker must help the group deal with an ending. One is when the group terminates, and the other is when a member leaves but the group continues.

When the group has reached its final meetings, the worker must help with a series of issues. The order in which these are dealt with is not an arbitrary one but should be determined by the circumstances of the particular group.

Feelings About the Ending

As was true of group beginnings, members experience a variety of feelings, often contradictory ones, about endings. They often feel regret because they are likely to lose contact with the worker and the other members of whom they have become fond. They also may miss the group meetings. Some fear that they will lose the gains they have made through the group experience. On the other hand, they may be happy to have the meeting time free and relieved that they will no longer have to pay fees for the group. Some will still have mixed feelings, or even negative ones, about how much the group has helped them. The members will benefit from a discussion of all these issues. Such discussions may help free them to pursue new relationships and other opportunities for growth and change.

Maintaining Changes

Members who have accomplished their goals can benefit from help in finding ways of maintaining these changes once the group ends. This can be aided by helping these members identify their gains and plan ways to continue to use their new competencies. One principle that can be employed in this is overlearning, in which members try out new behaviors, especially under a variety of circumstances, before the group ends. They can also be helped to identify others in their lives who will provide them with encouragement and reinforcement.

Seeking Out New Opportunities for Growth and Change

It is important to remind members that learning is a lifelong process, and that this is especially true with respect to learning about relationships. Some members will benefit by using a different kind of treatment group. Others should try out one of the many kinds of self-help groups that now exist. Still others may benefit by joining a social, educational, recreational, or political movement group.

EVALUATION

The worker can use almost any assessment measure in the group that has been developed for one-on-one helping. It is often important, however, for the worker to secure feedback after each session to help in planning the next session. Rose (1984) has developed a simple instrument for this purpose. Some of the questions he asks are as follows:

- How useful was today's session for you?
- Describe your involvement in today's session.
- Rate the extent to which you were able to disclose relevant information about yourself or your problem.
- How important to you were problems or situations you discussed (or that others discussed) in the group today?
- Circle the number on the scale that best describes the interrelationships among group members and workers in the group.
- Circle all the words that best describe you at today's session (excited, bored, depressed, interested, comfortable).
- How satisfied were you with today's session?

An evaluation process should be part of every group's termination. The members should be asked to indicate the progress they made (or failed to make) in accomplishing their goals, the extent to which the group was or was not helpful, and the ways in which the worker was or was not helpful to the group and its members.

RESEARCH ON GROUP TREATMENT

Research on the effectiveness of group treatment is very difficult because of the problems in maintaining an equivalent control condition, in monitoring process events that affect outcomes, and in ensuring that the treatment plan is implemented in the intended manner. Burlingame et al. (2004) have done a great deal of work in examining all the literature they could locate that reported on the question of effectiveness of group treatment. They began with 1,823 reports. They applied stringent criteria regarding the design of these studies, and the result was a reduction in the size of this sample to 107 studies and 14 meta-analyses. They subsequently grouped these studies as to the types of research questions posed and the nature of the group members, primarily in terms of psychiatric diagnoses. Their final conclusions were as follows:

> After reviewing hundreds of group psychotherapy outcomes and process studies, we are guardedly optimistic. The literature has become stronger and deeper and is capable of supporting evidence-based treatment recommendations for some patient populations. On the other hand, we face considerable challenges in bolstering our treatment models for some patient populations and refining our understanding of mechanisms of action to explain the change associated with group treatment. . . . We hope that the recommendations herein provide useful guidance for current and future investigations as we enter a new millennium of group research. (p. 684)

There have been few examinations of studies of group treatment in social work settings. Tolman and Molidor (1994), however, looked at 54 studies, of which 37 reported the outcome of a cognitive-behavioral group intervention. These cognitive-behavioral interventions included groups for parenting, woman abuse, child abuse, depression, and coping with physical disabilities. Two major deficiencies in the research literature were the absence of research on other practice approaches and the paucity of studies on groups whose members' presenting problems were heterogeneous. A recent summary of research on group work may be found in Garvin (2010).

An important development is the emergence of an emphasis on evidence-based group work. A leader in defining and explicating this approach is Mark J. Macgowan, who published what is likely to become the major reference on this topic. In his book *A Guide to Evidence-Based Group Work,* Macgowan (2008b) discusses in detail how to formulate practice questions in a way that facilitates a research literature search; how to conduct such a search; how to evaluate the rigor, impact, and applicability of sources; and how to apply and evaluate the achievement of outcomes related to a real-life application of these findings.

CONCLUSION

This chapter begins with a discussion of how group work emerged in social work practice as well as current group work approaches. The approaches described are the mediational model; the remedial model; the task-centered model; feminist, social justice, and empowerment models; and group psychotherapy models. The change theories drawn on by group work writers are also described, and these consist of psychodynamic theory, cognitive-behavioral theory, social-psychological and small-group theories, ecological theories, and theories that bear on the operation of therapeutic factors in groups.

Presented next were the activities of group workers during each phase of the group work process. The first phase is that of assessment, in which the worker and client determine whether a group experience is desirable and, if so, what type of group will be the most appropriate one. Some types that were discussed were open versus closed groups, short-term versus long-term groups, and support versus therapy groups. The worker can also use assessment information to determine how to compose a group; some principles of group composition were then described. Assessments conducted for group work purposes have some features that distinguish those used for other modalities of treatment, and these features were noted. An important compositional issue presented is the proportion of men and women in the group as well as of people from different ethnic backgrounds.

The beginning, middle, and termination phases of the group were then described, along with appropriate worker activities during each phase. Beginning phase issues include clarifying group purpose, determining member goals, strengthening relationships among members and between members and the worker, establishing group norms, dealing with feelings about the group, and selecting the group's initial activities.

The kinds of processes that occur in the group's middle phases were then detailed. These include problem solving, skill development, process illumination, program utilization, employment of group structures and role assignments, and interpretation. Important issues of transference and countertransference were noted.

The next section of the chapter described the process of termination. Aspects of termination that were described were handling feelings about ending, facilitating the maintenance of member change, and seeking new opportunities for change and growth. The following section of the chapter presented means for evaluating the group work experience. The chapter concluded by describing the current situation with respect to group work research.

A number of developments in group work practice and theory have become more pronounced just in the last several years. Foremost among these is an exploration of how social justice principles can infuse all of group work practice.[1] Secondly, more work is being done to empirically test the effects and processes of group work, research which uses quantitative, qualitative, and mixed methodological approaches. Group work methods are being used and tested in many fields of practice from which they had been absent, especially in the health and mental health fields. Finally, group workers are becoming appreciative of various ways of *knowing*, such as those of indigenous peoples, citizens of the countries in the southern hemispheres, and of the many ethnic groups in the economically developed nations,

and how these contribute to group work theory and practice.

REFERENCES

Adolph, M. (1983). The all-women's consciousness raising group as a component of treatment for mental illness. *Social Work With Groups, 6,* 117–132.

American Psychiatric Association. (1994). *Diagnostic and statistical manual of mental disorders* (4th ed.). Washington, DC: Author.

Bion, W. (1959). *Experiences in groups and other papers.* New York, NY: Basic Books.

Bloch, S., & Crouch, E. (1985). *Therapeutic factors in group psychotherapy.* New York, NY: Oxford University Press.

Burlingame, G. M., MacKenzie, K. R., & Strauss, B. (2004). Small group treatment: Evidence for effectiveness and mechanisms of change. In M. J. Lambert (Ed.), *Bergin and Garfield's handbook of psychotherapy and behavior change* (5th ed., pp. 647–696). New York, NY: Wiley.

Chu, J., & Sue, S. (1984). Asian/Pacific Americans and group practice. *Social Work With Groups, 7,* 23–36.

Dass-Brailsford, P. (2012). Culturally sensitive therapy with low-income ethnic minority clients: An empowering intervention. *Journal of Contemporary Psychotherapy.* 42 (1), 37-44.

Davis, L. (1984). Essential components of group work with black Americans. *Social Work With Groups, 7,* 97–109.

Ezriel, H. (1973). Psychoanalytic group therapy. In L. R. Wolberg & E. K. Schwartz (Eds.), *Group therapy* (pp. 191–202). New York, NY: Intercontinental Medical Book Corporation.

Finn, J. L., & Jacobson, M. (2008). *Just practice: A social justice approach to social work* (2nd ed.). Peosta, IA: Eddie Bowers.

Forsyth, D. R. (2010). *Group dynamics* (5th ed.). Belmont, CA: Wadsworth Cengage Learning.

Foulkes, S. H. (1965). *Therapeutic group analysis.* New York, NY: International Universities Press.

Freire, P. (1973). *Education for critical consciousness.* New York, NY: Seabury Press.

---

[1]This author is presently at work with Robert Ortega on a book on how social justice principles can be drawn upon in all aspects of group work.

Gant, L. (2004). Evaluation of group work. In C. D. Garvin, L. M. Gutiẽrrez, & M.J. Galinsky (Eds), *Handbook of social work with groups* (pp. 461–476). New York, NY: Guilford Press.

Garvin, C. D. (1974). Task-centered group work. *Social Service Review, 48,* 494–507.

Garvin, C. D. (1985). Group process: Usage and uses in social work practice. In M. Sundel, P. Glasser, R. Sarri, & R. Vinter (Eds.), *Individual change through small groups* (pp. 203–225). New York, NY: Free Press.

Garvin, C. D. (1987). Group theory and research. In A. Minahan (Ed.), *Encyclopedia of social work* (18th ed., pp. 50–75). Silver Spring, MD: National Association of Social Workers.

Garvin, C. D. (1991). Social learning and role theories. In R. Greene & P. H. Ephross (Eds.), *Human behavior theory and social work practice* (pp. 151–176). New York, NY: Aldine de Gruyter.

Garvin, C. D. (1997). *Contemporary group work* (3rd ed.). Boston, MA: Allyn & Bacon.

Garvin, C. D. (2009). Task-centered model. In A. Gitterman & R. Salmon (Eds.), *Encyclopedia of social work with groups* (pp. 55–58). New York, NY: Routledge.

Garvin, C.D. (2010). Group work research: Past, present, and future. In A. E. Fortune, P. McCallion, & K. Briar-Lawson (Eds) *Social work practice research for the twenty-first century* (pp. 121–135). New York, NY: Columbia University Press.

Garvin, C. D., Glasser, P. H., Carter, B., English, R., & Wolfson, C. (1985). Group work intervention in the social environment. In M. Sundel, P. Glasser, R. Sarri, & R. Vinter (Eds.), *Individual change through small groups* (pp. 273–293). New York, NY: Free Press.

Garvin, C. D., & Reed, B. G. (1983). *Groupwork with women/groupwork with men: An overview of gender issues in social groupwork practice.* New York, NY: Haworth Press.

Garvin, C. D., & Reed, B. G. (1995). Sources and visions for feminist group work: Reflective processes, social justice, diversity, and connection. In N. Van Den Berg (Ed.), *Feminist practice in the 21st century* (pp. 41–69). Washington, DC: National Association of Social Workers.

Germain, C. B., & Gitterman, A. (2008). *The life model of social work practice: Advances in theory and practice* (3rd ed.). New York, NY: Columbia University Press.

Gitterman, A. (2004). The mutual aid model. In C. D. Garvin, L. M. Gutiérrez, & M. J. Galinsky (Eds.), *Handbook of social work with groups* (pp. 93–110). New York, NY: Guilford Press.

Gitterman, A., & Shulman, L. (Eds.). (1994). *Mutual aid groups, vulnerable populations, and the life cycle* (2nd ed.). New York, NY: Columbia University Press.

Gutiérrez, L. (1990). Working with women of color: An empowerment perspective. *Social Work, 35,* 149–153.

Hall, J.C. (2011). A narrative approach to group work with men who batter. *Social Work with Groups, 34*(2), 175-189.

Konopka, G. (1949). *Therapeutic group work with children.* Minneapolis: University of Minnesota Press.

Levine, B. (1979). *Group psychotherapy: Practice and development.* Englewood Cliffs, NJ: Prentice Hall.

Macgowan, M. J. (2008a). Group dynamics. In T. Mizrahi & L. E. Davis (Eds.), *Encyclopedia of social work* (20th ed., pp. 279–287). New York, NY: Oxford University Press.

Macgowan, M. J. (2008b). *A guide to evidence-based group work.* New York, NY: Oxford University Press.

Macgowan, M. J. (2012). A standards-based inventory of foundation competencies in social work with groups. *Research on Social Work Practice, 22*(5), 578–589.

Martin, G., & Pear, J. (1999). *Behavior modification: What it is and how to do it* (6th ed.). Upper Saddle River, NJ: Prentice Hall.

Middleman, R. (1968). *The non-verbal method in working with groups.* New York, NY: Association Press.

Napier, R., & Gershenfeld, M. (1987). *Groups: Theory and experience* (3rd ed.). Boston, MA: Houghton Mifflin.

National Association of Social Workers. (1960). *Use of groups in the psychiatric setting.* New York, NY: Author.

Nixon, H. (1979). *The small group.* Englewood Cliffs, NJ: Prentice Hall.

Nurius, P., & Brower, A. (1993). *Social cognition and individual change: Current theory and counseling guidelines.* Newbury Park, CA: Sage.

Reed, B.G., Ortega, R.M., & Garvin, C. (2009). Small group theory and social work: Promoting diversity and social justice or recreating inequities. In R.R Green & N. Kropf (Eds.). *Human behavior theory: A diversity framework* (pp. 201-230). New Brunswick, NJ: Aldine Transaction.

Reid, W., & Epstein, L. (1972). *Task-centered casework.* New York, NY: Columbia University Press.

Rose, S. (1984). Use of data in identifying and resolving group problems in goal-oriented treatment groups. *Social Work With Groups, 7,* 23–36.

Rose, S. D. (1998). *Group therapy with troubled youth: A cognitive-behavioral interactive approach.* Thousand Oaks, CA: Sage.

Rutan, J. S., Stone, W. N., & Shay, J. J. (2007). *Psychodynamic group psychotherapy* (4th ed.). New York, NY: Guilford Press.

Sarri, R., & Galinsky, M. (1985). A conceptual framework for group development. In M. Sundel, P. Glasser, R. Sarri, & R. Vinter (Eds.), *Individual change through small groups* (pp. 70–86). New York, NY: Free Press.

Schiller, L. Y. (1997). Rethinking stages of development in women's groups: Implications for practice. *Social Work With Groups, 20*(3), 3–19.

Schwartz, W. (1994). The social worker in the group. In T. Berman-Rossi (Ed.), *Social work: The collected writings of William Schwartz* (pp. 257–276). Itasca, IL: Peacock.

Steinberg, D.M. (2010). Mutual aid: A contribution to best-practice social work. *Social Work with Groups: A Journal of Community and Clinical Practice*, *33*(1), 53–68.

Sundel, M., Glasser, P., Sarri, R., & Vinter, R. (Eds.). (1985). *Individual change through small groups.* New York, NY: Free Press.

Tolman, R. M., & Molidor, C. E. (1994). A decade of social group work research: Trends in methodology, theory, and program development. *Research on Social Work Practice, 4,* 142–159.

Tolson, E., Reid, W., & Garvin, C. (2003). *Generalist practice: A task-centered approach* (2nd ed.). New York, NY: Columbia University Press.

Toseland, R., & Rivas, R. (2012). *An introduction to group work practice* (7th ed.). Boston, MA: Allyn & Bacon.

Vinter, R. (1985). Program activities: An analysis of their effects on participant behavior. In M. Sundel, P. Glasser, R. Sarri, & R. Vinter (Eds.), *Individual change through small groups* (pp. 226–236). New York, NY: Free Press.

Whitaker, D. S., & Lieberman, M. A. (1965). *Psychotherapy through the group process.* New York, NY: Atherton Press.

Wilson, G., & Ryland, G. (1949). *Social group work practice.* Boston, MA: Houghton Mifflin.

Yalom, I., & Leszcz, M. (2005). *The theory and practice of group psychotherapy* (5th ed.). New York, NY: Basic Books.

12

THE CHALLENGE OF CLINICAL WORK WITH SURVIVORS OF TRAUMA

ROBERTA GRAZIANO

Folk wisdom is filled with ghosts who refuse to rest... until their stories are told.... Remembering and telling the truth about terrible events are prerequisites both for the restoration of the social order and for the healing of individual victims.

—J. Herman (1992, p. 1)

Psychic trauma has probably existed since the beginning of humankind. Although the term *posttraumatic stress* and its related diagnostic classifications have become a recognizable part of the mental health vocabulary only in the past two decades, as well as gaining increasing notice in the media and among the public at large more recently, the concepts underlying the current nomenclature have been observed, described, and studied for many centuries.

BACKGROUND

Long before there were psychiatrists, there were accounts, both factual and fictional, of catastrophic events and their effects on people. Trimble (1985) traces some of these, from Shakespeare's Hotspur (in *Henry IV*), who, following battle, suffered from sleep disturbance, intrusive memories, startle reactions, and depression, among other symptoms, to Samuel Pepys's description of the aftereffects, on him, of the Great Fire of London in 1666 (which included terror and nightmares), to Dickens's account of a railway accident in which he was involved in 1865 and his subsequent development of a phobia. More widespread scientific interest in the behavioral, physiological, and emotional phenomena engendered by trauma arose, beginning in the mid-19th century, in connection with medicolegal issues surrounding the compensation of victims of railway and industrial accidents and, early in the 20th century, with the spread of workers' compensation legislation.

Interest also arose in the military sphere. During and following the Civil War, attention was given to the idea that the emotional stress of wartime experiences could generate a spectrum of symptoms; Da Costa (1871) labeled it "irritable heart." Later in the century, Janet described the symptoms of his traumatized patients as "memory disruption" (1889). During World War I and again in World War II, this interest was renewed as ways were sought to treat soldiers exhibiting "shell shock," "combat fatigue," and "physioneurosis" (Kardiner, 1941) so that they might rapidly return to service (Albucher, Van Etten-Lee, & Liberzon, 2002).

The women's movement of the 1970s enabled many women to speak for the first time of the traumatic aftereffects of sexual abuse, rape, and domestic violence (Herman, 1992). Over the past century and a half, a variety of terms have been used to describe the symptoms exhibited following various traumatic events, including *railway spine disorder*, *hysteria*, *compensation neurosis*, (Holocaust) *survivor's syndrome*, *rape trauma syndrome*, *battered wife syndrome*, *post-Vietnam syndrome*, and *child abuse syndrome*, among many others (Meichenbaum, 1994).

Freud believed at first that many of the psychiatric difficulties he encountered in his patients, including hysteria, were the result of early trauma (Breuer & Freud, 1893–1895/1957; Freud, 1896/1962). However, after he began to theorize, more than a century ago, that childhood fantasies, rather than actual occurrences, were responsible for his patients' symptoms, there began a marked shift, first in psychoanalysis and then in psychiatry in general, away from a consideration of the role of overwhelming life experiences in the etiology of mental illness.

It is only in the past three decades that both those who are a part of the recent move toward a biomedical, genetic model and those who adhere to the more traditional focus on the dynamic and intrapsychic components of mental functioning have begun to accommodate to the idea that a wide variety of traumatic events, at any period in life, can have a crucial impact on people's emotional and physical selves. As more attention has been paid to examining both the spectrum of these experiences and the similarities among their effects, the realization has arisen that "the human response to overwhelming and uncontrollable life events is remarkably consistent" (van der Kolk, 1987, p. 2).

DEFINITIONS AND THEORY BUILDING

Although the *general* response to overwhelming events may be consistent, there has been debate as to the definition of trauma and other terms, as well as about the cohesiveness of the symptomatology of those who have undergone such experiences. For our purposes, we will compare two definitions of trauma. The first is by Figley (1985): "an emotional state of discomfort and stress resulting from memories of an extraordinary, catastrophic experience which shattered the survivor's sense of invulnerability to harm" (p. xviii). This definition emphasizes the extraordinary *nature of the event*. In contrast, Meichenbaum (1994) emphasizes the extraordinary *effort needed to cope* with the event(s): "extreme or severe events that are so powerful, harmful and/or threatening that they demand extraordinary coping efforts. Such traumatic events are neither very rare, nor unusual" (p. 32). These two definitions may reflect a changing outlook on the nature of trauma, to include not only one-time, unusual, shattering occurrences such as natural disasters or hostage situations but also everyday ongoing situations such as domestic violence.

Traumatic events that are unexpected, single occurrences, surprising and devastating but of limited duration (e.g., rape, car accident) are likely to lead to symptoms of intrusive ideation, avoidance, and hyperarousal. Long-term stressors associated with sustained and repeated ordeals, more likely to be intentional and of human design (e.g., combat, ongoing abuse), may eventuate in feelings of helplessness, dissociation, characterological and interpersonal problems, and the use of self-protective mechanisms such as detachment, constricted affect, and substance abuse, among other symptoms (Meichenbaum, 1994; Terr, 1991).

Regardless of the ordinary or extraordinary nature of the event or ongoing experience,

> The natural consequent behaviors and emotions of a trauma during a catastrophe is the traumatic stress reaction and can be defined as a set of conscious and unconscious actions and emotions associated with dealing with the stressors of the catastrophe and the period immediately afterwards.... Posttraumatic stress reactions are defined as a set of conscious and unconscious behaviors and emotions associated with dealing with the memories of the stressors. (Figley, 1985, p. xix)

Those who have followed discussions of trauma and its sequelae have noted with interest first the inclusion of the diagnostic category of posttraumatic stress disorder (PTSD) in the *Diagnostic and Statistical Manual of Mental Disorders*, third edition (*DSM-III*; American Psychiatric Association, 1980); then the inclusion of the clinical presentation of PTSD in children in the *DSM-III*, revised edition (*DSM-III-R*; American Psychiatric Association, 1987); followed by the struggle over whether to include additional categories, such as complex PTSD (Herman, 1992) and disorders of extreme stress (van der Kolk, Roth, Pelcovitz, & Mandel, 1993), in the fourth edition (*DSM-IV*; American Psychiatric Association, 1994). These latter efforts, though unsuccessful, may have helped broaden the original stressor criteria to include in the *DSM-IV*, the concept of vicarious traumatization, as well as to suggest revisions for the upcoming *DSM-V* (Brewin, Lanius, Novac, Schnyder, & Galea, 2009). In all this, however, the diagnosis is virtually the only one in which, as Pynoos (1994) notes,

> The diagnostic gateway is the occurrence of a specific personal experience. In a dramatic fashion, PTSD reopened the psychiatric door to the serious vicissitudes of life, and there has been tremendous clinical pressure to push through this opening an enormous backlog of human experience that otherwise seems to have no place in an "etiologically free" classification system. (p. ix)

The same event may have very different effects on different people, and PTSD is by no means the inevitable outcome. "Specific details need to be understood about each experience, including characteristics of the event itself and the perceptions, affects and interpretations on the part of the victim" (Davidson, 1994, p. 1). Despite the foregoing, however, "although the nature of the trauma, the age of the victim, predisposing personality, and community response all have an important effect on ultimate posttraumatic adaptation, the core features of the posttraumatic syndrome are fairly constant across these variables" (van der Kolk, 1987, p. 2).

POSTTRAUMATIC STRESS DISORDER

These core features have been identified in a number of ways and are described by van der Kolk (1987) as "a phasic reliving and denial, with alternating intrusive and numbing responses" (p. 3). Herman (1992), perhaps more poetically, depicts the syndrome as follows: "The conflict between the will to deny horrible events and the will to proclaim them aloud is the central dialectic of psychological trauma" (p. 1). A simpler explanation is that these features consist of "intense reexperiencing of the inciting trauma, persistent avoidance of reminders of the event, and heightened arousal" (*DSM-IV*, text revision [*DSM-IV-TR*], American Psychiatric Association, 2000). According to Katz and Yehuda (2006), "PTSD has an acute subtype, which is presumed to last less than three months. It has a chronic subtype that persists beyond that duration" (p. 68). Perhaps the definitive current description is provided in *DSM-IV*. A brief version is presented here:

> The essential feature of Posttraumatic Stress Disorder is the development of characteristic symptoms following exposure to an extreme traumatic stressor involving direct personal experience of an event that involves actual or threatened death or serious injury, or other threat to one's physical integrity; or witnessing [such] an event . . . ; or learning about [such an event] experienced by a family member or other close associate. The person's response . . . must

involve intense fear, helplessness, or horror (or in children, the response must involve disorganization or agitated behavior). The characteristic symptoms . . . include persistent reexperiencing of the traumatic event, persistent avoidance of stimuli associated with the trauma and numbing of responsiveness, and persistent symptoms of increased arousal. (American Psychiatric Association, 1994, p. 424)

The symptoms can include recurrent and intrusive recollections of the event, recurrent dreams in which the event is replayed, dissociation, intense psychological distress, physiological reactivity in response to triggers that resemble or in some way are symbolic of an aspect of the original event, avoidance of stimuli associated with the trauma, amnesia for an aspect (or aspects) of the event, diminished responsiveness or psychic numbing, feelings of detachment from others, reduced ability to experience emotions, a sense of a foreshortened future, persistent symptoms of anxiety, sleep disturbances, hypervigilance, exaggerated startle response, irritability or anger outbursts, and/or difficulty concentrating.

A number of questions have been raised as to the prevalence of PTSD in the general population, and a recent estimate points out that the "incidence of PTSD after a traumatic event ranges from as low as 6 percent to as high as 20 percent" (Yehuda, 2002, p. 108).

Many studies, most recently those of Terhakopian, Sinaii, Engel, Schnurr, and Hoge (2008) and Darves-Bornoz et al. (2008), have attempted to measure the prevalence rates of exposure to traumatic events, and actual PTSD, in various populations in the United States and Western Europe, but this is an extremely complex process (Dickstein, Suvak, Litz & Adler, 2010). As to whether the characteristic effects of PTSD occur regardless of ethnicity, culture, or gender, Marsella, Friedman, and Spain (1994), in their review of studies of various ethnocultural groups, victim populations, traumatic events, and clinical topics, suggest that this is the case:

The results of these studies are generally consistent with the results of existing biological research, which suggests that there is a universal biological response to traumatic events . . . However, although the response to a traumatic event may share some universal features, especially as the trauma becomes more severe, ethnocultural features may play an important role in the individual's vulnerability to PTSD, the expression of PTSD, and the treatment responsivity to PTSD. (p. 34)

Gusman et al. (1996) add the following caveat: "Ethnicity and trauma in America are likely to overlap increasingly in the future. . . . In this evolving context, the challenges for PTSD treatment are formidable" (p. 454). In fact, it has been suggested that "Trauma survivors comprise one large, diverse target group, marginalized by a dominant culture that wishes to obscure the realities of human capacities for cruelty" (Brown, 2009, p. 168). To provide the most effective treatment (Morsette, 2006) for each individual, then, it is most important for the worker or therapist to develop transcultural competency, to be aware of ethnocentrism, and to be open to learning from the client; otherwise, treatment may be more hurtful than helpful:

Symptoms differ among ethnic groups, as do definitions of a "problem," of mental health and disability, of physical illness, and of psychic pain. Therefore, the clinician needs to comprehend the various cultural accommodations to mental illness characteristic of the ethnic groups in question, and ethnic group members' help-seeking behavior and expectations. (Parson, 1985, p. 334)

COGNITIVE, AFFECTIVE, AND SOMATIC EFFECTS

Those who have studied trauma have looked at it from varying perspectives, depending on their own backgrounds, orientation, and professional education. Clinical social workers, using a biopsychosocial framework, have long been aware of the need to take a multitude of factors into account in their direct work with individuals, families, groups, and communities and must now be prepared to add concepts of traumatic stress to these elements. There is mounting evidence that traumatic events are associated with the development of various disorders and conditions:

1. It has been estimated that 40% to 60% of psychiatric outpatients and 50% of psychiatric inpatients report histories of early-childhood victimization (e.g., physical and sexual abuse) (Herman, 1992).

2. A majority of American women (68.9%) have experienced at least one type of traumatic event during their lifetimes (Resnick, Kilpatrick, Dansky, Saunders, & Best, 1993). "Being female is a risk factor, not a prerequisite, for PTSD. . . . [I]t is important that women's heightened risk for experiencing interpersonal violence accounts for much of their higher prevalence of PTSD" (Kimerling, Ouimette, & Wolfe, 2002, pp. 32–33).

3. There is an association between somatization disorder, dissociation, and a history of abuse in female psychiatric patients. This was noted more than a century ago by Janet and recently supported by Pribor, Yutzy, Dean, and Wetzel (1993). Women who have chronic pelvic pain are likely to have been sexually assaulted as children (Scaer, 2001; Walker, Katon, Nerras, Jemelka, & Massoth, 1992). Somatization disorders are widespread among Holocaust victims and former prisoners of war and increase over time in rape victims, and there is a strong association between chronic PTSD and physical illness (Barsky, Wool, Barnett, & Cleary, 1994; Scaer, 2001; Shalev, Bleich, & Ursano, 1990; White & Faustman, 1989).

4. Of those individuals who have borderline personality disorder, roughly one third fulfill the criteria for PTSD. There are high rates of traumatic childhood experiences, including physical and sexual abuse and exposure to violence, in adolescent and adult patients with borderline personality disorder (Gunderson & Chu, 1993).

5. According to Kulka et al. (1990), 15.2% of all male Vietnam veterans currently have PTSD; the incidence is 21% among African Americans and 28% among Hispanics (cited in Meichenbaum, 1994, p. 58). Falk, Hersen, and Van Hasselt (1994) note, "The general consensus in the literature is that PTSD currently exists in many World War II and Korean War veterans 4 or 5 decades after their actual combat experiences" (p. 384). Evidence from the 1.64 million military personnel deployed in Operation Enduring Freedom (OEF) and Operation Iraqi Freedom (OIF) suggests that approximately 300,000 individuals currently suffer from PTSD or major depression. Those with PTSD are more likely to have other psychiatric diagnoses (e.g., substance abuse disorder) and are at increased risk for suicide (Tanielian & Jaycox, 2008). The RAND Corporation's Center for Military Health Policy and Research estimates that at least 25% to 30% of returning veterans have PTSD, and that women soldiers are doubly traumatized by combat trauma and rape trauma, with nearly one third reporting having been sexually assaulted or raped by the men with whom they serve (H. Fancher, project PROVE, personal communication, January 9, 2009).

6. Researchers estimate that 1.3 million American women have rape-related PTSD and approximately 211,000 will develop it each year (Calhoun & Resick, 1993). Rape victims may constitute the largest single group of PTSD sufferers (Foa, Rothbaum, & Steketee, 1993).

7. There is a clear link between spouse abuse and familial child abuse. Survivors of physical assault by male partners evidence high levels of depression, suicidal ideation, substance abuse, and PTSD symptoms.

8. Survivors of ongoing, long-term trauma, such as that experienced under conditions of spousal or partner abuse, child sexual and/or physical abuse, political terrorism and genocide, prolonged combat, or being a prisoner of war, among others, are vulnerable to developing *Complex PTSD*: "In addition to often being life-threatening or physically violating, these experiences are typically chronic rather than one-time or limited, and they compromise the individual's personality development and basic trust in primary relationships" (Ford & Courtois, 2009, p. 14).

We are also increasingly aware of the coexistence of depression, eating disorders, panic attacks, self-mutilation, and other phenomena that are linked to trauma and to resulting PTSD. A growing body of epidemiological research (Chilcoat & Menard, 2003; Stewart & Conrod, 2003, Kingston & Raghavan, 2009) now points to considerable comorbidity of posttraumatic stress disorder and substance use disorder, a phenomenon that has been reported anecdotally, for many years, by those working with survivors of trauma.

Trauma that occurs early in life can have adverse effects on " . . . the fundamental psychological and biological foundations necessary for all subsequent development: (1) attention and learning; (2) working (short-term), declarative (verbal), and narrative (autobiographical) memory; (3) emotion regulation; (4) personality formation and integration; and (5) relationships (attachment)" (Ford, 2009, p. 31).

Trauma's lasting effects on the mind and body must be taken into consideration when we try to understand a client's somatic symptoms, behavior, and ways of thinking about the world, the future, and relationships. The age or developmental stage at which the traumatic event occurred (Brennen et al., 2010); frequency, intensity, and duration of the trauma; and gender (Gill, Page, Sharps, & Campbell, 2008; Kimerling et al., 2002) and ethnocultural features (Gusman et al., 1996) of the survivor are among the variables that can shape responses. So too are factors such as whether the situation was one that affected a large group or community (e.g., a flood, combat) or one in which the victim was alone or isolated (e.g., rape, torture). "What distinguishes people who develop PTSD from people who are merely temporarily overwhelmed is that people who develop PTSD become 'stuck' on the trauma and keep reliving it in thoughts, feelings, or images" (van der Kolk, van der Hart, & Burbridge, 2002, p. 24).

In general, one can speculate that the human tendency to construct stories, or narratives, to explain or make sense of experiences is called into action during and after traumatic events. Each individual constructs a unique narrative that may have a crucial influence on the subsequent development of posttraumatic symptomatology. Moreover, the meaning that the event has for the individual is a determining factor: A child may ascribe very different meanings to

being molested by a stranger than to being molested by a trusted family member.

Traumatic memories may be imprinted in the mind in vivid, indelible images and sensations. These visual, aural, and bodily encodings of fragments of intolerable happenings may be inaccessible to cognitive and verbal retrieval. It is possible that in states of high sympathetic nervous system arousal, the ability to encode memory in words fails, and the central nervous system is thrown back to earlier, predominantly sensory and iconic, forms of memory (Herman, 1992).

The inability to express in words the sensations and images attendant on traumatic memories may develop when the following occurs:

> An individual is confronted with overwhelming affects: in other words, his affective responses produce an unbearable psychic state which threatens to disorganize, perhaps even destroy, all psychic functions. . . . The capacity to tolerate emotions becomes diminished. In addition, there is a regression in the affects themselves, both their cognitive and expressive aspects. This regression accounts for the high incidence of psychosomatic disorders, and the disturbance in affectivity and capacity for verbalization . . . called "alexithymia." (Krystal, 1978, pp. 108–109)

In *alexithymia,* which literally means "without words for feelings," emotional arousal is responded to by a denial of the emotions aroused by the triggering event, rather than a denial of the event itself (Jones, 1991). This disavowal severs the connection between incident and affect.

> This failure to translate somatic states into words and symbols causes [some trauma survivors] to experience emotions simply as physical problems. This naturally plays havoc with intimate and trusting interpersonal communications. These people have somatization disorders and relate to the world through their bodies. (van der Kolk et al., 2002, p. 31)

What all this might mean is that the narrative constructed following a traumatic experience may not be told in words. Instead, it may be expressed in actions or somatic symptoms.

Ella, a 40-year-old woman of Cuban descent, who had recently begun outpatient therapy following a brief hospitalization for depression and suicidal ideation, was waiting for me in the interview room at the mental health clinic, but seemed far away. When I entered, she was visibly startled, and a few moments later, she fainted. She revived after a few moments and complained that she had hurt her back, and I accompanied her to the emergency room to be checked. The following week, Ella told me that the reason that she had been so "terrified" when I came into the room was that I "reminded her of a nun." At that point, I knew only that she had spent many years in an orphanage as a child. It took many months of very gentle listening, in bits and pieces, to uncover the fact that in this setting, isolated from the outside world and cut off from her remaining family members, Ella had been abused—physically, psychologically, and sexually—by the nuns, and that one of the ways she had "escaped" (or interrupted the abuse) was by fainting. My appearance in the interview room had apparently been quiet and unexpected, and in that way it resembled the manner in which the nuns used to appear (seemingly out of nowhere), grab her, and beat and sexually abuse her.

Traumatic memories may also appear in the form of flashbacks, triggered by any reminder of the original situation or experience. These flashbacks, which are vivid mental or sensory images of a fragment or moment during the overwhelming, terrifying event, may set off verbal or physical reactions or reenactments that are inexplicable in terms of the present but quite understandable in light of what has gone before.

Joan had been frequently and severely physically abused, and sometimes sexually abused, by her father from early childhood into her teens, when she made a suicidal gesture. This action galvanized her mother into leaving home with Joan and her younger brother. Joan's mother, who was addicted to alcohol and painkillers, was experienced as more nurturing than her father but was unpredictable, verbally abusive, and often physically and emotionally unavailable. Joan entered therapy in her early 30s, by which time she had already achieved substantial progress in recovery from substance abuse, and it soon became clear that she suffered from major dissociative episodes, of which she was aware, and pervasive and overwhelming anxiety. The dissociation took the form of several different personalities, some protective, some terrified, and some aggressive, and Joan would point each out to me as they emerged during sessions. Frequent flashbacks to her father's abuse occurred when Joan and her husband, Roger, a gentle and thoughtful man, began to get intimate. "It's like the minute Roger touches me sexually, my father's right back in the room," Joan said during a couples session. Therapy consisted of working within a trauma framework in which she recognized the psychic fragmentation and gradually reintegrated the dissociated personalities into a more whole self. At one point, a referral for medication was necessary to help Joan deal with the anxiety and panic that accompanied facing the realities of her past.

Joan eventually resumed her education, which had been interrupted when she had to go to work to support her mother. She graduated from college and a graduate program with honors, terminated therapy, and began a professional career in which she became a highly valued attorney. Several years later, Joan called in a panic: Her mother had died, as a result of complications of substance abuse that had resulted in diabetes and dementia, and Joan was unable to concentrate at work. As we resumed therapy, this time with Roger present at her request, Joan revealed that she had become involved, emotionally and psychologically (but not sexually), in a professional relationship that she had no desire to continue, with a person, "Mr. X," who threatened alternately to "ruin" her for "unprofessional" behavior and to commit suicide if Joan broke off contact. The parallels to Joan's mother, who had been extremely manipulative and used emotional blackmail as one of her main methods of keeping Joan close, were striking.

This time, however, a new dissociated personality, the "wise guy," who rejected any discussion, introspection, or attempt to link Joan's current plight with past experiences, seemed to rule the roost. Roger, who had been extremely patient in the past and understood Joan's issues, was now at the end of his rope because Joan continued to phone Mr. X, whom she avowed she wanted to escape from, and he felt their marriage was threatened. Joan, meanwhile, felt she had no choice but to continue to be in contact with Mr. X for a period of time. Both therapy and her marriage seemed to be at a stalemate, and she felt her job was in jeopardy. After initially dismissing suggestions regarding adjunctive treatments, such as medication, which had had disturbing side effects in the past, or cognitive-behavioral interventions (and acknowledging that the "wise guy" was behind her refusal to consider them), Joan finally underwent several eye movement desensitization and reprocessing (EMDR) sessions with a therapist certified in that modality whom she had found on her own. This led to marked diminution of the anxiety and a stronger sense of self-efficacy regarding the relationship with Mr. X. The reenactment of Joan's relationship with her mother, and the reemergence of fragmented parts of her younger self, were extraordinarily powerful, and trauma-focused psychodynamic psychotherapy needed to be augmented by another modality (which Joan sought out herself) to break the impasse.

Somatic symptoms may be manifestations of the biochemical and neurophysiological accompaniments to traumatic stress that have been discovered during recent research, where it has been found that "extreme threat to the organism, whether a laboratory animal or an individual exposed to extreme stress, may result in long-term changes in behavior and neurobiological systems" (Bremner, Davis, Southwick, Krystal, & Charney, 1994, p. 43; see also Krystal et al., 1989). Recent research into the neurobiological process of response to trauma (Katz & Yehuda, 2006) posits the following:

1. Sensory information floods into the region of the brain known as the amygdala. The amygdala then initiates a cascade of physiological reactions characteristic of fear responses: heightened arousal and alertness; elevated heart rates; depressed breathing; widened pupils to permit receipt of as much visual information as possible; and a rise in blood sugar to fuel the muscles of flight and action. These are known collectively as the fight-or-flight reaction (p. 62).

2. Since the visual cortex is involved, "It is possible that the flashbacks and nightmares of PTSD reflect a failure to encode these memories in semantic terms" (p. 75).

3. Another structure of the brain, the hippocampus, plays a role in determining the context in which an event arises (Katz & Yehuda, 2006, p. 63). A hippocampus damaged by elevated levels of stress hormones is less able to put *new* experiences into appropriate context, leading trauma survivors "to see otherwise nontraumatic

events as though they were threats akin to the initial trauma" (p. 75).

4. When the immediate threat passes, the body works to contain the stress reaction. Norepinephrine (NE), which initiates and maintains the fight-or-flight reaction, elevates heart rate and blood sugar to deliver energy to muscles, and also contributes to forming memories of the emotion-laden events in the amygdala. Cortisol, another stress hormone, which is simultaneously released in response to stress, helps diminish the levels of NE, and thus the state of alert. If the effort to contain the stress response fails, the results may include "significant emotional and mental disequilibrium and eventual psychiatric disorder" (Katz & Yehuda, 2006, p. 64; see also Yehuda, 2002). In addition, "an abnormally prolonged NE response can lead to the overconsolidation of bad memories" (Katz & Yehuda, 2006, p. 71).

5. PTSD seems to be biologically different from normal stress reactions

> because the system regulating the release of the adrenal stress hormones functions at a threshold that maintains unexpectedly low cortisol levels. . . . Given that stress-induced release of cortisol is hypothesized to be vital to turning off the fear response . . . the possible failure of this mechanism in PTSD sufferers may permit the fear response to proceed unchecked. (Katz & Yehuda, 2006, p. 69)

6. This may, in turn, lead to sustained arousal of the sympathetic nervous system and possibly to PTSD.

More specific connections between trauma and systems of the body are reported by Scaer (2001):

> Although much of the scientific data associating traumatic stress with adverse health effects is circumstantial and subject to debate and interpretation, many studies show physiological alterations in PTSD that correlate with predictable diseases seen in its victims. There also appears to be a small cluster of poorly understood syndromes that have a compelling link to the physiology and incidence of trauma, including irritable bowel syndrome, interstitial cystitis, chronic pain syndrome, fibromyalgia/ chronic fatigue syndrome, and reflex sympathetic dystrophy. Other so-called diseases of stress, including hypertension, peptic ulcer disease, ulcerative colitis, and atherosclerotic coronary artery disease, probably also can be added to the list of diseases of trauma. The trauma therefore changes the brain, which changes the body. (p. 83)

Similarly, van der Kolk and Greenberg (1987) note that while activation of the autonomic nervous system is necessary to cope with major stress, many traumatized people "continue to respond even to minor stimuli with an intensity appropriate only to emergency situations. . . . Autonomic arousal, no longer a preparation to meet external threat, becomes itself a precipitant of fear and emergency responses" (p. 66). Thus, we find that those who have suffered a traumatic experience often display reminders of the original event in the form of "body memories," which replicate or reenact the original injury or physical disorder, or they may exhibit somatic symptoms triggered by reminders of the original trauma.

As an adult, Ella suffered from frequent headaches, ear infections, and sinus problems, which would arise during times of interpersonal stress. Many of these physical symptoms seemed to have no organic basis. When Ella returned to school in midlife to earn a college degree, her headaches and earaches intensified, and she experienced recurrent panic attacks as well. Several flashbacks during therapy sessions led to Ella's realization that the physical abuse of her childhood had often occurred in the classroom, where Ella had been hit in the face, had her ears boxed, and had her head banged against the blackboard. This discovery was a turning point in both the diminution of the symptoms and the improvement of Ella's academic performance.

Of course, many survivors of trauma do not remember at all; instead, they use amnesia, disavowal, and dissociation to defend against unspeakable memories and protect themselves from experiencing intolerable feelings. Both client and worker may then be astonished at the various ways in which these memories surface and may indeed be unable to connect the various symptoms (somatic, emotional, etc.) with earlier occurrences, which, because of their dangerous or life-threatening content, had to be forgotten, at the time, for the individual to continue to function.

Zita's older sister, Annie, had been sexually abused by their father from early childhood until she left home as an adolescent. Zita, however, insisted that this had never happened to her. After several months in treatment, she mentioned that she had had an "image" of herself, age 4, and Annie, both being treated with an ointment on their genitals, administered by their mother. On hearing this, Annie told Zita that this treatment had been for a venereal disease. Zita continued to have no memory of being sexually molested in any way.

Dissociation is described in *DSM-IV* (American Psychiatric Association, 1994) as "a disruption in the usually integrated functions of consciousness, memory, identity, or perception of the environment" (p. 424). Amnesia (the "inability to recall important personal information, usually of a traumatic or stressful nature" [p. 424]), fugue (suddenly traveling away from home or work, with an inability to remember one's past and confusion about one's identity or assumption of a new identity), multiple personality disorder (more formally referred to as dissociative identity disorder), and depersonalization (a "feeling of being detached from one's mental processes or body" [p. 424]) are all aspects of dissociation. But just what is "disrupted" or "detached" and from what?

Allen (1995) suggests that aspects of the self are separated and walled off from the self's own experiences. Recent studies indicate that dissociation is strongly linked to trauma and that different kinds of traumatic experiences may be linked to varying symptoms or syndromes along the dissociative continuum. Awareness of the potential for dissociation in one or more forms should be an integral ingredient in the assessment and treatment of trauma:

> Dissociation is more likely to happen during and in the aftermath of physical trauma. Depersonalization, derealization, and psychogenic amnesia are common symptoms during natural disasters, combats, and other forms of physical trauma. In turn, a history of trauma has been found to be an almost universal etiology of such extreme chronic dissociative disorders as multiple personality disorder. In these cases the failure of integration of memory and identity serves a defensive purpose—against painful affect, recognition of physical helplessness, and physical pain. While such defenses can be quite adaptive, they carry with them a risk of failure to work through traumatic events, leading to chronic and severe posttraumatic dissociative symptoms in some instances. (Spiegel, 1993, p. 132)

Thus, whereas some individuals will communicate via words, others through somatic phenomena, and still others through flashbacks, those who dissociate tell their stories, paradoxically, through creating gaps in the continuity of their personal narrative.

ASSESSMENT AND TREATMENT STRATEGIES IN CLINICAL SOCIAL WORK

Although the array of features described may seem daunting when considering the assessment and treatment of survivors of trauma, the experience itself can be exhilarating as well as challenging. The most liberating feature of trauma work is the opportunity to depathologize the client and to view treatment as a way of helping a person (or people) emerge from the aftereffects of real incidents that would have been painful, terrifying, or overwhelming to almost anyone. Once the existence of traumatic events in the past (and/or present) has been established, both client and worker can trace the connection between the original occurrences and current symptoms or behavior and collaborate on strategies for change. (That is not to say, however, that establishing the existence of the trauma, tracing the connection, and/or collaboration are necessarily simple processes.)

Until recently, the average assessment or clinical interview did not target trauma factors, and often no information regarding traumatic experiences was elicited. Alternatively, clients would mention events that, if one were using a trauma framework, had been clearly traumatic, but these references were either overlooked, ignored, misunderstood, or misinterpreted by the interviewer. Many clients, of course, seek (or are referred or mandated to) treatment because of events or situations that may be, at least on the surface (or in the client's or the clinician's mind), a far cry from overwhelming, catastrophic events, but during the course of therapy, treatment, or recovery, trauma-related issues may surface, often with disturbing results. Still other clients, even if asked, may deny the existence of any traumatic events in their past, yet their behavior, symptoms, or ways of thinking or relating may point to the possibility of trauma as an etiological factor.

In any assessment, both symptoms and experiences must be weighed to determine whether there exists a basis for trauma or PTSD as the principal factor, whether the person suffers from PTSD (or a related disorder) in conjunction with another psychological disorder, or whether trauma should be ruled out altogether. What this implies is that questions or strategies for appraising trauma need to be included as a matter of course: we must "[e]mbed assessment of trauma within a standard psychosocial assessment" (Courtois, Ford & Cloitre, 2009, p. 88). An

open-ended clinical interview in any setting can be supplemented with specific questions; a self-report scale can be added to the assessment process; measures of comorbidity (i.e., the occurrence of PTSD or a related disorder along with another diagnosis, such as schizophrenia, substance abuse, or a personality disorder) can be an additional feature of the assessment. Alternatively, an assessment can be structured so as to include both an interview and a number of the many questionnaires and rating scales that measure PTSD symptoms, adjustment, cognitive skills, strengths, and comorbidity, among other factors (Briere, 2004; Meichenbaum, 1994). For excellent overviews of assessment instruments and recommendations for their use, see Briere (2004); Briere & Spinazzola (2009); and Flack, Litz, Weathers, and Beaudreau (2002).

Briere (2004) cautions that to be successful, the interviewer must consider

> the quality of the evaluation environment, the need to assess both trauma-related and more generic symptoms, the potential for the client to under- or overreport traumatic events and symptoms, and potential constraints on the interpretation of trauma-related psychological assessment data . . . [t]he effects of assessor interactional style on the client . . . the occasional need to stabilize the client who is overwhelmed by the assessment stimuli or environment. (p. 83)

The most important elements are the manner in which questions are asked and asking the right questions—questions tailored to clients who know at the outset that they have had traumatic experiences or to those who do not raise the issue of trauma initially but whose awareness of having been victimized or having survived a traumatic experiences surfaces later in treatment.

Meichenbaum (1994) provides an excellent review of ways in which to ask questions so as to give the client control, elicit information, enlist the client in a collaborative process, analyze the problem or situation, establish goals, assess coping efforts, and develop strategies for moving ahead. He points out that, in general, "why" questions tend to be unanswerable and lead to self-doubt, further self-preoccupation, intrusive ideation, and poorer adjustment. Instead . . . clinicians can focus on "what" and "how" questions" (p. 126). These might include, for example, "What would you be doing differently to be on track?" or "How will you let someone else know that?"

Another tactic is to ask clients to put the story of their victimization trauma on a timeline, which also includes positive events, as well as to visualize a future timeline:

> Starting with general developmental topics that are (presumably, although not inevitably) less affect-laden enables patients to experience themselves as competent autobiographers who are capable of taking an active role in the . . . evaluation. . . . [T]he trauma, once it is broached in detail, is situated within the developmental context of the person's life. (Flack et al., 2002, p. 11)

Encouraging clients to offer suggestions as to what can be done (in the present or the future) may result in better follow-through than suggestions made by the clinician.

What must also be added, in considering both assessment and treatment approaches, is the likelihood that once the issue of having lived through events that may have been catastrophic, terrifying, or life threatening has been raised, the affective, cognitive, behavioral, and somatic baggage that accompanied the original event will resurface during the assessment process as well as in the treatment relationship. Therefore, from the very beginning, it is essential to have on hand, in addition to a working knowledge of the various manifestations of posttraumatic distress, a philosophy of treatment and a repertoire of techniques or interventions that can serve to diminish anxiety and help the client regain his or her equilibrium.

The establishment of an environment where the client will begin to feel comfortable and safe is a cardinal rule in any therapeutic situation. Strengths-based and empowerment strategies are an integral part of treatment, as is a philosophical and ethical commitment to self-determination, while a systematic and shared

plan of organized interventions is essential (Courtois et al., 2009, pp. 86-87). However, when working with individuals whose basic assumptions about safety and security have been shattered and who may believe that there is no predictability in life, that events occur at random, and that they have no control over anything (Janoff-Bulman, 1985, 1992; McCann & Pearlman, 1990; McCann, Pearlman, Sakheim, & Abrahamson, 1985), the maintenance of a safe place is even more important. Whenever possible, interviews or sessions should take place in an environment that allows for privacy, has a minimum of interruptions, and is reasonably free of outside distractions. (At the same time, this kind of setting may actually raise anxiety for some clients, especially if the traumatic events for them were related to child sexual abuse or a situation where they were isolated or trapped. It is important to check with the client periodically as to whether anything about the location, or about the worker's appearance or manner, is causing discomfort.) Clients should know that they are

> the sole arbiters regarding what information they divulge and the pace at which they do so. This overt sharing of control reinforces the collaborative character of the clinical relationship, and often helps to decrease the anxiety that is almost always associated with direct discussion of traumatic events. (Flack et al., 2002, p. 12)

From the beginning, the emphasis must be on the client's ability to stop a particular line of questioning or discussion at any time he or she begins to feel unsafe. The client and worker may devise their own code, whether it is a word or a gesture, to signify "no more." A confrontational approach on the part of the worker, which might prove successful in other settings or with other client populations, may well retraumatize the client with a trauma history. Courtois (1988, 1992) notes that survivors of trauma are likely to fear being abandoned, rejected, disbelieved, blamed, and/or shamed by the therapist, as they have been by others in reality, and that these concerns must be discussed directly in treatment and reassurance provided. She likens treatment to the process of completing a giant jigsaw puzzle of memory fragments that may be terrifying.

The issue of trust is a difficult one for survivors of trauma. If their early lives were secure, their previous assumptions about an "average expectable environment" or "good-enough" world have now been splintered, and they may fear ever trusting again. If they grew up in an atmosphere that disregarded or could not fulfill their needs for security and nurturance (e.g., child abuse, wartime, famine), they may not only not trust others but also disregard their own perceptions, needs, and wishes and instead become overly responsive to the needs of the "other" (including the therapist or worker). The latter phenomena have been noted not only by those studying trauma but also by psychodynamic investigators such as Khan (1963), Winnicott (1965), Kohut (1971, 1977, 1984), and Ferenczi (1933/1955). Consequently, clients may use defenses and ways of relating, even in treatment, that were originally designed to protect themselves against further traumatization. These include compliance, denial, and dissociation.

The therapist needs to establish enough trust to engage in a working relationship, which will then entail the client's verbalizing or experiencing feelings that may be perceived internally as deadly. Yet the therapist must also serve the crucial function of bearing witness to the unspeakable experiences clients have undergone, which are always struggling to be expressed. Therapists may have to make provisions for listening that are somewhat different from the usual ones, including letting a person stay longer in a session (if a particularly distressing flashback has just occurred, the client is extremely anxious, or self-control is tenuous). They may need to be available by telephone between appointments, to help deal with intrusive thoughts, flashbacks, or panic attacks that may result from material uncovered or discussed in a session. They may need to help get a client out of a flashback, or reground him or her in reality, when overwhelming feelings or memories threaten to destroy from within. They may need to provide a physical environment that offers a choice of closeness or distance (more than one client chair, in different parts of the room) and that can be altered or talked about if any element seems to arouse distress (Graziano, 1992).

Sara came into a session with a criticism of my choice of music on the waiting room radio. I explained that the radio was on to ensure privacy and that she could choose whatever station she liked while she was sitting there. Sara went on to say that the music I played reminded her of her foster father; she thought of it as "old people's music." She added that it was the radio as background noise that she really objected to. In tracing the concept of background noise and what that meant to her, Sara mentioned that it was noise that seemed to go on endlessly, like a washing machine. I asked her where the washing machine had been located in her foster home. She became increasingly uncomfortable and began to dissociate, but we were able to establish, by collaborating on drawing a floor plan, that the washing machine had been in the basement, where her foster brother had his room, and it was next to the bathroom where he had sexually abused her over a period of many years. She had thought as a child that the abuse, like the noise of the washing machine, would go on forever. Sara came out of the flashback visibly relieved and can now either reassure herself in situations where background noise exists or take steps to eliminate it.

Sometimes spoken words will not come, and a client will need to be encouraged to use nonverbal means, such as drawing, poetry, journals, photographs, movement, body work, or music, to express parts of the story that cannot yet be talked about aloud. (e.g., Joan produced two videotapes on incest and child abuse that told her story through her drawings, writings, and poetry. Ella revealed in journals and poems brought to her sessions previously unspeakable memories; she was also able to use guided imagery to escape from horrifying flashbacks.) From time to time, the worker too will need to make connections through actions or symbolic gestures rather than verbally.

> In this way, we may address experiences which are either unavailable in the verbal realm or too "dangerous" to be spoken aloud. Understanding the "meanings" may have to wait. Once the connections become clearer, however, the symptoms may not need to be relied upon, as we and our clients find more effective ways to construct the story of their reality. (Graziano, 1996, p. 200)

Rachel entered treatment in her early 40s, several years after she had developed Graves' disease, a disorder of the thyroid. She was suffering from severe panic attacks, could hardly go out of her house or ride the bus, and had physical sensations of "worms inside her arms," in addition to migraines and asthma. She attributed her anxiety and distress to the Graves' disease; her symptoms persisted despite high doses of Synthroid and antianxiety medication. Rachel reported that she had been helped very much by a therapist, Joe, whom she had seen some 15 years previously for "primal therapy," which she described as "lying on the floor curled up and uttering the primal scream." A few months after we began treatment, Rachel developed a perforated intestine and underwent emergency surgery, including a colostomy. I visited her in the hospital, where her anxiety was maximal, and later at home, where she reported that not only did she have no pain but she was already (1 week postsurgery) walking 2 miles a day, something she had not done even before she became ill. The same pattern recurred when she had further surgery to reverse the colostomy; she felt no pain and immediately engaged in strenuous physical activity. I was disconcerted by her seeming inability to feel pain, but Rachel dismissed my concerns. Later, she asked me to accompany her on a visit to Joe: She needed a letter from him to support her application for supplementary security income. When we arrived, Rachel was clearly shocked at Joe's appearance and functioning, though she had already known that Joe, now elderly, had been quite ill.

On the way home, she denied any distress, but in our next session, she brought in poetry that she had written during the time she was in therapy with Joe. She also began to show me poetry she had written since she had started treatment with me. I remarked that the poetry appeared to be written in a variety of voices; this precipitated a period of severe fragmentation and anxiety of nearly psychotic proportions and led to the uncovering of numerous other "people" behind the voices and a tentative diagnosis of dissociative identity disorder. During this period, Rachel was frequently unable to talk coherently in our sessions but, at my suggestion, kept a journal, wrote poetry, drew pictures, and spoke into a tape recorder; she then brought the journal, poems, drawings, and tapes to our sessions. What they all revealed was a childhood of constant physical abuse by her father, emotional distance and verbal abuse by her mother, and sadistic emotional, verbal, and physical abuse by her older sister.

(Continued)

(Continued)

Specific elements included her father repeatedly throwing her on the floor and kicking her in the stomach and her sister sitting on her chest and punching her in the nose. To survive in this milieu, Rachel had created a world of "others" (her term) who protected her from physical and emotional pain. Some were older females who were tough and self-reliant; one had the specific job of absorbing pain; at least one was a boy (a strong and valued figure in Rachel's culture). Their purpose was to shield the vulnerable "young one" from the terrifying anguish of emotional abandonment and physical suffering.

Once we had identified many of the "others" and their functions and discussed them within a framework of trauma and its effects on children, Rachel's symptoms began to abate, the "others" receded into the background, and Rachel was better able to deal with the reality of her current physical condition. This included tracing the connections between her father's abuse and the feelings aroused by her stomach surgery and her sister's physical attacks and her asthma. Eventually, she was able to reduce her antianxiety medications, discontinue attendance at a group for psychiatric patients with chronic medical conditions (where she was consistently the highest-functioning member), seek better medical care, and attain her bachelor's degree with honors, despite her many physical disabilities. Without the traumatic stress framework, I would have assessed and treated Rachel as a person with a chronic psychiatric disorder, as had the other mental health personnel she had encountered (except Joe). Working with Rachel necessitated my educating both Rachel and myself, as well as many medical and mental health professionals, about trauma, posttraumatic stress, and dissociation.

Many clients function normally for years before an event or trigger reveals the existence of a single, earlier trauma; others will have experienced many different kinds of trauma over the years, starting with their early lives. Working with a client who has had a multitude of traumatic experiences, beginning in childhood, can present special problems because of the difficulty of determining the meaning (or layers of meaning) of a particular symptom, trigger, or reenactment. Even if the individual has not developed a dissociative disorder, there may be instances of inexplicable behavior that can be understood only within the context of an early need for self-protection, which may have been compounded or intensified by later experiences.

Heidi grew up in eastern Germany in the 1930s. Her mother was verbally and physically cruel: On one occasion, her mother had locked her in her room after a severe beating, and Heidi had been so terrified that, rather than ask to be let out to go to the bathroom, she defecated on the floor and threw her feces out the window. Heidi enjoyed various activities with her father, especially attending the local Protestant church, taking walks in the woods, and going to opera performances.

When Heidi was 12 (which corresponded with the time when Hitler became extremely powerful), she experienced a great change at school: Her teachers began to be mean and punitive, and she was forbidden to join the school youth group. When she asked why, she was told it was because her mother was Jewish. This was astonishing to Heidi; she had not known it before. Heidi was sent to a nearby city at age 16, to be a companion to an elderly woman, who eventually denounced her to the Gestapo on learning that she was half Jewish. Heidi was placed in a slave labor camp, where she was raped by a fellow inmate. When the Russians invaded Germany, Heidi was able to escape from the camp, to find her mother and sister, and, after surviving for several weeks in the woods by eating berries and roots, to find refuge on an isolated farm, where she managed to fight off a sexual assault by two American soldiers. She fled the farm and made her way to a large city, where she narrowly escaped death in an Allied bombing attack.

After the war, Heidi came to the United States, where she married an older Jewish man, who was verbally and physically abusive. His family called her a "Nazi" because she considered herself Christian and spoke German. By the time Heidi sought treatment for "depression," she was about 50 years old. She had migraines, terrifying anxiety attacks, and claustrophobia; smoked and drank to excess; had few friends and was socially phobic; and was working in a menial job where her boss was verbally demeaning.

Shortly after beginning therapy, Heidi talked about her frequent episodes of leaving home: She would pack a suitcase and take a bus or train, not having a destination; would disembark in a strange town and stay for a few days, feeling frightened and lonely; and would return home, where her husband would be angry and abusive. She was also deeply distressed about the fact that whenever she attended the opera (her only recreation), she would develop a headache and feelings of suffocation and would have to run out of the theater.

After a few months in treatment, Heidi (who had already demonstrated her tendency to leave home—and therapy—abruptly) announced that she was going back to Europe to revisit her hometown, which she had left some 35 years previously. She had no advance plans; she just intended to arrive there and stay for an unspecified amount of time. She seemed unconcerned (even after I verified with her that her hometown was now in fact part of Czechoslovakia instead of Germany) as to how she would manage in a country whose language and customs she did not know and that, at the time, was still firmly under Soviet domination. I presented Heidi with a map, and together, we located the town where she had lived and the city where she had worked (both now renamed). I asked her to keep track of her journey on the map and assured her that I would be thinking about her while she was gone; I would want to know about her trip and would be waiting for her when she got back.

Heidi returned angry and confused: Nothing was the same; her hometown had been resettled by Czechs, and nobody spoke German; and even the Protestant church had been reconsecrated as a Catholic church. Mindful of her German heritage, I said that it seemed to make her very sad that her fatherland (a term Germans use for their native country) no longer existed as she had known it. Later she was able to tell me, with considerable shame, of sexual abuse by her father, beginning when she was 5 or 6 years old. This was a very different picture from the one she had given initially. Eventually, Heidi was also able to connect her trips to the opera with her father, and the betrayal by the old woman (a retired singer), to her physical symptoms and claustrophobia. In addition, she began to piece together the many connections between abuse, betrayal, imprisonment (or being "locked up"), and fear of death, which were the components of her need to "run away." She also spent a long time

(Continued)

(Continued)

struggling with the issues around her father's warmth and supportiveness of her versus his using her sexually and the links between these items and her enjoyment of various activities (church, opera, hiking) and distress around sex. Heidi became increasingly aware of the fact that she had received both life-sustaining and destructive things from him.

Had it not been for the outdoor skills she had learned from him, she would not have been able to survive in the woods; her aesthetic and spiritual life was rooted in experiences she had first had with him; her difficulties around sex and fear of betrayal in relationships were strongly tied to his sexual molestation of her and his failure to protect her from her abusive mother. Many of these themes resonated even more strongly because of her later experiences of betrayal, rejection, sexual assault, abuse, and narrow escapes from death, both during the war and afterward with her husband, his family, and her employer.

In addition to the work of making connections between the various pieces of Heidi's puzzle, therapy included elements such as helping her find a German-language Protestant church, where she enjoyed both religious and social activities; supporting her in taking well-planned vacations, where her destination, length of time away, and accommodations were set ahead of time; encouraging her to learn to drive, especially after her husband became ill, so that she could more easily get to the places she planned to go, and working out with her, after his death, ways in which she could overcome her phobia of highway driving; including her in a support group for survivors of child abuse so as to minimize her feelings of isolation, shame, and guilt; sustaining her efforts to find a better job and helping her find ways to assert herself at work; and, finally, after many years where our contact was only of the sporadic, touching-base variety, wishing Heidi well as she moved to another region after retirement and reassuring her that we could continue to stay in touch.

TREATMENT MODALITIES

Most of the discussion so far has focused on individual casework with trauma victims and survivors. This treatment includes the establishment of a supportive relationship; careful detective work to create meaning out of what may appear to be a fragmented experience of a shattered self; a psychoeducational component, which provides information about trauma and its aftereffects on the mind, emotions, and body and serves to normalize and legitimize the client's feelings and beliefs about self, others, and experiences; empathic listening; nurturing hope and supporting the client's efforts at healing; providing constancy and containment in the face of the client's flashbacks, terror, and other reactions;

and a solid understanding of the dynamics underlying the symptoms, affects, and various behavioral manifestations of the survivor's trauma. In addition to individual treatment, family therapy, group treatment, and other adjunctive approaches (such as psychopharmacology) are often extremely helpful, and sometimes essential.

Family Treatment

Family work can assist the survivor's significant others to understand the workings and aftereffects of trauma and its impact on their family member, as well as the impact on the family, both over time and in the present. Survivor, worker, and family members can collaborate on issues such as decreasing retraumatization in everyday life, reducing blame when the survivor is experiencing symptoms of PTSD, eliciting support and (if necessary) containment, and establishing trust. It must also be remembered that traumatization, in the form of spousal battering and child abuse, can begin in the family and that patterns of family violence can be transmitted across many generations. Thus, the family is a critical component of the survivor's vulnerability, resilience, and recovery, and the whole family can suffer when one or more members are affected by overwhelming events (Krugman, 1987). Boss (2006), who did groundbreaking work with family members of union workers lost in the terrorist attacks of 9/11, makes the connection between trauma and *ambiguous loss* (where a family member can be either physically absent but psychologically present—as happened with families of victims of 9/11—or physically present but psychologically absent—such as a family member with Alzheimer's disease being a different person from before). She notes that ambiguous loss, a relational disorder that results from an external stressor, meets a PTSD criterion as an experience beyond the normal range of human suffering. With the families of disaster victims, returning combat veterans, and other trauma survivors, family work can play a crucial role in prevention of trauma as well as in alleviating some of its effects.

Group Treatment

A number of group treatment approaches have been used with survivors of trauma. "The appeal of group interventions for PTSD rests, to a large extent, on the clear relevance of joining with others in therapeutic work when coping with a disorder marked by isolation, alienation, and diminished feelings" (Foy et al., 2000, p. 155). Group approaches that have proved helpful include self-help support groups, such as those that use a 12-step approach (e.g., Survivors of Incest Anonymous); support groups facilitated by a worker or therapist; psychoeducational groups; and a variety of structured, time-limited groups designed specifically for survivors of a particular kind of trauma, as well as groups composed of family members or significant others of survivors. These groups may emphasize a variety of approaches: cognitive-behavioral, crisis intervention, task-oriented, psychodrama, and others (Boss, 2006; Danieli, 1988; Ford, Fallot, & Harris, 2009; Herman & Schatzow, 1984; McCann, Sakheim, & Abrahamson, 1988; Mennen & Meadow, 1992; Scurfield, 1985; Scurfield, Corker, & Gongla, 1984; Solomon, 1992; van der Kolk, 1987).

Groups can develop healing rituals, ceremonies, and other activities to symbolize or celebrate the transformation of victims into survivors or demonstrate their emergence into fuller and healthier lives:

> Ceremonies compartmentalize the review of the trauma, provide symbolic enactments of transformation of previously shattered relationships, and reestablish connections among family and with society in general. . . . Ritual and ceremony are highly efficient vehicles for accessing and containing intense emotions evoked by traumatic experience. (Johnson, Feldman, Lubin, & Southwick, 1995, p. 283)

A social work student working in a Veterans Administration hospital noticed that many of the veterans of World War II who attended the mental health clinic were former prisoners of war. Though they were by then quite elderly, they were still exhibiting various symptoms of PTSD. On inquiry, she discovered that each felt ashamed of his nightmares and anxiety attacks, but none of them had ever talked to other World War II veterans, even other ex– prisoners of war, about their reactions. She

(Continued)

(Continued)

formed a support group, which she co-led with her supervisor. After an initial period of distrust, the men were able, often with great distress, to talk about their experiences in Japanese or German prison camps. They shared their feelings of guilt over having survived when so many of their buddies had been killed as well as their shame at returning home after the war and being ignored by the public at large, at not being "heroes." They had always had to hide their stories, as they felt (sometimes correctly) that their friends and families would be turned off, alarmed, or disgusted by the details. After several months, the group, which named themselves the Ex-POWs, staged a fund-raising event. They used some of the profits to buy a flag and other materials, which were used in a ceremony they developed that became part of each meeting, and donated the rest of the proceeds to a fund for use by other former prisoners of war. Most of the group members reported that their symptoms had abated considerably and that they now felt that they too should be accorded the same respect (by society and by the armed forces) that their nonprisoner of war comrades had received.

Other Adjunctive Therapies

Other treatments that have been used for traumatic stress include psychological debriefing, hypnosis, EMDR, and other cognitive-behavioral interventions. Psychological debriefing, with its roots in crisis intervention, catharsis, narrative, and psychoeducation, is a semistructured intervention immediately after a traumatic event (such as a natural disaster). Participants (individually or as a group) state the facts of the event, discuss their thoughts and impressions of what happened, and respond to questions about their emotions. The debriefer then stresses that their reactions are entirely normal, given the situation, and helps participants focus on future planning and coping. This approach has yielded a mixed bag of results; the quality of studies as to their efficacy has been poor, and there is little evidence that this method prevents the development of PTSD. In fact, it may retraumatize participants, according to some researchers (Bisson, McFarlane, & Rose, 2000). "One-shot interventions for all, such as critical incident stress debriefing (CISD), are also seen as contradicting available risk and resilience research" (Litz, 2008, p. 503). Instead, most practice guidelines, especially those for disaster trauma, now recommend *psychological first aid*,

a "flexible conversational approach that provides comfort, support, connectedness, information, and fosters coping in the immediate interval" (Litz, 2008, p. 504).

Hypnosis, in one form or another, has been used to treat trauma for over 150 years, and hypnotic techniques

> may facilitate the important task of working through traumatic memories and increase coping skills and sense of competency. . . . They may also be of particular help for patients who exhibit such symptoms as anxiety, dissociation, pain, and sleep problems, for which hypnosis has been effective. And . . . hypnosis has enhanced the efficacy of various therapeutic approaches. (Cardena, Maldonado, van der Hart, & Spiegel, 2000, p. 270)

Effective cognitive-behavioral approaches include exposure therapy and cognitive therapy (Rothbaum, Meadows, Resick, & Foy, 2000; Ford & Cloitre, 2009). *Exposure therapy* is a technique whereby the therapist helps the person to confront traumatic memories through repeated written or verbal narratives and through being exposed to situations that are safe in reality but are avoided or fear-evoking because of their association with a trauma. Cognitive therapy techniques are often used in combination with exposure. Stress management techniques, such as relaxation training and breathing retraining, are often used as well (Bisson et al., 2000). A new type of exposure therapy, *virtual therapy*, which uses high-tech, multimedia software coupled with relaxation and tension reduction exercises, is now being tested with combat veterans:

> This experimental treatment is designed to desensitize veterans by leading them into gradual confrontation with their traumatizing experiences. Wearing special virtual reality goggles, veterans feel they are again in a war zone, but this time there is a therapist to gradually lead them through the stressful, fearful scenarios. (H. Fancher, project PROVE, personal communication, January 9, 2009)

EMDR focuses on changing one's reactions to the memories of the trauma. The client, after extensive discussion and preparation, holds in mind a disturbing image while the clinician moves his or her fingers back and forth in front of the client's face or uses finger tapping or sounds; this is supposed to reduce the client's sensitivity to the traumatic memory and is thus a form of desensitization. An analysis of numerous studies of the efficacy of EMDR found that this treatment was more helpful than wait-list, routine-care, and active-treatment controls but that it seemed more useful for one-time, civilian occurrences of trauma than for multiply traumatized, chronically ill veterans. The advantages may be treatment efficiency and client tolerance and comfort (Chemtob, Tolin, van der Kolk, & Pitman, 2000).

In considering the adjunctive use of any of these approaches, of course, it is of utmost importance that the therapist be fully trained (and certified, when indicated) in the method used.

Psychopharmacology

The issue of medication for clients with PTSD is a matter of ongoing debate, and research is ongoing and intensive. In general, those considering the use of medication for PTSD have concluded that pharmacotherapy, in and of itself, rarely provides complete remission of PTSD but can be helpful in controlling or ameliorating symptoms such as insomnia, flashbacks, trouble concentrating, intrusive memories, physiological hyperreactivity, impulsivity, hypervigilance, depressed mood, and explosiveness, among others. It may also help concentration and decrease anxiety and depression, which are often comorbid symptoms. Finally, medication may ameliorate alterations of the neurobiological systems that are caused by trauma (Albucher et al., 2002), given the effects on the central nervous system mentioned earlier (Katz & Yehuda, 2006; Yehuda, 2002).

Among the many classes of medication that have been used to treat clients with symptoms of traumatic stress, selective serotonin reuptake inhibitors (SSRIs), including Prozac, Zoloft, and Paxil, are widely used because they appear to target the entire PTSD syndrome most closely (Yehuda, Marshall, Penkower, & Wong, 2002). Other antidepressants, such as tricyclics (e.g., Elavil, Sinequan, Norpramin) and monoamine oxydase (MOA) inhibitors (such as Nardil and Parnate) have been used in the past but are currently less popular, in part because of severe side effects, toxicity, and life-threatening food-drug and drug-drug interactions. And most recently, "The National Institute of Mental Health is experimenting with the drug d-cycloserine (DCS) which binds to the neurotransmitter receptors that regulate the fear response in the amygdala. The hope is that DCS will help deactivate the fear response" (H. Fancher, project PROVE, personal communication, January 9, 2009). Excellent reviews of psychopharmacology and trauma by Rudin, Volpp, and Marshall (2006), Albucher et al. (2002), Opler, Grennan & Ford (2009), and Friedman, Davidson, Mellman, and Southwick (2000) should prove extremely helpful to social workers dealing with questions of medication. "Psychosocial treatment and pharmacotherapy have been shown to be effective in all three symptom clusters of PTSD: reexperiencing, avoidance/ numbing, and hyperarousal" (Rudin et al., 2006, p. 156). Furthermore, therapy alone may not suffice for some:

Psychotherapy alone may not be effective for reducing avoidance symptoms in PTSD patients with alexithymia. . . . [M]edications may therefore have a particularly critical role, in agreement with previous studies of alexithymic psychosomatic patients, who do not respond to psychodynamic therapy and benefit from antidepressants. (Kosten, Krystal, Giller, Frank, & Dan, 1992, p. 570)

Collaboration between psychopharmacologist, worker, and client is most important, and explanations and information will both assist the client in understanding the purpose of the medication and its effects and facilitate client cooperation. "The clinician should foster an atmosphere of *collaborative empiricism* . . . a treatment situation in which the patient assumes an active part in the decision-making process" (Rudin et al., 2006, p. 159). Care must also be taken that ethnic and cultural issues are taken into account, as it has been shown, for example, that

Caucasian versus Asian patients exhibit different pharmacokinetic responses to the same dose of the same drug. Furthermore, dietary habits, beliefs about drug efficacy, and social/familial factors affecting compliance all suggest that ethnocultural concerns must be considered when prescribing a drug for PTSD. (Friedman et al., 2000, p. 97)

The age of the client is also an important factor; older adults often cannot tolerate the same dosages as younger adults, and interactions with other medications (polypharmacy) are also an important consideration (Graziano, 2003).

Countertransference and Vicarious Traumatization

Regardless of treatment modality and therapist orientation, however, the matter of therapist reactions to clients' traumatization will surface, with attendant countertransference reactions. It is essential that the worker not contribute to or mirror the denial, avoidance, rejection, shaming,

blaming, reification of theory, and self-deception prevalent not only in society at large but in the mental health professions. Though "this denial which has been observed in many settings stems from a fundamental human difficulty in comprehending and acknowledging our own vulnerability" (Solomon, 1995, p. 280), professionals must do everything possible to combat these difficulties, so as to provide the kind of help that clients who have suffered overpowering and life-threatening experiences so urgently need.

In addition to confronting denial of trauma, which may be disheartening and frustrating, clinicians working with trauma survivors are also exposed to the painful details of their traumatization, whether they are dealing with survivors of 9/11, combat veterans, rape victims, or the myriad other survivors of traumatic events and conditions (Bride, 2007; Pulido, 2007). Repeated instances of listening to stories of violence, terror, torture, and abuse put the worker at risk of developing

vicarious traumatization . . . the transformation in the inner experience of the therapist that comes about as a result of empathic engagement with clients' trauma material. This material includes graphic descriptions of violent events, exposure to the realities of people's cruelty to one another, and involvement in trauma related reenactments, either as a participant or as a bystander. It includes being a helpless witness to past events and sometimes present reenactments. . . . [W]e view it as an occupational hazard, an inevitable effect of trauma work. (Pearlman & Saakvitne, 1995, p. 31)

Ironically, then, the clinician's ethical commitment, as well as wishes and efforts to help, can hurt the helper: *"VT is the negative transformation in the helper that results from empathic engagement with trauma survivors and their trauma material, combined with a commitment or responsibility to help them"* (Pearlman & Caringi, 2009, pp. 202-203). In the vicarious traumatization process, the personal characteristics, life circumstances, and trauma history of the worker interact with the material presented by the client. The resulting disruption of the worker's cognitive schemas (ideas about safety, trust, esteem, control, and intimacy) or worldview can lead to depression and/or anxiety (Cunningham, 2003), as well as disconnection from friends and loved ones, lack of energy, and hopelessness. To mitigate the effects of vicarious traumatization, self-care, in the form of consultation, education (Bussey, 2008), and support (particularly peer support from others also engaged in trauma work, whether it be formal or informal, structured or open-ended), is vitally necessary to do the work well and responsibly (Dane, 2002; Miller, 2003).

Four therapists, who also were survivors of childhood sexual abuse, met as a result of a professional conference on incest. They formed a peer support group and met regularly for several years. They used this forum to discuss the ways in which their own experiences affected the therapy they did with incest survivors (a major part of their professional work), as well as a place where they could safely discuss personal issues related to their own traumatization. They made a presentation at a conference on child sexual abuse that was instrumental in the formation of other peer support groups. They also established what eventually became a large network of mental health professionals (social workers, psychologists, psychiatrists, psychiatric nurses, art and activities therapists, etc.) who worked with survivors of child sexual abuse. Meetings of the network featured presentations by members on innovative aspects of their work, as well as workshops and lectures on topics such as psychopharmacology, movement therapy, art therapy, and dissociation. Most of the members of the network had never had an opportunity to meet with other professionals who were doing trauma work and felt that their skills, knowledge base, and personal ability to deal with issues of trauma had been enhanced by the information, support, and networking opportunities provided by the group.

CONCLUSION

This chapter has explored basic concepts of trauma and provided definitions of traumatic stress and posttraumatic stress disorder. The effects of trauma on mind, body, and memory have been discussed, and treatment strategies and modalities have been outlined. An attempt has been made to link the discussion of treatment to the theoretical constructs in such a way as to illustrate the main ideas with appropriate clinical vignettes. Since the study of trauma and approaches to its treatment are both relatively new territory (despite their historical antecedents) and since, in some ways, using a trauma framework is so different from more traditional psychodynamic approaches, there is much room for innovation in working with the varied populations that can be thought of as survivors of trauma.

In many ways, the treatment of survivors of trauma is demanding and difficult. If the worker is not cognizant of the theories underlying the concept of traumatic stress and is not alert to the various workings and manifestations of trauma in the somatic, affective, cognitive, and behavioral realms, the work can also become bewildering and frustrating. However, once a framework for understanding trauma is established and the basic principles of treatment are understood, a new realm unfolds, in which some of the more pathology-oriented approaches may have to be put on the sidelines but where the potential exists for helping a client struggle free from the nightmarish captivity of past events.

Among the most important characteristics of the therapist throughout assessment and treatment are an understanding of concepts of trauma, including PTSD; a willingness to hear what the client is trying to say, although the presentation may not be in words; an ability to tolerate descriptions, images, and reenactments of truly horrifying, and often hardly imaginable, events; a capacity for empathy without overidentification; a belief in the resilience of the human spirit in the face of tremendous odds; and knowledge that therapy can help clients cope more effectively but cannot erase their pasts. This will mean learning to master one's own impatience at the sometimes achingly slow progress of treatment; advocating for that treatment to take as long as it needs to (a formidable challenge in an era of budget reductions, regulations, limitations, and managed-care restrictions); living with uncertainty as to whether one is doing the right thing, especially as it will sometimes appear (because the individual is feeling the intense affects that had been dissociated or the emotional pain that had been somatized) that the client is getting worse instead of better; daring to be creative; understanding and working through one's own traumatic past and its effects, if they exist; and obtaining support and consultation when the transitory exhaustion, despair, and hopelessness that are occasional by-products of doing trauma work threaten to traumatize the helper. In essence, understanding and using the principles underlying the concept of trauma can both return us to and provide a new perspective on our grounding in social work, with its emphasis on the person-in-situation and the biopsychosocial perspective that trauma workers in other disciplines are beginning to discover.

A final word is necessary on the subject of bearing witness. One of social work's core principles is that of client advocacy. In the face of society's (and some professionals') reluctance to allow knowledge of trauma to enter awareness, we must support our clients' efforts to make sure that events such as the Holocaust and phenomena such as the torture of political prisoners are not forgotten.

The determination to bear witness is reflected in a massive outpouring of survivor memories, in public gatherings for commemoration, and in the initiation and support of programs and institutions that focus on the tragedy. In working with victims of severe, massive trauma, these and other culturally syntonic ways of remembrance and mourning must be understood and integrated into society's consciousness and into our conceptual orientation for clinical practice. These activities help fill fragments of memory, enhance an understanding of oneself, and facilitate the long-delayed process of grieving. The emotional benefits of these "self-healing" approaches must be understood and integrated into clinical practice (Graziano & Rosenbloom, 1995).

REFERENCES

Albucher, R., Van Etten-Lee, M., & Liberzon, I. (2002). Psychopharmacological treatment in PTSD. In M. B. Williams & J. F. Sommer Jr. (Eds.), *Simple and complex post-traumatic stress disorder* (pp. 47–72). New York, NY: Haworth Maltreatment and Trauma Press.

Allen, J. G. (1995). Dissociative processes: Theoretical underpinnings of a working model for clinician and patient. In J. G. Allen & W. H. Smith (Eds.), *Diagnosis and treatment of dissociative disorders.* Northvale, NJ: Jason Aronson.

American Psychiatric Association. (1980). *Diagnostic and statistical manual of mental disorders* (3rd ed.). Washington, DC: Author.

American Psychiatric Association. (1987). *Diagnostic and statistical manual of mental disorders* (3rd ed., rev.). Washington, DC: Author.

American Psychiatric Association. (1994). *Diagnostic and statistical manual of mental disorders* (4th ed.). Washington, DC: Author.

American Psychiatric Association. (2000). *Diagnostic and statistical manual of mental disorders* (4th ed., text rev.). Washington, DC: Author.

Barsky, A. J., Wool, C., Barnett, B. A., & Cleary, P. D. (1994). Histories of childhood trauma in adult hypochondriachal patients. *American Journal of Psychiatry, 151,* 397–401.

Bisson, J. I., McFarlane, A. C., & Rose, S. (2000). Psychological debriefing. In E. B. Foa, T. M. Keane, & M. J. Friedman (Eds.), *Effective treatments for PTSD* (pp. 317–319). New York, NY: Guilford Press.

Boss, P. (2006). *Loss, trauma, and resilience: Therapeutic work with ambiguous loss.* New York, NY: W. W. Norton.

Bremner, J. D., Davis, M., Southwick, S. M., Krystal, J. H., & Charney, D. (1994). Neurobiology of posttraumatic stress disorder. In R. Pynoos (Ed.), *Posttraumatic stress disorder: A clinical review* (pp. 43–64). Lutherville, MD: Sidran Press.

Brennen, T., Hasanovic, M., Zotovic, M., Blix, I., Skar, A S., Prelic, N.K., Mehmedovic, I., . . . Gavrilov-Jerkovic, V. (2010). Trauma exposure in childhood impairs the ability to recall specific autobiographical memories in late adolescence. *Journal of Traumatic Stress, 23*(2), 240–247.

Breuer, J., & Freud, S. (1957). *Studies on hysteria.* New York, NY: Basic Books. (Original work published 1893–1895)

Brewin, C. R., Lanius, R. A., Novac, A., Schnyder, U., & Galea, S. (2009). Refomulating PTSD for *DSM-V*: Life After Criterion A. *Journal of Traumatic Stress, 22*(5), 366-373.

Bride, B. E. (2007). Prevalence of secondary traumatic stress among social workers. *Social Work, 52*(1), 63–70.

Briere, J. (2004). *Psychological assessment of adult posttraumatic states: Phenomenology, diagnosis, and measurement* (2nd ed.). Washington, DC: American Psychological Association.

Briere, J., & Spinazzola, J. (2009). Assessment of the sequelae of complex trauma: Evidence-based measures. In C. A. Courtois & J. D. Ford (Eds.), *Treating complex traumatic stress disorders* (pp. 104–123). New York, NY: Guilford Press.

Brown, L. (2009). Cultural competence. In C. A. Courtois and J. D. Ford (Eds.), *Treating complex traumatic stress disorders* (pp. 166–182.). New York, NY: Guilford Press.

Bussey, M. C. (2008). Trauma response and recovery certificate program: Preparing students for effective practice. *Journal of Teaching in Social Work, 28*(1/2), 117–144.

Calhoun, K. S., & Resick, P. A. (1993). Post-traumatic stress disorder. In D. Barlow (Ed.), *Clinical handbook of psychological disorders* (pp. 48–98). New York, NY: Guilford Press.

Cardena, E., Maldonado, J., van der Hart, O., & Spiegel, D. (2000). Hypnosis. In E. B. Foa, T. M. Keane, & M. J. Friedman (Eds.), *Effective treatments for PTSD* (pp. 247–249). New York, NY: Guilford Press.

Chemtob, C. M., Tolin, D. F., van der Kolk, B. A., & Pitman, R. K. (2000). Eye movement desensitization and reprocessing. In E. B. Foa, T. M. Keane, & M. J. Friedman (Eds.), *Effective treatments for PTSD* (pp. 139–154). New York, NY: Guilford Press.

Chilcoat, H. D., & Menard, C. (2003). Epidemiological investigations: Comorbidity of posttraumatic stress disorder and substance use disorder. In P. Ouimette & P. J. Brown (Eds.), *Trauma and substance abuse* (pp. 9–27). Washington, DC: American Psychological Association.

Courtois, C. A. (1988). *Healing the incest wound: Adult survivors in therapy.* New York, NY: W. W. Norton.

Courtois, C. A. (1992). The memory retrieval process in incest survivor therapy. *Journal of Child Sexual Abuse, 1,* 15–31.

Courtois, C. A., Ford, J. D., & Cloitre, M. (2009). Best practices in psychotherapy for adults. In C. A. Courtois & J. D. Ford, (Eds.), *Treating complex traumatic stress disorders* (pp. 82–103). New York, NY: Guilford Press.

Cunningham, M. (2003). Impact of trauma work on social work clinicians: Empirical findings. *Social Work, 48*(4), 451–459.

DaCosta, J. (1871). On irritable heart: A clinical study of a form of functional cardiac disorder and its consequences. *American Journal of Medical Science, 16,* 17–52.

Dane, B. (2002). Duty to inform: Preparing social work students to understand vicarious traumatization. *Journal of Teaching in Social Work, 22*(3/4), 3–20.

Danieli, Y. (1988). Treating survivors and children of survivors of the Nazi Holocaust. In F. M. Ochberg (Ed.), *Post-traumatic therapy and victims of violence* (pp. 278–294). New York, NY: Brunner/Mazel.

Darves-Bornoz, J.-M., Alonso, J., de Girolamo, G., de Graaf, R., Haro, J.-M., Kovess-Masfety, V., et al. (2008). Main traumatic events in Europe: PTSD in the European study of the epidemiology of mental disorders survey. *Journal of Traumatic Stress, 21*(5), 455–462.

Davidson, J. R. (1994). Issues in the diagnosis of posttraumatic stress disorder. In R. S. Pynoos (Ed.), *Posttraumatic stress disorder: A clinical review* (pp. 1–16). Lutherville, MD: Sidran Press.

Dickstein, B. D., Suvak, M., Litz, B.T., & Adler, A.B. (2010). Heterogeneity in the course of posttraumatic stress disorder: Trajectories of symptomatology. *Journal of Traumatic Stress, 23*(3), 331–339.

Falk, B., Hersen, K., & Van Hasselt, V. B. (1994). Assessment of post-traumatic stress disorder in older adults: A critical review. *Clinical Psychology Review, 14,* 383–416.

Ferenczi, S. (1955). Confusion of tongues between adults and the child. In *The selected papers of Sandor Ferenczi: Vol. 3. Final contributions to the problems and methods of psychoanalysis* (pp. 156–167). New York, NY: Basic Books. (Original work published 1933)

Figley, C. (1985). Introduction. In C. Figley (Ed.), *Trauma and its wake: The study and treatment of post-traumatic stress disorder* (pp. xvii–xxvi). New York, NY: Brunner/Mazel.

Flack, W., Litz, B., Weathers, F., & Beaudreau, S. (2002). Assessment and diagnosis of PTSD in adults: A comprehensive psychological approach. In M. B. Williams & J. F. Sommer, Jr. (Eds.), *Simple and complex post-traumatic stress disorder: Strategies for comprehensive treatment in clinical practice* (pp. 9–22). New York, NY: Haworth Press.

Foa, E. B., Rothbaum, B. O., & Steketee, G. S. (1993). Treatment of rape victims. *Journal of Interpersonal Violence, 8,* 256–276.

Ford, J.D. (2009). Neurobiological and developmental research: Clinical implications. In C. A. Courtois & J. D. Ford (Eds.), *Treating complex traumatic stress disorders* (pp. 31-58). New York, NY: Guilford Press.

Ford, J. D., & Cloitre, M. (2009). Best practices in psychotherapy for children and adolescents. In C. A. Courtois, & J. D. Ford (Eds.), *Treating complex traumatic stress disorders* (pp. 59–81). New York, NY: Guilford Press.

Ford, J. D., & Courtois, C. A. (2009). Defining and understanding complex trauma and complex traumatic stress disorders. In C. A. Courtois & J. D. Ford (Eds.), *Treating complex traumatic stress disorders* (pp. 13–30). New York, NY: Guilford Press.

Ford, J. D., Fallot, R. D., & Harris, M. (2009). Group therapy. In C. A. Courtois & J. D. Ford (Eds.), *Treating complex stress disorders* (pp. 415–440). New York, NY: Guilford Press.

Foy, D. W., Glynn, S. M., Schnurr, P. P., Jankowski, M. K., Wattenberg, M. S., Weiss, D. S., et al. (2000). Group therapy. In E. B. Foa, T. M. Keane, & M. J. Friedman (Eds.), *Effective treatments for PTSD* (pp. 155–175). New York, NY: Guilford Press.

Freud, S. (1962). The aetiology of hysteria. In J. Strachey (Ed. & Trans.), *The standard edition of the complete psychological works of Sigmund Freud* (Vol. 3, pp. 91–122). London, UK: Hogarth Press. (Original work published 1896)

Friedman, M. J., Davidson, J. R. T., Mellman, T. A., & Southwick, S. M. (2000). Pharmacotherapy. In E. B. Foa, T. M. Keane, & M. J. Friedman (Eds.), *Effective treatments for PTSD* (pp. 84–105). New York, NY: Guilford Press.

Gill, J. M., Page, G. G., Sharps, P., & Campbell, J. C. (2008). Experiences of traumatic events and associations with PTSD and depression development in urban health care-seeking women. *Journal of Urban Health, 85*(5), 693–706.

Graziano, R. (1992). Treating women incest survivors: A bridge between "cumulative trauma" and "post-traumatic stress." *Social Work in Health Care, 17,* 69–85.

Graziano, R. (1996). The adult survivor of childhood sexual abuse: Linking inner and outer world. In J. Sanville & J. Edward (Eds.), *Fostering healing and growth: A psychoanalytic social work approach* (pp. 195–211). Northvale, NJ: Jason Aronson.

Graziano, R. (2003). Trauma and aging. *Journal of Gerontological Social Work, 40*(4), 3–21.

Graziano, R., & Rosenbloom, M. (1995, July). *Body, mind and trauma: Beyond words.* Paper presented at the 34th Annual Meeting International Conference for the Advancement of Private Practice of Clinical Social Work, Victoria, British Columbia, Canada.

Gunderson, J. G., & Chu, J. A. (1993). Treatment implications of past trauma in borderline personality disorder. *Harvard Review of Psychiatry, 1,* 75–81.

Gusman, F., Stewart, J., Young, B. H., Riney, S., Abueg, F., & Blake, D. D. (1996). A multicultural developmental approach for treating trauma. In A. J. Marsella, M. J. Friedman, E. T. Gerrity, & R. M. Scurfield (Eds.), *Ethnocultural aspects of post-traumatic stress disorder* (pp. 452–469). Washington, DC: American Psychological Association.

Herman, J. L. (1992). *Trauma and recovery.* New York, NY: Basic Books.

Herman, J. L., & Schatzow, E. (1984). Time-limited group therapy for women with a history of incest. *International Journal of Group Psychotherapy, 34,* 605–616.

Janet, P. (1889). *L'automatisme psychologique: Essai de psychologie experimentale sur les formes inferieures de l'activite humaine* [Psychological automatic behavior: Essay about experimental psychology on the lower forms of human activity]. Paris, France: Alcan.

Janoff-Bulman, R. (1985). The aftermath of victimization: Rebuilding shattered assumptions. In C. R. Figley (Ed.), *Trauma and its wake: The study and treatment of post-traumatic stress disorder* (pp. 15–35). New York, NY: Brunner/Mazel.

Janoff-Bulman, R. (1992). *Shattered assumptions: Towards a new psychology of trauma.* New York, NY: Free Press.

Johnson, D. R., Feldman, S. C., Lubin, H., & Southwick, S. M. (1995). The therapeutic use of ritual and ceremony in the treatment of post-traumatic stress disorder. *Journal of Traumatic Stress, 8,* 283–298.

Jones, D. M. (1991). Alexithymia: Inner speech and linkage impairment. *Clinical Social Work Journal, 19,* 237–249.

Kardiner, A. (1941). *The traumatic neurosis of war.* Washington, DC: National Research Council.

Katz, C. L., & Yehuda, R. (2006). Neurobiology of trauma. In L. A. Schein (Ed.), *Psychological effects of catastrophic disasters: Group approaches to treatment* (pp. 61–81). New York, NY: Haworth Press.

Khan, M. M. (1963). The concept of cumulative trauma. In *The privacy of the self* (pp. 42–58). New York, NY: International Universities Press.

Kimerling, P., Ouimette, P., & Wolfe, J. (2002). *Gender and PTSD.* New York, NY: Guilford Press.

Kingston, S., & Raghavan, C. (2009). The relationship of sexual abuse, early initiation of substance use, and adolescent trauma. *Journal of Traumatic Stress, 22*(1), 65–68.

Kohut, H. (1971). *The analysis of the self.* New York, NY: International Universities Press.

Kohut, H. (1977). *The restoration of the self.* New York, NY: International Universities Press.

Kohut, H. (1984). *How does analysis cure?* (A. Goldberg & P. Stepansky, Eds.). Chicago, IL: University of Chicago Press.

Kosten, T. R., Krystal, J. H., Giller, E. R., Jr., Frank, J., & Dan, E. (1992). Alexithymia as a predictor of treatment response in post-traumatic stress disorder. *Journal of Traumatic Stress, 5,* 563–573.

Krugman, S. (1987). Trauma in the family: Perspectives on the intergenerational transmission of violence. In B. A. van der Kolk (Ed.), *Psychological trauma* (pp. 127–151). Washington, DC: American Psychiatric Press.

Krystal, H. (1978). Trauma and affects. *Psychoanalytic Study of the Child, 33,* 81–116.

Krystal, J. H., Kosten, T. R., Southwick, S., Mason, J. W., Derr, B. D., & Giller, E. L. (1989). Neurobiological aspects of PTSD: Review of clinical and preclinical studies. *Behavior Therapy, 20,* 177–198.

Kulka, R. A., Schlenger, W. E., Fairbank, J. A., Hough, R. L., Jordan, B. K., Marmar, C. R., et al. (1990). *Trauma and the Vietnam generation: Findings from the National Vietnam Veterans readjustment study.* New York, NY: Brunner/Mazel.

Litz, B. T. (2008). Early intervention for trauma: Where are we and where do we need to go? A commentary. *Journal of Traumatic Stress, 21*(6), 503–506.

Marsella, A. J., Friedman, M. J., & Spain, E. H. (1994). Ethnocultural aspects of posttraumatic stress disorder. In R. S. Pynoos (Ed.), *Posttraumatic stress disorder: A clinical review* (pp. 17–42). Lutherville, MD: Sidran Press.

McCann, I. L., & Pearlman, L. A. (1990). *Psychological trauma and the adult survivor: Theory, therapy and transformation.* New York, NY: Brunner/Mazel.

McCann, I. L., Pearlman, L. A., Sakheim, D. K., & Abrahamson, D. J. (1985). Assessment and treatment of the adult survivor of childhood sexual abuse within a schema framework. In S. M. Sgroi (Ed.), *Vulnerable populations* (Vol. 1, pp. 77–101). Lexington, MA: Lexington Books.

McCann, I. L., Sakheim, D. K., & Abrahamson, D. J. (1988). Trauma and victimization: A model of psychological adaptation. *Counseling Psychologist, 16,* 531–594.

Meichenbaum, D. (1994). *A clinical handbook/practical therapist manual for assessing and treating adults with post-traumatic stress disorder (PTSD).* Waterloo, Ontario, Canada: Institute Press.

Mennen, F. E., & Meadow, D. (1992). Process to recovery: In support of long-term groups for sexual abuse survivors. *International Journal of Group Psycho-Therapy, 42,* 29–44.

Miller, M. (2003). Working in the midst of unfolding trauma and traumatic loss: Training as a collective process of support. *Psychoanalytic Social Work, 10,* 7–26.

Morsette, A. (2006). Cultural differences influence trauma treatment in Native American population.

Traumatic stress points: News for the International Society for Traumatic Stress Studies, 20(1), 3.

Opler, L. A., Grennan, M. S., & Ford, J. D. (2009). Pharmacotherapy. In C. A. Courtois & J. D. Ford (Eds.), *Treating complex traumatic stress disorders* (pp. 329–350). New York, NY: Guilford Press.

Parson, E. R. (1985). Ethnicity and traumatic stress: The intersecting point in psychotherapy. In C. R. Figley (Ed.), *Trauma and its wake: The study and treatment of post-traumatic stress disorder* (pp. 314–337). New York, NY: Brunner/Mazel.

Pearlman, L. A., & Saakvitne, K. W. (1995). *Trauma and the therapist.* New York, NY: W. W. Norton.

Pearlman, L. A., & Caringi, J. (2009). Living and working self-reflectively to address vicarious trauma. In C. A. Courtois & J. D. Ford (Eds.), *Treating complex traumatic stress disorders* (pp. 202-224). New York, NY: Guilford Press.

Pribor, E. F., Yutzy, S. H., Dean, J. T., & Wetzel, R. D. (1993). Briquet's syndrome, dissociation and abuse. *American Journal of Psychiatry, 150,* 1507–1511.

Pulido, M. L. (2007). In their words: Secondary traumatic stress in social workers responding to the 9/11 terrorist attacks in New York City. *Social Work, 52*(3), 279–281.

Pynoos, R. S. (1994). Introduction. In R. S. Pynoos (Ed.), *Posttraumatic stress disorder: A clinical review* (p. vii). Lutherville, MD: Sidran Press.

Resnick, H. S., Kilpatrick, D. G., Dansky, B. S., Saunders, B. E., & Best, C. L. (1993). Prevalence of civilian trauma and posttraumatic stress disorder in a representative sample of women. *Journal of Consulting and Clinical Psychology, 61,* 984–991.

Rothbaum, B. O., Meadows, E. A., Resick, P., & Foy, D. W. (2000). Cognitive-behavioral therapy. In E. B. Foa, T. M. Keane, & M. J. Friedman (Eds.), *Effective treatments for PTSD* (pp. 60–83). New York, NY: Guilford Press.

Rudin, S. B., Volpp, S. Y., & Marshall, R. D. (2006). Clinical issues in the psychopharmacology of PTSD. In L. A. Schein (Ed.), *Psychological effects of catastrophic disasters: Group approaches to treatment* (pp. 155–202). New York, NY: Haworth Press.

Scaer, R. C. (2001). *The body bears the burden: Trauma, dissociation, and disease.* New York, NY: Haworth Medical Press.

Scurfield, R. M. (1985). Post-trauma stress assessment and treatment: Overview and formulations. In

C. R. Figley (Ed.), *Trauma and its wake: The study and treatment of post-traumatic stress disorder* (pp. 219–231). New York, NY: Brunner/Mazel.

Scurfield, R. M., Corker, T. M., & Gongla, P. A. (1984). Three post-Vietnam "rap therapy" groups: An analysis. *Group, 8,* 3–21.

Shalev, A. Y., Bleich, A., & Ursano, R. J. (1990). Posttraumatic stress disorder: Somatic co-morbidity and effort tolerance. *Psychosomatics, 31,* 197–203.

Solomon, S. D. (1992). Mobilizing social support networks in times of disaster. In C. R. Figley (Ed.), *Trauma and its wake: The study and treatment of post-traumatic stress disorder* (Vol. 2, pp. 232–263). New York, NY: Brunner/Mazel.

Solomon, Z. (1995). Oscillating between denial and recognition of PTSD: Why are lessons learned and forgotten? *Journal of Traumatic Stress, 8,* 271–282.

Spiegel, D. (1993). Afterword. In D. Spiegel (Ed.), *Dissociative disorders: A clinical review* (p. 32). Lutherville, MD: Sidran Press.

Stewart, S. H., & Conrod, P. J. (2003). Psychosocial models of functional associations between posttraumatic stress disorder and substance use disorder. In P. Ouimette & P. J. Brown (Eds.), *Trauma and substance abuse* (pp. 29–55). Washington, DC: American Psychological Association.

Tanielian, T., & Jaycox, L. H. (2008). *Invisible wounds of war.* Santa Monica, CA: RAND Center for Military Health Policy Research.

Terhakopian, A., Sinaii, N., Engel, C. C., Schnurr, P. P., & Hoge, C. W. (2008). Estimating population prevalence of posttraumatic stress disorder: An example using the PTSD checklist. *Journal of Traumatic Stress Studies, 21*(3), 290–300.

Terr, L. (1991). Childhood trauma: An outline and overview. *American Journal of Psychiatry, 148,* 10–20.

Trimble, M. R. (1985). Post-traumatic stress disorder: History of a concept. In C. R. Figley (Ed.), *Trauma and its wake: The study and treatment of post-traumatic stress disorder* (pp. 5–14). New York, NY: Brunner/Mazel.

van der Kolk, B. A. (1987). The psychological consequences of overwhelming life experiences. In B. A. van der Kolk (Ed.), *Psychological trauma* (pp. 1–30). Washington, DC: American Psychiatric Press.

van der Kolk, B. A., & Greenberg, M. S. (1987). The psychobiology of the trauma response: Hyperarousal, constriction, and addiction to traumatic reexposure. In B. A. van der Kolk

(Ed.), *Psychological trauma* (pp. 63–87). Washington, DC: American Psychiatric Press.

van der Kolk, B. A., Roth, S., Pelcovitz, D., & Mandel, F. A. (1993). *Complex post-traumatic stress disorder. Results from the DSM IV field trial of PTSD.* Unpublished manuscript, Harvard Medical School.

van der Kolk, B. A., van der Hart, O., & Burbridge, J. (2002). Approaches to the treatment of PTSD. In M. B. Williams & J. F. Sommer Jr. (Eds.), *Simple and complex posttraumatic stress disorder: Strategies for comprehensive treatment in clinical practice* (pp. 23–46). New York, NY: Haworth Press.

Walker, E. A., Katon, W. J., Nerras, K., Jemelka, R. P., & Massoth, D. (1992). Dissociation in women with chronic pelvic pain. *American Journal of Psychiatry, 149,* 534–537.

White, P., & Faustman, W. (1989). Coexisting physical conditions among inpatients with posttraumatic stress disorder. *Military Medicine, 154,* 66–71.

Winnicott, D. W. (1965). Ego distortion in terms of true and false self. *The maturational processes and the facilitating environment* (pp. 140–152). New York, NY: International Universities Press.

Yehuda, R. (2002). Current concepts: Post-traumatic stress disorder. *New England Journal of Medicine, 346*(2), 108–114.

Yehuda, R., Marshall, R. M., Penkower, A., & Wong, C. M. (2002). Pharmacological treatments for posttraumatic stress disorder. In P. E. Nathan & J. M. Gorman (Eds.), *A guide to treatments that work* (2nd ed., pp. 411–445). New York, NY: Oxford University Press.

13

CLINICAL SOCIAL WORK WITH SURVIVORS OF DISASTER AND TERRORISM

A Social Ecological Approach[1]

MARTHA BRAGIN

The word *disaster* is derived from the Italian *disastro* or "unfavorable star" and implies a random act of wanton destruction by nature or by human intervention. Yet, in reality, disasters are a regular part of human experience. They occur in every part of the world, taking different forms and touching many lives. Planning to mitigate their effects and acting effectively to help communities to recover is not only possible but necessary (Kasi, Bhadra, & Dryer, 2007). As social workers, we appreciate that disasters disproportionately affect physically, socially, economically, and politically vulnerable populations (Mathbor, 2007; UN General Assembly, 2007). As clinicians, we appreciate the ways in which experiencing a disaster, as well as every aspect of relief and recovery, can affect the emotional well-being of vulnerable survivors (Inter-Agency Standing Committee [IASC], 2007). We understand that compromised well-being increases vulnerability, so the role that we play is crucial in supporting a population's ability to survive, thrive, and struggle as active participants in building the future.

This chapter discusses clinical social work intervention following natural disasters and terrorism (see Appendix A).[2] The purpose of the chapter is to compile, clarify, and discuss what has been

---

[1]*Editor's Note:* Although this chapter shares certain themes with those on trauma survivorship ("The Challenge of Clinical Work With Survivors of Trauma," Chapter 12, this volume) and grief and loss (Mourning and Loss: A Life Cycle Perspective," Chapter 16, this volume), it also addresses unique forms of these phenomena.

[2]This chapter will not discuss clinical social work in situations of sustained armed conflict, including war, state and community violence, or genocide. While some of the principles discussed in this chapter may be useful, elucidating the response of clinical social workers to these events would require a separate chapter.

learned in various countries and situations in order to integrate and build upon that knowledge to create opportunities for effective clinical response. Clinical social work theories inform interventions that preserve well-being, support psychosocial development, and facilitate reconstruction as well as address mourning, loss, and care of the mentally ill. They do so using the biopsychosocial model that forms an essential unit of clinical social work analysis, using an ecological framework to examine individual, biological, and intrapsychic life as it is situated in the sociocultural sphere. The chapter refers specifically to social ecological theories of resilience, psychodynamic theories that support resilience, as well as the new study of community resilience and the neurobiological principles that underpin it.

COMMONLY USED TERMS IN DISASTER RELIEF AND RECOVERY

The field of disaster relief and recovery has been closely linked to the humanitarian community. Over the years, the field has developed its own commonly used terms. Clinical social workers likely will find these concepts quite familiar, although they may find that they have used slightly different language.

Disaster

A *disaster* is "a serious disruption of the functioning of a community or a society involving widespread human, material, economic or environmental losses and impacts, which exceeds the ability of the affected community or society to cope using its own resources" (United Nations International Strategy for Disaster Reduction [UNISDR], 2009. p. 9).

Disasters are often described as a result of the combination of (a) exposure to a hazard, (b) the conditions of vulnerability that are present, and (c) insufficient capacity or measures to reduce or cope with the potential negative consequences (UNISDR, 2009 p. 9).

According to this definition, disasters can be either natural or created by human beings. This chapter is limited to coverage of single-incident disasters, including natural disasters and terrorism.[3]

Terrorism

Terrorism can be defined as the "instrumental use or threatened use of violence by an organization or individual against innocent civilian targets in furtherance of a political, religious, or ideological objective" (Halpern & Tramontin, 2007, p. 34). We do not include terrorist violence that is part of an ongoing, active armed conflict or political occupation, as these are considered "complex emergencies" requiring additional strategies of care that are beyond the scope of this chapter.

What Do We Mean by *Psychosocial?*

The term *psychosocial* was coined by the international relief and development community to define approaches informed by the ecological or biopsychosocial perspective. It is the name given by the relief and development community to the biopsychosocial approach central to clinical social work theory.

The prefix *psycho* refers to the psychological dimension of the individual, and it has to do with the inner world of thoughts, feelings, desires, beliefs, values, cognition, and the ways in which people perceive themselves and others.

The suffix *social* refers to the relationships and environment of the individual. It includes the

---

[3]A complex emergency is a humanitarian crisis in which there is total breakdown of authority resulting from internal or external conflict, which requires an international response that goes beyond the mandate or capacity of any single agency and/or the ongoing United Nations country program. These emergencies are characterized by extensive loss of life; widespread damage to society and the economy; the need for large-scale multifaceted humanitarian assistance; hindrance of such assistance by armed groups or factions; and danger to those providing such assistance (OCHA, 2004).

material world as well as the social and cultural context in which people live, ranging from the network of their relationships to cultural manifestations, to the community, and to the state. It is also used to refer to the socioeconomic resources and material conditions of life.

The term *psychosocial* is used to explain the way these aspects of the person are inseparable, with each continuously influencing the other, so that it is impossible to tease them apart (Duncan & Arnston, 2004).

Psychosocial well-being is a state in which one is able to master life tasks of love and work, family and community, and ascribe meaning to daily life so that one can raise the next generation in an atmosphere of hope. Every culture has its own, more specific definition of psychosocial well-being and how it should be represented, maintained, and acquired (Wurzer & Bragin, 2009).

Psychosocial interventions support people who are affected by disaster to create solutions that promote, rather than destroy, their well-being. They do so by increasing protective factors and reducing risks in the biological, social, and psychological realms.

THE PSYCHOSOCIAL SEQUELAE OF DISASTER AND TERRORISM

One of the most important characteristics of natural disasters and terrorism is that they occur in the public sphere. No matter how highly individualized a society, disasters and terror happen to all its members together. Therefore, it is important that clinical interventions address whole communities and work within the commonality of the experience. The very fact of acknowledging the shared nature of the experience can help break down fear and isolation, in order to begin to support a sense of capacity, connection, and hope for the future (Erikson, 1976).

The term *natural disaster* is in a sense a misleading one, for natural disasters are never exclusively natural. They affect communities differently, depending on the quality of the infrastructure, the quality and proximity of emergency services, and

the ways in which authorities respond to community needs and organizational representatives. Poor and marginalized communities are more likely to suffer more severely than wealthy communities or those whose citizens are well connected (Halpern & Tramontin, 2007; Pyles, 2007).

Disaster and terrorism have two distinct categories of psychosocial outcome that we discuss here. In disaster, there are massive, almost unimaginable levels of loss; in terrorism, there is exposure to extreme violence; and in some instances there are both.

THE PSYCHOSOCIAL CONSEQUENCES OF DISASTER AND TERRORISM: MASSIVE LOSS

Disaster disrupts almost every aspect of life, so losses are not only of the loved ones actually killed but also the loss of home, possessions, community and social fabric, historic continuity, and plans for the future. Therefore, each social and economic loss has psychological aspects, and each psychological loss has broader social consequences, as society's fabric is profoundly altered.

Losing Family, Friends, and Familiar Faces

In the first instance, there is the loss of people: family members, friends, and members of the community, from teachers to storekeepers. This is complicated by the fact that it takes some time to determine who has died and who is missing, a slow process in which, for many, hopefulness gives way to fear and then to the realization of death.

In disaster and terrorism, deaths are sudden and unexpected. When people die of illness, old age, or even war, the death is expected, though tragic. When people die in a disaster or terror attack, friends, family, and colleagues do not expect the person to die; they expect to see them again very soon. The death is a shock, leaving unfinished interpersonal business. When death is unexpected, regrets may come unbidden: One may have had an argument with the person, forgotten to say good-bye, failed to remember an important occasion, or neglected to pay a well-deserved compliment. Now there is no chance to complete this unfinished business. Survivors are often left with a particular sorrow related to the circumstances of the last encounter (Halpern & Tramontin, 2007).

Furthermore, deaths are confirmed slowly, so there is a process that begins with a search for lost relatives, leading to the discovery of the person or to the identification of the body and burial. People move through a series of emotions from fear and anxiety to loss, grief, and bereavement (Jones, 2008; Wurzer & Bragin, 2009).

Complicated Grief and Ambiguous Loss

Sometimes, the body is not intact, so more time goes by until the remains are identified scientifically and the results are given to the family. In still other instances, the remains are never found. This leads to a situation of ambiguous loss, in which the survivors never really know for sure whether the person is actually gone. While grief and sadness are present, the bereavement process is truncated as it is hard to give up hoping when there is no evidence to contradict the fantasy that one day, the loved one will return (Coates, Schechter, & First, 2003; Robins, 2010).

Loss of Material Things

Simultaneously, the losses are practical. People lose their homes, their clothing, their documents, their medicines and prescriptions, plus all the possessions that they may have accumulated in life or inherited. To the extent that there are remnants of their homes and possessions, there is the overwhelming task of salvaging what one can, a process made even more difficult when accompanied by grief and the loss of the practical assistance of a husband, wife, parent, or even child (Halpern & Tramontin, 2007).

I found a mother in Sri Lanka sitting in a half-ruined house and crying over a mud-soaked pile of silks. She lamented, "My mother had saved these for me, and I for my daughter, for her marriage trousseau. . . they cannot be made with this detail any more, they cannot be replaced. . . ." A vital link between past and future was gone (Bragin, 2011).

Loss of Hopes and Dreams

The losses may include the hopes and dreams of survivors, who are forced by necessity to replace everything that they have owned from basic supplies to any luxury items. This can have serious consequences on life savings, businesses, and educational possibilities, or a future beyond survival (Coates et al., 2003; Erikson, 1976; Halpern & Tramontin, 2007).

Change in Relationships: Loss of Familiar Experience

When people and possessions are lost, human relations suffer. Family interactions are disrupted as the stresses of coping with postdisaster adjustments affect the way people behave toward one another. Children find that parents and teachers are preoccupied, short-tempered, and distracted (Bragin, 2005; Jones, 2008).

Loss of Certainty

While some disasters, such as floods and hurricanes, are yearly occurrences and disaster is a constant worldwide, certain disasters, as well as terror attacks, are surprises that shatter the assumptions of daily life. Major earthquakes, tsunamis, and terror attacks are new to the families who first experience them, even though history shows that they are in some sense regular occurrences (IASC, 2007; UNIDSR, 2007). All of these occurrences, when they have devastated a particular family or community, compromise the assumptions upon which daily life is based (Halpern & Tramontin, 2007). "I send my children to school, I go to the sea to fish, I take the elevator to my office, and the day will end and the next one will begin." Suddenly, such reflexive assumptions of daily life are replaced with uncertainty.

EXPOSURE TO EXTREME VIOLENCE

Extremely violent events, whether terror attacks, earthquakes, or tsunamis, have specific psychological consequences.

When people are exposed to extremely violent events, frequently their minds cannot accept the information. The experiences that they are undergoing seem fantastic, although in fact they are only too real. The mind retains the information presented by the experience but only in an unintegrated, unsymbolized form. Laub and Auerhahn (1993) described this phenomenon as "knowing and not knowing" simultaneously.

Recent developments in cognitive neuroscience explain how this happens. Very violent events do not enter the memory in the same way as other experiences do, through the meaning-making apparatus of the brain's prefrontal cortex. Instead, they are retained in an unsymbolized form and remembered differently (Siegel, 1999).

People exposed to extremely violent events find their minds haunted by the experience. They normally try to block out the experience, only to find that it returns in the form of nightmares and flashbacks. Those who are more successful in blocking out violent experiences completely often find that they have difficulty being able to think clearly about anything at all (van der Kolk, McFarlane, & Weisaeth, 1996).

When many are exposed to the same events, yet no one can properly process the information, the whole of society is affected. Meaning making in such circumstances cannot occur, thus making normal adaptations impossible. In effect, personal responses in situations involving disaster or terrorism have distinctly social implications (Bragin, 2011, Ungar, 2012).

The theories discussed below inform clinical social work practice and help address (a) massive and multiple losses, as well as exposure to extreme violence, characteristic of the psychological responses to disaster and terrorism, and (b) the social context in which such phenomena occur.

CLINICAL SOCIAL WORK THEORIES THAT SUPPORT BEST PRACTICES IN DISASTER AND MASS VIOLENCE

Clinical social work is especially qualified to address these consequences because of the profession's fundamental understanding of the integrated nature of the material, the social, the cultural, and the intrapsychic. The theoretical foundations of clinical social work in an ecological systems model make clinical social workers especially qualified to work in a community context while keeping the needs of the individual human psyche in mind. Since disasters happen to whole communities, this perspective is crucial.

In addition, aspects of psychodynamic theory help us understand, and therefore act on, those elements of psychological functioning that support resilience.

Ecological Systems Theory

Duncan and Arnston (2004) use Figure 13.1 to describe the context in which people experience life and, with it, disaster.

This perspective allows us to look at emergency situations of disaster or terrorism in a biopsychosocial context. It also enables us to imagine our interventions holistically, as events that affect and are affected by multiple layers of experience. This leads us to address the situation on all levels or choose a particular level as appropriate. This differentiates clinical social work interventions from some more place-specific interventions, such as critical stress debriefing, which have been found to be unhelpful at best and even harmful in some instances when applied to diverse environments (Jones, 2008; van Ommeren & Wessells, 2007). At the same time, it keeps us mindful of the role of individual development and helps us seek solutions that are developmentally appropriate and contextualized relative to family, community, and culture (Ungar, 2012).

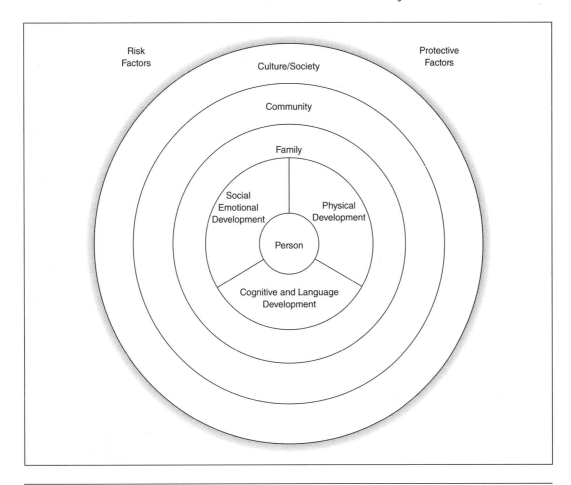

Figure 13.1   The Social Ecology of the Person

Source: Adapted from Duncan and Arnston (2004).

Dr. Timothy Sim (2009, 2011) is a systemic family therapist teaching at Hong Kong Polytechnic University. Following the 2008 earthquake in Sichuan China, Dr. Sim led faculty student teams to help establish social work support in the affected area. Using his skills in systemic family therapy, Dr. Sim used mapping exercises to determine needs, resources, strengths, and points of intervention with the diverse affected communities. Having mapped the communities' vulnerabilities and assets, both individually and as a group, his team was able to target their interventions effectively.

Community Resilience to Disasters: An Emerging Paradigm in the Social Ecological Framework

In keeping with global consensus on the need for comprehensive, culturally and locally determined care for people affected by disasters; the knowledge that such disasters are recurring and should be the subject ongoing of study and plan; and the fact that disasters affect communities as a whole, a new paradigm, community resilience, has developed around disaster health and mental health. Adopted by the U.S. Department of Health and Human Services and the United Nations Office for Disaster Risk Reduction (UNISDR), it addresses the need to work with community partners to strengthen their hardiness before, during, and following disasters (Chandra et al., 2011).

Community resilience theory falls under the social ecological perspective on understanding recovery from disaster and terrorism. Community resilience is defined as "the sustained ability of a community to withstand and recover from adversity" (Chandra et al., 2011; p. 1). An additional factor is the capacity of a community to develop and grow in the face of adversity (Hall & Zautra, 2010). The underlying assumption is that the creation of resilient communities will facilitate community members' ability to care for the most vulnerable members and to help all community members to recover more quickly.

Community resilience has been seen as a function of resource robustness and adaptive capacity (Longstaff, Armstrong, Perrin, Parker, & Hidek, 2010). Social work literature has already identified underresourced and marginalized communities as those most negatively affected by disaster (Mathbor, 2007). Connectedness, institutional memory, and innovative learning comprise adaptive capacity in this model (Longstaff et al., 2010, p. 6). These are the factors that can be most readily strengthened to build the capital needed for robust community resilience. However, community resilience is ideally built before the next disaster occurs.

To build community resilience in resource poor communities, clinical social workers should advocate for:

- Engagement of community organizations and structures, including religious, cultural, civic, and medical
- Partnership and reciprocity between these structures and formal governmental institutions providing health and mental health care
- Development of an understanding of the specific elements that support community resilience among specific populations
- Empowerment of community institutions to provide ongoing subclinical care (Chandra et al., 2011)

Protective Factor Research: Supporting Resilience of Individuals and Families

Figure 13.1 illustrates how some factors in the environment create risk, such as living in a region prone to fires, floods, or hurricanes or being exposed to a terrorist attack. Yet other factors mitigate risk. They are referred to in the literature as *protective factors.* The capacity to survive and even to thrive psychologically in the presence of risk is known as *resilience* and can best be understood in an ecological context (Ungar, 2005, 2012).

Resilience is not magic. Resilience occurs when protective measures are sufficient to counter risks. Psychosocial interventions create programs designed to increase protective factors and attempt to reduce risk whenever possible. This is an essential part of the ecosystem in which people grow (Wurzer & Bragin, 2009). Ungar (2012) expresses this in an equation by which resilient behaviors result from interaction of the person in the environment divided by adaptive outcomes in the presence of adversity.

Protective-factor research studies resilient people to learn what they have in common and which biopsychosocial factors promote the capacity to thrive, despite the effects of severe stress. It also studies people exposed to serious risks over time, to learn which characteristics those who survived well had in common. These are known as *protective factors.* Protective-factor research shows that the presence of these in combination is what helps people survive extreme risk (Ungar, 2005, 2012).

Key Risk Factors That Exacerbate the Effects of Disaster
- Poverty
- Membership in a socially excluded group
- Preexisting mental or physical illness or disability
- Residence in group facilities: prisons, nursing homes, hospitals
- Lack of family or community connections
- Previous exposure to danger, violence, or abuse
- An attachment style that makes creating connections difficult or unlikely

- Inflexible intellectual style, emotional difficulty tolerating uncertainty
- Despair (Ungar, 2005, 2012)

Key Protective Factors
- Close interpersonal connections and an attachment style that makes it possible to create more
- A sense of self-worth (as a person or as a group member)
- A sense of self-efficacy (a sense that one is able to be effective in the world, that one's actions matter, either as an individual or as part of the group)
- Connection to the community and culture, whether in a community of origin or the chosen one
- Ability to think flexibly and creatively
- Ability to access available resources
- Transcendent spiritual belief (religious, political, or other)
- Altruism
- Hopefulness (Ungar 2005, 2012)

Contemporary neuroscience has begun to shed light on the ways that some protective factors work to promote resilience, specifically, secure attachment style, purpose or meaning in life, the ability to think creatively, and transcendent spiritual belief. These appear to give rise to other protective factors, including hopefulness or altruism, which in turn support the ability (or strength) to access available resources (Rutten et al., 2013).

The Role of Psychodynamic Theory in Supporting Resilience

In addition to the ecological systems perspective, clinical social work is also informed by a psychodynamic perspective, which helps clinicians understand the emotions underlying people's behavior. Additionally, it helps us understand the meaning of grief and loss and the effects of overwhelming experience on mind and body. It can help us understand aggression and the effects of violence on our capacity to think. Moreover, recent developments in attachment theory can help us understand the importance of human connection and the role it can play in developing and strengthening resilience, creating a useful clinical correlate to what we are learning from neurobiology.

One such protective factor is the ability to think and reflect in the midst of crisis. It has now been well established that stressful experiences affect the thought processes (Perry, 2002; Siegel, 1999), none more so than exposure to extreme violence. It is difficult for people to process the information they receive and make proper use of knowledge and information while being exposed to violence. As a result, panic can feed on itself and exacerbate the situation.

Attachment-based research suggests that thinking about thinking is a neuropsychological capacity that is cocreated with caregivers, allowing for the capacity, over time, to reflect on the minds and ideas of others (Fonagy & Target, 1996, 1997; Fonagy & Allison, 2012). People with "reflective function" "mentalize," that is, think about what they are thinking and what others might be thinking (Fonagy & Target, 1996; Siegel, 1999). This capacity may be lost in the midst of disaster, leading to public harm (Fonagy & Bateman, 2012).

By understanding the origins of mentalization and reflective function in human connectedness, and the harm that comes from losing this capacity, and by supporting the creation of community connections and using those connections to build mentalizing capacity, even under the most difficult of circumstances (Fonagy & Allison, 2012; Bragin, 2012), clinical social workers are better equipped to assist clients who have been exposed to extreme violence.

Psychodynamic theory also helps clinical social workers to address people's specific reactions to the violence of terrorism and the despair of disaster-born loss. Specifically, object relations theory addresses human emotions and behaviors that are disturbing for people to think about— such as aggression and violence. One object relations theorist, D. W. Winnicott, wrote about the role of aggression in human life. Winnicott

(1939/1984a, 1964/1984b, 1960/1984c) suggests that we are all born with aggression, and that it is as essential to our "going on being" as are love and care. Exposure to excessive violence, loss, or terror leaves people feeling helpless and often very, very angry. It is hard for them to understand and tolerate how angry they feel. Aggression turned inward can lead to despair, increasing the effects of stressful experiences on thought processes. Psychodynamic theory suggests that the ability to do good things "repairs" the effects of violence and helps people manage aggression provoked by experiencing violence and loss (Winnicott, 1939/1984a, 1964/1984b, 1960/1984c). We can use this information to help build programmatic responses in community as well as individual settings (Bragin, 2012).

Trauma Theory and the PTSD Controversy

The diagnosis of posttraumatic stress disorder (referred to as PTSD) formally entered the nomenclature in 1980. Prior to the development of this diagnosis, survivors of extremely violent events, from rape victims or war veterans to those who survived disasters, were considered by some psychiatrists in the global north[4] to have a character defect if they reacted with symptomatic behavior to the events that they had experienced (Herman, 1992). The new diagnostic category emphasized that strong responses after experiencing extreme situations were *normal* reactions to events that were beyond the capacity of the mind to endure them (Herman, 1992; van der Kolk et al., 1996).

Researchers soon discovered that symptoms suffered by survivors vary, not so much by the nature of the survivor's history but rather by the severity of the trauma they have suffered and the duration of the suffering (Hovens, Falger, Op den Veld, & Shouten, 1992). This revelation is important in understanding reactions to disasters

and terrorism. The experiences of many of these survivors may differ from those of people who have lived through torture, war, repression, and community violence over a long period.

An additional and equally important discovery made by trauma researchers was the fact that many people who appeared not to have an adverse reaction immediately after the experience, did so later, sometimes after many years (Herman, 1992; van der Kolk et al., 1996).

Once professionals understood that the symptoms were in fact normal responses, they were able to develop programs to help survivors integrate their reactions and begin a return to normal life. Thus, trauma therapists in the global north were able to obtain treatment for their patients without fear of stigmatizing them (Bragin, 2007).

In addition, trauma-focused research facilitated the study of the effects of extreme experiences on the survivors. It also pointed the way for studying those who appeared more resilient than others, so that the protective factors that made their resilience possible could be replicated for others (Bragin, 2005, Wurzer & Bragin, 2009).

International Criticism of the Concept of PTSD

This diagnostic category, and the understandings that followed from its development, led to a proliferation of programs around the world that used some version of the Western model to address trauma symptoms. This application of PTSD theory to people in countries and cultures in the midst of, or immediately following, single violent incidents or natural disasters was greeted with dismay by many local experts. This view came from a number of different geographical locations and a number of differing viewpoints (IASC, 2007; Jones, 2008).

A most common concern was that any diagnosis, even one designed to do the opposite, could be used to pathologize entire populations as traumatized. Furthermore, it appeared to individualize

---

[4]This designation refers to the socioeconomic and political division that exists between the wealthy developed countries, known collectively as "the global north" and the poorer developing countries, or "the global south."

problems that were essentially social and communal in nature, fragmenting people and the resources available to help them (Bracken & Petty, 1998). Inasmuch as the expression and meaning of psychological distress is culturally constructed, it may be harmful to impose ideas about internal experience from external sources while ignoring indigenous ones (Wessells, 1999). Alcinda Honwana (2006), a Mozambican medical anthropologist, pointed out that PTSD was, in itself, a culturally constructed diagnosis, developed to explain the symptoms of American soldiers fighting a war in a foreign country who came home unable to adjust to "normal life," and then applied to disparate populations in which stress and distress were signaled in different ways and whose reactions to disasters in their home countries must be understood through their own lens.

In the 1980s, when PTSD theorists made many of their contributions, some of the current information from neurobiology was unavailable. We now know that the creation of a coherent narrative is a vital part of helping the brain and body to heal (Schore & Schore, 2008; Siegel, 1999). The original PTSD theorists wanted to emphasize that survivors of extreme events were likely to show symptoms of distress unrelated to any character pathology from the past. However, this led to a format for treatment that addressed the events themselves without regard to their historical context. This unwittingly created a climate for fragmentation and decontextualization rather than for the connection that promotes healing.

Furthermore, Jones (2008) found that the majority of the more severe psychological effects experienced by survivors of disasters and terrorism were related to the massive losses that they had experienced. Survivors both wanted and needed to talk about what their lives and communities were like before they were destroyed. Clinicians therefore felt that, instead of pathologizing survivors, talking about the past was critical to connecting them to the possibilities of the future. Allowing survivors to talk about their memories and their hopes, while assuming that their reactions to the stress of change are normal, may be helpful to most survivors in restoring a coherent narrative that helps them to include the disaster or incident of mass violence in their life stories as they move forward (Wurzer & Bragin, 2009).

In addition, it is important to note that those 6% to 7% of survivors with debilitating symptoms following disaster or terrorism, along with people already under treatment for psychological distress and serious and persistent mental illness, require a full range of appropriate treatments. PTSD treatment alone was seen as too narrow (Jones, 2008). For some survivors, that will mean treatment for trauma-related symptoms. For others, clinically sound and culturally competent care for complicated grief and depression will be required. The clinical social work theories presented earlier in this section may prove particularly useful for many of these patients. For still others, appropriate care may involve continuing the treatment they were receiving prior to the disaster for preexisting mental disorders (IASC, 2007; Jones, 2008).

EMERGING CONSENSUS ON BEST PRACTICES TO SUPPORT WELL-BEING IN DISASTER AND MASS VIOLENCE

The 21st century began with a series of high-profile and large-scale disasters and terrorist attacks, including the September 11, 2001, attacks in New York City; the Asian tsunami; hurricanes Katrina and Rita; and devastating earthquakes in India, Pakistan, Iran, and China. In some of these situations, the care for affected families and communities was quite good. In others, the care itself, and the relief arrangements thereafter, caused more psychosocial suffering than it prevented (IASC, 2007). Kasi et al. (2007), writing from India, pointed out that the social work community needed to prepare for the inevitability of events such as these taking place every year. They cited the Indian example following the tsunami in which clinical social workers had positioned themselves to work with government at every level to plan and implement psychosocial and mental health responses. For this to work well there had to be some sort of consensus on best practices.

Originally, there was tension between clinicians, who focused on psychological distress, and humanitarian workers, who focused on the social aspects. However, through practice, research, and discussion, a consensus has emerged within the humanitarian community (IASC, 2007).

How did this consensus emerge? Because of the very nature of emergency situations, it is extremely difficult to conduct clinical trials to determine the best intervention. Originally, this led to the implementation of practices that imposed a Western medical model of care, one that marginalized both indigenous and holistic, psychosocial models. Frequently, psychologists and psychiatrists took the lead, with focused approaches on individual mental health that ignored the broader social and cultural domain. Later, follow-up research indicated that some of the practices popularized by these disciplines, such as critical incident debriefing, were ineffective at best and harmful at worst (Hobfoll et al., 2007) in preventing adverse psychological reactions and promoting long-term readjustment.

Responding to these criticisms, and to begin the process of compiling information on best practices, Stevan Hobfoll and his colleagues at the Summa-Kent State University Center for the Treatment and Study of Traumatic Stress brought together experts with experience in disaster and mass violence from Israel, Europe, and the United States to extrapolate from their own research. The result was a consensus document laying out five empirically supported intervention principles in the immediate and early to midterm stages of disaster. They mandate promoting (1) a sense of safety, (2) calming, (3) a sense of self and community efficacy, (4) connectedness, and (5) hope (Hobfoll et al., 2007, p. 284). Not surprisingly, these principles promote the same factors that mitigate psychosocial risk and support resilience.

At the same time, the Office for the Coordination of Humanitarian Affairs (OCHA) saw a need to develop guidelines that could be used worldwide to support psychosocial well-being and address issues of mental health in emergency situations. This too was a response to the problem of popular psychological practices being ineffective, harmful practices being imported, and local best practices from affected communities being marginalized.

International humanitarian coordination efforts are directed by the IASC. The IASC, which issued the guidelines, was established in response to General Assembly Resolution 46/182 (Office for the Coordination of Humanitarian Affairs [OCHA], 1999; UN General Assembly 2007; UNISDR, 2007), with the mandate to coordinate humanitarian action around the world and establish and advocate for best practice in humanitarian assistance. It is headed by the Director of the UNOCHA and is made up of the heads of United Nations agencies, the Federation of Red Cross/Red Crescent Societies, the International Committee of the Red Cross, and the consortia of international nongovernmental organizations (NGOs).

In 2005, the IASC established a working group to develop guidelines on mental health and psychosocial support in emergencies.[5] The purpose of the guidelines was to outline a set of responses to be employed during and immediately after emergencies, support psychosocial well-being, increase resilience, minimize risk, and provide care for mentally ill persons and those who are severely affected by the disaster. The guidelines highlight the importance of mobilizing disaster-affected persons to organize their own supports and participate fully in every aspect of the relief and recovery effort (van Ommeren & Wessells, 2007). The guidelines were launched for implementation in 2007. Their effectiveness is monitored and evaluated by an ongoing body called a *reference group*.

The majority of people affected by disaster or mass violence, while changed in many ways, appear to be able to endure their experiences and even to find a measure of meaning and happiness in life following their ordeal, while others, about 5% to 6%, suffer from severe stress reactions (Jones, 2008). Therefore, a simultaneous,

---

[5]The author served on this working group representing CARE International.

multilayered approach to the way services are provided is called for, one that targets every aspect of biopsychosocial well-being and not simply the prevention and response to psychological trauma (Bragin, 2011).

The guidelines outline the layers of care that should be provided, ensure the maintenance of psychosocial well-being, and include all members of the affected population. The pyramid in Figure 13.2 outlines the layers.

The rest of this chapter highlights the role of clinical social work and clinical social workers in providing care at each layer of the pyramid, ensuring that our skills inform every aspect of the effort to safeguard and restore well-being, even

as professionally sound and culturally competent clinical care is provided to those who need it.

THE ROLES OF CLINICAL SOCIAL WORK DURING AND AFTER DISASTER AND TERRORISM: A MULTILAYERED APPROACH

A natural disaster has struck. You don't know where your family members are, where you can go to be safe, where you can find a bathroom (and your 5-year-old needs one badly), let alone where you will sleep tonight, and how long it

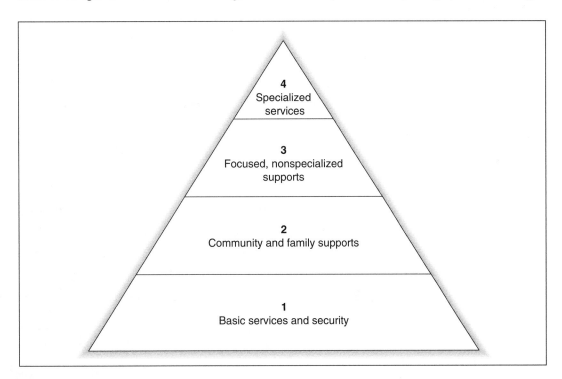

Figure 13.2 Intervention Pyramid for Mental Health and Psychosocial Support in Emergencies

Source: IASC (2007).

Note: (1) *Basic services and security:* These are the supports needed by the entire population and must be provided to all survivors immediately. (2) *Community and family supports:* These supports are group oriented and subclinical. They involve many members of the community. Often, they are designed by community members, and supports are brought to bear as requested. (3) *Focused, nonspecialized supports:* The third layer represents the supports necessary for the still smaller number of people who additionally require focused individual, family, or group interventions by trained and supervised workers. This layer also includes psychological first aid. (4) *Specialized services:* The top layer of the pyramid is for those members of the community who are mentally ill and need access to medication and continued care and those who are having a severe reaction to the events and require professional treatment.

will be until you are safe. You certainly don't know what will happen next.

You hear that there is transport to safety and that food and water are being distributed, but you, your infant, and the 5-year-old are literally running from place to place trying to find them. Rumors are flying, and you don't know what to believe. Some of the scariest may be true.

At one point, denied safe passage at every turn, and with flood waters rising around you, you simply put your baby in the arms of strangers on a bus to safety. You try to do the same with the 5-year-old, but she shrieks and clings to you, so you hang on for dear life and hope for the best. No one takes the trouble to record the information for you and tell you how to find your baby again when you are safe.

You find your spouse at the crowded, chaotic shelter, where they say the bathrooms are unsafe, and the little one is crying. Your spouse can't forgive you for putting the baby on the bus, you are mad with worry, and meanwhile you have lost everything that you ever owned. As you struggle to locate your baby, support your child, and search for grandma among the unmarked dead, you must face the recrimination of family members as well as try to find a home and a means to make a living. You begin to despair and think that you can't go on.

The provision of basic information and basic services is a clinical issue!

TIER I: BASIC SERVICES AND SECURITY[6]

Develop Coordinating Structures From the Local to the Larger-Community Level

By getting information from all those who can help and ensuring that no one is working alone, coordinated efforts ensure maximum inclusion. Such coordination will make the next

steps possible. This is hard work, and all our clinical skills will be needed to coordinate the multiple systems and personalities.

Participate in the immediate development of a central coordinating body and, within it, a psychosocial working group that can help ensure that everyone knows who is doing what and where.

Get Clear, Accurate, and Coordinated Information to the Population

People in the midst of disaster need the following information:

- What is known and not known about the nature of the disaster
- Where they can go to be safe
- Where they *cannot* go to be safe
- Where services are being provided
- Who can get the services
- How to register to locate missing family members

Ensure that information on these issues is disseminated clearly, consistently, regularly, and in all locally spoken languages.

Build the Capacity of Existing Health, Education, and Social Welfare Systems: Support Local Practitioners in Doing Their Jobs Well

One of the most important roles a clinician can play is to keep local health, welfare, and education systems in the lead and to provide health professionals, social workers, and teachers with the material and psychosocial support that they need to continue their work. Even though they are suffering the effects of the disaster themselves, it is important to recognize that they have valuable knowledge, skills, and experience. They are the ones who know exactly

---

[6]These correspond to Hobfoll et al.'s (2007) *safety, calm,* and *connections.*

what materials and information they already have and what is needed. They are the ones who know what will be useless or superfluous.

But, by definition, disasters overwhelm the available capacity of local systems. Therefore, outside help is needed. However, the most effective use of outside resources is to support the existing systems regardless of how overwhelmed they seem. To bolster their sense of empowerment and capacity, they must be assured that they retain their positions of authority and that necessary resources identified by these systems will be brought in, from equipment to personnel. At the same time, it is equally important to furnish the providers with psychosocial supports, so that they are able to carry on. (This is discussed in greater detail in the section Tier IV: Specialized Care.)

Support Skilled Workers, Merchants, and All Others in Being Useful at Their Work

When people have lost everything, it is important for them to remember that they have not lost their skills and capacities. They should assess the damage and take the lead in obtaining contracts for repair. Existing merchants should be consulted and given contracts to provide supplies to emergency workers whenever possible. When they have a role to play, they will cope better. This is best accomplished by daily meetings of the coordinating committee whose members will work with the concerned logistics managers.

Involve Community Members in Defining Their Own Well-Being and That of Their Children

The best information comes from the source, and poor information or external definitions of well-being may increase feelings of stress and inadequacy. Mental health and psychosocial support assessments in emergencies provide

(a) an understanding of the emergency situation, (b) an analysis of threats to and capacities for mental health and psychosocial well-being, and (c) an analysis of relevant resources to determine, in consultation with participants, whether a response is required and, if so, what the nature of the response should be.

An assessment should include documenting people's experiences of the emergency, how they react to it, and how this affects their mental health and psychosocial well-being. The assessment should include how individuals, communities, and organizations respond to the emergency. It must measure resources, as well as needs and problems. Resources include individual coping/life skills, social support mechanisms, community action, and capacities of government and nongovernment organizations. Understanding how to support affected populations to more constructively address Mental Health and Psychosocial Support (MHPSS) needs is essential. An assessment must also be part of an ongoing process of collecting and analyzing data in collaboration with the affected community and all those providers and support persons who understand their community well.

This assessment can guide the work that clinicians perform after the emergency and the types of specialized supports they may provide. In some instances, the assessment itself helps affected persons feel safe, secure, and calm.

A coordinated participatory assessment process should begin immediately.

Community members should be encouraged to identify their own coping mechanisms:

- What is in place? What is missing? What more/new is needed?
- Which traditional practices or ways of doing things make people invisible?
- Who needs to be involved in creating change where change is needed?

Community-based monitoring and evaluation of clinical interventions can begin early as well, forming part of the assessment.

The Haitian Community Resilience Project: Engaging the Strengths of a Diaspora Community

The Haitian Community Resilience Project did not take place in Haiti, but in the diaspora communities of Brooklyn and Queens in New York City. These communities were known for their strengths; the excellent school performance of the children, the high community representation in the health care workforce, and the unfailing financial contributions to family members on the island. Further, Haiti itself seemed to many the embodiment of resilience. Born out of a slave rebellion, the newly born republic paid every penny of the price needed to purchase its freedom, despite economic boycott from Europe and the United States and isolation imposed by the Vatican. Through the spirit of community solidarity known as *Kombit*, and a deep spirituality, Haiti somehow survived all of this adversity, as well as a history of hurricanes, earthquakes, and environmental degradation (Nicolas, Schwartz, & Pierre, 2009).

The earthquake that struck Haiti on January 12, 2010, at 7.3 on the Richter scale, was the most powerful to occur in that country for 200 years; 1.5 million people were directly affected, including 220,000 who lost their lives, 330,000 injured, and 1.3 million forced to live in temporary shelter. The unprecedented size and damaging sequelae of this earthquake placed an unprecedented burden on members of the Haitian-American diaspora, including the estimated 86,687 Haitian-American residents of Brooklyn and Queens. Of these it was estimated that 60% had lost immediate family members, with the entire community supporting survivors either in their homes temporarily or on the island.

New York City's Department of Health and Mental Hygiene (DOHMH) launched a massive outreach effort in churches and community centers to learn from the existing community institutions what factors supported their resilience and where resources should best be placed to support existing structures or to reach people who those structures were not reaching. Beginning with a participatory assessment, DOHMH professionals engaged all levels of the community, from leaders to earthquake refugees, to indicate what was needed to support resilience, what was in place, what needed strengthening, and what more was needed.

The community members were able to recommend capacity building initiatives that would allow for ongoing community supports—psychological, social, and economic —provided at churches, schools, and community centers. The interventions supported both the Kombit and spiritual traditions of the community. Participatory evaluation revealed high use of these supports and a sense that they had succeeded in restoring and building capacity, connectedness, and the ability to adapt. Now New York's DOHMH intends to use this as an opportunity to jump-start community resilience-building measures (Bragin & Prince, 2012).

Community members can also be asked to target specific vulnerable groups; success is measured in part by the capacity of the community members to include such groups and get that information to those distributing relief. (This entire section is from IASC, 2007, Action Sheets 2.1 and 2.2.[7])

---

[7]More on participatory monitoring and evaluation and the entire assessment sequence can be found in the following key Web sites: www.who.int/mental_health/emergencies/guidelines_iasc_mental_health_psychosocial_june_2007.pdf (IASC, 2007) and www.interventionjournal.com/downloads/31pdf/03_24%20Bragin%20.pdf (Bragin, 2005).

Ensuring the Protection of Vulnerable Groups

Very often in an emergency, those who are normally disenfranchised in a society remain invisible until their problems reach acute proportions. For example, after the events of September 11, 2001, in the United States, the families of the undocumented workers of color who were killed during the disaster were not supported to the same level as were others, until advocates sought them out and worked on their behalf. Problems such as this can occur in any society.

Learning about structures of power and historic discrimination are critical parts of any assessment so that even when cultural traditions are being honored and maintained, those that support discrimination and injury are not.

Supporting providers should include community standards of well-being in the design of all basic services, so that bathrooms are usable and safe, shelters are the same, and food and water cannot be exchanged for sex or money. (See IASC, 2007, Action Sheets 9–11 for details on this section.)

Identifying the Dead Before They Are Buried and Informing Families as Soon as Possible

One of the greatest sources of psychosocial distress is uncertainty about whether a loved one is dead or alive. It makes grief and mourning difficult and renders getting on with life almost impossible. Therefore, identification of the dead and notification of the living are essential for the restoration of well-being.

Fortunately, when healthy people die in a disaster or a terrorist attack, their bodies can be preserved for a day or two prior to burial, so that identification and registration can be made and, if possible, family members can be located and notified. There is no health-related need for immediate mass burial, unlike situations in which people die of disease (Wisner & Adams, 2002).

Clinicians can coordinate with health workers to ensure that bodies are identified before they are buried or cremated. Whenever possible, surviving relatives should be able to dispose of the identified bodies in accordance with their cultural traditions. Coordination meetings can help ensure this.

TIER II: COMMUNITY AND FAMILY SUPPORTS AND TIER III: FOCUSED NONSPECIALIZED SUPPORTS

These supports also provide some of the basic building blocks of well-being after disaster and terrorism (described by Hobfoll et al., 2007); that is, they build connections, promote self-efficacy and capacity, and begin to support the creation of hope.

Tier III supports, that is, those targeted to people who have suffered from specific types of devastation (e.g., loss of parents or children), are often nestled into family and community supports and will thus be presented here together with Tier II supports.

Support for Mourning Rituals and Ceremonies

It is normal to feel great sadness and anger in the wake of terrible calamities. These feelings do not require treatment unless they affect functioning over time. It is important to remember that losing a loved one in an untimely way changes the mourner forever. It will take at least 12 to 18 months to learn to live with the loss. This is not the same as moving on and getting over it.

Wherever possible, clinicians should support participation in traditional mourning rituals. In the case of death and mourning, even the nontraditional have traditions. Families should be permitted to define what they want to do, provided help to do it, and helped to create new traditions if old ones don't work.

Sam's Feast: A Ritual for Atheists

Everyone loved Sam, mostly because of the way that he loved life. Sam was an irreverent, foul-mouthed, smoking, and drinking 78-year-old who commented to everyone who would listen that he would womanize a bit more if only he could. He had no use for religion and had ceased to be an orthodox Marxist. Sam was a U.S. veteran of many conflicts for social justice, from the Spanish Civil War and World War II, to the civil rights movement in the South, to the struggles of immigrant workers in New York. That struggle brought him to the World Trade Center on September 11, 2001, where he was organizing undocumented workers at Windows of the World.

Sam would have hated all of the official ceremonies having to do with September 11. His partner in life, Esther, stated she wanted no part of any of this—not even the mention of his name—once it was clear that he was among those killed. (Conspiracy theorists still say that since his body was never found, he actually escaped and somehow made it to Cuba, where he remains in hiding, still organizing to this day.)

Esther, who was not his legal widow because she and Sam did not believe in marriage, had nothing to hold on to. At 60, Esther felt that she was living in a world in which nothing felt real at all. She couldn't own the ceremonies, and she was not acknowledged by official organizations because they didn't consider her a widow. Her sadness was complicated by this intensifying feeling of dissociation.

Members of the immigrant community that Sam had been organizing contacted their outreach worker to ask that someone visit Esther. Together with the outreach worker, they planned a huge memorial party, celebrating a small victory in gaining benefits for the workers.

There was a lot of Spanish wine, dancing, music, and an enormous feast. The songs of the Spanish Civil War were sung, Esther wore a dress from the Spanish war days, and an honor guard sang the anthem of the international brigades, standing at attention, left arms clenched. Young people Sam and Esther had mentored led the dancing and pledged to continue Sam's work. They collect Esther every year to march together with them in immigrants' rights marches and carry a banner in Sam's name.

Esther embraced this ritual as a way of beginning to think about Sam's death as a reality and how to rebuild her life.

Dancing Our Way From the Past to the Future: A Chinese Community Copes With Loss

The fact that every single child was in school that day was a source of pride to this small ethnic minority community in western China. Not so long ago, the rural schools were of poor quality and did not continue past grade four. Consequently, few students went beyond an elementary education. The perceived complication of an ethnic minority language spoken at home posed further educational challenges.

But by 2007, there were three schools in the nearby large town: elementary, middle, and high school. No one kept children at home. There were several regional universities and technical schools from which to choose. The school buildings were tall and well equipped, unlike the one-story pre-fabricated structures common in rural communities in other countries. This hardworking ethnic minority felt that they had really "made it." Many families sent the children to school happily the morning of the earthquake, but some had to argue and insist. All the schools in that town collapsed, killing all the students and teachers inside.

Families lost their only child. Everyone had to wait for two days until the army came with helicopters, rescuing the living and exhuming and helping to cremate the dead.

The community was devastated. Words were totally inadequate comfort. Parents who thought that they were helping their children by insisting that they go to school had instead sent them to their deaths.

The community had a custom: traditional dancing. Each generation taught the dances to the next, and they practiced them together with their children week after week. Slowly, they began to revive their dance troupe. With the support of the Hong Kong Polytechnic University Department of Social Work, the local social work teams were helped to understand that the weekly dancing was a way for the community to connect to their past as they slowly began to rebuild their future. At the first anniversary of their children's deaths, and the destruction of their community, the troupe danced for an international audience.

They wept, they remembered, but then they danced, with the surviving children (those too old or young to have been at school) dancing along.

The loss of a child is forever, and the grief may be lifelong. However, through this unusual transgenerational creative process, those with unbearable guilt, pain, and grief drew strength from one another and began the slow process of healing.

Source: Adapted from Sim (2009).

Support for First Responders

There is nothing that feels as good as being able to help someone in need, whether it is pulling them out of the rubble of an earthquake or carrying them from a burning building. Doing such lifesaving work in the company of others is a high unlike any other—a memory people recall until their dying days. First responders differ from soldiers because their mission is to heal, rather than harm, and their tasks are universally praised.

The high rates of posttraumatic stress in first responders, although lower than that of the affected population, are still noteworthy (Halpern & Tramontin, 2007). As previously noted, short-term debriefing was found to be ineffective (Hobfoll et al., 2007).

At first, rescuers may be incapable of rendering what they have experienced into a symbolic form. However, when the suffering stops, they may find that those parts of the experience that have not been symbolized return to haunt them.

Typical symptoms are substance abuse or risk-taking behavior that attempts to replicate the high of the lifesaving experience.

Psycho-educational interventions, which are designed to explain how the brain processes extreme experience, can be helpful. These are best done as part of a training program in which responders (a) are given the information so that they can help others, (b) are asked to develop a plan to discuss the experiences together, and (c) are invited to lead the community in training new members of the team, so that they don't fall prey to substance abuse or to behaviors that put others at risk.

Support for Children and Adolescents

Disasters and terror attacks create situations that affect every aspect of social and emotional life. As described above, they create great distress among all affected members of society. Children are engaged in a dynamic process of development that won't hold still and wait for better times and more positive influences to shape outcomes. Therefore, communities must be assisted to create the most favorable conditions possible for the development of all children to move forward. This is separate from and precedes any treatment program designed for those who suffer from specific levels of distress.

The following steps review simple, community-based actions to support children's continuing growth and development when all the usual services are disrupted, where massive loss has occurred, and when families are distraught.

Support for Parents and Teachers

For children to develop normally, they need parents and teachers who are supported well enough to do a good job with the children in their care. This is a subclinical level of care requiring culturally competent intervention within the affected communities.

Supporting Parents

Some of the supports below designed for children will also support their parents. Though specialized supports for parents, independent of their children, may be helpful, structured groups, which require that appointments be regularly kept, are not as effective when people are under stress. Therefore, a service center that provides essential information can also have a drop-in corner where parents can come and talk, blow off steam, and receive psycho-educational materials. Peer-to-peer support can also be offered at schools.

Support for Teachers

At this level, we want to emphasize more specific supports for teachers that include providing group encouragement, places to talk and get coffee, and solid recognition. Teachers need to talk and freely exchange stories and experiences with one another in an environment of mutual support. Their needs must be recognized.

One of the most effective ways to accomplish this goal, apart from providing coffee breaks and downtime, is through experiential education sessions. Such sessions allow teachers and others directly involved in child care to find ways of discussing their own experiences so that they can help children to talk about theirs.

Helping Babies and Very Young Children

Keeping Families Together/Preventing Separations. Small children can be quite resilient in disaster because their family members are their safety and security mechanism. We know that losing family connection is a developmental disaster for children. The loss causes stress on the parents and the entire family system as well. Sometimes, misguided individuals may want to provide food and safety for children alone, not aware that this may lead to the destruction of family ties. Therefore, assistance must be offered to the entire family, including the children. (See Appendix B for a detailed guide to preventing separations in the midst of emergencies.)

If a child has been separated from his or her parents, ensuring continuity of care by surviving family members is critical until the parents are located and the family has been reunited.

Assist Parents in Caring for Small Children

If at all possible, a tent or other safe space for mothers and grandmothers of small children should be provided, thus assuring safety and emotional support, as well as nutritious food, diapers, and beverages. In the international community, these are sometimes called *child-friendly spaces* and are easily run by volunteers, since parents are there with the children. Psychosocial support in the form of active listening can also be offered. Often, it's possible to have toddlers and younger children playing there, as well. That helps people to regain their balance.

There is no need to keep track of attendance. Parents can simply walk in and spend time as needed, no questions asked. A volunteer can find out if anyone needs additional emergency services and refer them.

Kids' Corner at Pier 94: World Trade Center 2001

One of the most difficult tasks following the World Trade Center attack of September 11, 2001, involved recovering and turning over the remains of the deceased to the surviving family, a task further complicated by the arduous process of documentation and disbursement of benefits. These tasks were performed at Pier 94 in Manhattan. Many surviving parents arrived with young children in tow. They were distraught, and the place still smelled of burning debris and decomposing bodies.

A dedicated child psychoanalyst, Desmond Heath, set up the Kids' Corner. It was a small space in a corner of the pier, staffed by volunteers, many of whom were clinical social workers. Children could draw or play with dolls and trucks while their parents went inside and waited in line for service. A sand tray with miniature dolls was also provided for those who wished to use that medium to make up stories.

Before and after receiving the information that they needed, and an urn containing the deceased's remains, parents were offered an opportunity to meet with volunteer clinicians, while their children continued to play, supervised by other volunteers.

Though the intervention was very brief, it helped these parents in distress to gather themselves and receive support at a critical time. It was also helpful to know that their children were able to play in a safe, supervised setting.

It proved beneficial for these children to express themselves through play with someone able to make sense of their feelings, if only for a few moments, before returning to the fray.

Source: Coates, Schechter, and First (2003).

Support for School-Age Children

Children from ages 6 to 12 like to learn the rules of the community and follow them. Disruptions from normal activities are particularly upsetting to them and so is exposure to violence or other rule breaking by adults. Therefore, interventions to maintain the flow of development involve as many normalizing activities as possible, coupled with specialized support to teachers, parents, and youth workers. The list below gives some essential suggestions.

Participation in Mourning Rituals. Children must be told who has survived and who has died and be allowed to participate with others in mourning rituals, so that they can see that there is an order to the things that have happened.

Emergency School. It is important to resume school as quickly as possible. Teachers can be supplied with books of games and helpful activities, including guides for talking and playing with children following a disaster. Some programs focus on identifying traumatized children. This is not useful. Rather, children should come to school and find as much routine as possible. They should be able to talk about the disaster during a special talk time, but the rest of the day should be devoted to regular learning activities. The Web address of the International Network on Education in Emergencies is included at the end of this chapter. The website lists suggested activities for school-age children and available training for teachers.

Creating Space for Organized Sports and Games. Children need to know that it's okay to play, inasmuch as play helps them work out problems and feel better again. School-age children like to play games with rules, from sports to board games, because they are learning about the rules that govern the world in which they live and how to take their place within it. Both disasters and terrorism violate those rules, whether they are the rules of nature (a big wave should not come onto land and destroy everything in its wake), the social compact (the levees are kept strong by the engineers so that the river will not flood our city), or human behavior (people don't kill thousands of people just because they don't like what their government does). When games and sports are organized for children after a disaster or terror attack, it can help restore their sense of security. Learning the rules of the game and playing by them can help school-age children know that the world has not gone completely mad.

Participation in Age-Appropriate Helping Activities. School-age children can be helped to find age-appropriate ways of helping others. This will aid them in feeling important and more hopeful. It is important that the tasks be easy enough, so that they can feel successful. They can be involved in activities such as playing games with and telling stories to younger children and helping identify lost little ones. They can also help by creating art and music projects that parents and others can enjoy.

What Teachers Can Do to Work Effectively With School-Age Children

Because school-age children are learning the rules of society, and these rules have been broken by the natural disaster or terror attack, they will not feel safe unless they are sure that there are rules that everyone in the classroom agrees on, that will not suddenly be changed without warning. When they have difficulty with their own emotions, and fear an outbreak of inner feelings, they need reassurance that they are normal and that with help, normal life will return for them and their classroom:

- Make sure that the rules for behavior at school are clear and that everyone knows them.
- Make sure that children have access to good, clear factual information about the events and that this information is repeated as often as required.
- Provide opportunities to discuss feelings and fears, and offer reassurance that they are cared for and protected.
- Explain that it is normal to have trouble concentrating during difficult times, and help them do schoolwork as a team and homework working one-on-one with a volunteer.
- Explain that their reactions (poor concentration, worry, psychosomatic symptoms) are related to the disaster, and that they will feel better with time.
- Don't reward psychosomatic complaints by paying too much attention to them, or the child will develop a habit of seeking love and support this way. Instead, provide reassurance and help children with psychosomatic problems put their worries into words.
- Teach children the principles of conflict resolution to help them feel empowered to control their behavior and solve problems among themselves.

Talking About Difficult Issues With School-Age Children

- Recognize that school-age children want and need as much factual information as possible.
- Allow children to discuss their own theories and ideas about what happened, so that they can begin to master the events.

- Tell children how and where they can obtain information and assistance.
- Initiate group discussions about distressing events that they may (or may not) have experienced, since it may be assumed that even those who are not directly affected would have heard about them. This will help affected children feel less alone in their suffering.

- If a child brings you a rumor or false alarm, take time to find out what the facts are and inform the child, reminding him or her of accurate sources of information.
- Tell the children that it is okay to feel afraid, confused, angry, and guilty. These are all normal responses to an extraordinary situation.
- Use realistic terms with children, and avoid euphemisms.[8]

The Program for Underserved Schools: Principals, Kids, and Teachers Get Support

Carol Sedgwick (not her real name) was principal of a school very near the World Trade Center. Her school catered to poor immigrant kids. After the towers collapsed, a temporary shelter was set up in her school, and at first she was glad to be of help. Her students and teachers who lived in the neighborhood had to go through police barricades and have their IDs checked before they got to school. Attention was lavished on those schools directly affected. However, to these students and teachers, who lived near the site/ but were powerless and invisible, it seemed that no services were being offered and more and more was asked of them.

When the Program for Underserved Schools' workers came to talk to Ms. Sedgwick, she was angry and bitter. She wanted to talk about the burdens that she faced but claimed to have no time to do so. She certainly had no spare rooms for any outsiders.

One worker then responded by joining her for an early breakfast and a cup of coffee. After some time, Ms. Sedgwick began to feel she could trust her and felt able to discuss what was troubling her about the larger response. She agreed to meet with some of the other principals to talk about their difficulties. She also articulated ways in which she needed help with the school.

The teachers proved even more angry and hard to reach. Many were immigrants themselves and felt badly treated. Rap groups were started in the teachers' lounge with no rules as to what the teachers could talk about. They began with their anger about the school and their treatment by the larger society. Soon, they were talking about how hard it was to help students under extraordinary circumstances.

That gave the social workers an opening to advise them about ways to work with children affected by a terrorist attack or disaster in the classroom and how to talk with them about difficult issues.

As the teachers felt better equipped, they were able to reach out to their students. Attendance and morale started to improve, especially when the principal announced that they would not provide further services unless they received services themselves.

(Continued)

---

[8]These last two sections are adapted from the IRC (International Rescue Committee) *Training Manual for Teachers* (2003) and the Christian Children's Fund (2005) *Emergency Manual Part 3* (2005).

(Continued)

The teachers asked the psychosocial team to agree to take the most difficult children into the group. They wanted those children to be accepted regardless of their relation to the disaster. They just wanted help with difficult kids. The most unruly children turned out to be those whose families were the most distressed by the collapse of the towers, either because they had lost family members or because it reminded them of previous disasters that they had fled to come to the United States. As undocumented workers, they were unable to access help and were too afraid to ask questions.

Program staff spent 18 months holding rap groups for teachers and art groups for children and helping this principal (and others at similarly affected schools) to articulate and advocate for her school's needs.

For Adolescents

Adolescence involves a new burst of growth in both brain and body, not seen since early childhood. Psychodynamic theory tells us that adolescents, like all others affected by disaster and terrorism, are not really able to think about the events and so may be prone to act out in destructive ways, either against other people or property or against themselves. This is not only because such events have been stored differently in their developing brains but also because they may be very angry and very sad and unable to manage such feelings.

Involving adolescents in every aspect of rebuilding and program development is important for several reasons. First, it reinforces their sense of hope as well as the feeling that they can be of use. Furthermore, such involvement supports reparation, the psychic mechanism by which doing good things helps mitigate the guilt and rage that sometimes follow survival.

All the following activities, employed in combination, will help most adolescents begin to process and heal from their experience.

Participation in Mourning Ceremonies. Like their younger siblings, adolescents need to participate in mourning ceremonies. Many will want to question the values that they have been taught, the meaning of life and death, and whether or not there is a purpose in life.

Expressing these thoughts should not simply be allowed but actively supported. Special opportunities for adolescents to grieve for their friends and classmates can be provided through activities at school and at local religious or community centers.

Starting School as Quickly as Possible. Like younger children, adolescents need the routine of school to help reassure them that life will go on. Those who are scheduled to graduate or take qualifying exams should be reassured that those events will still occur and that they need not lose out.

Providing Opportunities to Participate in Community Service. Nothing feels better after a disaster or terrorism than being able to do something about it. This is particularly true for adolescents, who may feel helpless and betrayed at a vulnerable age. These young people can and should serve as community volunteers and be praised for their activities as they help build shelters, find lost children, and promote hygienic practices. They can be the "legs" that ease coordination and information sharing. Classes at school can be asked to create and execute specific projects in which all class members have a role.

Providing Opportunities for Artistic and Cultural Expression. These activities could take the form of entertaining sick children or the elderly or something to do to have fun. Adolescents can paint murals and decorate temporary shelters. Opportunities to portray the past should be linked with their own visions of the future.

Supporting the Process of Thinking and Understanding. Adolescents are at a stage of development where formal cognition is developing. Encouraging them to express their opinions, identify problems and needs, and create their own solutions aids in the development of this new capacity. Increasing their awareness that they possess a mind and a brain and helping them form their ideas, without censorship, is critically important.

Supporting Participation in Prosocial Cultural Activities That Allow Them to Learn About and Develop Cultural Identity. When these strivings are pushed underground, they can appear in dangerous ways, such as joining hate groups or being recruited into gangs. However, when such strivings are respected and young people are free to participate in their own cultures and identify with them, they learn tolerance, even in the face of crisis.

Giving Importance to Sports and Games. Making sure that adolescents have some time for organized games, sports, dances, and other fun activities lets them know that it is still okay to enjoy living.

Post-Tsunami Sri Lanka: Youth Clubs Make a Difference

Fifteen-year-old Nilusha felt alone and abandoned. Her father was lost at sea, her mother seemed lost at home in the wake of the tsunami, and little remained of their home. Her school was full of mud and disgusting smells. She'd never take her exams, and she'd never graduate. Life seemed about over. Her friends were all overwhelmed, with parents locking them away for fear of danger. Would the sea betray them again?

However, not an hour's bicycle journey away, life was completely normal. It was all so weird. Kids who were just as poor as Nilusha had been completely unaffected by the devastating wave. Was it her fate to be unlucky, she wondered, as she tried half-heartedly to help her mother?

Radha was a member of a local youth club for poor kids run by an INGO (international nongovernmental organization). Teens could gather together and study, have parties and dances, and volunteer for social projects. The club was primarily made up of kids who had been beneficiaries of social and economic support when they were small. They usually had a clubhouse. It was a place where you could hang out and not be hassled.

When the tsunami came, these young people were already organized! Radha convinced the others not to just sit back but to do something. The INGO offered them assistance if they desired it. These teenagers got on their bicycles and rode to the disaster area.

There Radha met Nilusha, whom she had asked for directions amid all the detritus. The girls talked and agreed that Nilusha and others in the community could join the youth club on Saturday, when they returned to the neighborhood. The groups worked together, with local young people identifying problems that the whole group could focus on with the others subsequently joining in.

(Continued)

(Continued)

They made maps of the camps for displaced people, showing where the problem areas were and where there were safe places to go. They got little kids to help in the drawing of the maps. They brought problems to the authorities and asked them to work on them.

They divided up as teams according to interests and went to the local authorities to volunteer. Their organization also helped them find places to be useful.

Some wanted to work with young children, others to work in construction. Some wanted to organize sports matches. Others wanted to use singing and acting talents to entertain old people who were in despair. Radha and Nilusha were both on the team to entertain old people.

Nilusha and her friends, who were affected by the tsunami directly, felt supported by the others. They felt that they were not alone. They also had an ongoing way to work toward improving their situation. The artistic activities they participated in helped them begin to think about the disaster and symbolize it in their minds. The sense of group solidarity helped members feel connected to one another.

At the end of 1 year, Nilusha and the other affected young people were back in school and feeling hopeful. They still identified many problems in the community and in their lives, but they felt that they could be effective in making a change. They felt greater levels of efficacy and had high hopes for the future.

PSYCHOLOGICAL FIRST AID: LISTENING IN THE FACE OF DISASTER

Anger, sorrow, and even helplessness are not clinical problems requiring treatment. On the other hand, it is important to train volunteers, such as Nilusha and Radha, or those who sit with parents and teachers, to be able to listen to people on the spot, when they need to talk, supporting and directing them to the proper care.

Very similar to medical first aid, psychological first aid involves providing care immediately after a critical incident has occurred. This care is intended first to address immediate issues of safety and comfort and then to facilitate planning for additional care. Psychological first aid is typically provided by the first to arrive or those who become aware of the critical incident quickly. It is an attempt to bring comfort and reassurance to victims and to ensure that they get adequate follow-up care. It is not to be confused with psychological assessments or treatment,

both of which can only be provided by trained professionals.

Guidelines for psychological first aid are contained in Appendix C.

TIER IV: SPECIALIZED CARE

Specialized care refers to clinical care and mental health treatment. This tier has two subcategories of clients: (1) those with ongoing, serious, and persistent mental illness and (2) those with acute reactions to the grief, loss, and exposure to violence they have experienced.

Support for the Serious and Persistently Mentally Ill

In all disasters, people suffering from serious and persistent mental illness are among those affected. It is important to ensure that these persons are protected from harm and receive clinically sound and culturally competent care by trained professionals with as little interruption as possible. This group will get only a brief mention here, since the basic intervention is to locate these people, ensure that they are safe, and restore them to the care that they need, including appropriate medications.

They fall into two groups: (1) those in institutions and (2) those residing in the community. It must be determined that those who are in institutional care are brought to safety away from the disaster and are not abandoned or endangered in any way.

Those who are ambulatory will often come to the attention of the police or others when they create disruptions in shelters or other public accommodations. The loss of stability caused by the disaster and the loss of all the structures of daily life may be profoundly distressing to this population. If they have been unable to take their medications, they will be reacting to that as well. Mentally ill persons will need to be seen in whatever medical facilities are available to determine their diagnosis, how long they have been ill, and what medications and other care they were receiving.

When Risk Overwhelms Resilience: People Who Require a Clinical Level of Intervention Following a Disaster or Terror Attack

Among the most vulnerable in times of disaster or terrorist attacks are those who have suffered complicated grief, those who are vulnerable due to factors originating in family or personal history, or a combination of the two.

Jiang, a member of the Sichuan dance troupe, had two daughters. The oldest, a teacher, named Ha, was pregnant with her first child. Her younger daughter had completed high school and gone to work in a business enterprise. On the morning of the earthquake, Jiang's older daughter phoned, saying that she did not want to go to work as she was having a bit of morning sickness and wanted to come to her mother's house to chat. Jiang scolded her daughter and reminded her of the old days when teachers in their district seldom came to school, and the students had a low level of education. She urged her daughter to eat a cracker and go along to school. She wouldn't stay home from work for such a little thing, and neither should her daughter. She was angry with her for being so "spoiled." Later, it was discovered that Ha was killed instantly when her school building collapsed.

Jiang joined the dance troupe and tried to put her hopes in her second daughter, but her grief became more intense with the passage of time. She found herself blaming her younger daughter for surviving when her oldest had died. She blamed herself every day. Nothing relieved her depression.

Jiang's grief, like many people's, was complicated by her belief that she herself had sent her daughter to her death. She felt unworthy to have another child who had survived, when so many of her friends had lost their only one. She felt that she did not deserve to feel better in any way, at any time. Her cultural club, which had proved sufficient for the rest of the members, was not enough for Jiang. Soon she began to feel ill and went to the doctor for her headaches and backaches. The doctor thought that these illnesses were due to a lack of balance in her emotional life and recommended psychotherapy.

(Continued)

(Continued)

Therapy for Jiang could not focus on removing her symptoms, for others would come in their place. Instead, she needed to face and accept the fact that she had not been able to control what happened to her daughter and that on a day when she was impatient, she had unwittingly sent her daughter to her death. This is a difficult process in therapy, as the therapist often wants to "make it better" or to "absolve" the patient of his or her feelings of self-loathing. But the reality is that no one can take the pain away.

The dance group provided a protective holding environment for Jiang while she dealt with her grief and guilt in treatment. Two issues merged here: (1) a malignant feeling of guilt over both her actions and the feelings underlying them, which had proved unbearable, and (2) the difficulty of contemplating those feelings and making mental use of them, inasmuch as they had been locked away inside.

Her therapist recommended family therapy, as a way for the entire family to speak of and then memorialize the dead together but away from the eyes and ears of the community.

Jiang and the therapist met with family members and asked their forgiveness. Other family members told Jiang that they would all have done the same, told their children to go to work and not be a baby, and that they did not blame her. They urged her to look at her remaining daughter and see her light and her love.

To tolerate her guilt, Jiang began to volunteer for the local women's committee, raising funds to help elderly people who had lost their only child. In this way, she began to feel that she was compensating for what she had done. She gradually became able to look fondly at her second daughter.

When I met Jiang and her therapist, she had completed her weekly family therapy and remained in the dance troupe. However, follow-up sessions were scheduled in 3 months. The expectation was not that she would forget her daughter but that she would be able to bear the pain and rejoin life again.

For some patients, the real issue is not guilt or loss or something that happened to them or something that they did; instead, it comes from their family history and the ways that history has made them vulnerable.

My colleague called for a consultation with a disturbing case. The client in question—I will call him Paul—was a precociously bright African American adolescent, barely 14, enrolled as a freshman at a competitive public high school. Paul had been referred because of his "defiant attitude." His mother was particularly concerned that Paul, in whose high school African Americans were a tiny minority, was placing himself at risk.

Trauma in his family had come down through the generations, with his own mother having witnessed the attempted lynching of her father by an angry mob. Her untreated psychological difficulties, and real-life economic stress, left her struggling to be empathic to her son but often with an unconsciously communicated need to be avenged by him.

According to the therapist, Paul was responding rather well to treatment until the events of September 11, 2001. Then, he began to decompensate in a variety of ways, spending all his time on the Internet, writing about his very specific and perfect view of the appropriate response to the events ("How dare you say tragedy—this was evil, this was war"), and raging at anyone, including his mother, who responded in any way that he considered incorrect. He no longer ate or slept well and was awake all night, pacing and writing and refusing medication. What was particularly interesting is that he had not seen the events, since his high school was located in a different borough.

When he returned home one day, Paul told his mother that the smell was of burning bodies and the ash was of the dead and, indeed, that they were breathing in the bodies of their neighbors. He was overwhelmed by the sense of the evil that had been done, worse than Hiroshima and Nagasaki, because it was not committed during an act of war. He began to develop a complex scheme of who was guilty, who was more guilty, and what was appropriate as an expression of grief. His mother, a devout Christian, was cursed for her lack of respect for the dead when she spoke of her compassion for the mothers of the boys who died while committing the act (though such compassion was important for her own psychic survival).

Every waking moment of Paul's life revolved around the careful construction of behavior and ideas that repudiated all possible connection to the terrorists.

There is a great deal more to say, in a long and complicated story. However, we will focus here on the uncanny. This young man had gotten stuck in his own fantasies of violent retribution—in this instance, enacted by bright young men who were older and wealthier but perhaps not so different from him (Osama bin Laden visited Disneyland as a child). They were smart, educated, and aggrieved. They acted on their worst fantasies of retribution. He felt in this enormous crime a frightening breakthrough of his most violent fantasies. He needed to remind himself and everyone else that he was no terrorist.

Paul's history had already taught him that violence can be enacted. The acts of terror in the present time made it clear that the world had not become safe.

His therapy was aimed at helping him reduce the abject dread he experienced in relation to his anger and in gaining facility in expressing these complex feelings in words. The goal was to help him channel his aggression into academic success, which could help him feel good about himself and about the world.

He had a talent for poetry and began to write, attending poetry slams, where he expressed his anger at those he felt were responsible for the terrorist attacks and also those responsible for the violence against his grandfather. In this way, he was able to make the links between his family's past and his own future. As he was able to write about his anger and talk about it, he was better able to tolerate it and use it to benefit himself and others.

Most of those who develop symptoms during or following a disaster or terrorist attack are close to the situation or have suffered a complicated loss, such as Jiang. Some have been directly involved as survivors. But people with a family history of violence and terror, such as the attempted lynching of Paul's grandfather, may find that a repeat incident opens these wounds. Others who struggle with emotional issues related to either anger or loss find that the events trigger great distress that needs to be addressed clinically. For these populations, a focus on symptom reduction will not help enough, and one must help them to tolerate the experience of living in a world where great loss or extreme violence are possible, through clinical interventions such as those described here.

CONCLUSION

The sea represents more to fish than merely the means for biological life. It is their whole world, and embodies what it means to be a fish. Imagine a disaster that tears them from the sea, and with survivors coming to rest in a goldfish bowl filled with tap water. In this environment they can subsist, for this is how they experience it, but it is no world. How can they be helped to get back to the sea, or to begin to turn tap water into something more resembling the sea, and on their terms? For the overwhelming majority of survivors the task seems comparable to this.

—Derek Summerfield (2001, p. 1)

The 21st century began with a series of disasters and terrorist attacks engulfing every part of the globe. With them came loss on a massive scale to whole populations, as well as exposure to death and destruction on a scale greater than the mind can conceive. International standards have now been developed to address the psychosocial consequences of these events.

Addressing the clinical aftermath of disaster and terror requires a multilayered and holistic response. In such circumstances, it is necessary to attend not only to individuals within the context of their lives, and to whom suffering and loss have come not individually, but also to communities as a whole.

Clinical social work is uniquely qualified to address these issues through its fundamental understanding of the integrated nature of the material, social, cultural, and intrapsychic worlds. This chapter attempts to facilitate the work of clinicians who wish to make the link between the theory and practice of their profession and the contemporary international standards for supporting resilience, mitigating risk, and supporting the well-being of survivors of disaster and terrorism.

APPENDIX A

Do's and Don'ts in Community Emergencies

Experience from many different emergencies indicates that some actions are advisable, whereas others should typically be avoided. These are identified below as "Do's" and "Don'ts" (IASC, 2007).

Do's	Don'ts
Establish one overall coordination group on mental health and psychosocial support.	Do not create separate groups on mental health or on psychosocial support that do not talk or coordinate with one another.
Support a coordinated response, participating in coordination meetings and adding value by complementing the work of others.	Do not work in isolation or without thinking how one's own work fits with that of others.
Collect and analyze information to determine whether a response is needed and, if so, what kind of response.	Do not conduct duplicate assessments or accept preliminary data in an uncritical manner.

Do's	Don'ts
Tailor assessment tools to the local context.	Do not use assessment tools not validated in the local, emergency-affected context.
Recognize that people are affected by emergencies in different ways. More resilient people may function well, whereas others may be severely affected and may need specialized supports.	Do not assume that everyone in an emergency is traumatized or that people who appear resilient need no support.
Ask questions in the local language(s) and in a safe, supportive manner that respects confidentiality.	Do not duplicate assessments or ask very distressing questions without providing follow-up support.
Pay attention to gender differences.	Do not assume that emergencies affect men and women (or boys and girls) in exactly the same way or that programs designed for men will be of equal help or accessibility for women.
Check references in recruiting staff and volunteers and build the capacity of new personnel from the local and/or affected community.	Do not use recruiting practices that severely weaken existing local structures.
After trainings on mental health and psychosocial support, provide follow-up supervision and monitoring to ensure that interventions are implemented correctly.	Do not use one-time, stand-alone trainings or very short trainings without follow-up if preparing people to perform complex psychological interventions.
Facilitate the development of community-owned, managed, and run programs.	Do not use a charity model that treats people in the community mainly as recipients of services.
Build local capacities, supporting self-help and strengthening the resources already present in affected groups.	Do not organize supports that undermine or ignore local responsibilities and capacities.
Learn about, and where appropriate, use local cultural practices to support the local people.	Do not assume that all local cultural practices are helpful or that all local people are supportive of particular practices.
Use methods from outside the culture where it is appropriate to do so.	Do not assume that methods from abroad are necessarily better or impose them on the local people in ways that marginalize local supportive practices and beliefs.
Build government capacities and integrate mental health care for emergency survivors in general health services and, if available, in community mental health services.	Do not create parallel mental health services for specific subpopulations.
Organize access to a range of supports, including psychological first aid, to people in acute distress after exposure to an extreme stressor.	Do not provide one-off, single-session psychological debriefing for people in the general population as an early intervention after exposure to conflict or natural disaster.

(Continued)

(Continued)

Do's	Don'ts
Train and supervise primary/general health care workers in good prescription practices and in basic psychological support.	Do not provide psychotropic medication or psychological support without training and supervision.
Use generic medications that are on the essential drug list of the country.	Do not introduce new, branded medications in contexts where such medications are not widely used.
Establish effective systems for referring and supporting severely affected people.	Do not establish screening for people with mental disorders without having in place appropriate and accessible services to care for identified persons.
Develop locally appropriate care solutions for people at risk of being institutionalized.	Do not institutionalize people (unless an institution is temporarily an indisputable last resort for basic care and protection).
Use agency communication officers to promote two-way communication with the affected population as well as with the outside world.	Do not use agency communication officers to communicate only with the outside world.
Use channels such as the media to provide accurate information that reduces stress and enables people to access humanitarian services.	Do not create or show media images that sensationalize people's suffering or put people at risk.
Seek to integrate psychosocial considerations as relevant into all sectors.	Do not focus solely on clinical activities in the absence of a multisectoral response.

Source: IASC (2007).

APPENDIX B

Preventing Separations in Acute Emergencies: A Guide for First Responders

Losing family care, after losing life and limb, is among the most serious consequences of surviving an emergency for children, especially those 5 years of age or younger. There are three situations in which separations are likely to take place:

1. Separations due to mass movement
2. Separations due to the necessity for sudden departure
3. Separations due to the family's incapacity to continue to care for the child

Preventing Separations During Mass Movement

- Keep parents and children together.
- Make child registration available with the International Committee of the Red Cross (ICRC) as the movement occurs.
- Provide all children and parents with identification tags (provide string, tags, writing implements, and people who can assist with writing).
- Have volunteers ensure that all children under 5 years old are tagged.
- Provide adults with flyers, and post notices in public places, showing in words and pictures whom to notify if a child is lost.
- Bring separated children to the front of any convoy or to a place where all adults can see them, so that they can be identified by family and community members en route.

If the movement is with vehicles, then do the following:

- Provide vehicle drivers with rosters of children and parents on the day of the move.
- Provide staff (or seek a literate volunteer) to assist with the tagging and listing of each child in each vehicle.
- If children under 5 are to be placed in a vehicle and it is impossible to take the entire family, make sure that they are accompanied by a parent or that parent's designee.
- If it is not possible to have the child accompanied, make sure his or her name and the names of parents or family members are recorded before the vehicle departs and the parent is given identifying information regarding the vehicle and its destination. This must be in writing even if the parent cannot read.

Preventing Separations Due to Sudden Departure

Sometimes we know that a population is under threat of displacement, either through attack or natural disaster, before the events actually happen. Families should be informed about what they can do to keep from losing children along the way.

Families can do the following:

- Use songs and rhymes to teach their children their own names and the names of their village.
- Attach an identifying name tag to babies' clothes or jewelry or even paste such information on the child's head with a Band-Aid.
- If the parent becomes sick, weak, or tired and fears that she will let go of the child's hand or drop the child, stop and label the child or, if that is not possible, attach an identifying bit of clothing or jewelry before handing the child to someone else.

Preventing Separations Due to the Incapacity to Continue Care

Some families leave babies and young children behind because they do not have the resources to care for them anymore. These separations can be avoided by identifying vulnerable families and providing assistance. Assistance should never be provided to institutions for group care, as families who are poor or ill may feel forced to abandon their children in order to provide a better quality of care for them. Identify vulnerable families and provide assistance directly on the spot.

Especially vulnerable families may be found

- where the parents lack food and shelter,
- where the caregiver is either disabled or caring for one or more disabled children,
- where one or both parents are sick or dying,
- where one or more family members have already died, and
- where the caregiver appears exhausted for any reason and is unable to go on.

In these instances, parents should be given all possible support and be asked for a designated caregiver. Where extended family members are present, those members should be supported to see to the child or children's welfare within the community. Where strong community organizations are present, support them to support their community members to support families to support children.

Appendix C

Psychological First Aid

The following outline provides a general guideline for giving basic psychological first aid. As such, it gives only rudimentary information about how to talk to someone in distress. Use of this outline should be combined with good judgment, cultural sensitivity, and appropriate caution and respect. Consultation with a trained professional at the earliest opportunity following a critical incident is advised.

Although anyone may need assistance, psychological first aid should first be offered to those most likely to need it. Those needing prompt attention will include those requesting help, those visibly upset (crying, yelling, mute), those with a known history of tragic loss, those with a history of mental illness, and those apparently most significantly affected by what has occurred.

Preparing to deliver psychological first aid	1. Maintain a calm presence. 2. Be sensitive to culture and diversity.
Initiating contact	1. Ask about immediate needs. 2. Ask for permission to provide assistance.
Providing safety and comfort	1. Ensure immediate physical safety. 2. Attend to physical comfort. 3. Encourage interaction with others. 4. Attend to children first, if present. 5. Protect from additional traumatic experiences (media inquiries, lack of privacy, etc.). 6. Comfort those with a family member or close friend who has died. 7. Discuss relevant grief and spiritual issues. 8. Support those who receive a death notification by remaining with them. 9. Support those involved in body identification by accompanying them to the location of the body.
Being a calming presence	1. Sit and talk with those who are visibly upset. 2. Answer any questions about what has happened. 3. Provide someone to remain with those in distress during their time of greatest anguish. 4. Monitor or accompany those likely to harm themselves or others (based on your knowledge of their comments, behavior, or history).
Gathering information: Current needs and concerns	Through respectful conversation, gather information about the following: 1. Nature and severity of experiences during the traumatic event 2. Death of a loved one 3. Concerns about immediate post event circumstances and ongoing threat 4. Separations from or concern about the safety of loved ones 5. Physical illness, mental health conditions, and need for medications 6. Losses (home, school, neighborhood, business, personal property, and pets) 7. Extreme feelings of guilt or shame 8. Thoughts about causing harm to self or others 9. Availability of social support 10. Prior alcohol or drug use 11. Prior exposure to trauma and death of loved ones 12. Specific youth, adult, and family concerns
Providing practical assistance	Based on the information gathered, provide the following: 1. Identify the most immediate needs. 2. Clarify these needs. 3. Discuss an action plan for each need. 4. Act to address each need, including making a referral to a competent mental health professional for follow-up.
Connecting with social supports	1. Encourage contact with primary support persons (family and significant others). 2. Encourage use of immediately available support persons (colleagues and respected people in community) 3. Discuss support seeking and giving. 4. Model social support through your conversation.

Sharing information on coping	1. Provide basic information about stress reactions. 2. Review common psychological reactions to traumatic experiences and losses. 3. Provide basic information on ways of coping.
Linking with support services	1. Provide a direct link to additional needed services. 2. Promote ongoing use and coordination of helping relationships.

Source: Adapted from the National Child Traumatic Stress Network and National Center for PTSD (2006).

REFERENCES

Bracken, P., & Petty, C. (1998). *Rethinking the trauma of war.* London, UK: Free Association Press.

Bragin, M. (2005). The Community Participatory Evaluation Tool for psychosocial programs: A guide to implementation. *Intervention: International Journal of Mental Health, Psychosocial Work and Counseling in Areas of Armed Conflict, 3*(1), 3–24.

Bragin, M. (2007). Knowing terrible things: Engaging survivors of extreme violence in treatment. *Clinical Social Work Journal, 35*(4), 215–293.

Bragin, M. (2011). IASC Guidelines on Mental Health and Psychosocial Support: A quick guide for social workers. *Handbook of International Social Work.* New York, NY: Oxford University Press.

Bragin, M. (2012). So that our dreams will not escape us: Learning to think together in time of war. *Psychoanalytic Inquiry: A Topical Journal for Mental Health Professionals, 32*:2, 115–135. http://dx.doi.org/10.1080/07351690.2011.592740

Bragin, M., & Prince, J. (2012). *The Haitian Community Resilience Initiative 2011–2012: A mixed method evaluation.* New York, NY: DOHMH.

Chandra, A., Acosta, J., Stern, S., Uscher-Pines, L., Williams, M., Yeung, D., Garnett, J., & Meredith, L. (2011). *Building community resilience to disasters: A way forward to enhance national health security.* A technical report sponsored by the U.S. Department of Health and Human Services: TR-915-DHHS. Arlington, VA: Rand Corporation.

Christian Children's Fund. (2005). *Training manual for volunteers in child-centered spaces.* Richmond, VA: Author.

Coates, S. W., Schechter, D. S., & First, E. (2003). Brief interventions with traumatized children and families after September 11. In S. W. Coates, J. L. Rosenthal, & D. S. Schechter (Eds.), *September 11: Trauma and human bonds. Relational perspectives book series* (Vol. 14, pp. 23–49). Hillsdale, NJ: Analytic Press.

Duncan, J., & Arnston, L. (2004). *Children in crisis: Good practices in evaluating psychosocial programming* (p. 16.). Washington, DC: International Psychosocial Evaluation Committee and the Save the Children Federation.

Erikson, K. (1976). *Everything in its path: Destruction of community in the Buffalo Creek flood.* New York, NY: Simon & Schuster.

Fonagy, P., & Allison, E. (2012). What is mentalization? The concept and its foundations in developmental research. In Midgely & Vrouva (Eds), *Mentalization-based interventions with children, young people and their families.* London, UK: Routledge.

Fonagy, P., & Bateman, A. (2012). *Handbook of mentalizing in mental health practice.* Arlington, VA: American Psychiatric Publishers.

Fonagy, P., & Target, M. (1996). Playing with reality: I. Theory of mind and the normal development of psychic reality. *International Journal of Psychoanalysis, 77,* 217–233.

Fonagy, P., & Target, M. (1997). Attachment and reflective function: Their role in self-organization. *Development and Psychopathology, 9,* 679–700.

Hall, J., & Zautra, A. (2010). Indicators of community resilience: What are they and why bother? In J. Reich, A. Zautra, & J. Hall, (Eds.) *A handbook of adult resilience,* (pp. 350-375). New York, NY: Guilford Press.

Halpern, J., & Tramontin, M. (2007). *Disaster mental health: Theory and practice.* Belmont, CA: Thompson Brooks-Cole.

Herman, J. (1992). *Trauma and recovery.* New York, NY: Basic Books.

Hobfoll, S., Watson, P., Bell, C., Bryant, R., Brymer, M., Friedman, M. J., et al. (2007). Five essential elements of immediate and mid-term mass trauma intervention: Empirical evidence. *Psychiatry, 70*(4), 228–315.

Honwana, A. (2006). *Child soldiers in Africa.* Philadelphia: University of Pennsylvania Press.

Hovens, J., Falger, P., Op den Veld, W., & Shouten, E. (1992). Occurrence of current post traumatic stress disorder among Dutch World War II Resistance veterans according to the SCID. *Journal of Anxiety Disorder, 6,* 147–157.

Inter-Agency Standing Committee (IASC). (2007). *Guidelines on mental health and psychosocial support in emergency settings.* Geneva, Switzerland: Author. Retrieved September 22, 2009, from http://www.humanitarianinfo.org/iasc/pageloader.aspx?page=content-subsidi-tf_mhps-default

International Network for Education in Emergencies. (2006). *INEE good practice guide: Training teachers to meet psychosocial needs in emergencies.* Retrieved October 3, 2009, from www.ochaopt.org/cluster/ admin/output/files/inee_gpg_training_teachers_to_ meet_psychosocial_needs-20090220–134949.pdf

International Rescue Committee. (2003). *The IRC psychosocial teacher training guide.* New York, NY: The International Rescue Committee.

Jones, L. (2008). Responding to the needs of children in crisis. *International Review of Psychiatry, 20*(3), 291–303.

Kasi, S., Bhadra, S., & Dryer, A. (2007). A decade of disasters: Lessons from the Indian experience. *Southern Medical Journal, 100*(9), 929–931.

Laub, D., & Auerhahn, N. (1993). Knowing and not knowing in massive psychic trauma: Forms of traumatic memory. *International Journal of Psychoanalysis, 74,* 287–302.

Longstaff, P., Armstrong, N., Perrin, K., Parker, W., & Hidek, M. (2010). *Community resilience: A function of resources and adaptability.* White Paper: Institute for National Security and Counterterrorism: Syracuse University.

Mathbor, G. (2007). Enhancement of community preparedness for natural disasters: The role of social work in building social capital for sustainable disaster relief and management. *International Social Work, 50*(3), 357–369.

National Child Traumatic Stress Network and National Center for PTSD. (2006, July). *Psychological first aid: Field operations guide* (2nd ed.). Los Angeles, CA: Author.

Nicolas, G., Schwartz, B., & Pierre, E. (2009). Weathering the storms like bamboo: The strengths of Haitians in coping with natural disasters. In A. Kalayjian, D. Eugene, & G. Reyes (Eds.), *International handbook of emotional healing: Rituals and practices for resilience after mass trauma* (pp. 96–106). Westport, CT: Greenwood.

Office for the Coordination of Humanitarian Affairs. (1999). *OCHA orientation handbook on complex emergencies.* New York, NY: United Nations. Retrieved May 30, 2009, from www.reliefweb.int/library/ documents/ocha_orientation_handbook_on_.htm

Perry, B. (2002). Childhood experience and the expression of genetic potential: What childhood neglect tells us about nature and nurture. *Brain and Mind, 3,* 79–100.

Pyles, L. (2007). Community organizing for post-disaster social development: Locating social work. *International Social Work, 50*(3), 321–333.

Robins, S. (2010). Ambiguous loss in a non-Western context: Families of the disappeared in post-conflict Nepal. *Family Relations, 59,* 253–268. Doi:10.1111/j.1741-3729.2010.00600.x

Rutten, B. P. F., Hammels, C., Geschwind, N., Menne-Lothmann, C., Pishva, E., Schruers, K., van den Hove, D., Kenis, G., van Os, J., Wichers, M. (2013). Resilience in mental health: Linking psychological and neurobiological perspectives. *Acta Psychiatrica Scandinavia* Article first published online: 14 MAR 2013. Doi: 10.1111/acps.12095

Schore, J., & Schore, A. N. (2008). Modern attachment theory: The central role of affect regulation in development and treatment. *Clinical Social Work Journal, 36*(1), 9–20.

Siegel, D. (1999). *The developing mind: How relationships and the brain interact to shape who we are.* New York, NY: Guilford Press.

Sim, T. (2009, May). *Social work capacity building and professional support in post disaster reconstruction.* Paper presented at the Symposium on Sichuan Post-Quake Recovery and Reconstruction, Chengdu, People's Republic of China.

Sim, T. (2011). Developing an expanded school mental health network in a post-earthquake Chinese context. *Journal of Social Work, 11*(3), 326–330.

Summerfield, D. (2001). Discussion Guide 1: The nature of conflict and the implications for appropriate psychosocial responses. In *Refugee experience-psychosocial training module* (Rev. ed., p. 1). Oxford, UK: Refugee Studies Centre. Retrieved January 28, 2007, from http://earlybird.qeh.ox.ac.uk/rfgexp/ rsp_tre/welcome.htm

Ungar, M. (2005). Introduction: Resilience across cultures and contexts. In M. Ungar (Ed.), *Handbook for working with children and youth: Pathways to resilience across cultures and contexts* (pp. 211–226). Thousand Oaks, CA: Sage.

Ungar, M. (2012). Social ecologies and their contribution to resilience. In M. Ungar (Ed.), *The social ecology of resilience: A handbook of theory and practice.* New York, Heidelberg, and London: Springer.

UN General Assembly. (2007). *Natural disasters and vulnerability* (A/Res/61/200). Geneva, Switzerland: Author. Retrieved October 5, 2009, from www .unisdr.org/eng/about_isdr/basic_docs/GA-resolution/a-res-61–200-eng.pdfci

United Nations International Strategy for Disaster Reduction. (2007). *International strategy for disaster reduction: Global platform.* Retrieved September 22, 2009, from www.unisdr.org/index .php

United Nations International Strategy for Disaster Reduction. (2009). *UNISDR terminology on disaster risk reduction.* Geneva, Switzerland: UNISDR.

van der Kolk, B., McFarlane, A., & Weisaeth, L. (Eds.). (1996). *Traumatic stress: The effects of overwhelming experience on mind, body, and society.* New York, NY: Guilford Press.

van Ommeren, M., & Wessells, M. (2007). Interagency agreement on mental health and psychosocial support in emergency settings. *Bulletin of the World Health Organization, 85*(11), 822.

Wessells, M. (1999). Culture, power, and community: Intercultural approaches to psychosocial assistance and healing. In K. Nader, N. Dubrow, & H. Stamm (Eds.), *Honoring differences: Cultural issues in the treatment of trauma and loss* (pp. 98–121). Philadelphia, PA: Brunner/Mazel.

Winnicott, D. W. (1984a). Aggression and its roots: Aggression. In C. Winnicott, R. Shepherd, & M. Davis (Eds.), *Deprivation and delinquency: D. W. Winnicott* (pp. 84–91). London, UK: Tavistock. (Original work published 1939)

Winnicott, D. W. (1984b). Aggression and its roots: Roots of aggression. In C. Winnicott, R. Shepherd, & M. Davis (Eds.), *Deprivation and delinquency: D. W. Winnicott* (pp. 92–99). London, UK: Tavistock. (Original work published 1964)

Winnicott, D. W. (1984c). Aggression, guilt and reparation. In C. Winnicott, R. Shepherd, & M. Davis (Eds.), *Deprivation and delinquency: D. W. Winnicott* (pp. 136–144). London, UK: Tavistock. (Original work published 1960)

Wisner, B., & Adams, J. (2002). *Environmental health in emergencies and disasters: A practical guide* (pp. 198–202). Geneva, Switzerland: World Health Organization. Retrieved January 1, 2005, from www.who.int/water_sanitation_health/ hygiene/emergencies/emergencies2002/en/

Wurzer, J., & Bragin, M. (2009). *Integrating the psychosocial dimension in women's empowerment programming: A guide for CARE country offices.* Vienna: CARE Austria.

KEY WEBSITES

1. The International Federation of Red Cross and Red Crescent Societies: Psychosocial Support Centre. Available at http://psp.drk.dk:80/sw2955.asp

2. The Inter-Agency Standing Committee Guidelines on Mental Health and Psychosocial Work in Emergency Settings. Available at http://www.humanitarianinfo.org/iasc/pageloader.aspx?page=content-subsidi-tf_mhps-default

3. Psychceu.com's online course. *Disaster mental health services: A primer for practitioners.* Available at www.psychceu.com/disaster/disaster.asp

4. The United Nations Strategy for Disaster Risk Reduction publications includes many critical background documents. Available at www .unisdr.org/eng/ about_isdr/bd-isdr-publications .htm

5. Bragin, M. (2005). The community participatory evaluation tool for psychosocial programmes: A guide to implementation. *Intervention: International Journal of Mental Health, Psychosocial Work and Counselling in Areas of Armed Conflict, 3*(1), 3–24. Available at www .interventionjournal.com/downloads/31pdf/ 03_24% 20Bragin%20.pdf

6. International Network for Education in Emergencies. (2011). *INEE Minimum Standards Handbook.* Available at: http://www.ineesite .org/en/minimum-standards/handbook

14

DYNAMIC APPROACHES TO BRIEF AND TIME-LIMITED CLINICAL SOCIAL WORK

JERROLD R. BRANDELL

In a practice climate transformed by the requirements of managed health care and the ubiquitous use of biological interventions, brief and time-limited dynamic treatment approaches have become ever more attractive, both to agencies and to the clinicians who staff them. In fact, in many settings, the luxuries of limitless time and resources are often not available to social work practitioners and their clients, nor are these always necessary or even desirable. In this chapter, the essential characteristics of a dynamic approach to working with clients briefly are presented and discussed.

Historically speaking, the concept of brief treatment and the use of time limits have been neither revolutionary nor exceptional in the practice of social casework. In fact, it has been argued that most social casework has been short term in nature (Parad, 1971). The presumption of time limits, for example, is an almost invariant feature of certain social service settings, such as hospitals, the courts, or schools (Shechter, 1997), and in venues such as Traveler's Aid, the duration of contact has

rarely been longer than a single meeting. In recognition of this fact, a number of social work practice models have either treated the idea of brief or time-limited contact as a central organizing feature or may be easily adapted for such time-sensitive work (e.g., Golan, 1978; Goldstein & Noonan, 1999; Perlman, 1957; Rapoport, 1970; Reid & Shyne, 1969).

This chapter begins with a history of the concept of brief treatment in the psychoanalytic literature, focusing on Freud's use of brief and time-limited methods with several patients—among them "Katharina," the first published example of brief dynamic therapy. Others in the early psychoanalytic movement, most notably Sandor Ferenczi, Otto Rank, and Franz Alexander, subsequently experimented with brief dynamic interventions, and these contributions are also reviewed. In the past 40 years, several distinctive clinical models of brief dynamic psychotherapy have emerged, and in the next portion of the chapter, each is briefly summarized. Following this, a review of the principal techniques common to most contemporary models of brief dynamic psychotherapy is outlined. In the final portion of the chapter, a detailed discussion of Mann's integrative model of *time-limited psychotherapy* (TLP) is presented, followed by its application to a treatment case involving a female graduate student in her mid-20s seen at a university counseling center.

Source: From *Psychodynamic Social Work*, by Jerrold R. Brandell. Copyright © 2004. Reprinted with permission of Columbia University Press.

CLASSICAL PSYCHOANALYSIS AND THE IDEA OF BRIEF TREATMENT

Sigmund Freud

Although psychoanalysis has gradually come to be identified almost reflexively with terms such as *intensive* and *long term,* it may be instructive to note that historically, even within the psychoanalytic community, factors such as session frequency and the overall duration of treatment were far from being immutable givens. In fact, despite being conducted on a six-times-weekly basis, the average length of a psychoanalytic treatment in Freud's day was probably closer to 1 year than to the contemporary standard of 4 to 7 years. Furthermore, Freud had, himself, worked with at least several patients within what can be legitimately described as a brief-treatment framework. Miss Lucy R., a hysterical patient of Freud's whose complaints included chronic suppurative rhinitis, recurrent olfactory hallucinations, diminished energy, and dysphoria, was seen on a weekly basis for just nine sessions, although apparently with enduring results[1] (Breuer & Freud, 1893–1895/1955). In 1906, the pianist and conductor Bruno Walter consulted Freud when other specialists failed to

cure a partial paralysis of his right arm, presumably a conversion reaction. Freud met with Walter for a total of six sessions, following which the then 30-year-old musician was able to resume his duties as Gustav Mahler's assistant at the Vienna Court Opera. Whether this treatment can be termed *dynamic* is a matter of some dispute, however, inasmuch as Freud's approach with his patient may have been less interpretive than suggestive in nature and may have relied rather heavily on the patient's positive transference (Fonagy, 1999). A few years later, Freud met with Walter's mentor, the famed composer and conductor Gustav Mahler, for a single session of four hours' duration, most of which took place on a stroll through the town of Leyden, Holland. Evidently, Freud was able to quickly establish a connection between Mahler's presenting complaint, which was sexual impotence, and a powerful and conflict-laden, unconscious association the composer had made between his mother and his wife, Alma. Mahler's sexual potency, according to Jones (1957), was fully restored after his brief meeting with Freud.

Freud had actually conducted a single-session dynamic treatment some years earlier, most likely in the summer of 1893, which he later included in the *Studies on Hysteria* (Breuer & Freud, 1893–1895/1955). The case involved a young woman, Katharina, whom Freud had met while vacationing in the Austrian Alps. After discovering that Freud was a physician, the 18-year-old approached him, beseeching him for help with her "bad nerves." The origin of Katharina's panic attacks, which Freud was able to adduce from her story, lay in a traumatic experience in her 14th year, when her father had sexually molested her.[2] However, Katharina's symptoms only began 2 years later, after she had witnessed her father molesting a girl cousin. At that time, Katharina recognized the sexual nature of her father's behavior and

---

[1] Encountering his patient by chance some 4 months after treatment was concluded, Freud found Miss Lucy R. to be "in good spirits" and her recovery apparently maintained.

[2] In the original case history, Freud had disguised this fact, substituting Katharina's uncle for her father. In a postscript added to the case some 30 years later, this distortion was finally corrected.

made the connection to what she had experienced at the age of 14. She reported feeling disgust at this memory and soon thereafter developed a posttraumatic neurosis in which hysterical symptoms played a prominent part. Although Freud's contact with Katharina was limited to a single meeting, the case record reveals a fundamentally dynamic treatment encounter, in which latent meaning is derived from manifest content, the patient's associative material is encouraged, emotional catharsis is promoted, and genetic interpretation is employed. The effects were dramatically evident. As Gay (1988) has observed, Katharina's "artless recital helped to discharge her feelings, [and] her moody manner gave way to sparkling, healthy liveliness" (p. 73). Although Freud expressed the hope that Katharina might derive some enduring benefit from their brief encounter, he never again came into contact with her.

Sandor Ferenczi and Otto Rank

Ferenczi is generally acknowledged as being the first psychoanalyst to experiment more systematically with methods intended to shorten the duration of psychoanalytic treatment (Crits-Christoph & Barber, 1991). Ferenczi (1926/1950) first presented his ideas in a 1920 paper given at the Sixth International Congress of Psychoanalysis, concerned over what he regarded as a trend toward increasingly longer psychoanalyses and correspondingly greater passivity on the analyst's part. In his paper, he recommended that both analyst and analysand increase their activity so that the latter might be helped to "comply more successfully with the rule of free association," which, in Ferenczi's view, might facilitate "or hasten the exploring of unconscious material" (p. 198). The "active technique" that Ferenczi advocated might involve the analyst's prescription to the patient for the enactment of certain behaviors, or, conversely, it might involve injunctions made against their performance (Crits-Christoph & Barber, 1991). In fact, he believed that with certain kinds of patients, such as obsessional neurotics, the analyst's failure to intervene more actively would

likely culminate in the patient's use of the basic psychoanalytic method, free association, in the service of resistance (Tosone, 1997). He asked patients to associate to specific topics and themes and advocated that the analyst consciously and deliberately provoke affective experience in the transference (Messer & Warren, 2001). Ferenczi maintained that his "active technique" might serve as a basis for rapid amelioration of the patient's resistance, which could also contribute to shortening the overall duration of the analysis. Despite his contention that the active technique was intended to be employed judiciously and selectively, and only as a supplement to psychoanalysis, the psychoanalytic community was, generally speaking, rather unreceptive to Ferenczi's paper (Tosone, 1997).

Otto Rank has also been credited with introducing important ideas that are seen as developmental precursors to modern concepts of brief and, especially, time-limited therapy. Rank theorized that the whole of human development is characterized by a continuous tension between emotional attachment and dependency, on the one side, and separation and autonomy, on the other (Messer & Warren, 2001). In Rank's estimation, much that had been designated *resistance* by classical psychoanalytic theory could be defined more accurately as a natural opposition that existed between the "will" of the therapist and that of the patient. In his view, the therapeutic process in classical psychoanalysis, shaped by the analyst's confrontations and interpretations, might ultimately lead patients to the acceptance of a new view for their behavior but at the expense of their own "will" (Messer & Warren, 1995). Rank chose instead to assist patients to become more self-accepting, with an enhanced capacity to take responsibility for themselves without experiencing guilt (O'Dowd, 1986). As soon as the patient's will was sufficiently motivated for change, she or he might assume greater responsibility for the treatment, thereby leading to a more efficient and shorter analytic process (Crits-Christoph & Barber, 1991). Rank's theory, which emphasized the salience of the ongoing, immediate experience of the analytic relationship over that of past events, also introduced the idea of establishing an end point to treatment. However, termination, in the Rankian framework, was intimately associated with the patient's "will to individuate," so that a termination date was only finally set once Rank sensed the patient to be struggling with issues of dependency, separation, and relatedness. "The key aspect of this process," as O'Dowd (1986) has suggested in summarizing Rank's views on the topic of termination, "is maintaining the connection, the sense of belonging and attachment, along with a new-found capacity to will and to create a separate individual" (p. 146).

In 1925, Ferenczi and Rank published a jointly written book, *The Development of Psychoanalysis,* now widely acknowledged as the conceptual predecessor to Alexander and French's (1946) volume on brief treatment, *Psychoanalytic Therapy* (Crits-Christoph & Barber, 1991). Adumbrating many of the brief and time-limited models that were to follow, Ferenczi and Rank's work emphasized the immediate, "here-and-now" aspects of the patient's relationship with the analyst and placed less importance on reconstruction of events and experiences from the patient's childhood (Messer & Warren, 1995). Moreover, they maintained that the power of the unconscious was fully revealed to patients only after unconscious wishes and affects were revived in the context of the patient's ongoing transference to the analyst. It is at this juncture, they believed, that genetic reconstruction would be far more likely to be therapeutic and effective (Tosone, 1997). Ferenczi and Rank did acknowledge the significance of the genetic perspective and the self-understanding that might be derived from reconstructive work, but they also believed that undue emphasis on reconstruction of the past could lead to a strengthening of intellectual defenses (Tosone, 1997). Indeed, having identified the ultimate goal of an analysis as the substitution of "affective factors of experience for intellectual processes" (Ferenczi & Rank, 1925, p. 62), their work traverses a very different road than did classical conceptions of the psychoanalytic process prevailing in the mid-1920s.

This fact was not lost on others in the psychoanalytic movement, and Freud, despite certain misgivings, lent Ferenczi and Rank his qualified endorsement. He remained unconvinced that "one can penetrate to the deepest layers of the unconscious and bring about lasting changes in the mind" in 4 or 5 months, which he believed Ferenczi and Rank's modification of psychoanalytic technique sought to accomplish (Freud, as quoted in Jones, 1957, p. 61). However, he also believed such an experiment, with its aim of a shortened analysis, to be "entirely justified," and in any event, he felt it was undeserving of condemnation as a theoretical heresy (Jones, 1957, p. 61). Others, such as Karl Abraham (Jones, 1957), demonstrated far less equanimity in their appraisal of Ferenczi and Rank's work, and mounting criticisms of Rank's ideas within the psychoanalytic movement, particularly as these were developed in his controversial book on birth trauma, published in 1924 (Rank, 1973), added to the developing controversy. Ultimately, the modifications of technique proposed in *The Development of Psychoanalysis* (Ferenczi & Rank, 1925) seemed to suffer a fate similar to that of many other psychoanalytic innovations, namely marginalization.

Franz Alexander and Thomas French

Two decades after the publication of Ferenczi and Rank's (1925) controversial book, Franz Alexander and Thomas French, in collaboration with colleagues at the Chicago Institute for Psychoanalysis, published *Psychoanalytic Therapy* (1946). They readily acknowledged their intellectual debt to the authors of *The Development of Psychoanalysis,* noting their own work to be "a continuation and realization of ideas first proposed by Ferenczi and Rank" (p. 23). In particular, their work may be seen as an endorsement of Ferenczi and Rank's view of the comparatively greater importance of emotional experience over that of insight derived from intellectual understanding.

Alexander and French (1946) are arguably best known for their concept of "corrective emotional experience." This principle holds that the most important changes in psychotherapy occur when historical conflicts are revived in the context of a new relationship, that between analyst and patient. However, the potential for such change is only realized, in Alexander and French's view, insofar as the analyst's response offers something new to the patient:

> Because the therapist's attitude is different from that of the authoritative person of the past, he gives the patient an opportunity to face again and again, under more favorable circumstances, those emotional situations which were formerly unbearable and to deal with them in a manner different from the old. . . . This can only be accomplished through actual experience in the patient's relationship to the therapist; intellectual insight alone is not sufficient. (p. 67)

Thus, the corrective emotional experience is "corrective" only to the degree that the analyst understands the motives embedded in the patient's transference behavior and is able to assume an attitude toward the patient that is different from that of the original transference object (Crits-Christoph & Barber, 1991).

Alexander and French placed emphasis on the ongoing, contemporary aspects of the treatment relationship rather than viewing it from the classical vantage point, in which the relationship is principally a projection screen for patients' fantasies of the analyst. This feature, according to some, anticipates the perspective of modern relational therapies, in which the treatment relationship has assumed a central role for the overall improvement of the patient (Messer & Warren, 1995).

In their view of treatment as "a process of emotional reeducation," Alexander and French tended to be far more concerned with the patient's adjustment to the circumstances of the present, placing correspondingly less emphasis on the genetic origins of the patient's difficulties. While they did not dismiss such genetic understanding as unimportant, their interest in the patient's past was limited to the degree to which it illuminated the most immediate concerns in the present.

Indeed, much of what Alexander and French wrote in 1946 presages French's later work on the concept of "focal conflict" (French, 1954; French & Fromm, 1964). Alexander and French (1946) also believed that exclusive reliance on classical or "standard" technique might ultimately hinder therapeutic progress, and they adopted a flexible approach to the use of treatment techniques, in which tactics were adjusted in accordance with the requirements of individual cases. The following were among the modifications they proposed:

> Using not only the method of free association but interviews of a more direct character, manipulating the frequency of the interviews, giving directives to the patient concerning his daily life, employing interruptions of long or short duration in preparation for ending the treatment, regulating the transference relationship to meet the specific needs of the case, and making use of real-life experiences as an integral part of the therapy. (p. 6)

Such treatment strategies and techniques, Messer and Warren (1995) have suggested, can be linked to later developments in the brief-therapy field; these include the use of behavioral techniques and suggestions (Garfield, 1989); direct guidance, support, and advice giving (Bellak & Small, 1965); and a focus on the client's family circumstances (Gustafson, 1986).

Alexander and French's framework for brief treatment ultimately did exert a profound influence over the "next wave" in the brief-treatment field, those brief and time-limited systems that were introduced beginning in the late 1960s. However, at the time their book was published, condemnation from the psychoanalytic establishment was perhaps even sharper than the reaction Ferenczi and Rank's work had elicited 20 years earlier. The concept of the "corrective emotional experience" evoked a particularly strong reaction from many psychoanalysts, of which Phyllis Greenacre's criticism was representative. Greenacre (1954) dismissed the idea as "little more than the old-fashioned habit training with especially strong suggestive influencing" (p. 676; Tosone,

1997) and concluded that it involved a "working-out" rather than a "working-through" process. The former involved therapeutic procedures whereby the client's emotional reactions might be reshaped into new patterns "without paying too much attention to the old," while the latter aimed to loosen "neurotic tendencies at their source" (p. 676). Then too, Alexander and French's willingness to exchange the traditional role of analytic neutrality and abstinence for a far more active stance, in which the analyst makes specific therapeutic accommodations to the client's transference needs, seemed to further intensify opposition to their treatment model. With recommendations for once-weekly sessions, a far more flexible use of analytic technique, diminished importance attached to reconstruction of the past, and the seeming abdication of analytic neutrality, Alexander and French's ideas regarding brief treatment, however laudable, were destined to remain outside the psychoanalytic mainstream for nearly another generation.

THE "SECOND WAVE": MALAN, SIFNEOS, AND DAVANLOO

After the publication of Alexander and French's book, the psychoanalytic establishment appeared once again to close ranks in its dismissal of brief treatment as a legitimate form of dynamic psychotherapy. However, this negatively valenced reaction was not universal among psychoanalysts, and beginning in the early 1960s, several new approaches to brief dynamic treatment were introduced. These brief-therapy methods, each of which is grounded in the theoretical assumptions of classical psychoanalysis or psychoanalytic ego psychology, have been collectively referred to as the *drive/structure model* (Messer & Warren, 1995, 2001). This term is actually borrowed from Greenberg and Mitchell (1983), who, in their pioneering review of the psychoanalytic psychologies, made a distinction between psychoanalytic theories organized according to the classical schema of drive/structure and those

based on a relational/structure model. David Malan, Peter Sifneos, and Habib Davanloo are the principal exponents of this model, each of whom, independently, had developed an approach to brief treatment predicated on basic Freudian postulates such as drive and defense, the ubiquity of intrapsychic conflict and its mediation by the ego, the centrality of the Oedipus complex, the notion of symptoms as "compromise formations," and so forth (Messer & Warren, 2001).

Malan's approach, which he termed *brief intensive psychotherapy* (BIP), is perhaps the closest to "standard" psychoanalytic technique within the drive/structure group of brief-treatment approaches. It appears to be most effective with healthier clients who are motivated for insight, have attained a higher quality of object relations, and are able to employ "mature" or higher-level defenses (Messer & Warren, 1995; Piper, de Carufel, & Skrumelak, 1985). Unlike psychoanalysis or long-term psychoanalytic therapy, however, BIP imposes a time limit (20–30 sessions), has a specific dynamic objective (resolution of the conflict/s identified in the initial meeting), and applies specific therapeutic interventions to maintain a focus on the area of conflict (Malan, 1976). As a means of organizing treatment interventions, Malan (1976) developed two intersecting conceptual schemata: (1) the triangles of conflict and (2) the triangles of person (see Figure 14.1). The elements in the triangle of conflict are impulse or feeling (I/F), anxiety (A), and defensive reaction or response (D). The triangle of person includes the objects targeted by a client's impulses or feelings—the therapist (T), significant individuals in the current life of the client (C), and important figures from the past (P).

Malan's intent was to systematically link the pattern of conflict identified in the triangle of conflict with each corner in the triangle of person (Messer & Warren, 1995). Although the therapist makes active use of interventions tailored to address elements of the focal issue, Malan's treatment approach is not on that account a superficial one. Indeed, BIP is intended to "go as deeply as possible" into the psychodynamics and

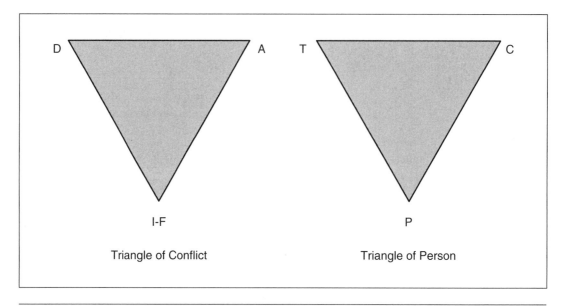

Figure 14.1 Triangles of Conflict and Person

origins of the client's core conflicts (Messer & Warren, 1995, p. 84). Research on this model has suggested "good evidence" for its efficacy, although this is apparently linked to the capacity for higher-level object relations as well as to the maturity of the defensive style (Messer & Warren, 1995).

Short-term anxiety-provoking psychotherapy (STAPP), the therapeutic approach developed by Sifneos, also seems most effective with healthier clients, in particular those with neurotic disorders or symptom constellations that include anxiety, mild depression, grief reactions, and interpersonal problems. Evidence of a capacity for insight or "psychological sophistication" is also judged to be important (Nielsen & Barth, 1991). One of the most striking features of this method of brief treatment is an unrelenting focus on triangular or oedipal issues, which Sifneos believed to be the focal issue in the majority of clients he treated (Nielsen & Barth, 1991). In stark contrast to the usual procedure in traditional psychoanalytic treatment, interpretation of the client's defense does *not* precede the therapist's interpretation

of the impulse or wish. In fact, therapists are encouraged to confront and interpret underlying wishes or impulses directly, and Sifneos consistently pushed clients to take responsibility for their fantasies, actions, wishes, and feelings. This represents a radical departure from psychoanalytic tradition, although, Sifneos claims, it is not without justification. In STAPP, the early effort to craft the therapeutic alliance and promote the client's positive transference makes possible a concentrated focus on those specific areas in which most of the client's dynamic conflicts reside (Nielsen & Barth, 1991). Moreover, Sifneos believed that the therapist's use of anxiety-provoking clarifications, confrontive questions, and direct interpretations often yielded significant new data. Although there has been some research on STAPP showing it to be effective in promoting client self-understanding, symptomatic relief, new learning, and the acquisition of problem-solving abilities (Sifneos, 1968, 1987; Sifneos, Apfel, Bassuk, Fishman, & Gill, 1980), methodological and other problems may cast doubt on the validity of these results (Messer & Warren, 1995).

Davanloo's *intensive short-term dynamic psychotherapy* (ISTDP; Davanloo, 1980) was developed as a confrontational method of breaking through a client's defensive structures to promote "the examination of repressed memories and ideas in a fully experienced and integrated affective and cognitive framework" (Laikin, Winston, & McCullough, 1991, p. 80). ISTDP is intended for use not only with higher-functioning neurotic clients but also with those suffering from personality disorders (e.g., avoidant, dependent, obsessive-compulsive, and passive-aggressive), as well as with some presenting with more severe psychopathology, such as borderline or narcissistic conditions. The duration of treatment varies, apparently according to the degree of client pathology, but in no case should it exceed 40 sessions. Davanloo adheres to a more or less traditional psychoanalytic model in which abstinence and analytic neutrality are observed, personal inquiries are deflected, and the therapist refrains from offering direct guidance, advice, and praise (Laikin et al., 1991). Davanloo's method is somewhat unique among drive/structure model brief-treatment approaches in its focus on "cognitive restructuring," a pre-interpretive phase of ISTDP in which the triangle of conflict is outlined for the client though without interpretation of the underlying psychodynamics. This variation in Davanloo's approach is intended principally for clients who are more resistant and difficult to treat—clients who would likely not be considered suitable candidates for either BIP or STAPP. Acknowledging his intellectual debt to both Malan and Sifneos, Davanloo also cites Wilhelm Reich's ideas regarding character resistance as an important influence. Like Malan, Davanloo's ISTDP is a dynamic model for intervention initially based on the therapist's understanding of the "two working triangles"—those of conflict and of person. Although outcome effectiveness research on this method of brief treatment has been limited to a single study (McCullough et al., 1991), results have been promising, particularly in light of the fact that certain personality-disordered cases deemed untreatable by other dynamic therapy approaches were included (Messer & Warren, 1995).

THE "THIRD WAVE": RELATIONAL APPROACHES TO BRIEF PSYCHOTHERAPY

The fact that all psychoanalytic theories, as Greenberg and Mitchell maintained, tend to be organized in conformity with either *drive/structural* or *relational/structure* assumptions points to the existence of a basic and fundamentally irreconcilable theoretical chasm (Greenberg & Mitchell, 1983; Messer & Warren, 1995; Mitchell, 1988). As we have noted previously, the relational/structure model, rather than accepting the classical notion of the primacy of the drives and the role they perform in the development of object relations, posits that psychic structure evolves from the interactions of the individual with other people. Or, put somewhat differently, in classical theory, the object was in a sense "created" to "suit the impulse," whereas in relational theories, the infant is *object seeking,* and the development of psychic structure is very intimately linked to a subject-environmental matrix.

Several important approaches based on the theoretical assumptions of the relational/structure model have been widely applied to the practice domain of brief treatment. These include the Penn Psychotherapy Project's *short-term expressive psychoanalytic psychotherapy,* closely linked to an overarching concept referred to as the *core conflictual relationship theme* (Luborsky & Mark, 1991); the model developed by Horowitz (1991) and the Center for the Study of Neuroses, *short-term dynamic therapy of stress-response syndromes*; the Vanderbilt Group's *time-limited dynamic psychotherapy* (Binder & Strupp, 1991); and the Mount Zion Group's method, which is based on the principles of *control-mastery therapy* (Weiss, Sampson, and the Mount Zion Psychotherapy Research Group, 1986).

Interestingly, none of the methods of treatment represented by these four psychotherapy research groups was originally conceived or promoted as a brief psychotherapy model. In fact, some authors have suggested that the distillation of brief-treatment principles and their application to this conceptual domain was, in each case, a by-product of a more general program of research on psychodynamic theory and psychoanalytic therapy. Nevertheless, all four are judged to have made important contributions to the brief-treatment field. Common themes seem to link these four methods with one another (Messer & Warren, 1995, pp. 119–120):

- With certain variations, each adopts the perspective that psychopathology is rooted in a maladaptive interpersonal matrix.
- Each accords a greater role to the real experience and to real failures of the environment.
- The adaptive function of defenses is emphasized, as contrasted with the more classical conceptualization of defense activation as a consequence of anxiety that arises from unacceptable impulses or wishes.
- The role of real experience, actual failures of the environment, and so forth are generally accorded greater importance in the formation of psychopathology.
- In varying degrees, each presumes the existence of internalized self and object representations in its theories of personality functioning and psychopathology.
- More emphasis is placed on the role of intercurrent variables in the perpetuation of psychopathology than on the classical notion of genetic causality.

THE "FOURTH WAVE": PSYCHODYNAMIC-EXPERIENTIAL TREATMENTS

Contemporary psychodynamic approaches to brief treatment, while adhering to the "traditional importance placed on the role of conflict, unconscious processes, transference, countertransference, and the regulation of anxiety" (Levenson, 2010, p. 28), factors common to all forms of psychodynamic therapy, appear in other respects to contrast sharply with many of their dynamic predecessors. In Levenson's view, the three features distinguishing these models from earlier psychodynamic approaches are

- the assimilation of concepts and/or techniques from a variety of sources external to psychoanalysis (e.g., cognitive-behavioral therapy,

child development, neuroscience) into more traditional perspectives, which makes these approaches more integrative;
- an emphasis on in-session experiential factors as critical components of the process of therapy; and
- a privileging of pragmatism and efficiency in response to powerful economic and sociopolitical forces (2010, pp. 25–26).

Several such models have been described in the recent literature on brief dynamic treatments. McCullough Vaillant's (1997; McCullough Vaillant, Kuhn, Wolf, & Hurley, 2003) *short-term anxiety-regulating psychotherapy* (STARP), integrates ideas from learning theory while simultaneously emphasizing the client's affectivity within the treatment sessions. Levenson has described a modified version of *time-limited dynamic psychotherapy* (TLDP), which is "integrative, attachment-based, and experiential" (Levenson, 2010, p. 26; Levenson, 2012). Yet another such model, exemplifying this emerging framework, is *brief dynamic interpersonal therapy* (Lemma, Target, and Fonagy, 2011), which has been developed as a specific, dynamically-grounded treatment approach for depressed clients. This form of dynamic psychotherapy, based on a "distillation of the evidence-based brief psychoanalytic/psychodynamic treatments pooled together from manualized approaches" (Lemma, Target, and Fonagy, 2010, p. 329), features an integrative focus on attachment, but is also anchored in arguably more traditional psychoanalytic ideas such as "the impact of internalized, unconscious 'self' and 'other' representations on current interpersonal functioning" (pp. 43–44).

TECHNICAL DIMENSIONS COMMON TO ALL METHODS OF BRIEF DYNAMIC TREATMENT

In the preceding sections, we have highlighted significant differences between brief-treatment approaches organized in accordance with the theoretical premises of the drive/structure model and those that are based on relational/structure assumptions. However, five technical dimensions common to all methods of psychodynamically based brief treatment have also been identified (Messer & Warren, 2001; Woods & Hollis, 2000). These are the (1) use of a central dynamic focus or issue, (2) setting of a time limit, (3) significance attached to termination, (4) active posture of the therapist, and (5) establishment of attainable goals and treatment objectives.

Use of a Central Dynamic Focus or Issue. The therapist's formulation of a central dynamic theme or issue is not unique to brief-therapy methods, but owing to the time-limited nature of such engagements of client and therapist, it is imbued with a special significance. Such a formulation, which is most usefully thought of as a clinical working hypothesis, accomplishes three objectives: (1) It conveys the therapist's understanding of the underlying meaning of a client's presenting complaints, (2) it provides an organizing framework for all subsequent clinical data collected over the course of treatment, and (3) it serves as a guide for specific clinical interventions.

Setting of a Time Limit. In some brief-therapy methods, the duration of the treatment and date of the terminal interview are established by the therapist in an explicit manner from the earliest point of contact, as exemplified by James Mann's *TLP,* which has a fixed number of sessions. Mann's treatment approach, however, differs from most others in specifying the total number of sessions and the date of the terminal interview and in its emphasis on the themes of separation and loss relative to the time limit (see next section). In other brief-therapy methods, the time limit may be implicit and subject to negotiation by therapist and client at some point after treatment is already under way. A basic assumption of all time-limited dynamic therapies is that a time limit, whether explicit or more implicit, serves to sharpen the focus on treatment objectives by heightening the "sense of urgency, immediacy, and emotional presence of the patient" (Messer & Warren, 2001, p. 76).

Significance Attached to Termination. It seems only natural for any treatment method in which a mutually acknowledged time limit exists that the issue of termination assumes great importance from the outset. In fact, therapy conducted briefly may afford unique opportunities for therapist and client to consider the impact of termination, with its attendant themes of separation, loss, and death, throughout the duration of therapy. In psychoanalysis or in psychotherapy, where therapeutic engagement is often of an indeterminate length, resistance to termination is rarely manifest until treatment is well under way; moreover, such resistance, frequently signifying issues of separation-individuation or loss, may be permitted to unfold gradually. In the context of brief treatment, however, such resistances may appear in the very first session and become an ongoing focus of the clinical discourse over the entire term of therapy.

Active Posture of the Therapist. Brief-therapy methods have long experimented with ways to hasten the pace of the clinical process, beginning with Ferenczi's (1926/1950) *active technique.* The establishment of time limits, confrontation, and direct interpretation of underlying wishes or impulses; early and aggressive interpretation of transference reactions; and direct suggestion and guidance are other techniques employed to attain treatment objectives within the abbreviated framework of time-sensitive treatment. More recent relational brief-treatment approaches have also tended to emphasize the therapist's awareness of transference patterns, as these are manifest in the evolving relationship with the client. With active reference to his or her experience of the client in the present, the therapist is then able to make "here-and-now" interpretative linkages between past relational patterns and the ongoing treatment relationship (Messer & Warren, 2001).

Establishment of Attainable Goals and Treatment Objectives. Another important difference between longer-term dynamic psychotherapy and brief dynamic treatment is in the setting of treatment goals and objectives. Owing in part to the use of a central dynamic focus, the therapist's and the client's awareness of a time limit, and the special meaning that attaches to termination in brief dynamic therapy, goals and objectives tend to be stated with more explicitness than in longer-term treatment. Even when goal setting is not formalized, however, it is often implied in brief treatment, which, in the main, tends to be more symptom or problem focused (Messer & Warrren, 2001). As a general rule, goals should also be realistic and attainable; time-sensitive treatment would not be an appropriate therapy in cases where significant alteration of character structure has been identified as the central treatment objective.

Mann's Time-Limited Psychotherapy

Each of the methods of brief dynamic treatment we have thus far reviewed possess certain strengths and weaknesses, although only James Mann's TLP offers a truly integrative transtheoretical framework. As Mann has previously articulated, TLP approaches psychopathology from four complementary theoretical vantage points: (1) the structural hypothesis, (2) the theory of narcissism and development of self-esteem, (3) object relations theory, and (4) the developmental perspective (Mann & Goldman, 1982). His treatment method also places a special emphasis on the concept of time and on the universal experience of loss as it is recapitulated within the framework of time-limited treatment.

Mann (1973, 1991) has observed that time is conceived in both "categorical" and "existential" terms. We measure the first, categorical or real time, with timepieces and calendars. The second, existential or limitless time, represents a more archaic mode of psychic experience and signifies both immortality and infinitude. Our understanding of categorical time evolves only gradually, as secondary-process thinking begins to supplant the primary-process experience and the reality principle claims a greater share of what was once the exclusive province of the pleasure principle.

An almost 6-year-old boy, in a quiet moment at bedtime, suddenly becomes painfully aware of his father's mortality. "I don't want you to die," he whispers. "Can't you and me always be together—forever?" Although categorical time gradually organizes our waking lives, our early pleasure of timelessness is never completely surrendered; indeed, we often seek to deny the effects of the passage of time, in ways both subtle and flagrant.

Unlike many other brief-treatment methods, Mann (1973) elevates the universal experience of separation and loss to programmatic status. In fact, he declares that "the recurring life crisis of separation-individuation is the substantive basis" on which TLP rests and proceeds to outline four "basic universal conflict situations," all of which are linked to the individual's lifelong efforts to manage object loss. These are (1) *independence versus dependence,* (2) *activity versus passivity,* (3) *adequate self-esteem versus diminished or loss of self-esteem,* and (4) *unresolved or delayed grief* (pp. 24–25). In keeping with the theme of object loss and separation-individuation, Mann's approach focuses on preoedipal rather than on oedipal issues, which reflects his belief that such issues are more amenable to time-limited treatment. At the same time, Mann has clearly noted that psychoanalysis continues to be the most effective method of treatment of oedipal issues, which cannot ordinarily be resolved without the establishment of a transference neurosis, consistent attention to resistance phenomena, and so forth (Mann & Goldman, 1982).

TLP, according to Mann, is suitable for clients who are judged to have the ego strength necessary for rapid affective engagement and equally rapid disengagement, with the latter considered a measure of their capacity for tolerating object loss. Beyond this, Mann believes that his approach may be of benefit to a variety of clients presenting with maturational crises, neurotic disorders (e.g., anxiety, hysterical, obsessional, and depressive problems), and some personality disorders (e.g., mild narcissistic and some borderline clients). Mann's (1991) treatment method is contraindicated, however, for more seriously disturbed character-disordered clients, severe psychosomatic problems, bipolar affective disorder, and schizoid disorders.

COMPONENTS AND PROCESS OF TLP

The Central Issue

As quickly as feasible, and almost always within the first or second meeting, Mann (1991) endeavors to formulate a statement of the client's *chronic and presently endured pain.* Such pain encompasses both a negative feeling about the self and also the client's fundamental belief of having been victimized. Because the central issue spans the client's entire experience "from the remote past to the immediate present and into the expectable future," its formulation by the therapist will, with rare exceptions, differ markedly from those problems the client has given as the motive for seeking help (Mann, 1986, p. 123). The therapist's formulation of the central issue includes three basic parts: (1) acknowledgment of the client's ongoing efforts to obtain recognition and to satisfy his or her needs, (2) the failure of these efforts, which has culminated in the client's negative feelings about herself or himself, and (3) some statement outlining the task of treatment (Mann, 1973, 1991; Messer & Warren, 1995). Eliciting the client's reactions, if they are not immediate, to the formulation of the central issue becomes the very next task of treatment.

Early Phase

In marked contrast to adherents of the drive/structure model (e.g., Davanloo or Malan), Mann's approach, particularly in the first several sessions, is nonconfrontative, with the intent of establishing a rapid working alliance and engaging the client through techniques such as mirroring, affirmation, and delicate probing (Mann & Goldman, 1982; Messer & Warren, 1995). Rather than interpreting aggressively, or challenging defenses, Mann endeavors to make the treatment experience a gentle, empathically attuned, and accepting one, which places the client at ease. In such an ambience, the therapeutic equivalent of the symbiotic orbit of mother and infant is (re)established (Rasmussen & Messer, 1986). In Mann's (1973) words, "The warm sustaining golden sunshine of eternal union" is restored, and the client reports significant diminution of the presenting complaints (p. 33). In this environment, it also becomes an increasingly difficult and a greater challenge for the therapist and the client to remain focused on the central issue.

Middle Phase

As therapy reaches the fourth or fifth session, the client begins to experience disappointment, and the "honeymoon" is over. There may be a recrudescence of the original symptoms or complaints and the recognition that not even the new relationship with the therapist, which seemed to hold so much promise, can solve all the client's problems. The prospect of yet another separation from a "meaningful, ambivalently experienced person" becomes painfully evident at this midpoint in the treatment, and manifestations of negative transference become more obvious (Mann, 1973). The task for the therapist at this stage is, through greater use of clarifications, mild confrontations, and interpretations, to encourage "further elaboration of the patient's ambivalence" so that associations to past separations and the feelings these evoked might be understood in relation to the individual's central issue (Mann, 1991).

Ending Phase

Mann (1991) has commented that termination may be considered satisfactory when the client leaves treatment feeling sad:

> Ambivalence, which previously had always led to feelings of anger or depression with concomitant self-derogation, has changed into awareness of positive feelings even in the face of separation and loss. Sadness in place of depression allows for separation without self-injury. (p. 36)

Mann assumes that by this juncture in treatment, the therapist has amassed a good deal of clinical data to support the link between the client's experience of past significant figures and the repetition of such feelings in the relationship with the therapist. In the final three or four sessions, therefore, Mann feels confident in stepping up the frequency of transference interpretations, all the while continuing to highlight the central issue with fairly explicit references. The therapist's use of direct suggestions and educational and supportive interventions also increases at this time. The intent of such interventions is to promote the client's self-esteem, as well as his or her efforts to master anxiety and to employ progressively more adaptive and independent actions.

LIMITATIONS AND RESEARCH SUPPORT FOR TLP

Several authors have been critical of TLP for its extension and generalization of the theme of separation loss to all forms of psychopathology. Westen (1986), in particular, has described Mann's model as a "single-cause theory of neurosis," problematic insofar as object loss may or may not be relevant to a given client's central dynamics. Others have noted that the concept of termination as a negatively valenced, anxiety-ridden time for clients—in effect, a time of crisis—may be lacking in empirical support in the psychotherapy research literature (Marx & Gelso, 1987). Mann's assumption that a definitive termination, with its accompanying

object loss, is necessary to promote the process of internalization has also been challenged. Some (Quintana, 1993; Quintana & Meara, 1990), for example, believe that the *dosing* of termination, where clients are invited to return for additional interviews on an as-needed basis, is more likely to lead to internalization than Mann's approach, which views relinquishment of the relationship as a necessary precondition for internalization.

Though relatively little systematic research on TLP exists, several studies offer support for its efficacy and for the durability of its therapeutic effects. Furthermore, retention of clinic patients seems to be enhanced through the use of a specified number of sessions and the setting of a terminal interview date (Messer & Warren, 1995). One study involved 33 psychiatric outpatients, between the ages of 23 and 42, who had completed their secondary education, worked in white-collar professions, and presented with symptoms of anxiety or depression (Shefler, Dasberg, & Ben-Shakhar, 1995). They were randomly assigned to an experimental group, which received TLP immediately, or to a control group, which received TLP but only after a delay of 3 months. Patients were evaluated on the basis of outcome measures at termination and subsequently at 6 and 12 months posttermination. Significant improvement was noted in the experimental group after TLP, but control group patients failed to demonstrate any systematic changes after 3 months; once TLP was initiated for the control group, however, these patients also improved significantly.

Carla, an attractive 24-year-old single woman of Welsh and Italian ancestry, sought treatment for anxiety and depression of approximately 6 weeks' standing at University of Y Counseling Service. When asked what she was seeking help for at that time, Carla, without hesitation, said that she had been feeling fine until her boyfriend had broken up with her 2 months earlier but now felt very depressed and discouraged. Furthermore, she wasn't sleeping well and was finding it increasingly difficult to concentrate on her schoolwork. At the time of her evaluation, she was completing a master's-level graduate program in engineering and anticipated leaving the area within several months to accept an out-of-state offer of employment. Carla, who was self-referred, had been in psychotherapy for approximately 4 months on one previous occasion several years earlier, an experience that she found helpful. At that time, she had also been depressed, and her treatment had focused on issues concerning her relationship with her father and with another boyfriend. Carla's parents were divorced when she was less than 2 years of age, at which time her father moved to a distant part of the country and, shortly thereafter, remarried. Although she visited her father during summers and other vacation periods, she typically had far more contact on these visits with her stepmother than with her father, a busy attorney who sometimes worked 60 hours or more. She often felt that he barely noticed her and reported that these visits were a "lonely time" for her, in contrast to the "happy times" she spent living with her mother, whom she now thought of as being almost like "a sister." At this time, her eyes welled up, and she began to cry softly, warning me with a laugh that there would probably be a lot more of this to come but that "it always looks worse than it is." Particularly when she was younger, Carla continued, the preparations for these visits with her father were an upsetting time, with tearful protests almost until the hour of her departure. But "each time," Carla sighed, "I ended up having to go. Even if she'd wanted to, Mom couldn't do anything about it," owing to the terms of the postdivorce custody arrangement.

When asked to say more about her parents, Carla first talked about her mother, who had recently turned 49. She and her mother had a "very close relationship," and this had been so "as far back as I can remember." Carla had decided to attend college very near her mother's home and then remained in the same geographical area (though she attended a larger university) for her graduate studies. Mother and daughter spent a good deal of time together and often confided in each other. In fact, Carla worried "a little" about her mother now that she was preparing to graduate, with a firm job offer from an engineering firm in the southeast, many hundreds of miles from her mother's Midwest home. Carla's father, now 55, led an active lifestyle and was a very well-respected public prosecutor in the northern California community where he and his family resided. He had one son, 7 years older than Carla, from a marriage antedating his relationship with Carla's mother; there were two other children, offspring of his current marriage, a 20-year-old son and a 17-year-old daughter. Carla continued to spend at least one vacation with him each year. Although she had long before stopped feeling anxious in preparation for these visits, she also observed, "You're pretty much on your own when you go out there. You just have to fit in; that's what I try and do, anyway."

I noted during this first meeting that although Carla often spoke of feeling sad, upset, or lonely both now and in the past, she often seemed to force a smile, playing down her distress. In fact, her disposition had been so cheerful when I greeted her in the reception area, and even during the first several minutes of our initial meeting, that I found it hard to imagine this young woman having any real problem at all. Even when she cried, the effect was minimized both by her laughter and her comment about having a penchant for such dramatic reactions.

Carla seemed highly motivated for time-limited treatment and appeared to be a strong candidate. This assessment was based on several factors: (1) She was able to engage rapidly, demonstrating a good capacity for an affective relationship; (2) generally speaking, she demonstrated good ego strength, including evidence of a capacity for tolerating both anxiety and guilt; (3) despite feeling anxious and depressed, she seemed reflective and appeared capable of introspection and insight; (4) she had reported having been helped by her previous experience in psychotherapy; and

(Continued)

(Continued)

(5) there were no obvious contraindications for TLP such as suicidality, the presence of a severe characterological disturbance, or bipolar affective disorder.

Following this initial evaluation, I suggested to Carla that we meet once a week on Fridays for 12 sessions, at which time we would conclude her therapy. She was agreeable to this, and so we decided on a regular meeting day and time as well as a specific date for termination. After our diagnostic session and prior to the first therapy session, I formulated Carla's central issue in this way:

> You have always tried very hard to please the men in your life, although their response is often disappointing, and that has caused you a great deal of pain. First there was your father, but there have been others, like your boyfriend, who've seemed to lose interest in you. Our job will be to figure out what's happening so that you always end up feeling hurt in this way.

With a clear statement regarding Carla's present and chronically endured pain, this formulation of the central issue also addresses the three components outlined earlier: (1) her ongoing efforts to obtain recognition and to meet interpersonal needs, (2) the apparent failure of these efforts, and (3) the task or objective of her therapy. It may be argued that the central issue can be reformulated in such a way as to acknowledge the importance of Carla's relationship with her mother, toward whom she has always felt overly responsible. Along these lines, one might understand Carla's relational difficulties with her father and boyfriend as being motivated by the need to remain loyal to her mother. If one were to proceed along these dynamic lines, the central issue could be restated as follows:

> From the time you were little, you and your mother have always had a very close relationship, and you've always felt a special sort of responsibility for her happiness. Sometimes, this concern has been so great that you haven't been able to enjoy other relationships or activities, and this makes you feel depressed and upset.

Such a problem, for which the clinical data offer a moderate level of support, is, however, largely unconscious. As such, it might be expected to arouse resistance, which, in the framework of TLP, becomes problematic. As Mann and Goldman (1982) have noted, "The central issue as posed by the therapist, must be one that, among other things, will bypass defenses, control the patient's anxiety, and stimulate the rapid appearance of a therapeutic or working alliance as well as a positive transference" (p. 20).

Session 1

When Carla arrived for her appointment, she noted right away that she had been feeling a little better since talking with me last week, despite having felt "sort of sad" after leaving the session. Although she had wanted very much to call her ex-boyfriend, Chris, she had managed to hold off, socializing with other friends over the weekend and trying to write a term paper. She then reported with sadness that her father had not sent her any flowers this year on Valentine's Day (which had fallen earlier in the week), which led to a memory of another disappointment dating to her senior year at high school. At that time, she had been admitted to X College, a rather prestigious school that she had convinced herself would not even seriously consider her application. When she received the letter of admission, she was elated and that evening called her father to tell him the good news. Carla was deeply hurt when her father, rather than responding with pride at her accomplishment, summoned little enthusiasm at the news, "which he knew meant so much to me." He then immediately focused on the cost and "began to tell me what he could and couldn't afford, how mom would have to pay for part of it, and stuff like that." Carla then did something very uncharacteristic that she had not done before and that she had not repeated since. Rather than simply holding onto her hurt or "trying hard to act nice" when she was feeling exactly the opposite, she instead became very angry with her father and accused him of not caring about her, of never being supportive, and so forth. "He said he wouldn't even dignify it with a response," and the conversation ended. Again, she became tearful but noted that it helped to be able to talk about this with someone other than her mother. At this juncture, I presented my formulation of the central issue to Carla, which she readily accepted.

Session 2

Carla talked more about her parents during this hour, filling in many details of her childhood, as well. She mentioned that her mother maintained very close ties with her family. She was the third oldest in a sibship of seven, and several brothers and a sister resided nearby. Her father was the oldest of three boys but was not particularly close to his family. She produced an early memory, dating from her 4th year, of spending the summer with her mother on Cape Cod at a "sleep-away" camp. Although her mother worked part-time as an administrator at the camp, Carla remembered getting "lots of attention" from the other staff members, who often played with her when her mother was unavailable. "I was always the number one priority in her life," Carla observed. She returned to the theme of feeling "cut loose" at her father's house. It was so hard for her as a little girl; her stepmother wasn't very helpful either. "They expected me to be able to do things that no 4- or 5-year-old should be expected to do. . . . Really, I tried so hard to do what I thought he wanted me to, but he never seemed happy." At this point, Carla began to sob. Referencing the central issue, we discussed how Carla might have interpreted her father's long absences during these visits as an indication that he was disappointed in her or didn't care about her, when in fact it was his professional responsibilities that drew him away. She hadn't considered this before, although it seemed to make some sense to her.

Session 3

During this hour, Carla seemed to focus once more on her ex-boyfriend. Although he had promised to call her, he had not contacted her. She waited for days hoping to hear from him, finally deciding that she couldn't wait any longer. He didn't seem pleased to hear from her, which was depressing to her. She kept trying to be accommodating but didn't know what she was doing wrong. I pointed out the connection between what she had discussed in our last session—her feeling that she could never

(Continued)

(Continued)

do enough or figure out what she was doing wrong in her relationship with her father—and the feeling that she has with Chris. This was beginning to make some sense to her. Almost as an aside, she told me that she remembered something following her last session that she thought might be worth mentioning. Following vacations spent with her father and his family in California, she would always feel "a little strange" coming back to her mother's house. Although she couldn't explain why, she had to "touch everything" in her bedroom. In this regard, we discussed how disconnected these two parts of her life were and how abrupt the transitions between her parents' homes must have felt to her. Possibly, the "touching" was a way of reestablishing this connection; it may also have signified that all these things, unlike the things in her father's house, belonged to her. Carla started looking forward to coming in for her weekly sessions. She was finding it a little easier to concentrate on schoolwork, even though things with Chris felt very unresolved.

Session 4

During the fourth session, I noted what seemed to be a pattern in the beginning of Carla's treatment sessions. Not only was she cheerful when I greeted her, but she would always ask, with genuine interest, how I had been. This seemed to go beyond the usual exchange of amenities, however, as though a more detailed response was anticipated. In fact, I had resisted the impulse on a couple of occasions to furnish her with more information than I would customarily provide a client in response to this query. As the hour began, she reported that her closest girlfriends had told her "It's time to move on" and to start dating other guys. She thought that maybe they had a point. Chris claimed that he just wanted more time apart from her to do things with his male friends, but she needed more from him; although she knew it was "unreasonable," she nevertheless felt jealous when he hung out with his roommates or partied with other friends. We discussed the parallel between this issue and Carla's childhood jealousies over her half siblings, with whom she always felt she was in competition while on visits to her father. I then commented, "So your dad wasn't just leaving you to go to work; you felt you couldn't hold your own against your half sibs, and this made it even more hurtful." Carla thought that this might be a possibility, since she has always felt this way with guys, not just with Chris. The conversation then shifted to a recent experience Carla had during a family get-together at her maternal grandmother's house. Her mother's older sister, Jenny, an unhappy woman in her mid-50s who had never enjoyed as close a relationship to Carla's grandmother as had Carla's mother, had been critical of Carla for not offering to help with the food preparation. As a matter of fact, Carla had earlier told an uncle that she would be happy to help but had been reassured that no further help was needed. Nevertheless, she felt "awful" when her aunt pulled her aside to lecture her, and she began to feel that she had been wrong. As we examined her reaction, however, it soon became clear that Carla didn't really feel the criticism to be a fair one; furthermore, she felt angry toward Aunt Jenny. We then talked about her need to "contain" and detoxify such angry feelings, even to the point where she punished herself for reacting normally to an unreasonable provocation. Carla found this idea intriguing and wondered how often she might be doing this with others, such as her father.

Session 5

In the evening before this session, a surprise winter storm had dumped six inches of snow on the ground. Carla arrived promptly for her session but asked whether any of my other clients had been unable to come in for their sessions. I had two thoughts about Carla's comment. The first was that here she was, whether or not anyone else showed up; she was reliable, committed, and so forth. I also recall thinking at the time that perhaps Carla had been concerned that I might not have been at my office when she arrived. She began the hour by talking about her recent tendency to behave in a sort of friendly though negativistic way. She found herself challenging things her friends said even when she was really in agreement with them. I suggested that perhaps she was displacing feelings that belonged elsewhere, such as toward her father or her boyfriend. Carla seemed slightly taken aback by this idea but admitted that it offered "some sort of explanation, anyway." Pausing for a moment, she continued:

Carla: I suppose I have a problem believing in relationships. Down deep, I feel that relationships don't last and that you can't count on guys.

Therapist: Perhaps you were wondering when you mentioned my clients not showing up whether I would be here when you arrived, whether you could count on me?

Carla: Oh. No, I don't . . . I hadn't . . . No, I guess I thought you'd call me. . . . I don't think I thought that.

Although Carla didn't accept my "here-and-now" interpretation of transference, her ambivalent reaction suggested that something had "hit home." In retrospect, this may have been the first indication that the positive transference was beginning to shift, revealing Carla's expectation that I, like her father, her boyfriend, and other men in her life, would sooner or later lose interest in her. In the remainder of the hour, Carla focused on the theme of "untrustworthy" men, in particular another former boyfriend she had dated during her freshman and sophomore years in college, who had "cheated" on her.

Session 6

Carla had been feeling a little more depressed recently. She would begin the session wondering what "therapy is all about." She had been feeling better a couple of weeks back, but she was having trouble sleeping again, couldn't concentrate as well, and so forth. She had had another conversation with Chris, and he seemed to be distancing himself from her. The more he distanced himself, the harder she tried. She then began to talk about her parents' marriage. Her mother was so accommodating toward her father before their divorce. When he was admitted to law school, she moved halfway across the country with him. She kept house, worked part-time to help make ends meet, and took care of his son, Sandy, when he would visit periodically. She really "put herself out." Carla then mentioned for the first time that her father had been involved in an affair just before he broke up with her mother, the woman he eventually married following their divorce. I commented that her mother had seemed to want to keep the momentum in the marriage going at virtually any cost; yet this somehow wasn't enough. I asked

(Continued)

(Continued)

Carla if she felt a parallel existed between her description of her own tendency to make accommodations and her mother's behavior while she was married to her father. "Yeah," she replied with a long sigh, "and look what happened to her. She says she's happy and all, but I mean, after she and my dad got divorced, well…she's never gotten seriously involved with another guy." I suggested that Carla's mother had good reason to feel betrayed by her father, although her solution—steering clear of deep commitments altogether—may not have been a terribly adaptive one. I also suggested that these solutions seemed to represent two extremes: either a woman behaves in an incredibly accommodating and self-sacrificing fashion or she has no relationships at all with men. Carla didn't reject this idea, but neither did she seem to embrace it. Toward the end of the hour, I asked her whether she knew how many sessions we had remaining. Carla paused for a moment and then, sounding just a bit surprised, said, "Six. I guess we're at the halfway point, right? Don't worry, I still have things to talk about."

Beginning in the fifth session and intensifying in this hour, Carla's reactions seemed to embody what Mann and Goldman (1982) characterize as the "return of ambivalence both about the therapist and the possible outcome of treatment" (p. 11). The anxiety revealed in her last comment suggests that (a) she will try hard to keep me interested even though she may be feeling that there is less to say and (b) the end of treatment and of the treatment relationship is not far off, although unresolved issues remain.

Session 7

Carla was feeling increasingly desperate about the relationship with Chris. They went out to talk about their relationship ("It wasn't really a date") and wound up at a bar that Chris frequented. They ran into two of Chris's friends and spent an hour or so chatting with them. Carla wanted to spend more time together afterward, but Chris decided to go home. I suggested that just as Carla could not "give up" on her father, even when he seemed so preoccupied with other things, she was unwilling to relinquish her relationship with Chris. On the other hand, it felt hurtful to her that she was not as important to Chris as he was to her. She then revealed that when Chris was a junior in high school, his mother developed a serious illness that left her bedridden for many months, and she became very dependent on Chris, her only child. Although he wasn't resentful, once the time came to look for schools, he applied only to colleges that were out of the state. I commented that perhaps Chris felt as though an important part of his adolescence was, somehow, derailed due to his mother's illness and that he was making up for lost time. She then observed, "Yeah, maybe that's one of the reasons he's afraid to get too involved with me. Maybe it's less about me and more about some sort of fear of involvement he has . . . but it still doesn't make me feel good."

Carla's insight was a poignant one, since it involved a dawning realization that Chris's reactions to her also reflected his own unique history, which made it harder for Carla to attribute them simply to a recapitulation of her past experience with her father. In fact, the contrast between Chris and Carla was rather striking: Chris needed to escape from the regressive pull of his mother and her illness, while Carla had tried to hold onto the relationship with her father in constant fear that his interest in her would otherwise wane. Her comment that it "doesn't make me feel good" to have arrived at this understanding is also important, since it represents both a more realistic appraisal of the relationship and a decline in the strength of the magical fantasy that she alone was responsible for keeping men interested in her.

Session 8

Carla began this hour by discussing a vacation she was going to be taking with two girlfriends to Miami Beach (which she had mentioned several weeks previously). It was spring break week, and she felt "determined" to have a good time. Both the other girls had boyfriends, but this was to be just a "girl thing." She then reported a dream in which "I was trying on a pair of socks. The socks were black with gray squares, definitely men's socks. But then, after I got them on, the color changed, and they seemed to have pink polka dots, like the socks I'd wear." I encouraged Carla to associate to the dream, and she began to talk about her older half brother, Sandy, whom she had previously described as being "a lost soul," having been married and divorced by his mid-20s, drifting from one job to the next, without a steady girlfriend, and so forth. The socks reminded her of the kind he might own, with sort of an argyle pattern. She had always found it hard to understand him before, and they had never been especially close. In fact, she felt that he resented her, and when they were younger, he had considered her "spoiled," perhaps because he knew how close a relationship Carla had with her own mother. But she knew that he had suffered; Sandy's mother had severe emotional problems, he had often been on his own during his childhood and adolescence, and he didn't seem comfortable during visits to his father's California home. In my interpretation, I emphasized her newly emerging capacity for trial identification, first with Chris, reflecting on her comments during the last session, and now with Sandy. She was, in effect, "trying his socks on" for size. This is further underscored when the socks temporarily morph into "girl's socks" as she pulls them onto her feet; it is as though this is her experience, at least for the moment. She seemed to confirm the accuracy of this interpretation by noting, "I guess I do want to know what guys think and feel."

Session 9

Carla reported that her trip had been a lot of fun and that she had actually met a guy one night while with her girlfriends in Miami Beach. He was very good-looking and also very attentive and interested in her; the two "hung out" together on and off for a couple of days, although Carla also wanted to spend time with her girlfriends.

I asked her how it had felt to be in the position of telling a guy that she had other friends to hang out with and wouldn't be able to spend all her time with him. Carla smiled, looking only slightly embarrassed, and said, "It was okay. Actually, it felt sort of good. One of the nicest parts was that I didn't feel like I was working that hard. It was more . . . spontaneous." She continued to think about Chris but was beginning to feel that maybe things would have to wait, especially since it looked as though they would be living in different parts of the country after they graduated. (Chris was also completing a master's degree, though in a different field.) Perhaps they would become reinvolved, although maybe not. In any event, she wasn't feeling nearly as desperate at the prospect of moving on and not being

(Continued)

(Continued)

with Chris. The night after she returned, she was still feeling very good about herself and decided to go to a singles bar downtown, where she met yet another interesting and attractive man, also in his mid-20s. He had been calling her ever since, although she didn't want "to encourage him too much." Making reference to the central issue once again, I commented that Carla didn't seem to be experiencing the old anxiety with either of these two men and sounded far more relaxed and self-confident than she typically reported having felt in similar situations in the past. Perhaps most important, she had also been able to enjoy herself "in the moment." She replied that while this was possibly true, she wasn't ready to give up on her idea of finding a "true love," as silly as that might sound. However, she now accepted the possibility that the time might not be right for this.

Session 10

Carla began this hour by telling me that although she had been feeling better, she was beginning to realize that there were still significant issues that she had not worked through. She was about to graduate, yet she still felt very confused about Chris; he had e-mailed her a very nice note a few days back, and it stirred up all sorts of feelings she thought she had finally put aside. She also mentioned feeling upset as she began to think about leaving the area and moving away. She felt concerned about her mother. For the first time, they wouldn't be within a few hours' drive of each other. She then wondered if maybe some of her problems with men could be related in some way to how she felt about her mother. I sensed that Carla was introducing what was, in essence, a new theme. It was actually somewhat along the lines of the alternate central issue mentioned earlier. However, its introduction at this time, along with her renewed anxiety, was more likely related to Carla's awareness of the approaching termination date. She seemed to be presenting me with new problems and a recrudescence of her original concerns as a sort of unconscious protest over our contract, as if to say, "Can't we continue to meet while I sort these things out?" However, since Carla had introduced the topic of her relationship with her mother, I thought it might be worthwhile to pursue it.

Therapist: It's a big responsibility when someone tells you that you're "the number one priority" in their life.

Carla: You know, sometimes, it wasn't that bad at my father's house. Actually, they do a lot of hiking, camping, and outdoorsy kind of things. As I got a little older, it could even be fun.

Therapist: Did you tell your mom about those parts?

Carla: Well, I think she knew. . . . But, no, I mostly complained to her; I'd tell her how much I'd missed her.

Therapist: So maybe you felt as though it would be hurtful to your mom if you were to have positive experiences with your dad?

Session 11

By the time we met for the 11th session, Carla had graduated from University of Y and spent the first part of the hour discussing this. Her mother, as well as a number of other relatives from her mother's family, came to see her graduate, although her father had told Carla he wouldn't be able to because "he was trying a very big case or something like that." Carla's eyes filled with tears, and sobbing, she said, "It's still hard at times like this not to have him there. I don't know, I just really wanted him to see me graduate. I don't think that's asking too much, is it?" We then discussed her wish to be seen as special in her father's eyes. On this occasion, however, the desire for recognition appeared much less tied to the childhood rivalries with her half siblings than to Carla's desire for affirmation, or mirroring. I commented that she had experienced many such disappointments in this relationship and that such a need for recognition, to be seen as "special" in her father's eyes, struck me as being both reasonable and healthy. Carla agreed that this was true, reflecting that this also seemed to be an important theme in her relationships with other men. She paused and then said, "I guess maybe I'm so convinced that other guys are going to act just like my dad that even when they don't, I can't really believe it. Like it's going to happen, sooner or later." I commented that this seemed to be an important insight and wondered whether Carla might yet expect a similar outcome in her relationship with me. She replied that this might have been true in our first few meetings; she had been aware of feeling slightly apprehensive prior to those first several appointments, wondering if I were really interested in her and so forth. However, she had gradually become more comfortable talking with me and now actually looked forward to coming in for her sessions. This theme, which of course had brought us back to the central issue, was then elaborated.

Carla observed that although she now understood herself much better than she had when therapy began and had begun to notice changes in the way she behaved with her family as well as with male friends, she was anxious at the prospect of falling back into her old routines. Without dismissing this possibility, I told her that I believed that she had made a good deal of progress and that she was now armed with knowledge about herself and the strength and courage to put it to good use. She smiled weakly but said, "Maybe, but I don't feel like I have very much courage." I told her that I had to disagree and not just based on the hard work that she had done in therapy. In fact, when I thought of Carla as a 4- or 5-year-old, flying 2,000 miles across the country to spend vacations with her father in an unfamiliar place, where she often felt isolated and alone—this took courage. She registered surprise at this, noting that she would never have thought of this as courageous but thought that perhaps I was right. As the session drew to a close, I mentioned that the next session was to be our last one. Although Carla appeared sad, she smiled and in a soft voice said simply, "I know."

Final Session

Although Carla had always been talkative in our therapy sessions, she confessed that she felt there wasn't as much to say today. She did offer that, for the most part, she wasn't feeling very anxious or depressed, nor was she having much difficulty sleeping, the problems that originally brought her into therapy. But there seemed little else to say. This seemed just a bit odd to her, inasmuch as just 2 weeks ago, she was feeling that much remained unresolved and also because this was to be our last meeting. I commented that perhaps she was now beginning the posttreatment task of relying more on herself to work through her problems and didn't need me in the same way. I took the opportunity to review some

(Continued)

(Continued)

of what she had accomplished in therapy. She now understood the basis of her chronic feeling of disappointment in her father. Although it saddened her, she could now recognize that this was the result of his limitations in combination with environmental factors that were beyond her control. Furthermore, her wish to feel "special" in his eyes represented a healthy entitlement, not the unreasonable reaction of a "spoiled" child. She had gradually come to understand that this dynamic had persisted in a largely unmodified form and was present in other important relationships, particularly with boyfriends. I also commented on Carla's concern that she must not betray her mother, both with respect to any positive aspects of her relationship with her father and in her own relationships with men. I suggested that she might now find it more difficult to blame herself for the shortcomings of others. Furthermore, she now possessed a greater range of adaptive solutions and strategies, so that "bad" feelings, such as anger, no longer needed to be "contained" at all costs or turned into their opposite.

Carla found this review helpful, although as we neared the end of the hour, she became very tearful and told me how much she would miss her sessions with me. I, too, felt moved and told her I would miss her as well. She embraced me warmly, handing me a card as she left my office for the last time. The card thanked me for helping her rediscover the inner strength she must have had all along and for being such a good listener. She also wrote that she had noticed a gradual change in her relationships, with which she was pleased, and that she hoped would continue to evolve. Finally, she felt much better able to take on the challenges that lay ahead.

CONCLUSION

Beginning with a historical overview of the concept of short-term treatment in the psychoanalytic literature, this chapter has examined a number of different approaches to the challenge of conducting therapy briefly. The pioneering contributions of writers such as Sigmund Freud, Sandor Ferenczi, and Franz Alexander were discussed in some detail, followed by summaries of the work of those representing the next several generations of brief-treatment theorists. The various treatment methods associated with recent theories of brief dynamic therapy appear to reflect the more generally observable trends in psychoanalytic theory formulation and can be ascribed to two basic conceptual models: (1) the *drive/structure* model and (2) the *relational/structure* model. In the next portion of the chapter, technical parameters common to all forms of time-limited and brief dynamic psychotherapy were summarized.

Following this, James Mann's TLP, which has been termed the only truly "integrative" model of brief dynamic treatment, was presented in greater depth. Finally, a case illustrating this method of time-limited treatment was offered in substantial detail, complete with process summaries of each treatment session.

REFERENCES

Alexander, F., & French, T. (1946). *Psychoanalytic therapy: Principles and application.* New York, NY: Ronald Press.

Bellak, L., & Small, L. (1965). *Emergency psychotherapy and brief psychotherapy* (2nd ed.). New York, NY: Grune & Stratton.

Binder, J., & Strupp, H. (1991). The Vanderbilt approach to time-limited dynamic psychotherapy. In P. Crits-Christoph & P. Barber (Eds.), *Handbook of short-term dynamic psychotherapy* (pp. 137–165). New York, NY: Basic Books.

Breuer, J., & Freud, S. (1955). Studies on hysteria. In J. Strachey (Ed. & Trans.), *The standard edition of the complete psychological works of Sigmund Freud* (Vol. 2). London, UK: Hogarth Press. (Original work published 1893–1895)

Crits-Christoph, P., & Barber, J. (Eds.). (1991). *Handbook of short-term dynamic psychotherapy.* New York, NY: Basic Books.

Davanloo, H. (1980). *Short-term dynamic psychotherapy.* New York, NY: Jason Aronson.

Ferenczi, S. (1950). The further development of an active therapy in psychoanalysis. In E. Jones (Ed.) & I. Suttie (Trans.), *Further contributions to the theory and technique of psycho-analysis* (pp. 198–217). London, UK: Hogarth Press. (Original work published 1926)

Ferenczi, S., & Rank, O. (1925). *The development of psychoanalysis.* New York, NY: Nervous and Mental Diseases.

Fonagy, P. (1999, April 16). *The process of change and the change of processes: What can change in a "good" analysis.* Keynote address to the Spring Meeting of Division 39 of the American Psychological Association, New York.

French, T. (1954). *The integration of behavior* (Vol. 3). Chicago, IL: University of Chicago Press.

French, T., & Fromm, E. (1964). *Dream interpretation: A new approach.* New York, NY: Basic Books.

Garfield, S. (1989). *The practice of brief therapy.* New York, NY: Pergamon Press.

Gay, P. (1988). *Freud: A life for our time.* New York, NY: W. W. Norton.

Golan, N. (1978). *Treatment in crisis situations.* New York, NY: Free Press.

Goldstein, E., & Noonan, M. (1999). *Short-term treatment and social work practice.* New York, NY: Free Press.

Greenacre, P. (1954). The role of transference: Practical considerations in relation to psychoanalytic therapy. *Journal of the American Psychoanalytic Association, 2,* 671–684.

Greenberg, J., & Mitchell, S. (1983). Object relations in psychoanalytic theory. Cambridge, MA: Harvard University Press.

Gustafson, J. (1986). *The complex secret of brief psychotherapy.* New York, NY: W. W. Norton.

Horowitz, M. (1991). Short-term dynamic therapy of stress response syndromes. In P. Crits-Christoph & P. Barber (Eds.), *Handbook of short-term dynamic psychotherapy* (pp. 166–198). New York, NY: Basic Books.

Jones, E. (1957). *The life and work of Sigmund Freud, 1919–1939: The last phase* (Vol. 3). New York, NY: Basic Books.

Laikin, M., Winston, A., & McCullough, L. (1991). Intensive short-term dynamic psychotherapy. In P. Crits-Christoph & P. Barber (Eds.), *Handbook of short-term dynamic psychotherapy* (pp. 80–109). New York, NY: Basic Books.

Lemma, A., Target, M., & Fonagy, P. (2010). The development of a brief psychodynamic protocol for depression: Dynamic Interpersonal Therapy (DIT). *Psychoanalytic Psychotherapy, 24,* 329–46.

Lemma, A., Target, M., & Fonagy, P. (2011). *Brief dynamic interpersonal therapy: A clinician's guide.* Oxford, England: Oxford.

Levenson, H. (2010). *Brief dynamic therapy.* Washington, D.C: American Psychological Association.

Levenson, H. (2012). Time-limited dynamic psychotherapy. In M. Dewan, B. Steenbarger, & R. Greenberg (Eds.), *The art and science of brief psychotherapies: An illustrated guide* (pp. 195–237). Washington, DC: American Psychiatric Press.

Luborsky, L., & Mark, D. (1991). Short-term supportive-expressive psychoanalytic psychotherapy. In P. Crits-Christoph & P. Barber (Eds.), *Handbook of short-term dynamic psychotherapy* (pp. 110–136). New York, NY: Basic Books.

Malan, D. (1976). *The frontier of brief psychotherapy.* New York, NY: Plenum Press.

Mann, J. (1973). *Time-limited psychotherapy.* Cambridge, MA: Harvard University Press.

Mann, J. (1986). Transference and countertransference in brief psychotherapy. In H. Myers (Ed.), *Between analyst and patient: New dimensions in countertransference and transference* (pp. 119–127). Hillsdale, NJ: Analytic Press.

Mann, J. (1991). Time-limited psychotherapy. In P. Crits-Christoph & P. Barber (Eds.), *Handbook of short-term dynamic psychotherapy* (pp. 17–44). New York, NY: Basic Books.

Mann, J., & Goldman, R. (1982). *A casebook in time-limited psychotherapy.* New York, NY: McGraw-Hill.

Marx, J., & Gelso, C. (1987). Termination of individual counseling in a university counseling center. *Journal of Counseling Psychology, 34,* 3–9.

McCullough, L., Farber, B., Winston, A., Porter, F., Pollack, J., Vingiano, W., et al. (1991). The relationship of patient-therapist interaction to outcome in brief psychotherapy. *Psychotherapy, 28,* 525–533.

McCullough Vaillant, L. (1997). *Changing character: Short-term anxiety-regulating psychotherapy for restructuring defenses, affects, and attachment.* New York, NY: Basic Books.

McCullough Vaillant, L., Kuhn, S., Kaplan, A., Wolf, J., & Hurley, C. (2003). Treating affect phobia: A manual for short-term dynamic psychotherapy. New York, NY: Guilford Press.

Messer, S., & Warren, C. (1995). *Models of brief psychodynamic therapy: A comparative approach.* New York, NY: Guilford Press.

Messer, S., & Warren, C. (2001). Brief psychodynamic therapy. In R. Corsini (Ed.), *Handbook of innovative therapy* (pp. 67–85). New York, NY: Wiley.

Mitchell, S. (1988). *Relational concepts in psychoanalysis.* Cambridge, MA: Harvard University Press.

Nielsen, G., & Barth, K. (1991). Short-term anxiety-provoking psychotherapy. In P. Crits-Christoph & P. Barber (Eds.), *Handbook of short-term dynamic psychotherapy* (pp. 45–79). New York, NY: Basic Books.

O'Dowd, W. (1986). Otto Rank and time-limited psychotherapy. *Psychotherapy, 23,* 140–149.

Parad, L. (1971). Short-term treatment: An overview of historical trends, issues, and potentials. *Smith College Studies in Social Work, 41,* 119–146.

Perlman, H. (1957). *Social casework: A problem-solving process.* Chicago, IL: University of Chicago Press.

Piper, W., de Carufel, F., & Szkrumelak, N. (1985). Patient predictors of process and outcome in short-term individual psychotherapy. *Journal of Nervous and Mental Disease, 173,* 726–733.

Quintana, S. (1993). Toward an expanded and updated conceptualization of termination: Implications for short-term, individual psychotherapy. *Professional Psychology: Research and Practice, 24,* 426–432.

Quintana, S., & Meara, N. (1990). Internalization of therapeutic relationships in short-term psychotherapy. *Professional Psychology: Research and Practice, 21,* 123–130.

Rank, O. (1973). *The trauma of birth.* New York, NY: Harper & Row. (Original work published in 1924)

Rapoport, L. (1970). Crisis intervention as a mode of brief treatment. In R. Roberts & R. Nee (Eds.), *Theories of social casework* (pp. 265–311). Chicago, IL: University of Chicago Press.

Rasmussen, A., & Messer, S. (1986). A comparison and critique of Mann's time-limited psychotherapy and Davanloo's short-term dynamic psychotherapy. *Bulletin of the Menninger Clinic, 50,* 163–184.

Reid, W., & Shyne, A. (1969). *Brief and extended casework.* New York, NY: Columbia University Press.

Shechter, R. (1997). Time-sensitive clinical social work practice. In J. Brandell (Ed.), *Theory and practice in clinical social work* (pp. 529–550). New York, NY: Free Press.

Shefler, G., Dasberg, H., & Ben-Shakhar, G. (1995). A randomized controlled outcome and follow-up study of Mann's time-limited psychotherapy. *Journal of Consulting and Clinical Psychology, 63,* 585–593.

Sifneos, P. (1968). Learning to solve emotional problems: A controlled study of short-term anxiety-provoking psychotherapy. In R. Porter (Ed.), *The role of learning in psychotherapy* (pp. 87–96). Boston, MA: Little, Brown.

Sifneos, P. (1987). *Short-term dynamic psychotherapy: Evaluation and technique* (2nd ed.). New York, NY: Plenum Press.

Sifneos, P., Apfel, R., Bassuk, E., Fishman, G., & Gill, A. (1980). Ongoing outcome research on short-term dynamic psychotherapy. *Psychotherapy and Psychosomatics, 33,* 233–241.

Tosone, C. (1997). Sandor Ferenczi: Father of modern short-term psychotherapy. *Journal of Analytic Social Work, 4,* 23–41.

Weiss, J., Sampson, H., & Mount Zion Psychotherapy Research Group. (1986). *The psychoanalytic process: Theory, clinical observation, and empirical research.* New York, NY: Guilford Press.

Westen, D. (1986). What changes in short-term psychodynamic psychotherapy? *Psychotherapy, 23,* 501–512.

Woods, M., & Hollis, F. (2000). *Casework: A psychosocial therapy.* New York, NY: McGraw-Hill.

15

SOCIAL WORK INTERVENTIONS WITH ALCOHOL AND OTHER DRUG PROBLEMS

MARYANN AMODEO AND LUZ MARILIS LÓPEZ

Too often, when clinicians think of intervening with alcohol and other drug (AOD) problems, they think of chronic alcoholics, heroin addicts, and women with crack cocaine habits. These populations constitute only a fraction of the clients seen in social work settings who have AOD problems. The majority of alcohol- and drug-involved clients have not reached the stage where functioning is dramatically impaired. They are living in families, attending school, holding jobs, and maintaining households.

They often come to human services agencies with presenting problems related to family life, health or employment status, and educational or career goals. Most often, they have not recognized that their drinking or drug use either contributes to or is the cause of the problems for which they seek help. Consequently, they do not bring up drinking or drug use as an aspect of the presenting problem and, if asked about it, would say that it does not interfere in their lives. Such clients often continue on workers' caseloads for long periods, as the AOD problem remains hidden from both worker and client. Unidentified, it undermines the achievement of therapeutic goals. Thus, a major challenge for social work is to acquire the screening and brief intervention skills necessary to identify and motivate these clients to seek help.

RATIONALE FOR SOCIAL WORK INTERVENTION

In a report by the Substance Abuse and Mental Health Services Administration's (SAMHSA) National Survey on Drug Use and Health in 2006, 23.6 million persons aged 12 or above needed treatment for an illicit drug or alcohol abuse problem (9.6% of the persons aged 12 or above). Of these, only 2.5 million (10.8% of those who needed treatment) received it at a specialty alcohol/drug treatment facility (see www.nida.gov). There is a huge unmet treatment need in the United States. This may be changing as health care settings, driven by cost containment efforts, implement early-screening

427

and brief-intervention methods. But AOD problems are currently pandemic in society and in virtually every setting where social workers see clients: family service, health, mental health, child welfare, school, employment, court, and correctional settings.

If AOD problems are not identified in mental health settings, they can masquerade as other diagnoses (e.g., cocaine dependence can create symptoms of depression; alcoholism withdrawal can create symptoms of panic attacks), leading to inappropriate treatment, for example, the prescribing of psychotropic drugs. Thus, clients who use AOD regularly and come to sessions high are unlikely to benefit from the sessions because the chemicals cause distortions in perception, new learning, memory, and affect. When clients have developed tolerance to these drugs, their use may not be discernible to the worker; thus, the worker and the client may spend many hours designing and trying to implement a service plan that ultimately comes to nothing.

AOD problems can be life threatening, especially when they have progressed to the chronic stage, but death can also be caused in the earlier stages or with only occasional use by particularly vulnerable individuals such as the elderly, teens and preteens, and those with medical conditions exacerbated by alcohol and other drug use.

Finally, alcoholism and drug dependence are conditions that often involve intergenerational transmission. For many families, if no intervention occurs, intergenerational transmission is almost certain.

POTENTIAL FOR SPECIAL CONTRIBUTIONS BY SOCIAL WORK

Social workers can be found in a variety of settings designed to help healthy populations lead a full and satisfying life: schools, day care centers, youth recreation programs, adoption agencies, and health centers, among others. This access to healthy populations provides the opportunity for unique contributions in the area of prevention of AOD problems. This means that social workers

are in an ideal position to facilitate primary prevention (promote health before problems begin) and secondary prevention (screening, identification, and brief intervention when problems are in the early stages and have not progressed into full-blown conditions), as well as tertiary prevention (treatment of the full-blown condition) and rehabilitation (intervention designed to limit the debilitation caused by the chronic condition).

Social work's ecological perspective increases the likelihood that workers will adopt a holistic approach in assessing and intervening with AOD problems. Rather than assuming that the problem resides only in the individual or only in the environment, the ecological perspective looks at the interaction between them. It is a person-in-environment and environment-in-person perspective (van Wormer, 1995).

Social work training provides specific skills that are needed for effective work with alcohol- and drug-involved clients. Among those skills are family outreach and intervention; group therapy skills; working with a range of defenses, including denial, avoidance, and intellectualization; working through loss and grief to resolution and recovery; the ability to use differential approaches to treatment, including cognitive, behavioral, psychodynamic, and family systems; and an appreciation of the role of self-help programs, natural support networks, and indigenous healers in client recovery.

SCOPE OF THE PROBLEM

Consequences of Abuse and Dependence

If a thorough discussion of the scope of AOD problems in the United States were to be undertaken, this chapter would be so long as to preclude attention to any other clinical issue. Thus, only a few aspects of the problem will be highlighted.

Alcohol use disorders are the third leading cause of premature death in the United States (Freiberg & Samet, 2005), and substance use disorders are the number one cause of preventable death (Gold & Jacobs, 2005). Between 24% and 31% of patients seen in emergency rooms have an alcohol use disorder (D'Onofrio & Degutis, 2004), and alcohol or illicit drug abuse is a factor in 50% to 75% of all psychiatric admissions (Miller, 2004). Concerning drug abuse only, truancy, school dropout, and absence from the labor force increase with use. Drug-using adolescents tend to leave school earlier, start work earlier in low-paying jobs, and form families earlier. Entry into other forms of criminal activity is more likely (Kail, 1992). Significant health problems are associated with adulterants in the drugs, the drugs themselves, the use of needles that are not sterile, and lifestyle issues associated with drug use. Between 30% and 40% of homeless Americans are alcohol abusers, and 10% to 15% are drug abusers (Caslyn & Morse, 1991; McCarty, Argeriou, Huebner, & Lubran, 1991).

Intravenous drug abuse has played a major role in the spread of the AIDS epidemic. Intravenous drug abusers compose the second largest group that has contracted AIDS in the United States. Human immunodeficiency virus (HIV) infection is spread among intravenous drug abusers primarily through the sharing of needles, but it can also be spread through sexual contact. Worldwide, HIV/AIDS continues to threaten not only intravenous drug users but also their sexual partners and children (Amil et al., 2004; Hilton, Thompson, Moore-Dempsey, & Janzen, 2001).

Drugs of Abuse

Alcohol is the drug most misused in the United States, but there is still much societal resistance to accepting it as a drug. Alcohol's legal status contributes to denial about its characteristics as a drug and its devastating effects. Polydrug use (regular use of more than one drug) is the most common pattern seen among clients in treatment in the United States and often includes taking drugs with different or opposite physical effects on the same occasion (Maisto, Galizio, & Connors, 1991). For example, cocaine users may switch to alcohol and other sedative drugs when they feel overstimulated

from cocaine. They may also combine substances such as cocaine and heroin, commonly known as "speedball" (Cornish, Lontos, Clemens, & McGregor, 2005).

The major categories of drugs of abuse are as follows:

1. Alcohol

2. Other depressants, including barbiturates (sleeping medications), benzodiazepines (minor tranquilizers such as Valium, Xanax, and Klonopin), and methaqualone

3. Stimulants, including cocaine, amphetamine, methamphetamine (crystal meth), and 3,4-methylenedioxymethamphetamine (MDMA, Ecstasy)

4. Cannabinoids, including marijuana and hashish

5. Hallucinogens, including lysergic acid diethylamide (LSD) and mescaline

6. Opioids and morphine derivatives, including heroin, codeine, oxycodone hydrochloride (oxycontin), vicodin, and fentanyl

7. Dissociative anesthetics such as phencyclidine (PCP) and ketamine (Special K)

8. Inhalants such as paint thinner, gasoline, and glue

9. Anabolic steroids

Patterns of drug abuse vary from one region of the country to another. However, some abuse patterns have become more prevalent nationally in recent years. For example, abuse of prescribed pain medication has become a widespread problem among adolescents and adults; abuse of medications for attention deficit hyperactivity disorder (ADHD), such as Ritalin and Aderall, has become more common among adolescents and college students. Date rape drugs such as rohypnol, ketamine, and gamma hydroxybutyrate (GHB) are more available now, as are anabolic steroids for bodybuilding. For a comprehensive discussion of drugs of abuse, we recommend Harold E. Doweiko's (2009) *Concepts of Chemical Dependency* (seventh edition).

DEFINITIONS AND DIAGNOSTIC ISSUES

Much of the research and writing on alcohol and other drug abuse has focused on alcoholism rather than on drug dependence, but many researchers and clinicians believe that explanatory models for alcoholism are applicable to other drug dependencies. Although there are significant differences in the psychoactive qualities of various drugs and their potential for dependence and physical addiction, there are also significant similarities. For the purposes of this chapter, the frameworks developed to describe alcoholism are also applied to drug dependence.

DSM-IV Criteria for Abuse and Dependence

The Diagnostic and Statistical Manual of Mental Disorders, fourth edition text revised (*DSM-IV-TR*), American Psychiatric Association (2000), provides criteria for substance abuse and dependence, as well as specific information on various drugs of abuse and their addiction course. The primary feature is a maladaptive pattern of use, occurring within a 12-month period, leading to failure to meet major role obligations; legal, interpersonal, or social problems; or use in situations that are physically hazardous.

Dependence is characterized by three or more of the following occurring at any time in the same 12-month period: tolerance, withdrawal, impaired control, restructuring of activities to facilitate drug taking, and continued use despite persistent negative consequences.

An Addiction Continuum

Doweiko (2009) has developed a continuum of degrees of drinking and drug use:

1. Total abstinence from drug use

2. Rare/social use of drugs (using one or more drugs on a social basis)

3. Heavy social use/early problem use (abusing one or more drugs on an episodic basis)

4. Heavy problem use/early addiction (abusing one or more drugs on a continual basis)

5. Clear addiction to drugs (p. 9)

Such a continuum is helpful because it allows for the classification of drug use of various intensities and patterns and it minimizes the tendency to think of alcohol and other drug dependency as an all-or-nothing phenomenon.

Alcoholism and Drug Dependence as Diseases

Alcoholism and drug dependence have been defined as diseases by the American Medical Association (Doweiko, 2009). Like other diseases, they have identifiable signs and symptoms, are chronic, are progressive in the sense that they become worse if untreated, can be fatal if untreated, and result in tissue damage. Although much of the general public understands that alcoholism and drug dependence are treated as diseases, this concept has met with some controversy over the years.

In 1960, *The Disease Concept of Alcoholism* (Jellinek, 1960) was published. Based on a survey of Alcoholics Anonymous (AA) members, it described alcoholism in behavioral and psychological terms, with identifiable stages and progressive symptoms, including loss of control or the inability to limit drinking, a pattern of negative consequences, and, finally, withdrawal symptoms and the psychological and physical devastation that often accompanies chronic alcoholism. This schema made a significant contribution to explaining alcoholism but was based on key concepts that have since been challenged: that progression occurs inevitably, that the progression of symptoms occurs in the order that Jellinek delineated, and that a total lack of control occurs. Vaillant (1983) found that drinking patterns change over time so that some individuals who have a pattern of abuse are able to move back to social use and that alcoholics are more likely to experience impaired control (Vaillant, 1990) rather than a total loss of control over their drinking.

These and other challenges (Fingarette, 1988; Peele, 1989) notwithstanding, Jellinek's model continues to have utility in identifying the types of symptoms that often appear as individuals move from moderate, nonproblem use, to abuse, to dependence. A benefit of the disease conceptualization is that clients, family members, and the general public can see that addiction has biological and physiological aspects, which make it more than willful acting out. The model conveys that the sufferer did not seek the condition, which can lead to reduced moralism and stigma, facilitating the securing of help. However, a drawback is that this medicalization of addiction emphasizes the biological over the psychological and social. It minimizes the influences of culture and societal forces in the development of AOD problems and can lead to myopia in the choice of intervention approaches.

ALCOHOLISM AND DRUG DEPENDENCE AS MULTICAUSAL AND MULTIVARIANT CONDITIONS

Alcoholism and drug dependence can be thought of as biopsychosocial illnesses (Wallace, 1989). They are considered to be multicausal conditions involving a range of factors, including genetic and/or biological (e.g., inherited predisposition to dependence), psychological (e.g., experiences of early trauma or repeated losses, or existence of a preexisting psychiatric disorder), familial (e.g., lack of parental limits on use or parental role modeling of excessive use), and cultural (e.g., cultural norms reinforcing drinking and drug use as a rite of passage or measure of masculinity). (For theories of etiology, see Doweiko, 2009; Frances, Miller, & Mack, 2005; Galanter & Kleber, 1999.)

These factors make a differential contribution to the development of AOD problems for various individuals. Alcoholism and drug dependence can also be thought of as multivariate conditions in that they display themselves in diverse patterns of dysfunction (Pattison & Kaufman, 1982). Thus, for some individuals, medical consequences and

physical symptoms predominate and result in the diagnosis. For others, it is a persistent pattern of negative social consequences such as employment, relationship, and legal problems that result in the diagnosis. For still others, it is the inability to limit or control the amount consumed that results in the diagnosis.

Alcoholism and Drug Dependence as Primary Illnesses

The prevalent view in the mental health field 25 years ago was that alcoholism and drug dependence should be viewed as primary illnesses rather than as symptoms of other disorders. While use may begin in response to another disorder or personal problem, these conditions take on lives of their own as a person progresses into alcoholism or drug dependence. Regardless of precipitants, a cycle of dependence has been established that will generate negative consequences of its own.

Alcohol and Drug Abuse and Dependence Among Adolescents

Adolescents deserve special attention as a population at high risk of developing AOD problems and as a group that often experiences AOD problems in ways that differ from the progression described for adults. The challenge for clinicians who work with adolescents is to neither underestimate nor overestimate the severity of the AOD problem for any individual client. The former mistake is common among workers who assume that drinking and drug use represent a normal phase of adolescent development and will spontaneously disappear as teens mature and find other interests. The latter mistake is common among workers who assume that the behavior exhibited by teens will invariably persist into later years. Neither assumption is borne out by research (Doweiko, 2009).

McNeece and DiNitto (1994) recommend that the presenting symptoms of a substance-abusing child or adolescent be considered from a developmental framework, that is, how much damage is likely to occur from this behavior based on the individual's age and developmental level. They suggest that clinicians examine the level of medical risk for the child or adolescent, for example, from sexual practices and the risk of HIV infection when using substances. They also recommend an examination of the meaning of the substance use to the child or adolescent. Are substances being used to cope with dysphoric states? Are they exacerbating more serious emotional disorders? (Research suggests that substance abuse may be a causative or contributing factor in conditions such as conduct disorders, affective disorders, attention deficit hyperactivity disorder, and anxiety disorders.)

McNeece and DiNitto (1994) also recommend that clinicians pay close attention to the contexts of the AOD problem, including legal, social, familial, and educational. Because they are minors, children and adolescents must function within these contexts, and ideally, it is within these contexts that incentives for behavior change can be identified. Clinicians would do well to examine the forces within these spheres that act to intensify or diminish the drinking and drug use behaviors, assess the overall severity of the situation, and mobilize individuals and resources to motivate the child or adolescent to get help.

ASSESSMENT AND INTERVIEWING METHODS

Countertransference and Transference

Potent and negative countertransference is often generated in workers facing clients who have AOD problems. In part, this is the consequence of living in a society that has a long history of moralism toward such individuals, viewing them as morally weak, lacking in self-discipline, unwilling to change, and untreatable. In part, this also results from the personal experiences many clinicians have had using alcohol and other drugs themselves and/or interacting with family members and loved ones with AOD problems.

These life experiences can be thought of as filters or lenses through which clinicians see AOD-troubled clients, and they often intensify workers' difficulties in viewing clients objectively and responding to their needs. For example, a clinician who has used alcohol and other drugs and was able to control the use without trouble or found it easy to reduce the use when problems began may be impatient or angry about the compulsive nature of the client's use. The clinician whose own use of alcohol or other drugs is excessive may resist labeling a client's use as abuse or dependence unless it far exceeds the clinician's own pattern and has become debilitating. Growing up in an alcoholic or drug-dependent family provides another filter, which may leave the clinician feeling cynical, overwhelmed, or defeated when faced with clients with AOD problems (Amodeo & Drouilhet, 1992).

In addition to these forms of direct countertransference, indirect countertransference, or the worker's responses to influences outside the worker-client relationship, is common for workers who see AOD-troubled clients, particularly involuntary clients. Referral agencies such as courts, schools, and child welfare organizations often convey the expectation that it is the worker's responsibility to see that the client becomes clean and sober. Responding to the real or perceived pressure of a third party watching over the treatment process, workers often become directive, over controlling, and confrontational (Amodeo & Drouilhet, 1992). In response, clients often defend against any acknowledgment that behavior change is necessary. They perceive that the worker is allied with or is an agent of the referring institution, that the worker is engaged in an effort to force them to relinquish something that has become central to their existence, and that admission of a problem may result in further losses, such as placement of children in foster care. The clinician's ability to identify his or her countertransference responses and manage them appropriately is key to working effectively with this population.

Identifying Risk Factors and Indirect Indicators

Assessment is the cornerstone of effective prevention and intervention with AOD problems. Since clients often do not correlate their drinking and drug use with the presenting problem, it will be through workers' careful assessments that AOD problems will be identified. Routine screening for AOD problems should occur as part of every psychosocial history since, in some settings (e.g., psychiatric, child welfare, courts, domestic violence), AOD problems may affect 60% to 80% of the clients seen.

A number of formats have been recommended for conducting assessments (Doweiko, 2009; Freeman & Landesman, 1992; Freshman, 2004; Liftik, 1995; Orlin & Davis, 1993; van Wormer, 1995; Washton & Zweben, 2006). These formats provide guidance for clinicians about the aspects of the client's life to be examined, the order in which the assessment should occur, specific questions to be raised, and methods for determining severity. One of the most useful of these is described by Liftik (1995), who recommends that prior to asking specific questions about drinking and drug use, clinicians should be alert both to risk factors in clients' backgrounds and current circumstances that make them particularly vulnerable to developing such problems and to indirect or hidden indicators of alcohol or other drug problems in clients' family, educational, employment, health, and relationship histories. Risk factors can

include parental and extended-family attitudes about drinking and drug use, a family history of alcoholism and drug dependence, age when drinking and drug use first started, experiences of early trauma, and peer group involvement with AOD.

Risk factors can be discussed with clients in the context of helping them determine whether they are currently at risk of developing a dependence on AOD and, if so, how they can limit current problems and prevent more serious ones. Clients are often familiar with discussions of risk factors from medical settings, where they have heard about their risks for conditions such as heart disease depending on family history and individual status with regard to smoking, cholesterol, or weight gain. Such a discussion can be supportive to clients, since it is focused not on demonstrating that clients have problems but on offering assistance in preventing the further development of problems.

Indirect indicators, or red flags, often consist of the negative consequences of drinking or drug use. They may include behavioral signs, such as personality changes, erratic job performance, unexplained memory lapses, or the smell of alcohol during appointments; medical signs such as gastritis (from drinking), hepatitis (from drugs), or dripping nose (from intranasal cocaine use); or social indicators, such as having a heavy-drinking and drug-using peer group or engaging in social activities that revolve around AOD.

Mrs. Kent, a 30-year-old African American woman, applied to the state child welfare agency to take responsibility for her cousin's daughter, Gemini, who was 3 years old. Gemini's mother was cocaine dependent and was unable to care for the child. Mrs. Kent was a single parent who was separated from her husband.

The worker conducting the home study could see that Mrs. Kent cared about Gemini's well-being. She had taught Gemini how to dress herself and fix food for herself when she was hungry. When she had time, Mrs. Kent played with Gemini and read to her.

(Continued)

(Continued)

During home visits, Mrs. Kent often looked haggard and depressed. When the worker mentioned this to her, Mrs. Kent became angry and defensive, saying she often had trouble falling asleep or woke up during the night and could not go back to sleep. She went on to say that if she finally fell asleep, she would not be able to get up until noon or early afternoon. She was vague about how long the pattern had been going on and dismissed the worker's questions with statements that it was "nothing for the worker to worry herself about."

Mrs. Kent also seemed to have little energy to clean the apartment or fix meals and delegated these tasks to her two biological children, who were 10 and 8. She relied on the children to care for themselves. Even Gemini was in the habit of going by herself to Mrs. Kent's mother's apartment on the top floor of the building. Using the fire escape, Gemini would climb three flights of rickety metal stairs in daylight and darkness, good weather and bad, to see "grandma." Witnessing this and hearing that it was not unusual, the worker was alarmed that Mrs. Kent did not see the danger. Gemini could fall several stories if she lost her foothold; she was out of sight for hours at a time in a building with occupants Mrs. Kent did not know; and the building was in a neighborhood known for its share of violence.

There were a number of red flags to raise the worker's suspicion that Mrs. Kent had an AOD problem. Each of these indicators appearing alone in a case might mean little. It is the accumulation or constellation of factors that should alert the worker to the likely presence of AOD problems:

- *Problems sleeping and awakening, appearing haggard and fatigued:* AOD use could be involved in various ways. Heavy drinking can lead to interrupted sleep; users of stimulants such as cocaine may have trouble falling asleep, then feel fatigued and depleted when they "crash."
- *Inconsistent parenting of young children and parentification of older children:* AOD-involved individuals often have difficulty with consistent parenting. When drug free, they can be attentive and involved; when high, they tend to be self-involved and preoccupied with drug seeking. Their children learn early in life to care for themselves.
- *Defensive responses to innocuous comments or questions:* AOD-involved clients are often

hyperalert to criticism. Comments that could be seen as covert references to the individual's addiction will be met with defensiveness and hostility.
- *Relatives who are AOD dependent.* Because heredity plays a role in AOD dependence, having relatives who are AOD dependent may put a person at greater risk. Also, drug-dependent relatives may initiate other family members into drug use, introduce family members to dealers, pressure family members to keep them company in their drug taking, and portray drug taking in a positive light.

The worker would need to do a detailed AOD history here, given the number of indirect indicators and risk factors. Such an AOD history requires more time when alcoholism or drug dependence are present, due to denial and other defenses common to addictions. A full session or multiple sessions may be needed (Amodeo, 1995a; Liftik, 1995).

The following case of Mrs. Abraham provides another example.

Mrs. Abraham is a 78-year-old woman who lives alone in a farmhouse in a rural area. The house was the family home until her husband died, and her children married and had families of their own. She is in fairly good health, still drives, and goes to the supermarket and town library at least once a week. Recently, she had a car accident that brought her to the attention of her primary-care physician. Driving home from the supermarket on a two-lane country road, she encountered oncoming traffic and couldn't keep her car in her own lane. She hit two cars in the oncoming lane and crashed into a stop sign. Her car was totaled. Since Mrs. Abraham sounded confused and disoriented when the police arrived, they called her daughter Carolyn, who drove Mrs. Abraham to her doctor.

After a medical exam and interview with Mrs. Abraham, the doctor asked to speak to Carolyn alone. To Carolyn's astonishment, the doctor said he believed that Mrs. Abraham had a serious drinking problem. He came to this conclusion because she was currently intoxicated (evidenced by a very high blood alcohol level on her blood test), she had elevated readings on recent liver tests, and he suspected that she had suffered memory blackouts in the past, since he had had lengthy conversations with her that she couldn't recall. She had also recently had a few falls that the doctor said were unusual for someone with her good balance and coordination.

Carolyn was so surprised because she had never suspected that her mother was drinking more than an occasional glass of wine or brandy. She had never seen her mother intoxicated, and her mother always had a good explanation if she couldn't remember conversations, if she had a fall, or if she dented her car.

The doctor explained that he had tried to talk about the situation with Mrs. Abraham when her lab tests showed that drinking had affected her liver, but she was so humiliated and angry that he decided to drop the subject for the time being. He told Carolyn that the car accident was a blessing in disguise because it would allow him to insist that she get help to stop drinking. He also planned to explore with her whether spending so much time alone, when she had been used to having a large family around her, was contributing to the drinking problem. Carolyn agreed to help in any way she could and offered to discuss the situation with her brother and sisters to see if they also could be helpful.

Confusing Diagnostic Picture

When alcohol/drug problems occur in an older adult, they often present a confusing picture because many of the symptoms resemble those that occur during the normal aging process. For example, deteriorating memory, balance, coordination, and judgment may be signs of substance abuse or aging or both.

Another complicating factor is that so many older adults are on a variety of medications for medical conditions such as heart, circulatory, and respiratory problems. These medications can affect memory, balance, coordination, and judgment if taken in the wrong doses, if taken in a way that was not prescribed, or if doses are skipped.

If the older adult drinks or takes illicit drugs while also taking prescribed medications, the combination can have a synergistic or exaggerated effect (causing an increased impact so that $1 + 1 = 5$ instead of $1 + 1 = 2$).

When symptoms of substance abuse are seen in an older adult, the cause may be a *combination of the factors* above. Experienced substance abuse specialists can tell the difference, as can geriatric medical specialists. A careful drinking/drug evaluation, a general medical history, a medical examination, and a family history provide the necessary data for these professionals to determine the cause of the problem.

Other Considerations With Older Adults

- It may be difficult to get reliable information about drinking and drug use patterns or the taking of prescribed medications because the older adult's memory may be poor.
- If the older adult lives alone, there may be no other people to provide reliable information about daily patterns.
- Small amounts of alcohol and other drugs have a more profound effect on an older adult because the person's body is deteriorating with age. Thus, small amounts of alcohol, for example, can result in intoxication. Family members may be unsuccessful in persuading the older adult that drinking is dangerous under certain circumstances because the older adult may be drinking small amounts that he or she considers to be inconsequential.
- Many older adults were raised in an era when there was great shame associated with having a drinking or drug problem. Thus, they are reluctant to discuss their drinking and drug use behavior and often find it humiliating and devastating if others discover that they have a problem.
- Treatment resources are often more limited than they are for other adults.

Maintaining the Therapeutic Alliance During Assessment

Clients are often convinced that no drinking or drug problem exists in spite of comments to the contrary from others in their lives. Involuntary clients are particularly determined to prove to the worker that no problem exists and to have this message conveyed back to the referring agency—the court, employer, child welfare agency, school, or similar other organization. Inexperienced workers commonly fall into the trap of prematurely discussing whether there is a drinking or drug problem and what should be done about it. Clients begin these discussions by asserting that changes in their lives are unnecessary. Workers, focusing on why the clients have been sent to treatment, often respond by pointing out that behavior change is necessary to prevent future trouble. They would like to see clients avoid the negative consequences they know are likely, such as arrests, accidents, loss of significant relationships, having children sent to foster care, or disability or death. Workers may also feel pressured if they sense that the referring institution expects the worker to get the client clean and sober quickly.

When workers declare that a problem exists and that clients need to change, they are seen as adversaries. Hence, clients withhold important personal information or engage in defensive debate and dismissal of the workers' ideas and concerns. In the following vignette, the worker avoids this trap by refocusing the assessment to provide an opportunity for the development of rapport and trust prior to discussing alcohol and other drug issues.

Kevin was a 22-year-old Irish American male mandated by his company to have an evaluation at a substance abuse clinic. In a random urine screening, Kevin had tested positive for marijuana. During the initial session with the worker, Kevin contended that he was only a "social user," smoking marijuana whenever friends came over. He told the worker that she would never convince him otherwise. The worker knew she needed to avoid discussing such a charged issue so soon in the therapeutic relationship since it was likely that they would become polarized over it.

Instead, she told Kevin that she needed more background information to help her see his situation as a whole and asked Kevin to describe his educational, family, work, and social life and talk about his goals for himself in counseling and in life in general. She knew that this background information would help her see if there were indirect indicators of a substance abuse problem. Also, this approach would be less likely than a direct discussion of drinking and drug use to mobilize the denial, avoidance, and other defenses that would be there if Kevin was indeed in trouble with AOD.

The worker learned that Kevin lived at home with his parents and two brothers. He described his family as close and said his parents were concerned about and involved with their children. His mother still made sure there was a hot meal on the table if Kevin planned to be home for the evening. He had lived in the same neighborhood through his elementary, junior high, and high school years. He enjoyed school because he was able to hang out with friends, but said that in high school, he was singled out by teachers as a wise guy. This led to his frequently skipping school.

Kevin said his goal for counseling was to keep his job. He believed his only problem was that he was unfairly singled out due to random drug testing. He believed that most of the other employees used AOD in a way similar to him.

Before the first session ended, the worker told Kevin that their task would be to explore the role drinking and drug use played in his life and to determine whether there was anything about his drinking and drug use that he wished to change. The worker stated that a decision about change would be entirely up to Kevin and that the worker was prepared to accept whatever conclusion Kevin came to about this. This was said to underscore the fact that the worker did not intend to force Kevin to give anything up and would not serve in the role of an agent of coercion.

Integrating Drinking and Drug Use Questions Into the Psychosocial Assessment

Clients will be less defensive if drinking and drug use are discussed as part of the exploration of other aspects of the client's history. This minimizes the possibility that the client will feel singled out or interrogated. Also, clients are generally more able to acknowledge past than current problem behavior. Following are examples of questions about childhood and adolescence in the psychosocial history that can help bring the client's experiences with AOD to the surface. In parentheses are issues the worker should be thinking about:

- *Extended family:* Did your family have much contact with your extended family—grandparents, aunts, uncles, and cousins? What were these relationships like? (Was there alcoholism, depression, suicide, social isolation, or estrangement in the extended family?) What were family gatherings like? Was there lots of eating, drinking, dancing, and athletics? (Did these occasions end in drunkenness, arguments, brawls?)

- *Parental discipline:* Was it strict or loose? What were the issues: dating, sex, drinking? (Was there permissiveness around drinking and drug use? Was there subtle encouragement of drinking and drug use? Was there neglect of the children so that the parents were unaware of what the children were doing?) What were parental attitudes and rules?

- *Peer group:* How connected were you with peers? What type of kids did you hang around with? Were they into sports, cars, sex, drugs, outdoor activities, good grades, going to college? Where did you fit in? Did you begin experimenting with drinking and drugs with your peer group? At what age? What were those experiences like: exciting, scary? Did you feel out of control? Did you get physically ill? Did you get punished? What types of drugs did you try?

- *School performance:* How did you do in school socially and academically? What were the factors contributing to your performance? If it was poor, did drinking or drug use play any role?

- *Coping methods:* When things went badly for you at home, in school, or with your friends, how did you deal with the situation?

Kevin's assessment continues.

Having learned that Kevin often skipped school and had been singled out as a wise guy, the worker commented that many teens had experimented with drinking and drug use by this point in their school experience, and she wondered what Kevin's experience had been by the time he got to junior high. Kevin acknowledged that by the time he was 12 or 13, he was drinking and had tried drugs and sometimes went to school when he was high. The worker then asked what drugs he had used. He said, "Pretty much only alcohol and marijuana." The worker noted that he had said "pretty much," which she interpreted to mean that there were other drugs, but she decided to move away from drinking and drug use questions because Kevin had become tense. She believed that he would become more defensive if she pressed the issue at that point.

Instead she returned to general questions, asking about his high school experience, including whether teachers continued to see him as a wise guy, whether there were parts of the school experience he enjoyed, and his grade point average at graduation. He volunteered that as a high school senior, he was using cocaine and selling small amounts to get money to buy his own. Within a year of graduation, he was stopped, but not arrested, for drunk driving by a police officer who was also a neighbor. Kevin was incredibly relieved because he had cocaine in the car, but the car was never searched. After this close call, he stopped using cocaine. This latter statement he made with pride, as if demonstrating that he was not a person who became dependent on drugs.

In describing his social life, Kevin said that he and his friends often went to a local bar. Still cautious about asking directly about AOD, the worker decided to return to this after learning more about Kevin's social life. Asked to talk about his relationships with women, Kevin said he had had several girlfriends since age 16, but the relationships had ended in conflict. He found that girls tried to control him and were jealous of his close relationships with his buddies.

The worker wondered to herself if Kevin's girlfriends were concerned about his AOD use and were thus seen as "trying to control him." Since Kevin had talked about the local bar as a place where he spent much of his time, the worker asked how often he and his friends gathered at the bar and how long they typically stayed. Kevin said most nights they stopped in at least for a while. The worker then said, "Tell me about your drinking." Kevin said on a typical evening he drank one or two six-packs and had a mixed drink or a shot. In response to the worker's probing, he said that he drank more on some evenings and might return home intoxicated a few times a week, usually on weekends.

Taking a Focused Drinking and Drug History

Having noted risk factors and indirect indicators, the clinician may need to go on to take a focused drinking and drug history. Liftik (1995) recommends that the clinician avoid mobilizing denial and defensiveness by asking a series of questions about drinking and drug use when the client has already indicated through the more general assessment that these topics are off limits.

He recommends, as do other authors (Amodeo, 1995a; Brown, 1985), that the focus of the interview be shifted at least temporarily to other aspects of the presenting problem. AOD problems are usually so persistent and pervasive that they surface again soon, albeit in disguised form. When issues come up that sound AOD related—for example, panic attacks, intense or extended arguments, verbal abuse, violence, medical emergencies, memory problems, or performance problems at work—the clinician should ask directly,

"Were you high when this occurred?" "What role did drinking play in this incident?" "Had you used cocaine in the day or two before this occurred?"

One of the benefits of taking a drinking and drug history is that it gives clients an opportunity to hear themselves report on the role of AOD in their lives. Clients see that what they perceived to be isolated incidents or random drinking and drug-using behavior falls into a pattern. Workers should strive to engage clients in a dialogue that provides a picture of the client's typical pattern and also atypical experiences or one-time events. The following six parameters can be kept in mind by workers as they engage clients in a dialogue: (1) quantity (amount used), (2) frequency (regularity of use), (3) duration (length of time the pattern has continued, in years, months, weeks, or days), (4) precipitants (factors that trigger use, including thoughts, feelings, bodily sensations, interactions, or situations), (5) consequences (effects or results of use), and (6) control (extent to which there have been efforts to limit use by reducing amounts or frequency or by establishing external controls such as asking others to hide the drugs or take charge of money that could be used for drugs).

If clients evidence a pattern of repeated negative consequences, there is a likelihood of substance abuse. If clients evidence both repeated negative consequences and impaired control (i.e., taking the substance in larger amounts or over a longer period than intended), there is a likelihood of substance dependence. The *DSM-IV-TR* criteria for each should be examined carefully.

Considered together, the parameters are especially helpful in identifying opportunities for prevention and early identification, that is, in identifying patterns where no diagnosis would be made but clients could be warned that their use was heavy or hazardous and could lead to eventual trouble.

The salience of AOD in a person's life should also be considered in an assessment (Babor & Grant, 1992). *Salience* means prominence, importance, or conspicuousness. Reframed, salience reflects the nature and intensity of a person's relationship with AOD. Salience is the extent to which this relationship dominates the thoughts and actions of the person, affects the person's sense of self-esteem and well-being, and results in the sacrificing of other relationships in preference for this one. The following case illustrates this dynamic.

Saul was a 29-year-old second-year medical student when he initiated therapy with a social worker in private practice. He was from an upper-middle-class Jewish family. His father was a physician and had exceedingly high expectations of Saul. Saul reported that his problems began when he started medical school 1½ years ago. He became depressed and anxious, fearing that he would not succeed. He spent much of his time alone and had no close friends.

The therapist agreed to work with Saul on his adjustment to medical school, his father's expectations of him, and his own expectations of himself. The worker suggested they meet for eight sessions.

During the fifth session, the therapist noticed the smell of alcohol while meeting with Saul and realized that he had smelled alcohol before. He had not included AOD questions in his assessment, so he could not rule out a substance abuse problem. In the next session, when Saul talked about persistent anxiety related to his academic performance, the worker asked Saul if he ever used AOD to manage this anxiety. Saul said he had not used drugs since college, and then he had used only marijuana, but that he generally had a few drinks during the evening when studying. He said he

(Continued)

(Continued)

had never associated this with his feelings of anxiety. The worker asked him what types of drinks he preferred and how many he typically had. Saul said he usually had three or four gin and tonics. The worker asked whether Saul usually drank at times when he was not studying. Saul said he would often have a few drinks when watching television, listening to music, or reading.

The worker told Saul that exploring drinking was important because, without Saul's recognizing it, his drinking might have increased to the point where it was having a negative effect. The worker said that it was important to identify any factors that might contribute to Saul's feelings of anxiety, lack of productivity, and poor self-esteem. The worker was aware that alcohol is well-known for affecting all three.

The worker then explored whether there were days when Saul drank more than four drinks and the maximum consumed on those days, how long the pattern had continued, whether Saul had experienced memory lapses, and how Saul felt physically and emotionally on the days he did not drink. The worker learned that Saul seldom had more than four drinks per night, but on mornings when he felt especially anxious, he also drank one to three drinks just before leaving for school. Daily drinking had continued for over a year, but there were no blackouts and no withdrawal symptoms.

When the worker asked Saul to picture spending evenings without drinking, Saul said he felt isolated and restless, with nothing to look forward to. The worker pointed out that moderate, non-problem drinkers do not develop an intense relationship with alcohol and that Saul needed to consider whether his drinking pattern should be changed. Saul was frightened by the idea that he might be psychologically hooked on drinking.

ADDRESSING CO-OCCURRING PSYCHIATRIC CONDITIONS IN ASSESSMENT

It is thought that between 40% and 64% of clients seeking substance abuse treatment have one or more co-occurring psychiatric disorders (Karageorge, 2002; SAMHSA, 2006). These clients have special treatment needs (Horgan, 1997; Miller, Leukefeld, & Jefferson, 1994, 1996; Ouimette, Gima, Moos, & Finney, 1999); they are more difficult to assess, have more complex health needs, and often require services for a variety of systems (e.g., mental health, substance abuse, medical) that may not be connected (Horgan, 1997). They relapse more frequently, and their care tends to be more episodic (Goodman, Hankin, & Nishiura, 1997).

One of the most difficult and crucial clinical tasks is to determine the interface between substance abuse and psychiatric symptoms, that is, whether there are *two separate* conditions or only one condition that is masquerading as another, since substance abuse problems tend to mimic psychiatric conditions. An inaccurate diagnosis will result in misapplication of treatment. The following guidelines (Nace, 1995; Washton & Zweben, 2006) can assist in this process:

- *Use multiple sources of information*, as clients with co-occurring disorders are often not accurate reporters. The use of substances has interfered with memory and self-perception. Psychiatric symptoms such as anxiety, depression, or psychotic symptoms may play an additional role in this. Thus, interviews with family members and significant others are extremely valuable in history taking. In addition, information from collaterals such as physicians or case managers, case records, and urine screens can be invaluable.

- *Determine the chronology of symptom initiation for both sets of symptoms* to answer the question "Did psychiatric symptoms precede substance use during adolescence or early adulthood, or did drinking and drug use precede the psychiatric symptoms?" Use a timeline that is unique to that client, breaking the periods into sections that facilitate the client or family's memory, and record the history of each drug used and psychiatric symptoms.

- *Observe client symptoms during abstinence* (for at least a few weeks) to see whether the psychiatric symptoms increase or decrease. If they increase, this could be an indication of two separate conditions. If they decrease, this would suggest that substance abuse is mimicking (creating) the psychiatric symptoms, the most common of which are depression and anxiety in early abstinence.

- *Examine the family history* to determine whether first- or second-degree relatives suffered from either a substance abuse or a psychiatric condition; while this is not conclusive, it may lend weight to a hypothesis about the diagnosis.

- *Conduct drug-screening tests periodically* to ensure that the client's reporting of drug use or abstinence is accurate.

- *Monitor functioning in major life spheres* (e.g., work, family, health, social relationships) to determine how even small amounts of alcohol or other drugs affect behavior. With the chronically mentally ill, look for poor money management, unstable housing, violence, and legal problems; low-quantity use is common but with high disruption.

- *Assess responsiveness to psychotropic drugs* to see if there is a reduction in psychiatric symptoms; this may add weight to the hypothesis about the diagnosis. If you seek a psychiatric consultation, try to do so with a psychiatrist who is board certified in addiction psychiatry.

Addressing Cultural Issues in Assessment

In the United States, there are few differences in the overall rates of substance abuse between Whites, Blacks, and Hispanics, yet the public stereotype of this is quite different, with many members of the general public viewing drug problems as primarily associated with racial and ethnic minorities. Furthermore, racial and ethnic minorities in the United States have often suffered discrimination as the result of their minority status and/or their addiction status, and this may have contributed to the severity of the addiction. In spite of fairly equivalent addiction rates, racial and ethnic minorities have differential access to drug treatment; thus, minorities are often underserved in terms of their substance abuse treatment needs.

Talking with clients about their racial, ethnic, and cultural background and identity is an essential part of engagement, assessment, and treatment. Cultural identity refers to all those characteristics that define a person as part of a broader cultural group, including a person's race, ethnicity, country of origin, gender, age, religion, social class, sexual orientation, physical ability, and citizenship. Ignoring these issues can leave clients feeling isolated and misunderstood. Clinicians can benefit by the following:

1. *Understanding the client's self-perception:* Cultural identity may be "who the client is"— the most important ways the client sees himself or herself. Clinicians who avoid this aspect of the client may never be able to get close enough to the client to assist with recovery issues.

2. *Appreciating the client's worldview related to addiction:* Worldview affects the way people view addiction, the point at which help is needed, the type of help that is preferred, and the need for abstinence or behavior change.

3. *Assessing cultural issues as a source of stress:* Being caught in intergenerational tension around acculturation or experiencing discrimination due to race/ethnicity could contribute to the drug problem or relapse.

4. *Determining whether cultural concerns are causing difficulty in treatment engagement:* Examples might be lack of a peer group in residential treatment or in the neighborhood or community that is ethnically/racially similar to the client or having a clinician who comes from a racial/ethnic group toward which the client holds negative stereotypes.

5. *Exploring refugee or immigrant experiences:* These may have led to traumatic experiences that are exacerbating drug use and need to become a part of treatment.

Culturally responsive care includes practitioner self-awareness, a basic understanding of the ethnoculture of one's clients, and an ability to adapt one's practice to fit the client's ethnocultural background (Amodeo & Jones, 1997; Lum, 1996; Orlandi, Weston, & Epstein, 1992; Straussner, 2001). Factors such as the client's level of acculturation, the culture's view of the causes and remedies of AOD problems, and the level of shame associated with AOD problems influence the client's and family's ability to respond to typical or mainstream treatment methods (Amodeo & Jones, 1997). Effective treatment for some clients may include use of an indigenous community healer, joining the neighborhood Pentecostal church, residing at the local Buddhist temple, or going to a sweat lodge (Amodeo, Robb, Peou, & Tran, 1996; Delgado, 1994, 1995). Talking about cultural traditions, experiences, and preferences also assists clients in the treatment process, since it helps them identify coping and recovery methods that are consistent with their cultural identity; finding activities that reinforce important aspects of their cultural identity and seeking out recovering individuals from their cultural group who can serve as role models are also important.

The following vignettes illustrate culture-related questions that would be relevant for the clinician to ask himself or herself or to raise with clients during the assessment and in discussions of treatment planning.

Marie Xavier is a 43-year-old Haitian woman who came to the United States about 7 years ago. She has just completed detoxification and was referred for outpatient substance abuse treatment. She has a diagnosis of alcohol dependence and wants to try to remain abstinent from alcohol and other drugs

- To what extent is Ms. Xavier identified with the Haitian community in the United States?
- To what extent does Ms. Xavier fear stigma and social isolation due to this condition? What would be the experience of alcoholic women in Haiti? What about in the U.S. community in which Ms. Xavier has now resettled?
- What recovery or healing methods for this condition does Ms. Xavier know about? Which are used in Haiti and which are used in the U.S. communities where Haitians have resettled?
- In the process of coming to this country, did Ms. Xavier experience trauma? Might this be related to her drinking, and if so, how?

Liam O'Malley is a 55-year-old Irish immigrant who came to Philadelphia about 10 years ago. He's been sent to an employee assistance program by his boss because of intoxication on the job. He does not believe that he has any problem and feels that he's been singled out by his boss.

- What was his experience with drinking in Ireland? What was drinking like for the men in his peer group, among his friends, and in his family?
- At what point now or in the future would he judge drinking to be a problem? What current or future behavior or consequences would make him think that his drinking warranted attention?
- How does he view men who abstain from drinking or drink very little? How would his current peer group and his peer group in Ireland view such men?

Yen Thranh is a 23-year-old Vietnamese college student. She has come to the college counseling center for help with heavy, often daily (perhaps dependent) marijuana use. She was caught smoking pot in the dorm. Although she was born in the United States, her parents came from Vietnam as refugees.

- How long were her parents in the country before she was born?
- How traditional or acculturated is the family? How does Yen see herself on this continuum?
- How do her peers at the college view marijuana use? Is this similar or different from the way her parents view marijuana use?
- Did her parents' immigration to the United States cause them hardship? Did they suffer from traumatic experiences? Might Yen have experienced trauma secondary to their experiences? If so, how has this manifested itself, and is it related in any way to her marijuana use?

CONTINUED ASSESSMENT USING A REDUCED-USE EXPERIMENT

To determine whether clients meet the *DSM-IV* dependence criterion related to impaired control, workers can suggest that clients engage in a reduced-use experiment or, alternatively, an abstinence experiment: preplanned, time-limited attempts by clients to modify their drinking and

drug use patterns. Details are worked out with the clinician to ensure that the experiment is a real test of the criterion. Such experiments work only if clients are receptive to trying them. If clients are pressured into them, especially under circumstances where clients are mandated to attend treatment, there is a high likelihood that clients will convey the idea that the experiments were successful, whether this is true or not.

The worker suggested that treatment be extended to work on the drinking issue. He suggested that Saul try to cut down on his drinking for a 2-week period, limiting himself to no more than two per night and none at any other time of the day. Saul tried this for 2 weeks and was unsuccessful. The worker suggested he try for another several weeks, asking him every session or two about his progress on this goal. He reported fairly close adherence to the goal at times but acknowledged going over the limit about half the time. Within 8 weeks, Saul realized he would need to remain abstinent for the long haul, since even one or two drinks triggered the desire to keep on drinking.

Determining Readiness for Change

Prochaska and DiClemente (DiClemente, 1991; Prochaska & DiClemente, 1983) have developed a stages of readiness for change model that provides a method for assessing clients' readiness to alter addictive behavior. Six stages that mark the individual's progress through the change process are outlined:

1. *Precontemplation:* The individual has never considered changing the addictive behavior

because he or she does not believe that the behavior is a problem.

2. *Contemplation:* The individual begins to think about changing the behavior but is not convinced that it needs to be changed.

3. *Determination:* The individual recognizes that change is necessary and makes plans to change (e.g., setting a date for the change and announcing to others that the change will occur or reducing the frequency of the behavior targeted for change).

4. *Action:* The individual stops the addictive behavior.

5. *Maintenance:* The individual continues the action over the long term, integrating the new behavior into the course of daily living.

6. *Relapse:* The individual fails to maintain the behavior change.

Individuals in the relapse stage who do not remain there over the long term will return to contemplation and perhaps progress again through the other stages. Success has often been preceded by movement through the sequence several times.

Miller and Rollnick (1991, 2002) have used this framework as part of their motivational enhancement therapy or motivational interviewing method based on reflective listening. Client ambivalence is seen as a predictable dynamic, and clinicians are encouraged to validate its presence and assist clients in examining the content and feelings related to it as a necessary step toward action. The choice to change behavior rests with the client. Clinicians are advised to adopt a nondirective stance in negotiating goals and assisting clients with them. This means that abstinence may or may not be the goal.

Client in Precontemplation

The dialogue that follows shows the clinician's use of motivational interviewing methods, specifically reflective listening and the Importance Ruler and Confidence Ruler, with a drug-dependent client who is HIV-positive. The worker's goal is to help this client consider a change to always having protected sex. The client is in the precontemplation stage concerning this behavior. The worker uses methods to help the client engage in "change talk" (Miller & Rollnick, 2002, p. 53). Unlike some addiction counseling approaches that try to convince clients to change, in this approach the clinician elicits *from the client* statements about the importance of changing unsafe sexual behavior and confidence about changing. Although the client may assign a somewhat low level of importance to changing or a low level of confidence about changing, the clinician asks, "Why not a lower number?" to prompt the client to express aspects of internal motivation.

Clinician:	Let's return to something you mentioned at the end of last session—that you've been having unsafe sex. I know that you're HIV-positive. Can you tell me more about this—how often, with whom, under what circumstances?
Client:	I don't know . . . different people, maybe once a month, after getting together and drinking . . .
Clinician:	What do you think are the chances you could be infecting others?
Client:	Low chance.
Clinician:	What makes you think that?
Client:	I try not to think about it much. I know people who have sex with other people who are positive, and they don't get infected.
Clinician:	Then it's your impression that infecting people doesn't happen very often.
Client:	Well, it happened to me. I got infected, and I'm sure it was from someone who was positive, because I don't use needles, so I certainly don't use dirty needles.
Clinician:	From your experience, you can see that it happens sometimes—people can get infected.

Client: Yes, but it's always risky to have sex anyway—whether it's getting an STD, getting pregnant, getting the virus . . . whatever. One way to be safe is to avoid ever having sex, but that doesn't make any sense to me.

Clinician: You're pointing out two choices—never having sex or living with the risk of infecting someone. Are those the only two choices that you see?

Client: No, if you follow the rules and always use a condom or you never have sex with someone who's got the virus, you won't get infected. Still, condoms break, they fall off, and always worrying about having safe sex isn't a real turn-on.

Clinician: You think that even "following the rules," a person can still get infected if something goes wrong. You've mentioned condoms . . . Have you considered using them?

Client: Yeah, I've used them at times, but if you've had a few drinks or had a line or two of coke . . . the last thing you're thinking about is condoms.

Clinician: So sometimes you've used condoms, but there are times when it's too inconvenient or you just aren't thinking about it.

Client: I can't always stop to think about this when I want to have sex. And I certainly don't want to think about being positive when I'm having sex. If I can't have sex once in a while without wearing a condom, what's the point of living? It's the one time when I can forget about being positive and just do what I want—put it out of my mind.

Clinician: It sounds like having sex without a condom happens impulsively. It sounds like it's an escape and a glimpse of freedom or a little time to be without the worries of living with the virus.

Client: Yeah, it does feel like that sometimes.

Clinician: I can understand how you feel burdened by the virus. It must be a heavy weight to carry. Are you willing to continue talking about this, or should we shift gears for today?

Client: No, I don't mind. What's on your mind?

Clinician: How many times have you had what you'd consider unsafe sex in the past 3 months?

Client: Two or three times.

Clinician: You mentioned that having sex is an outlet for you to not think about the burden of being HIV-positive. So it's been helpful to you in this way. How concerned are you about the fact that you might be infecting others?

Client: I guess it bothers me a little.

Clinician: How important is it to you to change this? To only have sex when you know the other person can't be infected? To wear a condom every time you have sex or to not have sex if you can't get ahold of a condom? On a scale from 1 to 10, 1 being not at all important to 10 being very important?

Client: I'd like to say it's important, but sometimes I just don't care. About a 6.

(Continued)

(Continued)

Clinician: Why so high? Why not lower?

Client: I know I shouldn't be doing it—doing something that puts another person at risk. But if it's late at night and I've been drinking, it doesn't seem so important.

Clinician: When you say you know you're putting someone else at risk and you shouldn't be doing it, it sounds like you're saying that you have ethical or moral feelings about it.

Client: Yeah, I guess I do. I was raised a Catholic, and I think it's wrong to do harm to anyone else. . .

Clinician: If you decided at some point in the future that you wanted to change this—only have safe sex, how confident are you that you would be able to do it? On a scale from 1 to 10, 1 being not at all confident and 10 being very confident?

Client: I'd say about a 3.

Clinician: Why a 3 and not a 2?

Client: Well, I know I can do it sometimes. One time, I was at a party, and I was going to have sex, and I knew the guy pretty well, and I don't think he's positive, and I just decided not to have sex at all. . . . All of a sudden, I told him I wasn't feeling well and I was going home. He was surprised, but it was OK.

TREATMENT GOALS: ABSTINENCE, CONTROLLED USE, AND HARM REDUCTION

Abstinence

Most treatment programs in the United States have operated on a treatment goal of abstinence from all alcohol and drug use, viewing this as the only path to recovery. Some individuals, especially young people, may be treated for misuse of AOD and return to moderate, nonproblem use, but for those who have developed symptoms that meet the criteria for alcohol or drug dependence, practice experience supports the need for abstinence as a treatment goal (Hester & Miller, 1995; Washton & Zweben, 2006).

Controlled Use or Moderation

In recent years, efforts have been made to address the needs of individuals who intend to continue drinking and drug use but want help in controlling their use. Moderation approaches based on cognitive-behavioral therapy methods have been developed and are being used with some limited success (Miller & Munoz, 2005; Miller & Page, 1991). Some clients who work with clinicians to achieve moderation have been successful; for others, the effort to adopt this approach has shown them that moderation is an unrealistic goal.

Harm Reduction

Harm reduction is a term encompassing a variety of approaches designed to reach individuals who might otherwise avoid, refuse, or drop out of treatment because they perceive that expectations are too high (Denning, 2000; Marlatt, 1996; McMaster, 2004). Harm reduction approaches that are community focused include needle exchange programs that distribute clean syringes to injection drug users, designated driver campaigns that ask groups of adolescents who engage in drinking to identify someone in the group who will remain sober enough to be able to drive, and HIV education and condom distribution to sex workers to reduce the spread of HIV. Such programs are primarily designed to address the health of the public (e.g., reduce the spread of AIDS, reduce traffic accidents) rather than stop or reduce substance abuse. Research evidence is excellent for the effectiveness of these programs in accomplishing the goals for which they were designed.

When harm reduction is individually focused, the clinician develops a partnership with the client to help him or her set the treatment goals. For example, a client might agree to try to maintain abstinence from alcohol and other drugs with the exception of marijuana, which the client plans to use regularly. A clinician who agreed to this treatment contract would avoid efforts to change the client's marijuana use but would actively help the client maintain abstinence from the other drugs. If the client were able to achieve stable abstinence from other drugs, the clinician might eventually encourage the client to work on the marijuana use, but the clinician who is effective at implementing a harm reduction approach would halt efforts to address the marijuana use if the client were unresponsive. Principles include working closely with the stated goals of the client rather than pressuring the client to change, valuing small accomplishments (e.g., the client uses drugs in a safe place rather than a shooting gallery or uses clean rather than dirty needles to inject), and assisting clients in making more substantial changes when and if they choose to do so.

Harm reduction is used when clients perceive themselves to be unable to achieve abstinence or feel too defeated to try. It is especially helpful with clients who have multiple diagnoses (e.g., substance abuse, psychiatric problems, HIV-positive) and limited emotional and material resources to deal with them.

A harm reduction approach *keeps open the dialogue* between client and clinician about possible future change. Clients are not forced to commit to change right now, and clinicians are not forced to abandon the possibility that the client may be interested in change in the future.

Although the harm reduction clinician would make no demands for abstinence or behavior change, abstinence is seen as an ideal outcome and long-range goal for clients who can achieve it. It recognizes that some clients will never be able to achieve it, but the work should always be headed in that direction. Clients need *not* be left in their comfort zone at all times.

FRAMEWORKS FOR VIEWING THE TASKS OF TREATMENT

Many theoretical and intervention frameworks—cognitive-behavioral, psychodynamic, family systems, and person-in-environment—have been used to view the treatment of AOD problems. Each has made a valuable contribution to understanding the helping process and has a place in the treatment of AOD problems.

Bean (1984) outlines eight tasks of recovery that incorporate both cognitive and psychodynamic theory and help clinicians focus on abstinence and recovery in a sequenced way. The worker's role is initially educational. Grief work related to loss of alcohol is seen as a necessary step in achieving and maintaining abstinence. Psychotherapy is helpful in achieving long-term recovery, since the addiction process is viewed as one that profoundly changes identity. Understanding alcoholism from three perspectives—medical, psychological, and moral—is seen as essential in the treatment. Workers are encouraged to help clients see the disease aspects of their condition so they will accept medical treatment, the cognitive distortions and self-defeating patterns that have developed so they will accept psychotherapy, and the internalized societal moralism toward alcoholics that they themselves experience so they can begin to forgive themselves for having the condition.

Brown (1985) describes a developmental model of recovery incorporating cognitive, behavioral, psychodynamic, and family systems theory. Like Prochaska and DiClemente (1983) and Bean (1984), Brown's model guides the clinician to work on tasks in a sequenced fashion. The model describes four stages:

1. *Drinking:* When clients come for treatment for other reasons and are unaware of their alcohol or other drug problem

2. *Transition:* When clients experiment with abstinence but have not yet made a commitment to it

3. *Early recovery:* Marked by a commitment to abstinence, a time when acquiring the tools of abstinence is the central issue and cognitive methods and 12-step programs are most essential

4. *Ongoing recovery:* When identity, intimacy, and examining life goals are the central issues and psychotherapy can be most useful

Although the framework explicitly addresses only alcoholism, it is equally applicable to other drug-dependent clients. It is based on a perspective that views alcoholism as having profound emotional consequences for the alcohol-dependent drinker. It reminds the clinician to be aware of the emotional vulnerability of the alcoholic and the elaborate defenses erected to cope with the vulnerability.

Finally, the model demonstrates how to integrate psychotherapy and abstinence work, providing guidance on addressing trauma and responding to increases in environmental stresses. Specific methods for working with denial and other defenses during these stages are described by Amodeo (1995a, 1995b) and Zweben (1995).

Following detoxification from heroin and prescription pain medication, Laura, a 44-year-old White, divorced woman, began treatment to prevent relapse and deal with symptoms of anxiety and panic, which sometimes made it difficult for her to get out of bed in the morning. She worked as an administrative assistant for an advertising agency. There was considerable pressure on the job. She functioned efficiently on the job through her 3-year opiate addiction, but her work began to deteriorate at the point she entered the detoxification program.

The outpatient therapist recommended that Laura attend at least three meetings of AA or Narcotics Anonymous (NA) each week and find a temporary sponsor until she got to know enough people in the program to choose her own permanent sponsor. Therapy sessions were spent practicing cognitive and behavioral techniques for managing anxiety, and Laura often called AA and NA friends for support during an especially stressful workday. Eventually, the worker recommended that Laura be medicated for her panic symptoms, since they continued unabated for some weeks.

Within 6 months, Laura no longer experienced daily anxiety. Within a year, the panic symptoms had diminished almost entirely. She began to consider applying to graduate school. She also began dating Devlin, a man who lived in her apartment building. Therapy focused on Laura's improved self-esteem, her self-image as a woman, and her career goals.

She then became preoccupied with her relationship with Devlin and whether he would make a permanent commitment to her. All discussions returned to this subject. The worker knew that intense emotional involvements could threaten early abstinence.

Although Laura had been drug free for a year, she had periodically experienced impulses to return to drug use. The worker saw Laura as still managing the tasks of early abstinence and was concerned about how Laura would handle rejection. Furthermore, Laura had discovered that drinking was an important activity in Devlin's life. The worker saw Laura as vulnerable to relapse from spending time with someone whose life was organized around drinking. When she alluded to this, Laura dismissed her concern, saying that Devlin would soon give up drinking.

When the worker asked Laura to comment on the risks and satisfactions of her intense level of involvement with Devlin, Laura became furious and defensive, saying that the worker did not trust her judgment and had not observed her progress. The worker then engaged in "hand wringing" (Bean, 1984), a demonstration of worry and concern on the part of the therapist related to the client's physical and emotional safety and ability to engage in self-care. The worker "worried aloud with Laura" about her seeming preoccupation with a partner whose drinking could restimulate her own addiction.

Within a few months, Laura began getting intense headaches, had her doctor prescribe pain medication, and relapsed to using heroin. She struggled to control her use, then tried to taper off and stop. Over a 3-month period, she called frequently to cancel appointments because she was too "dope sick" to come in. The worker offered to arrange detoxification, but Laura declined. Finally, Laura called from a detoxification unit to which she had admitted herself. She was getting "clean" and had decided that, following her detoxification stay, she would go to a recovery home until her abstinence was solid.

In retrospect, the worker could see that she had allowed the therapy to "move too far from the AOD focus" (Brown, 1995) once Laura's anxiety had diminished, and she had had several months of abstinence. Instead, therapy had focused on the feasibility of graduate school, career goals, and identity issues. When Laura became involved with Devlin, the worker realized that she should have responded to this environmental demand by shifting back to the AOD focus. She and Laura should have reexamined the tools Laura would use to maintain abstinence, Laura's definition of high-risk situations at this new juncture in her life, and Laura's backup plan for abstinence if her typical coping methods failed and she found herself thinking about the possibility of using drugs again.

Case Illustration: Home-Based Family Services

Rhonda Miller, MSW, was hired by the State's Child Protective Services Agency to do home-based intervention with multistressed families. The program goal was to prevent out-of-home placement of children living in chaotic and unsafe home environments. The Abbott family was referred following a supported 51-A report alleging neglect due to the children's poor school attendance. The child protective worker told Rhonda that collateral reports suggested that Mrs. Abbott was abusing prescription medications and probably alcohol, and that her husband might be back in the home and physically violent toward her. Four years earlier, due to these same issues, the children had been removed and put in foster care for 3 months.

(Continued)

(Continued)

The children (ages 15, 10, 9, and 7) all had significant learning, behavioral, and emotional problems. Mrs. Abbott cancelled her first visit with Rhonda because she had admitted her 10-year-old son to a psychiatric hospital for smashing windows in the apartment and threatening to kill his 9-year-old sister for breaking his Sony PlayStation. A month and a half later, he was rehospitalized due to death threats toward his mother and siblings. He had not attended school in a month and had been truant intermittently throughout the academic year. He was the identified client for Rhonda's intervention; however, the program believed that effective work could only take place through family treatment and careful coordination with collateral providers.

Mrs. Abbott denied that her husband was back in the household, but Rhonda found out through the 9-year-old daughter that he was back, and that this was a secret that she had been asked to keep. Mrs. Abbott gave conflicting reports about his whereabouts.

Mrs. Abbott had said that Rhonda could help her most by teaching her how to handle the boys. Although Rhonda was most concerned about Mrs. Abbott's substance abuse problem, Mrs. Abbott had denied any use of alcohol or other drugs. Rhonda wanted to join with her by making the therapeutic work relevant to her needs. Although she was dismayed and intimidated by the level of chaos in the household during home visits (e.g., the 7- and 10-year-old boys repeatedly engaged in impulsive and unsafe behaviors), Rhonda decided to focus on a few small goals. Helping Mrs. Abbott arrange for a psychological evaluation for the two boys was one of these goals (the 7-year-old had been diagnosed with ADHD, but the school felt that he might have Asperger's syndrome); helping her set limits on the children was another.

About 4 weeks after the initial home visit, Mrs. Abbott signed releases of information so that treatment could be coordinated with other service providers (mental health clinicians, school staff, doctors, court personnel), a major breakthrough—the mother was beginning to develop trust. (Weeks later, Rhonda facilitated a successful meeting involving many of these collaterals to address the family's complex needs.) During this same visit, the 10-year-old had been flinging various objects around the room, then held a heavy space heater over his 7-year-old brother's head in a threatening manner. Rhonda had been coaching Mrs. Abbott for some time on appropriate ways to set limits on the children. In this situation, Mrs. Abbott was able to intervene with the boys, diffuse the tension, and experience a rare sense of competence in parenting. She was grateful to Rhonda.

Rhonda told Mrs. Abbott that her children were probably especially needy because they had special learning needs, had been away from her for some months in foster care, and might be afraid of losing her again. Furthermore, her husband's behavior toward her may have caused a level of anxiety or fear that they could only express in aggressive behavior. Rhonda pointed out that this would be a very challenging parenting situation even for mothers who were very experienced in setting limits; anyone would have difficulty coping with so many needs.

Rhonda asked how she had tolerated the feeling of not being able to meet everyone's needs at one time, saying that some mothers would escape by tuning out, watching a lot of television, turning over responsibility to the oldest child, or using other methods to gain relief. Feeling supported, Mrs. Abbott acknowledged that she had a few drinks whenever she had a moment to herself and took pills so she could sleep or "just get the racing in my head to stop." Rhonda explained that sometimes the drugs that give us relief can also cause us trouble because we depend on them when we need to cope. She wondered whether this might be so for Mrs. Abbott as the pressures mounted, with the children getting older and harder to handle, her husband being abusive and coming and going in the household, and her fears that she might not be able to salvage the situation (e.g., keep the children out of foster care). Mrs. Abbott acknowledged that this was true in her case, and that she had seen her drinking and pill taking increase. On occasion, she even used cocaine when she could get her hands on it because it helped her feel energetic and get the household straightened out.

Rhonda explored Mrs. Abbott's family history as a way of leading into Mrs. Abbott's own history. She learned that Mrs. Abbott's father had died of cirrhosis of the liver, and that one brother had died in jail from a heroin overdose. Her husband, she stated, was an alcoholic who had been violent and abusive toward her.

Rhonda named a number of treatment methods (e.g., detoxification, AA and NA, outpatient substance abuse counseling, and group approaches) that might help Mrs. Abbott with her escalating drinking and drug problems and said that she believed that Mrs. Abbott's parenting would improve considerably if she could get help with alcohol and other drugs. Mrs. Abbott acknowledged that she was "tormented" by the guilt and shame of losing her children once already as a result of her addiction. She decided to try AA, since she had a friend a few years ago who went regularly and had benefited greatly. Rhonda supported this decision, saying that it would help her take care of herself and set appropriate limits with the children and her husband.

Within 4 months, she was attending regularly, had gotten a sponsor, and had a telephone list of other members she could call when she felt like using again. By 6 months, with Rhonda's help, she had talked to her husband about his own drug taking and told him he needed to go to treatment.

Rhonda continued to implement several service plan recommendations; chief among them was the regular convening of meetings of the collateral providers. Rhonda could see that such a multi-stressed family needed the participation of multiple service systems to maintain stability.

TREATMENT METHODS

In many communities, services to treat AOD problems include detoxification centers, inpatient and outpatient programs, long-term residential settings, and specialized services for high-risk groups such as pregnant and parenting women, individuals with HIV or AIDS, youth, the elderly, and linguistic minorities and clients of color for whom traditional services may have been ineffective. A number of treatment methods are used within these settings, including didactic education about addiction, individual counseling, group therapy, family education and treatment, urine testing, psychotropic medications, exposure to 12-step programs, and relapse prevention training (Doweiko, 2009; Frances et al., 2005; Galanter & Kleber, 1999; Washton & Zweben, 2006). When offering treatment options, workers should consider the gender, age, ethnicity, culture, and sexual orientation of the client. These factors influence the client's ability to respond to typical or mainstream treatment methods, which were often designed for middle-aged, White, heterosexual males.

Drug Abuse Treatment Principles: What Does the Research Evidence Tell Us?

In the past, the AOD field endorsed a narrow range of treatment approaches. In contrast, social work practitioners are now encouraged to consider a range of counseling methods and modalities, choosing the ones that best meet the needs of the AOD client, couple, or family. The National Institute on Drug Abuse (NIDA; 2000) publication, *Principles of Drug Addiction Treatment: A Research-Based Guide*, a valuable guide for practitioners working with AOD clients, provides the scientific evidence for a range of currently accepted treatment approaches. Organized around treatment principles, it discusses issues such as appropriate treatment goals and optimum length of treatment. The importance of medication for AOD and co-occurring psychiatric conditions is stressed. Methadone and similar-acting medications are now the treatment of choice for long-term opiate-addicted individuals. Due to brain changes from long-term opiate use, it is the preferred treatment for many, and as a medication-assisted drug treatment, it is considered akin to abstinence. Research is examining the effectiveness of matching clients to particular treatments before treatment begins. This is likely to be especially useful for groups such as adolescents, older adults, clients with co-occurring psychiatric disorders, criminal justice populations, and the homeless.

Twelve-Step Programs

An increasing amount of research on 12-step programs indicates that consistent and long-term AA attendance leads to positive outcomes. For example, for those using AA as an adjunct to formal treatment, intensive use of AA modestly improves abstinence (Emrick, Tonigan, Montgomery, & Little, 1993; Nowinski, 1999). When AA is used alone, abstinence rates are equal to the abstinence rates for individuals attending formal treatment over the long term (3- to 4-year outcomes). For men, improvement in a range of psychosocial

outcomes (e.g., family, employment, interpersonal relationships) has also been found. Longer and more intensive involvement leads to better outcomes (Tonigan & Hiller-Sturmhofel, 1994). While there is less research on other 12-step programs, there is clinical evidence to suggest that this may be true of Al-Anon and NA as well. What is intensive involvement? Many experts describe ideal participation as including frequent attendance at meetings, speaking at meetings, using the 12 steps for guidance, getting a sponsor, sponsoring others, and finding a "home group" to meet consistently with the same group of members, who can provide feedback and support.

Workers often suggest that clients attend these programs without preparing clients for what they might find when they arrive and without exploring clients' apprehensions about attending. To maximize the success of the referral, workers are advised to read literature on the programs and attend meetings themselves (many are open to the public). This will help workers confront their own stereotypes of the program—the most significant barrier to making an effective referral. The client's ideas and concerns about the type of people who attend, the requirements for membership, the philosophy, and what will be expected of the client at meetings and afterward should be thoroughly explored. Meetings in different locations should be suggested so clients can sample the personality of different groups. If clients reject these programs as an option, a power struggle should be avoided. If clients have difficulty initiating or maintaining abstinence by other means, 12-step programs can be reintroduced later as a resource. The suggestion can be made that clients try again to work on recovery in their own way but agree to attend a specified number of future AA or NA meetings if their method fails.

Family Intervention Approaches

Many alcoholics have extensive marital and family problems. Although there is significant evidence that problem drinking leads to marital and family conflict, it is also likely that marital and family factors play a role in the development and maintenance of alcohol problems (O'Farrell, 1995; O'Farrell & Fals-Stewart, 2006). Family members of alcoholics and addicts develop their own maladaptive patterns to survive, and these include an increased risk for AOD problems themselves, chronic health disorders, depression and anxiety, and difficulties with intimacy (Bepko & Krestan, 1985; Brown, 1995; Dulfano, 1992; Jackson, 1954; Steinglass, 1987).

AOD problems in the family can be viewed from the perspective of the family life cycle, with some types of alcoholic families impaired in their ability to offer a positive legacy to their children (Steinglass, 1987). Interventions for families and couples have also been described in terms of stages, with specific therapist tasks intended for each stage. Usher (1991) presents four stages:

1. *Treatment initiation:* When the alcohol is removed and the family accepts the problem and contracts for change

2. *Learning:* When the family confronts the "emotional desert" of family life

3. *Reorganization:* When ruptures in relationships are repaired and growth and change occur

4. *Consolidation:* When intimacy develops

Bepko and Krestan (1985) and Brown and Lewis (1995) offer different schemata but also use the stages of recovery to guide interventions.

Behavioral interventions focusing on marital interaction have been studied more extensively than family systems and psychodynamic approaches, and they currently have the greatest empirical support. O'Farrell (1995; O'Farrell & Fals-Stewart, 2006) has made major contributions to this area of practice by developing behavioral couples therapy for alcoholics and their significant others. O'Farrell summarizes a number of behavioral interventions within three stages of recovery: (1) the initial commitment to change, (2) the change itself, and (3) the long-term maintenance of change. He warns clinicians of typical obstacles encountered during the initial stage, including alcohol-related crises, the potential for violence between the partners, and the dynamic of blaming. Focusing on the change itself, he reviews methods such as behavioral contracting, structuring the spouse and the alcoholic's role in the recovery process, decreasing family members' behaviors that trigger or enable drinking, and dealing with drinking that occurs during treatment. Among the interventions recommended to improve marital and family relationships are planning shared recreational and leisure activities and homework titled, "Catch Your Partner Doing Something Nice," a technique involving the daily recording of caring behaviors performed by the partner. These methods increase the couple's awareness of benefits from the relationship and increase the frequency with which spouses acknowledge and initiate pleasing or caring behaviors in the relationship. He concludes by pointing out that the most promising marital and family therapy method is a behavioral approach that combines a focus on the drinking and drinking-related interactions with work on more general marital relationship issues.

Use of Evidence-Based Practices (EBPs) in Substance Abuse Treatment

Manuel, Hagedorn, and Finney (2011) examined whether such evidence-based practices (EBPs) were being used by substance abuse treatment programs. They found that EBPs have proliferated in the United States in part because funders (state and federal) have required that treatment programs use them. They note that clients exposed to these interventions (specifically, behavioral couples therapy, cognitive-behavioral therapy, contingency management, motivational enhancement/motivational interviewing, 12-step facilitation, brief interventions for alcohol misuse or alcohol use disorders) had significantly better outcomes at the end of treatment or after follow-up than comparison populations. Organizational factors have played a key role in use of the practices (National Institute on Drug Abuse, 2012), that is, readiness of the organization to adopt the innovative practice, ongoing training to help clinicians integrate the skills, and clinical supervision to provide feedback and mentoring so clinicians can address particularly difficult client situations (Amodeo et al., 2011; Lundgren, Chassler, Amodeo, D'Ippolito, & Sullivan, 2012).

SPECIAL TREATMENT CONSIDERATIONS

The Role of Gender-Specific Treatment

Women often bring special needs to treatment, including intense shame about the addiction, victimization due to sexual or physical violence, co-occurring psychiatric disorders, substance-abusing partners, and efforts to secure drugs that include dealing in and selling sex for drugs (Brady & Randall, 1999; Straussner, 1997). Furthermore, many women have young children, from whom they do not want to be separated during treatment. When women receive services, they encounter service agencies that focus on separate aspects of the problem (e.g., housing, domestic violence, health, mental health, child care, job training, criminal involvement). Women must apply separately for these services and often have separate case managers in each agency, sometimes as many as 5 to 10 separate case managers at the same time. Medical and psychiatric reimbursement mechanisms do not respond to the need to provide "family care" (Brown, 2002), a system that might bring some of these services together, at least for mother and child. Women benefit as much as men when they remain in treatment (Hubbard et al., 1989; Institute of Medicine 1990; Sanchez-Craig, Leigh, Spivak, & Lei, 1989). Because of the dearth of women-only programs, most women are still treated in mixed-gender settings with a male-oriented treatment approach that some authors feel impedes women's ability to benefit fully

(Amaro, Raj, & Reed, 2001; Palacios, Urmann, Newel, & Hamilton, 1999).

Culturally Adapted Evidenced-Based Interventions

There is a growing demand for culturally adapted evidence-based interventions in response to the increasing diversity of the U.S. population. Questions about how and when to make cultural adaptations have also increased with the realization that cultural adaptations may be essential for certain subcultural groups and unnecessary for other subcultural groups (e.g., translation from English to Spanish, or explanation of U.S. holidays, for low-acculturated Latinos vs. high-acculturated Latinos) (Castro, Barrera, & Steiker, 2010; Holleran Steiker, L. K. H., 2008). Thus, cultural adaptations must be planned and organized in a collaborative process with members of the target population, taking into account surface adaptations (e.g., language, food) and deep structural adaptations (e.g., understanding of cultural, historical, environmental, and psychological factors that influence the health and well-being of the target population) (Castro et al., 2010). In cognitive-behavioral therapy (CBT) for Asian American clients (Hwang, 2006), the EBP adapters highlighted several aspects of the therapeutic process that therapists might need to modify due to cultural differences: orienting clients to the therapy, managing the client-therapist relationship, communicating verbally and nonverbally; and addressing specific cultural issues (e.g., shame and stigma, acculturative stress). The cultural competence of the EBP adapters and EBP clinicians is also a key aspect of this work.

Approaches to Posttraumatic Stress Disorder and Substance Abuse Treatment

Many women in addiction treatment have extensive trauma histories, and the substance abuse field is discovering that many men suffer from traumatic histories as well. Individuals who have experienced posttraumatic stress disorder (PTSD) are 4 times more likely to have a diagnosis of substance use disorder than individuals who have not experienced PTSD (Ouimette & Brown, 2002). For many individuals, the traumatic events preceded the substance use disorder, for example, in childhood sexual or physical abuse or witnessing parental violence (Ouimette & Brown, 2002). For others, the traumatic events may have occurred during adolescence or adulthood, for example, serving in active combat, being held up at knifepoint on the street, or crashing a car in which a passenger is killed. Furthermore, in recent years, communities and nations have experienced shared trauma as a consequence of events such as terrorist attacks and natural disasters that have resulted in widespread suffering. A final level of trauma that many substance users experience is related to activities necessary to maintain the addiction. These include interacting with drug dealers, fear of overdose and contracting AIDS and other communicable diseases, periodic arrests and exposure, or confronting the dangers of living on the street.

For at least some individuals, alcohol and other drugs have been a primary coping method and have suppressed the traumatic memories and provided temporary relief from the accompanying symptoms of anxiety, panic, depression, and/or sexual dysfunction (Khantzian & Albanese, 2008). Thus, relapse is likely if the trauma work is done too soon, for example, in the first 3 months of abstinence, without helping clients acquire recovery tools. On the other hand, some clients may relapse if trauma work is avoided. A differential assessment is necessary, and clinical tools and guidelines are still evolving.

Finkelstein and colleagues (2004) recommend that clinicians use *trauma-informed* approaches to substance abuse treatment, including (a) seeing trauma as a defining and organizing experience that can shape the survivor's sense of self and others; (b) necessitating a collaborative relationship between providers and consumers; (c) avoiding practices that may be physically intrusive and potentially retraumatizing, including shame-inducing confrontations; and (d) simultaneously addressing the trauma and substance abuse.

These authors also describe five trauma-specific approaches to intervention that are group models with various levels of evidence for effectiveness: (1) Addictions and Trauma Recovery Integrated Model (ATRIUM; Miller & Guidry, 2001), (2) Helping Women Recover (HWR; Covington, 1999), (3) Seeking Safety (Najavits, 2002), (4) Trauma Recovery Empowerment Model (TREM; Harris, 1998), and (5) TRIAD Women's Group Model (Clark & Fearday, 2003). There is also the Men's Trauma Recovery Empowerment (M-TREM; Harris & Fallot, 2001), adapted specifically for groups of men and integrating the trauma and drug use treatment. Finkelstein and colleagues (2004) encourage clinicians to choose the one that best fits their treatment setting.

Providing guidelines for clinicians working in addiction treatment, Najavits (2006) identifies four highly salient client dilemmas: (1) a tendency for parts of the self to be fragmented (splitting), (2) intense reactivity to trauma-related and substance-use-related situations (triggering), (3) enacting relationships that are too close or too distant (boundaries), and (4) intense feelings of personal failure from which it is difficult to recover (demoralization). The trauma-specific approaches listed above are designed to address these dilemmas. Common elements include educating clients about the interface between substance abuse and trauma, empowering clients to participate actively in their treatment, and teaching stress reduction methods common to cognitive-behavioral therapy, such as thought containment and visualization. These latter methods are especially recommended in early abstinence until clients are emotionally and physically stable (Najavits, 2002, 2004; Najavits, Weiss, & Shaw, 1997, 1999; Rosenthal, Lynch, & Linehan, 2005). A key recommendation is that clinicians not ask clients to engage in lengthy descriptions of the traumatic event(s). Such descriptions should be kept to a minimum in early treatment due to the likelihood of treatment dropout and the lack of specialized trauma training among many clinicians. Processing traumatic memories can cause damage to the client if done poorly (Foa, Keane, & Friedman, 2004).

RELAPSE AND RECOVERY

A *relapse* is a return to use after a period of abstinence and recovery. Relapse is a common problem in AOD treatment, and research has focused more intensely in recent years on determining methods for relapse prevention. In general, AOD-involved clients are considered to be at high risk for relapse during the first year of abstinence.

Specific relapse prevention methods have been identified to assist clients in early and ongoing recovery. Such methods include avoiding high-risk situations, developing a drug-free peer group, identifying personal signs of impending relapse (physical, emotional, and cognitive), and using a predesigned plan to avoid acting on relapse impulses. Relapses can serve as opportunities for learning if clients can be helped to reflect on situations that preceded or seemed to trigger the relapse (Daley, 1987; Gorski & Miller, 1986; Marlatt & Gordon, 1985). Cognitive-behavioral methods have been used widely in relapse prevention and have been shown to increase positive treatment outcomes (Beck, Liese, & Najavits, 2005; Carroll, 2005).

Case Illustration: Marisa Ramirez

Background: Mrs. Marisa Ramirez, 32 years old, came to the United States from the Dominican Republic when she was 5 years old. Her father is from Montserrat Island in the Caribbean, and her mother was born in the Dominican Republic. Her mother was 19 years old when she gave birth to Marisa. Her father did not want the birth and urged her mother to get an abortion. Marisa describes a painful childhood with an alcoholic mother (now in recovery) who was very strict, constantly angry, and verbally abusive. Her father, also an alcoholic, disrespected her mother, sometimes verbally and physically abusing her.

Marisa did well in school, graduating from high school with good grades. She also attended business school for a year to become an executive secretary. She is widowed—her husband died suddenly from a heart attack 5 years ago—and has three children, 6-year-old twin boys and a 9-year-old daughter.

Substance abuse history: She has been in 10 detoxification programs spanning more than 10 years and in four other substance abuse treatment facilities. She has just entered a residential program for Latinas, where she is expected to remain for 6 to 12 months. At times in the past, she has quit drug use for 6 to 18 months at a time, but she has always started again. Her addiction has caused her to lose many jobs. She began smoking and drinking at age 12, using marijuana by age 14, and using cocaine by age 16.

Psychological functioning: Marisa states that she has always felt different; she never felt loved by her family or others. She feels detached from people and cannot trust anyone. She was diagnosed with depression about 4 years ago; her doctor had her see a psychiatrist because she reported always feeling sad. She is currently taking Celexa.

She describes herself as the failure of the family, the "black sheep"—she has several cousins who have good jobs and never had alcohol or drug problems. When Marisa was 12, her hair started falling out. She states that it was her nerves because her mother would always yell and she was very scared of her. Her father was always high and at this time also started sexually abusing her. Her mother found them together on one occasion and then left the house abruptly; when she returned, she acted as if nothing had happened. The father's behavior continued.

Residential treatment: On entering the program 2 months ago, Marisa was withdrawn and reluctant to participate, even with support and urging from staff. She stated that she wanted to leave the program and was anxious about what the treatment would involve.

Her mother is currently taking care of the children. Mother stated that she does not want to participate in her daughter's treatment, and this made Marisa very sad. Mother also told staff that she is getting tired of handling her daughter's responsibilities and sees her daughter as irresponsible.

Treatment Approach

The history of sexual and physical abuse and the repeated relapses raise the question of whether Marisa suffers from PTSD. The worker will assess for specific *DSM-IV-TR* (American Psychiatric Association, 2000) PTSD symptoms.

Marisa's drinking and drug use began around the age of 12; this coincides with the sexual abuse by her father and what Marisa describes as her hair falling out. To understand the level of trauma Marisa may have experienced, the worker will ask Marisa about the specific chronology of these events, speculating that the trauma of molestation, which could not be discussed in the family and was not stopped by the mother, resulted in the child's profound and visible physical reaction.

Past substance abuse treatment seems to have been somewhat effective in that Marisa maintained abstinence for substantial periods of time. However, the repeated relapses suggest that trauma symptoms may have resurfaced during these periods and that Marisa reverted to using alcohol and other drugs for their numbing effects. A key part of treatment planning must be to address the trauma if a PTSD diagnosis is verified.

Treatment should focus on the impact on Marisa's current functioning rather than on the traumatic events themselves. Focusing on the traumatic events may cause Marisa to further isolate herself from other people and may intensify her low self-esteem, since she does not yet have an array of coping methods to use to deal with these memories.

Teaching Marisa grounding exercises is important so that when she feels herself beginning to dissociate, she can engage in a visualization (picturing herself in a quiet, safe place) or thought-stopping exercise (picturing her children's faces as a substitute for other thoughts).

(Continued)

(Continued)

Acknowledging the impact of the mother's silence and lack of protection would be another important aspect of treatment. Eventually, while Marisa is still in residential treatment, it may be helpful for the worker to have a family meeting between Marisa and her mother during which Marisa can talk about the effects of her mother's silence on her. Such a meeting would need to be carefully rehearsed with Marisa so that she could convey this message without being aggressive toward her mother or alienating her.

Referring Marisa to a trauma group for substance-abusing women, where she could talk with others who have had this experience, would also be key to her recovery.

Case Illustration: Myra

Myra is a 32-year-old Latina diagnosed as cocaine dependent. The drug problem was identified by a protective-service worker responding to a report of neglect related to Myra's 3-year-old daughter, Angelina. The worker referred Myra to an inpatient program. The program, reluctant to accept cocaine-dependent clients unless they had first tried less costly outpatient treatment, accepted Myra because her repeated efforts to quit on her own had been unsuccessful, her apartment building was a mecca for drug deals, and the worker advocated strongly for this service plan. Angelina was placed in foster care.

As a condition for Angelina's return, Myra was mandated to attend outpatient counseling and undergo regular urine screening following discharge. Myra developed a positive relationship with the clinician assigned to her and attended sessions regularly. Myra relapsed several times during her initial months in treatment. Urine screens were helpful in alerting the worker to these relapses, but the worker asked Myra to agree to tell the worker about relapses prior to receipt of the urine test results. This strengthened the therapeutic alliance and kept the worker out of the watchdog role.

After several months of "dirty" urines, Myra established 8 months of abstinence. She received badly needed dental care, moved to a safer neighborhood, and began to plan for Angelina's return to live with her. Then Myra's mother died unexpectedly, and the foster family alerted Myra that they suspected that Angelina had been sexually abused by a teenager in their neighborhood. Myra's feelings of loss, guilt, and anger about both incidents precipitated a relapse. The worker increased her sessions with Myra to twice per week and referred Myra to a local addictions program for daily acupuncture treatments designed to help clients avoid relapse. Nevertheless, Myra continued to relapse about every 5 weeks.

In a case review, a program administrator raised the question of whether Myra should continue in the program, since she had established little abstinence. The worker was adamant that Myra should remain in the program if she chose, since she had made considerable progress in treatment. She had come regularly to sessions, visited regularly with Angelina and managed the visits in a healthy way, established 8 months of continuous abstinence in slightly more than 18 months, notified the worker when relapses occurred, and examined precipitants and ways to avoid them in the future. She had also completed long-needed dental care, moved to a safer neighborhood, and used more frequent counseling sessions and acupuncture when they were offered.

While the worker saw abstinence as a crucial measure of recovery, she emphasized that it should not be seen as the sole measure of progress in someone such as Myra, for whom drug dependence had been a way of life.

Eventually, the worker decided to recommend that Myra enter a substance abuse day treatment program where she would be involved in relapse prevention activities for several hours every day. If Myra resisted, the worker would point out that the current treatment plan seemed to offer insufficient support. Myra could recommend methods she thought would be better—for example, daily AA or NA meetings or getting on a waiting list for a long-term residential program—but some change seemed necessary to reduce the frequency of relapse. Myra's safety was the agency's primary concern, and with such frequent relapses, she was not physically or emotionally safe.

Recovery is a developmental process occurring over time and involving certain biopsychosocial benchmarks. Personnel in the addictions field often use the terms *recovering alcoholic* or *recovering addict* to describe individuals in recovery. The term *recovering* emphasizes that although individuals have made a commitment to abstinence and have demonstrated an ability to move in that direction, they continue to be vulnerable to relapse. Since the work of recovery is viewed as never fully done, the past tense of the word, *recovered*, is carefully avoided.

Recovery is also seen by many as involving necessary life changes above and beyond abstinence: repairing relationships damaged through years of drinking and drug use, dealing with shame and self-hatred, addressing experiences of early trauma, and giving up patterns acquired during addiction, including the "addict mentality" and a personality of secretiveness, manipulation, and self-absorption.

Effective Technology-Based Tools

The substance abuse field needs more effective recovery-oriented ways to provide ongoing support to clients following treatment. An emerging trend is the use of mobile technology-based tools (e.g., cell phone applications, text messages) to help clients maintain social support and engage in self-care (Gustafson et al., 2011). Marcsh (2011) views these tools as "clinician extenders" because they reach beyond geographic boundaries and can accompany clients wherever they go. These tools have been used for assessment, intervention, and research purposes. For example, a treatment program may send an automatic daily text to clients at the time of day when the clients feel most vulnerable to relapse, asking them what coping methods they are currently using. Upon the client's request, the treatment program may generate a list of alternative coping methods clients could employ at that time (Bickel, Christensen, & Marsch, 2011).

Federal Initiatives to Improve Substance Abuse Treatment

Several relatively recent national policies are designed to improve care for substance use disorders (Humphreys, McLellan, & Thomas, 2010). These include President Obama's National Drug Control Strategy and budget emphasizing routine screening, brief intervention and referral to treatment (SBIRT) for alcohol and drug-troubled individuals, greater integration of substance abuse treatment into community health centers, more funds for prisoner reentry programs and drug courts, and the creation of a quality-treatment initiative where organizations are reimbursed based on positive patient outcomes (Humphreys et al., 2010).

CHALLENGES FOR THE PROFESSION

Two particular challenges face social work in this decade and beyond. The medical profession has taken the leadership in spearheading a movement toward prevention and early intervention. Social workers will need to catch up by acquiring the SBIRT skills necessary to identify and motivate a range of more intact clients—not only those diagnosed with AOD abuse or dependence but also those whose hazardous or harmful use could lead to physical, psychological, or social problems. Such prevention and early-intervention work is changing the face of substance abuse treatment so that clients and families can be helped at a point when they are more functional. These screening and brief-intervention methods are now being reimbursed by health insurance, but many social service settings and social workers are untrained in these methods.

Another significant challenge will be finding better ways to integrate research-based practices such as cognitive-behavioral therapy, behavioral couples therapy, dialectical behavioral therapy, contingency management, medication-assisted treatment, and trauma interventions, along with ensuring that the methods are applied with fidelity and that they are culturally adapted to fit the target populations for whom they are intended. Many social workers are trying to learn about these evidence-based approaches so they can decide how to apply them judiciously, but certain barriers prevail. Some workers believe that these are simply cookbook approaches to therapy and that clinical wisdom should prevail. Other workers believe that research evidence on treatment effectiveness should guide practice but they are not in settings that have access to databases that would allow them to research best practices or review high-quality research evidence. Finally, it is not yet common practice for social workers to engage in an evidence-based practice process in which the worker combines knowledge of the best evidence for a particular client system with clinical wisdom, then educates the client about the possible interventions and involves the client in decision making about what approach would best meet the client's needs. It is hoped that this type of process will help integrate research evidence, practice-based wisdom, and the client's perspective for more informed clinical decision making across the social work field.

REFERENCES

Amaro, H., Raj, A., & Reed, E. (2001). Women's sexual health: The need for feminist analyses in public health in the decade of behavior. *Psychology of Women Quarterly, 25*(4), 324–334.

American Psychiatric Association. (2000). *Diagnostic and statistical manual of mental disorders* (4th ed., text rev.). Washington, DC: Author.

Amil, A., Gómez, M., Fernández, D. M., Bangdiwala, S. I., Ríos, E., & Hunter, R. F. (2004). Changing profiles of injecting drug users with AIDS in a Hispanic population. *Society for the Study of Addiction, 99,* 1147–1156.

Amodeo, M. (1995a). The therapist's role in the drinking stage. In S. Brown (Ed.), *Treating alcoholism* (pp. 95–132). San Francisco, CA: Jossey-Bass.

Amodeo, M. (1995b). The therapist's role in the transitional stage. In S. Brown (Ed.), *Treating alcoholism* (pp. 133–162). San Francisco, CA: Jossey-Bass.

Amodeo, M., & Drouilhet, A. (1992). Substance-abusing adolescents. In J. R. Brandell (Ed.), *Countertransference in psychotherapy with children and adolescents* (pp. 285–314). Northvale, NJ: Jason Aronson.

Amodeo, M., & Jones, L. K. (1997). Viewing alcohol and other drug use cross-culturally: A cultural framework for clinical practice. *Families in Society, 78*(3), 240–254.

Amodeo, M., Lundgren, L., Cohen, A., Rose, D., Chassler, D., Beltrame, C., & D'Ippolito, M. (2011). Barriers to implementing evidence-based practices in addiction treatment: Comparing staff reports on Motivational Interviewing, Adolescent Community Reinforcement Approach, Assertive Community Treatment, and Cognitive-Behavioral Therapy. *Evaluation and Program Planning, 34,* 382–389.

Amodeo, M., Robb, N., Peou, S., & Tran, H. (1996). Adapting mainstream substance abuse interventions for Southeast Asian clients. *Families in Society, 77*(7), 403–412.

Babor, T. F., & Grant, M. (Eds.). (1992). *Project on identification and management of alcohol-related problems. Report of Phase II: A randomized clinical trial of brief interventions in primary health care.* Geneva, Switzerland: World Health Organization, Programme on Substance Abuse.

Bean, M. (1984). Clinical implications of models for recovery from alcoholism. *Addictive Behaviors, 3,* 91–104.

Beck, J. S., Liese, B. S., & Najavits, L. M. (2005). Cognitive therapy. In R. J. Frances, S. I. Miller, & A. H. Mack (Eds.), *Clinical textbook of addictive disorders* (3rd ed., pp. 474–501). New York, NY: Guilford Press.

Bepko, C., & Krestan, J. A. (1985). *The responsibility trap.* New York, NY: Free Press.

Bickel, W. K., Christensen, D. R., & Marsch (2011). A review of computer-based interventions used in the assessment, treatment, and research of drug addiction. *Substance Use and Misuse, 46*(1), 4–9.

Brady, K. T., & Randall, C. L. (1999). Gender differences in substance use disorders. *Psychiatric Clinics of North America, 22,* 241–252.

Brown, S. (1985). *Treating the alcoholic: A developmental model of recovery.* New York, NY: Wiley.

Brown, S. (Ed.). (1995). *Treating alcoholism.* San Francisco, CA: Jossey-Bass.

Brown, S. (2002). Women and addiction: Expanding theoretical points of view. In S. L. A. Straussner & S. Brown (Eds.), *The handbook of addiction treatment for women: Theory and practice* (pp. 26–50). San Francisco, CA: Jossey-Bass.

Brown, S., & Lewis, V. (1995). The alcoholic family: A developmental model of recovery. In S. Brown (Ed.), *Treating alcoholism* (pp. 279–315). San Francisco, CA: Jossey-Bass.

Carroll, K. M. (2005). Matching and differential therapies: Providing substance abusers with appropriate treatment. In R. J. Frances, S. I. Miller, & A. H. Mack (Eds.), *Clinical textbook of addictive disorders* (3rd ed., pp. 637–664). New York, NY: Guilford Press.

Caslyn, R. J., & Morse, G. A. (1991). Correlates of problem drinking among homeless men. *Hospital and Community Psychiatry, 42,* 721–724.

Castro, F. G., Barrera, M., & Steiker, L. K. H. (2010). Issues and challenges in the design of culturally adapted evidence-based interventions. *Annual Review of Clinical Psychology, 6,* 213–239.

Clark, C., & Fearday, F. (Eds.). (2003). *Triad women's project: Group facilitator's manual.* Tampa: Louis de la Parte Florida Mental Health Institute, University of South Florida.

Cornish, J. L., Lontos, J. M., Clemens, K. J., & McGregor, I. S. (2005). Cocaine and heroin ("speedball") self-administration: The involvement of nucleus accumbens dopamine and d-opiate, but notδopiate receptors. *Psychopharmacology, 180*(1), 21–32.

Covington, S. S. (1999). *Helping women recover: A program for treating addiction.* San Francisco, CA: Jossey-Bass.

Daley, D. (1987). Relapse prevention with substance abusers: Clinical issues and myths. *Social Work, 32*(2), 138–142.

Delgado, M. (1994). Hispanic natural support systems and the AOD field: A developmental framework for collaboration. *Journal of Multicultural Social Work, 3*(2), 11–37.

Delgado, M. (1995). Natural support systems and AOD services: Challenges and rewards for practice. *Alcoholism Treatment Quarterly, 12*(1), 17–31.

Denning, P. (2000). *Practicing harm reduction psychotherapy: An alternative approach to addictions.* New York, NY: Guilford Press.

DiClemente, C. C. (1991). Motivational interviewing and the stages of change. In W. R. Miller & S. Rollnick (Eds.), *Motivational interviewing* (pp. 191–202). New York, NY: Guilford Press.

D'Onofrio, G., & Degutis, L. C. (2004). Screening and brief intervention in the emergency department. *Alcohol Research and Health, 28*(2), 63–72.

Doweiko, H. (2009). *Concepts of chemical dependency* (7th ed.). Belmont, CA: Brooks/Cole.

Dulfano, C. (1992). *Families, alcoholism, and recovery.* San Francisco, CA: Jossey-Bass.

Emrick, C. D., Tonigan, J. S., Montgomery, H., & Little, L. (1993). Alcoholics Anonymous: What is currently known? In B. S. McCready & W. R. Miller (Eds.), *Research on Alcoholics Anonymous: Opportunities and alternatives* (pp. 41–76). New Brunswick, NJ: Rutgers University Press.

Fingarette, H. (1988). *Heavy drinking: The myth of alcoholism as a disease.* Berkeley: University of California Press.

Finkelstein, N., VandeMark, N., Fallot, R., Brown, V., Cadiz, S., & Heckman, J. (2004). *Enhancing substance abuse recovery through integrated trauma treatment.* Washington, DC: U.S. Department of Health and Human Services (DHHS), Center for Substance Abuse Treatment, Substance Abuse and Mental Health Services Administration (SAMHSA).

Foa, E. B., Keane, T. M., & Friedman, M. J. (2004). *Effective treatments for PTSD: Practice guidelines from the International Society for Traumatic Stress Studies.* New York, NY: Guilford Press.

Frances, R. J., Miller, S. I., & Mack, A. H. (Eds.). (2005). *Clinical textbook of addictive disorders* (3rd ed.). New York, NY: Guilford Press.

Freeman, E. M., & Landesman, T. (1992). Differential diagnosis and the least restrictive treatment. In E. Freeman (Ed.), *The addiction process: Effective social work approaches* (pp. 27–42). New York, NY: Longman.

Freiberg, M. S., & Samet, J. H. (2005). Alcohol and coronary heart disease: The answer awaits a randomized controlled trial. *Circulation, 112,* 1379–1380.

Freshman, A. (2004). Assessment and treatment of adolescent substance abusers. In S. L. A. Straussner (Ed.), *Clinical work with substance-abusing clients* (2nd ed., pp. 305–331). New York, NY: Guilford Press.

Galanter, M., & Kleber, H. D. (1999). *Textbook of substance abuse treatment* (2nd ed.). Washington, DC: American Psychiatric Press.

Gold, M. S., & Jacobs, W. S. (2005). Cocaine and crack: Clinical aspects. In J. H. Lowinson, P. Ruiz, R. B. Millman, & J. G. Langrod (Eds.), *Substance abuse: A comprehensive textbook* (4th ed., pp. 218–251). New York, NY: Lippincott, Williams & Wilkins.

Goodman, A. C., Hankin, J. R., & Nishiura, E. (1997). Drug abuse treatment costs: An interpretive essay. In J. A. Egertson, D. M. Fox, & A. I. Leshner (Eds.), *Treating drug abusers effectively* (pp. 159–186). Malden, MA: Blackwell.

Gorski, T., & Miller, H. (1986). *Staying sober: A guide for relapse prevention.* Independence, MO: Independence Press.

Gustafson, D. H., Shaw, B. R., Isham, A., Baker, T., Boyle, M. G., & Levy, M. (2011). Explicating an evidence-based, theoretically informed, mobile-technology-based system to improve outcomes for people in recovery for alcohol dependence. *Substance Use & Misuse, 46*(1), 96–111.

Harris, M. (1998). *Trauma recovery and empowerment: A clinician's guide for working with women in groups.* New York, NY: Free Press.

Harris, M., & Fallot, R. D. (Eds.). (2001). *Using trauma theory to design service systems: New directions for mental health services series.* San Francisco, CA: Jossey-Bass.

Hester, R. K., & Miller, W. R. (1995). *Handbook of alcoholism treatment approaches: Effective alternatives.* Boston, MA: Allyn & Bacon.

Hilton, B. A., Thompson, R., Moore-Dempsey, L., & Janzen, R. G. (2001). Harm reduction theories and strategies for control of human immunodeficiency virus: A review of the literature. *Journal of Advanced Nursing, 33*(3), 357–370.

Holleran Steiker, L. K. H. (2008). Making drug and alcohol prevention relevant: Adapting evidence-based curricula to unique adolescent cultures. *Family and Community Health* 31(1S), S52–60.

Horgan, C. (1997). Need and access to drug abuse treatment. In J. A. Egertson, D. M. Fox, & A. I. Leshner (Eds.), *Treating drug abusers effectively* (pp. 75–97). Malden, MA: Blackwell.

Hubbard, R. L., Marsden, M. E., Rachal, J. V., Harwood, H. J., Cavanaugh, E. R., & Ginzburg, H. M. (1989). *Drug abuse treatment: A national study of effectiveness.* Chapel Hill: University of North Carolina Press.

Humphreys, K., McLellan, & Thomas, M. A. (2010). Brief intervention, treatment, and recovery support services for Americans who have substance use disorders: An overview of policy in the Obama administration. *Psychological Services, 7*(4), 275–284.

Hwang, W. (2006). The psychotherapy adaptation and modification framework: Application to Asian Americans. *American Psychologist, 61,* 702–715.

Institute of Medicine. (1990). *Broadening the base for alcohol problems.* Washington, DC: National Academies Press.

Jackson, J. K. (1954). The adjustment of the family to the crisis of alcoholism. *Quarterly Journal of Studies on Alcohol, 15*(4), 562–586.

Jellinek, E. M. (1960). *The disease concept of alcoholism.* New Haven, CT: College & University Press.

Kail, B. L. (1992). Recreational or casual drug use: Opportunities for primary prevention. In E. M. Freeman (Ed.), *The addiction process: Effective social work approaches* (pp. 96–407). New York, NY: Longman.

Karageorge, K. (2002). Identification of clients with co-occurring disorders in the substance abuse and mental health treatment systems. *NEDS Fact Sheet 148.* Retrieved January 14, 2005, from www.icpsr.umich.edu/SAMHDA/NTIES/ NTIES-PDF/SHEETS/ 148_identification.pdf

Khantzian, E. J., & Albanese, M. J. (2008). *Understanding addiction as self-medication: Finding hope behind the pain.* Lanham, MD: Rowman & Littlefield.

Liftik, J. (1995). Assessment. In S. Brown (Ed.), *Treating alcoholism* (pp. 57–94). San Francisco, CA: Jossey-Bass.

Lum, D. (1996). *Social work practice and people of color: A process-stage approach* (3rd ed.). Pacific Grove, CA: Thompson Brooks/Cole.

Lundgren, L., Chassler, D., Amodeo, M., D'Ippolito, M., & Sullivan, L. (2012). Barriers to implementation of evidence-based addiction treatment: A national study. *Journal of Substance Abuse Treatment, 42*(3), 231–238.

Maisto, S. A., Galizio, M., & Connors, G. J. (1991). *Drug use and misuse.* Fort Worth, TX: Holt, Rinehart & Winston.

Manuel, J. K, Hagedorn, H. J., Finney, J. W. (2011). Implementing evidence-based psychosocial treatment in specialty substance use disorder care. *Psychology of Addictive Behaviors, 25*(2), 225–237.

Marlatt, G. A. (1996). *Harm reduction: Pragmatic strategies for managing high-risk behaviors.* New York, NY: Guilford Press.

Marlatt, G. A., & Gordon, J. R. (1985). *Relapse prevention: Maintenance strategies in the treatment of addictive behaviors.* New York, NY: Guilford Press.

Marsch, L.A. (2011). Technology-based interventions targeting substance use disorders and related issues: An editorial. *Substance Use and Misuse, 46*(1), 1–3.

McCarty, D., Argeriou, M., Huebner, R. B., & Lubran, B. (1991). Alcoholism, drug abuse, and the homeless. *American Psychologist, 46,* 1139–1148.

McMaster, S. A. (2004). Harm reduction: A new perspective on substance abuse services. *Social Work, 49*(3), 356–363.

McNeece, C. A., & DiNitto, D. M. (1994). *Chemical dependency: A systems approach.* Englewood Cliffs, NJ: Prentice Hall.

Miller, D., & Guidry, L. (2001). *Addictions and trauma recovery: Healing the body, mind and spirit.* New York, NY: W. W. Norton.

Miller, N. S. (2004). Prescription opiate medications: Medical uses and consequences, laws and controls. *Psychiatric Clinics of North America, 27,* 689–708.

Miller, T. W., Leukefeld, C., & Jefferson, B. (1994). Dual diagnosis: Clinical issues in substance abuse treatment. *Journal of Contemporary Psychotherapy, 24*(3), 169–178.

Miller, T. W., Leukefeld, C., & Jefferson, B. (1996). Dual diagnosis: Clinical issues in the treatment of substance abuse, and affective, personality, and psychotic disorders *Journal of Contemporary Psychotherapy, 26*(1), 73–82.

Miller, W. R., & Munoz, R. F. (2005). *Controlling your drinking: Tools to make moderation work for you.* New York, NY: Guilford Press.

Miller, W. R., & Page, A. C. (1991). Warm turkey: Other routes to abstinence. *Journal of Substance Abuse Treatment, 8,* 227–232.

Miller, W. R., & Rollnick, S. (1991). *Motivational interviewing: Preparing people to change addictive behavior.* New York, NY: Guilford Press.

Miller, W. R., & Rollnick, S. (2002). *Motivational interviewing: Preparing people for change.* New York, NY: Guilford Press.

Nace, E. (1995). The dual diagnosis patient. In S. Brown (Ed.), *Treating alcoholism* (pp. 163–196). San Francisco, CA: Jossey-Bass.

Najavits, L. M. (2002). *Seeking safety: A treatment manual for PTSD and substance abuse.* New York, NY: Guilford Press.

Najavits, L. M. (2004). Implementing seeking safety therapy for PTSD and substance abuse: Clinical guidelines. *Alcoholism Treatment Quarterly, 22,* 43–62.

Najavits, L. M. (2006). Managing trauma reactions in intensive addiction treatment environments. *Journal of Chemical Dependency Treatment, 8,* 153–161.

Najavits, L. M., Weiss, R. D., & Shaw, S. R. (1997). The link between substance abuse and posttraumatic stress disorder in women: A research review. *American Journal on Addictions, 6,* 273–283.

Najavits, L. M., Weiss, R. D., & Shaw, S. R. (1999). Clinical profile of women with posttraumatic stress disorder and substance dependence. *Psychology of Addictive Behaviors, 13*(2), 98–104.

National Institute on Drug Abuse. (2000). *Principles of drug addiction treatment: A research-based guide.* Washington, DC: National Institutes of Health, National Institute on Drug Abuse.

National Institute on Drug Abuse. (2012). *Report of the Adoption of NIDA's Evidence-based Treatments in Real World Settings Workgroup.* National Advisory Council on Drug Abuse.

Washington, DC: National Institutes of Health, National Institute on Drug Abuse.

Nowinski, J. (1999). Self-help groups for addictions. In B. S. McCready & E. E. Epstein (Eds.), *Addictions: A comprehensive guidebook* (pp. 328–346). New York, NY: Oxford University Press.

O'Farrell, T. J. (1995). Marital and family therapy. In R. K. Hester & W. R. Miller (Eds.), *Handbook of alcoholism treatment approaches: Effective alternatives* (2nd ed., pp. 160–175). Boston, MA: Allyn & Bacon.

O'Farrell, T. J., & Fals-Stewart, W. (2006). *Behavioral couples therapy for alcoholism and drug abuse.* New York, NY: Guilford Press.

Orlandi, M. A., Weston, R., & Epstein, L. G. (Eds.). (1992). *Cultural competence for evaluators: A guide for alcohol and other drug abuse prevention practitioners working with ethnic/racial communities.* Rockville, MD: U.S. Department of Health and Human Services, Alcohol, Drug Abuse and Mental Health Administration, Office for Substance Abuse Prevention, Division of Community Prevention and Training.

Orlin, L., & Davis, J. (1993). Assessment and intervention with drug and alcohol abusers in psychiatric settings. In S. L. A. Straussner (Ed.), *Clinical work with substance-abusing clients* (pp. 50–68). New York, NY: Guilford Press.

Ouimette, P., & Brown, P. J. (Eds.). (2002). *Trauma and substance abuse: Causes, consequences, and treatment of co-morbid disorders.* Washington, DC: American Psychological Association.

Ouimette, P. C., Gima, K., Moos, R. H., & Finney, J. W. (1999). A comparative evaluation of substance abuse treatment IV: The effect of co-morbid psychiatric diagnoses on amount of treatment, continuing care, and 1-year outcomes. *Alcoholism: Clinical and Experimental Research, 23,* 552–557.

Palacios, W., Urmann, C., Newel, R., & Hamilton, N. (1999). Developing a sociological framework for dually diagnosed women. *Journal of Substance Abuse Treatment, 17*(1–2), 91–102.

Pattison, E. M., & Kaufman, E. (1982). The alcoholism syndrome: Definitions and models. In E. M. Pattison & E. Kaufman (Eds.), *Encyclopedic handbook of alcoholism* (pp. 3–26). New York, NY: Gardner Press.

Peele, S. (1989). *Diseasing of America.* Lexington, MA: Heath.

Prochaska, J. O., & DiClemente, C. C. (1983). Stages and processes of self change of smoking: Toward an integrative model of change. *Journal of Consulting and Clinical Psychology, 51,* 390–395.

Rosenthal, M. Z., Lynch, T. R., & Linehan, M. M. (2005). Dialectical behavior therapy for individuals with borderline personality disorder and substance use disorders. In R. J. Frances, S. I. Miller, & A. H. Mack (Eds.), *Clinical textbook of addictive disorders* (3rd ed., pp. 615–636). New York, NY: Guilford Press.

Sanchez-Craig, M., Leigh, G., Spivak, K., & Lei, H. (1989). Superior outcome of females over males after brief treatment for the reduction of heavy drinking. *British Journal of Addiction, 84,* 395–404.

Steinglass, P. (1987). *The alcoholic family.* New York, NY: Basic Books.

Straussner, S. L. A. (1997). Gender and substance abuse. In S. L. A. Straussner & E. Zelvin (Eds.), *Gender and addictions: Men and women in treatment* (pp. 3–27). Northvale, NJ: Aronson.

Straussner, S. L. A. (Ed.). (2001). *Ethnocultural factors in substance abuse treatment.* New York, NY: Guilford Press.

Substance Abuse and Mental Health Services Administration (SAMHSA). (2006). *National survey on drug use and health.* Retrieved October 13, 2009, from www.oas.samhsa.gov/NSDUH/2k6NS DUH/ tabs/TOC.htm

Tonigan, J. S., & Hiller-Sturmhofel, S. (1994). Alcoholics Anonymous: Who benefits? *Alcohol Health and Research World, 18*(4), 308–309.

Usher, M. L. (1991). From identification to consolidation: A treatment model for couples and families complicated by alcoholism. *Family Dynamics of Addictions Quarterly, 1*(2), 45–58.

Vaillant, G. (1983). *The natural history of alcoholism.* Cambridge, MA: Harvard University Press.

Vaillant, G. (1990). We should retain the disease concept of alcoholism. *Harvard Medical School Mental Health Letter, 9*(6), 4–6.

van Wormer, K. (1995). *Alcoholism treatment: A social work perspective.* Chicago, IL: Nelson-Hall.

Wallace, J. (1989). A biopsychosocial model of alcoholism. *Social Casework, 70,* 325–332.

Washton, A. M., & Zweben, J. E. (2006). *Treating alcohol and drug problems in psychotherapy practice: Doing what works.* New York, NY: Guilford Press.

Zweben, J. E. (1995). The therapist's role in early and ongoing recovery. In S. Brown (Ed.), *Treating alcoholism* (pp. 197–229). San Francisco, CA: Jossey-Bass.

16

LOSS AND MOURNING

A Life Cycle Perspective

MARGARET O'KANE BRUNHOFER

Loss and mourning are universal human experiences, integral to the human condition. Movement through the life cycle naturally involves substantial change and separation, loss of what was and adaptation to what is. Individuals and families are continually confronted with new life experiences, developmental tasks, and life cycle alterations that require adjustment to loss. Sometimes the loss is through death or loss of health, while other losses involve change in role, status, or life circumstance. All transitions over the life cycle pose some degree of loss, either real or symbolic. Children lose the illusions of childhood as they develop and grow into adolescence. Young adults lose the security of their family of origin as they move toward increased reliance on themselves. Young couples experiencing parenthood lose the personal freedom they enjoyed during their single years. Midlife adults lose the family unit, as they once knew it, as their children grow and leave the family home. Later-life adults lose their mate, their occupational role, and ultimately their health. Indeed, the longer we live, the greater the number of losses we sustain and the more we must mourn.

We are not usually aware of the loss and mourning dynamics associated with life transitions. Typically, we conceive of loss and mourning as reactions to death, a taboo subject in U.S. society. Neimeyer (1988) used the term *death anxiety* to describe the typical reactions to the issues of death and dying in our society. He suggests that death anxiety is the fear of one's own death and of others', and that this anxiety inhibits our ability to cope with the final phase of life. Kamerman (1988) noted our characteristic responses to death as indexes of death anxiety. In our culture, we seclude the dying, allowing most of them to die in hospitals, away from family and friends. We employ professionals, funeral directors, to make the corpse appear lifelike. Our death rituals commence immediately, so we can dispose of the body quickly. If we talk about death, we typically use euphemisms, saying one has "passed away" or "gone to a better place." This allows us to avoid the reality of death. Recent examples are drive-through visitation and long-distance disposal of cremated remains sent by crematoriums via postal delivery to surviving loved ones.

We frequently deny the dying person the opportunity to acknowledge the awareness of his

465

or her own death. We also avoid discussion of the person's reactions to the dying process. As for those left behind, the bereaved, we discourage the outward expression of their emotion and equate a good reaction to the loss as a composed, stoic one. The mourner is expected to manage a brief transition period between the death ritual and daily routine. Finally, the mourner is not expected to dwell on the death or to mention the loss.

Individuals and families must confront loss and mourning experiences within a death-denying ecological context. Since we have difficulty acknowledging loss through death, other types of losses are often not acknowledged. Without recognition of their loss enabling them to resolve and adapt to loss, mourners may have significant difficulty grieving and resolving their loss.

Mourning, the period following loss, is characterized by varying degrees of painful grieving and a range of intense emotions: feelings of shock, panic, anxiety, sadness, and anger, among others. Working through these feelings is the task of the mourning process. The mourner must accept and resolve the loss and adapt to a changed life.

Social workers invariably work with clients coping with loss. Some losses are identified by clients, while others are unarticulated and unresolved. Goldsworthy (2005) suggests that the identification of grief and loss issues is a central and basic competency for social workers since all loss experiences influence the psychosocial functioning of the individual and the family. For effective practice, social workers need to recognize the myriad losses clients experience across the life cycle and the consequent grief reactions. Practitioners also need to understand the characteristics of the mourning process and methods for facilitating the grief reactions of individuals and families.

ATTACHMENT AND LOSS

The Concept of Attachment

Attachment theory provides a useful framework for understanding the concept of loss and life span development (Sable, 2008). Bowlby (1980), a British psychiatrist and psychoanalyst, is well-known for his research and writings on attachment theory. Bowlby studied human separation and loss and developed a theory of attachment. He believed that attachment resulted from our human need for safety and security, both required to support our physical and psychological development, and social and emotional well-being. Bowlby noted the enduring affectional bonds associated with significant relationships. Motivation to maintain proximity to those who show concern for us is characteristic of these "affectional relations." When the attachments are threatened or lost, intense feelings of distress result. Bowlby (1973) identified universal responses to the loss or disruption of the focus of our attachment. Anger, protest, despair, and anxiety are the emotions typically associated with separation. One must reorganize one's life, strengthened by "an abiding sense of the lost person's continuing and benevolent presence" (Bowlby, 1980, p. 243). Detachment from one's attachment figure is no longer viewed as a goal of mourning. Rather, grievers experience a continuing sense of the deceased's presence. Acceptance and adaptation to a loss can occur once the individual is able to modify his or her internal world, concede that the external world has changed, and develop a continuing bond with the deceased while investing affectional energy with others in the environment (Baker, 2001).

The Concept of Loss

Loss is experienced at all stages of the individual and family life cycles. It is understood and resolved in differing ways, depending on many factors. Personality, age and life stage, social support, previous loss experiences, and circumstances related to the loss will influence the mourner's experience. The nature of the loss, its symbolic meaning to the mourner, and whether it is expected or unexpected, normative or nonnormative are important factors contributing to the loss experience (Walsh & McGoldrick, 1991).

Rando (1984, 1993) categorized loss as comprising physical losses and psychosocial losses.

Physical losses are tangible losses, including persons or objects evident to others—for example, the death of a loved one or cherished belongings. Psychosocial losses are symbolic, intangible losses not necessarily evident to others—for example, one's child leaving home or immigration to a new country. Positive life events may also involve a symbolic loss. Chemically dependent individuals, new to recovery programs, must confront the loss of their former lifestyle and the chemical that formerly played a significant role in their everyday life.

Physical losses are more frequently acknowledged by others, whereas symbolic losses are less often understood. As a result, they may not be viewed by others as legitimate loss experiences. Doka (1989, 2002) introduced the concept of disenfranchised grief to describe those loss experiences where one is deprived of the "right to grieve" openly, to gain acknowledgment of one's loss and, consequently, support from others.

The timing of the loss in the life cycle and the opportunity to prepare for a loss are significant factors affecting the experience. An expected, normative loss is the death of one's parents, inasmuch as children generally outlive their parents. The normative timing of such a loss is thought to be during one's adult years. If the death occurs earlier in the life cycle, it is viewed as a nonnormative loss because it occurs unexpectedly relative to time. An example of an unexpected loss would be the diagnosis of a chronic illness during the young adult years, a period when one expects to enjoy good health. This type of loss is viewed as nonnormative as well. Exposure to early traumatic loss, for example, abandonment by one's primary caretaker, can mitigate one's capacity to develop the requisite ego capacities to mourn later losses (McCarthy, 2006).

Every loss causes a degree of disruption and pain in our lives, but the more profound the loss is, the more intense are the disruption and the affective reactions. O'Connor (1984) proposed a "circle of loss" as a model to outline the relationship of the threat of the loss to oneself. Factors that contribute to the significance of the loss are the intensity of emotional pain and the upheaval associated with the loss. The most painful losses are those associated with our own physical status, and these are represented in the model as the core of the circle. Losses of health or a body part are the most significant and are associated with the most intense mourning reactions. Social workers can expect that individuals who have been informed of a terminal illness or a chronic health condition will confront an acute loss of self and experience severe anguish. The next ring in the circle of loss is loss associated with the separation from significant others, such as abandonment by an important person, the loss of a parent, the death of a spouse, or marital dissolution. Clients confronting abandonment, widowhood, parental death, or divorce experience a significant grief response.

Life experiences that require adjustment to our ways of living are included in the third ring. Examples are the loss of special acquaintances and retirement. When working with clients who have recently relocated to a new city or who leave the workforce, social workers should appreciate the losses and grief work clients need to address.

The fourth and outer ring of the circle involves the loss of desired opportunities, lost objects, and changes in one's social network. An individual dealing with a rejection from a desired school program or the emotional sequelae of a home burglary are examples. O'Connor (1984) suggests that every significant loss is experienced as a loss of oneself and as an end. As a result, loss threatens our sense of survival, always causing some disruption in our lives.

DYNAMICS OF MOURNING AND GRIEF

Mourning and Grief in Individuals

An understanding of loss and its impact on psychological functioning has been provided by Freud in his classic paper "Mourning and Melancholia" (1917/1957). This was the first comprehensive study of bereavement (Stroebe, Hansson, Stroebe, & Schut, 2008). Freud described the psychological dynamics of object loss, the loss of a loved one. Mourning results from this loss and is characterized by distinct differences in one's usual behavior and psychological functioning. The mourner experiences considerable psychic pain, in varying degrees, throughout the bereavement period and must expend considerable time and energy to incorporate the reality of the loss. Typical reactions to loss are dejection, withdrawal, and disinterest in one's world for a period following the loss. In the classic psychoanalytic perspective, the work of mourning is completed bit by bit, and resolution of the loss occurs only after the bereaved individual successfully withdraws the libidinal energy attached to the loved object. Following the loss of his daughter, Freud suggested that enduring attachments remain, as one does not wish to relinquish one's connection to the love object (Jones, 1957). Freud noted that denial of a loss may result in a "hallucinatory wish psychosis," a form of incomplete mourning whereby object decathexis is unresolved. Freud's observations have been developed by others (e.g., Abraham) who have studied individuals coping with loss.

Lindemann (1944) was one of the first researchers to investigate acute grief reactions. He studied the reactions of victims of the Coconut Grove fire in Boston. From his research, he identified the typical and atypical, and physical and psychological reactions to loss. He described the process of grief and mourning reactions and proposed that the grief response comprises a definite syndrome. Lindemann proposed three important tasks that must be addressed to resolve the loss successfully. Initially, one must detach oneself from the loved one or the loss. This involves emancipating oneself from the attachment to the loss. While one is not expected to forget the loved one, one must divest the emotional energy that is bound up in the attachment. The next task of grief requires readjustment and environmental accommodation to the loss. For a recent widow, this typically requires a redefinition of identity. The widow or widower must begin to experience himself or herself as a "me" rather than a "we." Developing new relationships is the focus of the third task.

Bereaved individuals must now invest their energies into other important relationships and develop a means for incorporating the memory of the loss into their current lives.

Intense feelings of distress and painful emotions are associated with the mourning period. Somatic symptoms (e.g., gastric distress), respiratory disturbances (sighing), fatigue, and mental distress are all experienced. One may have difficulty eating and sleeping and may speak of having a heavy heart and of feeling mental anguish. Shock and disbelief are common reactions. Grieving individuals may report that they cannot believe the loss has occurred. Feelings of guilt are present, with the bereaved examining their behavior to decide if through commission or omission they somehow contributed to the occurrence of the loss. Irritability and anger are characteristic, along with difficulties in expressing warmth and appreciation to those who attempt to provide comfort to the bereaved.

Building on the work of these pioneers, current research in the field of grief and loss focuses more on empirical studies from a range of disciplines rather than the clinical reports of practitioners. Researchers are investigating a wide range of grief and loss issues that include normal and pathological grief responses, models of coping, cultural variations, and intervention strategies (Stroebe et al., 2001, 2008).

Normal Grief and Mourning Reactions

Due to the range and intensity of emotions experienced by the bereaved, grief reactions are both physically and psychologically taxing. Rando (1984) suggests that "grief is work," with physical and emotional strain. She described the psychological reactions to grief and proposed three phases: (1) avoidance, (2) confrontation, and (3) reestablishment. Rando stressed that grief responses do not progress in stages in an orderly, linear fashion but may be seen in varying intensity over the course of the mourning period. Other writers in the field agree that grief is best described as a process, characterized by phases (Parkes, 2006; Sanders, 1999).

Mourners in the avoidance phase experience shock and numbness as they attempt to acknowledge that a significant loss has occurred. Individuals usually respond with disbelief, experiencing confusion and an inability to act. They may seem dazed and deny the significance of the loss. This is a predominant response with sudden loss experiences. One client reported a sense of disbelief that "this cannot be happening" when informed by doctors that her child had been diagnosed with a progressive muscle disease that usually resulted in death during the teenage years. Another client, 6 months following the sudden death of her teenage daughter, reported that she was "just waking up" and recognizing what had occurred in her life and that of the family. These feelings of disbelief may be present for days, weeks, or months following the loss and are often prominent during the period when the bereaved's support network initially offers emotional support and comfort. The numbness may be mistaken for doing well in accepting the loss or holding up. In reality, these emotions constitute the initial psychological reaction to the trauma that the bereaved are not yet able to incorporate.

The confrontation phase is often characterized by intense and painful emotions. Panic and extreme anxiety are felt as the numbness wears off and restlessness and irritability are often experienced. Mourners may report anguish and despair. As the reality of the loss is incorporated, depressive affect is common, with characteristic feelings of hopelessness, helplessness, and sadness. A profound yearning and pining for the deceased may be felt, sometimes followed by frantic efforts to search for and recover the deceased. Anger may be present and may be displaced onto others. In a death, the caregivers of the deceased or the deceased himself or herself may be the focus of the anger. Pollock (1961) noted that mourners may express hostility toward the professionals (e.g., medical staff, funeral personnel, clergy) who attend to the deceased. In one treatment session, a recently widowed woman reported to the social worker that she was feeling intense anger toward her recently deceased husband. She felt that he had abandoned her at a very difficult time in their lives, leaving her to cope with the difficulties their children had been presenting to them. Guilt reactions may also be present, often triggered by the disagreements and ambivalent feelings the bereaved may recall having for the departed one.

During this phase, mourners have difficulty concentrating and are distractible due to the emotional and physical energy that is bound up in the grief work. Behavioral manifestations of grief may include decreased energy and extreme fatigue. Mourners may have sleep difficulties and experience vivid dreams of the deceased. Changes in normal eating patterns, difficulty experiencing pleasure in daily activities, and periods of intense crying and sobbing may also be reported.

Rando (1993) describes the subsequent, temporary upsurges of grief (STUG) responses that mourners often experience. These are sudden, brief episodes of intense emotional reactions mourners may feel as they attempt to manage their daily activities. A client described an experience in the grocery store when she came across her recently deceased husband's favorite cereal on the grocery shelf. She began to cry uncontrollably, fleeing the store and feeling confused and embarrassed. Another client who had delivered a stillborn infant 5 years earlier described the anguish that she felt when her neighbor, pregnant at the same time, described her own daughter's first day at kindergarten. The client was reminded of her own dead infant and her unrealized hopes and dreams for the child. These reactions are examples of STUG responses.

Mourners often have difficulty initiating social activity and requesting emotional support from significant others while experiencing these emotions. Their social withdrawal should not be interpreted as a desire to be left alone. They need the attention and comfort of others to cope successfully with their emotional distress. The bereaved often feel that they lack control and are confused and frightened by the range and intensity of the emotions that surface during the mourning period.

The reestablishment phase, the third and final phase, is characterized by the gradual return to one's interests and social involvements. Psychological distress is less intense and less frequent. The mourner is now able to invest energy and interest in new relationships and experiences. Acceptance of the loss occurs, culminating in the establishment of a satisfactory method for remembering the deceased and the gradual adaptation to the changes that the loss has effected.

The concept of the anniversary reaction is frequently mentioned in the grief-and-loss literature and is an expected dimension of the grief process. Typically, the reaction is considered a temporal event when the more intense feeling associated with a loss surfaces and results in distress to the mourner. There are differing perspectives on the reaction: a normative reaction or a symptom of complicated grief. Freud (1895) was the first to identify the anniversary reaction. He described this reaction as a temporal event, seen at particular times of the year, coincident with the death of a beloved family member. Corr, Nabe, and Corr (2000) describe the anniversary reaction much like Freud and underscore the normative nature of the reaction. Similarly, Parkes (2001) suggests that the anniversary reaction is an expected event and describes it as a "rite of passage." During an intake assessment, a client who lost his wife the previous year complained of significant distress and felt like he "was starting all over again with his grief." When asked about his loss, he identified that he was confronting the anniversary of his wife's death as well as their wedding anniversary and the Christmas holidays within a 2-month time period. Indeed, he was coping with intense feelings resulting from a number of anniversaries and responding in an understandable manner.

In some cases, the anniversary reaction can be one of a number of symptoms of a complicated grief reaction. Pollock (1970) proposed that the reaction is likely a manifestation of a traumatic loss, indicative of incomplete mourning. Likewise, Engel (1975) underscored the unconscious nature of the anniversary reaction that may be manifested in somatic or psychiatric symptomatology. Rando (1993) suggested that there are a range of precipitating triggers for anniversary reactions that include particular dates; holiday times; special rituals, for example, weddings; age-correspondent or experience-associated factors; or meaningful points in one's development. Clinicians should undertake a comprehensive clinical assessment to determine whether the reaction is normative or symptomatic of unresolved loss.

Current loss experiences often trigger thoughts and feelings associated with prior losses. Pollock (1961) suggested that "psychological lesions" may develop after a significant loss, with the lost one becoming a part of one's psychic world. "New mourning experiences can serve to revive past mourning reactions that may still have bits of unresolved work present. In the instance of a very significant object, the total mourning process may never be complete" (p. 167). Bowlby (1980), Parkes (1998), and Roos (2002) support the notion that the resurgence of grief is often a normative phenomenon. Recent significant losses naturally revive mourning reactions due to identification, introjection, and attachment processes.

A 70-year-old woman, a retired nurse, reported that her 40-year-old son had been recently diagnosed with a malignant brain tumor and given 6 months to live. The client was bereft that her son had so little time left and felt very angry that he had more pain to endure. During his early 20s, he had been diagnosed with a mental illness and, consequently, had experienced limited social and occupational success during his adulthood. Because of these limitations, she had been very involved in his life and spent considerable leisure time with him.

The client recognized that she was having significant difficultly coping with her son's impending death and sought treatment to help her manage her anticipatory grief and to have the strength to accompany him through the dying process. In the months before his death, the client used treatment sessions to process her fears, sadness, and anger. She benefitted from the opportunity to share her anxiety, confusion, and disbelief.

Sessions, scheduled biweekly, focused on supporting her efforts to provide care for him, to process her intense emotions, and to anticipate life without him.

Following her son's death, the client was seen for sessions every few weeks. She discussed her sadness about her son's life and all the losses she and the family endured due to his mental illness. She never grieved the loss of a healthy son during his lifetime, since these were issues the family never openly discussed. She shared her grief reactions about his life and death during her sessions. At times of anniversaries and special occasions, for example, her son's birthday or Mother's Day, she scheduled weekly appointments to process and work through her feelings of loss and disillusionment. The treatment ended shortly after the first anniversary of her son's death.

A year later, the client experienced considerable irritability and agitation. She feared that she was destroying her relationship with her husband, a kind, supportive man who functioned as a friend and confidant. During treatment sessions, she recognized her displaced feelings were related to her anger over her son's life and death. She was seen for several months and came to accept that her grief would not be resolved but rather she would likely experience some degree of sadness and yearning for her son throughout her life. We focused on how she could live with her grief, maintain a continuing bond with her son, and have a meaningful life.

Following the client's mother's death, some 5 years later, the client returned again for treatment. She worried that she was alienating family and friends with her angry comments and impatience. As she discussed her feelings about this recent loss, she recognized that she was grieving for her mother and for her son. The resurgence of grief was normalized, and the client came to accept that she would likely experience these upsurges of grief when confronted with new loss experiences.

Many factors influence grief reactions. Parkes (2002) suggests that those with a secure attachment with their loved one may experience less distress while grieving than those with insecure attachments. The circumstances of the loss will have a significant effect on the grief process. The expected or sudden nature of the loss has an impact on the mourner's experience. Expected losses are often accompanied by some anticipatory grieving. While such individuals do have the opportunity to prepare psychologically for the loss, their grief reactions are nonetheless painful since the actual loss must still be mourned. When a loss is expected, individuals have the opportunity to address unresolved issues in the relationship and to say good-bye. This provides for some degree of closure and the resolution of unresolved aspects of the relationship.

Sudden losses are often followed by an intense experience of shock and disbelief. The mourner must cope with an unanticipated loss and feels considerable confusion and denial. The avoidance phase is often longer and replete with intense emotions and disorganization. Since there has been no opportunity to prepare for the loss and consider the needed adaptations in one's life, mourners initially require more support. A client whose husband abruptly left her and her three children reported her difficulty believing that her husband was not returning home. She continued to prepare the family dinner, setting a table for five family members for several months, until she could acknowledge that her husband was gone and that she would have to alter her usual daily routine.

Dynamics of Grief and Mourning in Families

Loss in families, particularly loss through death, is experienced uniquely by each family member. Factors such as age, gender, and role function in the family affect an individual's response. Family members often differ in the range and intensity of emotional responses. The length of time needed to accept and resolve the loss is also related to one's coping methods and the survivor's unique relationship with the deceased (McGoldrick & Walsh, 1991; Walsh & McGoldrick, 1991).

Major family tasks following a loss require family members to give permission to mourn openly and to modulate their emotional response to their loss (Folkman & Moskowitz, 2000). Bowen (1976) stressed the importance of family communication following a loss. Families that allow for open, reciprocal communication and the freedom to express their thoughts and feelings are better able to grieve. Bowen suggests that closed or fused family systems—those that block communication—are vulnerable to long-term dysfunction following a death. Fused family systems often experience an "emotional shock wave" or "a network of underground 'after shocks' of serious life events that can occur anywhere in the extended family system in the months and years following serious emotional events in the family" (Bowen, 1976, p. 339). These long-term sequelae often hamper role functioning and interpersonal relations in and outside the family system and influence relationships across generations.

While communication patterns and tolerance for differences in the mourning process support healthy adaptation to loss, other factors also influence the family's response and adjustment to loss. Death in the family represents the loss of important relationships. The nature of the family's grief reaction to this loss is influenced by how and when the family relationship was lost. The expected or sudden occurrence of death in the family is a significant factor to consider. The role held by the deceased family member also has an important impact on the survivors (Worden, 2009).

The nature of death, whether expected or unexpected, has ramifications for the family. Expected deaths that follow terminal illness can cause emotional and financial strain on the family. Anticipatory-grief responses, or grieving before the death, may result in emotional distancing from the terminally ill family member. To protect one another from painful emotions, family members may become detached and remote. Expected deaths do allow the family to prepare for the loss and provide time to discuss unresolved relationship issues, along with an opportunity to say good-bye. Conversely, sudden death in the family does not allow for any preparation or for time to finish unfinished business, and it is characterized by intense emotional distress. It is not unusual to see long-term negative effects following sudden deaths in families (Herz, 1980). If violence was associated with the death, the grief response can be exacerbated (Walsh & McGoldrick, 1991).

Certain illnesses (e.g., AIDS) can influence the family's mourning. The stigma associated with the cause of death may reinforce feelings of shame and guilt in family members and result in abbreviated death rituals and mourning responses. Death from suicide may cause overwhelming, intense reactions in family members; bewilderment and disbelief, along with anger and guilt, are often paramount as families try to search for clues to the death. Blaming and scapegoating of family members may result. Families may not receive adequate support as friends and acquaintances may feel significant discomfort in acknowledging the loss. It is not unusual for chronic anxiety and a sense of insecurity to follow sudden death as families learn that a catastrophe can occur without warning (Rando, 1984).

Just as the timing of a loss affects the individual's mourning experience, the expected or untimely loss of a family member also has implications for future family functioning. Death is usually associated with and expected during the later stages of the family life cycle, and a lesser degree of family stress is related to such deaths. Death at early life stages is considered nonnormative because the life cycle has been interrupted. Prolonged mourning responses may follow untimely death, and survivor guilt may frequently be present (Walsh & McGoldrick, 1991).

The role status of the deceased family member is another important dynamic in family adaptation to the loss. The more pivotal the role of the deceased family member within the family unit, the more difficulty the surviving family members will experience following the death. Both the functions of the deceased member's role in the family and the level of emotional dependence on that family member will influence the reactions to the loss (Herz, 1980). If the roles assigned to the deceased were pivotal to the family's functioning (e.g., wage earner), reorganization of the family system will be more difficult. Vess, Moreland, and Schwebel (1985–1986) suggest that "child-present" families will experience more stress than "child-absent" families because child-rearing demands and economic issues will tax the family system.

Since 60% of households in the United States own one or more pets, families frequently confront pet loss (American Veterinary Medical Association [AVMA], 2002). Pet loss is a significant loss since one's attachment to one's pet is often strong. Wrobel and Dye (2003) suggest that the psychological impact of this loss is similar to that experienced with human loss and results in a grief reaction comparable with that felt for a human person. Unfortunately, this loss often results in lack of acceptance and understanding by others (Field, Orsini, Gavish, & Packman, 2009). When completing a loss history, clinicians should include the loss of pets and legitimize the loss. Pet loss is a loss for the whole family and, most often, the first loss a child experiences. Parents should assist the child in mourning the loss, validating the sadness, and providing a family ritual to memorialize the loss.

A well-functioning family system is a central moderator of adjustment to loss. While other support networks facilitate coping with loss, families can counteract the isolation often felt by the bereaved and provide a nurturing environment (Kissane & Lichtenthal, 2008).

Unresolved Loss and Grief

Social workers frequently work with individuals and families who are having difficulty coping with loss. Many losses are unacknowledged and unresolved, never grieved by the mourner. Social and psychological factors can contribute to such losses, resulting at times in complicated grief reactions.

Lindemann (1944) described pathological grief reactions as those that distorted the normal grief response. Delayed grief reactions are those characterized by no apparent emotional response to the loss.

A 15-year-old girl was brought for treatment by her mother who was concerned with serious parent-child conflict in the home. The girl reported that her father had been killed 6 months earlier in a car crash. When the social worker asked the 15-year-old about the death, the girl reported the details of her father's accident, expressing little emotion. She said that her friends seemed to feel more sadness about her father's death than she did. During treatment, she was able to acknowledge that she felt the need to take care of her mother during the months following her father's death. She believed that

(Continued)

(Continued)

her mother was devastated by the loss and required her support, and she therefore denied the expression of her own feelings and reactions to protect her mother from additional strain.

In this case, the daughter had not been able to express her own grief over the loss of her father. Later, when her mother was better able to manage her own grief, the daughter was finally able to grieve her father's death, a response that she had suppressed for some time.

Distorted grief can include exaggerated grief responses where the mourner's excessive reactions may begin to interfere significantly with daily functioning (Rando, 1993). Such individuals may experience disabling panic attacks or profound despair.

A 42-year-old client reported to her social worker that she could barely leave her bed in the morning since her divorce 5 months earlier. Most days she arrived at her job several hours late. On the weekends, she stayed in bed all day and through the night. While family and friends were calling her and encouraging her to spend time with them, she consistently refused their support and became quite angry with them. She cried for hours each day, ate little, and had ruminative thoughts of her former spouse.

This client's behavior suggests a distorted grief response. The client was unable to manage her life activities and expressed hopelessness and deep despair. After assessing the degree of her depression, the social worker referred her for a psychiatric evaluation. Once the client began to take the prescribed antidepressant medication and became more functional, treatment focused on discussing the loss and the pain the client had experienced with the failure of her marriage.

Chronic grief reactions are marked by a prolonged mourning period. Grief is experienced for a lengthy period without a lessening of the intensity and range of emotions seen during the initial months following the loss (Rando, 1993). Families coping with an adult child with a chronic mental illness often experience chronic grief as they arrive at the realization that their hopes and dreams for their child will never be fulfilled. Families experience multiple losses, for example, expectations for the present and for the future, and must cope with guilt, blame, and self-reproach (Bland, 1998).

More recently, bereavement researchers have focused on the concept of complicated grief, the inability to successfully mourn a loss, resulting in ongoing intense symptoms of grief that undermine adjustment to the loss and the life changes necessitated by the loss. Symptoms of complicated grief include prolonged sadness, refusal to acknowledge or discuss the loss, excessive anxiety, and preoccupation with the loss as well as other emotional, cognitive and behavioral signs that interfere with adaptive functioning (Stroebe, Schut, & van den Bout, 2012). Lobb et al. (2013) attempted to identify predictors of complicated grief. From their systemic review of the research, they identified adverse experiences in childhood/psychiatric history, excessive dependent relationships, negative cognitive styles, traumatic deaths, and stressful caregiving experiences.

Facilitating Grief

Facilitating grief reactions and helping individuals cope with loss requires an active involvement with the bereaved. The clinician must be a nonjudgmental listener and be able to appreciate that the client will express intense, painful affects. Genuine concern for the bereaved should be expressed, acknowledging the significance of the loss to them. Social workers should not minimize the importance of the loss or suggest that the loss is minor compared with what others have experienced. At times, clients try to minimize their own losses as a way to escape the pain associated with loss. As with all other clinical situations, social workers should attempt to remain empathically attuned to the client, always endeavoring to understand the client's unique perspective of the loss. Practitioners should never propose their own philosophical or religious understandings as methods to resolve the loss (Rando, 1993). Respect for the mourner's philosophical or belief system and his or her beliefs regarding life after death, future reunions, and so on can provide the mourner with a sense of peace and inner comfort.

Worden (2009) proposed principles to guide treatment with the bereaved. These principles provide a broad framework for social workers engaged in grief therapy and include interventions focused on education, habilitation, rehabilitation, and maintenance of social functioning. In the beginning stages of treatment, the social worker should emphasize that the loss actually happened. Discussion of the loss with the bereaved helps actualize this reality. Educating the bereaved and his or her support network about the grief process and normative reactions to loss early in the treatment is useful and may need to be repeated at other points in the therapy. The range and intensity of feelings experienced by grievers are often confusing and overwhelming. Mourners often report that they "feel crazy," are flooded with thoughts and feelings about the loss, and feel unable to cope with daily life as they had prior to the loss. Mourners profit from learning that the grief process is characterized by many intense emotions and with preoccupation over the loss, factors that can undermine their usual coping capacities. Learning that these feelings will diminish in intensity and range over the course of the mourning period can assuage the mourner's anxiety about loss of control and ineffective coping.

The clinician must also acknowledge the likelihood of differences in grieving styles. Individuals cope with their grief in varying ways. One's culture, race/ethnicity, religiosity, and gender influence one's response to loss and grief (Irish, Linquist, & Nelsen, 1993). The clinician's respect for these differences and acknowledgment of their normality is important.

The mother of a recently deceased 8-month-old infant described her frustration with her husband. He seemed to have resolved his feelings within several months of the infant's sudden death. The wife, however, believed that her husband should have been as preoccupied and despairing as she continued to feel. Discussion of gender differences helped her accept the differences between her husband's and her own style of grieving. She noted that her husband's tendency to spend considerable time at his basement work bench, fixing broken appliances and toys, as his unique method for dealing with his feelings of loss. She came to understand this behavior as representing his efforts to "make things right for the family."

Bereaved individuals need the involvement of a supportive network (Hall & Irwin, 2001). They require others to listen to them verbalize their thoughts and feelings about their loss. Clinicians should help the bereaved clarify their thoughts and feelings and allow for the ventilation of ambivalence, anger, and guilt associated with the deceased. Particular attention should be given to the individual's anxiety and sense of helplessness. The bereaved often require assistance to manage life without the deceased. Feelings of sadness and despair must also be discussed and related to the meaning of what has been lost.

The social worker should support the coping capacities of the bereaved to further the management of their daily lives and help mourners clarify how the roles and responsibilities assumed by the deceased can now be managed. Because bereaved individuals are experiencing considerable emotional distress, they can benefit from assistance in problem solving. They may require help with certain decisions, which is most usefully approached by clarifying the issues that require resolution.

Meaning making/reconstruction is viewed as a significant aspect of the mourning process and one that is given increasingly more attention in the bereavement literature. Individuals attempt to make meaning of their loss, "make sense of it," and incorporate the loss into their prior "worldview" (Neimeyer, Prigerson, & Davies, 2002). This process entails the development of cognitive understandings of the loss, which can further a sense of coherence and control for the bereaved (Neimeyer, Burke, Mackay, & Van Dyke Stringer, 2010; Davis, Wortman, Lehman, & Silva, 2000).

The provision of active, ongoing support to the bereaved is a critical aspect of the treatment. This is particularly important during the first year following the loss. Holiday times, special family occasions, and the anniversary of the loss are critical times to contact the bereaved and offer comfort to them. Throughout the treatment process, the social worker should clarify both adaptive and nonadaptive coping patterns. The use of alcohol and drugs during the mourning period can interfere significantly with grieving, since these substances numb feelings and provide an escape from the pain of the loss. Assessment of the mourner's use of alcohol and drugs should be done routinely. Along with this, behavior that complicates the normal process of mourning and potentially leads to pathological grief reactions should be identified and assessed. Clinicians should clarify earlier losses that the mourner has experienced and the methods used to accept and grieve these prior losses.

A critical aspect of the grief process requires the bereaved to accept and adapt to the loss and focus on the present while remembering the past. Mourners transform their attachment to the loved one from a physical presence into an internal presence, that is, a continuing bond with the lost loved one (Field, 2006; Klass, Silverman, & Nickman, 1996; Silverman & Klass, 1996). Examples might include keepsakes/possessions of the deceased, introjection of the deceased's values and beliefs, or an ongoing experience of the deceased's presence in one's life. These bonds help mourners cope with loss and provide a sense of comfort and security (Baker, 2001; Field, 2006; Field, Gao, & Paderna, 2005).

Bennett and Bennett (2000) refer to another type of continuing bond, the "social ghost." Mourners may report the presence of the dead, experienced in dreams, memories, and visions of the deceased that provide comfort and guidance.

Bereaved individuals find that new relationships can coexist with the transformed relationship without their feeling disloyal to the deceased loved one. The social worker must also appreciate the griever's need to have sufficient time to mourn a loss and identify ways to commemorate the loss. For some individuals, depending on the nature of their loss, grief resolution may require up to 2, 3, or more years before acceptance and adaptation have been achieved.

Stroebe and Schut (1999) propose the dual-process model (DPM) of grief counseling. This model emphasizes both loss-oriented and restoration-oriented coping. Loss-oriented coping encourages the processing of grief feelings, while restoration-oriented coping promotes distraction, engaging one's energies in new tasks and relationships. The oscillation between these two helps grievers tolerate the demands of the grief process and adapt to the loss (Richardson, 2007).

A 28-year-old client reported that she had recently delivered a stillborn baby girl. This was her first child, and she was overwhelmed with sadness, anxiety, and confusion. Three months following her delivery, she planned to resume her position on a bowling team. However, she felt guilty for "taking time off" from her grieving. After some discussion, she recognized that this distraction helped her tolerate the difficult feelings she continued to experience over the death of her first-born daughter.

Spirituality and religion often offer comfort to mourners and contribute to the meaning they make of their loss (Walsh, 2012). Religious practices and convictions may provide methods for engaging the support of other like-minded believers and for maintaining a spiritual bond with the deceased. Johnson (2010) suggests religiosity provides a coping strategy for many African-Americans in their search for "making-sense" of loss, especially traumatic loss.

These principles provide a broad overview of the factors that social workers engaged in grief counseling should consider in their work. Offering some understanding of the behavior of significant others can also be therapeutic. Mourners report a range of reactions from their support network, from consistent concern and interest to a pretense that nothing significant has occurred. Family and friends who are silent about the loss rarely appreciate the message the mourner may infer from their silence. Mourners may feel that others are insensitive to their feelings and needs or are unwilling to extend themselves. Hearing that others are often unaware of the needs of the bereaved or are uncomfortable expressing their own feelings of loss can assist the bereaved in understanding the behavior of others better.

Social workers should be particularly sensitive to the feelings of mourners during the termination phase of treatment. Termination represents loss of the therapist and the therapeutic relationship and involves further grief work. Since this additional loss may be difficult for the mourner to manage, termination should be well planned and openly discussed.

Transference and Countertransference Considerations

Clinical work with mourners is demanding and may be stressful. Since clinicians often see themselves as helpers and gain gratification from this role, they may have difficulty dealing with their own powerlessness in helping mourners. Therapists experience a range of intense, painful affects in mourners. They cannot alter the mourner's circumstances or assuage the mourner's painful feelings. Indeed, such efforts can be detrimental in that they can undermine the therapeutic work.

Rando (1993) refers to the changes that may occur in the therapists' "assumptive world" as she or he witnesses the trauma of mourners. The death and loss experience of mourners can arouse significant anxiety in therapists and heighten their own sense of vulnerability. Clinicians may also be reminded of their own losses when engaged in grief therapy. Those who have unresolved losses or who experience concurrent loss may experience difficulty helping mourners.

The management of transference and countertransference reactions may be difficult for clinicians engaged in grief therapy. The clinician may experience intense emotional reactions to the content, the affect, and the process of the mourner's therapeutic work. Mourners may express a range of intense emotions during the confrontation phase of grief work. Therapists may feel frustration, anger, and hopelessness in reaction to the mourner's feelings and to the repetitive nature of the material discussed by the mourner. They may attempt to thwart the expression of the mourner's feelings or minimize the significance of the loss in order to guard against the mourner's grief reactions. Clinicians should monitor and examine their reactions to the mourner to further the therapeutic process. Clinical supervision and peer support can provide good opportunities for this examination. Social workers who work intensively with trauma victims should arrange for regular supervision/consultation to manage the affects experienced and encountered in this type of treatment (Dalenberg, 2000).

Grief Therapy With Families

Families might not enter treatment with unresolved mourning as their presenting concern, but it may be uncovered during the diagnostic process as one dynamic impeding healthy family functioning. Once uncovered, the major focus of the initial therapeutic work should be sanctioning the grief of the family. Fulmer (1983) suggested that therapists should support enactment of the grief feelings and provide education about the mourning process to help normalize the feelings of the family members. The social worker should be active in the sessions, clarifying whether family interactions are meant to support or suppress the expression of grief.

Stierlin, Rucker-Embden, Wetzel, and Wirsching (1980) and Worden (2009) suggest that therapists should note the dates and causes of death in the multigenerational family system during the early phases of treatment. The use of a genogram (see Chapter 1, "System Theory," this volume) facilitates this process (Walsh & McGoldrick, 1991). Other significant events in the family (e.g., births, relocation) should be noted since they can directly influence the family's movement through the mourning process (Walsh, 1978). These connections should be examined once the therapeutic alliance has been developed. Clarification of the roles played by the deceased family member and how they are currently being filled should also be included in the assessment process. Renegotiation of role assignment may be one aspect of the therapeutic work. Alliances and triangles in the family system should also be examined. At times, one family member may be the focus of the unresolved

feelings the family carries for the deceased member (Worden, 2009).

To uncover unresolved family issues related to the death, the therapist must engage the family in a direct and open discussion of the deceased, exploring miscommunications and misperceptions (Bosticco & Thompson, 2005). The therapist must be comfortable with the subject of death and assume a calm, nonreactive posture. Hare-Mustin (1979) and Bowen (1976) suggested that the therapist must not collude with the family by avoiding the painful topic of death or by using euphemisms that reinforce the taboo of death. In family meetings, the therapist should raise the family's awareness of communication patterns and relationship strains that have resulted from the death. Dysfunctional patterns of behavior can be reframed as methods that family members use to protect one another from their pain (Fulmer, 1983). The therapist should expect frequent resistance to opening the channels of communication but should nevertheless persist with open discussion.

Paul and Grosser (1991) proposed that treatment should provide a "corrective mourning experience" (p. 96). They suggested that therapists should ask direct questions about the loss. This approach can activate mourning by encouraging family members to reminisce, express feelings, and empathize with one another. Such a therapeutic approach can also reduce the disequilibrium in the family and result in better understanding, communication, and a new level of emotional closeness (Paul, 1967).

Walsh (2002) proposed the use of family consultations prior to or following a loss to address and resolve conflicts on difficult, sensitive family issues and to help estranged family members to reconcile. Family life review sessions, another method Walsh suggested, can provide family members the opportunity to reflect on the family's history and gain new perspectives and understandings of disappointments, which will make them more able to begin the process of healing.

McBride and Simms (2001) offer a brief family intervention model that includes an appraisal of the death-denying context in which the family interacts, clarification of the impact the death has for each family member, and strategic timing of sessions related to the family's movement through the grief process. Family therapists should have their own support network, for example, supervision/consultation or peer supervision to process clients' losses and their countertransference.

When working with families with young children, the use of family drawings can also be a valuable tool in treatment (Schumacher, 1984). Asking the family members to draw a picture of the family before and following the death may enhance an understanding of the impact of the death on the family unit. This technique can be particularly useful for children since their drawings often communicate alliances and feelings among family members. Herz (1980) suggests that therapists be sensitive to "sideshows," or behavior that is symptomatic of unresolved loss. Separate sessions with parents may allow the unfolding of toxic issues and lessen the frequency of sideshows. Such opportunities may also help the therapist gain an understanding of the parents' perception of the children's adaptation to the loss and the degree of shame and guilt that the parents may themselves be experiencing. Normalizing such feelings of guilt for the parents can be useful, since they often view it as pathological (Miles & Demi, 1991–1992). Separate sessions with the children can provide an opportunity to explore feelings and issues openly that children fear may upset their parents. In a case where a child has died, it is important to allow siblings the opportunity to explore the guilt they may experience in surviving the sibling's death. Fantasies about causing the sibling's death and fears about their own mortality should be carefully explored. Using therapeutic play activities for children under age 11 can permit children to enact and ultimately to resolve ambivalent feelings experienced toward the deceased family member (Baker, Sedney, & Gross, 1992).

Families that cope with ambiguous losses, for example, surrendering a child for adoption or a parent slowly deteriorating with amyotrophic lateral sclerosis (ALS), may benefit from a narrative therapy approach (Betz & Thorngren,

2006). The therapist should help family members identify the loss, normalize their respective reactions to the loss, clarify the methods members use to cope with the loss, and encourage sharing of their beliefs and perceptions about the loss.

Prescribing rituals can be another useful and powerful therapeutic tool in family treatment (Imber-Black, 1991). Rituals give the family a shared activity where open emotional expression and support are encouraged, permitting the family to acknowledge their loss publicly. Such rituals are particularly useful on holidays and anniversaries of the death or birth of the deceased family member. "Besides helping to resolve contradictions, face anxiety, and strong emotions, rituals support transitions" (Imber-Black, Roberts, & Whiting, 1988, p. 19).

If rituals were not held at the time of death, the therapist can help the family in structuring a farewell ritual. This can allow the family to acknowledge their loss, reminisce, and move on. Therapists can help families create their own unique rituals by emphasizing the need for innovation and flexibility (Imber-Black, 1991). Looking at a family picture or visiting the grave site as a family unit may have meaning for the family and support grief resolution (Fulmer, 1983).

Hare-Mustin (1979) has issued a warning to therapists who take on family grief work. She suggests that therapists need to resolve their own unfinished business, their unresolved mourning experiences. In other words, to be effective, therapists must deal with their own death anxiety and the multiple losses they have experienced during their lifetimes. Therapists should give particular attention to the potential for compassion fatigue and vicarious traumatization (Becvar, 2003).

Social workers provide services to families across the life span, in a range of practice settings where end-of-life care issues arise. Due to the aging of the population, clinicians encounter families more often who are confronted with these issues. Practitioners require knowledge and skill in the range of concerns end-of-life care presents. Palliative, "comfort care" vs. "life-extension" care frequently entails difficult, emotionally laden decisions for families along with the painful experience of watching a loved one die. Rabow, Hauser, and Adams (2004) describe a number of caregiving burdens faced by families. These include the burdens of protracted time demands and logistical concerns related to coordinating schedules, medical appointments, and additional ancillary services. Oftentimes, caregiving is provided by older adults who themselves have chronic medical conditions and risk physical injury in the provision of care. Family caregiving presents an economic burden given the financial costs of care and for some, lost income. The emotional burden of caregiving is another consideration for families providing end-of-life care. While many may derive satisfaction caring for their loved one, family members also endure many painful feelings, for example, sadness, guilt, resentment, anger, and powerlessness arising from their role and responsibilities. Lack of needed sleep, loss of leisure and restorative time, and neglect of their own medical/ health care needs may result in physical health decline for caregivers. Social workers can assist families with many of these burdensome issues with therapy and referral to needed community resources. Walsh (2012) suggests social workers complete a comprehensive family assessment to clarify the preexisting family dynamics, conflict-laden relationships, and unresolved issues that may cause additional caregiver strain during the end-of-life process.

Grief Therapy With Groups

Various forms of group treatment can be useful for certain mourners. For individuals with limited support networks, groups offer the opportunity to share feelings and concerns with other grievers and identify methods for resolving the loss. Grief groups in school settings provide opportunities to process feelings and build on strengths and coping capacities (Eppler, 2008). Videka-Sherman (1982) studied the role of support group membership for bereaved parents. Her findings supported the value of self-help groups for parents coping with a child's death. Involvement with bereavement support groups, available in many communities, may provide grievers with an important adjunct to individual or family grief counseling.

As with all treatment groups, it is essential to screen members to determine their appropriateness for group intervention. Groups composed of grievers who have sustained similar losses are most beneficial (Piper, McCallum, & Hassan, 1992). Piper, Ogrodniczuk, Joyce, Weideman, and Rosie (2007) suggest that short-term groups with a high percentage of members with well-developed object relations are optimal for the treatment of complicated grief. Group cohesion and therapeutic progression result from the sense of "universality" members experience in a group and contribute to the group process and meeting of therapeutic goals (Yalom, 1985).

The timing of the griever's involvement in a group is another factor to consider. Group membership is useful during the confrontation phase, when grievers have acknowledged that a loss has occurred and are more able to cope with their distress.

OVERVIEW OF LIFE CYCLE LOSSES

Loss, both tangible and psychosocial, occurs throughout the life cycle. When the loss involves the death of a family member early in the life cycle, it can be more difficult to resolve. We consider such early deaths unnatural, denying individuals their expected long lives (Walsh & McGoldrick, 1991). Loss in the later years is considered normative; indeed, anyone who lives long enough confronts many substantial losses.

Childhood Losses

Loss experiences are understood and resolved differently, depending in part on one's age and life stage. Children have differing capacities to understand and to cope with loss compared with adults, and they depend more on adults to help them grieve their losses. Children's loss experiences are less understood and are frequently unacknowledged (Doka, 1989). However, children must cope with a range of losses beginning in their early years. As they develop and are expected to behave in more adult ways, children are confronted with tangible losses, such as their favorite blanket or other transitional object. They may have to cope with the death of a pet or a move to a new home and the concomitant loss of neighborhood friends and the security of their school and teachers. The death of a parent or grandparent or separation from a parent following a parental divorce is a significant, tangible loss that children increasingly encounter. Entering the foster care system represents substantial loss to children as they cope with the loss of their parents and, sometimes, of their siblings and much else that was familiar to them in their daily lives. Even with normal life events, such as the birth of a sibling, children confront the loss of parental time and attention as these important commodities come to be shared with the newborn.

When working with children who are coping with loss, social workers can begin by acknowledging the loss and the feelings associated with it, both to the child and to the child's parents. Parents may have a limited appreciation of the child's experience of the loss and the underlying dynamics the loss represents. Educating parents about the child's capacity to understand the concept of loss is an essential part of the treatment. In her study of childhood bereavement, Furman (1974) noted the value of parental discussions with children about death and loss. Such acknowledgment and responsiveness to the children's feelings about the loss were believed to help them grieve their current loss as well as significant losses that occurred in their later years.

Children's age and level of cognitive functioning influence their understanding and response to loss (Waas & Stillion, 1988). Infants and toddlers are incapable of a cognitive understanding of the concepts of death and loss, yet they may have acute awareness of separation from important adults in their lives and respond with distress when these adults are unavailable. From ages 3 to 5, children are unable to comprehend the finality of death, viewing it as a reversible event, such as sleep or being away on a trip. For these reasons, phrases such as "final rest" or "gone to a better place" are of little use when explaining death to young children and can actually be damaging. The child may begin to develop a fear of going to sleep or being separated even briefly from parents. Providing the child with honest, concrete details of the death and reassurance of continued parental support in dealing with the loss are useful interventions. Around ages 5 to 9, children are better able to understand the finality of death but have difficulty relating it to themselves and to important people in their lives. At this age, they are also better able to understand the causative factors contributing to death and have an awareness that serious illness or old age increases the likelihood of death.

Along with their differing cognitive capacities for understanding death and loss, children's grief responses also differ. Children frequently manifest their grief through behavioral expression rather than through verbal discussion. Physical aggression, overactivity, clinging behavior, and detachment from previously enjoyed activities may serve as expressions of grief. Frequent crying, sleep difficulties, and nightmares may also be noted. School-age children may develop academic difficulties when, in consequence of their grief, they become distracted and less able to concentrate on their schoolwork.

An 11-year-old girl had recently been hospitalized in the pediatric unit complaining of severe stomach pain. Extensive medical testing could not identify a physiological basis for her complaints. The psychosocial assessment completed by the hospital social worker identified the recent death of her aunt as a precipitant to her physical complaints. Medical staff determined that her condition was

(Continued)

(Continued)

psychosomatic and referred her to a social worker. After completing a comprehensive assessment of the girl with her mother, other symptoms of the child's grief were noted. She was having difficulty sleeping and had frequent nightmares. She was clinging to her mother and often attempted to stay home from school. Her parents were particularly worried about their daughter's condition. They had been planning a special weekend away from home in several months, and they believed that their daughter might have considerable difficulty coping with their absence.

The death of this child's maternal aunt was the first significant loss she had experienced. She was particularly close to her aunt and had spent considerable time with her. The aunt was several years younger than the child's mother and had been ill for a brief time before her death. The 11-year-old had not been included in the family's death rituals, and they had provided little explanation to her about the specifics of her aunt's condition, either before or following the death. The hospital social worker believed that the aunt's death had triggered the girl's fears of losing her own parents.

The treatment focused on work with this child and her parents. The parents were advised to begin to discuss the details of the aunt's death with their daughter, allowing her to ask whatever questions she might have regarding her aunt's condition. They were also advised to reminisce about the times their child had spent with her aunt and to share their own feelings of loss with their daughter. The social worker recommended that the child visit her aunt's grave site. Children's books about death and loss were suggested as another vehicle to permit the child to acknowledge the loss and feelings natural to the grief process. Individual play sessions augmented by discussion helped the child express her confusion about the loss. The therapist also encouraged the child to express her conflictive feelings about separation from her parents and further encouraged her to talk with her parents about their planned trip. Over a 12-week period, the child's stomach cramps remitted, she reported that she was sleeping better, and she planned where she would spend the weekend while her parents were away from home. She stayed overnight at a girlfriend's house and reported that she had enjoyed the experience. A final session with the child following her parents' trip revealed that she had tolerated their absence well, enjoying the time she spent with a schoolmate's family.

Once the child's grief reaction and fears were acknowledged and addressed, she was able to mourn her aunt's death with the assistance of her parents. The parents' sensitivity to their daughter's separation fears and the comfort that they were then able to provide permitted her to mount the loss of her aunt and gradually resume her normal activities.

Rando (1984) offers several useful suggestions for adults involved with bereaved children, some of which may also be appropriate for children who must cope with other types of losses. She suggests that adults be open and honest with the child regarding the circumstances of the loss, since this can reduce the child's tendency toward magical thinking. Young children may believe that their thoughts and behavior somehow have contributed to a loss. Providing rational, truthful explanations can dispel these beliefs.

Children should be informed of the reality of the loss soon after it occurs. This lessens the chances of their learning of the loss from someone else. Considerable reassurance and attention from adults will be necessary to assuage the child's sadness and anxiety. The child should also be reassured that his or her needs will continue to be met.

In the case of loss through death, it is important to involve children in memorial services and funeral rituals. Children learn about grief and mourning from the significant adults in their lives. Exclusion from grief rituals is confusing to children and denies them opportunities to receive comfort for their own grief. They are also deprived of the opportunity for ritual closure that such ceremonies offer older family members. Of course, it is important that children be prepared for what they may see at a funeral or memorial service. This allows the child the opportunity to decide if he or she wishes to be involved in the ritual. It is also important that children be provided with ways to remember the deceased, whether through pictures or special objects that can facilitate the process of grief resolution.

Grief reactions in children frequently follow parental divorce. When the custodial parent becomes preoccupied with his or her own grief and new role responsibilities, that parent's ability to attend to the child's needs and to understand the child's behavior may also be diminished.

A 4-year-old boy was brought for treatment by his mother, who had recently separated from her husband. The mother expressed concern about the child's increasingly aggressive and oppositional behavior. He was destroying his toys, hitting his younger sibling, and refusing to accept parental limits. Over the 4 months of play therapy sessions, this child typically focused on the dollhouse and family figures. He provided a story about the doll family, often recreating conflicts between the mother and father figures. The social worker offered interpretations of these stories, acknowledging the fear and confusion a child feels when his parents separate. During parent guidance sessions, his mother was helped to understand her son's behavior as an expression of his sadness, confusion, and anger over the separation and approaching divorce. His mother began to talk with the child about his feelings, allowing him to verbalize a range of emotions and to ask questions about what family life would be like following the divorce. The child's father was also seen for several individual sessions. Visitation plans were discussed and explanations for his son's behavior were provided during these sessions. The importance of regular visitation with the father was stressed, and both parents were able to develop an amicable plan for visitation. His parents purchased several books about family divorce and frequently read these to their son. The child's behavior began to change as both parents were increasingly able to acknowledge his feelings of loss. His parents provided him a number of opportunities to ask about the changes in family life and were able to reassure him of their ongoing involvement in his life. Frequent, regular visitation with the father then began, and both parents reported improved family interactions.

The loss of daily contact with a parent is a significant loss indeed for a child. Young children often fear abandonment by their custodial parent after a divorce. It is critical that they receive substantial reassurance that the adults in their lives will continue to be available to them (Wallerstein, 2005; Wallerstein & Kelly, 1980).

Therapeutic work with child grievers should always include work with the parents or significant adults in the child's life. Providing guidance and resources to the parents helps the therapeutic efforts with the child. Many children's books dealing with the themes of death and loss are available (Goldman, 1994). Crenshaw (2005) suggests that latency-age children, especially those dealing with traumatic loss, may respond best to projective techniques, for example, drawings and storytelling. These clinical tools can evoke varied, intense emotions in the child griever, who often cannot directly express his or her feelings and thoughts.

Clinical work with the child who has lost a sibling presents a significant challenge to the therapist. The death of a child in the family is considered almost universally to be the most devastating loss. In such tragedies, parents lose the hopes and dreams they held for their child, as well as a part of themselves. Hare-Mustin (1979) has noted the sense of emptiness and profound grief reactions that parents experience. Guilt is a common response in parents and may constitute one of the most prominent, intense reactions (Rando, 1986). Parents may feel that their behavior, whether through commission or omission, was responsible for the child's death. Parents also experience "recovery guilt" as they begin to work through the mourning process and experience some renewed enjoyment in their lives. Any pleasure may be experienced as a sign of unfaithfulness to the deceased child. One mother whose first baby had died from sudden infant death syndrome noted the guilt she felt on the birth of her second child. She was ecstatic caring for her newborn, yet felt her feelings reflected a lack of love for her deceased child.

Grief reactions following a child's death are prolonged and complicated for the parents. Arnold and Gemma (2008) suggest that parental grief is the most devastating loss one could experience, characterized by a grief that is lifelong. Self-identity and one's worldview are profoundly changed by this incomprehensible loss.

The surviving children are also deeply affected and often overlooked. Their needs may be unmet as their parents are consumed by their own grief. The surviving children gain a new status, that of a survivor, which can impose a significant hardship for them. Krell and Rabkin (1979) noted a number of maladaptive reactions in families following a child's death. A surviving child may try to replace the dead sibling, taking on special attributes of the deceased. "The absent child thus remains in some sense alive, a misbegotten restoration protecting the family from having to fully face their loss" (p. 473). This can impede the child's own sense of identity as she or he tries to represent not one but two children to the parents. Such children may become "precious children," bound to the parents, who have become vigilant and overprotective. Or they may be "haunted children," who collude in the family's conspiracy of silence, where little is ever said about the deceased child. Family members may suppress details of the child's death and their feelings about the loss when significant guilt and shame are present. These family interaction patterns impede the psychosocial development of the surviving children and the mourning experience for the entire family.

Families need time to heal and to adapt to their altered family unit. Family rituals that promote sharing memories and openly acknowledge the loss contribute to healing for the surviving family members (Gudmundsdottir & Chesla, 2006).

Marital relations are also affected and strained following a child's death. Each partner has had a different relationship with the child, and most likely their methods for coping with the loss will also differ. Gender differences appear to account for the typically greater emotional expressiveness shown by mothers than by fathers over the loss of a child (Bohannon, 1990; Rando, 1986). Research by Miles and Demi (1991–1992) and Rando (1986) suggests that spouses are out of sync with one another, often unable to support the needs of their partner. Over time, however, most couples are able to resume satisfactory marital relations (Bohannon, 1990).

Adolescent Loss

Both tangible and psychosocial losses are experienced during the adolescent period. Tangible losses might include rejection by a romantic interest, exclusion from membership on a desired team or squad, or lack of acceptance by a preferred peer group. Teenagers may lose friends to death, through suicide or homicide. Many psychosocial and symbolic losses are also experienced during this stage. Adolescents are expected to give up their dependencies on their families and take on increased responsibility for themselves. Biological growth results in body image changes and therefore the loss of the former image of oneself; identity issues require the loss of one's former vision of oneself and an adaptation to a complex, altered understanding of self.

Cognitive development occurring during this period equips adolescents to discern death from other kinds of losses. Death is now conceived of as a final, irreversible event that affects everyone. As a result, when death occurs, adolescents have a heightened awareness of their own mortality. Gender differences in grief work may now be clearly seen, as compared with younger children (Crenshaw, 1990). Social workers should be aware that adolescent males may engage in increased aggressive behaviors and are more likely to use alcohol or drugs to cope with their loss. Females are usually more verbal about their feelings, soliciting attention and consolation from others.

The separation-individuation process may complicate grief reactions for adolescents (Rosen, 1991). Ambivalent feelings experienced toward one another by both adolescents and their parents may result in complicated grief reactions for both the adolescent and the parents. When a death occurs in the family, adolescents may respond in ways that undermine their own developmental needs and tasks. The teenager may adopt a family role as the perfect child, failing to engage in the challenging and questioning of authority that is so typical of adolescent behavior. Mishne (1992) observes that adolescents often feel rage when a parental death occurs, displacing their rage onto the surviving parent and idealizing the dead parent. Fearing a contagion effect, adults sometimes disregard an adolescent's grief. Social workers should encourage adults involved with grieving adolescents to discuss the tragedy and to mourn their loss.

A 17-year-old girl complained of significant anxiety and depression. She explained that she lived with her mother, who was widowed 2 years earlier. This teenager had adopted the role of "mother's companion." She rarely engaged in social activities with her peers and instead worked diligently on her academics. She reflected on the pride her father would have felt over her school performance, since he had valued education and had saved for her college tuition. When confronted with the sacrifices she had made in her social life, the teenager acknowledged that she felt lonely and isolated. Treatment focused on increasing her awareness of her own needs and feelings. Over the course of the treatment, she could acknowledge the anger she felt toward her mother, who relied on her for support and companionship. The daughter became better able to disagree with her mother on meaningful issues and increasingly was able to schedule time with friends. She came to recognize the rage she felt toward her father for leaving her without his support and for the increased responsibility she had been feeling for her mother since his death.

Suicide is a major cause of death in adolescents (Bursztein & Apter, 2009). Bolton (1986) describes the reaction that parents often experience when a teenage child takes his or her own life. They feel that they have failed their child, and this sense of parental failure is magnified further if the suicide is experienced as a rejection or punishment of the parent. These are painful emotions that parents must cope with during the mourning process, and resolution of their grief is generally a long, slow process. Parents must be able to forgive themselves for not being perfect parents, which, in turn, lessens their guilt feelings. If they can gain a better understanding of the factors that contributed to the hopelessness and despair of their child, then parents may be better able to resolve their own grief. Finally, parents should be encouraged to be open with others about their loss. This openness can help decrease the stigma associated with death by suicide and signal to family and friends the intense grief the parents are experiencing.

A group of seven 10th- and 11th-grade teenage girls were assessed as high risk for self-destructive behavior following the deaths of two classmates, one a suicide and the other a homicide. The school social worker offered an 8-week grief resolution group to the survivors to support their mourning and reduce the potential for self-destructive sequelae. During the first session, the girls were quiet and listened to the social worker briefly describe the mourning process, acknowledging that the girls were mourning two significant losses. The girls were initially passive but then became hostile toward the social worker, confronting her with the fact that they believed their families and school personnel were insensitive in refusing to discuss the deaths. In the following sessions, the teenagers began to describe their confusion and sadness about their deceased friends and their own feelings of vulnerability. They reminisced about their friends and expressed a range of feelings about their deaths. One session was used to write farewell letters to both friends. A meeting with the girls' parents was scheduled to provide the parents with an understanding of the mourning process, but few parents responded. The social worker admitted to the girls the difficulty that adults often have in dealing with death, particularly when it is violent death. At the last session, the girls expressed their appreciation for having had their feelings acknowledged and for being given the opportunity to deal with their grief.

Young Adult Losses

Leaving home, choosing an occupational role and a life partner, and becoming a parent are the major normative tasks of young adulthood. In adapting to an adult role and its attendant responsibilities, young adults sustain many real and symbolic losses. Gould (1978) identifies the illusions and false assumptions that must be resolved during the adult years, the foremost among which is the symbolic loss of one's parents as providers of safety and security. Young adults are expected to leave the financial security and emotional comfort of their families and to develop increased autonomy and an adult identity. Parents are no longer perceived as experienced caretakers and rescuers, and childhood dependencies and beliefs regarding parental omnipotence are given up.

Choosing a life partner often entails involvement with several potential love interests. The resulting disappointments and rejections, which are universal, are experienced as both real and symbolic losses. Young adults coping with estranged relationships grieve the loss of their potential companion and the life they had anticipated sharing with their partner. Marriage results in the loss of one's prior identity and requires that self-interest and self-concern be expanded and augmented to include another. Parenthood demands the individual's adaptation to significant time constraints as well as other major changes in daily activities. Couples confronted with miscarriage, stillbirth, or neonatal death must mourn their lost infant. Those coping with infertility issues must grieve the loss of the ability to conceive a child of their own. Certain chronic illnesses, such as diabetes or rheumatoid arthritis, are initially diagnosed during the young adult years. Young adults so diagnosed must cope with the loss of function, often debilitating, and then begin to make life adjustments to accommodate to a chronic health problem.

It is not infrequent that the unexpected death of a parent or parental divorce occurs during this stage. Multiple changes in family roles, responsibilities, and activities may result from such losses.

A 30-year-old married woman initiated treatment following the sudden death of her recently divorced mother. She was having difficulty grieving the loss of her mother's death and adapting to her new responsibilities for a disabled sibling, previously cared for by her mother. She reported overwhelming sadness over the loss of her mother, with whom she had had a warm and loving relationship. She longed for her mother's companionship and for the guidance and assistance her mother had provided her in raising her own children. Over the course of the treatment, she expressed anger toward her deceased mother, both for leaving her too early and for the increased responsibility that she had inherited for her disabled sibling. The treatment facilitated the expression of these thoughts and feelings and helped her identify the symbolic losses that had also resulted from her mother's death. Therapy also enabled her to clarify her responsibilities for her sibling and to develop methods for managing these responsibilities. She was eventually able to find a meaningful way of commemorating her mother and to reminisce about her with her own children.

This client had sustained multiple losses when her mother died. Not only had she lost an important relationship but she had also lost her mother's presence in the lives of her own children. With new responsibilities for her sibling, she lost both the time and the flexibility to attend to her own children's needs.

Divorce is a common experience in our society and replete with real and symbolic losses. Divorce can be more painful than death, since death truly ends a relationship while divorce may change the relationship but not end it (Hooyman & Kramer, 2006). Individuals may obtain a legal divorce but never gain an emotional divorce, harboring bitterness, hostility, and anger for years. Williams and Dunne-Bryant (2006) suggest that divorce has significant negative consequences on one's psychosocial functioning, particularly for mothers of young children.

A 29-year-old client entered treatment to discuss fears that her husband was having an affair. She reported that she would confront her spouse with her suspicions and become irate when he would deny the validity of her accusations. The client became highly anxious and more and more enraged with her husband's emotional distance. Over the course of the first 6 months of treatment, she

(Continued)

(Continued)

processed her fears and concerns about her deteriorating marriage. When her husband filed for divorce, she felt relieved but also highly anxious and depressed.

During the next year, while the client, a mother of three young children, was coping with the divorce process, she reported limited patience with her children and frequent use of a punitive approach with them. While she regretted her behavior and the difficulty it caused her children, she felt unable to rectify it. Over time, the patient began to discuss her own childhood and the painful experiences she had endured as a child of divorced parents. She had never felt safe and had longed to be in her father's custody, since her mother suffered from a mental illness and was unable to provide a stable home life.

In treatment sessions, the client came to recognize that her husband's infidelity and subsequent desire for a divorce represented a number of losses for her. First, there was the loss of her spouse and the marital relationship that once had been loving and gratifying. She felt abandoned by him and questioned her attractiveness and capacity to sustain an intimate relationship in the future. Her self-esteem was assaulted by his rejection of her. During the course of the marriage, her husband had been a good provider, and she had felt a degree of security in the marriage that she had never experienced in her childhood. Following the divorce, she recognized that she would need to adjust to a new life style with limited financial resources, another loss to endure. She recognized that she was grieving the end of the hopes and dreams she had embraced since her teenage years—that she would someday raise her own children in a stable, two-parent family. Now, her children would need to endure a degree of upheaval, just as she had in her childhood. This symbolic loss was very painful and required a reworking of her assumptions about her future, her identity, and her fantasies about adult life. During sessions, the client shared and processed these painful feelings and grieved the multiple losses. Her parenting skills improved, and she agreed to seek treatment for her children, recognizing that they were experiencing fear and sadness and needed help to grieve the loss of the family unit.

Couples coping with the death of an infant through miscarriage, stillbirth, or neonatal death often receive minimal support and recognition while mourning their loss (Nichols, 1990). Loss of a child, whatever the age of the child, always represents a loss of self, of one's hopes and dreams for one's offspring (Rubin & Malkinson, 2001). Yet this loss is frequently misunderstood and may be minimized by the couple's support network. When a significant loss is negated by others, complicated mourning may be the result. Couples require an adequate explanation of the medical factors that contributed to the loss, acknowledgment of the loss, and support and comfort from family and friends (DeFrain, 1991).

Midlife Losses

During the middle adulthood years, children leave home, causing alterations in family life and in role functioning for midlife parents. Women who have primarily invested their energies in a maternal role lose their primary role identification and may experience this separation from their children as a major calamity. Midlife adults may have limited involvement with their children if these relationships become strained. During this period, midlife couples are faced with more time together so that partners begin to refocus on each other. Divorce sometimes results when couples are unable to negotiate satisfying relations, the result being the loss of one's long-term partner and companion.

Another loss associated with this period is related to time. Midlife adults experience time differently, with more awareness of the finite nature of time, of "time left" (Neugarten, 1976), leading to a heightened awareness of one's mortality. Women face menopause, signifying the end of their childbearing capacities. Disappointments with one's work status and prior expectations of occupational success are often confronted during the middle years (Levinson,

1978). Role loss and identity changes may be the result of forced early retirement or job loss for some midlife workers.

A normal decline in physical stamina and abilities occurs during this period, with some midlife adults experiencing the onset of significant health problems that may require adjustments in lifestyle and lead to changes in the individual's self-image. Frail, elderly parents may require care by their midlife children, resulting in the loss of time and freedom. Adaptation to new, more demanding daily routines may be the result, particularly for midlife women.

All these life changes involve some degree of grief and mourning, as illustrated by the following example.

A 43-year-old divorced father of two entered treatment. He had been feeling sad, had little energy, and reported experiencing little enjoyment in his daily life. He could not identify any recent events that triggered his depression. In discussing his situation, he said that he had tense relations with his two young adult children. He had no hope for more frequent and gratifying contact with his children but deeply wanted a more significant role in their lives. He reported experiencing intense feelings of guilt over his decision to divorce the children's mother during their early adolescence. The initial phase of treatment focused on helping him identify his losses and provided clarification and validation of his feelings about them. Once he was able to mourn the loss of expectations for a warm family, this client was able to understand and begin to deal with his feelings. As he worked through his grief, he was able to begin problem solving to reestablish his relationship with his children.

Other losses surfaced during the treatment, particularly those related to his occupational standing and intimate relationships. This client's occupational goals had never been realized. He felt angry and bitter about his work status, often ruminating about his situation. Gradually, it became possible for him to discuss his unrealized dreams and mourn his lost expectations. He was also experiencing dissatisfaction in his third marriage yet desperately wanted to preserve it. He was assisted in understanding the strains in this marriage, as well as his contribution to these problems. Subsequently, he decided to seek marital therapy with his wife to resolve these marital difficulties.

Social work treatment with this client involved the identification and resolution of both current and past losses that he had not been able to mourn. His depression was the result of these unresolved losses.

Complicated mourning may occur when grief reactions are delayed or absent. When life events involving loss are not acknowledged, the mourner is at much greater risk of experiencing depression.

A 47-year-old woman reported a long history of personal dissatisfaction and unhappiness. She had recently engaged in several incidents of hitting and punching herself and became alarmed when her husband threatened to leave her if she did not seek treatment. Fearing the loss of her spouse, she reluctantly scheduled an appointment with a social worker. In discussing her past experience, she mentioned that she had given up her only child for adoption over 25 years earlier when she was a single woman. Only one of her siblings and a close friend were aware of her pregnancy and the adoption, neither of whom had ever again mentioned this event. The woman felt sadness in never having had the opportunity to be a parent and in not knowing her child. She poignantly described the anger and jealousy she felt when seeing families together, enjoying one another's company. She began to recognize that her long-standing depression reflected this loss that she had sustained and never had any opportunity to mourn. Treatment focused on helping her grieve the loss of her child. She revealed the guilt and anguish that she had felt for so many years and was able to recognize that her inability to talk about the adoption and her fantasies about the child she never knew had been a principal cause of her despair and anger.

Chronic depression or dysthymic conditions often result when significant losses are never mourned. When a loss is discounted, the mourner is unable to express associated painful thoughts and affects and remains incapable of completing the grief work.

Later-Life Losses

Older adults sustain many losses of a physical, social, and psychological nature. While such losses are normative and expected, they are nonetheless painful and can result in significant mourning experiences.

Retirement represents permanent leave from the occupational world. The retiree often experiences substantial loss with this transition. One loses the occupational role, which is a source of identity. The daily rhythms of life revolve around work and define one's time schedule. Work also provides a social network with coworkers, with whom the worker often spends more time than with family members and friends. In our society, occupational standing provides a source of prestige, and those who do not participate in the workforce are often viewed as having lesser social status.

While retirement is generally regarded as a reward for one's life of labor, leaving the workforce requires a significant adaptation to loss, which is inherent in this experience. If older adults are unable to compensate adequately for such losses by developing new daily rhythms and furthering their interests and their social contacts, they may have significant difficulty with this transition. Cox (1988) refers to the concept of "retirement syndrome" as an experience that male retirees in particular may face if unable to compensate for such losses.

As older adults lose their physical vigor, relocating from the family home to smaller living quarters may become necessary. Such a move may allow for continued independence and self-sufficiency, but it also represents a significant loss. The family home and neighborhood are important ties to one's family history, and neighborhood surroundings are reminders of life events involving children, friendships, and daily-life patterns.

At times, older adults who are faced with debilitating health conditions must move to nursing homes, a placement that symbolizes a major loss. Decline in health, inevitable in the later years, represents one of the most difficult losses to sustain (Hooyman & Kramer, 2006). A loss of autonomy often accompanies this decline in health status.

Married couples inevitably lose their life partner, often considered the most significant life loss for the surviving spouse and one of life's most stressful events (Lopata, 1972; Somhlaba & Wait, 2008). One loses one's primary support person, confidant, and partner in leisure. Social and emotional needs formerly met by the spouse must be met through relationships with others. Living patterns, reflecting the long-term relationship, are altered, and significant adjustments are required by the widow or widower to cope with these major life changes.

A 68-year-old retired carpenter seemed unable to develop a satisfying daily schedule since leaving his employment 8 months earlier. His wife noticed her husband's sadness and apparent boredom. She had become concerned about his increased drinking, irritability, and excessive sleeping. She told the social worker at the senior citizens' center of her concerns. The social worker encouraged her to bring her husband with her to a weekly lunch at the center, where the social worker could meet with them. When the couple came, the social worker encouraged the man's wife to verbalize her concerns to him and to express her worry about his limited daily activity and alcohol intake. The husband became tearful, acknowledging the difficulty he was having with his retirement and the depression he was experiencing. The social worker helped the husband identify activities that might interest him, as well as provide structure for his day. Over several sessions, the husband identified various activities, both at home and in the community, that he would initiate. He discussed his former work and how gratifying it had been for him. He then decided to contact his fellow retirees once he was able to acknowledge that he missed their companionship.

The focus of treatment for this client addressed the losses associated with his retirement. He was assisted in identifying substitute activities. Efforts to increase his self-esteem and to help him expand his social network were major treatment goals.

CONCLUSION

Individuals experience a multiplicity of losses as they move through the life cycle. Although all loss experiences are characterized by some degree of pain, these experiences can also result in opportunities for growth. Following acceptance and adaptation to their loss, mourners often report a heightened sensitivity to others and an increased appreciation for life and human relationships. They may more readily acknowledge others' losses and offer needed support and compassion to mourners. Pollock (1989) suggests that the outcome for some mourners may be the "ability to feel joy, satisfaction, and a sense of accomplishment" (p. 28). Some individuals may experience posttraumatic growth, that is, a positive change in one's psychological functioning, following a highly painful loss. This growth can result from one's efforts to understand and find value in the loss experience (Taku, Calhoun, Cann, & Tedeshi, 2008). Clinicians who work with mourners may also develop new understandings and sensitivities toward individuals and the human experience.

REFERENCES

American Veterinary Medical Association. (2002). *U.S. pet ownership and demographic sourcebook.* Schaumburg, IL: Author (Membership and Field Services).

Arnold, J., & Gemma, P. B. (2008). The continuing process of parental grief. *Death Studies, 32,* 658–673.

Baker, J. E. (2001). Mourning and the transformation of object relationships: Evidence for the persistence of internal attachments. *Psychoanalytic Psychology, 18*(1), 55–73.

Baker, J. E., Sedney, M., & Gross, E. (1992). Psychological tasks for bereaved children. *American Journal of Orthopsychiatry, 68*(11), 105–116.

Becvar, D. S. (2003). The impact on the family therapist of a focus on death, dying, and bereavement. *Journal of Marital and Family Therapy, 29*(4), 469–477.

Bennett, G., & Bennett, K. M. (2000). The presence of the dead: An empirical study. *Mortality, 5*(2), 139–157.

Betz, G., & Thorngren, J. M. (2006). Ambiguous loss and the family grieving process. *Family Journal, 14,* 359–365.

Bland, R. (1998). Understanding grief and guilt as common themes in family response to mental illness: Implications for social work practice. *Australian Social Work, 51*(4), 27–34.

Bohannon, J. (1990). Grief responses of spouses following the death of a child: A longitudinal study. *Omega, 22,* 109–121.

Bolton, I. (1986). Death of a child by suicide. In T. Rando (Ed.), *Parental loss of a child* (pp. 201–212). Champagne, IL: Research Press.

Bosticco, C., & Thompson, T. (2005). The role of communication and storytelling in the family grieving system. *Journal of Family Communication, 5*(4), 255–278.

Bowen, M. (1976). Family reaction to death. In P. Guerin (Ed.), *Family therapy: Theory and practice* (pp. 335–348). New York, NY: Gardner Press.

Bowlby, J. (1973). *Attachment and loss: Vol. 2. Separation, anxiety, and anger.* New York, NY: Basic Books.

Bowlby, J. (1980). *Attachment and loss: Vol. 3. Loss, sadness, and depression.* New York, NY: Basic Books.

Bursztein, C., & Apter, A. (2009). Adolescent suicide. *Current Opinions in Psychiatry, 22*(1), 1–6.

Corr, C. A., Nabe, C. M., & Corr, D. M. (2000). *Death and dying: Life and living* (3rd ed.). Belmont, CA: Wadsworth.

Cox, H. G. (1988). *Later life: The realities of aging.* Englewood Cliffs, NJ: Prentice Hall.

Crenshaw, D. A. (1990). *Bereavement: Counseling the grieving through the life cycle.* New York, NY: Continuum Books.

Crenshaw, D. A. (2005). Clinical tools to facilitate treatment of childhood traumatic grief. *Omega, 51*(3), 239–255.

Dalenberg, C. (2000). *Countertransference and the treatment of trauma.* Washington, DC: American Psychological Association.

Davis, C. G., Wortman, C. B., Lehman, D. R., & Silva, R. C. (2000). Searching for meaning in loss: Are clinical assumptions correct? *Death Studies, 24*(6), 497–541.

DeFrain, J. (1991). Learning about grief from normal families: SIDS, stillbirth, and miscarriage. *Journal of Marital and Family Therapy, 17*(8), 215–232.

Doka, K. J. (Ed.). (1989). *Disenfranchised grief: Recognizing hidden sorrow.* Lexington, MA: Lexington Books.

Doka, K. J. (2002). *Disenfranchised grief: New directions, challenges and strategies for practice.* Champaign, IL: Research Press.

Engel, G. (1975). The death of a twin: Mourning and anniversary reactions. Fragments of 10 years of self-analysis. *International Journal of Psychoanalysis, 56,* 23–40.

Eppler, C. (2008). Explaining themes of resilience in children after the death of a parent. *Professional School Counselor, 11,* 189–196.

Field, N. P. (2006). Continuing bonds in adaptation to bereavement: Introductions. *Death Studies, 30*(8), 709–714.

Field, N. P., Gao, B., & Paderna, L. (2005). Continuing bonds in bereavement: An attachment theory based perspective. *Death Studies, 29*(4), 277–299.

Field, N. P., Orsini, L., Gavish, R., & Packman, W. (2009). Role of attachment in response to pet loss. *Death Studies, 33*(4), 334–355.

Folkman, S., & Moskowitz, J. T. (2000). Positive affect and the other side of coping. *American Psychologist, 55,* 647–654.

Freud, S. (1895). Studies in hysteria. In J. Strachey (Ed.), *The standard edition of the complete works of Sigmund Freud* (Vol. 2, pp. 1–305). London, UK: Hogarth Press.

Freud, S. (1957). Mourning and melancholia. In J. Strachey (Ed.), *The standard edition of the complete works of Sigmund Freud* (Vol. 14, pp. 243–258). London, UK: Hogarth Press. (Original work published 1917)

Fulmer, R. H. (1983). A structural approach to unresolved mourning in single parent family systems. *Journal of Marital and Family Therapy, 5,* 51–58.

Furman, E. (1974). *A child's parent dies: Studies in childhood bereavement.* New York, NY: Yale University Press.

Goldman, L. (1994). *Life and loss: A guide to help grieving children.* Muncie, IN: Accelerated Development.

Goldsworthy, K. K. (2005). Grief and loss theory in social work practice: All changes involve loss, just as all losses require change. *Australian Social Work, 58*(2), 167–178.

Gould, R. L. (1978). *Transformations: Growth and change in adult life.* New York, NY: Simon & Schuster.

Gudmundsdottir, M., & Chesla, C. A. (2006). Building a new world: Habits and practices of healing following the death of a child. *Journal of Family Nursing, 12*(2), 143–164.

Hall, M., & Irwin, M. (2001). Physiological indices of functioning in bereavement. In M. S. Stroebe, R. O. Hansson, W. Stroebe, & H. Schut (Eds.), *Handbook of bereavement research and practice* (pp. 473–492). Washington, DC: American Psychological Association.

Hare-Mustin, R. (1979). Family therapy following the death of a child. *Journal of Marital and Family Therapy, 5,* 51–58.

Herz, F. (1980). The impact of death and serious illness on the family life cycle. In M. McGoldrick & E. Carter (Eds.), *The family life cycle: A framework for family therapy* (pp. 223–240). New York, NY: Gardner Press.

Hooyman, N. R., & Kramer, B. J. (2006). *Living through loss: Interventions across the life span.* New York, NY: Columbia University Press.

Imber-Black, E. (1991). Rituals and the healing process. In F. Walsh & M. McGoldrick (Eds.), *Living beyond loss: Death in the family* (pp. 207–223). New York, NY: W. W. Norton.

Imber-Black, E., Roberts, J., & Whiting, R. (1988). *Rituals in families and family therapy.* New York, NY: W. W. Norton.

Irish, D. P., Linquist, K. F., & Nelsen, V. J. (1997). *Ethnic variations in dying, death and grief.* Washington, DC: Taylor & Francis.

Johnson, C. M. (2010). African-American teen girls grieve the loss of friends to homicide: Meaning making and resilience. *Omega, 61*(2), 121–143.

Jones, E. (1957). *The life and work of Sigmund Freud* (Vol. 3). New York, NY: Basic Books.

Kamerman, J. B. (1988). *Death in the midst of life.* Englewood Cliffs, NJ: Prentice Hall.

Kissane, D. W., & Lichtenthal, W. G. (2008). Family focus grief therapy: From palliative care into bereavement. In M. S. Stroebe, R. O. Hannson, H. Schut, & W. Stroebe (Eds.), *Handbook of bereavement research and practice* (pp. 485–510). Washington, DC: American Psychological Association.

Klass, D., Silverman, P., & Nickman, S. L. (Eds.). (1996). *Continuing bonds: New understandings of grief.* London, UK: Taylor & Francis.

Krell, R., & Rabkin, L. (1979). The effects of sibling death on the surviving child: A family perspective. *Family Process, 10,* 471–479.

Levinson, D. J. (1978). *The seasons of a man's life.* New York, NY: Ballantine Books.

Lindemann, E. (1944). Symptomatology and management of acute grief. *American Journal of Orthopsychiatry, 101,* 141–148.

Lobb, E., Kristjanson, L. J., Aoun, S. M., Monterosso, L., Halkett, C. K., & Davies, A. (2013). Predictors of complicated grief: A systemic review of empirical studies. *Death Studies, 34,* 673–698.

Lopata, H. Z. (1972). *Widowhood in an American city.* Cambridge, MA: Schenkman.

McBride, J., & Simms, S. (2001). Death in the family: Adapting a family systems framework to the grief process. *American Journal of Family Therapy, 29,* 59–73.

McCarthy, J. (2006). A framework for healing from loss: A further integration of psychodynamic and social work theory. *Journal of Human Behavior in the Social Environment, 14*(3), 45–79.

McGoldrick, M., & Walsh, F. (1991). A time to mourn: Death and the life cycle. In F. Walsh & M. McGoldrick (Eds.), *Living beyond loss: Death in the family* (pp. 30–49). New York, NY: W. W. Norton.

Miles, M. S., & Demi, A. S. (1991–1992). A comparison of guilt in bereaved parents whose children died by suicide, accident or chronic illness. *Omega, 24*(3), 203–215.

Mishne, J. (1992). The grieving child: Manifest and hidden losses in childhood and adolescence. *Child and Adolescent Social Work Journal, 9*(6), 471–490.

Neimeyer, R. A. (1988). Death anxiety. In H. Waas, F. Berardo, & R. A. Neimeyer (Eds.), *Dying: Facing the facts* (pp. 97–136). Washington, DC: Hemisphere.

Neimeyer, R. A., Burke, L. A., Mackay, M. M., & van Dyke Stringer, J. G. (2010). Grief therapy and the reconstruction of meaning: From principles to practice. *Journal of Contemporary Psychotherapy, 40*: 73–83.

Neimeyer, R. A., Prigerson, H. G., & Davies, B. (2002). Mourning and meaning. *American Behavioral Scientist, 46*(2), 235–251.

Neugarten, B. L. (1976). Adaptation and the life cycle. *Counseling Psychologist, 6*(1), 16–20.

Nichols, J. A. (1990). Perinatal grief: Bereavement issues. In J. A. Nichols (Ed.), *Unrecognized and unsanctioned grief: The nature and counseling of unacknowledged loss* (pp. 19–29). Springfield, IL: Charles C Thomas.

O'Connor, N. (1984). *Letting go with love: The grieving process.* Apache Junction, AZ: La Mariposa Press.

Parkes, C. M. (1998). *Bereavement: Studies of grief in adult life* (2nd ed.). Madison, CN: International Universities Press.

Parkes, C. M. (2001). *Bereavement: Studies of grief in adult life* (3rd ed.). Philadelphia, PA: Taylor & Francis.

Parkes, C. M. (2002). Grief: Lessons from the past, visions for the future. *Death Studies, 26,* 367–385.

Parkes, C. M. (2006). *Love and loss: The roots of grief and its complications.* New York, NY: Routledge.

Paul, N. (1967). The role of mourning and empathy in conjoint marital therapy. In G. Zuk & I. Boszormenyi (Eds.), *Family therapy and disturbed families* (pp. 186–205). Palo Alto, CA: Science & Behavioral Books.

Paul, N., & Grosser, G. (1991). Operational mourning and its role in conjoint family therapy. In F. Walsh & M. McGoldrick (Eds.), *Living beyond loss: Death in the family* (pp. 93–103). New York, NY: W. W. Norton.

Piper, W. E., McCallum, M., & Hassan, F. (1992). *Adaptation to loss through short-term group therapy.* New York, NY: Guilford Press.

Piper, W. E., Ogrodniczuk, J. S., Joyce, A. S., Weideman, R., & Rosie, J. S. (2007). Group composition and group therapy for complicated grief. *Journal of Consulting and Clinical Psychology, 75*(1), 116–125.

Pollock, G. H. (1961). Mourning and adaptation. In R. V. Frankel (Ed.), *Essential papers on object loss* (pp. 142–179). New York: New York University Press.

Pollock, G. H. (1970). Anniversary reactions, trauma, and mourning. *Psychoanalytic Quarterly, 39,* 347–371.

Pollock, G. H. (1989). The mourning process, the creative process, and the creation. In D. Deitrich & P. C. Sabad (Eds.), *The problem of loss and mourning: Psychoanalytic perspectives* (pp. 27–60). Madison, CT: International Universities Press.

Rabow, M. W., Hauser, J. M., & Adams, J. (2004). Supporting family caregivers at the end-of-life: They don't know what they don't know. *Journal of the American Medical Association* (0098-7484), *291*(4), 483–491.

Rando, T. (1984). *Grief, dying and death: Clinical interventions for caregivers.* Champaign, IL: Research Press.

Rando, T. (1986). *Parental loss of a child.* Champaign, IL: Research Press.

Rando, T. (1993). *Treatment of complicated mourning.* Champaign, IL: Research Press.

Richardson, V. E. (2007). A dual process model of grief counseling: Findings from the changing lives of older couples (CLOC) study. *Journal of Erotological Social Work, 48*(3/4), 311–329.

Roos, R. (2002). *Chronic sorrow.* New York, NY: Brunner-Routledge.

Rosen, H. (1991). Child and adolescent bereavement. *Child and Adolescent Social Work Journal, 8*(1), 5–16.

Rubin, S. S., & Malkinson, R. (2001). Parental response to child loss across the life cycle: Clinical and research perspectives. In M. Stroebe, R. O. Hansson, W. Stroebe, & H. Schut (Eds.), *Handbook of bereavement research* (pp. 219–240). Washington, DC: American Psychological Association.

Sable, P. (2008). What is adult attachment? *Clinical Social Work Journal, 36,* 21–30.

Sanders, C. (1999). *Grief: The mourning after: Dealing with adult bereavement* (2nd ed.). New York, NY: Wiley.

Schumacher, J. (1984). Helping children cope with a sibling's death. In J. Hansen (Ed.), *Death and grief in the family* (pp. 82–94). Rockville, MD: Aspen.

Silverman, P., & Klass, D. (1996). Introduction: What's the problem? In D. Klass, P. R. Silverman, & S. L. Nickman (Eds.), *Continuing bonds: New understandings of grief* (pp. 3–23). Washington, DC: Taylor & Francis.

Somhlaba, N. Z., & Wait, J. W. (2008). Psychological adjustment to conjugal bereavement: Do social networks aid coping following spousal death? *Omega, 57*(4), 341–366.

Stierlin, H., Rucker-Embden, I., Wetzel, N., & Wirsching, M. (1980). *The first interview with the family.* New York, NY: Brunner/Mazel.

Stroebe, M., & Schut, H. (1999). The dual process model of coping with bereavement: Rationale and description. *Death Studies, 23,* 197–224.

Stroebe, M. S., Hansson, R. O., Stroebe, W., & Schut, H. (Eds.). (2001). *Handbook of bereavement research: Consequences, coping and caring.* Washington, DC: American Psychological Association.

Stroebe, M. S., Hansson, R. O., Stroebe, W., & Schut, H. (Eds.). (2008). *Handbook of bereavement research and practice.* Washington, DC: American Psychological Association.

Stroebe, M. S., Schut, H., & van den Bout, J. (Eds.). (2012). *Complicated grief.* New York, NY: Routledge.

Taku, K., Calhoun, L. G., Cann, A., & Tedeshi, R. G. (2008). The role of rumination in the coexistence of distress and posttraumatic growth among bereaved Japanese university students. *Death Studies, 32,* 428–444.

Vess, J., Moreland, J., & Schwebel, A. (1985–1986). Understanding family role reallocation following a death: A theoretical framework. *Omega, 19*(2), 116–127.

Videka-Sherman, L. (1982). Coping with the death of a child: A study over time. *American Journal of Orthopsychiatry, 52,* 688–698.

Waas, H., & Stillion, J. M. (1988). Death in the lives of children and adolescents. In H. Waas, F. Berardo, & R. A. Neimeyer (Eds.), *Dying: Facing the facts* (pp. 201–229). Washington, DC: Hemisphere.

Wallerstein, J. S. (2005). Growing up in the divorced family. *Clinical Social Work Journal, 33*(4), 401–418.

Wallerstein, J. S., & Kelly, J. B. (1980). *Surviving the breakup: How children and parents cope with divorce.* New York, NY: Basic Books.

Walsh, F. (1978). Concurrent grandparent death and birth of a schizophrenic offspring: An intriguing finding. *Family Process, 17,* 457–463.

Walsh, F. (2002). A family resilience framework: Innovative practice applications. *Family Relations, 51*(2), 130–137.

Walsh, F., & McGoldrick, M. (1991). Loss and the family: A systemic perspective. In F. Walsh & M. McGoldrick (Eds.), *Living beyond loss: Death in the family* (pp. 1–29). New York, NY: W. W. Norton.

Walsh, K. (2012). *Grief and loss: Theories and skills for the helping professional* (2nd ed.). Upper Saddle River, NJ: Pearson.

Williams, K., & Dunne-Bryant, A. (2006). Divorce and adult psychological well-being: Clarifying the role of gender and child age. *Journal of Marriage and Family, 68*(5), 1178–1197.

Worden, J. (2009). *Grief counseling and grief therapy* (4th ed.). New York, NY: Springer.

Wrobel, T. A., & Dye, A. L. (2003). Grieving pet death: Normative, gender, and attachment issues. *Omega, 47*(4), 385–393.

Yalom, I. D. (1985). *The theory and practice of group psychotherapy.* New York, NY: Basic Books.

INDEX

Page numbers in *italics* indicate figures and tables.

psychoanalytic therapy with adults and, 225
relational thought and, 76–76
AGT (activity-group therapy), 278
Aichorn, A., 43
Aims, and childhood wishes, 48
Akhtar, S., 71n
Alcohol and other drug problems (AOD). *See also* Assessments, for AOD (alcohol and other drug problems)
overview and challenges in, 427–427, 460
addiction continuum and, 430
adolescents and, 431–431
consequences of, 428–428
countertransference and, 431
diagnoses confusion in older adults and, 435–435
diagnostic issues and, 430–430, 435–435
diseases classification and, 430–430
drugs of abuse described and, 429
DSM-IV and, 430
multicausal and multivariant conditions and, 431–431
older adults issues and, 435–435
transference and, 431
Alexander, F., 43, 127, 145, 405–405
Alexithymia, 343
Alloplastic adaptation, 57
Alter ego (partnering selfobjects), 70
Ambiguous (complicated grief loss), 369
Amodeo, M., 448
Amygdala, 85
Anaclitic depression, 57–57
Analysand (client). *See* Client (analysand)
Anderson, C. M., 177
Anniversary reaction, and loss, 470
Anomie, 5–5
Anonymity principle, 237
AOD (alcohol and other drug problems). *See* Alcohol and other drug problems (AOD)
APA (Association for Play Therapy), 280
Applegate, J., 85
Arbitrary inference, 205
Archaeological metaphor, for psychoanalytic process, 231–231
Archer, J. C., 279
Arlow, J., 47
Arnston, L., 370, 371
Aron, L., 77, 105
Artistic expression (cultural expression activities, for children of disasters and terrorism), 388–388

Artistic (cultural) expression activities, for children of disasters and terrorism, 388–388
Assessments. *See also* Assessments, for AOD (alcohol and other drug problems)
CBT or cognitive-behavioral therapy with adults and, 195–195
developmental assessment for group treatment with children or adolescents and, 280–280
family functioning, 164–164
group treatment with adults and, 318–318
individual therapy with adolescents and, 131–131
individual therapy with children and, 114–114
processes in family resilience and, 165, *166,* 167–167
trauma survivors support and, 347–347
Assessments, for AOD (alcohol and other drug problems). *See also* Alcohol and other drug problems (AOD); Assessments
co-occuring psychiatric conditions and, 440–440
cultural issues and, 441–441
drinking and drug use history in, 438–438
drinking and drug use questions in, 437–437
indirect indicators and, 433–433
precontemplation by clients and, 444–444
readiness for change and, 443–443
reduced-use experiment and, 443–443
risk factors and, 433–433
therapeutic or helping alliance during, 436–436
Assisting interventions, 268
Association for Play Therapy (APA), 280
At-risk (vulnerable) survivors, and disasters survivors support, 381, 391–391, 397
Attachment concept, and loss, 466–466
Attachment experiences, 85
Auerhahn, N., 370
Autobiographical memory, 89
Autonoetic consciousness, 130–130, 131n
Autoplastic adaptation, 57
Axline, V., 278

Babies, and disasters survivors support, 384
Bacal, H., 72
Bacon, F., 32
Badenoch, B., 85, 87–87, 92, 98
Baer, J. S., 281
Bagarozzi, D. A., 34
Balint, A., 60
Balint, M., 60, 66–66
Bandura, A., 37

client's communications and, 246–246
psychoanalytic therapy with adults and, 222,
    246–246
Clinical social work. *See also specific models,
    theories and therapies*
    BT and, 22–22, 37–37
    CBT or cognitive-behavioral therapy and, 22, 38
    clinical assessment instruments and, 35
    clinical examples of neurobiology in, 91–91, 93n
    cognitive theory and, 35, 37–37
    relational psychoanalysis tenets of, 77
    social work defined and, 18
Closed systems, 4, 9
    open versus closed groups and, 320
Cognitive-behavioral therapy (CBT). *See also
    Behavior theory (BT, or behaviorism);
    Cognitive-behavioral therapy (CBT), with
    adults; Cognitive theory*
    ABC theory of cognitive theory and, 34–34
    active theory and, 193
    behavior therapy in comparison to cognitive
        therapy and, 34–34
    client assessment elements and, 33–33
    clinical assessment instruments and, 35
    clinical social work and, 22, 35, 37–37
    "cognitive sets" and, 35
    collaborative effort and, 192
    directive theory and, 193
    education theory and, 193
    effectiveness of, 187–187, 188n
    empirical focus and, 194
    family therapy and, 175
    features of, 191–191
    group treatment with adults and, 317–317,
        328–328
    idiosyncratic subjective experience and, 192
    interventions in, 34
    organizations and, 35–35
    publications about, 36
    publications and, 35–35
    rational emotive therapy or rational emotive
        behavior therapy and, 34
    REBT or rational emotive behavior therapy and, 34
    relapse prevention and, 194
    RET or rational emotive therapy and, 33, 34–34
    SLT or social learning theory and, 33, 36, 38
    Socratic method and, 193–193
    structural theory and, 193
    time-limited treatment and, 194

trauma survivors support and, 356–356
unconditional regard for self and others and,
    192–192
Cognitive-behavioral therapy (CBT), with adults.
    See also Psychoanalytic therapy, with adults;
    Psychoanalytic therapy technique, with adults
    overview of, 186–186, 208–208
    ABCDE theory and, 202
    ABC theory or expanded ABC theory and,
        199–199
    absolutistic/dichotomous thinking and, 204
    active theory and, 193
    ACT or acceptance and commitment therapy
        and, 189
    arbitrary inference and, 205
    assessments and, 195–195
    behavioral techniques and, 203–203
    BT and, 188–188
    cognitive content or cognitive products and, 196
    cognitive homework and, 202–202
    cognitive process and, 196
    cognitive psychotherapies and practice and,
        188–188
    cognitive restructuring and, 198
    collaborative effort and, 192
    constructivist theory and practice and, 189–189
    CT and, 186–186, 189, 204–204
    derivatives of irrational beliefs and, 200–200
    detection of irrational beliefs and, 201–201
    directive theory and, 193
    disputing irrational beliefs and, 201–201
    downward arrow technique and, 197
    education theory and, 193
    effectiveness of CBT or cognitive-behavioral
        therapy and, 187–187, 188n
    emotive techniques and, 203
    empirical focus and, 194
    features of CBT or cognitive-behavioral therapy
        and, 191–191
    idiosyncratic subjective experience and, 192
    interventions and, 198–198
    irrationality and, 198, 199
    Leahy Emotional Schema Scale and, 197–197
    magnification and, 205
    minimization and, 205
    overgeneralization and, 204–204
    personalization and, 205
    problem-solving and, 207–207
    rationality and, 198, 199

Self-cohesion (cohesion), 71–71
Selfobjects, 70
Self psychology (psychology of self)
    overview of, 69–69, 71n, 72
    cohesion or self-cohesion and, 71–71
    cohesive self and, 70–70
    compensatory structures and, 72
    empathy and, 71
    false self and, 67–67
    grandiose self and, 70–70
    nuclear self and, 70–70
    psychoanalytic theories and, 69–69
    selfobjects and, 70
    self types and, 70–70
    transmuting internalization and, 71, 71n
    tripolar self and, 70
    true self and, 67–67
    virtual self and, 70–70
Self-system, 63
Self types, 70–70
Semantic (factual memory), 89
Separations prevention, and disasters survivors
    support, 384, 396–396
Set time limit by therapists, 411
Setting for therapy (situation for therapy, or
    therapeutic situation), 114, 235
Sexual drive
    infantile sexuality and, 49
    psychoanalytic theories and, 49–49
    psychoanalytic therapy with adults and, 225
    relational thought and, 76–76
    sex as term of use and, 49
    sexual as term of use and, 49
    sexuality as term of use and, 49
Sexually addictive behavior, 99–99
Shakespeare, W., 338
Shame, 97
Shapiro, J., 85
Shay, J. J., 316
Sheldon, B., 36
Short-term anxiety-regulating psychotherapy
    (STARP), 410
Short-term expressive psychoanalytic
    psychotherapy, 409
Siegel, D., 85, 89, 148
Siegel, J. P., 148
Sifneos, P., 408
Signal affect, 52
Signal anxiety, 51, 52

Sim, T., 371
Sinaii, N., 341
Situation for therapy (setting for therapy, or
    therapeutic situation), 114, 235
Skinner, B. F., 21, 23, 30, 37
Slavson, S. R., 278, 280
SLT (social learning theory). *See* Social learning
    theory (SLT)
Smalley, R., 44
Small-group theory, 317–317
Smead, R., 296
Social anxiety (social phobias), 101
Social context, for group treatment with children and
    adolescents, 285–285
Social diagnosis, 43
Social ecological theory (ecological systems theory).
    See Ecological systems theory (social ecological
    theory; Systems theory (general systems theory)
Social justice theory, 316
Social learning theory (SLT)
    overview of, 33, 38
    behavior theory and, 22–22, 33, 38
    cognitive theory and, 33, 36, 38
    negative punishment and, 29–29
    negative reinforcement and, 28
    observational learning or modeling and, 32–32
    operant extinction and, 30–30
    operant learning and, 27–27
    positive punishment and, 28–28
    positive reinforcement and, 27–27
    PR or progressive relaxation and, 26–26
    punishment and, 27
    reinforcement and, 27
    relief and, 27
    respondent learning or respondent conditioning
        and, 25–25
    rewarding and, 27
Social network map, 17–17, *19*
Social phobias (social anxiety), 101
Social-psychological theory, 317–317
Social treatment, 43
Social work, 18. *See also* Clinical social work
Sociometric (affectional) structure, and group
    treatment with adults, 331
Solution-focused theory, in family therapy, 177
Somatic effects of trauma, 341–341
Sort-term anxiety-provoking psychotherapy
    (STAPP), 408
Spain, E. H., 341